Zeroing Neural Networks

Zeroing Neural Networks

Finite-time Convergence Design, Analysis and Applications

Lin Xiao
Hunan Normal University

Lei Jia
Hunan Normal University

IEEE PRESS

WILEY

Published by John Wiley & Sons, Inc., Hoboken, New Jersey. All rights reserved.
Published simultaneously in Canada.

For general information on our other products and services or for technical support, please contact our Customer Care Department within the United States at (800) 762-2974, outside the United States at (317) 572-3993 or fax (317) 572-4002.

Wiley also publishes its books in a variety of electronic formats. Some content that appears in print may not be available in electronic formats. For more information about Wiley products, visit our web site at www.wiley.com

Library of Congress Cataloging-in-Publication Data is Applied for:

Hardback ISBN: 9781119985990

Cover design: Wiley
Cover image: © BAIVECTOR/Shutterstock

Set in 9.5/12.5pt STIXTwoText by Straive, Chennai, India

To our parents and ancestors, as always

Contents

List of Figures

List of Tables

Author Biographies

Lin Xiao received the B.S. degree in Electronic Information Science and Technology from Hengyang Normal University, Hengyang, China, in 2009, and the Ph.D. degree in Communication and Information Systems from Sun Yat-sen University, Guangzhou, China, in 2014. He is currently a Professor with the College of Information Science and Engineering, Hunan Normal University, Changsha, China. He has authored over 100 papers in international conferences and journals, such as the IEEE-TNNLS, the IEEE-TCYB, the IEEE-TII, and the IEEE-TSMCA. He is an Associate Editor of IEEE-TNNLS. His main research interests include neural networks, robotics, and intelligent information processing.

Lei Jia received the B.S. degree in Information and Computing Science from InnerMongolia Normal University, Hohhot, China, in 2018. She is currently studying toward the Ph.D. degree in Operations Research and Control from College of Mathematics and Statistics, Hunan Normal University, Changsha, China. Her main research interests include neural networks and image processing.

Preface

Computational problems usually play an important role in various fields. For example, matrix inversion problem is widely used in graph estimation, cloud computing, robotics, and image processing; matrix square root finding is widely applied in various scientific and engineering areas; linear matrix equations are widely used in control theory, optimization, signal processing, robotics, and multi-agent systems; Lyapunov equation widely appears in many scientific and engineering fields, e.g. linear algebra, disturbance decoupling, and multi-agent systems. For these computational problems, there are generally two kinds of solving methods: serial processing and parallel processing. In the previous studies, many numerical algorithms with the serial processing method are researched to solve the computational problems, such as Newton iteration and its variants, Meini iteration, singular value decomposition, and Greville recursive method. However, numerical algorithms have many limitations. For example, the computational complexity is usually proportional to the cube of the matrix dimension, which leads to the failure of solving large-scale matrix problems in view of the limitations of numerical algorithms to solve constant matrix problems, let alone the efficiency for addressing time-varying matrix problems. Actually, the time-varying problems are more general in the real world, and thus their practical applications are more extensive. In recent years, due to the hardware-implementation ability and parallel distributed nature of neural networks, they are developed vigorously by many researchers to solve computational problems, especially time-varying problems.

Recurrent neural network (RNN) as a powerful computational tool has important applications, particularly in the fields of system identification, optimization, speech processing, and robotics, after the seminal work on Hopfield neural network. In algebraic computation, the RNN is divided into two classes: gradient neural network (GNN) and zeroing neural network (ZNN). The GNN method mainly adopts the norm of the error matrix, which is defined by the specific problems, as the performance indicator and designs a neural network evolving along the negative gradient-descent direction to make the error norm decrease to zero with time. Based on the parallel processing characters, the GNN is extensively applied to settling various computational problems, such as Lyapunov equations, Sylvester equations, matrix inversion, and so on. However, the GNN is not suitable for computing time-varying problems due to the lack of compensation to the velocity components of the time-varying coefficients. Thus, it is known that any methods designed specifically for settling the time-invariant problems cannot ensure the decrease of the performance indicator related to the time-varying problems, and a relatively larger residual error always exists. As a breakthrough in solving time-varying computational problems, the ZNN method was firstly proposed by Zhang *et al.* in 2003, and it has been studied deeply and extensively in recent years. The ZNN as a kind of efficient neurodynamic approach is mainly aimed at addressing time-varying problems, such as linear matrix equation, nonlinear equation, quadratic programming, matrix Moore–Penrose inversion, and various complex-valued problems. Generally speaking, designing a ZNN model for a specific time-variant problem needs three steps including: (i) define a matrix error function; (ii) design an evolutionary formula; and (iii) substitute the matrix error function into the evolutionary formula. Then the ZNN model can be obtained by these design steps. The main idea of the ZNN is to define a matrix error-monitoring function, instead of the scalar-valued cost function, to make the computational error decrease globally and asymptotically.

Nowadays, many researchers devote themselves to studying the ZNN, and the scopes of the study include the time-varying problems to be solved, design parameters, evolutionary formulas, and activation functions. The main purpose of these studies is to improve the properties of the ZNN, such as stability, convergence, and noise tolerance (i.e. robustness). The previous design parameters are usually constants, that is to say, the value is fixed and cannot vary as time changes, which leads to the convergence time of the ZNN as it can only depend on the selected activation function. Based on this limitation, various time-varying design parameters are investigated and proposed. However, the time-varying design parameters have the disadvantage that the corresponding value always consistently increases as time increases. As a result, when the time is large, the calculation will overflow. Thus, an adaptive fuzzy parameter generated from a pre-designed fuzzy logic system was further studied, which can adaptively adjust the convergence rate of the ZNN and avoid the inadequacy of time-varying design parameters. In a word, through the study of the design parameters, the convergence of the ZNN can be improved in finite time to some extent. In addition to design parameters, many nonlinear activation functions and evolutionary formulas are also researched and proposed to enhance the convergence and noise tolerance of the ZNN. The basic linear activation function with its transformations can only realize exponential convergence. This kind of convergence has the deficiency that the convergence rate will decrease as the residual error approaches zero. In order to avoid this deficiency, the concept of finite time is generated, and then a variety of nonlinear activation functions are put forward, such as the classical sign-bi-power function. Moreover, based on the inevitability of noise pollution in realistic environment, some nonlinear activation functions also possess the ability of the noise tolerance. Besides, some improved evolutionary formulas have certain inherent noise tolerance in themselves. These improved evolutionary formulas perform much better than the traditional evolutionary formula both in convergence and noise tolerance. That is to say, the improved evolutionary formulas have much faster convergence rate and stronger noise tolerance compared to the traditional evolutionary formula under the same conditions. Especially, several evolutionary formulas can possess finite-time convergence and noise tolerance simultaneously.

In this book, finite-time zeroing neural network (FTZNN) is designed, analyzed, and verified for all kinds of time-varying problems, including matrix square root, matrix inversion, linear matrix equation, optimization, Lyapunov equation, Sylvester equation, and inequality. The finite-time convergence property of the ZNN is mainly achieved from three aspects: enhancing the design parameter, activation function, and evolutionary formula. Even more to the point, when the time increases, the residual errors of the FTZNN models can directly converge to zero. As a result, the convergence rate is much faster than the exponential convergence. Further, the fixed-time convergence is presented, and this kind of modified finite-time convergence has a remarkable advantage that the convergence time is independent of the initial state of the FTZNN models. This character is more in line with the practical requirements. In addition to analyzing the convergence of the FTZNN models, the noise tolerance is also taken into account, because the noise interference cannot be avoided in the real world.

The idea of FTZNN in this book mainly comes from laboratory discussions, academic conference communications, and scientific research. This book is supported by materials from the authors' academic papers published in international journals, such as *IEEE Transactions on Industrial Informatics*, *IEEE Transactions on Fuzzy Systems*, and *IEEE Transactions on Neural Networks and Learning Systems*, and these studies have been widely applied and developed. In fact, since the early 1980s, the neural network has been developed greatly, with many novel concepts being proposed (including the authors' researchers). Importantly, these analytical studies have been successfully applied to practical problems. Thus, our prior considerations are to involve every central theme in a detailed manner to make the materials clear and coherent. That is to say, each part or even each chapter is written in a relatively self-contained form.

This book contains 21 chapters which are classified into the following 8 parts.
Part I: Application to Matrix Square Root (Chapters 1 and 2)
Part II: Application to Matrix Inversion (Chapters 3–5)

Part III: Application to Linear Matrix Equation (Chapters 6 and 7)
Part IV: Application to Optimization (Chapters 8–10)
Part V: Application to Lyapunov Equation (Chapters 11–13)
Part VI: Application to Sylvester Equation (Chapters 14–16)
Part VII: Application to Inequality (Chapters 17 and 18)
Part VIII: Application to Nonlinear Equation (Chapters 19–21).

Chapter 1 – In this chapter, we present a new design formula and apply it to zeroing neural network (ZNN). Further, a finite-time zeroing neural network (FTZNN) model is proposed and investigated for finding the time-varying matrix square root. Theoretical analyses of the novel design formula and the FTZNN model are proposed in detail. Besides, simulative experiments verify the advantages of the proposed FTZNN model to the original zeroing neural network (OZNN) model for finding the time-varying matrix square root.

Chapter 2 – In this chapter, a finite-time zeroing neural network (FTZNN) model is proposed and studied for finding the matrix square root. The FTZNN model fully utilizes a nonlinearly activated sign-bi-power function, and thus possesses faster convergence ability. The upper bound of convergence time of the FTZNN model is theoretically derived and estimated by solving differential inequalities. Simulative experiments of the FTZNN model are conducted, and the results validate the effectiveness and superiority of the FTZNN model for finding the matrix square root.

Chapter 3 – In this chapter, online solution to time-varying matrix inverse is investigated by proposing a finite-time zeroing neural network (FTZNN) model, which is evolved by a new design formula. The purpose of presenting the novel design formula is to accelerate the convergence of the FTZNN model to further achieve the finite-time convergence. Theoretical analyses of the design formula and the FTZNN model are given in detail. Simulative experiments substantiate the effectiveness and superiority of the proposed FTZNN model for online time-varying matrix inversion problem.

Chapter 4 – In this chapter, a new noise-tolerant finite-time zeroing neural network (NT-FTZNN) model using a versatile activation function (VAF) is presented and introduced for solving time-dependent matrix inversion (TVMI) problem. The convergence and robustness of the NT-FTZNN model are mathematically analyzed in detail. Two comparative numerical simulations with different dimensions are conducted to test the efficiency and superiority of the NT-FTZNN model. In addition, two practical application examples (i.e. a mobile manipulator and a real Kinova JACO 2 robot manipulator) are presented to validate the applicability and physical feasibility of the NT-FTZNN model in a noisy environment. Both simulative and experimental results demonstrate the effectiveness and tolerant-noise ability of the NT-FTZNN model.

Chapter 5 – In this chapter, an improved varying parameter finite-time ZNN (IVP-FTZNN) model is established and researched to solve the time-varying matrix inversion (TVMI) problem. Specifically, the value of the proposed novel time-varying parameter in the IVP-FTZNN model can grow rapidly over time, which can better meet the needs of ZNN in hardware implementation. Theoretical analyses of the novel time-varying parameter and the proposed IVP-FTZNN model are given to guarantee the global super-exponential convergence and finite-time convergence. Experimental results verify the superior property of the established IVP-FTZNN model for addressing the TVMI problem.

Chapter 6 – In this chapter, a superior design formula activated by noise-tolerant nonlinear functions is proposed to achieve the denoising and finite-time convergence of zeroing neural network (ZNN). According to this design formula, a robust finite-time zeroing neural network (R-FTZNN) is developed and applied to robotic motion tracking illustrated via time-varying linear equation system solving. Furthermore, theoretical analyses on the global stability, the finite-time convergence, and the denoising ability of the proposed design formula and the corresponding R-FTZNN model are presented in detail. The upper bound on the convergence time is also analytically derived. A numerical example is supplied to verify the superiority of the R-FTZNN model according to the results of computing a time-varying linear equation system in the presence of additive noises. Finally, an application to robotic motion tracking is successfully applied to the R-FTZNN model.

Chapter 7 – This chapter designs two finite-time zeroing neural network (FTZNN) models for time-varying linear matrix equation through taking two new activation functions into consideration. Theoretical analysis proves that two new activation functions can not only accelerate the convergence rate of the FTZNN models but also come true through the finite-time convergence. Besides, after adding the differential error and the model-implementation error into the models, the theoretical upper bounds of the steady state residual errors are calculated, which demonstrates the certain robustness of the proposed two FTZNN models. Finally, comparative simulations show the excellent performance of the proposed two FTZNN models for solving time-varying linear matrix equation.

Chapter 8 – In this chapter, we propose a unified finite-time zeroing neural network (U-FTZNN) model for solving time-varying quadratic programming (QP) problems subject to equality or inequality constraints. The proposed U-FTZNN model mainly has advantages in the following three aspects: (i) solving QP problems with or without inequality constraints in a unified model; (ii) converging to the optimal solution of QP problems within a predefined time that can be determined in advance; and (iii) resisting many external noises with tiny and predictable residual error. These improvements have been rigorously proved in theory. By conducting both qualitative and quantitative simulations with comparisons, the superior properties of the U-FTZNN model are further validated. Finally, the application of the U-FTZNN model to image fusion task illustrates the efficiency together with its applicability.

Chapter 9 – In this chapter, a robust finite-time zeroing neural network (R-FTZNN) is devised and presented to solve time-dependent nonlinear minimization under various external disturbances. The proposed R-FTZNN model simultaneously possesses two characteristics, i.e. finite-time and noise suppression. Besides, rigorous theoretical analyses are given to prove the superior performance of the R-FTZNN model when adopted to solve time-dependent nonlinear minimization under external disturbances. Comparative results also substantiate the effectiveness and advantages of R-FTZNN via solving a time-dependent nonlinear minimization problem.

Chapter 10 – In this chapter, a nonlinear finite-time zeroing neural network (N-FTZNN) model is proposed and studied for real-time solution of the equality-constrained quadratic optimization with nonstationary coefficients. The proposed N-FTZNN model possesses the much superior convergence performance (i.e. finite-time convergence). Furthermore, the upper bound of the finite convergence time is derived analytically according to Lyapunov theory. Both theoretical and simulative results verify the efficacy and superior of the N-FTZNN model.

Chapter 11 – In this chapter, a finite-time zeroing neural network (FTZNN) is proposed and investigated for solving online Lyapunov equation. The proposed FTZNN model adopts a sign-bi-power activation function and thus possesses the best convergence performance. Furthermore, we prove that the FTZNN model can converge to the theoretical solution of Lyapunov equation within finite time, instead of converging exponentially with time. Simulative results also verify the effectiveness and superiority of the FTZNN model for solving online Lyapunov equation.

Chapter 12 – In this chapter, based on a new evolution formula, a novel finite-time zeroing neural network (FTZNN) is proposed and studied for solving a non-stationary Lyapunov equation. The convergence performance has a remarkable improvement for the proposed FTZNN model and can be accelerated to finite time. Besides, by solving the differential inequality, the upper bound of the convergence time of the FTZNN model is computed theoretically and analytically. Simulations are conducted and compared to validate the superiority of the FTZNN model for solving the nonstationary Lyapunov equation. Further, the FTZNN model is successfully applied to online tracking control of a wheeled mobile manipulator.

Chapter 13 – In this chapter, we present a systematic and constructive procedure on using zeroing neural network (ZNN) to design control laws based on the efficient solution of dynamic Lyapunov equation. To do so, a novel formula is first designed in a unified manner of ZNN. Differing from the conventional formula appearing in ZNN, the proposed formula simultaneously has finite-time convergence and noise robustness properties. According to this novel formula, a novel nonlinear finite-time zeroing neural network (N-FTZNN) is established to compute dynamic Lyapunov equation in the presence of various additive noises. Both theoretical and simulative results ensure the finite-time convergence and noise robustness properties of the N-FTZNN model for computing dynamic Lyapunov equation in front of various additive noises.

Chapter 14 – In this chapter, to solve dynamic Sylvester equation in the presence of additive noises, a novel finite-time zeroing neural network (N-FTZNN) with finite-time convergence and excellent robustness is proposed and analyzed. The proposed N-FTZNN is based on an ingenious integral design formula activated by nonlinear functions, which are able to expedite the convergence speed and suppress unknown additive noises during the solving process of dynamic Sylvester equation. In addition, the global stability, finite-time convergence, and denoising property of the N-FTZNN model are theoretically proved, with the upper bound of the finite convergence time for the N-FTZNN model being also estimated. Simulative results further verify the efficiency of the N-FTZNN mode for the dynamic Sylvester equation in front of additive noises. At last, the proposed design method for establishing the N-FTZNN model is successfully applied to the noise-polluted kinematical control of robotic manipulator.

Chapter 15 – In this chapter, two noise-tolerant predefined-time zeroing neural network (NT-PTZNN) models are established by devising two novelly constructed nonlinear activation functions (AFs) to find the accurate solution of the time-variant Sylvester equation in the presence of various noises. The proposed two NT-PTZNN models are activated by two novel AFs, therefore possessing the excellent predefined time convergence and strong robustness even in the presence of various noises. Besides, the detailed theoretical analyses of the predefined-time convergence and robustness abilities for the NT-PTZNN models are given by considering different kinds of noises. Simulation comparative results further verify the excellent performance of the proposed NT-PTZNN models, when applied to online solution of the time-variant Sylvester equation.

Chapter 16 – In this chapter, for obtaining better convergence performance when zeroing neural network (ZNN) is applied to solve time-varying Sylvester equation (TVSE), three different types of adaptive design coefficients for the sign-bi-power activation function are developed and investigated. Based on these adaptive coefficients, three new adaptive finite-time (FTZNN) models are proposed for solving the TVSE. For better analysis, the effect of two parts constituting the sign-bi-power activation function on the convergence of the standard ZNN model is discussed. Then, detailed theoretical derivations and proofs are provided to verify excellent performance of the proposed FTZNN models. Finally, illustrative comparison experiments are presented to show the enhanced finite-time convergence performance of the FTZNN models for addressing the TVSE.

Chapter 17 – In this chapter, three novel finite-time zeroing neural network (FTZNN) models are designed and analyzed to solve time-varying linear matrix inequalities (LMIs). To make the Matlab toolbox calculation processing more convenient, the matrix vectorization technique is used to transform the matrix-valued FTZNN models into the vector-valued FTZNN models. Furthermore, the sign-bi-power activation function (AF), the improved sign-bi-power AF, and the tunable sign-bi-power AF are explored to activate the FTZNN models. Theoretical analysis shows that the FTZNN models not only can accelerate the convergence speed, but also can achieve finite-time convergence. Numerical examples ulteriorly confirm the effectiveness and advantages of the FTZNN models for finding the solution set of time-varying LMIs.

Chapter 18 – In this chapter, we propose a novel integral design scheme for finding the robust solution of time-varying matrix inequalities. The core idea of this method is to add an integral term in the construction of the error function to make the model have error memory, so as to eliminate static difference. Meanwhile, appropriate activation functions (AFs) are used in the noise tolerance finite-time zeroing neural network (NT-FTZNN) model, which can also make error function accomplish finite-time convergence. The noise tolerance property of the NT-FTZNN model is proved by theoretical analysis, and the upper limit of convergence time is obtained. Numerical examples ulteriorly verify the finite time and noise-tolerant properties of the NT-FTZNN model.

Chapter 19 – In this chapter, a finite-time zeroing neural network (FTZNN) model, together with a specially constructed activation function, is proposed and investigated for finding the root of nonlinear equation. The FTZNN model in the form of implicit dynamics has the following advantages: (i) has better consistency with actual situations; (ii) has a greater ability in representing dynamical systems; and (iii) can achieve superior convergence performance (i.e. finite-time convergence). Both theoretical analysis and computer-simulation results substantiate the effectiveness and superiority of the FTZNN model for solving nonlinear equation in real-time.

Chapter 20 – In this chapter, we propose a nonlinearly activated finite-time zeroing neural network (FTZNN) model to solve time-varying nonlinear equations in real time. In the theory part, the upper bound of convergence time is estimated analytically. Simulations are performed to evaluate the performance of the proposed FTZNN model, which substantiates the effectiveness and superiority of the FTZNN model for solving time-varying nonlinear equations in real time.

Chapter 21 – In this chapter, by suggesting a new nonlinear activation function, a robust and fixed-time zeroing neural network (R-FTZNN) model is proposed and analyzed for time-variant nonlinear equation (TVNE). The R-FTZNN model not only converges to the theoretical solution of TVNE within a fixed time (a kind of finite-time convergence), but also rejects external disturbances to show good robustness. In addition, the upper bound of the fixed-time convergence is theoretically computed in mathematics, which is independent of initial states of the R-FTZNN model. At last, computer simulations are conducted under external disturbances, and comparative results demonstrate the effectiveness, robustness, and advantages of the R-FTZNN model for solving TVNE.

In a word, this book studies and summarizes the finite-time convergence of the ZNN from different aspects, with the characters guaranteed by the theoretical analysis and simulative experiments. This book is written for researchers who are developing in the fields of neural networks, neurodynamics, numerical computation, control, simulation and modeling, and time-variant dynamic systems. It provides a full-scale perspective for the previous researches of this field. We expect that readers can learn abundant knowledge about this direction with curiosity and pleasure from this book, and spur novel consideration to further study. At the end of the preface, it is worth pointing out that, in this book, some important figure ranges are presented in various forms so as to make them easier for reading and identifying. Any comments or suggestions are welcome. The authors can be contacted via e-mail: xiaolin860728@163.com and ljia@smail.hunnu.edu.cn.

Hunan Normal University, Changsha, Hunan   *L. Xiao and L. Jia*

Acknowledgments

This book basically comprises the results of many original research papers of the authors' research group, in which many authors of these original papers have done a great deal of detailed and creative research work. Therefore, we are much obliged to our contributing authors for their high-quality work and the continuous support of our research by the National Natural Science Foundation of China (under grants 61866013 and 61503152), and the Natural Science Foundation of Hunan Province of China (under grants 2021JJ20005, 2019JJ50478, 2016JJ2101, 18A289, 15B192, 2018TP1018, and 2018RS3065). Besides, we are very grateful to the editors for their time and effort in dealing with this book and for their constructive comments on it. Also, we sincerely thank the people in Wiley and IEEE for their strong support during the preparation of this book. Finally, we would like to say thanks again deeply to the editors and supporters for their contributions to this book.

L. Xiao and L. Jia

Part I

Application to Matrix Square Root

1

FTZNN for Time-varying Matrix Square Root

1.1 Introduction

In the past several decades, there are many techniques in the literature for the computation of the matrix square root because of its usefulness as a tool in computers [1–4]. In order to solve the matrix square root problem, most of the approaches are based on the following definition in mathematics [3–5]:

$$U^2 - B = 0, \tag{1.1}$$

where coefficient $B \in \mathbb{R}^{n \times n}$ is a known matrix. If $B \in \mathbb{R}^{n \times n}$ has no non-positive real eigenvalues, then there is a unique solution, which is denoted by $B^{1/2}$ and called the principal square root of B [1]. In general, there are two classes of methods for solving the matrix square root problem: One is the direct method in which a Schur decomposition of the matrix B is first computed, then a square root of the triangular factor is done and is finally recovered [1]. The other is based on the iterative algorithms performed in a serial manner, such as Newton iteration and its variants [3], Meini iteration [4], and Denman and Beavers iteration [5]. However, because of the serial nature of the digital computer [6], these numerical algorithms may encounter serious speed bottleneck, and may not be efficient enough for large-scale online applications and its time-varying case.

In this chapter, a new design formula is skillfully proposed to accelerate the convergence speed of the original zeroing neural network (OZNN) model. Based on this new design formula, a finite-time zeroing neural network (FTZNN) model, as a hardware implementable approach, is proposed and investigated for time-varying matrix square root finding. Furthermore, theoretical analyses and simulative experiments of the FTZNN model are carried out to show the effectiveness and superiority of the proposed method.

Zeroing Neural Networks: Finite-time Convergence Design, Analysis and Applications,
First Edition. Lin Xiao and Lei Jia.
© 2023 The Institute of Electrical and Electronics Engineers, Inc. Published 2023 by John Wiley & Sons, Inc.

1.2 Problem Formulation and ZNN Model

Let us consider the more general time-varying matrix square root equation expressed in the following form in mathematics [7, 8]:

$$U^2(t) = B(t), \tag{1.2}$$

where t denotes time, $U(t) \in \mathbb{R}^{n \times n}$ denotes an unknown time-varying matrix to be obtained, and $B(t) \in \mathbb{R}^{n \times n}$ denotes a known time-varying coefficient matrix. Throughout this chapter, we assume that $B(t)$ at each time has no non-positive real eigenvalues so that (1.2) has an unique time-varying principal matrix square root. Without loss of generality, let $U^*(t) \in \mathbb{R}^{n \times n}$ denote the theoretical matrix square root of (1.2). For comparative purposes, the design process of the OZNN model for time-varying matrix square root is presented simply as follows [7–10].

To solve time-varying matrix square root, the following matrix-valued error function is firstly defined:

$$Y(t) = U^2(t) - B(t) \in \mathbb{R}^{n \times n}. \tag{1.3}$$

Then, the following design formula for $Y(t)$ is adopted:

$$\dot{Y}(t) = -\gamma \Phi(Y(t)), \tag{1.4}$$

where design parameter $\gamma > 0$ and activation function array $\Phi(\cdot) : \mathbb{R}^{n \times n} \to \mathbb{R}^{n \times n}$ is a matrix-valued mapping.

After that, expanding the aforementioned design formula (1.4), we can obtain the OZNN model for time-varying matrix square root finding:

$$U(t)\dot{U}(t) + \dot{U}(t)U(t) = -\gamma \Phi\left(U^2(t) - B(t)\right) + \dot{B}(t), \tag{1.5}$$

where $U(t)$, starting from initial state $U(0) \in \mathbb{R}^{n \times n}$, is the state matrix corresponding to the time-varying theoretical matrix square root $U^*(t)$. In addition, for the OZNN model (1.5), we have the following lemma to guarantee its exponential convergence when applied to time-varying matrix square root finding [7, 8].

Lemma 1.1 *Consider time-varying matrix square root Eq. (1.2), where $B(t)$ is assumed to have a unique time-varying principal matrix square root. If a monotone increasing odd function array $\Phi(\cdot)$ is used, state matrix $U(t)$ of the OZNN model (1.5), starting from a randomly generated initial state $U(0) \in \mathbb{R}^{n \times n}$, can exponentially converge to the time-varying theoretical square root $U^*(t)$ of (1.2).*

1.3 FTZNN Model

In Section 1.2, the OZNN model (1.5) has been presented for finding time-varying matrix square root and the lemma shows that it can converge ideally when time goes to infinity. However, due to in-depth research on the OZNN model (1.5), we find that its convergence speed can be further accelerated and even achieve finite time. Therefore, to improve the convergence speed of the OZNN model (1.5), a new design formula is proposed and analyzed first in this section. Then, based on this new design formula, the FTZNN model is proposed for solving time-varying matrix square root Eq. (1.2).

1.3.1 Model Design

First, as the same as the OZNN model (1.5), a matrix-valued error function $Y(t)$ is defined as follows:

$$Y(t) = U^2(t) - B(t) \in \mathbb{R}^{n \times n}.$$

Then, different from the OZNN model (1.5), a new design formula for $Y(t)$ is proposed as follows:

$$\frac{dY(t)}{dt} = -\gamma \Phi(\kappa_1 Y(t) + \kappa_2 Y^{q/p}(t)), \tag{1.6}$$

where $\Phi(\cdot)$ and γ are defined as before; design parameters $\kappa_1 > 0$; $\kappa_2 > 0$; p and q denote positive odd integer and satisfy $p > q$. For such a new design formula, we have the following theorem to show its superiority to the conventional design formula used in the OZNN model (1.5). Note that activation function array $\Phi(\cdot)$ is not the focus of this work, so we limit the discussion to the situation where linear activation function array is used for the purposes of simplicity and clarity.

Theorem 1.2 *Considering the new design formula (1.6) for $Y(t)$, if the linear activation function array is used, starting from a randomly generated initial error $Y(0)$, error function $Y(t)$ converges to zero in finite-time t_f:*

$$t_f = \frac{p}{\beta_1(p - q)} \ln \frac{\beta_1 Y(0)^{(p-q)/p} + \beta_2}{\beta_2},$$

where $\beta_1 = \gamma \kappa_1 > 0$, $\beta_2 = \gamma \kappa_2 > 0$, and $Y(0)$ stands for a randomly generated initial error matrix.

Proof: If the linear activation function array is used, the new design formula (1.6) is reduced to

$$\begin{aligned} \frac{dY(t)}{dt} &= -\gamma(\kappa_1 Y(t) + \kappa_2 Y^{q/p}(t)) \\ &= -(\beta_1 Y(t) + \beta_2 Y^{q/p}(t)), \end{aligned} \tag{1.7}$$

where $\beta_1 = \gamma \kappa_1 > 0$ and $\beta_2 = \gamma \kappa_2 > 0$. In order to solve design formula (1.7), the aforementioned differential equation can be equivalently expressed as follows:

$$Y^{-q/p}(t) \diamond \frac{dY(t)}{dt} + \beta_1 Y^{(p-q)/p}(t) = -\beta_2, \tag{1.8}$$

where the matrix-multiplication operator $\diamond$ denotes Hadamard product and is defined as

$$
G \diamond H = \begin{bmatrix} G_{11}H_{11}, & G_{12}H_{12}, & \cdots, & G_{1n}H_{1n} \\ G_{21}H_{21}, & G_{21}H_{21}, & \cdots, & G_{2n}H_{2n} \\ \vdots & \vdots & \ddots & \vdots \\ G_{m1}H_{m1}, & G_{m2}H_{m2}, & \cdots, & G_{mn}H_{mn} \end{bmatrix} \in \mathbb{R}^{m \times n}.
$$

Therefore, solving the dynamic response of design formula (1.7) is equivalent to solving the differential Eq. (1.8). Now, let us define $Z(t) = Y^{(p-q)/p}(t)$, and we have

$$
\frac{dZ(t)}{dt} = \frac{p-q}{p} Y^{-q/p}(t) \diamond \frac{dY(t)}{dt}.
$$

Thus, the differential Eq. (1.8) can be equivalent to the following first order differential equation:

$$
\frac{dZ(t)}{dt} + \frac{p-q}{p} \beta_1 Z(t) = -\frac{p-q}{p} \beta_2. \tag{1.9}
$$

It follows from the first order differential theory that the dynamic response of the resultant differential Eq. (1.9) can be derived as follows:

$$
Z(t) = \left(\frac{\beta_2}{\beta_1} + Z(0) \right) \exp\left(-\frac{p-q}{p} \beta_1 t \right) - \frac{\beta_2}{\beta_1}. \tag{1.10}
$$

Obviously, in this situation, $Z(t)$ can converge to zero in finite time t_f, i.e. $Z(t_f) = 0$. Then, we have

$$
\left(\frac{\beta_2}{\beta_1} + Z(0) \right) \exp\left(-\frac{p-q}{p} \beta_1 t_f \right) = \frac{\beta_2}{\beta_1}. \tag{1.11}
$$

Thus, starting from a randomly generated initial error matrix $Y(0)$, the new design formula (1.6) using the linear activation function array only needs the finite time t_f to converge to the equilibrium state (i.e. $Y(t_f) = 0$):

$$
t_f = \frac{p}{\beta_1(p-q)} \ln \frac{\beta_1 Y(0)^{(p-q)/p} + \beta_2}{\beta_2},
$$

which is an important progress, as compared with the infinite-time convergence. The proof is thus completed. ∎

Next, we continue to focus on the new design formula (1.6) for $Y(t)$. Expanding it leads to the following FTZNN model for solving time-varying matrix square root Eq. (1.2):

$$
\begin{aligned}
U(t)\dot{U}(t) + \dot{U}(t)U(t) \\
= -\gamma\Phi\left(\kappa_1 \left(U^2(t) - B(t) \right) + \kappa_2 \left(U^2(t) - B(t) \right)^{q/p} \right) + \dot{B}(t),
\end{aligned} \tag{1.12}
$$

where design parameters $\kappa_1 > 0, \kappa_2 > 0, p, q\, \gamma > 0$, and $\Phi(\cdot)$ are defined as before. Especially, if the linear activation function array is used, the FTZNN model is reduced to the linearly activated one:

$$U(t)\dot{U}(t) + \dot{U}(t)U(t) = \dot{B}(t) - \beta_1\left(U^2(t) - B(t)\right) - \beta_2\left(U^2(t) - B(t)\right)^{q/p},$$
(1.13)

where design parameters $\beta_1 = \gamma\kappa_1 > 0$ and $\beta_2 = \gamma\kappa_2 > 0$.

1.3.2 Theoretical Analysis

As mentioned earlier, activation function array $\Phi(\cdot)$ is not the focus of this work. Therefore, in this subsection, the linearly activated FTZNN model (1.13) is mainly discussed, and its finite-time convergence performance is presented through the following theorem.

Theorem 1.3 *Consider time-varying matrix square root Eq. (1.2), where $B(t)$ is assumed to have an unique time-varying principal matrix square root. Starting from a randomly generated initial state $U(0) \in \mathbb{R}^{n\times n}$, state matrix $U(t)$ of FTZNN model (1.13) converges to the theoretical time-varying matrix square root $U^*(t)$ of (1.2) in finite time t_f:*

$$t_f \leqslant \max\left\{\frac{p}{\beta_1(p-q)}\ln\frac{\beta_1 y^+(0)^{(p-q)/p} + \beta_2}{\beta_2}, \frac{p}{\beta_1(p-q)}\ln\frac{\beta_1 y^-(0)^{(p-q)/p} + \beta_2}{\beta_2}\right\},$$

where $y^+(0)$ and $y^-(0)$ are the largest and the smallest elements in the initial error matrix $Y(0)$, respectively.

Proof: Let us focus on the new design formula (1.7) once again:

$$\frac{dY(t)}{dt} = -\beta_1 Y(t) - \beta_2 Y^{q/p}(t).$$

Entry-wisely, we have

$$\dot{y}_{ij}(t) = -\beta_1 y_{ij}(t) - \beta_2 y_{ij}^{q/p}(t),$$
(1.14)

where $y_{ij}(t)$ denotes the ijth element of $Y(t)$ with $i, j = 1, 2, 3, \ldots, n$.

For such a scared-valued first order differential Eq. (1.14), let us define $y^+(t)$ to be the element in $Y(t)$ with the largest initial value $y^+(0) = \max\{y_{ij}(0)\}$ for all possible i and j; and define $y^-(t)$ to be the element in $Y(t)$ with the smallest initial value $y^-(0) = \min\{y_{ij}(0)\}$ for all possible i and j. Note that every $y_{ij}(t)$ in $Y(t)$ has the identical dynamics (1.14). Then, according to the comparison lemma, we have

$$y^-(t) \leqslant y_{ij}(t) \leqslant y^+(t),$$

for all possible i and j and all $t > 0$. This demonstrates that $y_{ij}(t)$ converges to zero for all possible i and j when both $y^+(t)$ and $y^-(t)$ decrease to zero. In other words, the convergence time of FTZNN model (1.13) is bounded by the larger one between the dynamics of $y^+(t)$ and $y^-(t)$, i.e. $t_f \leqslant \max\{t_f^+, t_f^-\}$, where t_f^+ and t_f^- represent the convergence time of the dynamics of $y^+(t)$ and $y^-(t)$, respectively.

To compute t_f, we have to estimate t_f^+ and t_f^- first. For t_f^+, according to the analysis of Theorem 1.2, there exists t_f satisfying

$$t_f \leqslant \frac{p}{\beta_1(p-q)} \ln \frac{\beta_1 y^+(0)^{(p-q)/p} + \beta_2}{\beta_2}$$

such that $y^+(t_f) = 0$ when $t > t_f$. In the same way, for t_f^-, there exists t_f satisfying

$$t_f \leqslant \frac{p}{\beta_1(p-q)} \ln \frac{\beta_1 y^-(0)^{(p-q)/p} + \beta_2}{\beta_2}$$

such that $y^-(t_f) = 0$ when $t > t_f$.

Therefore, the upper bound of the finite convergence time for FTZNN model (1.13) is derived as

$$t_f \leqslant \max \left\{ \frac{p}{\beta_1(p-q)} \ln \frac{\beta_1 y^+(0)^{(p-q)/p} + \beta_2}{\beta_2}, \frac{p}{\beta_1(p-q)} \ln \frac{\beta_1 y^-(0)^{(p-q)/p} + \beta_2}{\beta_2} \right\},$$

which shows that state matrix $U(t)$ of FTZNN model (1.13), starting from a randomly generated initial state $U(0)$, converges to time-varying theoretical matrix square root of (1.2) after a period finite time t_f. The proof is thus completed. ∎

1.4 Illustrative Verification

In the previous Sections 1.2 and 1.3, the OZNN (1.5) and FTZNN models (1.13) have been presented for finding time-varying matrix square root of Eq. (1.2). In this section, computer-simulation comparative results are presented for substantiating the superiority of FTZNN model (1.13) to the OZNN model (1.5).

Without loss of generality, the following example is considered to be solved (which is the same as the Example 1 of [8]) with design parameters $\gamma = 1$, $p = 5$ and $q = 1$:

$$B(t) = \begin{bmatrix} 3\sin(2t)\cos(2t) + 36 & 21\sin(2t) \\ 28\cos(2t) & 3\sin(2t)\cos(2t) + 64 \end{bmatrix}. \tag{1.15}$$

From [8], we can obtain the time-varying theoretical matrix square root of $U(t)$ in this situation as follows:

$$U^*(t) = \begin{bmatrix} 6 & 1.5\sin(2t) \\ 2\cos(2t) & 8 \end{bmatrix},$$

which can be used to verify the solution correctness of such two neural-network models.

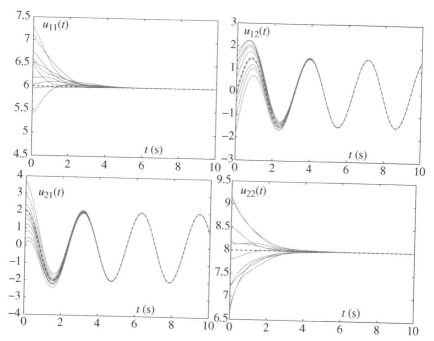

Figure 1.1 Transient behavior of $U(t)$ synthesized by the OZNN model (1.5) starting with 10 randomly generated initial states, where solid curves correspond to neural state $U(t)$, and dash curves correspond to theoretical matrix square root $U^*(t)$.

First, starting from 10 randomly-generated initial state $U(0) \in \mathbb{R}^{2\times2}$, we adopt the OZNN model (1.5) to compute the aforementioned time-varying matrix square root. The transient behavior of the neural-state solutions is shown in Figure 1.1, where solid curves correspond to the neural-state solution elements of $U(t)$, and dash curves correspond to the theoretical time-varying solution elements of $U^*(t)$. From this figure, we can observe that the neural-state solutions can exponentially converge to the theoretical time-varying matrix square root with time. Under the same conditions, FTZNN model (1.13) is applied to compute the same problem. From Figure 1.2, we can see that the neural-state solutions of FTZNN model (1.13) can fit with the theoretical time-varying matrix square root well only after a little finite time.

To more directly show the solution process of the OZNN model (1.5) and FTZNN model (1.13), the evolution of the corresponding residual errors, measured by the Frobenius norm $\|U^2(t) - B(t)\|_F$, is plotted in Figure 1.3. From Figure 1.3a, it can be seen that the residual errors $\|U^2(t) - B(t)\|_F$ of the OZNN model (1.5) can approximate to zero after about six seconds. From Figure 1.3b, we can obtain that the residual errors $\|U^2(t) - B(t)\|_F$ of FTZNN model (1.13) can

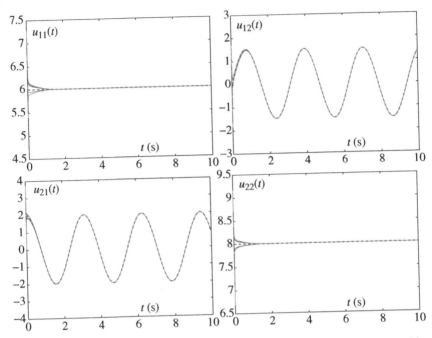

Figure 1.2 Transient behavior of $U(t)$ synthesized by FTZNN model (1.13) starting with 10 randomly generated initial states, where solid curves correspond to neural state $U(t)$, and dash curves correspond to theoretical time-varying matrix square root $U^*(t)$.

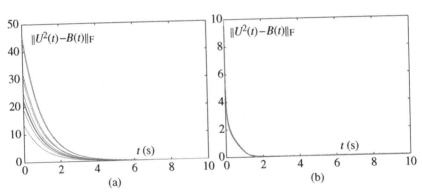

Figure 1.3 Transient behavior of the residual error $\|U^2(t) - B(t)\|_F$ corresponding to $U(t)$ synthesized by the OZNN model (1.5) and FTZNN model (1.13). (a) By the OZNN model (1.5) and (b) by FTZNN model (1.13).

directly decrease to zero within finite time two seconds. The convergence speed of FTZNN model (1.13) is more than three times as fast as the OZNN model (1.5). In summary, from the aforementioned comparison results, we can draw a conclusion that FTZNN model (1.13) is much better than the OZNN model (1.5) for finding online time-varying matrix square root.

1.5 Chapter Summary

A FTZNN model has been proposed and investigated for finding online time-varying matrix square root in this chapter. Different from the conventional acceleration method, the construction of the proposed FTZNN model is based on a new design formula, which plays an accelerated role for computation of the time-varying matrix square root. Besides, the upper bound of finite convergence time for the FTZNN model has been derived theoretically. Computer simulations are performed to evaluate and compare the performance of the OZNN model and the FTZNN model. The results show that the FTZNN model is a more effective solution model for finding time-varying matrix square root.

References

1 N. J. Higham, Stable iterations for the matrix square root, *Numer. Algor.*, 15 (1997) 227–242.

2 C. R. Johnson, K. Okubo, and R. Reams, Uniqueness of matrix square roots and an application, *Linear Algebra Appl.*, 323(1–3) (2001) 51–60.

3 Y. Shitov, A note on square roots of nonnegative matrices, *Linear Algebra Appl.*, 497 (2016) 62–65.

4 R. Brunnock, M. C. Lettington, and K. M. Schmidt, On square roots and norms of matrices with symmetry properties, *Linear Algebra Appl.*, 459 (2014) 175–207.

5 J. Long, X. Hu, and L. Zhang, Newton's method with exact line search for the square root of a matrix, *J. Phys.: Conf. Ser.*, 96 (2008) 012034.

6 J. H. Mathews and K. D. Fink, *Numerical methods using MATLAB*, Upper Saddle River, NJ: Pearson Prentice Hall, 2004.

7 Y. Zhang and W. Li *et al.*, Different Zhang functions leading to different ZNN models illustrated via time-varying matrix square roots finding, *Expert Syst. Appl.*, 40(11) (2013) 4393–4403.

8 Y. Zhang and Y. Yang *et al.*, Zhang neural network and its application to Newton iteration for matrix square root estimation, *Neural Comput. Appl.*, 21 (2012) 453–460.

9 Y. Zhang and L. Xiao *et al.*, *Zeroing dynamics, gradient dynamics, and Newton iterations*, CRC Press, 2018.

10 Y. Zhang, Y. Yang, and N. Tan, Time-varying matrix square roots solving via Zhang neural network and gradient neural network: Modeling, verification and comparison, Proceedings of 6th International Symposium on Neural Networks, (2009) 11–20.

2

FTZNN for Static Matrix Square Root

2.1 Introduction

The solving problem of matrix square root has been the subject of much research in recent years and widely applied in various scientific and engineering areas [1–4]. Much effort has been directed towards the matrix square root finding [4–9] because of its usefulness as a tool in computers. In mathematics, in order to solve the matrix square root problem, almost all algorithms/schemes are based on the following defining equation [1–9]:

$$U^2(t) - A = 0, \tag{2.1}$$

where coefficient matrix $A \in \mathbb{R}^{n \times n}$ is assumed to be known (or at least measurable accurately). If $A \in \mathbb{R}^{n \times n}$ has no non-positive real eigenvalues, then there is a unique solution $U(t)$, which is denoted by $A^{1/2}$ and called the principal square root of A [1–4]. For presentation convenience, let $U^*(t)$ denote the theoretical principal square root of matrix A, which corresponds to the actual $U(t)$ solved by various methods. In this chapter we assume that A has no non-positive real eigenvalues and we are interested in the computation of the principal square root.

Recently, based on the study of the finite-time convergence for continuous autonomous system [10–13], it is found that the sign-power function (generally expressed in the form of $\mathrm{sgn}^{q/p}$) can make the ordinary differential equation (ODE) converge to the equilibrium state within finite time. In view of this point, a finite-time zeroing neural network (FTZNN) model is proposed and studied for matrix square root finding in this chapter by adding a nonlinearly activated sign-bi-power function. Compared with the original zeroing neural network (OZNN) model, the FTZNN model possesses faster convergence ability. More importantly, the upper bound of convergence time for the FTZNN model is theoretically derived and estimated by solving differential inequalities. Now, in order to better show the novelties and differences of the FTZNN model, we would like to compare the FTZNN model with the gradient neural network (GNN)

Zeroing Neural Networks: Finite-time Convergence Design, Analysis and Applications,
First Edition. Lin Xiao and Lei Jia.
© 2023 The Institute of Electrical and Electronics Engineers, Inc. Published 2023 by John Wiley & Sons, Inc.

Table 2.1 The main novelties and differences of the FTZNN model from the GNN model and the OZNN model for matrix square root finding.

#	Item	GNN model	OZNN model	FTZNN model
1	Solution problems	Static	Time-varying	Time-varying
2	Theoretical errors	Yes	Yes	No
3	Activation functions	No	Yes	Yes
4	Dynamics forms	Explicitly	Implicitly	Implicitly
5	Convergence	Asymptotically	Exponentially	Finitely

model and the OZNN model through summarizing the related papers (i.e. [7–9]). The corresponding comparative results are shown in Table 2.1.

2.2 Solution Models

To lay a basis for further discussion, in this section, the OZNN model is first presented. Then, a specially constructed nonlinear activation function (called the sign-bi-power activation function) is presented to accelerate the OZNN model to converge in finite time. Thus, a FTZNN model is proposed for finding matrix square root of Eq. (2.1). In addition, the upper bound of the convergence time is derived analytically.

2.2.1 OZNN Model

For the purpose of finding matrix square root of Eq. (2.1), a matrix-valued error function (instead of a norm-based energy function usually associated with GNN [14]) is constructed by following Zhang *et al.*'s neural-network design method [5, 7–9]. That is,

$$Y(t) = U^2(t) - A \in \mathbb{R}^{n \times n}.$$

After that, the ZNN design formula [7–9] is adopted such that every element $y_{ij} \in \mathbb{R}$ of $Y(t)$ converges to zero, with $i, j = 1, 2, \ldots, n$. For readers' convenience, the ZNN design formula is presented and repeated as follows:

$$\dot{Y}(t) = -\gamma \Phi(Y(t)), \tag{2.2}$$

where design parameter $\gamma > 0$ is used to scale the convergence speed of the neural-network structure, and activation function array $\Phi(\cdot) : \mathbb{R}^{n \times n} \to \mathbb{R}^{n \times n}$ is a matrix-valued mapping with each processing element denoted by $\phi(\cdot) : \mathbb{R} \to \mathbb{R}$.

Then, expanding ZNN design formula (2.2), we can obtain the following ODE of the ZNN model (termed the original ZNN, OZNN):

$$U(t)\dot{U}(t) + \dot{U}(t)U(t) = -\gamma\Phi\left(U^2(t) - A\right),\tag{2.3}$$

where $U(t)$, starting from initial state matrix $U(0) \in \mathbb{R}^{n\times n}$, denotes the state matrix corresponding to the theoretical matrix square root $U^*(t)$ of Eq. (2.1).

2.2.2 FTZNN Model

After deep investigation and analysis of the OZNN, the convergence rate of the OZNN model can be remarkably increased by designing an effective activation function [15, 16]. Besides, by taking advantage of the nonlinearity, a properly designed nonlinear activation function often outperforms the linear one in convergence rate. For example, the following three types of nonlinear activation functions $\phi(\cdot)$ have been used and investigated in the previous work [5, 7–9, 15–17]:

(1) Bipolar-sigmoid activation function

$$\phi(x) = (1 - \exp(-\xi x))/(1 + \exp(-\xi x)), \quad \text{with } \xi \geqslant 2;$$

(2) Power-sigmoid activation function

$$\phi(x) = \begin{cases} x^m, & \text{if } |x| \geqslant 1, \\ \frac{1+\exp(-\xi)}{1-\exp(-\xi)} \cdot \frac{1-\exp(-\xi x)}{1+\exp(-\xi x)}, & \text{if } |x| < 1 \end{cases}$$

with design parameter $\xi \geqslant 2$ and odd integer $m \geqslant 3$.

(3) Power-sum activation function

$$\phi(x) = \sum_{k=1}^{m} x^{2k-1}, \quad \text{with integer parameter } m > 1.$$

It is worth pointing out that OZNN model (2.3) with the previously suggested activation functions can converge to the theoretical solution of matrix square root problem exponentially with time, but cannot converge within finite time, which may limit its large-scale applications in real-time computation. Therefore, in this section, we focus on developing a specially constructed nonlinear activation function, which can endow OZNN model (2.3) with a finite-time convergence for solving matrix square root problem.

Inspired by the study on finite-time control of autonomous systems and finite-time convergence of RNNs [10–13], we can present a sign-bi-power activation function to accelerate OZNN model (2.3) to finite-time convergence to theoretical matrix square root of Eq. (2.1). Specifically, the sign-bi-power activation function is consist of two different sign-power functions and defined as follows:

$$\phi(x) = \text{sgn}^m(x) + \text{sgn}^{1/m}(x),\tag{2.4}$$

where design parameter $m \in (0,1)$ and the power-sign function $\text{sgn}^m(\cdot)$ is defined as

$$\text{sgn}^m(x) = \begin{cases} |x|^m, & \text{if } x > 0, \\ 0, & \text{if } x = 0, \\ -|x|^m, & \text{if } x < 0. \end{cases}$$

Therefore, by adding the sign-bi-power activation function matrix array, the FTZNN for finding matrix square root of Eq. (2.1) is proposed as follows:

$$U(t)\dot{U}(t) + \dot{U}(t)U(t) = -\gamma \left(\text{SGN}^m \left(U^2(t) - A \right) + \text{SGN}^{1/m} \left(U^2(t) - A \right) \right), \tag{2.5}$$

where $\text{SGN}^m(\cdot)$ denotes the matrix mapping array of the power-sign function $\text{sgn}^m(\cdot)$. After giving out FTZNN model (2.5), the following theoretical result is presented to guarantee the finite-time convergence of FTZNN model (2.5).

Theorem 2.1 *Given nonsingular coefficient matrix $A \in \mathbb{R}^{n \times n}$ in (2.1), if the sign-bi-power activation function matrix array is used, then state matrix $U(t)$ of FTZNN model (2.5), starting from any randomly generated initial state $U(0) \in \mathbb{R}^{n \times n}$, converges to the theoretical matrix square root of Eq. (2.1) within finite time*

$$t_f < \max \left\{ \frac{|y^-(0)|^{1-m}}{\gamma(1-m)}, \frac{|y^+(0)|^{1-m}}{\gamma(1-m)} \right\},$$

where $y^+(0)$ and $y^-(0)$ denote the largest and the smallest initial error elements of the initial error function matrix $Y(0)$, respectively.

Proof: As a matter of convenience, $y^+(t)$ is used to denote the element of error function $Y(t)$ with the largest initial value $y^+(0) = \max\{Y(0)\}$, and $y^-(t)$ is used to denote the element of error function $Y(t)$ with the smallest initial value $y^-(0) = \min\{Y(0)\}$. In other words, $y^+(0) \geqslant y_{ij}(0)$ for all possible $i, j \in \{1, 2, \ldots, n\}$, and $y^-(0) \leqslant y_{ij}(0)$ for all possible $i, j \in \{1, 2, \ldots, n\}$. Besides, since all elements of error function $Y(t)$ have identical dynamical system $\dot{y}_{ij} = -\gamma \left(\text{sgn}^m(y_{ij}) + \text{sgn}^{1/m}(y_{ij}) \right)$, we can obtain $y^+(t) \geqslant y_{ij}(t)$ with $t \geqslant 0$ for all possible i and j. By the same token, we can obtain $y^-(t) \leqslant y_{ij}(t)$ with $t \geqslant 0$ for all possible i and j. Thus, it follows that $y^-(t) \leqslant y_{ij}(t) \leqslant y^+(t)$ for all possible i and j as time t goes on. This means that $y_{ij}(t)$ can converge to zero for all possible i and j when both $y^+(t)$ and $y^-(t)$ decrease to zero. That is, the convergence time of FTZNN model (2.5) is bounded by the larger one between the dynamics of $y^+(t)$ and $y^-(t)$, i.e. $t_f \leqslant \max\{t_f^+, t_f^-\}$ where t_f^+ and t_f^- denote the convergence time of the dynamics of $y^+(t)$ and $y^-(t)$, respectively.

In order to compute t_f, we must estimate t_f^+ and t_f^- firstly. For t_f^+, we have

$$\dot{y}^+(t) = -\gamma \left(\text{sgn}^m(y^+(t)) + \text{sgn}^{1/m}(y^+(t)) \right) \text{ with } y^+(0) = \max\{Y(0)\}. \tag{2.6}$$

Then, Lyapunov's direct method can be used to analyze the convergence performance of the aforementioned dynamical system (2.6). Thus, we can define firstly a Lyapunov function candidate $p(t) = |y^+(t)|^2$ with regard to the aforementioned dynamical system (2.6). Then, the time-derivative of $p(t)$ can be derived as follows:

$$\dot{p}(t) = 2y^+(t)\dot{y}^+(t)$$

$$= -2\gamma y^+(t)\left(\text{sgn}^m(y^+(t)) + \text{sgn}^{1/m}(y^+(t))\right)$$

$$= -2\gamma\left(|y^+(t)|^{m+1} + |y^+(t)|^{\frac{1}{m}+1}\right)$$

$$\leqslant -2\gamma|y^+(t)|^{m+1}$$

$$= -2\gamma p^{\frac{m+1}{2}}(t).$$

Therefore, according to the theory of differential inequality, the aforementioned differential inequality $\dot{p}(t) \leqslant -2\gamma p^{\frac{m+1}{2}}(t)$ with the initial value $p(0) = |y^+(0)|^2$ can be solved as follows:

$$p^{\frac{1-m}{2}}(t)\begin{cases} \leqslant |y^+(0)|^{1-m} - \gamma t(1-m), & \text{if } t \leqslant |y^+(0)|^{1-m}/\gamma(1-m), \\ = 0, & \text{if } t > |y^+(0)|^{1-m}/\gamma(1-m), \end{cases}$$

which means $p(t)$ can decrease directly to zero after a time period $|y^+(0)|^{1-m}/\gamma(1-m)$. Therefore, $y^+(t) = 0$ for $t > |y^+(0)|^{1-m}/\gamma(1-m)$, i.e. $t_f^+ < |y^+(0)|^{1-m}/\gamma(1-m)$. In the same way, we can conclude that $y^-(t) = 0$ for $t > |y^-(0)|^{1-m}/\gamma(1-m)$. That is to say, $t_f^- < |y^-(0)|^{1-m}/\gamma(1-m)$. In summary, we have

$$t_f < \max\left\{\frac{|y^-(0)|^{1-m}}{\gamma(1-m)}, \frac{|y^+(0)|^{1-m}}{\gamma(1-m)}\right\},$$

which means that, if the sign-bi-power activation function matrix array is used, state matrix $U(t)$ of FTZNN model (2.5), starting from any randomly generated initial state $U(0)$, converges directly to the theoretical matrix square root of Eq. (2.1) within finite time t_f. The proof is completed. ∎

2.3 Illustrative Verification

In the aforementioned section, both OZNN model (2.3) and FTZNN model (2.5) have been presented for finding the matrix square root of Eq. (2.1). Besides, the finite-time convergence of FTZNN model (2.5) has been proved by using Lyapunov method and the theory of differential inequality. In this section, OZNN model (2.3) and FTZNN model (2.5) are applied to online solution of matrix square root problem under the same conditions, and the corresponding simulative comparison would be provided for substantiating the efficacy of such two ZNN models, as well as the superior of FTZNN model (2.5) to OZNN model (2.3). Without loss of generality, we set design parameters $\gamma = 1$ and $r = 0.25$.

2.3.1 Example 1

Let us consider a simple matrix square root problem with the positive-definite matrix $A \in \mathbb{R}^{2 \times 2}$ being:

$$A = \begin{bmatrix} 7 & -2 \\ -3 & 10 \end{bmatrix}.$$

In order to check the correctness of the neural-network solution, the theoretical principal square root $U^*(t)$ of the aforementioned positive-definite matrix is presented as follows for comparative purposes:

$$U^* = \begin{bmatrix} 2.6112 & -0.3482 \\ -0.5222 & 3.1334 \end{bmatrix}.$$

Starting from a randomly generated initial state $U(0) \in \mathbb{R}^{2 \times 2}$ close to $U^*(t)$, we apply such two neural-network models to online solution of the aforementioned matrix square root problem. In addition, for OZNN model (2.3), linear and power-sigmoid activation functions are used for comparison purposes. The corresponding simulation comparative results are displayed in Figures 2.1–2.3. Specifically, from Figure 2.1a, we can see that the neural-state matrix $U(t) \in \mathbb{R}^{2 \times 2}$ synthesized by linearly activated OZNN model (2.3) can converge the principal square root $U^*(t)$ of the aforementioned matrix exponentially. In addition, It takes the linearly activated OZNN model about six seconds to complete this convergence process, which can be illustrated in Figure 2.1b.

For verifying the role of nonlinear activation functions played in OZNN model (2.3), the power-sigmoid activated OZNN model is synthesized under the same conditions. Figure 2.2 shows the transient behavior of state matrix $U(t)$ and

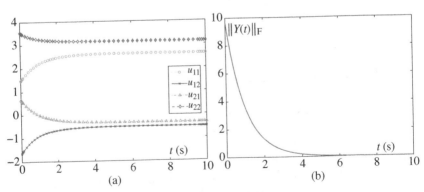

Figure 2.1 Simulative results of OZNN model (2.3) using linear activation functions under the condition of $\gamma = 1$ and a randomly generated $U(0) \in \mathbb{R}^{2 \times 2}$ close to $U^*(t)$. (a) Transient behavior of state matrix $U(t)$ and (b) transient behavior of residual error $\|Y(t)\|_F$.

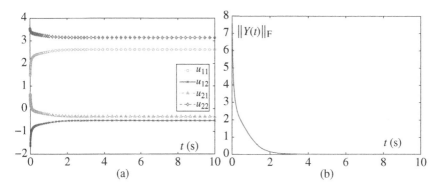

Figure 2.2 Simulative results of OZNN model (2.3) using power-sigmoid activation functions under the condition of $\gamma = 1$ and a randomly generated $U(0) \in \mathbb{R}^{2\times2}$ close to $U^*(t)$. (a) Transient behavior of state matrix $U(t)$ and (b) transient behavior of residual error $\|Y(t)\|_F$.

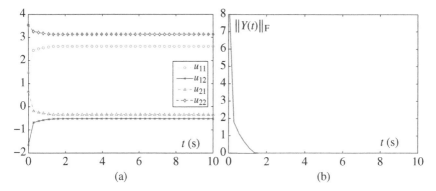

Figure 2.3 Simulative results of FTZNN model (2.5) under the condition of $\gamma = 1$, $m = 0.25$ and a randomly generated $U(0) \in \mathbb{R}^{2\times2}$ close to $U^*(t)$. (a) Transient behavior of state matrix $U(t)$ and (b) transient behavior of residual error $\|Y(t)\|_F$.

the corresponding residual error. As compared with results of Figure 2.1, we can conclude that the convergence time of the power-sigmoid activated OZNN model is shortened from six seconds to three seconds. The convergence speed is increased by two times. This means that nonlinear activation functions can accelerate the convergence speed of neural networks and play an important role in OZNN model (2.3).

Now and here, under the same conditions, we apply FTZNN model (2.5) to finding the principal square root of the aforementioned matrix and the corresponding simulative results are shown in Figure 2.3. As seen from Figure 2.3a, neural-state matrix $U(t) \in \mathbb{R}^{2\times2}$ converges directly and accurately to the principal square root after a very short finite time. In addition, Figure 2.3b shows the transient behavior of $\|Y(t)\|_F$ corresponding to neural-state matrix $U(t) \in \mathbb{R}^{2 \times 2}$. It follows from Figure 2.3b that $\|Y(t)\|_F$ decreases directly to zero within finite time 1.5 seconds. As compared with the previous results of OZNN model (2.3), the convergence speed of FTZNN model (2.5) is fastest, which verifies the superior of FTZNN model (2.5) to OZNN model (2.3) with suggested activation functions.

2.3.2 Example 2

In order to verify the superiority of FTZNN model (2.5) further, a more complex matrix square root equation is considered, of which the coefficient A is a Toeplotz matrix and has the following form:

$$A = \begin{bmatrix} a_1 & a_2 & a_3 & \cdots & a_n \\ a_2 & a_1 & a_2 & \cdots & a_{n-1} \\ a_3 & a_2 & a_1 & \cdots & a_{n-2} \\ \vdots & \vdots & \vdots & \ddots & \vdots \\ a_n & a_{n-1} & a_{n-2} & \cdots & a_1 \end{bmatrix},$$

where $a_1 = 1 + \sin(2)$ and $a_k = \cos(2)/(k-1)$ with $k = 2, 3, \dots, n$. In this example, we set $n = 6$, and only adopt FTZNN model (2.5) to solve such a complex matrix square root problem under the conditions of $\gamma = 1$ and $\gamma = 10$, of which the initial state $U(0) \in \mathbb{R}^{6 \times 6}$ is randomly generated and close to $U^*(t)$. The corresponding simulative results are shown in Figure 2.4. From this figure, we can see that, starting from a randomly generated initial state $U(0)$, the residual error $\|Y(t)\|_F$ synthesized by FTZNN model (2.5) can decrease directly within finite time. In addition, as the value of γ increases, the convergence performance of FTZNN model (2.5) can be modified remarkably.

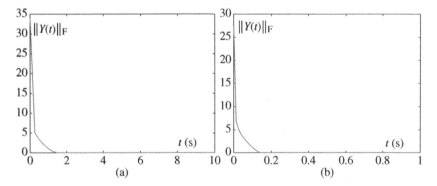

Figure 2.4 Transient behavior of residual error $\|Y(t)\|_F$ synthesized by FTZNN model (2.5) under the condition of $m = 0.25$ and a randomly generated $U(0) \in \mathbb{R}^{6 \times 6}$ close to $U^*(t)$. (a) With $\gamma = 1$ and (b) with $\gamma = 10$.

In summary, from the aforementioned comparative simulative results, either linear activation functions or nonlinear activation functions, OZNN model (2.3) is effective on finding the principal square root of Eq. (2.1). In addition, FTZNN model (2.5) possesses a superior finite-time convergence performance, as compared with OZNN model (2.3) with different activation functions.

2.4 Chapter Summary

A FTZNN model for finding the principal square root has been proposed in this chapter. Finite-time convergence performance of the FTZNN model has been proved, and the upper bound has also been estimated by solving differential inequalities. For comparative purposes, the OZNN model with different activation functions has been presented for finding the principal square root. Finally, comparative simulative results have been presented, which substantiated the theoretical analysis and effectiveness of FTZNN model (2.5) for finding the principal square root, as well as its superiority as compared with OZNN model (2.3) with suggested activation functions.

References

1 C. R. Johnson, K. Okubo, and R. Reams, Uniqueness of matrix square roots and an application, *Linear Algebra Appl.*, 323(1–3) (2001) 51–60.

2 B. Iannazzo, A note on computing the matrix square root, *Calcolo*, 40 (2003) 273–283.

3 B. Meini, The matrix square root from a new functional perspective: Theoretical results and computational issues, *SIAM J. Matrix Anal. Appl.*, 26(2) (2004) 362–376.

4 J. Long, X. Hu, and L. Zhang, Newton's method with exact line search for the square root of a matrix, *J. Phys.: Conf. Ser.*, 96 (2008) 012034.

5 Y. Zhang and D. Chen *et al.*, On exponential convergence of nonlinear gradient dynamics system with application to square root finding, *Nonlinear Dyn.*, 79 (2015) 983–1003.

6 M. A. Hasan, A. A. Hasan, and S. Rahman, Fixed point iterations for computing square roots and the matrix sign function of complex matrices, Proceedings of the 39th IEEE Conference on Decision and Control, 5 (2000) 4253–4258.

7 Y. Zhang and W. Li *et al.*, Different Zhang functions leading to different ZNN models illustrated via time-varying matrix square roots finding, *Expert Syst. Appl.*, 40(11) (2013) 4393–4403.

8 Y. Zhang and Y. Yang *et al.*, Zhang neural network and its application to Newton iteration for matrix square root estimation, *Neural Comput. Appl.*, 21 (2012) 453–460.

9 Y. Zhang and Z. Ke *et al.*, Time-varying square roots finding via Zhang dynamics versus gradient dynamics and the former's link and new explanation to Newton-Raphson iteration, *Inf. Process. Lett.*, 110(24) (2010) 1103–1109.

10 S. P. Bhat and D. S. Bernstein, Finite-time stability of continuous autonomous systems, *SIAM J. Control Optim.*, 38(3) (2000) 751–766.

11 M. Forti and M. Grazzini *et al.*, Generalized Lyapunov approach for convergence of neural networks with discontinuous or non-Lipschitz activations, *Phys. D Nonlinear Phenom.*, 214(1) (2006) 88–99.

12 W. Lu and T. Chen, Dynamical behaviors of delayed neural network systems with discontinuous activation functions, *Neural Comput.*, 18(3) (2006) 683–708.

13 M. Marco, M. Forti, and M. Grazzini, Robustness of convergence in finite time for linear programming neural networks, *Int. J. Circ. Theory Appl.*, 34(3) (2006) 307–316.

14 Y. Zhang, Revisit the analog computer and gradient-based neural system for matrix inversion, Proceedings of the 2005 IEEE International Symposium on, Mediterrean Conference on Control and Automation Intelligent Control, (2005) 1411–1416.

15 Y. Zhang and G. Ruan *et al.*, Robustness analysis of the Zhang neural network for online time-varying quadratic optimization, *J. Phys. A: Math. Theor.*, 43(24) (2010) 245202.

16 Y. Zhang and Z. Li, Zhang neural network for online solution of time-varying convex quadratic program subject to time-varying linear-equality constraints, *Phys. Lett. A*, 373(18–19) (2009) 1639–1643.

17 Y. Zhang and Z. Li *et al.*, Z-type and G-type models for time-varying inverse square root (TVISR) solving, *Soft Comput.*, 17(11) (2013) 2021–2032.

Part II

Application to Matrix Inversion

3

Design Scheme I of FTZNN

3.1 Introduction

The online inversion of a matrix arises in many scientific fields and is found in wide engineering applications, e.g. in multiple-input multiple-output (MIMO) systems [1, 2], graph estimation [3], cloud computing [4], and robot kinematics [5, 6]. Besides, as an essential step of many solutions, when we want to understand the physical mechanism of phenomena, exact solutions for the matrix inversion have to be obtained. Thus, much effort has been devoted to the fast and high accuracy solution of such a matrix inversion problem, and various methods have been presented and investigated for matrix inversion [4, 5, 7–10].

In this chapter, different from the previous processing method (i.e. choosing a better nonlinear activation to accelerate convergence speed), a new design formula is subtly proposed to accelerate the original zeroing neural network (OZNN) model and used to design a finite-time zeroing neural network (FTZNN) model for time-varying matrix inversion. In addition, theoretical analyses of the design formula and the FTZNN model are carried out to show the effectiveness and superiorness of the proposed method.

3.2 Problem Formulation and Preliminaries

The online matrix inversion is widely encountered in various engineering and scientific fields [1–5]. In mathematics, the time-varying case of matrix inversion can be defined as follows:

$$A(t)U(t) = I \in \mathbb{R}^{n \times n} \quad \text{or} \quad U(t)A(t) = I \in \mathbb{R}^{n \times n}, \tag{3.1}$$

where t stands for time, $U(t) \in \mathbb{R}^{n \times n}$ is an unknown time-varying matrix to be obtained, $A(t) \in \mathbb{R}^{n \times n}$ denotes a known time-varying coefficient matrix, and $I \in \mathbb{R}^{n \times n}$ denotes the identity matrix of an appropriate size. In this chapter,

Zeroing Neural Networks: Finite-time Convergence Design, Analysis and Applications,
First Edition. Lin Xiao and Lei Jia.
© 2023 The Institute of Electrical and Electronics Engineers, Inc. Published 2023 by John Wiley & Sons, Inc.

we limit the discussion to the situation where $A(t)$ is nonsingular at any time instant $t \in [0, +\infty)$ so that (3.1) has a unique time-varying solution. Without loss of generality, let $U^*(t) \in \mathbb{R}^{n \times n}$ denote the time-varying theoretical solution of (3.1).

For comparative purposes, the gradient-based neural network (GNN) for time-varying matrix inversion is directly presented as follows [11, 12]:

$$\dot{U}(t) = -\gamma A^{\mathrm{T}}(t)(U(t)A(t) - I),$$ (3.2)

where $A^{\mathrm{T}}(t)$ denotes the transpose of time-varying coefficient matrix $A(t)$, and design parameter $\gamma > 0$ is used to adjust the convergence rate of the GNN model (3.2). Besides, by following Zhang *et al.*'s design method, the OZNN model for time-varying matrix inversion can be given out directly as follows [13, 14]:

$$A(t)\dot{U}(t) = -\gamma \Phi(U(t)A(t) - I) - \dot{A}(t)U(t),$$ (3.3)

where $\Phi(\cdot)$ denotes an activation function array. For OZNN model (3.3), we have the following lemma to guarantee its exponential convergence when applied to time-varying matrix inversion [13, 14].

Lemma 3.1 *Consider time-varying Eq. (3.1), i.e. $A(t)U(t) = I \in \mathbb{R}^{n \times n}$, where $A(t)$ is assumed to be nonsingular. If a monotonically increasing odd function array $\Phi(\cdot)$ is used, state matrix $U(t)$ of OZNN model (3.3), starting from a randomly generated initial state $U(0) \in \mathbb{R}^{n \times n}$, can exponentially converge to the unique time-varying theoretical solution $U^*(t)$ of (3.1). In addition, by choosing different nonlinear activation functions, the convergence rate of OZNN model (3.3) can be accelerated accordingly.*

3.3 FTZNN Model

As discussed before, GNN model (3.2) has been developed to compute the inverse of time-varying matrix with considerable lagging errors. To eliminate the lagging errors and solve time-varying matrix inverse in real time, OZNN model (3.3) has been presented and has been proven to converge ideally when time goes to infinity. In addition, by choosing an elaborate activation function [15–18], the convergence rate of OZNN model (3.3) can be thoroughly accelerated. Different from the idea of improving activation functions, in this section, we aim at developing a new evolution formula and thus propose a FTZNN model for solving time-varying matrix inversion Eq. (3.1).

3.3.1 Model Design

To lay a basis for investigation on the FTZNN model, the design procedure of the FTZNN model is presented as follows.

First, as the same as OZNN model (3.3), an indefinite matrix-valued time-varying error function $Y(t)$ is defined as follows:

$$Y(t) = A(t)U(t) - I \in \mathbb{R}^{n \times n}.$$

Then, different from OZNN model (3.3), a new design formula for $Y(t)$ is proposed as follows:

$$\frac{dY(t)}{dt} = -\gamma \Phi(\kappa_1 Y(t) + \kappa_2 Y^{q/p}(t)), \tag{3.4}$$

where $\Phi(\cdot)$ and γ are defined as before; design parameters $\kappa_1 > 0$; $\kappa_2 > 0$; p and q denote positive odd integer and satisfy $p > q$. For such a new design formula, we have the following theorem to show its superiority to the conventional design formula used in OZNN model (3.3). Note that activation function $\Phi(\cdot)$ is not the focus of this research, so we limit the discussion to the situation where the linear activation function is used for the purposes of simplicity and clarity, although the extension to the nonlinear activation function array is possible.

Theorem 3.2 *Considering design formula (3.4) for $Y(t)$, if the linear activation function array is used, starting from any randomly generated initial error $Y(0)$, error function $Y(t)$ converges to zero in finite-time t_f:*

$$t_f = \frac{p}{\beta_1(p-q)} \ln \frac{\beta_1 y^+(0)^{(p-q)/p} + \beta_2}{\beta_2},$$

where $\beta_1 = \gamma \kappa_1 > 0$, $\beta_2 = \gamma \kappa_2 > 0$, and $y^+(0)$ denotes the largest element in the initial error matrix $Y(0)$.

Proof: If the linear activation function array is used, the new design formula (3.4) is reduced to

$$\begin{aligned}\frac{dY(t)}{dt} &= -\gamma(\kappa_1 Y(t) + \kappa_2 Y^{q/p}(t)) \\ &= -(\beta_1 Y(t) + \beta_2 Y^{q/p}(t)),\end{aligned} \tag{3.5}$$

where $\beta_1 = \gamma \kappa_1 > 0$ and $\beta_2 = \gamma \kappa_2 > 0$. In order to solve the dynamic response of the reduced design formula (3.5), the aforementioned differential equation can be written as follows:

$$Y^{-q/p}(t) \diamond \frac{dY(t)}{dt} + \beta_1 Y^{(p-q)/p}(t) = -\beta_2 I, \tag{3.6}$$

where the matrix-multiplication operator $\diamond$ denotes the Hadamard product and is defined as

$$Q \diamond V = \begin{bmatrix} Q_{11}V_{11} & Q_{12}V_{12} & \cdots & Q_{1n}V_{1n} \\ Q_{21}V_{21} & Q_{21}V_{21} & \cdots & Q_{2n}V_{2n} \\ \vdots & \vdots & \ddots & \vdots \\ Q_{m1}V_{m1} & Q_{m2}V_{m2} & \cdots & Q_{mn}V_{mn} \end{bmatrix} \in \mathbb{R}^{m \times n}.$$

Thus, solving the dynamic response of the reduced design formula (3.5) is equivalent to solving the differential Eq. (3.6). Let us define $Z(t) = Y^{(p-q)/p}(t)$. Then, we have

$$\frac{dZ(t)}{dt} = \frac{p-q}{p} Y^{-q/p}(t) \diamond \frac{dY(t)}{dt}.$$

Thus, the differential Eq. (3.6) can be equivalent to the following first order differential equation:

$$\frac{dZ(t)}{dt} + \frac{p-q}{p}\beta_1 Z(t) = -\frac{p-q}{p}\beta_2 I. \tag{3.7}$$

It follows from the first order differential theory that the dynamic response of the resultant differential Eq. (3.7) can be derived as follows:

$$Z(t) = \left(\frac{\beta_2}{\beta_1}I + Z(0)\right)\exp\left(-\frac{p-q}{p}\beta_1 t\right) - \frac{\beta_2}{\beta_1}I. \tag{3.8}$$

Evidently, in this situation, $Z(t)$ can converge to zero in finite time t_f, i.e. $Z(t_f) = 0$. Then, we have

$$\left(\frac{\beta_2}{\beta_1}I + Z(0)\right)\exp\left(-\frac{p-q}{p}\beta_1 t_f\right) = \frac{\beta_2}{\beta_1}I. \tag{3.9}$$

Thus, starting from any randomly generated initial error matrix $Y(0)$, and defining $y^+(0) = \max\{Y(0)\}$, the new design formula (3.4) using the linear activation function array only needs the finite time t_f to converge to the equilibrium state (i.e. $Y(t_f) = 0$), which is an important progress, as compared with the infinite-time convergence. The proof is thus completed. ∎

Now, we continue to discuss the new design formula (3.4) for $Y(t)$. Expanding it leads to the following FTZNN model for solving time-varying matrix inversion Eq. (3.1):

$$A(t)\dot{U}(t) = -\dot{A}(t)U(t) - \gamma\Phi\left(\kappa_1\left(A(t)U(t) - I\right) + \kappa_2(A(t)U(t) - I)^{q/p}\right), \tag{3.10}$$

where design parameters $\kappa_1 > 0, \kappa_2 > 0, p, q, \gamma > 0$, and $\Phi(\cdot)$ are defined as before. In addition, if the linear activation function array is used, the FTZNN model is reduced to the linearly-activated one:

$$A(t)\dot{U}(t) = -\dot{A}(t)U(t)(t) - \beta_1\left(A(t)U(t) - I\right) - \beta_2(A(t)U(t) - I)^{q/p}, \tag{3.11}$$

where design parameters $\beta_1 = \gamma\kappa_1 > 0$ and $\beta_2 = \gamma\kappa_2 > 0$. As mentioned earlier, activation function array $\Phi(\cdot)$ is not the focus of this research, so the linearly activated FTZNN model (3.11) is our main research content.

3.3.2 Theoretical Analysis

It is worth mentioning that convergence performance is of primary importance for a neural-network model to be successfully applied. Thus, we would analyze and discuss the finite-time convergence performance of FTZNN model (3.11), which is presented through the following theorem.

Theorem 3.3 *Consider time-varying Eq. (3.1), i.e. $A(t)U(t) = I \in \mathbb{R}^{n \times n}$, where $A(t)$ is assumed to be nonsingular. Starting from a randomly generated initial state $U(0) \in \mathbb{R}^{n \times n}$, state matrix $U(t)$ of FTZNN model (3.11) converges to the theoretical time-varying solution of (3.1) in finite time t_f:*

$$t_f \leqslant \max \left\{ \frac{p}{\beta_1 (p-q)} \ln \frac{\beta_1 y^+(0)^{(p-q)/p} + \beta_2}{\beta_2}, \frac{p}{\beta_1 (p-q)} \ln \frac{\beta_1 y^-(0)^{(p-q)/p} + \beta_2}{\beta_2} \right\},$$

where $y^+(0)$ and $y^-(0)$ are the largest and the smallest elements in the initial error matrix $Y(0)$, respectively.

Proof: Let $\tilde{U}(t) = U(t) - U^*(t)$ denote the difference between the time-varying solution $U(t)$ generated by FTZNN model (3.11) and the theoretical time-varying solution $U^*(t)$ of (3.1). Then, we can obtain

$$U(t) = \tilde{U}(t) + U^*(t) \in \mathbb{R}^{n \times n}. \tag{3.12}$$

Then, based on $A(t)U^*(t) - I = 0$ and its time-derivative $A(t)\dot{U}^*(t) + \dot{A}(t)U^*(t) = 0$, it can be followed that $\tilde{U}(t)$ is the solution to the following dynamics by substituting Eq. (3.12) into FTZNN model (3.11):

$$A(t)\dot{\tilde{U}}(t) = -\dot{A}(t)\tilde{U}(t) - \beta_1 \left(A(t)\tilde{U}(t) \right) - \beta_2 \left(A(t)\tilde{U}(t) \right)^{q/p}.$$

Besides, because $Y(t) = A(t)U(t) - I = A(t)\tilde{U}(t)$, the aforementioned differential equation for $\tilde{U}(t)$ can be reformulated equivalently as the formula (3.5). Then, based on the formula (3.5), entry-wisely, we have

$$\dot{y}_{ij}(t) = -\beta_1 y_{ij}(t) - \beta_2 y_{ij}^{q/p}(t), \tag{3.13}$$

where $y_{ij}(t)$ denotes the ijth element of $Y(t)$ with $i, j = 1, 2, 3, \ldots, n$.

For such a scalar-valued first order differential Eq. (3.13), let us define $y^+(t)$ to be the element in $Y(t)$ with the largest initial value $y^+(0) = \max \{y_{ij}(0)\}$ for all possible i and j; and define $y^-(t)$ to be the element in $Y(t)$ with the smallest initial value $y^-(0) = \min \{y_{ij}(0)\}$ for all possible i and j. Note that every $y_{ij}(t)$ in $Y(t)$ has the identical dynamics (3.13). Then, according to the comparison lemma, we have

$$y^-(t) \leqslant y_{ij}(t) \leqslant y^+(t),$$

for all possible i and j and all $t > 0$. This means that $y_{ij}(t)$ converges to zero for all possible i and j when both $y^+(t)$ and $y^-(t)$ decrease to zero. In other words, the convergence time of FTZNN model (3.11) is bounded by the larger one between the dynamics of $y^+(t)$ and $y^-(t)$, i.e. $t_f \leqslant \max\{t_f^+, t_f^-\}$ where t_f^+ and t_f^- represent the convergence time of the dynamics of $y^+(t)$ and $y^-(t)$, respectively.

To calculate t_f, we need to estimate t_f^+ and t_f^- first. For t_f^+, based on the analysis of Theorem 3.3, there exists t_f satisfying

$$t_f \leqslant \frac{p}{\beta_1(p-q)} \ln \frac{\beta_1 y^+(0)^{(p-q)/p} + \beta_2}{\beta_2},$$

such that $y^+(t_f) = 0$ when $t > t_f$. In the same way, for t_f^-, there exists t_f satisfying

$$t_f \leqslant \frac{p}{\beta_1(p-q)} \ln \frac{\beta_1 y^-(0)^{(p-q)/p} + \beta_2}{\beta_2},$$

such that $y^-(t_f) = 0$ when $t > t_f$.

Thus, we conclude that the upper bound of the finite-time convergence for FTZNN model (3.11) is derived as

$$t_f \leqslant \max\left\{ \frac{p}{\beta_1(p-q)} \ln \frac{\beta_1 y^+(0)^{(p-q)/p} + \beta_2}{\beta_2}, \frac{p}{\beta_1(p-q)} \ln \frac{\beta_1 y^-(0)^{(p-q)/p} + \beta_2}{\beta_2} \right\},$$

which shows that state matrix $U(t)$ of FTZNN model (3.11), starting from any randomly generated initial state $U(0)$, converges to the theoretical solution of time-varying matrix inversion Eq. (3.1) after a period finite time t_f. The proof is thus completed. ∎

3.4 Illustrative Verification

In Sections 3.2 and 3.3, GNN model (3.2), OZNN model (3.3), and FTZNN model (3.11) have been presented for solving online time-varying matrix inverse depicted in Eq. (3.1). In this section, computer-simulation results based on two illustrative examples are presented for substantiating the superiority of FTZNN model (3.11) to GNN model (3.2) and OZNN model (3.3). Without loss of generality, the values of design parameters are set to be $p = 5$ and $q = 1$.

3.4.1 Example 1: Nonrandom Time-varying Coefficients

In order to show the superior finite-time convergence of FTZNN model (3.11), the following time-varying matrix is considered to be inverted:

$$A(t) = \begin{bmatrix} \sin(4t) & -\cos(4t) \\ \cos(4t) & \sin(4t) \end{bmatrix}. \tag{3.14}$$

The theoretical inverse of $U(t)$ in this situation can be obtained as follows:

$$U^*(t) = \begin{bmatrix} \sin(4t) & \cos(4t) \\ -\cos(4t) & \sin(4t) \end{bmatrix},$$

which can be used to verify the solution correctness of such three neural-network models.

First, starting from 8 randomly generated initial state $U(0) \in \mathbb{R}^{2\times2}$ and with design parameter $\gamma = 1$, we adopt GNN model (3.2) to compute the aforementioned time-varying matrix inverse. The transient behavior of the neural-state solutions is shown in Figure 3.1, where solid curves correspond to the neural-state solution elements of $U(t)$, and dash curves correspond to the theoretical time-varying solution elements of $U^*(t)$. From this figure, we can observe that the neural-state solutions are not fit with the theoretical time-varying inverse, and there exists a lagging error between them. This demonstrates again that GNN model (3.2) cannot be used to solve effectively time-varying problems as mentioned before. Under the same conditions, OZNN model (3.3) is applied to solve this time-varying matrix inversion problem. The transient behavior of the corresponding neural-state solutions is displayed in Figure 3.2, from which we can conclude that, starting with 8 randomly generated initial states, the neural-state solutions can exponentially converge to the theoretical time-varying inverse with time. To more directly show the solution process of GNN model (3.2)

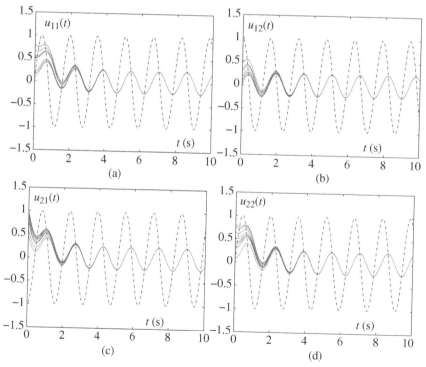

Figure 3.1 Transient behavior of $U(t)$ synthesized by GNN model (3.2) starting with 8 randomly generated initial states under the condition of $\gamma = 1$.

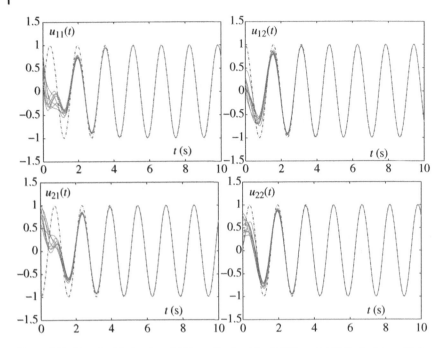

Figure 3.2 Transient behavior of $U(t)$ synthesized by OZNN model (3.3) starting with 8 randomly generated initial states under the condition of $\gamma = 1$.

and OZNN model (3.3), the evolution of the corresponding residual errors, measured by Frobenius norm $\|A(t)U(t) - I\|_F$, is plotted in Figure 3.3. From Figure 3.3a, it can be seen that the residual error $\|A(t)U(t) - I\|_F$ of GNN model (3.2) is always oscillating with time and never converges to zero. The results are consistent with those of Figure 3.1. From Figure 3.3b, we can see that the residual error $\|A(t)U(t) - I\|_F$ of OZNN model (3.3) can converge to zero after about six seconds. The results verify the effectiveness of OZNN model (3.3).

Second, under the same conditions (with $\kappa_1 = \kappa_2 = 1$), FTZNN model (3.11) is applied and the corresponding simulative results are shown in Figures 3.4 and 3.5a. From Figure 3.4, we can see that the neural-state solution of FTZNN model (3.11) can fit with the theoretical time-varying matrix inverse very well only after a little time. In addition, Figure 3.5a shows the transient behavior of the corresponding residual error $\|A(t)U(t) - I\|_F$, from which we can obtain that the residual error $\|A(t)U(t) - I\|_F$ of FTZNN model (3.11) can directly decrease to zero within finite time 2.6 seconds. The convergence speed of FTZNN model (3.11) is more than two times as fast as OZNN model (3.3). It is worth pointing out that the convergence speed of FTZNN model (3.11) can be accelerated by choosing large values of design parameters γ, κ_1, and κ_2 with time. For example, as shown in Figure 3.5b, with $\kappa_1 = \kappa_2 = 1$, the convergence time of FTZNN model (3.11) is shortened from 2.6 to 0.026 seconds when the value of design parameter γ

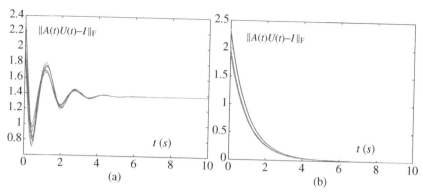

Figure 3.3 Transient behavior of the residual error $\|A(t)U(t) - I\|_F$ corresponding to $U(t)$ synthesized by GNN model (3.2) and OZNN model (3.3). (a) By GNN model (3.2) and (b) by OZNN model (3.3).

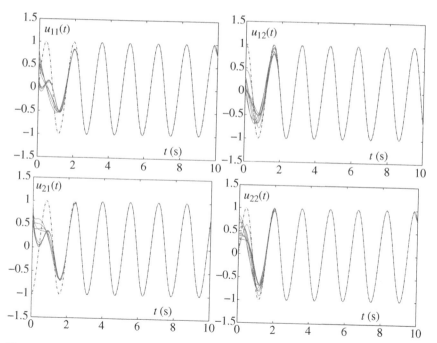

Figure 3.4 Transient behavior of $U(t)$ synthesized by FTZNN model (3.11) starting with 8 randomly generated initial states under the conditions of $\gamma = \kappa_1 = \kappa_2 = 1$.

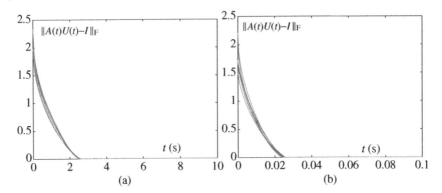

Figure 3.5 Transient behavior of the residual error $\|A(t)U(t) - I\|_F$ synthesized by FTZNN model (3.11) under the conditions of $\kappa_1 = \kappa_2 = 1$. (a) $\gamma = 1$ and (b) $\gamma = 100$.

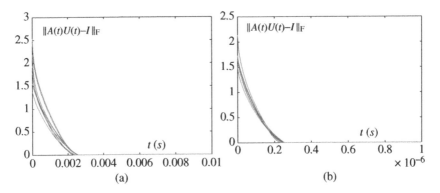

Figure 3.6 Transient behavior of the residual error $\|A(t)U(t) - I\|_F$ synthesized by FTZNN model (3.11) under the conditions of $\kappa_1 = \kappa_2 = 10$. (a) $\gamma = 100$ and (b) $\gamma = 10^6$.

increases from 1 to 100. Besides, as shown in Figure 3.6, with $\kappa_1 = \kappa_2 = 10$, the convergence time of FTZNN model (3.11) is shortened to 2.6×10^{-3} seconds and even to 2.6×10^{-7} seconds when the values of design parameter γ are set to be 100 and 10^6, respectively.

3.4.2 Example 2: Random Time-varying Coefficients

For further demonstrating the effectiveness of FTZNN model (3.11), a more complex matrix inversion equation is considered, where time-varying Toeplitz coefficients are expressed in the following form:

$$
A(t) = \begin{bmatrix}
a_1(t) & a_2(t) & a_3(t) & \cdots & a_n(t) \\
a_2(t) & a_1(t) & a_2(t) & \cdots & a_{n-1}(t) \\
a_3(t) & a_2(t) & a_1(t) & \cdots & a_{n-2}(t) \\
\vdots & \vdots & \vdots & \ddots & \vdots \\
a_n(t) & a_{n-1}(t) & a_{n-2}(t) & \cdots & a_1(t)
\end{bmatrix},
$$

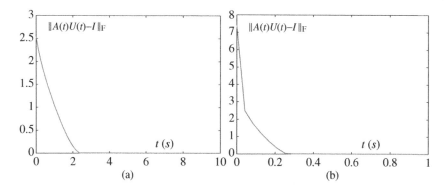

Figure 3.7 Transient behavior of the residual error $\|A(t)U(t) - I\|_F$ synthesized by FTZNN model (3.11) using random time-varying coefficients under the conditions of $\kappa_1 = \kappa_2 = 1$. (a) $\gamma = 1$ and (b) $\gamma = 10$.

where time-varying coefficient $a_1(t) := \rho_{11}\cos(\rho_{21}t)$, $a_j(t) := \rho_{1j}\sin(\rho_{2j}t)$ $(j = 2, 3, \ldots, n)$ with constants ρ_{1j} and ρ_{2j} (including ρ_{11} and ρ_{21}) being randomly generated. In this example, we set $n = 8$, $\kappa_1 = \kappa_2 = 1$, and only adopt FTZNN model (3.11) to solve such a complex time-varying matrix inversion equation under the conditions of $\gamma = 1$ and $\gamma = 10$. The corresponding simulative results are shown in Figure 3.7. From this figure, we can see that, starting from a randomly generated initial state $U(0)$, the residual error $\|A(t)U(t) - I\|_F$ synthesized by FTZNN model (3.11) can decrease to directly within finite time. In addition, as the value of γ increases, the convergence performance of FTZNN model (3.11) can be improved accordingly. It is worth pointing out that parameters κ_1 and κ_2 have the same effect with parameter γ when they are used to solve time-varying matrix inversion. Thus, the simulative results using different κ_1 and κ_2 are not presented.

In summary, from the aforementioned simulation comparison results, we can draw a conclusion that FTZNN model (3.11) is the most effective model for solving online time-varying matrix inversion problem, as compared with OZNN model (3.3) and GNN model (3.2).

3.5 Chapter Summary

In this chapter, a FTZNN model has been proposed and investigated for solving online time-varying matrix inversion problem. Different from the conventional design method, the construction of the proposed FTZNN model is based on a new design formula, which plays an accelerated role for computing the time-varying matrix inverse. The upper bound of convergence time for the FTZNN model has been derived and analyzed theoretically. For comparative purposes, the GNN model and the OZNN model have been developed for solving the same time-varying problem. Computer simulations are performed to evaluate and compare the performance of such three neural-network models. The results show that the FTZNN model is the most effective solution model for time-varying matrix inversion.

References

1 Z. Quan, Y. Zakharov, and J. Liu, DCD-based simplified matrix inversion for MIMO-OFDM, 2011 IEEE International Symposium of Circuits and Systems (ISCAS), (2011) 2389–2392.

2 Y. Wang and H. Leib, Sphere decoding for MIMO systems with Newton iterative matrix inversion, *IEEE Commun. Lett.*, 17(2) (2013) 389–392.

3 T. Zhao, K. Roeder, and H. Liu, Positive semidefinite rank-based correlation matrix estimation with application to semiparametric graph estimation, *J. Comput. Graph. Stat.*, 23(4) (2014) 895–922.

4 D. H. Bae, K. Bayartsogt, and J. S. Kim, An algorithm for solving massive matrix inversion in cloud computing systems, Proceedings of the 2011 ACM Symposium on Research in Applied Computation, (2011) 61–66.

5 D. Guo and Y. Zhang, Zhang neural network, Getz-Marsden dynamic system, and discrete-time algorithms for time-varying matrix inversion with application to Robots' kinematic control, *Neurocomputing*, 97(15) (2012) 22–32.

6 L. Jin and Y. Zhang, G2-type SRMPC scheme for synchronous manipulation of two redundant robot arms, *IEEE Trans. Cybern.*, 45(2) (2015) 153–164.

7 W. E. Leithead and Y. Zhang, $O(N^2)$-operation approximation of covariance matrix inverse in Gaussian process regression based on quasi-Newton BFGS methods, *Commun. Stat. Simul. Comput.*, 36(2) (2007) 367–380.

8 A. Storjohann and S. Yang, A relaxed algorithm for online matrix inversion, Proceedings of the 2015 ACM on International Symposium on Symbolic and Algebraic Computation, 48 (2015) 339–346.

9 G. Sharma, A. Agarwala, and B. Bhattacharya, A fast parallel Gauss Jordan algorithm for matrix inversion using CUDA, *Comput. Struct.*, 128 (2013) 31–37.

10 F. K. Haghani and F. Soleymani, An improved Schulz-type iterative method for matrix inversion with application, *Trans. Inst. Meas. Control*, 36(8) (2014) 983–991.

11 Y. Zhang, Revisit the analog computer and gradient-based neural system for matrix inversion, Proceedings of IEEE International Symposium on Intelligent Control, (2005) 1411–1416.

12 Y. Zhang and Y. Shi *et al.*, Global exponential convergence and stability of gradient-based neural network for online matrix inversion, *Appl. Math. Comput.*, 215(3) (2009) 1301–1306.

13 Y. Zhang and S. S. Ge, Design and analysis of a general recurrent neural network model for time-varying matrix inversion, *IEEE Trans. Neural Netw.*, 16(6) (2005) 1477–1490.

14 K. Chen and C. Yi, Robustness analysis of a hybrid of recursive neural dynamics for online matrix inversion, *Appl. Math. Comput.*, 273 (2016) 969–975.

15 L. Xiao and Y. Zhang, Different Zhang functions resulting in different ZNN models demonstrated via time-varying linear matrix-vector inequalities solving, *Neurocomputing*, 121(9) (2013) 246–251.

16 L. Xiao and R. Lu, Finite-time solution to nonlinear equation using recurrent neural dynamics with a specially-constructed activation function, *Neurocomputing*, 151 (2015) 246–251.

17 L. Xiao, A finite-time convergent neural dynamics for online solution of time-varying linear complex matrix equation, *Neurocomputing*, 167 (2015) 254–259.

18 S. Li, S. Chen, and B. Liu, Accelerating a recurrent neural network to finite-time convergence for solving time-varying Sylvester equation by using a sign-bi-power activation function, *Neural Process. Lett.*, 37 (2013) 189–205.

4

Design Scheme II of FTZNN

4.1 Introduction

The matrix inversion has been widely used in practical engineering applications, such as multiple-input multiple-output (MIMO) and robotics [1–3]. Besides, numerous principles of machine operation in real life can be explained by matrix inversion. For example, in robotics [4–6], the path tracking is a typical task for any robot manipulators. To achieve this task successfully, the Jacobian matrix of a robot manipulator has to be solved online according to the given path. When the Jacobian matrix has been obtained, the corresponding control law can be solved and described by joint-angle or joint-velocity variables, which can drive the robot manipulator to complete the path-tracking task. Obviously, the matrix inversion is closely related to the age of artificial intelligence that people are yearning for. It is very important to find a better method for matrix inversion with faster convergence and stronger robustness.

Considering the impact of external disturbances, which are inevitable in the real world, in this chapter, we are devoted to studying a versatile activation function (VAF) to design a new noise tolerant finite-time zeroing neural network (NT-FTZNN) model for time-independent matrix inversion. The proposed NT-FTZNN model not only has a strong noise capability but also has a predefined finite-time convergence. In addition, the upper bound of the predefined convergence time for the NT-FTZNN model is independent to its initial states (i.e. the upper bound of the predefined convergence time is known). More detailed comparisons about several models can be seen from Table 4.1. More importantly, the convergence and robustness of the NT-FTZNN model are mathematically rigorously demonstrated in theorems. In addition, to numerically verify the efficacy and generalization of the proposed NT-FTZNN model, two different dimensional time-independent matrix examples and a robotic application are presented in the simulation part. The simulation results also demonstrate the

Zeroing Neural Networks: Finite-time Convergence Design, Analysis and Applications,
First Edition. Lin Xiao and Lei Jia.
© 2023 The Institute of Electrical and Electronics Engineers, Inc. Published 2023 by John Wiley & Sons, Inc.

Table 4.1 The main differences of the NT-FTZNN model from other models (i.e. GNN model, ZNN model, and EIZNN model) for time-independent matrix inversion.

#	Item	GNN	ZNN	EIZNN	NT-FTZNN
1	Target	Static	Dynamic	Dynamic	Dynamic
2	Error	No-zero	Zero	No-zero	Zero
3	AF	No	Yes	No	Yes
4	Model	Explicitly	Implicitly	Implicitly	Implicitly
5	Speed	Asymptotically	Finitely	Exponentially	Predefined
6	Robustness	Weaker	Weak	Strong	Stronger

Source: Adapted from [7–10].

efficiency, superiority, and applicability of NT-FTZNN using VAF for solving time-dependent matrix inversion.

4.2 Preliminaries

In this section, in order to make the process of the proof and solution more convenient, some basic preparations for finding the inverse of the time-dependent matrix are given as follows.

4.2.1 Mathematical Preparation

In general, a recurrent neural network can be represented as a differential dynamic system in mathematics, which is formed by

$$\dot{u}(t) = s(u(t), t), \ t \in [0, +\infty), \tag{4.1}$$

where $u(t) \in \mathbb{R}^n$ represents an appropriately sized system state. Let $u(0) = u_0$ represent an appropriately sized initial state for this system, and assume that $u(t) = 0$ is the equilibrium state of the system. There are some concepts related to the convergence for this system (4.1), which are presented as follows for completeness of this work [11–17].

Definition The origin of system (4.1) is globally finite-time stable if it is globally and asymptotically stable; and there exists a locally bounded settling-time function $T : \mathbb{R}^n \to \mathbb{R}_+ \cup \{0\}$, such that $u(t, u_0) = 0$ for all $t \geqslant T(u_0)$.

Definition The origin of system (4.1) is globally predefined-time stable if the system is globally finite-time stable and the settling-time function T is globally bounded, i.e. there exists a constant $t_f \in \mathbb{R}_+$ satisfying $t_f \geqslant T(u_0)$ for all $u_0 \in \mathbb{R}^n$.

Lemma 4.1 *If there exists a continuous radially unbounded function* $V : \mathbb{R}^n \to \mathbb{R}_+ \cup \{0\}$ *such that* $V(\zeta) = 0$ *for* $\zeta \in S$ *and any solution* $\zeta(t)$ *satisfies*

$$\dot{V}(t) \leqslant -\tau V^\eta(\zeta(t)) - \rho V^w(\zeta(t)),$$

where parameters $\tau > 0$, $\rho > 0$, $0 < \eta < 1$, *and* $w > 1$ *are constants, then the set* S *is globally predefined-time attractive for system (4.1), and the upper bound for the predefined time convergence is*

$$t_f = \frac{1}{\tau(1 - \eta)} + \frac{1}{\rho(w - 1)}.$$

4.2.2 Problem Formulation

In mathematics, the time-dependent matrix inversion problem is generally formulated as the following dynamic matrix equation:

$$L(t)U(t) = I \in \mathbb{R}^{n \times n}, \quad \text{or} \quad U(t)L(t) = I \in \mathbb{R}^{n \times n}, \qquad t \in [0, +\infty), \qquad (4.2)$$

where $L(t) \in \mathbb{R}^{n \times n}$ represents an invertible time-dependent coefficient matrix, $U(t) \in \mathbb{R}^{n \times n}$ represents an unknown time-dependent matrix, and $I \in \mathbb{R}^{n \times n}$ represents an appropriately sized identity matrix. Without loss of generality, let $U^*(t) \in \mathbb{R}^{n \times n}$ represent the theoretical solution of (4.2). This current work focuses on finding an unknown $U(t)$ using the proposed NT-FTZNN model within finite time under the interference of various noises (such as constant noise, time-dependent bounded or unbounded noise).

4.3 NT-FTZNN Model

In this section, the NT-FTZNN model will be proposed for time-dependent matrix inversion. The detailed design process is presented as follows.

Considering problem (4.2), according to the design method of ZNN [7, 8, 17–19], a time-dependent error function $Y(t)$ is defined as follows:

$$Y(t) = L(t)U(t) - I \in \mathbb{R}^{n \times n}. \tag{4.3}$$

Then, a design formula for $Y(t)$ is given directly as

$$\frac{dY(t)}{dt} = -\gamma \Phi(Y(t)), \tag{4.4}$$

where $\Phi(\cdot)$ represents an activation function array with each element denoted by $\phi(\cdot)$ and $\gamma > 0$ represents a resizable design parameter to adjust the convergence rate of the neural network. Substituting Eq. (4.3) into formula (4.4), one can get the following initial ZNN model:

$$L(t)\dot{U}(t) = -\dot{L}(t)U(t) - \gamma \Phi(L(t)U(t) - I), \tag{4.5}$$

where the meanings of γ and $\Phi(\cdot)$ are the same as before. Considering that various noises may exist during the actual problem solving, it is better to study a noise-perturbed ZNN model, which is directly given as follows:

$$L(t)\dot{U}(t) = -\dot{L}(t)U(t) - \gamma\Phi(L(t)U(t) - I) + Z(t), \qquad (4.6)$$

where $Z(t)$ represents a universal noise.

Generally speaking, different activation functions for a neural network can lead to different convergence and stability. In the past few years, many activation functions (e.g. BPAF, SBPAF) have been studied to speed up the convergence of neural networks, and some of that even reach finite time convergence. However, the denoising capability of the ZNN models using these activation functions is not considered. That is to say, when perturbed by noises, these models may be no longer effective. In order to overcome this drawback, the following VAF will be added to the aforementioned presented ZNN model to solve the time-dependent matrix inversion problem under different noise pollution environments [15, 16]:

$$\phi(x) = (a_1|x|^\eta + a_2|x|^w)\text{sgn}(x) + a_3x + a_4\text{sgn}(x), \qquad (4.7)$$

where design parameters $0 < \eta < 1$, $w > 1$, $a_1 > 0$, $a_2 > 0$, $a_3 \geqslant 0$, $a_4 \geqslant 0$ and $\text{sgn}(\cdot)$ denotes the sign function. For better understanding, if ZNN model (4.5) is activated by VAF (4.7), this model is termed as the new noise tolerant finite-time ZNN (NT-FTZNN) model; and if noise-perturbed ZNN model (4.6) is activated by VAF (4.7), this model is termed as the noise-perturbed NT-FTZNN model. Besides, the main differences and formulations of the commonly used activation functions are compared and listed in Table 4.2. In addition, different from other activation functions for ZNN, when the VAF is used, the NT-FTZNN model

Table 4.2 Comparisons and differences of commonly used activation functions.

Activation function	Formulation
Linear activation function (LAF)	$\phi(x) = x$
Bi-Polar Sigmoid activation function (BPAF)	$\phi(x) = (1 - \exp(-\xi x))/(1 + \exp(-\xi x))$ with $\xi > 1$
Power activation function (PAF)	$\phi(x) = x^r$ with $r > 3$ indicating an odd integer
SAF	$\phi(x) = \begin{cases} x^r, & \text{if } |x| \geq 1 \\ \frac{1+\exp(-\xi)}{1-\exp(-\xi)} \cdot \frac{1-\exp(-\xi x)}{1+\exp(-\xi x)}, & \text{otherwise} \end{cases}$
Hyperbolic Sine activation function (HSAF)	$\phi(x) = (\exp(\xi x) - \exp(-\xi x))/2$ with $\xi > 1$
Sign-Bi-Power activation function (SBPAF)	$\phi(x) = (|x|^r + |x|^{1/r})\text{sgn}(x)/2$ with $0 < r < 1$
VAF (this work)	$\phi(x) = (a_1|x|^\eta + a_2|x|^w)\text{sgn}(x) + a_3x + a_4\,\text{sgn}(x)$

can converge to the theoretical solution within a predefined finite time when solving the time-dependent matrix inversion problem, regardless of whether there is bounded vanishing or non-vanishing noise. That is to say, the NT-FTZNN model has faster convergence speed and stronger robustness, as compared ZNN activated by other activation functions.

4.4 Theoretical Analysis

In the previous section, the NT-FTZNN model with finite time convergence performance is deduced step by step to find the time-dependent matrix inversion. In this section, the predefined-time convergence and robustness of the NT-FTZNN model will be theoretically analyzed in detail under different noise environments.

4.4.1 NT-FTZNN in the Absence of Noises

The following theorem guarantees the predefined-time convergence of NT-FTZNN model (4.5) activated by VAF (4.7) in the absence of noises.

Theorem 4.2 *Assume that time-dependent matrix $L(t)$ in Eq. (4.2) is smooth and invertible for $t \in [0, +\infty)$. If VAF (4.7) is used, then neural-state matrix $U(t)$ of NT-FTZNN model (4.5), starting from an arbitrary initial matrix $U(0) \in \mathbb{R}^{n \times n}$, converges to the theoretical time-dependent matrix inversion $U^*(t)$ of $L(t)$ in predefined time t_f:*

$$t_f \leqslant \frac{1}{\gamma a_1(1 - \eta)} + \frac{1}{\gamma a_2(w - 1)}.$$

Proof: Since $Y(t) = L(t)U(t) - I$, NT-FTZNN model (4.5) is simplified as $\dot{Y}(t) = -\gamma \Phi(Y(t))$ which entry-wisely consists of the following n^2 subsystems:

$$\dot{y}_{ij}(t) = -\gamma \phi(y_{ij}(t)) \quad \text{with} \quad i, j \in \{1, 2, \dots, n\},$$

where matrix $\dot{Y}(t)$ denotes the time derivative of matrix $Y(t)$ and scalars $y_{ij}(t)$ and $\dot{y}_{ij}(t)$ are the ijth elements of matrices $Y(t)$ and $\dot{Y}(t)$, respectively. Evidently, dynamics of each element in the error function $Y(t)$ is independent and self-autonomous.

Define a Lyapunov function candidate $p(t) = |y_{ij}(t)|$ for the ijth subsystem. The time derivative of $p(t)$ is

$$\dot{p}(t) = \dot{y}_{ij}(t)\text{sgn}(y_{ij}(t)) = -\gamma \phi(y_{ij}(t))\text{sgn}(y_{ij}(t)).$$

When VAF (4.7) is used, one can obtain

$$\dot{p}(t) = -\gamma(a_1|y_{ij}(t)|^\eta + a_2|y_{ij}(t)|^w + a_3|y_{ij}(t)| + a_4)$$
$$\leqslant -\gamma(a_1|y_{ij}(t)|^\eta + a_2|y_{ij}(t)|^w)$$
$$= -\gamma(a_1 p^\eta(t) + a_2 p^w(t)).$$

On basis of Lemma 4.1 mentioned in Section 4.2, one can obtain the convergence time of the ijth subsystem for NT-FTZNN model (4.5):

$$t_{ij} \leqslant \frac{1}{\gamma a_1 (1 - \eta)} + \frac{1}{\gamma a_2 (w - 1)}.$$

Since the upper bound is a constant that is independent on the initial conditions of the ijth subsystem of NT-FTZNN model (4.5) and time t, the maximum convergence upper bound of NT-FTZNN model (4.5) is obtained as

$$t_f = \max(t_{ij}) \leqslant \frac{1}{\gamma a_1 (1 - \eta)} + \frac{1}{\gamma a_2 (w - 1)}.$$

Hence, NT-FTZNN model (4.5) activated by VAF (4.7) exhibits a predefined-time convergence property. The predefined-time convergence of NT-FTZNN model (4.5) activated by VAF (4.7) is theoretically proved. ∎

4.4.2 NT-FTZNN in the Presence of Noises

In practical implementation of a neural network model, there always exist unavoidable additive noises. Hence, it is worth investigating the convergence performance of noise-perturbed NT-FTZNN model (4.6).

4.4.2.1 Dynamic Bounded Gradually Disappearing Noise

When perturbed by a dynamic bounded vanishing noise $Z(t)$, the following result can ensure the predefined-time convergence of noise-perturbed NT-FTZNN model (4.6).

Theorem 4.3 *Assume that time-dependent matrix $L(t)$ in Eq. (4.2) is smooth and invertible for $t \in [0, +\infty)$, and NT-FTZNN model (4.6) is perturbed by a matrix noise $Z(t)$ with its ijth entry satisfying $|z_{ij}(t)| \leqslant \delta |y_{ij}(t)|$ where $\delta \in (0, +\infty)$ and $|y_{ij}(t)|$ denotes the ijth absolute element of error function (4.3). If VAF (4.7) is used with $\gamma a_3 \geqslant \delta$, then neural-state matrix $U(t)$ of noise-perturbed NT-FTZNN model (4.6), starting from an arbitrary initial matrix $U(0) \in \mathbb{R}^{n \times n}$, converges to the theoretical time-dependent matrix inversion $U^*(t)$ of $L(t)$ in predefined time t_f:*

$$t_f \leqslant \frac{1}{\gamma a_1 (1 - \eta)} + \frac{1}{\gamma a_2 (w - 1)}.$$

Proof: As the same as Theorem 4.2, noise-perturbed NT-FTZNN model (4.6) can be simplified as $\dot{Y}(t) = -\gamma \Phi(Y(t)) + Z(t)$ that entry-wisely consists of the following n^2 subsystems:

$$\dot{y}_{ij}(t) = -\gamma \phi(y_{ij}(t)) + z_{ij}(t) \quad \text{with} \quad i, j \in \{1, 2, \dots, n\}, \tag{4.8}$$

where matrix $\dot{Y}(t)$ denotes the time derivative of matrix $Y(t)$ and scalars $y_{ij}(t)$, $\dot{y}_{ij}(t)$ and $z_{ij}(t)$ are the ijth elements of matrices $Y(t)$, $\dot{Y}(t)$ and $Z(t)$, respectively. Define a Lyapunov function candidate $p(t) = |y_{ij}(t)|^2$ for the ijth subsystem. The time derivative of $p(t)$ is

$$\dot{p}(t) = 2y_{ij}(t)\dot{y}_{ij}(t) = 2y_{ij}(t)(-\gamma\phi(y_{ij}(t)) + z_{ij}(t)).$$

When VAF (4.7) is used with $\gamma a_3 \geqslant \delta$, one can obtain

$$\begin{aligned}\dot{p}(t) &= -2\gamma(a_1|y_{ij}(t)|^{\eta+1} + a_2|y_{ij}(t)|^{w+1}) - 2\gamma a_4|y_{ij}(t)| \\ &\quad + 2(y_{ij}(t)z_{ij}(t) - \gamma a_3|y_{ij}(t)|^2) \\ &\leqslant -2\gamma(a_1|y_{ij}(t)|^{\eta+1} + a_2|y_{ij}(t)|^{w+1}) \\ &\quad + 2(\delta|y_{ij}(t)|^2 - \gamma a_3|y_{ij}(t)|^2) \\ &\leqslant -2\gamma(a_1|y_{ij}(t)|^{\eta+1} + a_2|y_{ij}(t)|^{w+1}) \\ &= -2\gamma(a_1 p(t)^{\frac{\eta+1}{2}} + a_2 p(t)^{\frac{w+1}{2}}).\end{aligned}$$

On basis of Lemma 4.1 mentioned in Section 4.2, the convergence time of noise-perturbed NT-FTZNN model (4.6) is

$$t_f \leqslant \frac{1}{\gamma a_1(1-\eta)} + \frac{1}{\gamma a_2(w-1)}.$$

Hence, NT-FTZNN model (4.6) activated by VAF (4.7) under a dynamic bounded vanishing noise exhibits a predefined-time convergence property. ∎

4.4.2.2 Dynamic Bounded Non-disappearing Noise

When noise-perturbed NT-FTZNN model (4.6) with dynamic bounded non-vanishing noises is involved, one has the following theorem to ensure the predefined-time convergence property.

Theorem 4.4 *Assume that time-dependent matrix $L(t)$ in Eq. (4.2) is smooth and invertible for $t \in [0, +\infty)$, and noise-perturbed NT-FTZNN model (4.6) is perturbed by a matrix noise $Z(t)$ with its ijth entry satisfying $|z_{ij}(t)| \leqslant \delta$ where $\delta \in (0, +\infty)$. If VAF (4.7) is used with $\gamma a_4 \geqslant \delta$, then neural-state matrix $U(t)$ of noise-perturbed NT-FTZNN model (4.6), starting from an arbitrary initial matrix $U(0) \in \mathbb{R}^{n \times n}$, converges to the theoretical time-dependent matrix inversion $U^*(t)$ of $L(t)$ in predefined time t_f:*

$$t_f \leqslant \frac{1}{\gamma a_1(1-\eta)} + \frac{1}{\gamma a_2(w-1)}.$$

Proof: Define a Lyapunov function candidate $p(t) = |y_{ij}(t)|^2$ for the ijth subsystem depicted in (4.8). The time derivative of $p(t)$ is

$$\dot{p}(t) = 2y_{ij}(t)\dot{y}_{ij}(t) = 2y_{ij}(t)(-\gamma f(y_{ij}(t)) + z_{ij}(t)).$$

When VAF (4.7) is used with $\gamma a_4 \geqslant \delta$, one would have

$$\dot{p}(t) = -2\gamma(a_1|y_{ij}(t)|^{\eta+1} + a_2|y_{ij}(t)|^{w+1}) - 2\gamma a_3|y_{ij}(t)|^2$$
$$+ 2(y_{ij}(t)z_{ij}(t) - \gamma a_4|y_{ij}(t)|)$$
$$\leqslant -2\gamma(a_1|y_{ij}(t)|^{\eta+1} + a_2|y_{ij}(t)|^{w+1})$$
$$+ 2(\delta|y_{ij}(t)| - \gamma a_4|y_{ij}(t)|)$$
$$\leqslant -2\gamma(a_1|y_{ij}(t)|^{\eta+1} + a_2|y_{ij}(t)|^{w+1})$$
$$= -2\gamma(a_1 p(t)^{\frac{\eta+1}{2}} + a_2 p(t)^{\frac{w+1}{2}}).$$

Therefore, the maximum convergence time for noise-perturbed NT-FTZNN model (4.6) is

$$t_f \leqslant \frac{1}{\gamma a_1(1-\eta)} + \frac{1}{\gamma a_2(w-1)}.$$

Thus, noise-perturbed NT-FTZNN model (4.6) activated by VAF (4.7) under a dynamic bounded non-vanishing noise exhibits a predefined-time convergence property. The proof is thus completed. ∎

It is worth pointing out that Theorems 4.3 and 4.4 indicate that noise-perturbed NT-FTZNN model (4.6) can not only converge to the theoretical inversion $U^*(t)$ of $L(t)$ in a predefined time, but also reject dynamic bounded vanishing and non-vanishing noises simultaneously. This is a remarkable improvement when compared with the previous ZNN models that require infinity long time or finite time to be convergent or cannot handle dynamic bounded noises completely.

4.5 Illustrative Verification

In Section 4.3, NT-FTZNN model (4.6) with the VAF is proposed for time-dependent matrix inversion. In Section 4.4, the predefined finite-time convergence and robustness of NT-FTZNN model (4.6) for time-dependent matrix inversion are theoretically analyzed in detail under various noises. In this part, two illustrative numerical examples and one robotic application will be used to authenticate the efficacy and prominent convergence of NT-FTZNN model (4.6) for solving time-dependent matrix problems (4.2). For the purpose of comparison, several commonly used activation functions (such as LAF, PSAF, SBPAF) are also used to construct the ZNN models for solving time-dependent matrix inversion problems (4.2) under the same noise-contaminated environment.

4.5.1 Example 1: Two-dimensional Coefficient

Let us first consider the following time-dependent invertible matrix to authenticate the efficacy of NT-FTZNN model (4.5):

$$L(t) = \begin{bmatrix} \sin(4t) & \cos(4t) \\ -\cos(4t) & \sin(4t) \end{bmatrix} \in \mathbb{R}^{2\times2}. \tag{4.9}$$

Through mathematical calculations, one can calculate the theoretical solution $L^*(t)$ of (4.9) as

$$U^*(t) = \begin{bmatrix} \sin(4t) & -\cos(4t) \\ \cos(4t) & \sin(4t) \end{bmatrix}. \tag{4.10}$$

Without loss of generality, one can set $\gamma = a_1 = a_2 = a_3 = a_4 = 1, \eta = 0.2, w = 5$, and it is easy to calculate the predefined time as $t_f \leq 1.5$ second. First, NT-FTZNN model (4.5) is employed to find the time-dependent matrix inversion of (4.9) without noise. The simulation consequences are shown in Figure 4.1, where the dash curves line in the figure represents the theoretical solution of the time-dependent matrix inversion problem (4.9), and the solid curves represents the state solution $U(t)$ from the randomly generated initial state $U(0)$. From Figure 4.1, one can see the solid curves in the four subgraphs can quickly coincide with the dash curves in a very short time (i.e. approximately 0.5 second that is less than $t_f = 1.5$ seconds), which means that when using NT-FTZNN model (4.5) to find the time-dependent matrix inversion (4.9) without noise, the state solution $U(t)$ from any randomly generated initial state $U(0)$ can quickly converge to the theoretical

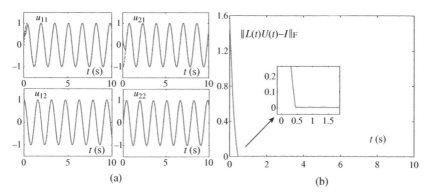

Figure 4.1 Transient behavior of NT-FTZNN model (4.6) activated by VAF for solving time-dependent matrix inversion (4.9) without noise. (a) State solutions and (b) residual error.

solution $U^*(t)$. That is, NT-FTZNN model (4.5) is effective when applied to finding the time-dependent matrix inversion of (4.9).

When noise is considered (we first set the noise $z_{ij}(t) = 1$), the NT-FTZNN model using the VAF and several other ZNN models using LAF, PSAF, and SBPAF are hired to solve the same problem (4.9). The corresponding simulation consequences are shown in Figures 4.2–4.5. When the ZNN model using LAF is hired to solve the problem (4.9), the corresponding simulation consequences are shown in Figure 4.2. From Figure 4.2a, one can see that there is always a certain distance between the solid curves and the dash curves, and there is no coincidence all the time. From Figure 4.2b, one can see that when the time reaches 10 seconds, the resultant residual remains stable at approximately 2 instead of 0. That's to say, the ZNN model using LAF cannot solve problem (4.9) accurately when there is a noise $z_{ij}(t) = 1$. When the ZNN models activated by PSAF and SBPAF are employed to solve problem (4.9) with noise $z_{ij}(t) = 1$, the corresponding state solution trajectories are shown in Figures 4.3a and 4.4a, respectively. One can see that all the state solutions of these two subfigures are not convergent to the theoretical solution as time going to infinity. From Figures 4.3b and 4.4b, one can see that the transient behavior of the residual error does not converge to 0 when the time reaches 10 seconds. Specifically, the residual error of the ZNN model activated by PSAF converges to approximately 1.8, and the residual error of the ZNN model activated by SBPAF converges to approximately 2. In addition, the simulation consequences of the NT-FTZNN model employed to solve problem (4.9) are shown in Figure 4.5. Figure 4.5a shows that the state solution $U(t)$ from the randomly generated initial state $U(0)$ converges to the theoretical solution in a very short period of time. Figure 4.5b shows that the transient behavior of the synthesized residual error converges to 0 rapidly in a very short time

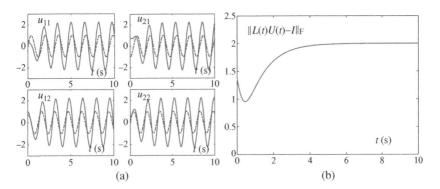

Figure 4.2 Transient behavior of the ZNN model activated by LAF for solving time-dependent matrix inversion (4.9) with noise $z_{ij}(t) = 1$. (a) State solutions and (b) residual error.

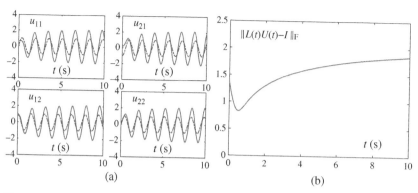

(a)   (b)

Figure 4.3 Transient behavior of the ZNN model activated by power-sum activation function (PSAF) for solving time-dependent matrix inversion (4.9) with noise $z_{ij}(t) = 1$. (a) State solutions and (b) residual error.

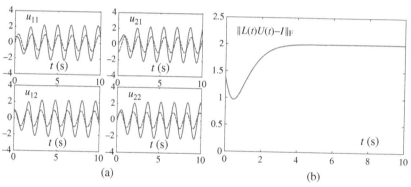

(a)   (b)

Figure 4.4 Transient behavior of the ZNN model activated by SBPAF for solving time-dependent matrix inversion (4.9) with noise $z_{ij}(t) = 1$. (a) State solutions and (b) residual error.

(i.e. approximately 0.6 second that is less than $t_f \leq 1.5$ second). By analyzing Figures 4.2–4.5, one can see that when the noise $z_{ij}(t) = 1$ is considered, only the NT-FTZNN model (4.6) activated by VAF can be employed to solve problem (4.9) accurately, while other ZNN models (activated by LAF, PSAF, and SBPAF) are employed to solve problem (4.9), there will be a larger error.

To further verify the superior predefined-time convergence and the denoising capability of the NT-FTZNN model (4.6) in solving problem (4.9), some more simulation results synthesized by NT-FTZNN model (4.6) activated by VAF and other ZNN models activated by LAF, PSAF, and SBPAF under different noise environments are shown in Figure 4.6. Figure 4.6a shows the transient behavior of the residual errors $\|L(t)U(t) - I\|_F$ synthesized by NT-FTZNN model (4.6) activated by VAF and other ZNN models activated by LAF, PSAF, and SBPAF can converge to

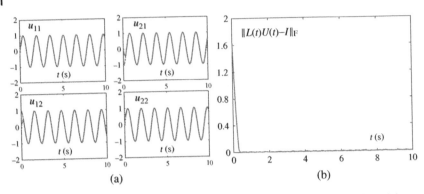

(a)

(b)

Figure 4.5 Transient behavior of NT-FTZNN model (4.6) activated by VAF for solving time-dependent matrix inversion (4.9) with noise $z_{ij}(t) = 1$. (a) State solutions and (b) residual error.

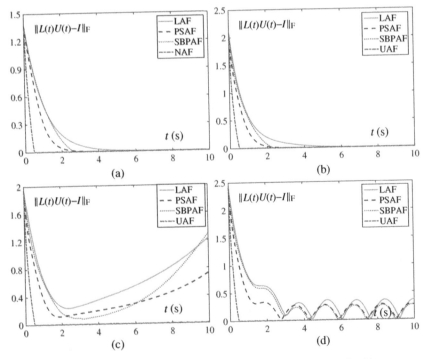

Figure 4.6 Transient behavior of residual errors $\|L(t)U(t) - I\|_F$ synthesized by NT-FTZNN model (4.6) activated by VAF and other ZNN models activated by different activation functions in different noise environments for solving time-dependent matrix inversion (4.9). (a) Noise $z_{ij}(t) = 0$ with $\gamma = 1$, (b) noise $z_{ij}(t) = 0.4|y_{ij}(t)|$ with $\gamma = 1$, (c) noise $z_{ij}(t) = 0.1\exp(0.2t)$ with $\gamma = 1$, and (d) noise $z_{ij}(t) = 0.4\cos(2t)$ with $\gamma = 1$.

0 when noise $z_{ij}(t) = 0$, noting that the time required for the residual error synthesized by NT-FTZNN model (4.6) to converge to 0 is the shortest (i.e. only approximately 0.5 second), while other ZNN models take longer time to converge to 0 (i.e. LAF takes approximately six seconds, PSAF takes approximately three seconds, and SBPAF takes approximately 2.5 seconds). Figure 4.6b considers a gradually disappearing noise disturbance. One can see that all the models can solve problem (4.9) effectively, but the NT-FTZNN model is the fastest compared with other ZNN models. Figure 4.6c considers an unbounded time-dependent noise $z_{ij}(t) = 0.1\exp(0.2t)$, from which we can see that only the residual error of NT-FTZNN model (4.6) activated by VAF can converge to 0 within approximately 0.5 second, while the residual errors of the ZNN models activated by other activation functions gradually diverge over time rather than converge to 0. The fact validates the accuracy of NT-FTZNN model (4.5) for problem (4.9) not only in a steady noise disturbance, but also in time-dependent noise interference. From Figure 4.6d, one can see that when there is time-dependent bounded noise interference, the residual error of NT-FTZNN model (4.6) for solving problem (4.9) can still converge to 0 in approximately 0.5 second, while the residual errors of the ZNN models activated by LAF, PSAF, and SBPAF for solving problem (4.9) are always fluctuating over time.

At last, let us consider different values of parameters for NT-FTZNN model (4.6) and other ZNN models to verify its effectiveness and advantage further. Specifically, we set $\gamma = 10$ and $\gamma = 20$ for these models under the injection of different external disturbances. First, let us consider a time-dependent unbounded noise $z_{ij}(t) = 2t$. As seen from Figure 4.7a, in this simulation, when one increases the value of design parameter $\gamma = 1$ to $\gamma = 10$, the residual error of NT-FTZNN

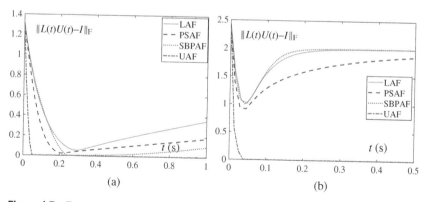

(a) (b)

Figure 4.7 Transient behavior of residual errors $\|L(t)U(t) - I\|_F$ synthesized by NT-FTZNN model (4.6) activated by VAF and other ZNN models activated by different activation functions in different noise environments for solving time-dependent matrix inversion (4.9) with different values of parameter γ. (a) Noise $z_{ij}(t) = 2t$ with $\gamma = 10$ and (b) noise $z_{ij}(t) = 20$ with $\gamma = 20$.

model (4.6) converges to 0 at approximately 0.05 second, while the residual errors of other ZNN models cannot converge to 0 over time. Then, let us consider a large noise $z_{ij}(t) = 20$. In this situation, one can set the design parameter $\gamma = 20$. As observed in Figure 4.7b, NT-FTZNN model (4.6) only takes approximately 0.05 second to accurately solve the problem (4.9), while other ZNN models cannot converge to 0.

4.5.2 Example 2: Six-dimensional Coefficient

To further verify the efficacy and generalization of NT-FTZNN model (4.6), a six-dimensional time-dependent Toeplitz matrix is considered as

$$L(t) = \begin{bmatrix} l_{11}(t) & l_{12}(t) & l_{12}(t) & \cdots & l_{1n}(t) \\ l_{21}(t) & l_{22}(t) & l_{13}(t) & \cdots & l_{2n}(t) \\ l_{31}(t) & l_{32}(t) & l_{33}(t) & \cdots & l_{3n}(t) \\ \cdots & \cdots & \cdots & \cdots & \cdots \\ l_{n1}(t) & l_{n2}(t) & l_{n3}(t) & \cdots & l_{nn}(t) \end{bmatrix} \in \mathbb{R}^{n \times n}, \tag{4.11}$$

with $l_{ij}(t)$ denotes

$$l_{ij}(t) = \begin{cases} 6 + \sin(2t), & i = j, \\ \cos(2t)/(i-j), & i > j, \\ \sin(2t)/(j-i), & i < j, \end{cases}$$

For comparison purposes, GNN and IEZNN models [7–10] are also used to solve the aforementioned time-dependent Toeplitz matrix under the same conditions. All design parameters are kept identical, and simulation results are shown in Figure 4.8.

As seen from Figure 4.8a, when there is constant noise $z_{ij}(t) = 1$, the residual error of NT-FTZNN model (4.6) activated by VAF from the randomly generated initial state can converge to zero rapidly (approximately one second). In contrast, residual errors synthesized by the GNN model and other ZNN models activated by LAF, PSAF, and SBPAF cannot converge to 0 over time. Note that the residual error of the IEZNN model can slowly converge to 0.1 when the time is $t = 10$ seconds. As seen from Figure 4.8b, when there is time-dependent bounded noise interference, the residual error of NT-FTZNN model (4.6) for solving problem (4.11) can still converge to 0 in approximately 0.5 second, while the residual errors of the GNN model, IEZNN model, and ZNN models activated by LAF, PSAF, and SBPAF for solving problem (4.11) are always fluctuating over time. Figure 4.6c considers an unbounded time-dependent noise $z_{ij}(t) = 0.15 \exp(0.2t)$, from which one can see that only the residual error of NT-FTZNN model (4.6) activated by VAF can converge to 0 within approximately 0.5 second, while the residual errors of the other neural models gradually diverge over time rather than

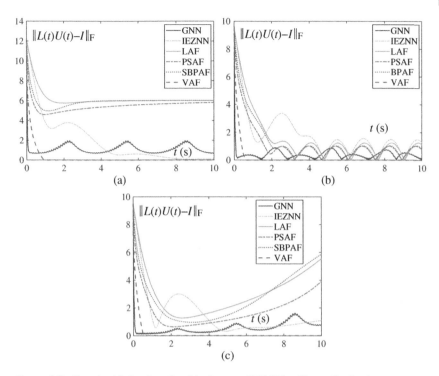

Figure 4.8 Transient behavior of residual errors $\|L(t)U(t) - I\|_F$ synthesized by NT-FTZNN model (4.6) activated by VAF, GNN model, IEZNN model, and other ZNN models activated by LAF, PSAF, and SBPAF under different noise environments for solving time-dependent matrix inversion (4.11). (a) $z_{ij}(t) = 1$, (b) $z_{ij}(t) = 0.5 \sin(2.2t)$, and (c) $z_{ij}(t) = 0.15 \exp(0.2t)$.

converge to 0. The observation validates the accuracy of NT-FTZNN model (4.5) for problem (4.11) not only in a steady noise disturbance, but also in time-dependent noise interference.

From the results of this example, one would have the remark to discuss how NT-FTZNN model (4.5) responds and converges for more training data.

Remark Different from the BP neural network, given the input (i.e. the initial value of neural state matrix $U(0)$), the proposed NT-FTZNN model (4.5) will fall into a dynamic process, repeatedly compute, and finally reach a steady state (i.e. the error function converges to 0). In this sense, the training procedure of the proposed NT-FTZNN model (4.5) can be viewed as global convergence of the error function. In addition, it is worth pointing out that the proposed NT-FTZNN model (4.5) can be solved by Matlab routines, such as "ode45," "ode15s," and so on. For more data (e.g. a larger matrix $X(t)$ shown in this example), the solving process and convergence for the proposed NT-FTZNN model will be acted just like before. Generally speaking, for a specific matrix, the weights of the corresponding NT-FTZNN model are fixed. Therefore, as long as a random initial state is given, the corresponding NT-FTZNN model will output an accurate solution. That is to say, no matter how many times the NT-FTZNN model executes, it always outputs an accurate solution (i.e. the execution is repeated). In this work, simulation results show the value of a single run calculation. In addition, as the NT-FTZNN model is globally convergent, the results generated by the NT-FTZNN model will reach the consensus whatever the initial value is.

As for the computational complexity, as shown in [20], the original ZNN model with LAF contains $4n$ addition operations, $3n^2 + n$ multiplication operations, and n integrator operations, and thus is of $O(n^2)$ operations. The complexity of a RNN is mainly dictated by its architecture. Therefore, as for the NT-FTZNN model, only the activation function $\Phi(\cdot)$ is different and increases its computational complexity, as compared with that of the original ZNN model with the linear activation function. If the VAF is regarded as a whole and realized by co-processors, it only increases one multiplication operation. Therefore, the computational complexity of the NT-FTZNN model is of $O(n^2)$ operations to some degree. Although the NT-FTZNN model possesses more operations on calculating, the computational complexity is on the same order of $O(n^2)$. In addition, the presented model will finally be implemented in hardware with a parallel processing nature, so the ability for real-time computation can be guaranteed.

4.5.3 Example 3: Application to Mobile Manipulator

In this example, the proposed NT-FTZNN model (4.6) would be applied to path tracking of a mobile manipulator [21] by solving inverse kinematical equation in a noisy environment. For comparison, the ZNN model activated by SBPAF is also explored under the same condition. The desired path is set as a circle with the radius being 2 m, and the external additive noise $z_{ij}(t) = 0.35$. Simulative comparison results are described in Figures 4.9 and 4.10. As seen from these two figures, it follows that the ZNN model activated by SBPAF does not complete the desired path tracking, while the proposed NT-FTZNN model (4.6) successfully fulfills the desired circular tracking task. These robotic application results further validate the efficacy and superior robustness of the proposed NT-FTZNN model (4.6).

4.5.4 Example 4: Physical Comparative Experiments

To further validate the real applicability of NT-FTZNN model (4.6), the Kinova JACO^2 manipulator is adopted as a test, and its detailed information can be referred to [22–25]. In this example, two physical comparative experiments

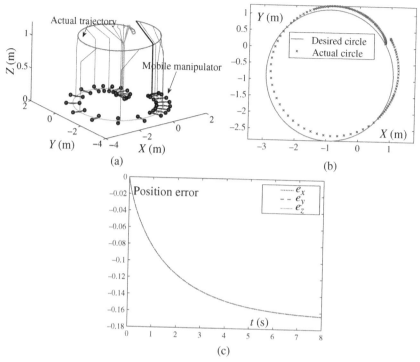

Figure 4.9 Circular task tracking synthesized by the original ZNN model activated by the SBP activation function in the presence of additive noise $z_{ij}(t) = 0.35$. (a) Whole tracking process, (b) task comparison, and (c) position error.

generated respectively by the SBPAF activated ZNN model and NT-FTZNN model (4.6) will be presented for comparison purposes in front of external noise via tracking a butterfly path. Without loss of generality, the external noise is set as $Z(t) = [1, 2, 3; 4, 5, 6; 7, 8, 9]$, $\gamma = 100$, the parameters of a butterfly path are the same as these of [22–24]. The whole process of comparative physical experiments are snapshoted and integrated in Figure 4.11. Observed from Figure 4.11a produced by the SBPAF activated ZNN model, when the external noise disturbance is presented, the end-effector of the robot deviates from the desktop occasionally when tracking the given butterfly path. Therefore, the tracking experiment in this situation is fail, which can be verified by the last snapshot of Figure 4.11a. In contrast, observed from Figure 4.11b produced by NT-FTZNN model (4.6), under the same conditions, the Kinova JACO² manipulator successfully completes the given butterfly-path tracking task.

Through the aforementioned comparative consequences, one can conclude that NT-FTZNN model (4.6) and other ZNN models can be employed to find

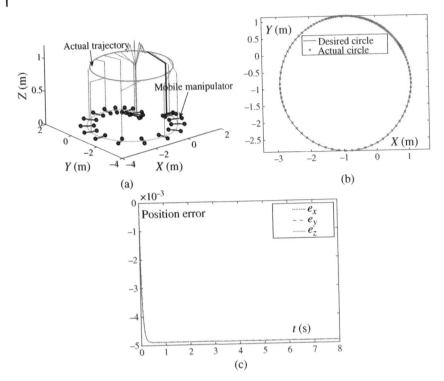

(a)

(b)

(c)

Figure 4.10 Circular task tracking synthesized by NT-FTZNN model (4.6) in the presence of additive noise $z_{ij} = 0.35$. (a) Whole tracking process, (b) task comparison, and (c) position error.

(a)

(b)

Figure 4.11 Physical comparative experiments of a butterfly-path tracking task generated by different ZNN models and performed on the Kinova JACO^2 robot manipulator when disturbed by external noise. (a) Failure by SBPAF activated ZNN and (b) success by NT-FTZNN.

time-independent matrix inversion accurately in the absence of noise, but the NT-FTZNN model (4.6) has the largest convergence rate (i.e. the predefined time convergence) when problem (4.9) is solved. When noise is considered, only NT-FTZNN model (4.6) can be hired to solve problem (4.9) accurately in a predefined time, while other ZNN models are not suitable for solving problem (4.9) due to excessive errors. The robotic application examples also validate this conclusion.

4.6 Chapter Summary

In this current work, a new NT-FTZNN model with a VAF is proposed and researched for finding time-dependent matrix inversion. Unlike the traditional ZNN models that can only be used to find time-dependent matrix inversion in a disturbance-free environment, the proposed NT-FTZNN model can still be used to find time-dependent matrix inversion under various external noises. In addition, the convergence time of the NT-FTZNN model for time-dependent matrix inversion problem can be calculated in advance (i.e. the upper bound of the predefined convergence time is known). In addition to this property, the excellent robustness of the NT-FTZNN model is also analyzed in detail under the injection of different external disturbances. The main reason for these excellent properties is to add a new sign function, which makes the NT-FTZNN model satisfy the requirement of the predefined time convergence. At last, two numerical simulations with different dimensions and two practical applications are used as test examples in a noisy environment, of which the final consequences further substantiated the effectiveness, excellence, and applicability of the NT-FTZNN model, as compared with the traditional ZNN models using existing activation functions (such as LAF, PSAF, and SBPAF).

References

1 H. Prabhu and J. Rodrigues *et al.*, Approximative matrix inverse computations for very-large MIMO and applications to linear pre-coding systems, 2013 IEEE Wireless Communications and Networking Conference (WCNC), (2013) 2710–2715.

2 D. Zhu, B. Li, and Z. Liang, On the matrix inversion approximation based on Neumann series in massive MIMO systems, 2015 IEEE international conference on communications (ICC), (2015) 1763–1769.

3 L. Xiao and S. Li *et al.*, Co-design of finite-time convergence and noise suppression: A unified neural model for time varying linear equations with robotic applications, *IEEE Trans. Syst. Man Cybern. Syst.*, 50(12) (2020) 5233–5243.

4 L. Xiao and Y. Zhang, A new performance index for the repetitive motion of mobile manipulators, *IEEE Trans. Cybern.*, 44(2) (2014) 280–292.

5 Z. Zhang and T. Fu *et al.*, A varying-parameter convergent-differential neural network for solving joint-angular-drift problems of redundant robot manipulators, *IEEE ASME Trans. Mechatron.*, 23(2) (2018) 679–689.

6 L. Xiao, Z. Zhang, and S. Li, Solving time-varying system of nonlinear equations by finite-time recurrent neural networks with application to motion tracking of robot manipulators, *IEEE Trans. Syst. Man Cybern. Syst.*, 49(11) (2019) 2210–2220.

7 Y. Zhang and S. S. Ge, Design and analysis of a general recurrent neural network model for time-varying matrix inversion, *IEEE Trans. Neural Netw.*, 16(6) (2005) 1477–1490.

8 Y. Zhang, W. Ma, and B. Cai, From Zhang neural network to Newton iteration for matrix inversion, *IEEE Trans. Circuits Syst. I Regul. Pap.*, 56(7) (2009) 1405–1415.

9 L. Jin, Y. Zhang, and S. Li, Integration-enhanced Zhang neural network for real-time-varying matrix inversion in the presence of various kinds of noises, *IEEE Trans. Neural Netw. Learn. Syst.*, 27(12) (2016) 2615–2627.

10 L. Jin, S. Li, and B. Hu, RNN models for dynamic matrix inversion: A control-theoretical perspective, *IEEE Trans. Ind. Inform.*, 14(1) (2018) 189–199.

11 L. Xiao, A finite-time convergent Zhang neural network and its application to real-time matrix square root finding, *Neural Comput. & Appl.*, 31(2) (2019) 793–800.

12 A. Polyakov, Nonlinear feedback design for fixed-time stabilization of linear control systems, *IEEE Trans. Autom. Control*, 57(8) (2012) 2106–2110.

13 L. Xiao and Y. Zhang *et al.*, A novel recurrent neural network and its finite-time solution to time-varying complex matrix inversion, *Neurocomputing*, 331 (2019) 483–492.

14 J. P. Mishra and C. Li *et al.*, Fixed-time converging terminal surface with non-singular control design for second-order systems, *IFAC-PapersOnLine*, 50(1) (2017) 5139–5143.

15 W. Li and B. Liao *et al.*, A recurrent neural network with predefined-time convergence and improved noise tolerance for dynamic matrix square root finding, *Neurocomputing*, 337 (2019) 262–273.

16 W. Li, A recurrent neural network with explicitly definable convergence time for solving time-variant linear matrix equations, *IEEE Trans. Ind. Inform.*, 14(12) (2018) 5289–5298.

17 Q. Xiang and B. Liao, A noise-tolerant Z-type neural network for time-dependent pseudoinverse matrices, *Optik*, 165 (2018) 16–28.

18 Y. Zhang, C. Yi, and W. Ma, Simulation and verification of Zhang neural network for online time-varying matrix inversion, *Simul. Model. Pract. Theory*, 17(10) (2009) 1603–1617.

19 D. Guo, Z. Nie, and L. Yan, Novel discrete-time Zhang neural network for time-varying matrix inversion, *IEEE Trans. Syst. Man. Cybern. Syst.*, 47(8) (2017) 2301–2310.

20 L. Xiao and Y. Zhang, Zhang neural network versus gradient neural network for solving time-varying linear inequalities, *IEEE Trans. Neural Netw.*, 22(10) (2011) 1676–1684.

21 L. Xiao and B. Liao *et al.*, Design and analysis of FTZNN applied to real-time solution of nonstationary Lyapunov equation and tracking control of wheeled mobile manipulator, *IEEE Trans. Ind. Inform.*, 14(1) (2018) 98–105.

22 Z. Zhang and Y. Lu *et al.*, A new varying-parameter convergent-differential neural-network for solving time-varying convex QP problem constrained by linear-equality, *IEEE Trans. Autom. Control*, 63(12) (2018) 4110–4125.

23 Z. Zhang and L. Zheng *et al.*, A new varying-parameter recurrent neural-network for online solution of time-varying Sylvester equation, *IEEE Trans. Cybern.*, 48(11) (2018) 3135–3148.

24 Z. Zhang, Z. Yan, and T. Fu, Varying-parameter RNN activated by finite-time functions for solving joint-drift problems of redundant robot manipulators, *IEEE Trans. Ind. Inform.*, 14(12) (2018) 5359–5367.

25 Z. Zhang and Z. Li *et al.*, Neural-dynamic-method-based dual-arm CMG scheme with time-varying constraints applied to humanoid robots, *IEEE Trans. Neural Netw. Learn. Syst.*, 26(12) (2015) 3251–3262.

5

Design Scheme III of FTZNN

5.1 Introduction

Matrix inversion problems are ubiquitous in scientific and engineering field [1, 2], such as multiple-input multiple-output (MIMO) [1], robots [2], and image processing [3]. For solving matrix inversion equations, some numerical algorithms such as iterative methods have been commonly used to find matrix inversions [4]. Although these methods can be effectively applied in matrix inversion, some unacceptable disadvantages such as high complexity and long time consuming [5] are inevitable. Therefore, when faced with large-scale real-time computing problems, these traditional numerical algorithms turn to be not so suitable for finding theoretical solutions in real time.

In this chapter, an improved varying parameter finite-time zeroing neural network (IVP-FTZNN) model for computing time-varying matrix inversion (TVMI) is proposed and investigated. Additionally, the global super-exponential convergence property of the proposed IVP-FTZNN model is strictly proved. When the sign-bi-power activation function (SBPAF) and tunable activation function (TAF) are employed, the upper bounds of the finite time convergence of the proposed IVP-FTZNN model are analyzed and estimated separately. Compared with the existed fixed parameter zeroing neural network (FPZNN) [6], exponential-enhanced-type varying parameter zeroing neural network (EVPZNN) [7], and varying-parameter zeroing neural network (VPZNN) [8] models, the proposed IVP-FTZNN model has faster speed and better robustness for solving the TVMI problem, regardless of whether external noise exists or not.

5.2 Problem Formulation and Neural Solver

The TVMI problem can be mathematically expressed as

$$H(t)U(t) = I \in \mathbb{R}^{n \times n} \quad \text{or} \quad U(t)H(t) = I \in \mathbb{R}^{n \times n}, \tag{5.1}$$

Zeroing Neural Networks: Finite-time Convergence Design, Analysis and Applications,
First Edition. Lin Xiao and Lei Jia.
© 2023 The Institute of Electrical and Electronics Engineers, Inc. Published 2023 by John Wiley & Sons, Inc.

where $H(t) \in \mathbb{R}^{n \times n}$ is a known time-varying matrix, $U(t) \in \mathbb{R}^{n \times n}$ is an unknown reversible matrix to be solved, and $I \in \mathbb{R}^{n \times n}$ is an identity matrix of appropriate size. In order to supervise the process of solving TVMI, let $U^{-1}(t) \in \mathbb{R}^{n \times n}$ represent the theoretical inversion of (5.1).

The purpose of this work is to construct an IVP-FTZNN model for TVMI (5.1) solving. For the purpose of comparison, the traditional FPZNN model is also established to calculate the TVMI, with the detailed design steps and common activation functions listed.

5.2.1 FPZNN Model

As a type of recurrent neural network, zeroing neural network (ZNN) is often employed for calculating time-varying problems. Generally, the design process of ZNN has the following three steps [5]:

1. Define an error function based on the problem to be solved.
2. Design an evolution formula for ensuring that the error function can converge to 0.
3. Obtain the corresponding ZNN model by substituting the error function into the evolution formula.

According to the ZNN model's design steps [5, 9], an error function for TVMI (5.1) can be given as follows:

$$Y(t) = H(t)U(t) - I \in \mathbb{R}^{n \times n}. \tag{5.2}$$

Apparently, when all elements in $Y(t)$ converge to zero, $U(t)$ can approach to the theoretical inverse $U^{-1}(t)$ of (5.1). To ensure that all elements in $Y(t)$ converge to 0, a design formula is studied and utilized as follows [9, 10]:

$$\frac{dY(t)}{dt} = -\gamma\Phi(Y(t)), \tag{5.3}$$

where $\Phi(\cdot) : \mathbb{R}^{n \times n} \to \mathbb{R}^{n \times n}$ is an odd activation function array with each element denoted by $\phi(\cdot) : \mathbb{R} \to \mathbb{R}$ and γ is a known scalable positive fixed parameter that can be hired to adjust the convergence speed of ZNN.

Then, substituting (5.2) into (5.3), and noting that the time derivative of $Y(t)$ in (5.2) is $\dot{Y}(t) = \dot{H}(t)U(t) + H(t)\dot{U}(t)$, the ZNN model for TVMI can be obtained:

$$H(t)\dot{U}(t) = -\dot{H}(t)U(t) - \gamma\Phi(H(t)U(t) - I). \tag{5.4}$$

Considering that $\gamma > 0$ in (5.4) is a fixed parameter, this ZNN model (5.4) is called the FPZNN model. Besides, different activation functions (AFs) for ZNN can result in different convergence properties. Some commonly employed odd activation functions are listed as follows:

1. linear activation function (LAF): $\phi(x) = x$;
2. bipolar sigmoid activation function (BSAF) ($\zeta > 1$):
   $\phi(x) = (1 - \exp(-\zeta x))/(1 + \exp(-\zeta x))$;

3. power activation function (PAF):
   $\phi(x) = x^\tau$ with $\tau \geq 3$ denoting an odd integer;
4. power-sigmoid activation function (PSAF):

$$\phi(x) = \begin{cases} x^\tau, & \text{if } |x| \geq 1, \\ \frac{1+\exp(-\zeta)}{1-\exp(-\zeta)} \cdot \frac{1-\exp(-\zeta x)}{1+\exp(-\zeta x)}, & \text{otherwise,} \end{cases}$$

with $\tau \geq 3$ and $\zeta > 1$;
5. hyperbolic sine activation function (HSAF) $(\zeta > 1)$:
   $\phi(x) = (\exp(\zeta x) - \exp(-\zeta x))/2$;
6. sign-bi-power activation function (SBPAF):
   $\phi(x) = (|x|^\varepsilon + |x|^{1/\varepsilon})\text{sgn}(x)/2$ with $0 < \varepsilon < 1$ and $\text{sgn}(\cdot)$ denoting the signum function.
7. tunable activation function (TAF):
   $\phi(x) = ((\kappa_1|x|^\varepsilon + \kappa_3|x|^{1/\varepsilon})\text{sgn}(x) + \kappa_2(x))/2$ with $0 < \varepsilon < 1$, $\kappa_1 > 0$, $\kappa_2 > 0$ and $\kappa_3 > 0$.

In this chapter, for convenience, SBPAF is hired to accelerate ZNN models for finding the theoretical inversion $H^{-1}(t)$ of TVMI equation (5.1).

5.2.2 IVP-FTZNN Model

It is noted that the design parameter γ in FPZNN model (5.4) is a constant real number. In general, the design parameter of the neural network should be set as large as possible in the actual engineering application. Therefore, in this subsection, the establishment process of a IVP-FTZNN model with time-varying increasing design parameters is shown next in detail.

Like the FPZNN model (5.4), we first define an error function $Y(t)$ that is exactly the same as (5.2). On the other hand, unlike the FPZNN model's evolution formula, where the design parameter γ is fixed, the IVP-FTZNN model has a time-varying design parameter $\gamma(t)$ as follows:

$$\frac{dY(t)}{dt} = -\gamma(t)\Phi(Y(t)). \tag{5.5}$$

In addition, another type of time-varying parameter is proposed in the literature [7] to establish the EVPZNN model:

$$\gamma_1(t) = k^t + k, \quad k > 0, \tag{5.6}$$

and the corresponding expression of the EVPZNN is

$$H(t)\dot{U}(t) = -\dot{H}(t)U(t) - \gamma_1(t)\Phi(H(t)U(t) - I). \tag{5.7}$$

Note that the expression of the time-varying parameter in the VPZNN model proposed in [8] is

$$\gamma_2(t) = t^k + k, \quad k > 0, \tag{5.8}$$

where $t > 0$ represents time variable and $k > 0$ represents a positive real number. Substituting (5.2) and the time-varying parameter (5.8) into (5.5), the following VPZNN can be derived:

$$H(t)\dot{U}(t) = -\dot{H}(t)U(t) - \gamma_2(t)\Phi(H(t)U(t) - I). \tag{5.9}$$

Inspired by using the time-varying parameter to build the VPZNN model, the following improved time-varying parameter is hired to design the IVP-FTZNN model in this work:

$$\gamma(t) = \begin{cases} t^k + k, & 0 < k \le 1, \\ k^{t+2} + 2kt + k^2, & k > 1. \end{cases} \tag{5.10}$$

Similarly, by substituting (5.2) into (5.5) with time-varying parameter (5.10), the IVP-FTZNN model is obtained as

$$H(t)\dot{U}(t) = -\dot{H}(t)U(t) - \gamma(t)\Phi(H(t)U(t) - I). \tag{5.11}$$

It is worth noting that when $0 < k \le 1$, the improved time-varying parameter $\gamma(t)$ becomes exactly the same as the time-varying parameter (5.8). That's to say, compared with VPZNN in [8], the superior performance of our studied IVP-FTZNN model (5.11) is mainly reflected in the case of $k > 1$.

5.3 Theoretical Analysis

The main theoretical results of IVP-FTZNN model (5.11) are shown in this section.

Theorem 5.1 *Given an invertible matrix $H(t) \in \mathbb{R}^{n \times n}$ defined in (5.1), when the SBPAF array $\Phi(\cdot)$ is hired, the state matrix $U(t) \in \mathbb{R}^{n \times n}$ of IVP-FTZNN model (5.11), starting from a random initial value $U(0)$, can globally and super-exponentially converge towards the theoretical inverse $H^{-1}(t)$.*

Proof: Let $\overline{U}(t) = U(t) - \tilde{U}(t)$, where $\tilde{U}(t) = H^{-1}(t)$. Considering $Y(t) = H(t)U(t) - I$, one can obtain:

$$\begin{aligned} Y(t) &= H(t)U(t) - I \\ &= H(t)(\overline{U}(t) + \tilde{U}(t)) - I \\ &= H(t)\overline{U}(t). \end{aligned} \tag{5.12}$$

Substituting design formula $\dot{Y}(t) = -\gamma(t)\Phi(Y(t))$ of IVP-FTZNN model (5.11) into Eq. (5.12), one can have

$$H(t)\dot{\overline{U}}(t) = -\dot{H}(t)\overline{U}(t) - \gamma(t)\Phi(H(t)\overline{U}(t)). \tag{5.13}$$

Usually, the Lyapunov theorem is often used to prove the stability and convergence property of a neurodynamic system. To facilitate analysis stability, a Lyapunov function candidate is defined as

$$p(t) = \frac{\|Y(t)\|_F^2}{2} = \frac{\mathrm{Tr}((Y(t))^\mathrm{T} Y(t))}{2}, \tag{5.14}$$

and its time derivative is

$$\begin{aligned} \dot{p}(t) &= \mathrm{Tr}((Y(t))^\mathrm{T} \dot{Y}(t)) \\ &= -\gamma(t)\mathrm{Tr}((Y(t))^\mathrm{T} \Phi(Y(t))). \end{aligned} \tag{5.15}$$

Since $\phi(\cdot)$ is a monotonically increasing odd activation function, one can obtain $\phi(-x) = -\phi(x)$, and

$$\phi(x) \begin{cases} > 0, & \text{if } x > 0, \\ = 0, & \text{if } x = 0, \\ < 0, & \text{if } x < 0. \end{cases} \tag{5.16}$$

Hence,

$$x\phi(x) \begin{cases} > 0, & \text{if } x \neq 0, \\ = 0, & \text{if } x = 0. \end{cases} \tag{5.17}$$

It follows that

$$\gamma(t)\mathrm{Tr}((Y(t))^\mathrm{T} \Phi(Y(t))) \geq 0. \tag{5.18}$$

That is to say, $\dot{p}(t) \leq 0$. According to the Lyapunov stability theory [10, 11], when IVP-FTZNN model (5.11) is employed for the TVMI (5.1), the error $Y(t)$ of IVP-FTZNN model (5.11) can globally converge to 0 as time goes to infinity. At the same time, the state solution $U(t)$ gradually converges to $\tilde{U}(t) = H^{-1}(t)$.

In addition, for the AF $\Phi(\cdot)$, if the LAF array is considered, one can obtain

$$\dot{p}(t) = -\gamma(t)\|Y(t)\|_F^2 = -2\gamma(t)p(t). \tag{5.19}$$

Hence,

$$p(t) \leq p(0)\exp(-2\gamma(t)), \tag{5.20}$$

$$\|Y(t)\|_F \leq \|Y(0)\|_F \exp(-\gamma(t)). \tag{5.21}$$

Thus, one can conclude that when it comes to a LAF, the error $Y(t)$ of the established IVP-FTZNN model (5.11) exponentially converges to 0. Better still, contributing to the nonlinearity and monotonicity of $\gamma(t)$, super-exponential convergence is achieved in the case of LAF. Noting that the abstract value of SBPAF keeps larger than the LAF, which leads to a faster speed for the decrease of $\|Y(t)\|_F$, thus the proposed IVP-FTZNN model (5.11) has super-exponential convergence performance.

That is to say, when the SBPAF array $\Phi(\cdot)$ is hired, the state matrix $U(t) \in \mathbb{R}^{n \times n}$ of the proposed IVP-FTZNN model (5.11), starting from a random initial value $U(0)$, can globally and super-exponentially converge toward the theoretical inverse $H^{-1}(t)$. This completes the proof. ∎

Theorem 5.2 *Given an invertible time-varying matrix $H(t) \in \mathbb{R}^{n \times n}$ defined in (5.1), when the SBPAF array $\Phi(\cdot)$ is hired, the state matrix $U(t) \in \mathbb{R}^{n \times n}$ of the proposed IVP-FTZNN model (5.11), starting from a random initial value $U(0)$, can converge towards the theoretical inverse $H^{-1}(t)$ in finite time. The convergence time satisfies*

$$
\begin{cases}
t^{k+1} + k(k+1)t \le \frac{(k+1)(y^+(0))^{1-\varepsilon}}{1-\varepsilon}, & 0 < k \le 1, \\
\frac{k^{t+2}}{\ln k} + kt^2 + k^2 t \le \frac{(y^+(0))^{1-\varepsilon} + \frac{(1-\varepsilon)k^2}{\ln k}}{1-\varepsilon}, & k > 1.
\end{cases}
$$

where $0 < \varepsilon < 1$, $y^+(0) = \max_{1 \le i,j \le n}\{y_{ij}(0)\}$ with $y_{ij}(0)$ being the ijth element of the initial error function $Y(0) = H(0)U(0) - I$ and $k > 0$ is defined as before.

Proof: Consider the following design formula:

$$
\dot{Y}(t) = -\gamma(t)\Phi(Y(t)), \tag{5.22}
$$

where

$$
\gamma(t) = \begin{cases} t^k + k, & 0 < k \le 1, \\ k^{t+2} + 2kt + k^2, & k > 1. \end{cases} \quad t \in [0, +\infty). \tag{5.23}
$$

The scalar form of (5.22) is

$$
\dot{y}_{ij}(t) = -\gamma(t)\Phi(y_{ij}(t)), \tag{5.24}
$$

with $\forall i,j \in \{1, \ldots, n\}$.

Defining Lyapunov functions $p_{ij}(t) = y_{ij}^2(t)$, and $p^*(t) = (y^+(t))^2$, we have $p_{ij}(t) \le p^*(t)$. Because the SBPAF array $\Phi(\cdot)$ is hired, the following result is got as

$$
\begin{aligned}
\dot{p}^*(t) &= -\gamma(t)y^+(t)\left(|y^+(t)|^\varepsilon + |y^+(t)|^{\frac{1}{\varepsilon}}\right)\operatorname{sgn}(y^+(t)) \\
&= -\gamma(t)|y^+(t)|\left(|y^+(t)|^\varepsilon + |y^+(t)|^{\frac{1}{\varepsilon}}\right) \\
&\le -2\gamma(t)|y^+(t)|\min\left\{|y^+(t)|^\varepsilon, |y^+(t)|^{\frac{1}{\varepsilon}}\right\} \\
&= -2\gamma(t)(p^*(t))^{\frac{1}{2}}\min\left\{(p^*(t))^{\frac{\varepsilon}{2}}, (p^*(t))^{\frac{1}{2\varepsilon}}\right\} \\
&= -2\gamma(t)(p^*(t))^{\frac{1+\varepsilon}{2}},
\end{aligned} \tag{5.25}
$$

where $0 < \varepsilon < 1$, $y^+(0) = \max\{y_{ij}(0)\}$ with $y_{ij}(0)$ being the ijth element of the initial error function $Y(0) = H(0)U(0) - I$ and $k > 0$ is defined as before.

■ For $0 < k \le 1$, i.e. $\gamma(t) = t^k + k$, one can obtain

$$\dot{p}^*(t) \le -2\left(t^k + k\right)(p^*(t))^{\frac{1+\varepsilon}{2}}.$$

Calculating this differential inequality leads to

$$0 \le (p^*(t))^{\frac{1-\varepsilon}{2}} \le (1-\varepsilon)\left(-\frac{t^{k+1}}{k+1} - kt\right) + (y^+(0))^{1-\varepsilon}.$$

So, the convergence upper bound for t satisfies

$$t^{k+1} + k(k+1)t \le \frac{(k+1)y^+(0)^{1-\varepsilon}}{1-\varepsilon}.$$

In other words, $p^*(t) \equiv 0$ after the following constraint condition is satisfied:

$$t^{k+1} + k(k+1)t > \frac{(k+1)y^+(0)^{1-\varepsilon}}{1-\varepsilon}.$$

■ For $k > 1$, i.e. $\gamma(t) = k^{t+2} + 2kt + k^2$, then

$$\dot{p}^*(t) \le -2\left(k^{t+2} + 2kt + k^2\right)(p^*(t))^{\frac{1+\varepsilon}{2}}.$$

Hence, the following inequality holds

$$0 \le (p^*(t))^{\frac{1-\varepsilon}{2}} \le (1-\varepsilon)\left(-\frac{k^{t+2}}{\ln k} - kt^2 - k^2t\right) + y^+(0)^{1-\varepsilon} + \frac{(1-\varepsilon)k^2}{\ln k},$$

from which one can obtain

$$\frac{k^{t+2}}{\ln k} + kt^2 + k^2t \le \frac{y^+(0)^{1-\varepsilon} + \frac{(1-\varepsilon)k^2}{\ln k}}{1-\varepsilon}.$$

In other words, $p^*(t) \equiv 0$ after the following constraint condition is satisfied:

$$\frac{k^{t+2}}{\ln k} + kt^2 + k^2t > \frac{y^+(0)^{1-\varepsilon} + \frac{(1-\varepsilon)k^2}{\ln k}}{1-\varepsilon}.$$

Therefore, we have

$$\begin{cases} t^{k+1} + k(k+1)t \le \frac{(k+1)y^+(0)^{1-\varepsilon}}{1-\varepsilon}, & 0 < k \le 1, \\ \frac{k^{t+2}}{\ln k} + kt^2 + k^2t \le \frac{y^+(0)^{1-\varepsilon} + \frac{(1-\varepsilon)k^2}{\ln k}}{1-\varepsilon}, & k > 1. \end{cases}$$

Thus, one can conclude that the proposed IVP-FTZNN model (5.11) possesses the finite time convergence property when SBPAF is explored. This completes the proof. ■

Theorem 5.3 *Given an invertible matrix $H(t) \in \mathbb{R}^{n \times n}$ defined in (5.1), when the TAF array $\Phi(\cdot)$ is hired, the state matrix $U(t) \in \mathbb{R}^{n \times n}$ of the proposed IVP-FTZNN model (5.11), starting from a random initial value $U(0)$, can converge towards the theoretical inverse $H^{-1}(t)$ in finite time. The convergence time satisfies the following results.*

- *When $0 < k \le 1$, $\gamma(t) = t^k + k$, then*

$$\begin{cases} \frac{t^{k+1}}{k+1} + kt \le t_1, & p_1(0) \ge 1, \\[2mm] \frac{t^{k+1}}{k+1} + kt \le t_2, & p_1(0) < 1, \end{cases}$$

- *and when $k > 1$, $\gamma(t) = k^{t+2} + 2kt + k^2$, then*

$$\begin{cases} \frac{k^{t+2}}{\ln k} + kt^2 + k^2 t \le t_1 + \frac{2k^2}{\ln k}, & p_1(0) \ge 1, \\[2mm] \frac{k^{t+2}}{\ln k} + kt^2 + k^2 t \le t_2 + \frac{k^2}{\ln k}, & p_1(0) < 1, \end{cases}$$

with

$$t_1 = \frac{2\varepsilon \ln\left[\frac{\kappa_2 + \kappa_3}{\kappa_2 p_1(0)^{\frac{\varepsilon-1}{2\varepsilon}} + \kappa_3}\right]}{\kappa_2(1-\varepsilon)} + \frac{2\ln\left(1 + \frac{\kappa_2}{\kappa_1}\right)}{\kappa_2(1-\varepsilon)},$$

$$t_2 = \frac{2\ln\left[1 + \frac{\kappa_2}{\kappa_1}p_1(0)^{\frac{1-\varepsilon}{2}}\right]}{\kappa_2(1-\varepsilon)},$$

where $0 < \varepsilon < 1$, κ_1, κ_2, and κ_3 are positive parameters of the TAF array $\Phi(\cdot)$, $p_1(0) = (y^+(0))^2$, $y^+(0) = \max\{y_{ij}(0)\}$ with y_{ij} being the ijth element of the initial error function $Y(0) = H(0)U(0) - I$ and $k > 0$.

Proof: Define Lyapunov functions $p_{ij}(t) = y_{ij}^2(t)$ and $p_1(t) = (y^+(t))^2$. Considering that $\dot{y}_{ij}(t) = -\gamma\phi(y_{ij}(t))$ and $y^+(0) = \max\{y_{ij}(0)\}$, $p_{ij}(t)$ naturally converges to zero when $p_1(t)$ converges to zero. Since the TAF $\phi(\cdot)$ is employed, we get

$$\begin{aligned} \dot{p}_1(t) &= -2\gamma(t)y^+(t)\phi(y^+(t)) \\ &= -\gamma(t)|y^+(t)|\left(\kappa_1|y^+(t)|^\varepsilon + \kappa_2|y^+(t)| + \kappa_3|y^+(t)|^{\frac{1}{\varepsilon}}\right) \\ &= -\gamma(t)\left(\kappa_1|y^+(t)|^{\varepsilon+1} + \kappa_2|y^+(t)|^2 + \kappa_3|y^+(t)|^{\frac{1+\varepsilon}{\varepsilon}}\right) \\ &= -\gamma(t)\left(\kappa_1 p_1(t)^{\frac{\varepsilon+1}{2}} + \kappa_2 p_1(t) + \kappa_3 p_1(t)^{\frac{\varepsilon+1}{2\varepsilon}}\right). \end{aligned} \qquad (5.26)$$

- If $0 < k \le 1$, $\gamma(t) = t^k + k$. For $p(0) = (y^+(0))^2 \le 1$, one can consider the following:

$$\dot{p}_1(t) = -\left(t^k + k\right)\left(\kappa_1 p_1(t)^{\frac{\varepsilon+1}{2}} + \kappa_2 p_1(t)\right). \qquad (5.27)$$

Solving this Bernoulli equation, we have

$$\begin{aligned} p_1(t)^{1-s} y^{\kappa_2(1-s)\left(\frac{t^{k+1}}{k+1}+kt\right)} &+ \frac{\kappa_1}{\kappa_2} y^{\kappa_2(1-s)\left(\frac{t^{k+1}}{k+1}+kt\right)} \\ &= p_1(0)^{1-s} + \frac{\kappa_1}{\kappa_2}, \end{aligned} \qquad (5.28)$$

where $s = \frac{1+\varepsilon}{2}$. Since $p_1(0) \le 1$, one can have

$$\frac{\kappa_1}{\kappa_2} y^{\kappa_2(1-s)\left(\frac{k+1}{k+1}+kt\right)} \le p_1(0)^{1-s} + \frac{\kappa_1}{\kappa_2}. \tag{5.29}$$

Further,

$$\frac{t^{k+1}}{k+1} + kt \le \frac{2\ln\left[1 + \frac{\kappa_2}{\kappa_1} p_1(0)^{\frac{1-\varepsilon}{2}}\right]}{\kappa_2(1-\varepsilon)}. \tag{5.30}$$

For $p_1(0) = (y^+(0))^2 \ge 1$, one can consider

$$\dot{p}_1(t) = -\left(t^k + k\right)\left(\kappa_2 p_1(t) + \kappa_3 p_1(t)^{\frac{\varepsilon+1}{2\varepsilon}}\right). \tag{5.31}$$

By using the formula for general solution of the Bernoulli equation, when $p_1(0) > 1$, we have

$$\frac{t^{k+1}}{k+1} + kt \le \frac{2\varepsilon \ln\left[\frac{\kappa_2 + \kappa_3}{\kappa_2 p_1(0)^{\frac{\varepsilon-1}{2\varepsilon}} + k_3}\right]}{\kappa_2(1-\varepsilon)}. \tag{5.32}$$

Considering (5.30), when $p_1(0) = 1$,

$$\frac{t^{k+1}}{k+1} + kt = \frac{2\ln\left(1 + \frac{\kappa_2}{\kappa_1}\right)}{\kappa_2(1-\varepsilon)}. \tag{5.33}$$

Thus,

$$\frac{t^{k+1}}{k+1} + kt \le \frac{2\varepsilon \ln\left[\frac{\kappa_2 + \kappa_3}{\kappa_2 p_1(0)^{\frac{\varepsilon-1}{2\varepsilon}} + \kappa_3}\right]}{\kappa_2(1-\varepsilon)} + \frac{2\ln\left(1 + \frac{\kappa_2}{\kappa_1}\right)}{\kappa_2(1-\varepsilon)}.$$

- If $k > 1$, $\gamma(t) = k^{t+2} + 2kt + k^2$. When $p_1(0) = (y^+(0))^2 \le 1$, then

$$\dot{p}_1(t) \le -\left(k^{t+2} + 2kt + k^2\right)\left(\kappa_1 p_1(t)^{\frac{t+1}{2}} + \kappa_2 p_1(t)\right). \tag{5.34}$$

Since $p_1(0) \le 1$, one can get

$$\frac{k^{t+2}}{\ln k} + kt^2 + k^2 t \le \frac{2\ln\left[1 + \frac{\kappa_2}{\kappa_1} p_1(0)^{\frac{1-\varepsilon}{2}}\right]}{\kappa_2(1-\varepsilon)} + \frac{k^2}{\ln k}. \tag{5.35}$$

When $p_1(0) = (y^+(0))^2 \ge 1$, then

$$\dot{p}_1(t) \le -\left(k^{t+2} + 2kt + k^2\right)\left(\kappa_2 p_1(t) + \kappa_3 p_1(t)^{\frac{\varepsilon+1}{2\varepsilon}}\right). \tag{5.36}$$

Solving this differential inequality, one can obtain

$$\frac{k^{t+2}}{\ln k} + kt^2 + k^2 t < \frac{2\varepsilon \ln\left[\frac{\kappa_2 + \kappa_3}{\kappa_2 p_1(0)^{\frac{\varepsilon-1}{2\varepsilon}} + \kappa_3}\right]}{\kappa_2(1-\varepsilon)} + \frac{k^2}{\ln k}. \tag{5.37}$$

Considering (5.35), when $p_1(0) = 1$, it follows that

$$\frac{k^{t+2}}{\ln k} + kt^2 + k^2 t = \frac{2\ln\left[1 + \frac{\kappa_1}{\kappa_2}\right]}{\kappa_2(1-\varepsilon)} + \frac{k^2}{\ln k}. \tag{5.38}$$

Hence, for $p_1(0) \geq 1$, we have

$$\frac{k^{t+2}}{\ln k} + kt^2 + k^2 t \leq \frac{2\varepsilon\ln\left[\frac{\kappa_2+\kappa_3}{\kappa_2 p_1(0)^{\frac{\varepsilon-1}{2\varepsilon}}+\kappa_3}\right] + 2\ln\left(1 + \frac{\kappa_2}{\kappa_1}\right)}{\kappa_2(1-\varepsilon)} + \frac{2k^2}{\ln k}.$$

This completes the proof. ∎

5.4 Illustrative Verification

In Section 5.2, by employing a specially constructed time varying parameter, IVP-FTZNN model (5.11) is proposed to solve the TVMI (5.1). In Section 5.3, theoretical analyses of global super-exponential convergence and finite time convergence of IVP-FTZNN model (5.11) activated by SBPAF and TAF are given in detail. In this part, two test examples are employed to demonstrate the effectiveness and dominance of the proposed IVP-FTZNN model (5.11). For comparison, existing FPZNN model (5.4), EVPZNN model (5.7), and VPZNN model (5.9) are also applied to solve this TVMI (5.1).

5.4.1 Example 1: Two-Dimensional Coefficient

In the first place, one can set the design parameter $\gamma = k = 1.5$, and pick the coefficient matrices of TVMI (5.1) as

$$H(t) = \begin{bmatrix} \sin(4t) & -\cos(4t) \\ \cos(4t) & \sin(4t) \end{bmatrix} \quad \text{and} \quad I = \begin{bmatrix} 1 & 0 \\ 0 & 1 \end{bmatrix}.$$

Apparently, the corresponding theoretical inverse H^{-1} of the TVMI (5.1) can be easily calculated as

$$H^{-1}(t) = \begin{bmatrix} \sin(4t) & \cos(4t) \\ -\cos(4t) & \sin(4t) \end{bmatrix},$$

which can be used as a criterion for measuring the correctness of FPZNN (5.4), EVPZNN (5.7), VPZNN (5.9), and IVP-FTZNN (5.11) to solve TVMI (5.1).

First, let's set $\varepsilon = 1/3$, $\kappa_1 = 1$, $\kappa_2 = 1$, $\kappa_3 = 1$, $\zeta = 4$, $\tau = 3$. Employing FPZNN (5.4), EVPZNN (5.7), VPZNN (5.9), and the proposed IVP-FTZNN (5.11) for solving TVMI (5.1) activated by the same SBPAF, the corresponding calculation results are plotted in Figures 5.1–5.4. Figure 5.1 displays simulation results of the traditional FPZNN (5.4) for solving inequality (5.1). As seen from Figure 5.1a, all of

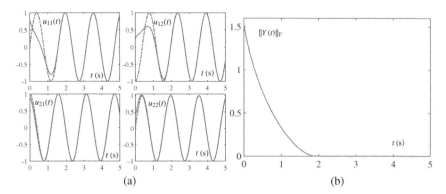

(a)   (b)

Figure 5.1 Simulative results using FPZNN model (5.4) with SBPAF when solving TVMI (5.1) of Example 1 with $k = 1.5$. (a) State solution $U(t)$ and (b) residual error $\|Y(t)\|_F$.

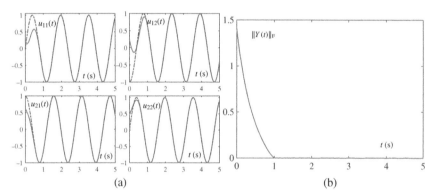

(a)   (b)

Figure 5.2 Simulative results using EVPZNN model (5.7) with SBPAF when solving TVMI (5.1) of Example 1 with $k = 1.5$. (a) State solution $U(t)$ and (b) residual error $\|Y(t)\|_F$.

these state solutions $U(t)$ (solid curves) starting from a random initial state $U(0)$ can converge towards the theoretical solution $U^{-1}(t)$ (dash curves) in a short time. The convergence performance of the related synthetic errors $\|Y(t)\|_F$ is illustrated by Figure 5.1b, where the synthetic residual errors $\|Y(t)\|_F$ of FPZNN (5.4) converge to 0 within approximately 1.8 seconds. In addition, simulation results for computing the TVMI (5.1) using EVPZNN (5.7) and VPZNN (5.9) are displayed in Figures 5.2 and 5.3, respectively. Both of the state solutions $U(t)$ in Figures 5.2a and 5.3a can quickly converge to the theoretical solution $U^{-1}(t)$. As illustrated in Figures 5.2b and 5.3b, the corresponding residual errors $\|Y(t)\|_F$ of EVPZNN (5.7) and VPZNN (5.9) for the TVMI (5.1) can converge towards 0 within a short time period. Specifically, EVPZNN (5.7) takes approximately one second, VPZNN (5.9) takes approximately 1.4 seconds. Besides, Figure 5.4 shows computation results

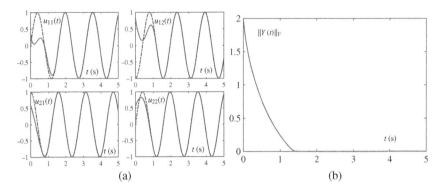

Figure 5.3 Simulative results using VPZNN model (5.9) with SBPAF when solving TVMI (5.1) of Example 1 with $k = 1.5$. (a) State solution $U(t)$ and (b) residual error $\|Y(t)\|_F$.

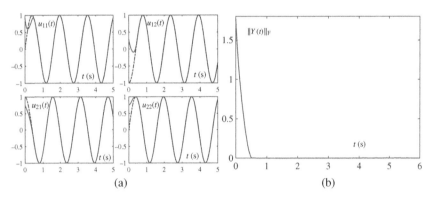

Figure 5.4 Simulative results using IVP-FTZNN model (5.11) with SBPAF when solving TVMI (5.1) of Example 1 with $k = 1.5$. (a) State solution $U(t)$ and (b) residual error $\|Y(t)\|_F$.

of the established IVP-FTZNN (5.11) for calculating the TVMI (5.1). As observed from Figure 5.4a, all state solutions $U(t)$ starting from any random initial state $U(0)$ can still converge quickly towards the theoretical solution $U^{-1}(t)$ (in approximately 0.5 second). The convergence of the synthetic errors $\|Y(t)\|_F$ of the proposed IVP-FTZNN (5.11) for calculating the TVMI (5.1) is displayed in Figure 5.4b. It clearly shows that residual error $\|Y(t)\|_F$ can converge towards 0 in approximately 0.5 second. Figure 5.5 further shows the logarithmic graph of the residual error $\|Y(t)\|_F$ of the four neural models for TVMI (5.1). By comparing the convergence time, one can find that when SBPAF is employed, the time required to calculate the TVMI (5.1) is the shortest for the proposed IVP-FTZNN (5.11). In addition, considering that different AFs lead to different convergence speeds of ZNNs, the residual errors $\|Y(t)\|_F$ of the proposed IVP-FTZNN (5.11) for calculating TVMI (5.1) when activated by different AFs are exhibited in Figure 5.6. From

Figure 5.5 Residual errors $\|Y(t)\|_F$ of FPZNN (5.4), EVPZNN (5.7), VPZNN (5.9), and IVP-FTZNN (5.11) with SBPAF when solving TVMI (5.1) of Example 1 with $\gamma = k = 1.5$.

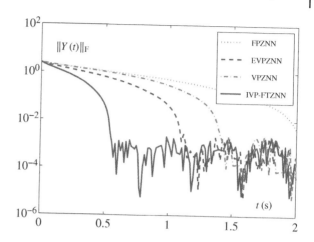

Figure 5.6 Residual errors $\|Y(t)\|_F$ of IVP-FTZNN model (5.11) with different activation functions when solving TVMI (5.1) of Example 1 with $k = 1.5$.

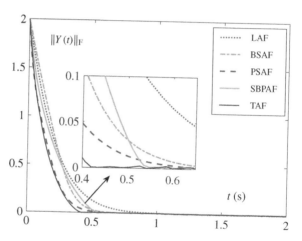

this figure, residual errors $\|Y(t)\|_F$ of the proposed IVP-FTZNN (5.11) activated by SBPAF and TAF can converge towards zero at 0.42 and 0.55, respectively.

5.4.2 Example 2: Three-Dimensional Coefficient

To further demonstrate the effectiveness and excellence of the constructed IVP-FTZNN (5.11) for calculating the TVMI (5.1), a higher dimensional example for (5.1) is considered:

$$H(t) = \begin{bmatrix} 2.1 + \sin(1.5t) & \cos(1.5t) & \cos(1.5t)/2 \\ \cos(1.5t) & 2.1 + \sin(1.5t) & \cos(1.5t) \\ \cos(1.5t)/2 & \cos(1.5t) & 2.1 + \sin(1.5t) \end{bmatrix}.$$

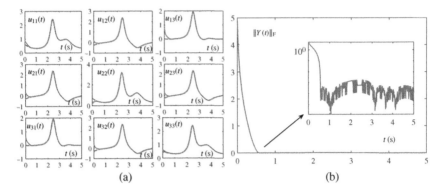

Figure 5.7 Simulative results using IVP-FTZNN model (5.11) with SBPAF when solving TVMI (5.1) of Example 2 with $k = 1.5$. (a) State solution $U(t)$ and (b) residual error $\|Y(t)\|_F$.

First of all, let's set the design parameter $k = 1.5$, i.e. $\gamma(t) = 1.5^{t+2} + 2 \times 1.5t + 1.5^2$ for IVP-FTZNN (5.11). When SBPAF is hired, simulation results of the proposed IVP-FTZNN (5.11) for (5.1) are revealed in Figure 5.7. Especially, Figure 5.7a displays each entry of the state solution $U(t)$ for the TVMI (5.1) by using the proposed IVP-FTZNN (5.11). It can be seen from Figure 5.7a that all state solutions of $U(t)$ can quickly converge towards the theoretical solution $U^{-1}(t)$, which further validates the efficacy of the established IVP-FTZNN (5.11) for solving TVMI (5.1). The corresponding residual error $\|Y(t)\|_F$ synthesized by IVP-FTZNN (5.11) is illustrated in Figure 5.7b. From Figure 5.7b, the residual error $\|Y(t)\|_F$ can accurately converge to 0 within approximately 0.6 (the order is 10^{-3}).

In the circuit implementation process of the neural network, it is generally required to make design parameters large enough as possible, and the larger the design parameters are, the higher the convergence rate is. To verify the dominance of the established IVP-FTZNN (5.11) for solving the TVMI (5.1), different values of p and γ are considered, and for comparison purposes, FPZNN (5.4), EVPZNN (5.7), and VPZNN (5.9) are also hired to compute the TVMI (5.1) under same conditions in this example. Since state solutions $U(t)$ of FPZNN (5.4), EVPZNN (5.7), VPZNN (5.9), and IVP-FTZNN (5.11) are too similar to each other, their dynamic behaviors are omitted here. Only the corresponding residual errors $\|Y(t)\|_F$ are shown in Figure 5.8. As seen from Figure 5.8a, when $\gamma = k = 0.5$, the residual error $\|Y(t)\|_F$ synthesized by the proposed IVP-FTZNN (5.11) can converge to 0 within about 2.1 seconds, while it takes about 3.6 seconds for EVPZNN (5.7) and 6 seconds for FPZNN (5.4). Since the time-varying parameter $\gamma(t)$ of VPZNN (5.9) and IVP-FTZNN (5.11) is the same when $k < 1$, the residual error $\|Y(t)\|_F$ of VPZNN (5.9) is omitted here.

As shown in Figure 5.8b, when $\gamma = k = 2$, all residual errors $\|Y(t)\|_F$ can converge towards 0, but the time required for IVP-FTZNN (5.11) to converge

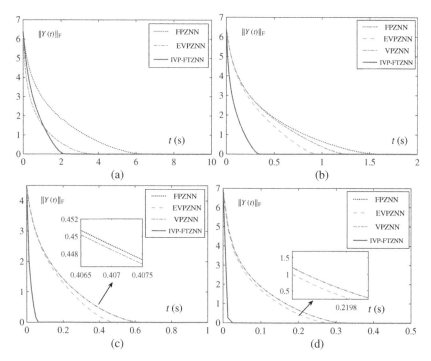

Figure 5.8 Simulative residual errors using FPZNN (5.4), EVPZNN (5.7), VPZNN (5.9), and IVP-FTZNN (5.11) with SBPAF when solving TVMI (5.1) of Example 2 with different γ and k. (a) With $\gamma = k = 0.5$, (b) with $\gamma = k = 2$, (c) with $\gamma = k = 5$, and (d) with $\gamma = k = 10$.

towards zero is the shortest. Specifically, FPZNN (5.4) takes about 1.6 seconds, EVPZNN (5.7) takes about 0.9 second, VPZNN (5.9) takes about 1.3 seconds, while IVP-FTZNN (5.11) takes about 0.32 second.

From Figure 5.8c, adjusting design parameters to $\gamma = k = 5$, all residual errors $\|Y(t)\|_F$ can still converge towards 0 rapidly, but the proposed IVP-FTZNN model (5.11) possesses the fastest convergence rate and only takes about 0.06 second, while FPZNN (5.4), VPZNN (5.9), and EVPZNN (5.7) take more time.

Continuing to adjust the parameters to $\gamma = k = 10$, the corresponding transient behavior of the residual errors $\|Y(t)\|_F$ is shown in Figure 5.8d. It takes about 0.0025 second to make the residual error $\|Y(t)\|_F$ of the proposed IVP-FTZNN model (5.11) converge to 0, while FPZNN (5.4) and VPZNN (5.9) take about 0.62 second, and EVPZNN (5.7) takes about 0.27 second. These four subfigures verify that IVP-FTZNN (5.11) has better convergence performance than FPZNN (5.4), EVPZNN (5.7), and VPZNN (5.9) when applied to solving the TVMI (5.1).

Noting that the value of the time-varying parameter $\gamma(t)$ will increase rapidly with respect to the time variable t, which might result in the better robustness of IVP-FTZNN (5.11) and the existing EVPZNN (5.7), VPZNN (5.9) than FPZNN (5.4). For the purpose of testing the efficacy about robustness, we can develop the corresponding noise-polluted versions of FPZNN (5.4), EVPZNN (5.7), VPZNN (5.9), and IVP-FTZNN (5.11) by adding an additive noise. The noise-polluted IVP-FTZNN model can be expressed as the following form:

$$H(t)\dot{U}(t) = -\dot{H}(t)U(t) - \gamma(t)\Phi(H(t)U(t) - I) + N(t), \tag{5.39}$$

where $N(t)$ denotes the additive noise. Note that if $\gamma(t) = \gamma$, the aforementioned model (5.39) becomes the noise-polluted version of FPZNN (5.4); if $\gamma(t) = \gamma_1(t)$, the aforementioned model (5.39) becomes the noise-polluted version of EVPZNN (5.7); and if $\gamma(t) = \gamma_2(t)$, the aforementioned model (5.39) becomes the noise-polluted version of VPZNN (5.9).

Then, several types of external noise $N(t)$ are considered, and the corresponding calculation results are shown in Figure 5.9. As displayed in Figure 5.9a, when

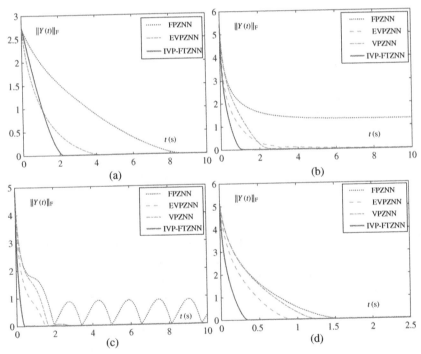

Figure 5.9 Simulative residual errors using FPZNN (5.4), EVPZNN (5.7), VPZNN (5.9), and IVP-FTZNN (5.11) with SBPAF when solving TVMI (5.1) of Example 2 with different γ, k and noises $n_{ij}(t)$. (a) With $\gamma = k = 0.5$ and $n_{ij}(t) = 0.2\|Y(t)\|_F$, (b) with $\gamma = k = 1.2$ and $n_{ij}(t) = 0.5$, (c) with $\gamma = k = 2$ and $n_{ij}(t) = 0.5\sin(2t)$, and (d) With $\gamma = k = 2$ and $-1 \leq n_{ij}(t) \leq 1$.

$\gamma = k = 0.5$ and a gradually disappearing noise $n_{ij}(t) = 0.2\|Y(t)\|_F$ is presented, the residual error $\|Y(t)\|_F$ produced by IVP-FTZNN (5.11) can still converge to 0 within about 2.2 seconds, while EVPZNN (5.7) takes about 4.1 seconds, and FPZNN (5.4) takes about 8.5 seconds. Besides, when $\gamma = k = 1.2$ and a constant noise $n_{ij}(t) = 0.5$ is presented, from Figure 5.9b, it follows that all of these residual errors $\|Y(t)\|_F$ for IVP-FTZNN (5.11), EVPZNN (5.7) and VPZNN (5.9) can converge towards 0, but the proposed IVP-FTZNN (5.11) has the fastest convergence rate and only takes about one second. In contrast, the residual error $\|Y(t)\|_F$ of FPZNN (5.4) gradually converges towards a fixed value (i.e. converges towards about 1.2 instead of 0). When $\gamma = k = 2$ and a time-varying bounded noise $n_{ij}(t) = 0.5\sin(2t)$ is presented, as plotted from Figure 5.9c, remarkably, the residual error $\|Y(t)\|_F$ of the established IVP-FTZNN (5.11) only needs about 0.3 second to converge to 0. The residual errors $\|Y(t)\|_F$ of EVPZNN (5.7) and VPZNN (5.9) can converge towards 0 within about three seconds. However, the residual error $\|Y(t)\|_F$ of FPZNN (5.4) fluctuates with time instead of converging towards 0. When $\gamma = k = 2$ and a bounded random noise $n_{ij}(t) = [-1,1]$ is presented, from Figure 5.9d, all of the residual errors $\|Y(t)\|_F$ can converge to 0, and the residual error $\|Y(t)\|_F$ of IVP-FTZNN (5.11) still holds the fastest convergence rate.

When the design parameters are adjusted to $\gamma = k = 5$ and two time-varying unbounded noises are considered, the corresponding residual errors $\|Y(t)\|_F$ for solving TVMI (5.1) are plotted in Figure 5.10. From Figure 5.10a, when external noise $n_{ij}(t) = 1.2t$ is presented, the residual error $\|Y(t)\|_F$ of FPZNN (5.4) cannot converge towards 0 and has a rising trend, while the others can converge to 0, and the residual error $\|Y(t)\|_F$ of IVP-FTZNN (5.11) converges to 0 with the fastest speed. It only takes about 0.05 second. From Figure 5.10b, when external noise

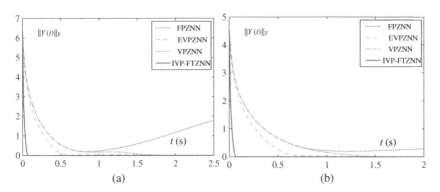

Figure 5.10 Simulative residual errors using FPZNN (5.4), EVPZNN (5.7), VPZNN (5.9), and IVP-FTZNN (5.11) with SBPAF when solving TVMI (5.1) of Example 2 with $\gamma = k = 5$ and different noises $n_{ij}(t)$. (a) With $n_{ij}(t) = 1.2t$ and with $n_{ij}(t) = 0.8\exp(0.2t)$.

$n_{ij}(t) = 0.8 \exp(0.2t)$ is presented, the residual error $\|Y(t)\|_F$ of FPZNN (5.4) converges to the value 0.3 and there is an increasing trend at two seconds. The residual error $\|Y(t)\|_F$ of IVP-FTZNN (5.11) can converge towards 0 after a time period (i.e. within about 0.05 second). While the residual errors $\|Y(t)\|_F$ of EVPZNN (5.7) and VPZNN (5.9) for converging towards 0 take about 0.8 and 1.6 seconds, respectively.

Based on the aforementioned simulation results, one can find that, compared with FPZNN (5.4), EVPZNN (5.7), and VPZNN (5.9), IVP-FTZNN (5.11) has better convergence performance when solving TVMI (5.1), whether or not external noises are presented.

5.5 Chapter Summary

By suggesting a time varying parameter, a IVP-FTZNN model has been established and researched for calculating the time varying matrix. The super-exponential convergence property of such an IVP-FTZNN model has been rigorously analyzed in detail. Besides, upper bounds of the convergence time corresponding to the proposed IVP-FTZNN model activated by SBPAF and TAF are respectively estimated in theory. For comparison purposes, the FPZNN, EVPZNN, and VPZNN models have also been hired to solve the TVMI problem. In numerical simulations, we have compared the established IVP-FTZNN model with the traditional FPZNN model as well as the existing EVPZNN, and VPZNN models for calculating the same TVMI problem. Comparative results indicate the better convergence performance and robustness of the IVP-FTZNN model than the FPZNN, EVPZNN, and VPZNN models.

References

1 D. Zhu, B. Li, and P. Liang, On the matrix inversion approximation based on Neumann series in massive MIMO systems, Proceedings of IEEE International Communications (ICC), (2015) 1763–1769.

2 W. Fang and Y. Zhen *et al.*, A simulation research on the visual servo based on pseudo-inverse of image Jacobian matrix for robot, *Appl. Mech. Mater.*, 494-495 (2015) 1212–1215.

3 I. Dobbins and T. James, Matrix inversion tomosynthesis improvements in longitudinal X-ray slice imaging, Google Patents, 1990.

4 F. Ding and T. Chen, Gradient based iterative algorithms for solving a class of matrix equations, *IEEE Trans. Autom. Control*, 50(8) (2015) 1216–1221.

5 L. Jin and S. Li *et al.*, Zeroing neural networks: A survey, *Neurocomputing*, 267 (2017) 597–604.

6 Y. Zhang and S. S. Ge, Design and analysis of a general recurrent neural network model for time-varying matrix inversion, *IEEE Trans. Neural Netw.*, 16(6) (2005) 1477–1490.

7 Z. Zhang, L. Zheng, and M. Wang, An exponential-enhanced-type varying-parameter RNN for solving time-varying matrix inversion, *Neurocomputing*, 338 (2019) 126–138.

8 Z. Zhang and L. Zheng, A complex varying-parameter convergent-differential neural-network for solving online time-varying complex Sylvester equation, *IEEE Trans. Cybern.*, 49(10) (2019) 3627–3639.

9 Y. Shi and B. Qiu *et al.*, Proposing and validation of a new four-point finite-difference formula with manipulator application, *IEEE Trans. Ind. Inform.*, 14(4) (2018) 1323–1333.

10 D. Chen, Y. Zhang, and S. Li, Tracking control of robot manipulators with unknown models: A jacobian-matrix-adaption method, *IEEE Trans. Ind. Inform.*, 14(7) (2018) 3044–3053.

11 Y. Shen and P. Miao *et al.*, Finite-time stability and its application for solving time-varying Sylvester equation by recurrent neural network, *Neural Process. Lett.*, 42(3) (2015) 763–784.

Part III

Application to Linear Matrix Equation

6

Design Scheme I of FTZNN

6.1 Introduction

In the past decades, robotic manipulators were widely applied in various areas from industrial engineering to scientific education [1–9]. The inverse kinematic resolution of these manipulators is perhaps the most vital step when exploited to execute a great diversity of tasks [10–12]. Generally speaking, this problem can be stated as [9]: if the end-effector desired Cartesian path $r(t) \in \mathbb{R}^m$ (or to say, the end-effector motion tracking task) is allocated, how to compute joint angle trajectory $\theta(t) \in \mathbb{R}^n$. Theoretically, the kinematical equation of robotic manipulators at the position level can be described in the following text [7–12]:

$$r = f(\theta), \tag{6.1}$$

where θ stands for the joint angle, r stands for the end-effector position, and $f(\cdot)$ represents a differentiable function, usually having the nonlinear character [7, 8, 12]. Thus, it may be more feasible to solve the kinematic equation at the velocity level, which can be derived by differentiating (6.1) as follows:

$$\dot{r} = J(\theta)\dot{\theta}, \tag{6.2}$$

where $\dot{\theta}$ and $\dot{r}$ respectively stand for the time derivative of θ and r, and $J(\theta) = \partial f(\theta)/\partial \theta$. Obviously, the kinematic equation (6.2) can be deemed as a linear system in this situation when $\dot{r}$ and $J(\theta)$ are known. Thus, the inverse kinematic resolution of these robotic manipulators is equivalent to solving a linear system [13–15]. In this chapter, a robust finite-time zeroing neural network (R-FTZNN) model is proposed and applied to robotic motion tracking in front of external noises via time-varying linear equation system solving. To do so, a noise-tolerant nonlinearly activated formula is devised and analyzed according to the time-varying linear system, which is able to suppress external disturbances and converge to its equilibrium point with finite time, and thus is completely different from and superior to the previous formula usually related to zeroing neural network (ZNN). The main

Zeroing Neural Networks: Finite-time Convergence Design, Analysis and Applications,
First Edition. Lin Xiao and Lei Jia.
© 2023 The Institute of Electrical and Electronics Engineers, Inc. Published 2023 by John Wiley & Sons, Inc.

Table 6.1 The main differences of the R-FTZNN model from the GNN model [16], the ZNN model [17] and the FTZNN model [18] for systems of linear equations.

#	Item	GNN [16]	ZNN [17]	FTZNN [18]	R-FTZNN (this work)
1	Solution problems	Static	Static	Static	Time-varying
2	Theoretical errors	Non-zero	Zero	Zero	Zero
3	Activation functions	No	Yes	Yes	Yes
4	Dynamic forms	Explicitly	Implicitly	Implicitly	Implicitly
5	Convergence	Asymptotically	Exponentially	Finitely	Finitely
6	Robustness	No	No	No	Yes

differences of R-FTZNN from gradient neural network (GNN) [16], ZNN [17], and FTZNN [18] for linear equations are listed in Table 6.1. Finally, simulative results (including the application to robotic motion tracking) also demonstrate the applicability and superiority of R-FTNN in front of external disturbances.

6.2 Convergence Speed and Robustness Co-design

In order to achieve the robustness and finite-time convergence of R-FTZNN for time-varying linear system, a noise-tolerant nonlinearly activated formula is devised and investigated in this part. Besides, the stability, finite-time convergence, and noise-suppressing property of such a new design formula are proved in details. For convenience, this new design formula is termed the finite-time robust (FTR) design formula.

On this basis, let us denote $J(\theta)$ by $A(t)$, $\theta(t)$ by $u(t)$, and $\dot{r}(t)$ by $b(t)$. Then, the kinematical equation (6.2) is converted to the following time-varying linear equations:

$$A(t)u(t) = b(t) \in \mathbb{R}^m. \tag{6.3}$$

The aim of the current work is to devise a neural model to find $u(t)$ in front of external disturbances within finite time such that (6.3) holds. Now, by defining an indefinite error function $y(t) = A(t)u(t) - b(t)$, the FTR design formula for $y(t)$ is proposed as follows:

$$\dot{y}(t) = -\gamma_1\Phi_1(y(t)) - \gamma_2\Phi_2\left(y(t) + \gamma_1\int_0^t \Phi_1(y(\tau))d\tau\right), \tag{6.4}$$

where argument t denotes time; $\gamma_1 > 0$ and $\gamma_2 > 0$ denote the scaling factors of $\lim_{t\to\infty}y(t) = 0$; and $\Phi_1(\cdot)$ and $\Phi_2(\cdot)$ denote two monotone increasing odd activation function arrays.

In addition, for FTR design formula (6.4), we have the following three theorems to respectively ensure its theoretical results.

Theorem 6.1 *Error function $y(t)$ generated by FTR formula (6.4) globally converges to 0 with time provided that $\Phi_1(\cdot)$ and $\Phi_2(\cdot)$ are monotone increasing odd activation functions.*

Proof: First, let us discuss the jth subsystem of FTR formula (6.4) with $\forall j \in 1, 2, \ldots, m$:

$$\dot{y}_j(t) = -\gamma_1 \phi_1(y_j(t)) - \gamma_2 \phi_2 \left(y_j(t) + \gamma_1 \int_0^t \phi_1(y_j(\tau)) d\tau \right), \tag{6.5}$$

where $\phi_1(\cdot)$ and $\phi_2(\cdot)$ respectively denote the elements of $\Phi_1(\cdot)$ and $\Phi_2(\cdot)$. For the jth subsystem (6.5), we can introduce an auxiliary variable $q_j(t)$, and define

$$q_j(t) = y_j(t) + \gamma_1 \int_0^t \phi_1(y_j(\tau)) d\tau. \tag{6.6}$$

Therefore, taking the time derivative of the previous equation from both sides, we have

$$\dot{q}_j(t) = \dot{y}_j(t) + \gamma_1 \phi_1(y_j(t)). \tag{6.7}$$

Then, combining (6.5), (6.6), and (6.7), we further have

$$\dot{q}_j(t) = -\gamma_2 \phi_2(q_j(t)), \tag{6.8}$$

which is obviously the same as the ZNN design formula by comparison [17, 19–22]. For (6.8), from the previous research results, we can easily know that $q_j(t)$ can converge to zero provided that $\phi_2(\cdot)$ is a monotone increasing odd function; and even drop to zero within finite time provided that $\phi_2(\cdot)$ belongs to a kind of sign-bi-power function [18, 23].

Now for proving the conclusion of Theorem 6.1, a Lyapunov function candidate $p_j(t)$ for the jth subsystem (6.5) is devised as follows (with $y_j(0)$ and $q_j(0)$ known):

$$p_j(t) = \frac{1}{2}\mu y_j^2(t) + \frac{1}{2}q_j^2(t), \tag{6.9}$$

where $\mu > 0$ and $p_0 = p_j(0) = \mu y_j^2(0)/2 + q_j^2(0)/2$. Obviously, this Lyapunov function $p_j(t)$ is positive-definite according to $p_j(t) > 0$ for any $y_j(t) \neq 0$ or $q_j(t) \neq 0$, and $p_j(t) = 0$ only for $y_j(t) = q_j(t) = 0$. The time derivative of the Lyapunov function is computed as follows:

$$\begin{aligned}
\frac{dp_j(t)}{dt} &= \mu y_j(t)\dot{y}_j(t) + q_j(t)\dot{q}_j(t) \\
&= \mu y_j(t)[\dot{q}_j(t) - \gamma_1 \phi_1(y_j(t))] - \gamma_2 q_j(t)\phi_2(q_j(t)) \\
&= -\mu\gamma_2 y_j(t)\phi_2(q_j(t)) - \mu\gamma_1 y_j(t)\phi_1(y_j(t)) \\
&\quad - \gamma_2 q_j(t)\phi_2(q_j(t)).
\end{aligned} \tag{6.10}$$

Now, let us show $\dot{p}_j(t) \leq 0$. When $p_j(t) \leq p_0$, we can obtain the following conclusions:

$$\frac{1}{2}\mu y_j^2(t) \leq p_0 \quad \text{and} \quad \frac{1}{2}q_j^2(t) \leq p_0, \tag{6.11}$$

from which we can further obtain

$$|y_j(t)| \leq \sqrt{2p_0/\mu} \quad \text{and} \quad |q_j(t)| \leq \sqrt{2p_0}. \tag{6.12}$$

Let us denote respectively the set S_1 for $y_j(t)$ and the set S_2 for $q_j(t)$. It follows that

$$\begin{aligned} S_1 &= \{y_j(t) \in R, \ |y_j(t)| \leq \sqrt{2p_0/\mu}\}, \\ S_2 &= \{q_j(t) \in R, \ |q_j(t)| \leq \sqrt{2p_0}\}. \end{aligned} \tag{6.13}$$

In the bounded region S_2 of $q_j(t)$, applying the mean-value theorem, we can easily have:

$$\phi_2(q_j(t)) - \phi_2(0) = (q_j(t) - 0)\frac{\partial \phi_2(q_j(\vartheta))}{\partial q_j}\bigg|_{q_j(\vartheta) \in S_2}. \tag{6.14}$$

In addition, $\phi_2(\cdot)$ is a monotone increasing odd function, therefore $\phi_2(0) = 0$ and $\partial \phi_2(q_j(t))/\partial q_j > 0$. Therefore, the following can be further derived from (6.14):

$$|\phi_2(q_j(t))| \leq C_0|q_j(t)|,$$

where $C_0 = \max\{\partial \phi_2(q_j(t))/\partial q_j\}|_{q_j(t) \in S_2} > 0$ is bounded. Thus, according to the conclusion $|\phi_2(q_j(t))| \leq C_0|q_j(t)|$ with C_0 denoting a positive constant, we have

$$\begin{aligned} |y_j(t)\phi_2(q_j(t))| &\leq |y_j(t)| \cdot |\phi_2(q_j(t))| \\ &\leq C_0|y_j(t)| \cdot |q_j(t)|. \end{aligned} \tag{6.15}$$

Substituting (6.15) back into (6.10), we can derive the following result:

$$\begin{aligned} \frac{dp_j(t)}{dt} =& - \mu\gamma_2 y_j(t)\phi_2(q_j(t)) - \mu\gamma_1 y_j(t)\phi_1(y_j(t)) \\ & - \gamma_2 q_j(t)\phi_2(q_j(t)) \\ \leq& \mu\gamma_2|y_j(t)\phi_2(q_j(t))| - \mu\gamma_1 y_j(t)\phi_1(y_j(t)) \\ & - \gamma_2 q_j(t)\phi_2(q_j(t)) \\ \leq& \mu\gamma_2 C_0|y_j(t)| \cdot |q_j(t)| - \mu\gamma_1 C_1 p_j^2(t) - \gamma_2 C_2 q_j^2(t) \\ =& -\mu\left(\sqrt{\gamma_1 C_1}|p_j(t)| - \frac{\gamma_2 C_0}{2\sqrt{\gamma_1 C_1}}|q_j(t)|\right)^2 - \mu\left(\frac{\gamma_2 C_2}{\mu} - \frac{\gamma_2^2 C_0^2}{4\gamma_1 C_1}\right)q_j^2(t), \end{aligned} \tag{6.16}$$

where $C_1 = \min\{\partial\phi_1(y_j(t))/\partial y_j\}|_{y_j(t)\in S_1} > 0$ and $C_2 = \min\{\partial\phi_2(q_j(t))/\partial q_j\}|_{q_j(t)\in S_2}$ > 0, which can be derived by using the mean-value theorem. In summary, we have $\dot{p}_j(t) \le 0$ provided that

$$\frac{\gamma_2 C_2}{\mu} - \frac{\gamma_2^2 C_0^2}{4\gamma_1 C_1} \ge 0 \quad \text{and} \quad \mu > 0, \quad \text{i.e. } 0 < \mu \le \frac{4\gamma_1 C_1 C_2}{\gamma_2 C_0^2}, \tag{6.17}$$

which guarantees the negative definiteness of $\dot{p}_j(t)$. In sense of Lyapunov, it follows that the jth subsystem (6.5) is globally stable and $y_j(t)$ converges to 0. Therefore, error function $\mathbf{y}(t)$ solved by the FTR design formula (6.4) is globally convergent to zero. The proof is thus completed. ∎

Theorem 6.2 *Error function $\mathbf{y}(t)$ generated by FTR design formula (6.4) converges to 0 within finite time, with the upper bound t_f being*

$$t_f < \frac{\gamma_1 + \gamma_2}{\gamma_1\gamma_2(1-r)} \max\left\{|y^-(0)|^{1-r}, |y^+(0)|^{1-r}\right\},$$

provided that $\phi_1(y_j) = \phi_2(y_j) = \phi^r(y_j) + \phi^{1/r}(y_j)$ with $r \in (0,1)$ and $\phi^r(\cdot)$ defined as

$$\phi^r(y_j) = \begin{cases} |y_j|^r, & \text{if } y_j > 0, \\ 0, & \text{if } y_j = 0, \\ -|y_j|^r, & \text{if } y_j < 0, \end{cases}$$

where the initial errors $y^+(0) = \max\{\mathbf{y}(0)\}$ and $y^-(0) = \min\{\mathbf{y}(0)\}$.

Proof: As proved before, we have $\dot{q}_j(t) = -\gamma_2\phi_2(q_j(t))$ via introducing the auxiliary variable $q_j(t) = y_j(t) + \gamma_1\int_0^t \phi_1(y_j(\tau))d\tau$. Especially, $q_j(0) = y_j(0)$ with $t = 0$. Besides, as for $\dot{q}_j(t) = -\gamma_2\phi_2(q_j(t))$, we can choose Lyapunov function as $p_j(t) = q_j^2(t)$, and $\dot{p}_j(t)$ is derived as follows:

$$\begin{aligned} \dot{p}_j(t) &= 2q_j(t)\dot{q}_j(t) \\ &= -2\gamma_2 q_j(t)\phi_2(q_j(t)) \\ &= -2\gamma_2\left(|q_j(t)|^{r+1} + |q_j(t)|^{\frac{1}{r}+1}\right) \\ &\le -2\gamma_2|q_j(t)|^{r+1} \\ &= -2\gamma_2 p_j(t)^{\frac{r+1}{2}}. \end{aligned}$$

Solving the inequality $\dot{p}_j(t) \le -2\gamma_2 p_j(t)^{\frac{r+1}{2}}$ with the initial value $p_j(0) = |y_j(0)|^2 = |y_j(0)|^2$, we can derive:

$$p_j(t)^{\frac{1-r}{2}} \begin{cases} \le |q_j(0)|^{1-r} - \gamma_2 t(1-r), & \text{if } t \le \frac{|q_j(0)|^{1-r}}{\gamma_2(1-r)}, \\ = 0, & \text{if } t > \frac{|q_j(0)|^{1-r}}{\gamma_2(1-r)}, \end{cases}$$

which implies that $p_j(t)$ is convergent to zero when $t > |q_j(0)|^{1-r}/\gamma_2(1-r)$. Owing to $p_j(t) = q_j^2(t)$ and $q_j(0) = y_j(0)$, we can also say $q_j(t)$ decreases to zero after $t > |y_j(0)|^{1-r}/\gamma_2(1-r)$.

Because every element of $q(t)$ is of the dynamics of $\dot{q}_j(t) = -\gamma_2\phi_2(q_j(t))$, $y(t)$ is capable of converging to 0 if $t > \max\left\{|y^-(0)|^{1-r}, |y^+(0)|^{1-r}\right\}/\gamma_2(1-r)$, where $y^+(0) = \max\{y(0)\}$ and $y^-(0) = \min\{y(0)\}$. Therefore, the upper bound t_1 for $q(t)$ is derived as

$$t_1 < \frac{1}{\gamma_2(1-r)} \max\left\{|y^-(0)|^{1-r}, |y^+(0)|^{1-r}\right\}.$$

The calculation time for the first step is thus completed. Now, we move to the second step.

After the time period t_1, $q(t) = 0$ and $\dot{q}(t) = 0$. Thus, according to (6.7), we have

$$\dot{y}_j(t) = -\gamma_1\phi_1(y_j(t)). \tag{6.18}$$

According to the expression of $\phi_1(\cdot)$, the upper bound t_2 for the aforementioned dynamics is similarly computed next:

$$t_2 < \frac{1}{\gamma_1(1-r)} \max\left\{|y^-(0)|^{1-r}, |y^+(0)|^{1-r}\right\}.$$

Summarizing the results of the aforementioned two steps, it follows that $y(t)$ solved by FTR design formula (6.4) is able to converge to 0 within finite time with the upper bound being $t_f = t_1 + t_2$:

$$t_f < \frac{\gamma_1 + \gamma_2}{\gamma_1\gamma_2(1-r)} \max\left\{|y^-(0)|^{1-r}, |y^+(0)|^{1-r}\right\},$$

provided that $\phi_1(y_j) = \phi_2(y_j) = \phi^r(y_j) + \phi^{1/r}(y_j)$. The proof is thus completed. ∎

Remark As mentioned in Theorem 6.1, we only need to guarantee that $\frac{\partial\phi_2(q_j(\theta))}{\partial q_j}$ is bounded on S_2 regardless of whether $\partial\phi_2(q_j(\theta))/\partial q_j$ is continuous or not. If this condition is satisfied, we can obtain that the inequality $|\phi_2(q_j(t))| \leq C_0|q_j(t)|$, where $C_0 = \max\{\partial\phi_2(q_j(t))/\partial q_j\}|_{q_j(t)\in S_2} > 0$. In addition, in order to ensure the stability of the FTR design formula (6.4), we only assume that the function $\phi_2(q_j(t))$ is a monotone increasing odd activation function. Obviously, the sign-bi-power activation function satisfies this criterion. Therefore, the finite-time stable results for the R-FTZNN model can be obtained.

Note that, in the proof process, we estimate the finite convergence time of the FTR design formula (6.4) by using the $\dot{p}_j(t) = -2\gamma_2 p_j(t)^{r+1/2}$. It is conservative to discard the term $|q_j(t)|^{1/r+1}$. Therefore, some improvements about the finite-time convergence upper bound and conservativeness will be done as a future research by considering the idea of [24, 25].

As mentioned before, the conventional finite-time design formula for $y(t)$ neglected influence of external disturbances. If these external disturbances are injected to these design formula, the effectiveness is hard to be guaranteed. Generally, external disturbances may cause a decrease in accuracy of RNN solutions. In order to investigate the noise-suppression property of FTR design formula (6.4), an additive constant noise η is adopted and integrated in (6.4). Thus, we can obtain the noise-disturbed FTR design formula as follows:

$$\dot{y}(t) = -\gamma_1 \Phi_1(y(t)) - \gamma_2 \Phi_2 \left(y(t) + \gamma_1 \int_0^t \Phi_1(y(\tau)) d\tau \right) + \eta, \tag{6.19}$$

where γ_1 and γ_2 are defined as before; $\Phi_1(\cdot)$ and $\Phi_1(\cdot)$ represent two monotone increasing odd activation function arrays; and η denotes an additive constant noise vector. Now, we can prove the robustness of FTR design formula (6.4) in front of the constant noise η via analyzing the noise-disturbed FTR design formula (6.19).

Theorem 6.3 *Error function $y(t)$ generated by FTR formula (6.19) converges to 0 in front of an unknown constant noise with time as long as $\Phi_1(\cdot)$ and $\Phi_2(\cdot)$ are monotone increasing odd functions.*

Proof: Let us discuss the jth subsystem of the noise-disturbed FTR design formula (6.19):

$$\dot{y}_j(t) = -\gamma_1 \phi_1(y_j(t)) - \gamma_2 \phi_2 \left(y_j(t) + \gamma_1 \int_0^t \phi_1(y_j(\tau)) d\tau \right) + \eta_j. \tag{6.20}$$

Then, we still introduce the auxiliary variable $q_j(t)$, which is defined as the same with (6.6). In consequence, the time derivative of $q_j(t)$ can be derived as $\dot{q}_j(t) = \dot{y}_j(t) + \gamma_1 \phi_1(y_j(t))$. Then, substituting the expressions of $q_j(t)$ and $\dot{q}_j(t)$ into (6.20), we have

$$\dot{q}_j(t) = -\gamma_2 \phi_2(q_j(t)) + \eta_j. \tag{6.21}$$

Hence, we can select a Lyapunov function to analyze the stability of the jth subsystem (6.20):

$$p_j(t) = \left(\gamma_2 \phi_2(q_j(t)) - \eta_j \right)^2 / 2. $$

Obviously, this Lyapunov function is positive definite. Next, solving process of $\dot{p}_j(t)$ is derived as

$$\begin{aligned} \frac{dp_j(t)}{dt} &= \left(\gamma_2 \phi_2(q_j(t)) - \eta_j \right) \gamma_2 \frac{\partial \phi_2(q_j(t))}{\partial y_j} \dot{q}_j(t) \\ &= -\gamma_2 \frac{\partial \phi_2(q_j(t))}{\partial y_j} \left(\gamma_2 \phi_2(q_j(t)) - \eta_j \right)^2. \end{aligned} \tag{6.22}$$

Since $\phi_2(\cdot)$ is a monotone increasing odd function, we know $\partial\phi_2(q_j(t))/\partial q_j > 0$. It follows that $\dot{p}_j(t)$ is negative definite and $\dot{p}_j(t) \leq 0$; i.e. $\dot{p}_j(t) < 0$ for any $\gamma_2\phi_2(q_j(t)) - \eta_j \neq 0$ and $\dot{p}_j(t) = 0$ only for $\gamma_2\phi_2(q_j(t)) - \eta_j = 0$. Thus, as time goes on, the Lyapunov function candidate $p_j(t)$ converges to zero. Otherwise, if $p_j(t)$ converges to a nonzero constant, we have $\gamma_2\phi_2(q_j(t)) - \eta_j \neq 0$ because $\dot{p}_j(t) = 0$ only for $\gamma_2\phi_2(q_j(t)) - \eta_j = 0$. If $\gamma_2\phi_2(q_j(t)) - \eta_j \neq 0$, according to the expression of (6.22), it must have $\dot{p}_j(t) \neq 0$. Therefore, in terms of Lyapunov theory, we can conclude that the Lyapunov function candidate $p_j(t)$ converges to zero as time goes on. At the same time, $\lim_{t\to\infty}\gamma_2\phi_2(q_j(t)) - \eta_j = 0$, i.e. $\lim_{t\to\infty}q_j(t) = \phi_2^{-1}(\eta_j/\gamma_2)$. That is to say, $q_j(t)$ converges to $\phi_2^{-1}(\eta_j/\gamma_2)$ and $\lim_{t\to\infty}\dot{q}_j(t) = -\gamma_2\phi_2(q_j(t)) + \eta_j = 0$.

Now, considering that $\dot{q}_j(t) = \dot{y}_j(t) + \gamma_1\phi_1(y_j(t))$ and $\lim_{t\to\infty}\dot{q}_j(t) = 0$, we can derive that $\dot{y}_j(t) = \dot{q}_j(t) - \gamma_1\phi_1(y_j(t))$. When $t \to \infty$, $\dot{y}_j(t) = \dot{q}_j(t) - \gamma_1\phi_1(y_j(t))$ falls into

$$\dot{y}_j(t) = -\gamma_1\phi_1(y_j(t)). \tag{6.23}$$

Based the aforementioned analysis, it is easy to conclude $\lim_{t\to\infty}y_j(t) = 0$ [17, 19–22].

From the aforementioned analysis, we come to a conclusion that error function $y(t)$ generated by FTR formula (6.19) converges to 0 in front of an unknown constant noise with time as long as $\Phi_1(\cdot)$ and $\Phi_2(\cdot)$ are monotone increasing odd functions. The proof on the noise-suppressing property of FTR design formula (6.4) is thus completed. ∎

In a word, the results of the aforementioned three theorems show the outstanding properties of the FTR design formula (6.4). In view of the superiority of these theoretical results, the FTR design formula (6.4) is applied to design a R-FTZNN model for robotic motion tracking via time-varying linear equation system solving.

6.3 R-FTZNN Model

Based on the FTR design formula (6.4), in this section, the R-FTZNN model is designed and applied to kinematical control of robotic manipulators via time-varying linear equation system solving. In addition, the mathematical theoretical results are supplied to ensure the outstanding performance of the R-FTZNN model in front of external disturbances.

6.3.1 Design of R-FTZNN

In this part, according to ZNN's method [17, 19, 20] and the proposed FTR design formula (6.4), the R-FTZNN model is established, and the specific design process is presented as follows.

First of all, let us denote $J(\theta)$ by $A(t)$, $\theta(t)$ by $\boldsymbol{u}(t)$, and $\dot{\boldsymbol{r}}(t)$ by $\boldsymbol{b}(t)$. Then, based on the kinematical equation of robotic manipulators, the Cartesian trajectory error function $\boldsymbol{y}(t)$ between the actual velocity trajectory $A(t)\boldsymbol{u}(t)$ and desired velocity path $\boldsymbol{b}(t)$ is defined as

$$\boldsymbol{y}(t) = A(t)\boldsymbol{u}(t) - \boldsymbol{b}(t), \tag{6.24}$$

which can be zero, positive, and negative, depending on the joint configurations of robot manipulators during the motion tracking of the desired task.

Second, as a paramount step, the proposed FTR design formula (6.4) is exploited to establish the R-FTZNN model by following the definition of the first step. For presentation convenience, FTR formula (6.4) is listed again as follows:

$$\dot{\boldsymbol{y}}(t) = -\gamma_1 \Phi_1(\boldsymbol{y}(t)) - \gamma_2 \Phi_2 \left(\boldsymbol{y}(t) + \gamma_1 \int_0^t \Phi_1(\boldsymbol{y}(\tau))\mathrm{d}\tau \right). \tag{6.25}$$

At last, by substituting (6.24) into (6.25), the R-FTZNN model for kinematical control of robotic manipulators illustrated via time-varying linear equation system solving is established as follows:

$$\begin{aligned}
A\dot{\boldsymbol{u}} = {} & -\gamma_1 \Phi_1(A\boldsymbol{u} - \boldsymbol{b}) - \dot{A}\boldsymbol{u} + \dot{\boldsymbol{b}} \\
& - \gamma_2 \Phi_2 \left((A\boldsymbol{u} - \boldsymbol{b}) + \gamma_1 \int_0^t \Phi_1(A\boldsymbol{u} - \boldsymbol{b})\mathrm{d}\tau \right),
\end{aligned} \tag{6.26}$$

where t is deleted for presentation continence. Note that R-FTZNN model (6.26) is consist of a set of ordinary differential equations, of which, starting an initial joint configuration, the actual joint trajectory $\theta(t)$ will achieve the desired motion tracking in front of external disturbances.

Besides, for comparative purposes, ZNN for this time-varying linear system is directly presented as follows [17, 18]:

$$A\dot{\boldsymbol{u}} = -\dot{A}\boldsymbol{u} + \dot{\boldsymbol{b}} - \gamma(A\boldsymbol{u} - \boldsymbol{b}), \tag{6.27}$$

where t is deleted for presentation continence and $\gamma > 0$ denotes a scaling factor.

6.3.2 Analysis of R-FTZNN

The main theoretical results are provided in this part to guarantee the advantages of the proposed R-FTZNN model (6.26) for kinematical control of robotic manipulators illustrated via time-varying linear equation system solving.

Theorem 6.4 *The R-FTZNN model (6.26) is stable provided that $\Phi_1(\cdot)$ and $\Phi_2(\cdot)$ are monotone increasing odd functions. Besides, the actual joint trajectory $\theta(t)$ makes the Cartesian trajectory error function $\boldsymbol{y}(t)$ converge to 0.*

Proof: First, it is easy to conclude that the R-FTZNN model (6.26) can be rewritten as (6.25). Then, according the proof and conclusion of Theorem 6.1 on the FTR design formula (6.4), we can conclude that the R-FTZNN model (6.26) is globally stable, and the actual joint trajectory $\theta(t)$ generated by the proposed R-FTZNN model (6.26) makes the Cartesian trajectory error function $y(t)$ converge to 0. This completes proof. ∎

Theorem 6.5 *The actual joint trajectory $\theta(t)$ generated by the R-FTZNN model (6.26) makes the Cartesian trajectory error function $y(t)$ converge to 0 in finite time, with upper bound t_f being*

$$t_f < \frac{\gamma_1 + \gamma_2}{\gamma_1 \gamma_2 (1 - r)} \max \left\{ |y^-(0)|^{1-r}, |y^+(0)|^{1-r} \right\},$$

provided that $\phi_1(y_j) = \phi_2(y_j) = \phi^r(y_j) + \phi^{1/r}(y_j)$ with $r \in (0, 1)$ and $\phi^r(\cdot)$ defined as

$$\phi^r(y_j) = \begin{cases} |y_j|^r, & \text{if } y_j > 0, \\ 0, & \text{if } y_j = 0, \\ -|y_j|^r, & \text{if } y_j < 0, \end{cases}$$

where the initial errors $y^+(0) = \max\{y(0)\}$ and $y^-(0) = \min\{y(0)\}$.

Proof: It can be derived by adopting the conclusions of Theorems 6.2 and 6.4, and thus not presented. ∎

Theorem 6.6 *The actual joint trajectory $\theta(t)$ generated by the R-FTZNN model (6.26) makes the Cartesian trajectory error function $y(t)$ converge to 0 in front of external disturbances with time as long as $\Phi_1(\cdot)$ and $\Phi_2(\cdot)$ are monotone increasing odd functions.*

Proof: It can be derived by adopting the conclusions of Theorems 6.3 and 6.4, and thus not presented. ∎

Remark Summarizing the previous results, we have that the R-FTZNN model (6.26) is an equivalent extension of FTR formula (6.4). In addition, we can further explain the R-FTZNN model (6.26) from the viewpoint of control. The R-FTZNN model (6.26) can be seen as a nonlinear controller, because it realizes the kinematical motion control of robot manipulators, and is consist of the proportional unit, derivative unit, and integral unit of the Cartesian velocity path $b(t)$. In addition, due to the role of the integral unit, the R-FTZNN model (6.26) is able to suppress the additive constant noises. On the other hand, the R-FTZNN model (6.26) is consist of a set of ordinary differential equations, and can start with the given initial value to evolve with time until the equilibrium state is achieved.

6.4 Illustrative Verification

In the aforementioned two sections, the novel FTR design formula (6.4) and R-FTZNN model (6.26) are proposed and investigated for kinematical motion tracking of robot manipulators illustrated via time-varying linear equation system solving. Besides, the superior theoretical results are presented in details. In this part, computer simulations are conducted to demonstrate the outstanding properties of the R-FTZNN model (6.26). First, a numerical example (i.e. a time-varying linear equation system) is first demonstrated. Then, a kinematical motion tracking task of a planar two-link manipulator is provided for validating the applicability of the R-FTZNN model (6.26).

6.4.1 Numerical Example

Without loss of generality, we simply select $A(t)$ and $b(t)$ as follows:

$$A(t) = \begin{bmatrix} \sin(t) & \cos(t) \\ -\cos(t) & \sin(t) \end{bmatrix} \quad \text{and} \quad b(t) = \begin{bmatrix} 2\sin(3t) \\ 3\cos(2t) \end{bmatrix}.$$

For correctness purposes, its corresponding theoretical solution is directly given as

$$u^*(t) = \begin{bmatrix} 2\sin(t)\sin(3t) - 3\cos(t)\cos(2t) \\ 2\sin(3t)\cos(t) + 3\sin(t)\cos(2t) \end{bmatrix}. \tag{6.28}$$

In addition, ZNN model (6.27) is also comparatively used to solve the aforementioned time-varying linear equation system. Note that $\Phi_1(\cdot)$ and $\Phi_2(\cdot)$ have the same expression, and each entry is selected as $\phi_1(y_j) = \phi_2(y_j) = \phi^r(y_j) + \phi^{1/r}(y_j)$.

6.4.1.1 No Noise Considered

First, with design parameters $r = 1/3$ and $\gamma_1 = \gamma_2 = \gamma = 1$, we apply R-FTZNN model (6.26) and ZNN model (6.27) to computing the aforementioned time-varying linear equation system in the ideal condition. Figure 6.1 plots the simulation results generated by R-FTZNN model (6.26). From this figure, we can conclude that the neural state output $u(t)$ can converge to the time-varying trajectory of the theoretical solution $u^*(t)$ within finite-time 2.25 seconds. In addition, the residual error $\|A(t)u(t) - b(t)\|_2$ corresponding to the neural state output $u(t)$ can rapidly converge to zero. The convergence speed of the residual error trajectory is very fast at the beginning, until it approaches to zero at about 0.5 seconds. The computation time for the residual error is consistent with that of the neural state output $u(t)$. Simulation results generated by ZNN model (6.27) are plotted in Figure 6.2, which implies ZNN model (6.27) can also effectively address

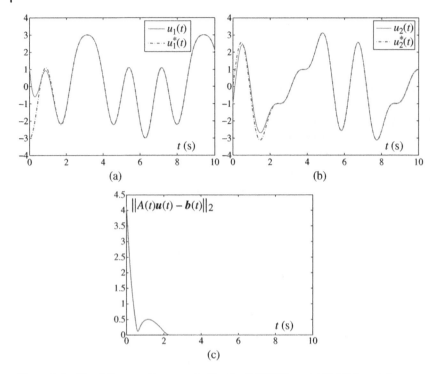

Figure 6.1 Simulative results generated by the R-FTZNN model (6.26) for solving the time-varying linear equation system with no noise. (a) The first element of the neural state $u(t)$ and the theoretical solution $u(t)$. (b) The second element of neural state $u(t)$ and the theoretical solution $u(t)$. (c) The residual error $\|A(t)u(t) - b(t)\|_2$ corresponding to the neural state $u(t)$.

this problem. However, it takes about five seconds to make the neural state output $u(t)$ keep pace with the time-varying trajectory of the theoretical solution $u^*(t)$. The aforementioned fact shows that R-FTZNN model (6.26) is better than ZNN model (6.27) for time-varying linear equation system.

6.4.1.2 With Noises Considered

In this part, let us study the influence of various different external disturbances on R-FTZNN model (6.26) and ZNN model (6.27). First, a constant noise $\eta_j = 0.5$ is injected into such two models. With $\gamma_1 = \gamma_2 = \gamma = 1$, the corresponding simulation results are shown in Figures 6.3 and 6.4. From Figure 6.3, we can conclude that, in front of the external disturbance $\eta_j = 0.5$, neural output $u(t)$ generated by R-FTZNN model (6.26) still keeps pace with the theoretical solution $u^*(t)$ within finite time 2. In addition, the corresponding residual error $\|A(t)u(t) - b(t)\|_2$ is also

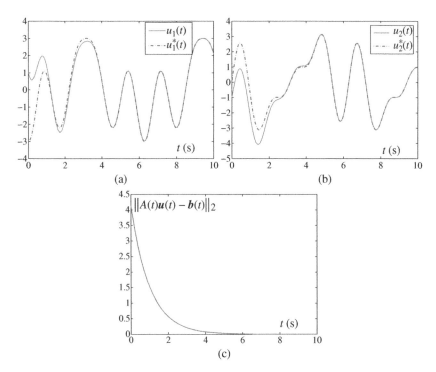

Figure 6.2 Simulative results generated by ZNN model (6.27) for solving the time-varying linear equation system with no noise. (a) The first element of the neural state $u(t)$ and the theoretical solution $u^*(t)$. (b) The second element of neural state $u(t)$ and the theoretical solution $u^*(t)$. (c) The residual error $\|A(t)u(t) - b(t)\|_2$ corresponding to the neural state $u(t)$.

rapidly decreasing to zero with finite time. That is to say, R-FTZNN model (6.26) is an inherently noise-tolerant model and simultaneously achieves finite-time convergence. In contrast, from Figure 6.4, we can conclude that, in front of the external disturbance $\eta_j = 0.5$, neural output $u(t)$ generated by ZNN model (6.27) is not able to keep pace with the theoretical solution $u^*(t)$ with time. Some certain errors are existing for them. In addition, as seen from Figure 6.4c, the corresponding residual error $\|A(t)u(t) - b(t)\|_2$ is not capable of converging to 0. The previous fact shows ZNN model (6.27) is not able to suppress external disturbances. Summarizing the aforementioned discussion, it is easy to come a conclusion that R-FTZNN model (6.26) is much better than ZNN model (6.27) in terms of convergence speed and noise tolerance.

In addition, both R-FTZNN model (6.26) and ZNN model (6.27) are applied to solve this problem in front of different kinds of external disturbances under

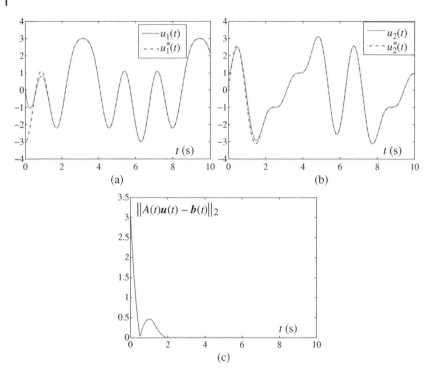

(a)

(b)

(c)

Figure 6.3 Simulative results generated by the R-FTZNN model (6.26) for solving the time-varying linear equation system with the constant noise $\eta_j = 0.5$. (a) The first element of the neural state $\boldsymbol{u}(t)$ and the theoretical solution $\boldsymbol{u}^*(t)$. (b) The second element of neural state $\boldsymbol{u}(t)$ and the theoretical solution $\boldsymbol{u}^*(t)$. (c) The residual error $||A(t)\boldsymbol{u}(t) - \boldsymbol{b}(t)||_2$ corresponding to the neural state $\boldsymbol{u}(t)$.

the conditions of different values of design parameters. The corresponding simulation results are plotted in Figure 6.5. Firstly, we set $\gamma_1 = \gamma_2 = \gamma = 10$ and take into account the bounded external noise (e.g. $\eta_j = 20$). The transient behavior of the residual errors $||A(t)\boldsymbol{u}(t) - \boldsymbol{b}(t)||_2$ produced by R-FTZNN model (6.26) and ZNN model (6.27) for solving time-varying linear equation system is plotted in Figure 6.5a, where the transient behavior of the neural state output is omitted due to the similarity. As seen from this subfigure, R-FTZNN model (6.26) is still effective to solve time-varying linear equation system even in front of the bounded external noise. Specifically, the residual error of R-FTZNN model (6.26) is able to converge to 0 within finite time 0.22 second. However, in the same conditions, ZNN model (6.27) losses efficacy, which is reflected in its residual error, not converging to 0 as time goes on. This fact shows that ZNN model (6.27) cannot solve time-varying linear equation system in front of the bounded external noise. On the other hand, we take into account the external disturbance that is dynamic

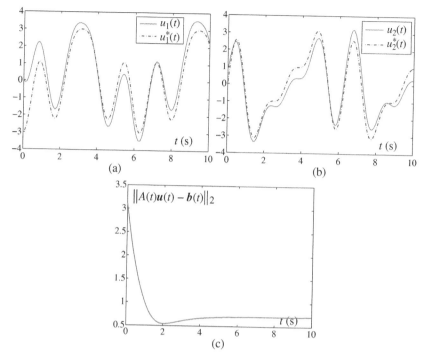

Figure 6.4 Simulative results generated by ZNN model (6.27) for solving the time-varying linear equation system with the constant noise $\eta_j = 0.5$. (a) The first element of the neural state $u(t)$ and the theoretical solution $u^*(t)$. (b) The second element of neural state $u(t)$ and the theoretical solution $u^*(t)$. (c) The residual error $\|A(t)u(t) - b(t)\|_2$ corresponding to the neural state $u(t)$.

with time (e.g. $\eta(t) = 5u(t)$). Keeping $\gamma_1 = \gamma_2 = \gamma$ unchanged, the transient behavior of the residual errors produced by such two neural-network models is plotted in Figure 6.5b. As seen from it, it can be concluded that R-FTZNN model (6.26) is still effective, while ZNN model (6.27) becomes worse in this situation.

At last, we set $\gamma_1 = \gamma_2 = \gamma = 100$ and still consider the bounded random noise $\eta_j = 20$. The simulative results synthesized by such two models are displayed in Figure 6.5c. As compared with the results of Figure 6.5a, it can be concluded that the computation time for the R-FTZNN model (6.26) is lower than ten times, i.e. decreasing from 0.22 to 0.022 seconds. For ZNN model (6.27), the residual error is still not convergent to 0, but the value of the residual error is becoming small. These results demonstrate that, by increasing the value of parameters, the solution efficiency of such two models can be improved accordingly.

All in all, summarizing the aforementioned facts, we are able to conclude that R-FTZNN model (6.26) and ZNN model (6.27) are both effective on solving

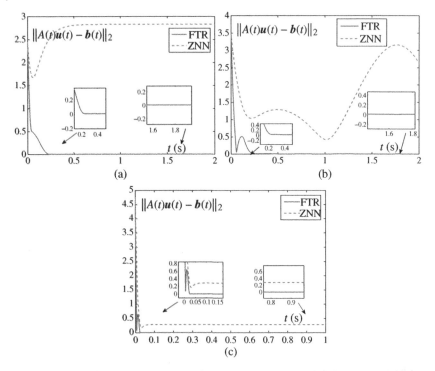

Figure 6.5 Residual errors $\|A(t)u(t) - b(t)\|_2$ generated by the R-FTZNN model (6.26) and ZNN model (6.27) for solving the time-varying linear equation system with the different noises and parameters. (a) The bounded noise $\eta_j = 20$ with $\gamma_1 = \gamma_2 = \gamma = 10$. (b) The time-varying noise $\eta_j(t) = 5u(t)$ with $\gamma_1 = \gamma_2 = \gamma = 10$. (c) The bounded noise $\eta_j = 20$ with $\gamma_1 = \gamma_2 = \gamma = 100$.

time-varying linear equation system with no external noises considered, but the convergence speed of R-FTZNN model (6.26) is faster than that of ZNN model (6.27). When the external disturbances are injected into such two models, ZNN model (6.27) is no longer effective on solving time-varying linear equation system, while R-FTZNN model (6.26) still generates the high accuracy solution of time-varying linear equation system. In a word, R-FTZNN model (6.26) is a better model for addressing the time-varying problem polluted by external disturbances.

6.4.2 Applications: Robotic Motion Tracking

In this subsection, we first consider the application of R-FTZNN model (6.26) to kinematic path tracking of a planar two-link manipulator shown in [20]. For comparative purposes, ZNN model (6.27) is also applied under the same conditions. For such a manipulator, the kinematical equations at the position level and at the velocity level can also be described as (6.1) and (6.2), respectively. Thus, we can use the R-FTZNN model (6.26) as a nonlinear controller to realize the kinematic path tracking of the planar two-link manipulator by allocating the specific path tracking task. Without loss of generality, the length of each link for the manipulator is 1 m, $x(0) = \theta(0) = [\pi/6, \pi/4]^T$ rad, $r = 0.5$, $\gamma_1 = \gamma_2 = 100$, and the additive noise is set as time-varying $\eta_j(t) = 2t$. In this simulation, the specific tracking task is allocated as a ellipse path with the major radius being 0.5 m and the minor radius being 0.25 m, and the task-tracking time is 10 seconds.

First, the ellipse-path tracking results synthesized by ZNN model (6.27) are displayed in Figure 6.6. From Figure 6.6a, we can see that, owing to the additive noise, the planar two-link manipulator is not able to perform the allocated ellipse-path tracking task successfully. In addition, by comparing the desired ellipse path shown in Figure 6.6b, the actual tracking trajectory starts to deviate from its normal motion path with time. In addition, the maximal error between them reaches about 9 cm, which can be supported by Figure 6.6c. The results

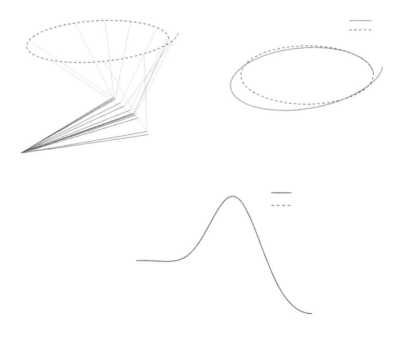

Figure 6.6 Actual ellipse-tracking results synthesized by ZNN model (6.27) in the presence of the additive noise $\eta_j = 2t$. (a) Actual ellipse-tracking process. (b) Desired ellipse path and actual ellipse-tracking trajectory. (c) Position error between desired ellipse path and actual ellipse-tracking trajectory.

show the invalidity of ZNN model (6.27) for kinematical motion tracking of robotic manipulators in the presence of the additive noise. Then, under the same conditions, we apply the R-FTZNN model (6.26) to kinematical motion tracking of the planar two-link manipulator, and the corresponding simulation results are displayed in Figure 6.7. As seen from this figure, we can conclude that the planar two-link manipulator completes the allocated ellipse-path tracking task successfully, and the maximal error is less than 1.5×10^{-5} m. Compared with the result of ZNN model (6.27), the solution accuracy of the R-FTZNN model (6.26) is greatly improved. The results demonstrate again the efficiency, superiority, and applicability of R-FTZNN model (6.26) even in front of external disturbances.

In addition, in order to illustrate the superiority, we further consider the application of R-FTZNN model (6.26) to kinematic path tracking of a 3D manipulator, of which its forward kinematic equation is given as

$$r(t) = f(\theta) = \begin{bmatrix} \cos\theta_1(32\cos\theta_3 + 27\sin\theta_2 + 3)/200 \\ \sin\theta_1(32\cos\theta_3 + 27\sin\theta_2 + 3)/200 \\ 27\cos\theta_2/200 - 4\sin\theta_3/25 + 103/1000 \end{bmatrix}.$$

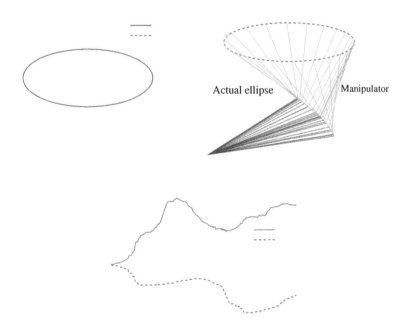

Figure 6.7 Actual ellipse-tracking results synthesized by R-FTZNN model (6.26) in the presence of the additive noise $\eta_j = 2t$. (a) Actual ellipse-tracking process. (b) Desired ellipse path and actual ellipse-tracking trajectory. (c) Position error between desired ellipse path and actual ellipse-tracking trajectory.

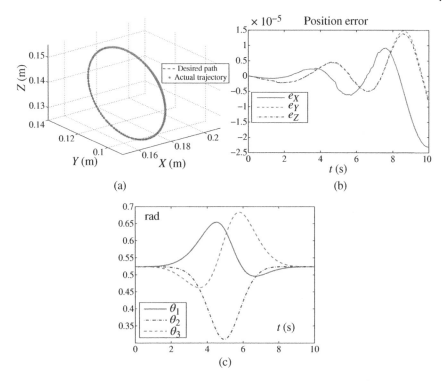

Figure 6.8 Actual circle-tracking results of the thee-dimensional (3D) manipulator synthesized by R-FTZNN model (6.26) in the presence of the additive noise $\eta_j = 1$. (a) Desired circle path and actual circle-tracking trajectory. (b) Position error between desired circle path and actual circle-tracking trajectory. (c) Dynamic behavior of joint angle.

In the simulation, the additive constant noise is $\eta_j(t) = 1$, and the initial angle of each link is set as $\pi/6$. The given tacking task is a circle in a 3D space, which has a 45° with X–Y plane. The radius is 2 cm, time duration is 10 seconds, and the parameters of R-FTZNN model (6.26) is set to $\gamma_1 = \gamma_2 = 50$. The circle-tracking task results are shown in Figure 6.8, which further validate the efficacy and applicability of R-FTZNN model (6.26) for 3D manipulators.

6.5 Chapter Summary

A noise-tolerant nonlinearly activated design formula is proposed and analyzed in details. Then, based on this new design formula, a R-FTZNN model is presented for robotic motion tracking illustrated via time-varying linear equation system solving in the presence of additive noises. Rigorous theoretical proofs are supplied to ensure the global stability, the finite-time convergence property, and the denoising ability of the new design formula and the R-FTZNN model. As compared with the previous ZNN model for time-varying linear equation system solving, our model makes great progress in terms of these outstanding properties. At last, we have conducted two typical simulative experiments. Simulation results have further validated the superiority of the R-FTZNN model for time-varying linear equation system solving and kinematical control of robotic manipulators in the presence of additive noises. As a final remark of this chapter, it worth pointing out that the work can handle finite-time convergence and noise suppression in a unified model in the field of ZNN research, making ZNN more robust and practical to address industrial problems with both timing constraints and noise pollution.

References

1 H. Xiao and Z. Li *et al.*, Formation control of leader-follower mobile robots' systems using model predictive control based on neuraldynamic optimization, *IEEE Trans. Ind. Electron.*, 63(9) (2016) 5752–5762.

2 W. He and W. Ge *et al.*, Model identification and control design for a humanoid robot, *IEEE Trans. Syst. Man Cybern. Syst.*, 47(1) (2017) 45–57.

3 L. Xiao, Z. Zhang, and S. Li, Solving time-varying system of nonlinear equations by finite-time recurrent neural networks with application to motion tracking of robot manipulators, *IEEE Trans. Syst. Man Cybern. Syst.*, 49(11) (2019) 2210–2220.

4 Z. Zhang and Z. Li *et al.*, Neural-dynamic-method based dual-arm CMG scheme with time-varying constraints applied to humanoid robots, *IEEE Trans. Neural Netw. Learn. Syst.*, 26(12) (2015) 3251–3262.

5 H. M. La, W. Sheng, and J. Chen, Cooperative and active sensing in mobile sensor networks for scalar field mapping, *IEEE Trans. Syst. Man Cybern. Syst.*, 45(1) (2015) 1–12.

6 L. Jin and S. Li *et al.*, Cooperative motion generation in a distributed network of redundant robot manipulators with noises, *IEEE Trans. Syst. Man Cybern. Syst.*, 48(10) (2018) 1715–1724.

7 L. Xiao and Y. Zhang, A new performance index for the repetitive motion of mobile manipulators, *IEEE Trans. Cybern.*, 44(2) (2014) 280–292.

8 Z. Zhang, A. Beck, and N. Magnenat-Thalmann, Human-like behavior generation based on head-arms model for tracking external targets and body parts, *IEEE Trans. Cybern.*, 45(8) (2015) 1390–1400.

9 D. Guo, Z. Nie, and L. Yan, The application of noise-tolerant ZD design formula to robots' kinematic control via time-varying nonlinear equations solving, *IEEE Trans. Syst. Man Cybern. Syst.*, 48(12) (2018) 2188–2197.

10 L. Xiao and Y. Zhang, Solving time-varying inverse kinematics problem of wheeled mobile manipulators using Zhang neural network with exponential convergence, *Nonlinear Dyn.*, 76(2) (2014) 1543–1559.

11 D. Chen and Y. Zhang, A hybrid multi-objective scheme applied to redundant robot manipulators, *IEEE Trans. Autom. Sci. Eng.*, 14(3) (2017) 1337–1350.

12 Z. Zhang and Y. Zhang, Acceleration-level cyclic motion generation of constrained redundant robots tracking different paths, *IEEE Trans. Syst. Man Cybern. Syst.*, 42(4) (2012) 1257–1269.

13 L. Xiao and S. Li *et al.*, A new recurrent neural network with noise-tolerance and finite-time convergence for dynamic quadratic minimization, *Neurocomputing*, 285 (2018) 125–132.

14 Y. Liu and S. Tong, Barrier Lyapunov functions-based adaptive control for a class of nonlinear pure-feedback systems with full state constraints, *Automatica*, 64 (2016) 70–75.

15 Y. Liu and S. Tong, Adaptive fuzzy identification and control for a class of nonlinear pure-feedback MIMO systems with unknown dead zones, *IEEE Trans. Fuzzy Syst.*, 23(5) (2015) 1387–1398.

16 J. Wang, Electronic realisation of recurrent neural work for solving simultaneous linear equations, *Electron. Lett.*, 28(5) (1992) 493–495.

17 K. Chen, Implicit dynamic system for online simultaneous linear equations solving, *Electron. Lett.*, 49(2) (2013) 101–102.

18 L. Xiao and B. Liao *et al.*, A finite-time convergent dynamic system for solving online simultaneous linear equations, *Int. J. Comput. Math.*, 94(9) (2017) 1778–1786.

19 L. Xiao and R. Lu, Finite-time solution to nonlinear equation using recurrent neural dynamics with a specially-constructed activation function, *Neurocomputing*, 151 (2015) 246–251.

20 Z. Zhang and T. Fu *et al.*, A varying-parameter convergent-differential neural network for solving joint-angular-drift problems of redundant robot manipulators, *IEEE ASME Trans. Mechatron.*, 23(2) (2018) 679–689.

21 Z. Zhang and Y. Zhang, Design and experimentation of acceleration-level drift-free scheme aided by two recurrent neural networks, *IET Control. Theory Appl.*, 7(1) (2013) 25–42.

22 D. Guo, Z. Nie, and L. Yan, Novel discrete-time Zhang neural network for time-varying matrix inversion, *IEEE Trans. Syst. Man Cybern. Syst.*, 47(8) (2017) 2301–2310.

23 S. Li, S. Chen, and B. Liu, Accelerating a recurrent neural network to finite-time convergence for solving time-varying Sylvester equation by using a sign-bi-power activation function, *Neural Process. Lett.*, 37 (2013) 189–205.

24 P. Miao and Y. Shen *et al.*, Solving time-varying quadratic programs based on finite-time Zhang neural networks and their application to robot tracking, *Neural Comput. Appl.*, 26(3) (2015) 693–703.

25 P. Miao and Y. Shen *et al.*, Finite-time recurrent neural networks for solving nonlinear optimization problems and their application, *Neurocomputing*, 177 (2016) 120–129.

7

Design Scheme II of FTZNN

7.1 Introduction

Solving linear matrix equation (matrix inversion can be regarded as a special linear matrix equation) is a basic problem in many scientific and engineering fields. This problem is widely used in signal processing [1], optimized algorithm [2], and robot kinematics [3]. The methods for solving linear matrix equation are usually divided into two directions: serial numerical algorithms [4–6] and parallel processing methods. The time complexity of numerical algorithms is the cube of the dimension of the matrix. This relationship will lead to a problem that it could spend much time to solve the equation when the dimension of the matrix is high. In this situation, the efficiency of solving problems is greatly reduced. In order to avoid this drawback, the idea of parallel processing [7] is presented and many researchers devoted themselves to this direction.

In this chapter, we design two finite-time zeroing neural network (FTZNN) models (called FTZNN1 and FTZNN2) for specific time-varying linear matrix equation problem. After two new finite-time activation functions (called NFTAF1 and NFTAF2) are applied to the models, we prove the finite-time convergence of the FTZNN1 and FTZNN2 models. At the same time, we also analyze that the Linear, Power, Bipolar Sigmoid, and Power-Sigmoid activation functions can not make the models converge in finite-time. Besides, when the differential error and the model-implementation error are injected into the FTZNN models, it is analyzed that the state solution of the models will converge to the theoretical solution with small residual error, and the upper bound of the steady-state residual state will be smaller as the parameter γ increasing. In general, FTZNN models have superior convergence and robustness.

Zeroing Neural Networks: Finite-time Convergence Design, Analysis and Applications,
First Edition. Lin Xiao and Lei Jia.

7.2 Problem Formulation

Take into account the smooth time-varying matrix $A(t) \in \mathbb{R}^{n \times n}$, $B(t) \in \mathbb{R}^{n \times n}$, $C(t) \in \mathbb{R}^{n \times n}$. Our purpose is to find a matrix $U(t) \in \mathbb{R}^{n \times n}$ such that the following matrix equation holds

$$A(t) U(t) B(t) = C(t). \tag{7.1}$$

In this chapter, we only consider $A(t)$, $B(t)$, and $C(t)$ as the smooth dynamic matrix with full rank. From Eq. (7.1), it is easy to get the theoretical solution $U^*(t) = A^{-1}(t) C(t) B^{-1}(t)$. For the following theoretical analysis, we should guarantee the existence of $A^{-1}(t)$, and $B^{-1}(t)$. So, based on [8], the following lemmas are introduced.

Lemma 7.1 *If there exists positive real numbers $\alpha > 0$ and $\beta > 0$ such that*

$$\min_{\forall i \in \{1,\ldots,n\}} |\lambda_i(A(t))| \geq \alpha,$$

$$\min_{\forall i \in \{1,\ldots,n\}} |\lambda_i(B(t))| \geq \beta,$$

where $t > 0$, $\lambda_i(\cdot)$ denotes the ith eigenvalue of matrix $A(t)$, $B(t) \in \mathbb{R}^{n \times n}$. Then the formula (7.1) exits a unique solution.

Lemma 7.2 *If $A(t)$, and $B(t)$ satisfy the Lemma 7.1 with $\|A(t)\|_F \leq \varepsilon_A$ and $\|B(t)\|_F \leq \varepsilon_B$, $\forall t \in [0, +\infty)$, where $\| \cdot \|_F$ denotes Frobenius norm. Then the boundedness of $\|A^{-1}(t)\|_F$ and $\|B^{-1}(t)\|_F$ are obtained,*

$$\|A^{-1}(t)\|_F \leq \varphi\left(\alpha, \varepsilon_A^2, n\right) = \sum_{i=0}^{n-2} \frac{C_n^i \cdot \varepsilon_A^{2(n-i-1)}}{\alpha^{n-i}} + \frac{n^{3/2}}{\alpha},$$

$$\|B^{-1}(t)\|_F \leq \varphi\left(\beta, \varepsilon_B^2, n\right) = \sum_{i=0}^{n-2} \frac{C_n^i \cdot \varepsilon_B^{2(n-i-1)}}{\beta^{n-i}} + \frac{n^{3/2}}{\beta},$$

where $C_n^i := \frac{n!}{i!(n-i)!}$.

7.3 FTZNN Model

According to the process of constructing a zeroing neural network (ZNN) model mentioned in [9], we define an error matrix $Y(U(t), t) \in \mathbb{R}^{n \times n}$ to replace the usual scalar-valued cost function:

$$Y(U(t), t) = A(t) U(t) B(t) - C(t), \tag{7.2}$$

where $A(t) \in \mathbb{R}^{n \times n}$, $B(t) \in \mathbb{R}^{n \times n}$, and $C(t) \in \mathbb{R}^{n \times n}$ are dynamic full rank matrix. Dynamic state matrix $U(t) \in \mathbb{R}^{n \times n}$ is unknown and wanted to be obtained.

The error-function derivative $\dot{Y}(U(t),t)$ should be defined to make every $y_{ij}(t)$ $(i,j = 1,\ldots,n)$ of $Y(U(t),t)$ converge to zero. Therefore, $\dot{Y}(U(t),t)$ is expressed in the following form:

$$\frac{dY(U(t),t)}{dt} = -\Gamma\Phi(Y(U(t),t)), \tag{7.3}$$

where Γ is a positive-defined matrix to adjust the convergence speed of the solution, and $\Phi(\cdot): \mathbb{R}^{n\times n} \to \mathbb{R}^{n\times n}$ is a matrix mapping. Combining (7.2) and (7.3), the following ZNN model is obtained:

$$\begin{aligned} &\dot{A}(t)U(t)B(t) + A(t)\dot{U}(t)B(t) + A(t)U(t)\dot{B}(t) - \dot{C}(t) \\ &= -\Gamma\Phi(A(t)U(t)B(t) - C(t)), \end{aligned} \tag{7.4}$$

where $U(t)$ with initial state $U(0) \in \mathbb{R}^{n\times n}$ is the state matrix, and corresponds to the output of the neural network. Besides, in order to analyze the character of this model simply, Γ is assumed as γI. As a result, every $y_{ij}(t)$ will have the same convergence rate at the time t. And the convergence rate could be adjusted by designing different values of parameter γ. So ZNN model (7.4) is rewritten as

$$\begin{aligned} A(t)\dot{U}(t)B(t) &= -\dot{A}(t)U(t)B(t) - A(t)U(t)\dot{B}(t) \\ &+ \dot{C}(t) - \gamma\Phi(A(t)U(t)B(t) - C(t)). \end{aligned} \tag{7.5}$$

According to the previous research, we know that the activation functions can influence the robustness and convergence rate of ZNN models. In general, any monotonically increasing odd function $\phi(\cdot)$ can be used as an element of $\Phi(\cdot)$ array. When different activation functions are added into neural network, the different methods can be used to analyze its character. Broadly speaking, there are three ways to prove the convergence and robustness of ZNN models. They are Lyapunov theory [10], ordinary differential equation (ODE), and Laplace transform. According to Lyapunov theory, the most important thing is to build a Lyapunov energy function $p(t)$ which must be positive definite. We calculate its differential $\dot{p}(t)$. If $\dot{p}(t)$ is negative definite then we can draw a conclusion that the equilibrium state of the system is asymptotically stable. That is to say, the residual error of the corresponding ZNN models asymptotically converges to zero. Lyapunov theory can be applied to ZNN models activated by not only linear functions but also nonlinear activation functions. The proof based on ODE and Laplace transform is usually used for linear activation functions. In this chapter we will use the Lyapunov theory to prove relative theory of FTZNN1 and FTZNN2 as usual.

For activation functions, there are several commonly used forms. (i) Linear activation function, $\Phi(x) = x$. ZNN models possess exponential convergence rate when the linear activation function is added. However, as we all known, for the character of exponential convergence rate, the convergence speed of ZNN models will become slowly with the error function getting to zero. In order to overcome this shortcoming, some nonlinear activation functions are put forward. (ii) Power activation function, $\Phi(x) = x_i^s$ with $s \geq 3$. (iii) Bipolar Sigmoid activation function, $\Phi(x) = (1 - \exp(-\xi x)) / (1 + \exp(-\xi x))$ with $\xi > 2$. (iv) Power-Sigmoid activation function, $\Phi(x) = x_i^q$ when $|x| \geq 1$ and $\Phi(x) = ((1 + \exp(-\xi)) / (1 - \exp(-\xi))) \cdot ((1 - \exp(-\xi x)) / (1 + \exp(-\xi x)))$ when $|x| < 1$, where $\xi > 2$ and $q \geq 3$. However, due to the further study, these three nonlinear activation functions cannot make ZNN models achieve finite-time convergence. Then, the sign-bi-power (Sbp) activation function is proposed in [11, 12] to accomplish this goal, and its formula is

$$\Phi(x) = \frac{1}{2}\text{sgn}^\tau(x) + \frac{1}{2}\text{sgn}^{\frac{1}{\tau}}(x), \quad 0 < \tau < 1. \tag{7.6}$$

Recently, based on Sbp activation function, two new activation functions are put forward in [13]. They are called new finite-time activation function 1 (NFTAF1) and new finite-time activation function 2 (NFTAF2). Their formulas are shown as follows:

$$\Phi(x) = \text{sgn}^\tau(x), \quad 0 < \tau < 1, \tag{7.7}$$

$$\Phi(x) = \beta_1 \text{sgn}^\tau(x) + \beta_2 x, \quad 0 < \tau < 1, \tag{7.8}$$

with $\beta_1 > 0$, and $\beta_2 > 0$. The function $\text{sgn}^\tau(x)$ mentioned earlier is defined as

$$\text{sgn}^\tau(x) = \begin{cases} |x|^\tau, & \text{if } x > 0, \\ 0, & \text{if } x = 0, \\ -|x|^\tau, & \text{if } x < 0. \end{cases}$$

In this chapter we will use NFTAF1 and NFTAF2 in ZNN (7.5), and the corresponding nonlinear activated models are named as the FTZNN1 model and the FTZNN2 model, respectively.

7.4 Theoretical Analysis

Based on the knowledge in the previous text, we will analyze the convergence and robustness of the FTZNN1 model and the FTZNN2 model.

7.4.1 Convergence

In this section, some conclusions are obtained from theoretical analysis, and the convergence rate of ZNN model (7.5) activated by different activation functions is compared.

According to Lemmas 7.1 and 7.2, if the given time-varying matrix $A(t) \in \mathbb{R}^{n \times n}$ and $B(t) \in \mathbb{R}^{n \times n}$ satisfy these conditions and the used activation functions have monotonous and odd character. Then, we can get the fact that the state matrix $U(t) \in \mathbb{R}^{n \times n}$ of ZNN model (7.5) with any initial state $U(0) \in \mathbb{R}^{n \times n}$ will converge to the time-varying theoretical solution of (7.1). From this analysis, some theorems can be concluded. In the following proof of theorems, $y_{ij}(t)$ represents the every element of $Y(t)$ at the time t, and $y_{\max}(t)$ represents the maximum among $y_{ij}(t)$. Besides, t_f and $t_{\max}$ are the convergence time of $Y(t)$ and $y_{\max}(t)$, respectively.

Theorem 7.3 *Given matrices $A(t)$ and $B(t)$ satisfying Lemmas 7.1 and 7.2, if NFTAF1 is used in ZNN model (7.5), the FTZNN1 model will converge to the time-varying theoretical solution of (7.1) in finite time $(|y_{\max}(0)|^{1-\tau})/(\gamma(1-\tau))$.*

Proof: Because the same dynamic equation exists in FTZNN1 for $y_{ij}(t)$ and NFTAF1 is an odd function, we have $|y_{ij}(t)| \leq |y_{\max}(t)|$, $\forall i,j = 1, 2, \ldots, n$. Then, according to the theory about nonlinear control, if we want every element $y_{ij}(t)$ to converge to zero, we only need to make $y_{\max}(t) = 0$. Therefore we could obtain $t_{\max}$ by solving the following dynamic equation:

$$\dot{y}_{\max}(t) = -\gamma \cdot \mathrm{sgn}^{\tau}(y_{\max}(t)), \quad 0 < \tau < 1. \tag{7.9}$$

The following three cases are considered according to the definition of $\mathrm{sgn}^{\tau}(\cdot)$.

(1) Under the condition of $y_{\max}(0) > 0$, (7.9) can be written as $\dot{y}_{\max}(t) = -\gamma \cdot (y_{\max}(t))^{\tau}$, which is further rewritten as

$$\frac{dy_{\max}(t)}{dt} = -\gamma(y_{\max}(t))^{\tau},$$

$$dt = -\frac{1}{\gamma}(y_{\max}(t))^{-\tau}dy_{\max}(t).$$

Integrate aforementioned equality from $t = 0$ to $t = t_{\max}$:

$$\int_0^{t_{\max}} dt = -\frac{1}{\gamma}\int_{y_{\max}(0)}^0 (y_{\max}(t))^{-\tau}dy_{\max}(t),$$

$$t_{\max} = \frac{(y_{\max}(0))^{1-\tau}}{\gamma(1-\tau)} = \frac{|y_{\max}(0)|^{1-\tau}}{\gamma(1-\tau)}.$$

(2) If $y_{\max}(0) < 0$, it can get the same result in a similar way. Thus, the derivative procedure is not presented.

(3) If $y_{\max}(0) = 0$, it is obvious that $t_{\max} = 0$, which satisfies $(|y_{\max}(0)|^{1-\tau}|)/(\gamma(1-\tau))$.

By combining the previous three cases, we can conclude that the state matrix $U(t)$ of the FTZNN1 model will converge to the time-varying theoretical solution of (7.1) in finite time $t_f \leq \frac{|y_{\max}(0)|^{1-\tau}}{\gamma(1-\tau)}$. ∎

Theorem 7.4 *Given matrices $A(t)$ and $B(t)$ satisfying Lemmas 7.1 and 7.2, if NFTAF2 is used in ZNN model (7.5), the FTZNN2 model will converge to the time-varying theoretical solution of (7.1) in finite time t_f:*

$$t_f \leq \frac{1}{(\tau - 1) \cdot \gamma\beta_2} \ln \frac{\gamma\beta_1}{\gamma\beta_2 \cdot |y_{\max}(0)|^{1-\tau} + \gamma\beta_1}.$$

Proof: In the same way, we only calculate t_{max} of $y_{max}(t) = 0$ to prove finite-time convergence of the FTZNN2 model that can be simplified as

$$\dot{y}_{max}(t) = -\gamma(\beta_1 \text{sgn}^\tau(y_{max}(t)) + \beta_2 y_{max}(t))$$

$$= -\gamma\beta_1 \cdot \text{sgn}^\tau(y_{max}(t)) - \gamma\beta_2 \cdot y_{max}(t). \tag{7.10}$$

(1) Under the condition of $y_{max}(0) > 0$, (7.10) can be written as $\dot{y}_{max}(t) = -\gamma\beta_1 \cdot (y_{max}(t))^\tau - \gamma\beta_2 \cdot y_{max}(t)$, which can be rewritten as

$$(y_{max}(t))^{-\tau} \cdot \frac{dy_{max}(t)}{dt} = -\gamma\beta_1 - \gamma\beta_2 \cdot y_{max}(t)^{1-\tau},$$

$$\frac{d(y_{max}(t))^{1-\tau}}{dt} = (\gamma\beta_1 + \gamma\beta_2 \cdot y_{max}(t)^{1-\tau}) \cdot (\tau - 1),$$

$$dt = \frac{dy_{max}(t)^{1-\tau}}{(\tau-1) \cdot (\gamma\beta_1 + \gamma\beta_2 \cdot (y_{max}(t))^{1-\tau})}.$$

Integrate aforementioned equality from $t = 0$ to $t = t_{max}$:

$$\int_0^{t_{max}} dt = \int_{y_{max}(0)}^0 \frac{dy_{max}(t)^{1-\tau}}{(\tau-1) \cdot (\gamma\beta_1 + \gamma\beta_2 \cdot (y_{max}(t))^{1-\tau})},$$

$$t\big|_0^{t_{max}} = \frac{1}{(\tau-1) \cdot \gamma\beta_2} \cdot \ln(\gamma\beta_2 \cdot (y_{max}(t))^{1-\tau} + \gamma\beta_1)\big|_{y_{max}(0)}^0,$$

$$t_{max} = \frac{\ln(\gamma\beta_1)}{(\tau-1) \cdot \gamma\beta_2} - \frac{\ln(\gamma\beta_2 \cdot (y_{max}(0))^{1-\tau} + \gamma\beta_1)}{(\tau-1) \cdot \gamma\beta_2},$$

$$t_{max} = \frac{1}{(\tau-1) \cdot \gamma\beta_2} \ln \frac{\gamma\beta_1}{\gamma\beta_2 \cdot (y_{max}(0))^{1-\tau} + \gamma\beta_1},$$

$$t_{max} = \frac{1}{(\tau-1) \cdot \gamma\beta_2} \ln \frac{\gamma\beta_1}{\gamma\beta_2 \cdot |y_{max}(0)|^{1-\tau} + \gamma\beta_1}.$$

(2) If $y_{max}(0) < 0$, we can get the same result, and thus delete the detailed derivative process.

(3) If $y_{max}(0) = 0$, it is easy to know that $t_{max} = 0$, which also satisfies requirement.

By combining the aforementioned three cases, we conclude that the state matrix $U(t)$ of the FTZNN2 model will converge to the time-varying theoretical solution of (7.1) in finite time t_f. ∎

Proposition 7.5 *Given matrices $A(t) \in \mathbb{R}^{n \times n}$ and $B(t) \in \mathbb{R}^{n \times n}$ satisfying Lemmas 7.1 and 7.2, if Linear activation function, Power activation function, Bipolar Sigmoid activation function and Power-Sigmoid activation function are used in ZNN model (7.5), the state matrix $U(t)$ will not converge to the time-varying theoretical solution of (7.1) in finite time.*

Proof: Firstly, Linear activation function $\Phi(x) = x$ is considered. Then, from ZNN model (7.5), we can get the equality $\dot{y}_{max}(t) = -\gamma y_{max}(t)$. Try to solve this equation with the same method which is used earlier. The following equality is obtained:

$$\frac{dy_{max}(t)}{dt} = -\gamma \cdot y_{max}(t),$$

$$dt = -\frac{1}{\gamma} \cdot \frac{1}{y_{max}(t)} dy_{max}(t).$$

Integrate aforementioned equality from $t = 0$ to $t = t_{max}$:

$$\int_0^{t_{max}} dt = \int_{y_{max}(0)}^0 -\frac{1}{\gamma} \cdot \frac{1}{y_{max}(t)} dy_{max}(t),$$

$$t_{max} = -\frac{1}{\gamma} \cdot \ln y_{max}(t)|_{y_{max}(0)}^0.$$

According to the character of function $f(x) = \ln x$, we can get that $\lim_{x \to 0} f(x) = -\infty$. Hence $Y(t)$ can not converge to zero in finite time.

Secondly, Power activation function $\Phi(x) = x_i^s$ with $s \geq 3$ is used in ZNN model (7.5). We assume every element $y_{ij}(t') \to 0$ at the time t'. Solving $\dot{y}_{ij}(t) = -\gamma \cdot (y_{ij}(t))^s$, we can obtain:

$$\frac{dy_{ij}(t)}{dt} = -\gamma \cdot (y_{ij}(t))^s,$$

$$dt = -\frac{1}{\gamma} \cdot y_{ij}(t)^{-s} dy_{ij}(t).$$

Integrate aforementioned equality from $t = 0$ to $t = t'$:

$$t|_0^{t'} = -\frac{1}{\gamma(1-s)} \cdot y_{ij}(t)^{1-s}|_{y_{ij}(0)}^{y_{ij}(t')},$$

$$t' = -\frac{1}{\gamma(1-s)} y_{ij}(t')^{1-s} + \frac{1}{\gamma(1-s)} y_{ij}(0)^{1-s}.$$

Due to $s \geq 3$, $\lim_{y_{ij}(t') \to 0} t' = -\infty$. Therefore, from this result, this activation function cannot make ZNN model (7.5) reach finite-time convergence.

Thirdly, we are concerned about ZNN model (7.5) activated by Bipolar Sigmoid activation function $\Phi(x) = (1 - \exp(-\xi x))/(1 + \exp(-\xi x))$ with $\xi > 2$. At the same way, we assume every element $y_{ij}(t') \to 0$ at the time t'. Then, the ZNN model is expressed by

$$\frac{dy_{ij}(t)}{dt} = -\gamma \cdot \frac{1 - e^{-\xi y_{ij}(t)}}{1 + e^{-\xi y_{ij}(t)}},$$

$$dt = -\frac{1}{\gamma} \cdot \frac{1 + e^{-\xi y_{ij}(t)}}{1 - e^{-\xi y_{ij}(t)}} dy_{ij}(t).$$

Integrate aforementioned equality from $t = 0$ to $t = t'$:

$$t|_0^{t'} = -\frac{1}{\gamma} \cdot (y_{ij}(t) + \frac{2\ln(e^{-\xi y_{ij}(t)} - 1)}{\xi})|_{y_{ij}(0)}^{y_{ij}(t')},$$

$$t = -\frac{1}{\gamma} \cdot (y_{ij}(t') - y_{ij}(0) + \frac{2}{\xi}(\ln(e^{-\xi y_{ij}(t')} - 1) - \ln(e^{-\xi y_{ij}(0)} - 1)))$$

Because $y_{ij}(t') \to 0$, $e^{-\xi y_{ij}(t')} \to 1$, and $\ln(e^{-\xi y_{ij}(t')} - 1) \to -\infty$, it follows that $\lim_{y_{ij}(t') \to 0} t' = +\infty$. It means that $y_{ij}(t) \to 0$ cannot be realized in finite time.

At last, Power-Sigmoid activation function is considered, which is a piecewise function. When $|x| \geq 1$, it becomes a power function, the theoretical analysis is the same as Power activation function; and if $|x| \leq 1$, because $\frac{1+\exp(-\xi)}{1-\exp(-\xi)}$ is an exact number and according to the proof about Bipolar Sigmoid activation function, $\lim_{y_{ij}(t) \to 0} t = +\infty$ can also be obtained. Therefore, the ZNN model activated by the power-sigmoid function cannot converge in finite time.

In general, we have proved the Proposition 7.5 that the neural network with these four activation functions will not realize finite-time convergence. ∎

By Theorem 7.3, Theorem 7.4, and Proposition 7.5, we conclude these activation functions in briefly. For Linear, Power, Bipolar Sigmoid, and Power-Sigmoid activation functions, they can make the state solution of ZNN model converge to the theoretical solution of the problem. Besides, Power, Bipolar Sigmoid, and Power-Sigmoid activation functions can overcome the disadvantages of exponential convergence which would be caused by Linear activation function. However, these functions can not make $y_{ij}(t)$ converge to zero in finite time. As compared with the upper bound of the ZNN model activated by Sbp activation function [14], the proposed two FTZNN models have lower upper bound of steady-state residual error, therefore they possess the superior performance about convergence in finite time.

7.4.2 Robustness

The ZNN model (7.5) aims to get the state matrix $U(t)$ in the ideal environment. However, we should pay attention to the realistic situation that always has unavoidable errors and noise. Thus, we will consider the differential error $\Delta d(t) \in \mathbb{R}^{n \times n}$ and the model-implementation error $\Delta m(t) \in \mathbb{R}^{n \times n}$ in ZNN model (7.5). Then, we can get the disturbed ZNN model:

$$\begin{aligned}
(\dot{A}(t) + \Delta d(t)) \, U(t) B(t) &+ A(t) \dot{U}(t) B(t) \\
&+ A(t) U(t) (\dot{B}(t) + \Delta d(t)) - \dot{C}(t) \\
&= -\gamma \cdot \Phi(A(t)U(t)B(t) - C(t)) + \Delta m(t),
\end{aligned} \tag{7.11}$$

which is transformed into:

$$\begin{aligned}
\dot{A}(t) U(t) B(t) + A(t) \dot{U}(t) B(t) &+ A(t) U(t) \dot{B}(t) - \dot{C}(t) \\
&= -\gamma \Phi(A(t)U(t)B(t) - C(t)) - \Delta d(t) U(t) B(t) \\
&- A(t) U(t) \Delta d(t) + \Delta m(t).
\end{aligned} \tag{7.12}$$

Considering error matrix $Y(t) = A(t)U(t)B(t) - C(t)$, and $U(t) = A^{-1}(t)Y(t)B^{-1}(t) + A^{-1}(t)C(t)B^{-1}(t)$, from the aforementioned equation, one can get:

$$\dot{Y}(t) = -\gamma \cdot \Phi(Y(t)) - \Delta d(t)A^{-1}(t)Y(t)$$
$$- \Delta d(t)A^{-1}(t)C(t) - Y(t)B^{-1}(t)\Delta d(t) \qquad (7.13)$$
$$- C(t)B^{-1}(t)\Delta d(t) + \Delta m(t).$$

In general, for matrix $A = [a_{ij}] \in \mathbb{R}^{m \times n}$, $B = [b_{ij}] \in \mathbb{R}^{s \times q}$. The Kronecker product of A and B is often defined as

$$A \otimes B = \begin{bmatrix} a_{11}B & \cdots & a_{1n}B \\ \vdots & \ddots & \vdots \\ a_{n1}B & \cdots & a_{nn}B \end{bmatrix} \in \mathbb{R}^{ms \times nq}.$$

And as stated in [15], the equation $AUB = C$ can be vectorized as $\text{vec}(AUB) = (B^T \otimes A)\text{vec}(U)$. Besides, for column vectorization of a matrix $U = [u_{ij}] \in \mathbb{R}^{m \times n}$, $\text{vec}(U)$ is defined as

$$\text{vec}(U) = [u_{11}, \ldots, u_{m1}, \ldots, u_{1n}, \ldots, u_{nn}]^T \in \mathbb{R}^{mn \times 1}.$$

Based on this notion, (7.13) can be vectorized as the following form:

$$\dot{y}(t) = -\gamma \cdot \Phi(y(t)) - S(t)y(t) - Q(t)y(t) + k(t), \qquad (7.14)$$

where $y(t) := \text{vec}(Y(t)) \in \mathbb{R}^{n^2 \times 1}$, $S(t) := I^T \otimes (\Delta d(t)A^{-1}(t))$, $Q(t) := (B^{-1}(t)\Delta d(t))^T \otimes I$, and $k(t) := \text{vec}(\Delta m(t) - \Delta d(t)A^{-1}(t)C(t) - C(t)B^{-1}(t)\Delta d(t))$.

Theorem 7.6 *For $\forall t \geq 0$, if $\|\Delta d(t)\|_F \leq \varepsilon_d$, and $\|\Delta m(t)\|_F \leq \varepsilon_m$ with $\varepsilon_d, \varepsilon_m \in (0, +\infty)$; $\|A^{-1}(t)\|_F \leq \beta_A$ and $\|B^{-1}(t)\|_F \leq \beta_B$ with $\beta_A, \beta_B B \in (0, +\infty)$; and $\|C(t)\|_F \leq \varphi_C$ with $\varphi_C \in (0, +\infty)$, then, under the condition of $\gamma > (\varepsilon_d \beta_A + \varepsilon_d \beta_B)/\rho$, the steady state residual error of the disturbed ZNN model (7.12) is bounded by*

$$\frac{(\sqrt{l}+l)(\varepsilon_m + \varepsilon_d \beta_A \varphi_C + \varphi_C \beta_B \varepsilon_d)}{2(\gamma \rho - \varepsilon_d \beta_A - \varepsilon_d \beta_B)},$$

where $l = n^2$, and $\rho = f(|y_i|)/|y_i| \geq 1$.

Proof: We define a Lyapunov function $p(t) = \|y(t)\|_2^2/2 = \sum_{i=1}^{n^2} y_i^2(t)/2 \geq 0$. According to the Lyapunov theory [10], we analyze $\dot{p}$ as follows, where for convenient, time t is omitted:

$$\dot{p} = y^T \dot{y}$$
$$= y^T(-\gamma \Phi(y) + Sy + Qy + k) \qquad (7.15)$$
$$= -\gamma y^T \Phi(y) + y^T Sy + y^T Qy + y^T k.$$

Every term of Eq. (7.15) will be taken into consideration, respectively. For the first term:

$$-\gamma y^T \Phi(y) = -\sum_{i=1}^{l} \gamma |y_i| f(y_i). \qquad (7.16)$$

For the second term, based on the mathematical characteristic $\max_{1\le i\le l}|\lambda_i(X)| \le \|X\|_F$, we can get:

$$
\begin{aligned}
\boldsymbol{y}^{\mathrm{T}} S \boldsymbol{y} &= \boldsymbol{y}^{\mathrm{T}}\frac{S+S^{\mathrm{T}}}{2}\boldsymbol{y} \\
&\le \boldsymbol{y}^{\mathrm{T}}\boldsymbol{y}\max_{1\le i<l}\left|\lambda_i\left(\frac{S+S^{\mathrm{T}}}{2}\right)\right| \\
&= \boldsymbol{y}^{\mathrm{T}}\boldsymbol{y}\max_{1\le i<l}\left|\lambda_i\left(\frac{I\otimes\left(\Delta dA^{-1}\right)+\left(I\otimes\left(\Delta dA^{-1}\right)\right)^{\mathrm{T}}}{2}\right)\right| \\
&= \boldsymbol{y}^{\mathrm{T}}\boldsymbol{y}\max_{1\le i<l}\left|\lambda_i\left(\frac{I\otimes\left(\left(\Delta dA^{-1}\right)+\left(\Delta dA^{-1}\right)^{\mathrm{T}}\right)}{2}\right)\right| \\
&\le \boldsymbol{y}^{\mathrm{T}}\boldsymbol{y}\|\Delta dA^{-1}\|_F \\
&\le \boldsymbol{y}^{\mathrm{T}}\boldsymbol{y}\|\Delta d\|_F\|A^{-1}\|_F \\
&\le \boldsymbol{y}^{\mathrm{T}}\boldsymbol{y}\varepsilon_d\beta_A.
\end{aligned}
\tag{7.17}
$$

For the third term, the following result can be obtained in a similar way:

$$
\boldsymbol{y}^{\mathrm{T}} Q \boldsymbol{y} \le \boldsymbol{y}^{\mathrm{T}}\boldsymbol{y}\varepsilon_d\beta_B.
\tag{7.18}
$$

For the last term, by $\max_{1\le i\le l}\left|[k]_i\right| \le \|[k]_i\|_2$, we can get:

$$
\begin{aligned}
\boldsymbol{y}^{\mathrm{T}} \boldsymbol{k} &\le \sum_{i=1}^{l}|y_i|\max_{1\le i\le l}|[k]_i| \le \sum_{i=1}^{l}|y_i|\|\boldsymbol{k}\|_2 \\
&\le \sum_{i=1}^{l}|y_i|(\|\Delta m\|_F + \|\Delta dA^{-1}C\|_F + \|CB^{-1}\Delta d\|_F) \\
&\le \sum_{i=1}^{l}|y_i|(\varepsilon_m + \varepsilon_d\beta_A\varphi_C + \varphi_C\beta_B\varepsilon_d).
\end{aligned}
\tag{7.19}
$$

According to (7.16)–(7.19), we can get:

$$
\begin{aligned}
\dot{p} &\le -\sum_{i=1}^{l}\gamma|y_i|f(y_i) + \boldsymbol{y}^{\mathrm{T}}\boldsymbol{y}\left(\varepsilon_d\beta_A+\varepsilon_d\beta_B\right) + \sum_{i=1}^{l}|y_i|\left(\varepsilon_m+\varepsilon_d\beta_A\varphi_C+\varphi_C\beta_B\varepsilon_d\right) \\
&= -\sum_{i=1}^{l}|y_i|(\gamma f(|y_i|) - |y_i|(\varepsilon_d\beta_A+\varepsilon_d\beta_B) - (\varepsilon_m+\varepsilon_d\beta_A\varphi_C+\varphi_C\beta_B\varepsilon_d)).
\end{aligned}
\tag{7.20}
$$

The aforementioned Eq. (7.20) has two situations to discuss about the value of $\dot{p}$. Firstly, considering $\gamma f(|y_i|) - |y_i|(\varepsilon_d\beta_A + \varepsilon_d\beta_B) - (\varepsilon_m + \varepsilon_d\beta_A\varphi_C + \varphi_C\beta_B\varepsilon_d) > 0$

with $\forall i \in 1, 2, \ldots, l$ holds in time interval, we have $\dot{p} < 0$. According to the Lyapunov theory, the error vector $Y(t)$ will be globally asymptotic stability, which indicates that the state matrix $U(t)$ of the disturbed ZNN model (7.15) will converge to the theoretical solution of (7.1). Secondly, considering $\gamma f(|y_i|) - |y_i|(\varepsilon_d\beta_A + \varepsilon_d\beta_B) - (\varepsilon_m + \varepsilon_d\beta_A\varphi_C + \varphi_C\beta_B\varepsilon_d) \leq 0$ with $\exists i \in (1, 2, \ldots, l)$ at any time point, then $\dot{p} \geq 0$, which implies $Y(t)$ may not converge toward zero. In this situation, $Y(t)$ will diverge, which makes $\gamma f(|y_i|) - |y_i|(\varepsilon_d\beta_A + \varepsilon_d\beta_B) - (\varepsilon_m + \varepsilon_d\beta_A\varphi_C + \varphi_C\beta_B\varepsilon_d)$ increase, until $\dot{p} = 0$ at t_0. That means the error vector $Y(t)$ reaches steady state at t_0 and when $t > t_0$.

By the analysis earlier, we will calculate the upper bound of $|y_i(t)|$. Due to the existence of $\rho = \frac{f(|y_i|)}{|y_i|} \geq 1$, Eq. (7.20) can be rewritten as

$$\dot{p} \leq - \sum_{i=1}^{l} |y_i|(\gamma f(|y_i|) - |y_i|(\varepsilon_d\beta_A + \varepsilon_d\beta_B) - (\varepsilon_m + \varepsilon_d\beta_A\varphi_C + \varphi_C\beta_B\varepsilon_d))$$

$$= - \sum_{i=1}^{l} |y_i|(\gamma\rho|y_i| - |y_i|(\varepsilon_d\beta_A + \varepsilon_d\beta_B) - (\varepsilon_m + \varepsilon_d\beta_A\varphi_C + \varphi_C\beta_B\varepsilon_d))$$

$$= - (\gamma\rho - \varepsilon_d\beta_A - \varepsilon_d\beta_B) \sum_{i=1}^{l} |y_i| \left(|y_i| - \frac{\varepsilon_m + \varepsilon_d\beta_A\varphi_C + \varphi_C\beta_B\varepsilon_d}{(\gamma\rho - \varepsilon_d\beta_A - \varepsilon_d\beta_B)} \right).$$

$$(7.21)$$

By the character of function $\dot{f}(x) = -x(x - a)$, we know it has two point $x = 0$ and $x = a$ which make $\dot{f} = 0$. Besides, $f(x)$ will get its maximum when $x = a$. We assume

$$\dot{p} = -(\gamma\rho - \varepsilon_d\beta_A - \varepsilon_d\beta_B) \sum_{i=1}^{l} |y_i| \left(|y_i| - \frac{\varepsilon_m + \varepsilon_d\beta_A\varphi_C + \varphi_C\beta_B\varepsilon_d}{(\gamma\rho - \varepsilon_d\beta_A - \varepsilon_d\beta_B)} \right) = 0.$$

$$(7.22)$$

The solution of the previous equation is

$$|y_l| = \frac{(\sqrt{l} + 1)(\varepsilon_m + \varepsilon_d\beta_A\varphi_C + \varphi_C\beta_B\varepsilon_d)}{2(\gamma\rho - \varepsilon_d\beta_A - \varepsilon_d\beta_B)},$$

$$(7.23)$$

with parameter requirement $\gamma > (\varepsilon_d\beta_A + \varepsilon_d\beta_B)/\rho$, where $|y_l|$ is maximal summation of all the elements $|y_i|, i \in 1, 2, \ldots, l$. Because $|y_l|$ can be upper bound of any $|y_i|$. Therefore,

$$\max_{1 \leq i \leq l} |y_i(t)| \leq \frac{(\sqrt{l} + 1)(\varepsilon_m + \varepsilon_d\beta_A\varphi_C + \varphi_C\beta_B\varepsilon_d)}{2(\gamma\rho - \varepsilon_d\beta_A - \varepsilon_d\beta_B)}.$$

$$(7.24)$$

If $\exists |y_i| > |y_l|$, $i \in 1, 2, \ldots, l$, then $\dot{p} < 0$ forcing v to decrease. In this situation, y_i will decrease until $|y_i| < |y_l|$ to stop v from decreasing. Therefore, every $|y_i(t)|$, $i \in 1, 2, \ldots, l$ in $Y(t)$ has the same upper bound. So, we have

$$
\begin{aligned}
\|Y(t)\|_F = \|y(t)\|_2 &= \sqrt{\sum_{i=1}^{l} y_i^2(t)} \\
&\leq \sqrt{l} \max_{1 \leq i \leq l} |y_i(t)| \\
&= \frac{(\sqrt{l} + l)(\varepsilon_m + \varepsilon_d \beta_A \varphi_C + \varphi_C \beta_B \varepsilon_d)}{2(\gamma \rho - \varepsilon_d \beta_A - \varepsilon_d \beta_B)}.
\end{aligned}
\tag{7.25}
$$

The proof is completed. ∎

Remark 7.7 Two conclusions about the upper bounds of steady-state residual error $\|Y(t)\|_F$ and entry error $|y_i(t)|$ can be obtained from Theorem 7.6. Then, we can get that the steady-state residual error $\|Y(t)\|_F$ will be smaller by increasing parameter γ. Besides, if we make

$$
\frac{\left(\sqrt{l} + 1\right)\left(\varepsilon_m + \varepsilon_d \beta_A \varphi_C + \varphi_C \beta_B \varepsilon_d\right)}{2\left(\gamma \rho - \varepsilon_d \beta_A - \varepsilon_d \beta_B\right)} \leq 1,
$$

i.e. γ satisfies following inequality:

$$
\gamma \geq \frac{\left(\sqrt{l} + 1\right)\left(\varepsilon_m + \varepsilon_d \beta_A \varphi_C + \varphi_C \beta_B \varepsilon_d\right) + (\varepsilon_d \beta_A + \varepsilon_d \beta_B)}{2\rho}.
$$

We can conclude that the entry error $|y_i(t)|$ will fall into the interval, $|y_i(t)| \in [0, 1]$, $\forall i \in \{1, 2, \ldots, l\}$.

Lemma 7.8 *Let $f_L(x)$, $f_{PS}(x)$, $f_{NFTAF1}(x)$, and $f_{NFTAF1}(x)$ denote Linear, Power-Sigmoid, NFTAF1, and NFTAF2, respectively. Then we can have the following property about these activation functions. $|f_L(x)| < |f_{PS}(x)| < |f_{NFTAF1}(x)| < |f_{NFTAF2}(x)|$, under the condition that $|x| < 1$, $\tau \leq \frac{2\xi e^{-\xi}}{1 - e^{-2\xi}}$ for $f_{NFTAF1}(x)$ and $\beta_1 = \beta_2 = 1$ for $f_{NFTAF2}(x)$.*

Proof: Firstly, we consider $|f_L(x)| < |f_{PS}(x)|$ under the condition of $|x| < 1$. Defining a function $\Phi(x) = \frac{1 + e^{-\xi}}{1 - e^{-\xi}} \cdot \frac{1 - e^{-\xi x}}{1 + e^{-\xi x}} - x$. If $x = 0$, and $x = 1$, it is easy to get $\Phi(0) = \Phi(1) = 0$. We take the derivative of $\Phi(x)$ and $\Phi'(x)$ with respect to x in turn:

$$
\Phi'(x) = \frac{1 + e^{-\xi}}{1 - e^{-\xi}} \cdot \frac{2\xi e^{-\xi x}}{\left(1 + e^{-\xi x}\right)^2} - 1,
$$

$$
\Phi''(x) = \frac{1 + e^{-\xi}}{1 - e^{-\xi}} \cdot \frac{-2\xi^2 e^{-\xi x}\left(1 - e^{-2\xi x}\right)}{\left(1 + e^{-\xi x}\right)^4}.
$$

If $0 < x < 1$, $\Phi''(x) < 0$. $\Phi(x)$ is a convex function with $0 < x < 1$, and because $\Phi(0) = \Phi(1) = 0$. Then we can get $\Phi(x) > 0$ in the domain field of $0 < x < 1$. So $\frac{1+e^{-\xi}}{1-e^{-\xi}} \cdot \frac{1-e^{-\xi x}}{1+e^{-\xi x}} > x$. Since $\frac{1+e^{-\xi}}{1-e^{-\xi}} \cdot \frac{1-e^{-\xi x}}{1+e^{-\xi x}} > 0$ and $x > 0$ in $0 < x < 1$. Therefore $|f_L(x)| < |f_{PS}(x)|$. Besides, $f_L(x)$ and $f_{PS}(x)$ are odd functions, so $|f_L(x)| < |f_{PS}(x)|$ hold true when $|x| < 1$.

Secondly, take $|f_{PS}(x)| < |f_{NFTAF1}(x)|$ into consideration and define a function $\Psi(x) = \frac{1+e^{-\xi}}{1-e^{-\xi}} \cdot \frac{1-e^{-\xi x}}{1+e^{-\xi x}} - \text{sgn}^\tau(x)$ with $\xi > 2$ and $0 < \tau < 1$. Clearly, $\Psi(0) = \Psi(1) = 0$. We take the derivative of $\Psi(x)$ and $\Psi'(x)$ with respect to x, respectively:

$$\Psi'(x) = \frac{1+e^{-\xi}}{1-e^{-\xi}} \cdot \frac{2\xi e^{-\xi x}}{\left(1+e^{-\xi x}\right)^2} - \tau x^{\tau-1},$$

$$\Psi''(x) = \frac{1+e^{-\xi}}{1-e^{-\xi}} \cdot \frac{-2\xi^2\left(1-e^{-\xi x}\right)}{\left(1+e^{-\xi x}\right)^4} - \tau(\tau-1)x^{\tau-2}.$$

From $\Psi'(x)$, we can get $\lim_{x\to 0^+}\Psi'(x) = -\infty$. Therefore, there must exist $\delta_1 > 0$, making $\Psi'(x) < 0$ in $x \in (0, \delta_1)$. And from $\Psi''(x)$, $\lim_{x\to 0^+}\Psi''(x) = +\infty$ can be obtained. So there must exist $\delta_2 > 0$, making $\Psi''(x) > 0$ in $x \in (0, \delta_2)$. Besides, another information, $\Psi''(x)$ increases as $x \in (0, 1)$ increasing, is obvious. We will discuss $\Psi''(x)$ in two different situation.

If $\Psi''(x) > 0$ with $x \in (0, 1)$. $\Psi(x)$ is a concave function, and because $\lim_{x\to 0^+}\Psi'(x) = -\infty$, there must exist a point x_0, where $\Psi(x)$ monotonically increasing in $(0, x_0)$ and monotonically decreasing in $(x_0, 1)$. And by $\Psi(0) = \Psi(1) = 0$, $\Psi(x)$ will satisfy $\Psi(x) < 0$ in $x \in (0, 1)$.

If $\Psi''(x) \leq 0$ with $x \in (x_0, 1)$ where x_0 is a inflection point. $\Psi(x)$ is a concave function in $x \in (0, x_0)$ and $\Psi(x)$ is a convex function in $x \in (x_0, 1)$. The value of $\Psi'(x)$ will decrease in $x \in (x_0, 1)$, but $\Psi'(1) = \frac{2\xi e^{-\xi}}{1-e^{-2\xi}} - \tau \geq 0$, $\Psi'(x)$ will not decrease below zero. Then due to $\Psi(0) = \Psi(1) = 0$, $\Psi(x) < 0$ holds true with $0 < x < 1$. Because of the properties of odd functions, when $-1 < x < 0$, $\Psi(x) < 0$ still satisfies. Therefore, $|f_{PS}(x)| < |f_{NFTAF1}(x)|$ in $|x| < 1$, $\tau \leq \frac{2\xi e^{-\xi}}{1-e^{-2\xi}}$ and $\beta_1 = \beta_2 = 1$.

Thirdly, it is obvious that $|f_{NFTAF1}(x)| < |f_{NFTAF2}(x)|$ in $|x| < 1$, where $\beta_1 = \beta_2 = 1$.

In a word, $|f_L(x)| < |f_{PS}(x)| < |f_{NFTAF1}(x)| < |f_{NFTAF2}(x)|$ with $|x| < 1$, $\tau \leq \frac{2\xi e^{-\xi}}{1-e^{-2\xi}}$ and $\beta_1 = \beta_2 = 1$. The proof of Lemma 7.8 is now complete. ∎

Theorem 7.9 *Let y_L, y_{PS}, y_{NFTAF1}, and y_{NFTAF2} denote steady-state residual functions that are activated by f_L, f_{PS}, f_{NFTAF1}, and f_{NFTAF2}, respectively. For $f_{NFTAF1}(x)$, $\tau \leq \frac{2\xi e^{-\xi}}{1-e^{-2\xi}}$, and for $f_{NFTAF2}(x)$, $\beta_1 = \beta_2 = 1$. If the design of parameter γ satisfy $\gamma \geq ((\sqrt{l}+1)\left(\varepsilon_m + \varepsilon_d\beta_A\varphi_C + \varphi_C\beta_B\varepsilon_d\right) + 2\left(\varepsilon_d\beta_A + \varepsilon_d\beta_B\right))/2\rho$. Then we can get $y_L > y_{PS} > y_{NFTAF1} > y_{NFTAF2}$.*

Proof: By Remark 7.7, we can get that if $\gamma \geq ((\sqrt{l}+1)(\varepsilon_m + \varepsilon_d \beta_A \varphi_C + \varphi_C \beta_B \varepsilon_d) + 2(\varepsilon_d \beta_A + \varepsilon_d \beta_B))/2\rho$, then the entry error $|y_i(t)| \in [0,1]$. In this case, the activation function defined in $|x| < 1$ will have an impact. According to Theorem 7.6, we know that the steady-state residual error will be smaller by increasing parameter ρ. However, ρ is decided by $\frac{|f(y_i(t))|}{|y_i(t)|}$. In order to compare y_L, y_{PS}, y_{NFTAF1}, and y_{NFTAF2}, we only need to compare the corresponding value of ρ. That is to say, only the activation functions should be compared. The smaller the activation function is, the bigger steady-state residual error is. Therefore, according to the result of Lemma 7.8, $|f_L(x)| < |f_{PS}(x)| < |f_{NFTAF1}(x)| < |f_{NFTAF2}(x)|$ with $|x| < 1$. We can get that $y_L > y_{PS} > y_{NFTAF1} > y_{NFTAF1}$. ∎

7.5 Illustrative Verification

In this section, we will give an example to illustrate the fantastic performance of the ZNN model with the activation functions NFTAF1 and NFTAF2. Time-varying coefficient matrices $A(t)$, $B(t)$, and $C(t)$ of the example are defined as

$$A(t) = \begin{bmatrix} \sin(t) & \cos(t) \\ -\cos(t) & \sin(t) \end{bmatrix}, \quad B(t) = \begin{bmatrix} \sin(2t) & \cos(2t) \\ -\cos(2t) & \sin(2t) \end{bmatrix},$$

$$C(t) = \begin{bmatrix} \sin(3t) & 0 \\ 0 & \cos(3t) \end{bmatrix}.$$

Therefore the Eq. (7.1) is written that

$$\begin{bmatrix} \sin(t) & \cos(t) \\ -\cos(t) & \sin(t) \end{bmatrix} \begin{bmatrix} u_{11} & u_{12} \\ u_{21} & u_{22} \end{bmatrix} \begin{bmatrix} \sin(2t) & \cos(2t) \\ -\cos(2t) & \sin(2t) \end{bmatrix} = \begin{bmatrix} \sin(3t) & 0 \\ 0 & \cos(3t) \end{bmatrix}.$$

$$(7.26)$$

Every element u_{ij}, $i,j = 1,2$, of the initial state matrix $U(0) \in \mathbb{R}^{2\times2}$ is generated from $[0,1]$ randomly.

7.5.1 Convergence

The theoretical solution of Eq. (7.1) will be a standard to compare with the state solution of (7.5). From Figures 7.1 and 7.2, it is clear that the state solution of ZNN model (7.5) with NFTAF1 and NFTAF2 can always converge to the theoretical solution quickly and precisely.

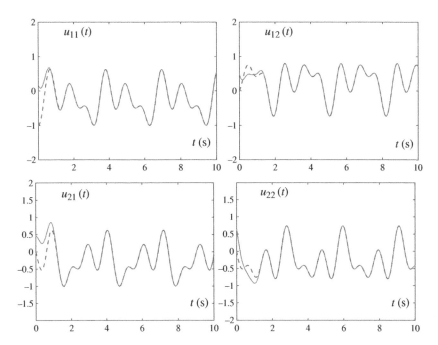

Figure 7.1 Solved by the FTZNN1 model with $\tau = 0.2$ and $\gamma = 1$, where dash curves represent theoretical solution of (7.1) and solid curves represent state solution of (7.5).

By Theorems 7.3 and 7.4, the upper bound of convergent time about FTZNN1 is $t_{f_1} = \frac{|y_{max}(0)|^{1-\tau}}{\gamma(1-\tau)}$ and about FTZNN2 is $t_{f_2} = \frac{1}{(\tau-1)\cdot\gamma\beta_2} \ln \frac{\gamma\beta_1}{\gamma\beta_2 \cdot |y_{max}(0)|^{1-\tau} + \gamma\beta_1}$. For Eq. (7.26), when $t = 0$, the initial error matrix $E(0)$ is

$$Y(0) = A(0)U(0)B(0) - C(0) = \begin{bmatrix} 0 & 1 \\ -1 & 0 \end{bmatrix} \begin{bmatrix} x_{11} & x_{12} \\ x_{21} & x_{22} \end{bmatrix} \begin{bmatrix} 0 & 1 \\ -1 & 0 \end{bmatrix} - \begin{bmatrix} 0 & 0 \\ 0 & 1 \end{bmatrix}$$

$$= \begin{bmatrix} -x_{22} & x_{21} \\ x_{12} & -x_{11} - 1 \end{bmatrix}.$$

Thus, $y_{max}(0) = 2$. We can compute t_{f_1} and t_{f_2} as

$$t_{f_1} = \frac{2^{1-0.2}}{1 \times (1 - 0.2)} \approx 2.17,$$

$$t_{f_2} = \frac{1}{(0.2 - 1) \cdot 1} \ln \frac{1}{2^{1-0.2} + 1} \approx 1.26.$$

Figure 7.3 shows that the convergent time of the FTZNN1 and FTZNN2 models are always less than t_f^1 and t_f^2. This result correctly proves Theorems 7.3 and 7.4.

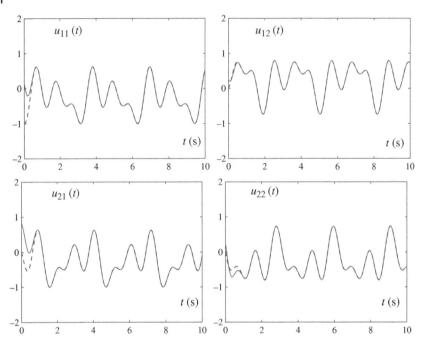

Figure 7.2 Solved by the FTZNN2 model with $\tau = 0.2$ and $\gamma = 1$, where dash curves represent theoretical solution of (7.1) and solid curves represent state solution of (7.5).

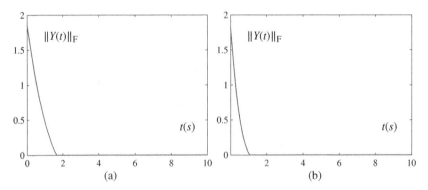

Figure 7.3 Steady-state error $||Y(t)||_F$ produced by proposed FTZNN models with $\tau = 0.2$ and $\gamma = 1$. (a) By FTZNN1. (b) By FTZNN2.

In order to show the superior performance of NFTAF1 and NFTAF2, the Linear, Power, Bipolar Sigmoid, and Power-Sigmoid activation functions are compared. Relative parameters of these functions are set as $p = 3$ and $\xi = 4$. Figure 7.4a has shown that the steady-state residual errors $||Y(t)||_F$ of ZNN model (7.5) activated by Linear, Power, Bipolar Sigmoid, and Power-Sigmoid activation functions

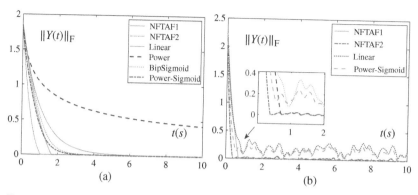

Figure 7.4 Steady-state error $||Y(t)||_F$. (a) By ZNN model (7.5) activated by different activation functions with $\tau = 0.2$ and $\gamma = 1$. (b) By the perturbed ZNN model (7.11) activated by different activation functions with $\tau = 0.2$ and $\gamma = 3$.

converge to zero exponentially. However, the FTZNN1 and FTZNN2 models always converge to zero directly in finite time. The convergent rate is more quickly.

7.5.2 Robustness

In order to show the robustness of the FTZNN1 and FTZNN2 models, the differential error $\Delta d(t) \in \mathbb{R}^{2 \times 2}$ and the model-implement error $\Delta m(t) \in \mathbb{R}^{2 \times 2}$ are added into these two models, and they are set as the following form:

$$\Delta d(t) = \begin{bmatrix} \sin(8t) & 0 \\ 0 & \cos(8t) \end{bmatrix}, \quad \Delta m(t) = \begin{bmatrix} 0 & -\sin(8t) \\ \cos(8t) & 0 \end{bmatrix}.$$

After we take perturbed ZNN models into consideration, the steady-state errors are compared with showing the effectiveness of activation functions. Figure 7.4b has demonstrated that NFTAF1 and NFTAF2 have superior performance at the same condition, as compared with Linear and Power Sigmoid activation functions. The convergent speed is more quickly and the steady-state error is much closer to zero. Figure 7.4b has shown the correctness of Theorem 7.9. If perturbed ZNN models are activated by NFTAF1 and NFTAF2, the theoretical upper bound of steady-state error $||Y(t)||_F$ could be obtained. Figure 7.5 has shown validity of Theorem 7.6, which implies the parameter γ influences the convergence rate of ZNN model. Remark 7.7 analyzes that $||Y(t)||_F$ will decrease with γ increasing, and Figure 7.5 has proved this conclusion by setting three different value of γ. In general, the results of these experiments illustrate the excellent performance of the FTZNN1 and FTZNN2 models and certify the relative theoretical analysis.

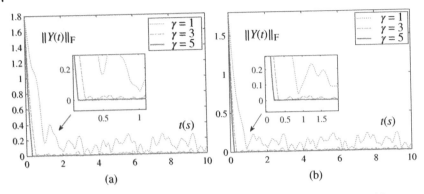

Figure 7.5 Steady-state error $\|Y(t)\|_F$ produced by perturbed ZNN model (7.11) activated by NFTAF activation functions with $\tau = 0.2$. (a) By NFTAF1 activation function with different γ. (b) By NFTAF2 activation function with different γ.

7.6 Chapter Summary

Based on ZNN, this chapter designs two novel FTZNN models to solve the time-varying linear matrix equation by exploiting two new activation functions. The purpose is to make the state solution of ZNN models converge to the theoretical solution of the problem in finite time. The maximum finite-time about FTZNN1 and FTZNN2 models has been calculated. Besides, it has analyzed that the other activations functions including Linear, Power, Bipolar Sigmoid, and Power-Sigmoid do not have such characters. In order to show the superior performance about robustness of FTZNN1 and FTZNN2 models. The differential error and implementation error are added into these models, and we have got the upper bounds of the steady-state residual error. In addition, two relative conclusions are also obtained that the upper bound of steady-state residual error decreases as the parameter γ increasing and it negatively correlated with $|f(\cdot)|$. Finally the results of simulative experiments have shown the validity of theoretical analysis.

References

1 R. J. Steriti and M. A. Fiddy, Regularized image reconstruction using SVD and a neural network method for matrix inversion, *IEEE Trans. Signal Process.*, 41(10) (1993) 3074–3077.

2 Y. Zhang, Towards piecewise-linear primal neural networks for optimization and redundant robotics, 2006 IEEE International Conference on Networking, Sensing and Control, (2006) 374–379.

3 R. H. Sturges, Analog matrix inversion (robot kinematics), *IEEE J. Robot. Automat.*, 4(2) (1988) 157–162.

4 Y. Wei, J. Cai, and M. K. Ng, Computing Moore-Penrose inverses of Toeplitz matrices by Newton's iteration, *Math. Comput. Model.*, 40(1–2) (2004) 181–191.

5 J. Zhou and Y. Zhu *et al.*, Variants of the Greville formula with applications to exact recursive least squares, *SIAM J. Matrix Anal. Appl.*, 24(1) (2002) 150–164.

6 H. Lu and L. Jin *et al.*, RNN for solving perturbed time-varying underdetermined linear system with double bound limits on residual errors and state variables, *IEEE Trans. Ind. Inform.*, 15(11) (2019) 5931–5942.

7 L. Xiao and B. Liao *et al.*, Nonlinear recurrent neural networks for finite-time solution of general time-varying linear matrix equations, *Neural Netw.*, 98 (2018) 102–113.

8 Y. Zhang and S. S. Ge, Design and analysis of a general recurrent neural network model for time-varying matrix inversion, *IEEE Trans. Neural Netw. Learn. Syst.*, 16(6) (2005) 1477–1490.

9 B. Liao and Y. Zhang, From different ZFs to different ZNN models accelerated via Li activation functions to finite-time convergence for time-varying matrix pseudoinversion, *Neurocomputing*, 133 (2014) 512–522.

10 Y. Zhang and Z. Li, Zhang neural network for online solution of time-varying convex quadratic program subject to time-varying linear-equality constraints, *Phys. Lett. A*, 373(18–19) (2009) 1639–1643.

11 S. Li, S. Chen, and B. Liu, Accelerating a recurrent neural network to finite-time convergence for solving time-varying Sylvester equation by using a sign-bi-power activation function, *Neural Process. Lett.*, 37(2) (2013) 189–205.

12 S. Li, Y. Li, and Z. Wang, A class of finite-time dual neural networks for solving quadratic programming problems and its κ-winners-take-all application, *Neural Netw.*, 39 (2013) 27–39.

13 L. Xiao, Z. Zhang, and S. Li, Solving time-varying system of nonlinear equations by finite-time recurrent neural networks with application to motion tracking of robot manipulators, *IEEE Trans. Syst. Man Cybern. Syst.*, 49(11) (2019) 2210–2220.

14 D. Guo and Y. Zhang, Li-function activated ZNN with finite-time convergence applied to redundant-manipulator kinematic control via time-varying Jacobian matrix pseudoinversion, *Appl. Soft. Comput.*, 24 (2014) 158–168.

15 R. A. Horn and C. R. Johnson, *Matrix analysis*, Cambridge University Press, (2012).

Part IV

Application to Optimization

8

FTZNN for Constrained Quadratic Programming

8.1 Introduction

Quadratic programming (QP) plays an important part in various applications including image processing [1, 2] and robot control [3, 4]. As a core analytical tool in many realistic problems, the QP problem is worth being investigated both for mathematical and practical purposes. Besides, solving time-varying quadratic programming (TVQP) problems have attracted more researchers' attention recently for its difficulty and broad usage.

For zeroing neural network (ZNN) models, one important thing that researchers focus on is the convergence time of the computation error converging to zero, and another element is the robustness property of the ZNN model since various noises in real application environment are inevitable [5]. Thus, a unified finite-time zeroing neural network (U-FTZNN) model with predefined-time convergence and robustness is proposed in this chapter to solve TVQP problems subject to equality or inequality constraints. In addition, we have selected two real-world applications to validate efficacy of our U-FTZNN model. One application is to achieve image denoising by image fusion and another application is to realize inverse-kinematics control of a redundant robotic manipulator. In [2], the image fusion task is modeled into a QP problem and is solved by a GNN model, and one disadvantage of this GNN method is its low convergence speed when compared with predefined-time ZNN models. For robot manipulator control task, there are various schemes such as obtaining Jacobian matrix pseudoinversion [6], solving TVQPE problem [4], and so on. However, most of the redundant robot manipulator control methods cannot handle joint limits, which is necessary in practice for avoiding obstacles or physical limits. In this chapter, our U-FTZNN model will overcome these shortcomings and demonstrate its superiorities in these applications.

Zeroing Neural Networks: Finite-time Convergence Design, Analysis and Applications,
First Edition. Lin Xiao and Lei Jia.

8.2 Preliminaries

8.2.1 Problem Formulation

In this chapter, we are mainly concerned with TVQP problems subject to equality or inequality constraints. Specifically, there are two types of TVQP problems: one is TVQP problems with equality constraints (TVQPE), and the other is TVQP problems with equality and inequality constraints (TVQPEI). In this chapter, we assume that each TVQP has a unique optimal solution. Firstly, let us consider the standard form of the TVQPEI problem:

$$\min \ \boldsymbol{u}(t)^{\mathrm{T}} S(t) \boldsymbol{u}(t)/2 + \boldsymbol{k}^{\mathrm{T}}(t) \boldsymbol{u}(t), \tag{8.1}$$

$$\text{s.t. } A(t)\boldsymbol{u}(t) = \boldsymbol{b}(t), \tag{8.2}$$

$$C(t)\boldsymbol{u}(t) \le \boldsymbol{d}(t), \tag{8.3}$$

where $\boldsymbol{u}(t) \in \mathbb{R}^n$ is an unknown vector and should be obtained; $S(t) \in \mathbb{R}^{n \times n}$ represents a Hessian matrix which is symmetric and positive definite; $A(t) \in \mathbb{R}^{m \times n}$ is a full rank matrix and $C(t) \in \mathbb{R}^{q \times n}$; other coefficient vectors are $\boldsymbol{k}(t) \in \mathbb{R}^n$, $\boldsymbol{b}(t) \in \mathbb{R}^m$ and $\boldsymbol{d}(t) \in \mathbb{R}^q$. Obviously, with these coefficient matrices and vectors all being time-varying, the optimal solution $\boldsymbol{u}^*(t) \in \mathbb{R}^n$ to the TVQPEI problems is also changing with time. Then, we consider the standard form of the TVQPE problem, which can be expressed as follows:

$$\begin{aligned} &\min \boldsymbol{u}(t)^{\mathrm{T}} S(t) \boldsymbol{u}(t)/2 + \boldsymbol{k}^{\mathrm{T}}(t) \boldsymbol{u}(t), \\ &\text{s.t. } A(t)\boldsymbol{u}(t) = \boldsymbol{b}(t), \end{aligned} \tag{8.4}$$

where $S(t), \boldsymbol{k}(t), A(t)$, and $\boldsymbol{b}(t)$ are the same definitions with TVQPEI (8.1) and (8.2).

Apparently, the major difference between TVPQEI and TVQPE lies in that TVQPE has no inequality constraints. In order to lay the foundation for the rest of this chapter, we can transform TVQPE into TVQPEI problem by adopting $C(t) = [I_n, -I_n]^{\mathrm{T}} \in \mathbb{R}^{2n \times n}$ and $\boldsymbol{d}(t) = [\infty_n^{\mathrm{T}}, \infty_n^{\mathrm{T}}]^{\mathrm{T}}$, where $I_n \in \mathbb{R}^{n \times n}$ is an identity matrix and ∞_n is n dimension column vector with each element being positive infinity. Because positive infinity is hard to represent in computer and digital circuit, a large enough positive real number is usually adopted to denote it.

8.2.2 Optimization Theory

According to Section 8.2.1, we conclude that the TVQPEI problem is the most generalized form among TVQP problems, since TVQPE problems can be easily reduced to the special case of TVQPEI problems. Therefore we apply the Karush–Kuhn–Tucker (KKT) theory to TVQPEI (8.1)–(8.3) and obtain the following lemma.

Lemma 8.1 *Vector $u^*(t) \in \mathbb{R}^n$ becomes the optimal solution of TVQPEI problems (8.1)–(8.3) if and only if the Lagrangian multipliers $\rho^*(t) \in \mathbb{R}^m$ and $\lambda^*(t) \in \mathbb{R}^q$ exist such that they satisfy the following KKT conditions [1, 7]–[9]:*

$$\begin{cases} S(t)u^*(t) + k(t) + A^{\mathrm{T}}(t)\rho^*(t) + C^{\mathrm{T}}(t)\lambda^*(t) = 0, \\ A(t)u^*(t) - b(t) = 0, \\ \lambda^*(t) \geq 0, \ d(t) - C(t)u^*(t) \geq 0, \\ \lambda^{*\mathrm{T}}(d(t) - C(t)u^*(t)) = 0, \end{cases} \tag{8.5}$$

where vectors $\rho^*(t)$ and $\lambda^*(t)$ are unknown and should be obtained to meet the constraints (8.2) and (8.3). Therefore $q^*(t) = [u^*(t)^{\mathrm{T}}, \rho^*(t)^{\mathrm{T}}, \lambda^*(t)^{\mathrm{T}}]^{\mathrm{T}} \in \mathbb{R}^{n+m+q}$ is solution vector of the TVQPEI problem.

In general, ZNN models are suitable for equality constrained instead of inequality constrained QP problems, so the vector type perturbed Fischer–Burmeister (PFB) function in [1, 8, 9] is introduced for converting the inequality constraints in (8.5). The PFB function is defined as follows:

$$\psi_{\mathrm{PFB}}(A, C) = A + C - \sqrt{A \circ A + C \circ C + \delta^+}, \ \delta^+ \to 0_+, \tag{8.6}$$

where A, C, δ^+ are all column vectors with the same dimension, and δ^+ is called the perturbed item. In addition, symbol $\circ$ denotes the Hadamrad product. According to [8], we have the following lemma.

Lemma 8.2 *Consider the scalar type of PFB function (8.6), we can conclude that*

$$\psi_{PFB}(a, c) = 0 \Leftrightarrow a \geq 0, c \geq 0, ac = \delta^+/2,$$

where $a, c, \delta^+ \in \mathbb{R}, \delta^+ > 0$. Besides, $\psi_{PFB}(a, c)$ is smooth with regard to a and c.

Therefore the vector valued PFB function (8.6) satisfies Lemma 8.2 by element. According to (8.5), we further have the following result.

Lemma 8.3 *The optimal solution $q^*(t) = [u^*(t)^{\mathrm{T}}, \rho^*(t)^{\mathrm{T}}, \lambda^*(t)^{\mathrm{T}}]^{\mathrm{T}} \in \mathbb{R}^{n+m+p}$ satisfies the following equations:*

$$\begin{cases} S(t)u^*(t) + k(t) + A^{\mathrm{T}}(t)\rho^*(t) + C^{\mathrm{T}}(t)\lambda^*(t) = 0, \\ A(t)u^*(t) - b(t) = 0, \\ \psi_{PFB}(d(t) - C(t)u^*(t), \lambda^*(t)) = 0, \end{cases}$$

for every $\delta^+ \to 0_+$ if and only if $u^*(t)$ is the KKT point of TVQPEI (8.1)–(8.3).

The previous equations can be reformulated as following nonlinear equation:

$$f(q(t), t) = G(t)q(t) + g(t) = 0, \tag{8.7}$$

with

$$G(t) = \begin{bmatrix} S(t) & A^{\mathrm{T}}(t) & C^{\mathrm{T}}(t) \\ A(t) & 0 & 0 \\ -C(t) & 0 & I \end{bmatrix}, \quad q(t) = \begin{bmatrix} u(t) \\ \rho(t) \\ \lambda(t) \end{bmatrix},$$

$$g(t) = \begin{bmatrix} g_1(t) \\ g_2(t) \\ g_3(t) \end{bmatrix} = \begin{bmatrix} k(t) \\ -b(t) \\ d(t) - \sqrt{h(t) \circ h(t) + \lambda(t) \circ \lambda(t) + \delta^+} \end{bmatrix},$$

where $h(t) := d(t) - C(t)u(t)$. Then, solving the TVQPEI problem is equivalent to finding a time-varying vector $q(t)$ that satisfies Eq. (8.7). In the following content of this chapter, we will propose a U-FTZNN model to tackle such a problem in predefined time and with strong robustness.

8.3 U-FTZNN Model

On the basis of the standard ZNN design routine, an error vector is defined as $y(t) = f(q(t), t)$ which is often defined to track the evolution of neural networks. Instead of using the conventional ZNN formula like

$$\dot{y}(t) = -\gamma \Phi(y(t)), \tag{8.8}$$

we adopt the following novel design formula [10, 11]:

$$\dot{y}(t) = -\gamma_1 \Phi_1(y(t)) - \gamma_2 \Phi_2 \left(y(t) + \gamma_1 \int_0^t \Phi_1(y(\tau)) \mathrm{d}\tau \right), \tag{8.9}$$

where $\gamma_1 > 0$ and $\gamma_2 > 0$ are design parameters used to tune the convergence speed, $\Phi_1(\cdot)$ and $\Phi_2(\cdot)$ are odd monotonically increasing activation function arrays that can be selected arbitrarily. By using design dynamic (8.9), $f(q(t), t)$ will be forced to converge to zero vector and the optimal solutions are obtained in the same time. Expanding Eq. (8.9) and we obtain the U-FTZNN model:

$$\dot{G}(t)q(t) + G(t)\dot{q}(t) + \dot{g}(t) = -\gamma_1 \Phi_1(G(t)q(t) + g(t))$$

$$- \gamma_2 \Phi_2 \left(G(t)q(t) + g(t) + \gamma_1 \int_0^t \Phi_1(G(\tau)q(\tau) + g(\tau)) \mathrm{d}\tau \right)$$

which can be further reformulated as the following expression:

$$J(t)\dot{q}(t) = -M(t)q(t) - v(t) - \gamma_1 \Phi_1(G(t)q(t) + g(t))$$

$$- \gamma_2 \Phi_2 \left(G(t)q(t) + g(t) + \gamma_1 \int_0^t \Phi_1(G(\tau)q(\tau) + g(\tau)) \mathrm{d}\tau \right), \tag{8.10}$$

where

$$J(t) = \begin{bmatrix} S(t) & A^{\mathrm{T}}(t) & C^{\mathrm{T}}(t) \\ A(t) & 0 & 0 \\ (K_1(t) - I)C(t) & 0 & I - K_2(t) \end{bmatrix},$$

$$M(t) = \begin{bmatrix} \dot{S}(t) & \dot{A}^{\mathrm{T}}(t) & \dot{C}^{\mathrm{T}}(t) \\ \dot{A}(t) & 0 & 0 \\ (-I + K_1(t))\dot{C}(t) & 0 & 0 \end{bmatrix},$$

$$v(t) = \begin{bmatrix} \dot{g}_1(t) \\ \dot{g}_2(t) \\ \dot{d}(t) - K_1(t)\dot{d}(t) \end{bmatrix},$$

with $n(t) := \sqrt{h(t) \circ h(t) + \lambda(t) \circ \lambda(t) + \delta^+}$, $K_1(t) := \Lambda(h(t) \oslash n(t))$, and $K_2(t) := \Lambda(\lambda(t) \oslash n(t))$. In addition, the symbol $\oslash$ denotes the Hadamard division and $\Lambda(\cdot)$ represents creating a diagonal matrix using corresponding vector.

In-depth researchers have already found that the nonlinear activation functions contribute greatly to the performance of ZNN models, especially their convergence speed. Traditional activation functions can only offer exponential convergence rate while sign-bi-power (SBP) [6, 12] and some other activation functions can achieve finite convergence time. To further enhance the performance of U-FTZNN model (8.10), we propose a novel piecewise predefined-time activation function (PPAF). The definition of PPAF is as follows:

$$\phi(x) = \begin{cases} \mathrm{sgn}^{r_1}(x), & |x| > 1, \\ \dfrac{r_1}{r_2}\mathrm{sgn}^{r_2}(x), & |x| \leq 1, \end{cases} \tag{8.11}$$

where $r_1 > 1, 0 < r_2 < 1$, and the function $\mathrm{sgn}^r(\cdot)$ is defined as

$$\mathrm{sgn}^r(x) = \begin{cases} |x|^r, & x \geq 0, \\ -|x|^r, & x < 0. \end{cases}$$

Besides, in order to accelerate the convergence speed of U-FTZNN model (8.10), both $\Phi_1(\cdot)$ and $\Phi_2(\cdot)$ use PPAF (8.11) in the following simulation part.

8.4 Convergence Analysis

In this section, we are going to prove that U-FTZNN model (8.10) is globally stable and can converge to the optimal solution of the TVQPEI problem in a predefined time. Considering the ith ($\forall i \in 1, 2, \ldots, n + m + p$) element of (8.9), we have the following subsystem:

$$\dot{y}_i(t) = -\gamma_1\phi_1(y_i(t)) - \gamma_2\phi_2\left(y_i(t) + \gamma_1\int_0^t \phi_1(y_i(\tau))\mathrm{d}\tau\right), \tag{8.12}$$

where $y_i(t)$ denotes the ith element of $y(t)$, $\phi_1(\cdot)$ and $\phi_2(\cdot)$ represent the ith element of $\Phi_1(\cdot)$ and $\Phi_2(\cdot)$, respectively. We introduce a new auxiliary function for analyzing (8.12):

$$z_i(t) = y_i(t) + \gamma_1\int_0^t \phi_1(y_i(\tau))\mathrm{d}\tau. \tag{8.13}$$

Then, seeking the derivative of (8.13) about time, we have

$$\dot{z}_i(t) = \dot{y}_i(t) + \gamma_1 \phi_1(y_i(t)). \tag{8.14}$$

Substituting (8.14) into (8.12), (8.12) can be reconstructed as $\dot{z}_i(t) = -\gamma_2 \phi_2(z_i(t))$ which is exactly the standard ZNN design formula for $z_i(t)$.

Theorem 8.4 *The new design dynamic (8.9) is globally Lyapunov stable, meaning that $\mathbf{y}(t)$ converges to $\mathbf{0}$ globally.*

Proof: We come to prove that any ith subsystem of (8.9) is globally stable. A Lyapunov function candidate for (8.12) is defined as $p_i(t) = \frac{1}{2}ky_i^2(t) + \frac{1}{2}z_i^2(t)$ where $k > 0$. Clearly, $p_i(t) > 0$ holds for any $y_i(t) \neq 0$ or $z_i(t) \neq 0$, $p_i(t) = 0$ come true if and only if $y_i(t) = z_i(t) = 0$. Thus, the aforementioned Lyapunov function is positive-definite. Calculating the time derivative of $p_i(t)$, we obtain

$$\begin{aligned}
\frac{\mathrm{d}p_i(t)}{\mathrm{d}t} &= ky_i(t)\dot{y}_i(t) + z_i(t)\dot{z}_i(t) \\
&= ky_i(t)\left[\dot{z}_i(t) - \gamma_1\phi_1(y_i(t))\right] - \gamma_2 z_i(t)\phi_2(z_i(t)) \\
&= -k\gamma_1 y_i(t)\phi_1(y_i(t)) - \gamma_2 z_i(t)\phi_2(z_i(t)) - k\gamma_2 y_i(t)\phi_2(z_i(t)).
\end{aligned} \tag{8.15}$$

Let $p_0 = p_i(0) = ky_i^2(0)/2 + z_i^2(0)/2$ and our first goal is proving that there exists k that makes $\dot{p}_i(t) \leq 0$. Suppose there exists any time instant $t_a \in [0, +\infty)$ that satisfies $p_i(t_a) \leq p_0$. We have $ky_i^2(t_a)/2 \leq p_0$ and $z_i^2(t_a) \leq p_0$, which leads to $0 \leq |y_i(t_a)| \leq \sqrt{2p_0/k}$ and $0 \leq |z_i(t_a)| \leq \sqrt{2p_0}$.

Let us define two domains:

$$D_1 := \{z_i(t) \in R, \quad |z_i(t)| \leq \sqrt{2p_0}\},$$

$$D_2 := \{y_i(t) \in R, \quad |y_i(t)| \leq \sqrt{2p_0/k}\}.$$

We use the mean-value theorem in D_1 and get:

$$\phi_2(z_i(t_a)) - \phi_2(0) = (z_i(t_a) - 0)\left.\frac{\partial\phi_2(z_i(\vartheta))}{\partial z_i}\right|z_i(\vartheta) \in D_1.$$

Because PPAF (8.11) satisfies $\phi_2(0) = 0$ and $\partial\phi_2(z_i(t))/\partial z_i > 0$, we can derive from the previous equation that $|\phi_2(z_i(t_a))| \leq W_0|z_i(t_a)|$, where $W_0 = \max\{\partial\phi_2(z_i(t))/\partial z_i\}|_{z_i(t)\in D_1} > 0$. Therefore, we have

$$\begin{aligned}
|y_i(t_a)\phi_2(z_i(t_a))| &\leq |y_i(t_a)| \cdot |\phi_2(z_i(t_a))| \\
&\leq W_0|y_i(t_a)| \cdot |z_i(t_a)|.
\end{aligned}$$

Combining (8.15) with aforementioned inequality, we have

$$\begin{aligned}
\dot{p}_i(t_a) &= -k\gamma_2 y_i(t_a)\phi_2(z_i(t_a)) - k\gamma_1 y_i(t)\phi_1(y_i(t_a)) - \gamma_2 z_i(t_a)\phi_2(z_i(t_a)) \\
&\leq k\gamma_2|y_i(t_a)\phi_2(z_i(t_a))| - k\gamma_1 y_i(t_a)\phi_1(y_i(t_a)) - \gamma_2 z_i(t_a)\phi_2(z_i(t_a)) \\
&\leq k\gamma_2 W_0|y_i(t_a)||z_i(t_a)| - k\gamma_1 W_1 y_i^2(t_a) - \gamma_2 W_2 z_i^2(t_a) \\
&= -k\left(\sqrt{\gamma_1 W_1}|y_i(t_a)| - \gamma_2 W_0|z_i(t_a)|/\left(2\sqrt{\gamma_1 W_1}\right)\right)^2 \\
&\quad - k\left(\gamma_2 W_2/k - \gamma_2^2 W_0^2/\left(4\gamma_1 W_1\right)\right)z_i^2(t_a),
\end{aligned} \tag{8.16}$$

where $W_1 = \min\{\partial\phi_1(y_i(t))/\partial y_i\}|_{y_i(t)\in D_2} > 0$ and $W_2 = \min\{\partial\phi_2(z_i(t))/\partial z_i\}|_{z_i(t)\in D_1} > 0$ that are also obtained using the mean-value theorem like calculating W_0. From (8.16) we know that $\dot{p}_i(t_a) \leq 0$ is guaranteed as long as k is selected that

$$\frac{\gamma_2 W_2}{K} - \frac{\gamma_2^2 W_0^2}{4\gamma_1 W_1} \geq 0, \quad k > 0 \Leftrightarrow 0 < k \leq \frac{4\gamma_1 W_1 W_2}{\gamma_2 W_0^2}.$$

After $\dot{p}_i(t_a) \leq 0$, the $p_i(t)$ will not increase for $t \geq t_a$ since $p_i(t) \leq p_0$ is always true. It is worth noting that $t_a = 0$ exists for all circumstances, the proof of $\dot{p}_i(t) \leq 0$ is finished. Therefore, (8.9) is globally stable in the sense of Lyapunov. ∎

Theorem 8.5 *Using PPAF (8.11) in $\Phi(\cdot)$, normal ZNN model (8.8) converges to 0 in predefined time $T(\gamma, r_1, r_2)$:*

$$T(\gamma, r_1, r_2) \leq \frac{1}{\gamma(r_1 - 1)} + \frac{r_2}{r_1} \cdot \frac{1}{\gamma(1 - r_2)},$$

where γ is defined in (8.8) and r_1, r_2 are defined in (8.11).

Proof: Take the ith ($\forall i \in 1, \ldots, n + m + p$) subsystem of ZNN model (8.8) into consideration:

$$\dot{y}_i(t) = -\gamma\phi(y_i(t)), \tag{8.17}$$

where $\phi(\cdot)$ is the PPAF, $y_0 = y_i(0)$ is unknown. Let us firstly consider the condition that $y_0 \geq 0$.

In the case of $y_0 > 1$, $y_i(t)$ should converge in two stages: from y_0 to 1 and from 1 to 0. Assuming that the first convergence stage takes time t_1, (8.17) becomes

$$y_i^{-r_1} dy_i = -\gamma dt.$$

Integrating the last equation of the aforementioned equations from $t = 0$ to $t = t_1$:

$$\int_{y_0}^1 y_i^{-r_1} dy_i = -\gamma \int_0^{t_1} dt.$$

Calculating the previous integral equation out gives us $t_1 = (1 - y_0^{1-r_1})/[\gamma(r_1 - 1)] \leq 1/[\gamma(r_1 - 1)]$. If the second converge stage takes time t_2, (8.17) becomes

$$y_i^{-r_2} dy_i = -\gamma \frac{r_1}{r_2} dt.$$

Similarly, we integrate the previous equality from $t = t_1$ to $t = t_1 + t_2$:

$$\int_1^0 y_i^{-r_2} dy_i = -\gamma \frac{r_1}{r_2} \int_{t_1}^{t_1+t_2} dt.$$

Solving the previous integral equation and we obtain $t_2 = r_2/[r_1\gamma(1 - r_2)]$. Therefore when $y_0 > 1$, $y_i(t)$ converges to 0 in predefined time $t_1 + t_2$. In other case of $0 \leq y_0 \leq 1$, the subsystem falls within the second convergence stage, which still satisfies the time upper bound $t_1 + t_2$.

As for the case of $y_0 < 0$, we can get the same convergence time upper bound $t_1 + t_2$ using the aforementioned technique. Thus, all subsystems of (8.8) converge to zero in predefined time $T(\gamma, r_1, r_2) = t_1 + t_2$. In other words, ZNN model (8.8) converges to 0 in predefined time $T(\gamma, r_1, r_2)$. ■

Theorem 8.6 *U-FTZNN model (8.9) will globally converge to 0 in predefined time* $T_p = T(\gamma_1, r_1, r_2) + T(\gamma_2, r_1, r_2)$:

$$T_p \leq \frac{\gamma_1 + \gamma_2}{\gamma_1 \gamma_2 (r_1 - 1)} + \frac{r_2}{r_1} \cdot \frac{\gamma_1 + \gamma_2}{\gamma_1 \gamma_2 (1 - r_2)}, \qquad (8.18)$$

using the same PPAF (8.11) in $\Phi_1(\cdot)$ *and* $\Phi_2(\cdot)$, *with* γ_1, γ_2 *defined in (8.9) and* r_1, r_2 *defined in (8.11).*

Proof: With the auxiliary function $z_i(t)$ defined in (8.13), we know that ith subsystem of U-FTZNN model (8.12) can be reformulated into the dynamic (8.14), which is equivalent to the ordinary ZNN model (8.17). Therefore, we conclude from Theorem 8.5 that $z_i(t)$ must converge to 0 in predefined time $t_3 = T(\gamma_2, r_1, r_2)$. Then, $z_i(t) = 0$ will hold after time period t_3, meaning $\dot{z}_i(t) = 0$ is satisfied for $t \geq t_3$. We thus have $\dot{y}_i(t) = -\gamma_1 \phi_1(y_i(t))$, $t \geq t_3$ according to Eq. (8.14). Evidently, the previous equality also conforms to normal ZNN model (8.17). Hence, $y_i(t)$ decreases to zero after another time period $t_4 = T(\gamma_1, r_1, r_2)$. Finally, U-FTZNN model (8.9) with its all subsystems converges to zero in predefined time $T_p = t_3 + t_4 = T(\gamma_1, r_1, r_2) + T(\gamma_2, r_1, r_2)$. The proof of Theorem 8.6 is now completed. ■

8.5 Robustness Analysis

The superiority of U-FTZNN model (8.9) lies not only in the fast and controllable convergence speed under ideal conditions, but also in its powerful noise suppression ability. In this section, we consider the additive noise polluted U-FTZNN model:

$$\dot{y}(t) = -\gamma_1 \Phi_1(y(t)) - \gamma_2 \Phi_2\left(y(t) + \gamma_1 \int_0^t \Phi_1(y(\tau))d\tau\right) + \xi(t), \qquad (8.19)$$

where $\xi(t) \in \mathbb{R}^{n+m+p}$ is unknown time-varying additive noise. The ith ($\forall i \in 1, \ldots, n + m + p$) subsystem of (8.19) can be expressed as

$$\dot{y}_i(t) = -\gamma_1 \phi_1(y_i(t)) - \gamma_2 \phi_2\left(y_i(t) + \gamma_1 \int_0^t \phi_1(y_i(\tau))d\tau\right) + \xi_i(t), \qquad (8.20)$$

where $\xi_i(t)$ is the ith element of $\xi(t)$. Similarly, the conventional ZNN model polluted by additive noise is

$$\dot{y}(t) = -\gamma \Phi(y(t)) + \xi(t). \qquad (8.21)$$

Theorem 8.7 *If time derivative of $\xi_i(t)$ in (8.20) exists and is bounded for any time $t \geq 0$, the residual error $\|\mathbf{y}(t)\|_2$ of the polluted U-FTZNN model (8.19) tends to converge to the bounded interval $[0, l|\dot{\xi}_{max}(t)|/(\gamma_1\gamma_2\phi)]$ when $t \to +\infty$, where $l = n + m + p$, $|\dot{\xi}_{max(t)}| = \max\{|\dot{\xi}_i(t)|\}$, and $\phi = \min\{\phi_i\}$ with $\phi_i = |\phi_1(y_i(t))|/|y_i(t)| \geq 1$.*

Proof: Defining a function $p_i(t) = z_i^2(t)/2 = |z_i(t)|^2/2$ for $z_i(t)$ in (8.13), the perturbed neural dynamic (8.20) is equivalent to $\dot{z}_i(t) = -\gamma_2\phi_2(z_i(t)) + \xi_i(t)$. Following this equation, the time derivative of $g_i(t)$ can be calculated:

$$\dot{p}_i(t) = \dot{z}_i(t)z_i(t) = \left(-\gamma_2\phi_2(z_i(t)) + \xi_i(t)\right)z_i(t).$$

In view of $\phi_2(z_i(t))z_i(t) \geq 0$, we have that $|z_i(t)|$ may increase only if $\xi_i(t)z_i(t) > 0$. If $|z_i(t)|$ is increasing under such condition, since $\xi_i(t)$ and $z_i(t)$ have the same sign, $|-\gamma_2\phi_2(z_i(t)) + \xi_i(t)|$ is decreasing in the same time. But the increasing of $|z_i(t)|$ stops when $-\gamma_2\phi_2(z_i(t)) + \xi_i(t) = 0$, i.e. $\dot{p}_i(t) = 0$. Therefore, with $t \to +\infty$, we have

$$0 \leq |z_i(t)| \leq |\phi_2^{-1}(\xi_i(t)/\gamma_2)|$$
$$-|\xi_i(t)/\gamma_2| \leq z_i(t) \leq |\xi_i(t)/\gamma_2|, \tag{8.22}$$

where $\phi_2^{-1}(\cdot)$ denotes the inverse function of $\phi_2(\cdot)$, and we have $|\phi_2(x)| \geq |x|$ meaning $|\phi_2^{-1}(x)| \leq |x|$ for PPAF (8.11).

Now, we continue to prove that with $t \to +\infty$, $\gamma_1\phi_1(y_i(t))$ converges to the bounded interval $[-|\dot{\xi}_i(t)/\gamma_2|, |\dot{\xi}_i(t)|/\gamma_2]$. We suppose there exists a time instant $t_a > 0$ that makes $E_1 = z_i(t_a)$ and $\gamma_1\phi_1(y_i(t)) \notin [-|\dot{\xi}_i(t)/\gamma_2|, |\dot{\xi}_i(t)|/\gamma_2]$. In order to use the contradiction technique, we suppose $\gamma_1\phi_1(y_i(t)) > |\dot{\xi}_i(t)|/\gamma_2 > 0$ holds true for $t \in [t_a, t_a + t_b]$. Thus, after a time period t_b, we get $E_2 = z_i(t_a + t_b)$. The difference between E_1 and E_2 in light of (8.13) is as follows:

$$E_2 - E_1 = (y_i(t_a + t_b) - y_i(t_a)) + \gamma_1 \int_0^{t_a+t_b} \phi_1(y_i(\tau))d\tau$$
$$- \gamma_1 \int_0^{t_a} \phi_1(y_i(\tau))d\tau$$
$$= (y_i(t_a + t_b) - y_i(t_a)) + \gamma_1 \int_{t_a}^{t_a+t_b} \phi_1(y_i(\tau))d\tau \tag{8.23}$$
$$\geq \gamma_1 \int_{t_a}^{t_a+t_b} \phi_1(y_i(\tau))d\tau - y_i(t_a).$$

It should be noted that we can obtain

$$|\xi_i(t_a + t_b)/\gamma_2| - E_1$$
$$\leq |\xi_i(t_a)/\gamma_2| + |\xi_i(t_a + t_b)/\gamma_2 - \xi_i(t_a)/\gamma_2| - E_1$$
$$= |\xi_i(t_a)/\gamma_2| + \left|\int_{t_a}^{t_a+t_b} (\dot{\xi}_i(\tau)/\gamma_2)d\tau\right| - E_1 \tag{8.24}$$
$$\leq |\xi_i(t_a)/\gamma_2| + \int_{t_a}^{t_a+t_b} |\dot{\xi}_i(\tau)/\gamma_2|d\tau - E_1.$$

Computing (8.23) and (8.24) leads to

$$E_2 - |\xi_i(t_a + t_b)/\gamma_2| \geq \int_{t_a}^{t_a+t_b} (\gamma_1\phi_1(y_i(\tau)) - |\dot{\xi}_i(\tau)/\gamma_2|)d\tau$$
$$- (|\xi_i(t_a)/\gamma_2| + y_i(t_a) - E_1).$$

With $t_a \to +\infty$, (8.22) tells us that $0 \geq E_2 - |\xi_i(t_a + t_b)/\gamma_2|$. It follows from the aforementioned inequality that

$$\int_{t_a}^{t_a+t_b} (\gamma_1\phi_1(y_i(\tau)) - |\dot{\xi}_i(\tau)/\gamma_2|)d\tau \leq |\xi_i(t_a)/\gamma_2| + y_i(t_a) - E_1. \tag{8.25}$$

For the left side of (8.25), $\gamma_1\phi_1(y_i(t)) - |\dot{\xi}_i(t)/\gamma_2| \geq 0$, $t \in [t_a, t_a + t_b]$ according to the previous assumption. Thus, the left side of (8.25) always increases with t_b increasing. Considering that the right side of (8.25) is a finite fixed value, we are able to conclude that $\gamma_1\phi_1(y_i(t)) - |\dot{\xi}_i(t)/\gamma_2| \to 0$ by the contradiction of (8.25) while $t_b \to +\infty$. Under another assumption when $\gamma_1\phi_1(y_i(t)) < -|\dot{\xi}_i(t)|/\gamma_2 < 0$, we can similarly have the conclusion that $\gamma_1\phi_1(y_i(t)) + |\dot{\xi}_i(t)/\gamma_2| \to 0$.

In brief, $\gamma_1\phi_1(y_i(t))$ can converge to the interval $[-|\dot{\xi}_i(t)/\gamma_2|, |\dot{\xi}_i(t)/\gamma_2|]$ under all circumstances, suggesting that $y_i(t)$ will converge to $[-|\dot{\xi}_i(t)|/(\gamma_1\gamma_2\phi_i),$ $|\dot{\xi}_i(t)|/(\gamma_1\gamma_2\phi_i)]$. Moreover, for the residual error $\|y(t)\|_2$, we get $0 \leq \|y(t)\|_2 = \sqrt{\sum_{i=1}^{l} y_i^2(t)} \leq l|y_{\max}(t)|$ where $|y_{\max}(t)|$ denotes the largest element among $|y_i(t)|$, $i \in 1, \ldots, l$. Eventually, $\|y(t)\|_2$ converges to the bounded interval

$$\|y(t)\|_2 \in [0, l|\dot{\xi}_{\max}(t)|/(\gamma_1\gamma_2\phi)]. \tag{8.26}$$

The proof is now completed. ∎

Remark Unlike convergence time, perturbations in realistic applications are usually unknown and we can only try to eliminate their negative impacts. For this reason, we provide Theorem 8.7 for U-FTZNN model (8.9) to help us evaluate and control the perturbed U-FTZNN model's residual error under nonstationary unknown noises, instead of studying only limited types of noises like in [10, 11]. We learn from Theorem 8.7 that, as long as the time derivative of unknown noises is bounded, steady error $\|y(t)\|_2$ is bounded for model (8.19) regardless of the size of noises. In addition, larger γ_1, γ_2 and ϕ in the activation function lead to smaller residual error.

8.6 Illustrative Verification

8.6.1 Qualitative Experiments

For validating previous theoretical results as well as further illustrating U-FTZNN's convergence and robustness advantages over conventional ZNN

model (8.8) for TVQP problems, a series of simulations are conducted in this section.
For the purpose of testing the predefined-time convergence performance of U-FTZNN model (8.10) on solving TVQP problems, both TVQPEI (8.1)–(8.3) and TVQPE (8.4) have been tested. It's worth noting that all elements in δ^+ are set to be 10^{-8} and the simulation duration is 10 seconds or 1 second in this section. The TVQPEI example is as follows:

$$\min (\sin(t)/4 + 1)/2 \cdot u_1^2(t) + (\cos(t)/4 + 1)/2 \cdot u_2^2$$
$$+ \cos(t)u_1(t)u_2(t)/2 + \sin(3t)u_1(t) + \cos(3t)u_2(t), \tag{8.27}$$

$$\text{s.t. } \sin(4t)u_1(t) + \cos(4t)u_2(t) = \cos(2t), \tag{8.28}$$

$$-1.2 \le u_1(t), u_2(t) \le 1.2, \tag{8.29}$$

where $u_1(0)$ and $u_2(0)$ are randomly generated in $[0, 1]$. Other parameters are $\gamma_1 = \gamma_2 = 1$ and $r_1 = 2, r_2 = 0.5$ in U-FTZNN model (8.10). The results of using U-FTZNN model (8.10) to solve (8.27)–(8.29) are presented in Figures 8.1a and 8.2a. We conclude from Theorem 8.6 that the residual error $\|\mathbf{y}(t)\|_2$ should converge to 0 in predefined time $T_p = 2 * T(1, 2, 0.5) \le 3$ seconds and it can be seen in Figure 8.2a that $\|\mathbf{y}(t)\|_2$ decreases to 0 within two seconds in the simulation. Clearly, U-FTZNN model (8.10) can handle the TVQPEI problem efficiently, and obtain the optimal solution in a predefined time.

For TVQPE problem simulation example, we consider

$$\min (\sin(t)/4 + 1)/2 \cdot u_1^2(t) + (\cos(t)/4 + 1)/2 \cdot u_2^2$$
$$+ \cos(t)u_1(t)u_2(t)/2 + \sin(3t)u_1(t) + \cos(3t)u_2(t), \tag{8.30}$$

$$\text{s.t. } \sin(4t)u_1(t) + \cos(4t)u_2(t) = \cos(2t). \tag{8.31}$$

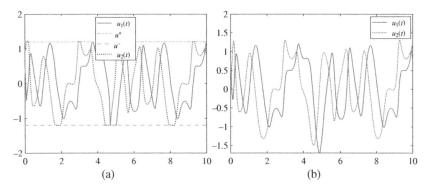

(a) (b)

Figure 8.1 The state solutions computed by U-FTZNN model (8.9) on solving different TVQP problems. (a) TVQPEI (8.27)–(8.29). (b) TVQPE (8.30)–(8.31).

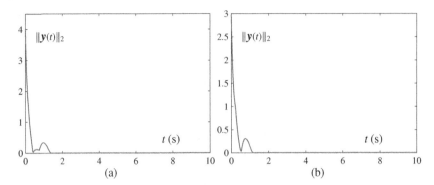

Figure 8.2 The residual error $\|\mathbf{y}(t)\|_2$ generated by U-FTZNN model (8.9) on solving different TVQP problems. (a) TVQPEI (8.27)–(8.29). (b) TVQPE (8.30)–(8.31).

From Section 8.2.1, we know that the TVQPE problem can be easily reconstructed into TVQPEI problem by adopting $C(t) = [I_n, -I_n]^T$ and $d(t) = [\infty_n^T, \infty_n^T]^T$ in (8.3). Therefore, we use real number 10^8 to denote the positive infinity, and other parameters are the same as in the aforementioned TVQPEI problem. Such experiment results can be found in Figures 8.1b and 8.2b. Figure 8.2b shows that the predefined-time convergence of U-FTZNN model (8.10) is validated again, in which $\|\mathbf{y}(t)\|_2$ drops to 0 within $2 \leq 3$ seconds. Furthermore, comparing the state solutions of TVQPE (8.30)–(8.31) in Figure 8.1b with that of TVQPEI (8.27)–(8.28) in Figure 8.1a, they strictly subject to inequality constraints and coincide with each other when the optimal solutions of (8.27/8.30) falls inside the feasible domain.

Consider the convergence time upper bound (8.18) in Theorem 8.6, the relationship between T_p and four parameters $\gamma_1, \gamma_2, r_1, r_2$ is so complicated that we can not validate it using only aforementioned conducted experiments. Hence, we shorten the designated upper bound T_p to one second and choose four different groups of design parameters to meet this restriction. In the first two groups, $r_1 = 2, r_2 = 0.5$ are kept unchanged and we set $\gamma_1 = 2, \gamma_2 = 6$ or $\gamma_1 = 6, \gamma_2 = 2$. For the last two groups, we keep $\gamma_1 = \gamma_2 = 1$ unchanged and make $r_1 = 4, r_2 = 0.4$ or $r_1 = 6$, $r_2 = 0.6$ instead.

Theorem 8.7 indicates that the stable computation error $\|\mathbf{y}(t)\|_2$ of the perturbed U-FTZNN model (8.19) is bounded and controllable even facing with time-varying additive noises. Thus, we have selected three representative noises: constant noise ξ_c, linear noise $\xi_l(t)$, and sinusoidal noise $\xi_s(t)$. All elements of ξ_c, $\xi_l(t)$, $\xi_s(t)$ are 3, t and $\sin(t)$, respectively. A linear noise $0.1\xi_l(t)$ is firstly used to demonstrate the superior robustness of the perturbed U-FTZNN model (8.19) against the normal perturbed ZNN model (8.21) for solving (8.27)–(8.29), where ZNN uses the same PPAF as in U-FTZNN (8.19) with $\gamma = \gamma_1 = \gamma_2 = 1, r_1 = 2, r_2 = 0.5$. Figure 8.3a

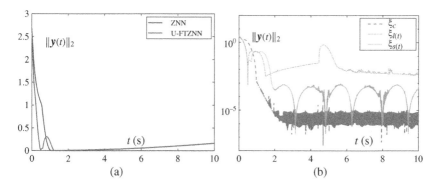

Figure 8.3 Comparisons of residual error $\|y(t)\|_2$ produced by different models with different noises. (a) by perturbed ZNN (8.21) and perturbed U-FTZNN (8.19) with $0.1\xi_1(t)$. (b) by perturbed U-FTZNN with $\xi_c, \xi_1(t)$ and $\xi_s(t)$.

depicts the results of this experiment, which shows that even with small noise pollution, the ordinary ZNN model performs much worse than U-FTZNN model (8.19). It's reasonable to assume that $\|y(t)\|_2$ of the ZNN model will continue to rise above 0.5 after 10 seconds while the one of U-FTZNN model (8.19) is always kept at a low and stable level.

In order to further verify the conclusion of Theorem 8.7, we apply all three larger noise $\xi_c, \xi_1(t), \xi_s(t)$ to U-FTZNN model (8.19) while keeping other parameters unchanged. The results of solving (8.27)–(8.29) by U-FTZNN model (8.19) are plotted in Figure 8.3b. Following the properties of those noises' time derivative, we can see in Figure 8.3b that: for ξ_c, the stable residual error $\|y(t)\|_2$ is nearly zero where the precision of this simulation is at level of 10^{-6}; for $\xi_1(t)$, $\|y(t)\|_2$ is slightly higher but still very small and stable (at the level of 10^{-2}), and for $\xi_s(t)$, due to the change of its time-varying time derivative, the stable computation error $\|y(t)\|_2$ is also changing, but always below that of the linear noise case. These inversely validate the correctness of Theorem 8.7.

8.6.2 Quantitative Experiments

Through the previous analysis, we have derived precise quantitative upper bound formulas for predefined convergence time (8.18) and stable residual error (8.26), and it is necessary to verify these formulas through more case studies and quantitative comparisons. Therefore, another example of TVQPEI problem called TVQPEI case 2 (TVQPEI-C2) is introduced as follows:

$$S = \begin{bmatrix} 2 * \sin(t) + 2 & \exp(\sin(t))/2 \\ \exp(\cos(t))/2 & \cos(t) + 3 \end{bmatrix},$$

$k(t) = [\cos(2t), \sin(t + 1)]^T, A(t) = [2 * \sin^2(t), \log(4 + \cos(t))], b = \cos(t) + \sin(3t),$
$C(t) = [I_2, -I_2]^T, d(t) = [\sin(t) + 2, \sin(t) + 2, \sin(t) + 2, \sin(t) + 2]^T$ and $u(t) \in \mathbb{R}^2$.

Compared with the TVQPEI problem used in Section 8.6.1, the TVQPEI-C2 has added more nonlinearity including exponential, power, logarithmic functions and the time-varying inequalities. Thus, the TVQPEI-C2 can better represent TVQPEI problems that we encounter in the real world. For controlling variables in the following experiments for solving TVQPEI-C2 problem, we have generated four different initial values $q(0) \in \mathbb{R}^4$ for the U-FTZNN model (8.10) in advance. They are denoted by $q_1(0), q_2(0), q_3(0)$, and $q_4(0)$ of which elements are randomly generated in interval $[-1, 1]$.

For TVQPEI-C2, let us firstly verify the predefined convergence time upper bound formula (8.18) with quantitative experiments. Note that due to simulation precision limit, we have shown in Figure 8.3 that the neural network can be deemed to converge to zero when its residual error approaches to about 10^{-6}. Therefore, the convergence time t_c in the following experiments is defined as the earliest time instant when $\|y(t_c)\|_2 \leq 10^{-5}$. According to formula (8.18), the predefined convergence time bound T_p of U-FTZNN model (8.9) is relevant to r_1, r_2, γ_1, and γ_2. Thus, we have conducted three experiments which validate roles of these variables, respectively. In these three experiments, the U-FTZNN model (8.10) is used to solve the TVQPEI-C2 problem. In the first experiment, we fix the last three model variables as $r_2 = 0.5, \gamma_1 = \gamma_2 = 1$ and change the first as $r_1 = 1.1, 1.2, 1.3, \ldots, 2.1$. Starting from different $q(0)$, results and corresponding T_p of U-FTZNN model (8.10) are plotted in Figure 8.4a. In the second experiment, we fix three model variables as $r_1 = 3, \gamma_1 = \gamma_2 = 1$ and change the other model variable as $r_2 = 0.4, 0.45, 0.5, \ldots, 0.9$. Starting from different $q(0)$, results of the U-FTZNN model (8.10) together with corresponding T_p are shown in Figure 8.4b. As for the third experiment, we keep $r_1 = 2, r_2 = 0.6, \gamma_1 = \gamma_2$ and change γ_1, γ_2 in $0.5, 0.6, 0.7, \ldots, 2$ with results illustrated in Figure 8.4c. In Figure 8.4a–c, convergence time of all simulations is clearly less than T_p predicted by formula (8.18). We also find that even if the convergence time may be slightly affected by the initial value $q(0)$, it still strictly conforms to our theoretical prediction. Another important observation of Figure 8.4a–c is that the changing direction of convergence time strictly conforms to the variable relationships reflected in formula (8.18) as well, which verifies the U-FTZNN model (8.10)'s tunable predefined-time convergence again.

Now, after verifying T_p in convergence time bound (8.18), we would like to quantitatively examine U-FTZNN model (8.10)'s stable residual error under time-varying noises, which should be coincide with bound (8.26). According to error bound formula (8.26) and Figure 8.3b, we conclude that $\|y(t)\|_2$ may be non-stationary due to the time-varying noise. Thus in the following experiments, the maximum steady-state residual error (MSSRE) is introduced for evaluation

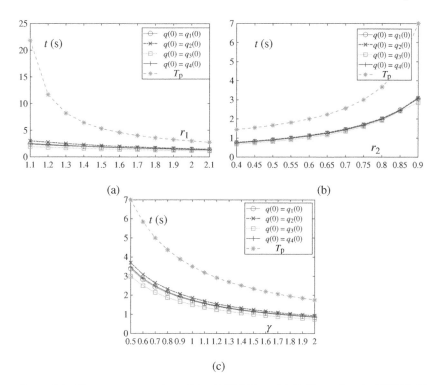

Figure 8.4 The convergence time of the U-FTZNN model (8.10) solving the TVQPEI-C2 problem starting from different initial condition $q(0)$ with different model variable settings. T_p is the predefined convergence time bound by Eq. (8.18). (a) $r_2 = 0.5$, $\gamma_1 = \gamma_2 = 1$ while changing r_1. (b) $r_1 = 3, \gamma_1 = \gamma_2 = 1$ while changing r_2. (c) $r_1 = 2, r_2 = 0.6$, $\gamma_1 = \gamma_2$ while changing γ_1 and γ_2.

and MSSRE is defined as max $\{ \|\mathbf{y}(t)\|_2 \}, \forall t \in [7, 10]$s (the duration of simulation experiments are 10 seconds). Moreover, a new type of time-varying noise is designed as $\xi_c(t, a_n) = \cos(a_n t), a_n \in \mathbb{R}^+$, of which the maximum value will not change with a_n but its time derivative $\dot{\xi}_c(t, a_n) = -a_n * \sin(a_n t)$ will. To validate the relationship between $\|\mathbf{y}(t)\|_2$ and $\dot{\xi}_{\max}(t)$ in inequality (8.26), we set $r_1 = 4, r_2 = 0.6, \gamma_1 = \gamma_2 = 1, \xi(t) = \xi_c(a_n, t)$ and change $a_n = 1, 1.5, 2, \ldots, 10$. The MSSREs of perturbed U-FTZNN model (8.19) when solving TVQPEI-C2 problem are presented in Figure 8.5a, where the linear relationship between MSSRE ($\|\mathbf{y}(t)\|_2$) and a_n ($\dot{\xi}_{\max}(t)$) is well illustrated. We also find that the initial condition of $q(0)$ has a slight influence on MSSRE. If we assume $\phi = 4 \times 10^3$ with known $l = n + m + p = 7$, MSSRE upper bounds (MSSRE$_{\text{pred}}$) predicted by (8.26) coincide with actual MSSREs in Figure 8.5a well, meaning noise resistance of U-FTZNN model (8.19) can be much stronger than the worst case when $\phi = 1$.

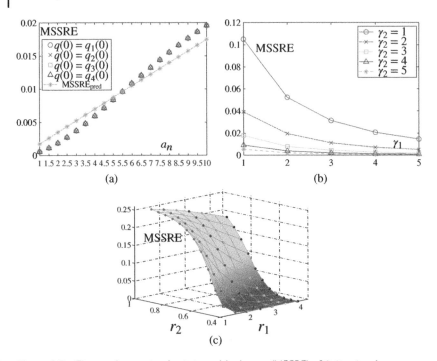

Figure 8.5 The maximum steady-state residual error (MSSRE) of $\xi_c(t, a_n)$ noise perturbed U-FTZNN model (8.21) solving the TVQPEI-C2 problem with different model variable settings, where MSSRE$_{pred}$ is the predicted MSSRE bound by inequality (8.26) when $\phi = 4 \times 10^3$. (a) $r_1 = 4, r_2 = 0.6, \gamma_1 = \gamma_2 = 1$ while changing a_n and $q(0)$. (b) $r_1 = 2$, $r_2 = 0.6, q(0) = q_1(0), a_n = 10$ while changing γ_1 and γ_2. (c) $\gamma_1 = \gamma_2 = 1, a_n = 10$ while changing r_1 and r_2.

Next, we want to validate how γ_1 and γ_2 contribute in bound (8.26). We have $r_1 = 2, r_2 = 0.6, q(0) = q_1(0), a_n = 10$. Changing γ_1, γ_2 individually and keeping other settings the same as previous noise simulations, the results are shown in Figure 8.5b. As can be observed in Figure 8.5b, the MSSREs of noise-perturbed U-FTZNN model (8.19) always decrease with the increasing of γ_1 or γ_2. Through this, it can be also verified that their decreasing curves match the fractional function about γ_1, γ_2 revealed in bound (8.26). Finally, based on the bound of $\|y(t)\|_2$ (8.26) and $\phi = \min \{ |\phi(y_i(t))| / |y_i(t)| \}$, we conjecture that r_1, r_2 in PPAF (8.11) may affect MSSRE as well by affecting ϕ. Thus, we keep $\gamma_1 = \gamma_2 = 1, \xi(t) = \xi_c(t, 10)$ unchanged and change r_1, r_2 individually, and the noise-perturbed U-FTZNN model (8.19) is used to solve TVQPEI-C2 with MSSREs plotted in Figure 8.5c. From Figure 8.5c, the MSSREs always drop with the increasing of r_1 or decreasing of r_2, meaning MSSRE will drop if we adjust activation function to increase ϕ.

Guided from aforementioned quantitative comparison experiments, we now conclude that our U-FTZNN model (8.10) can enhance convergence and noise suppression simultaneously by making r_1, γ_1, γ_2 as big as possible and r_2 as small as possible.

8.7 Application to Image Fusion

In this section, U-FTZNN model (8.10) is applied to solve image fusion problem, which receives several noisy images for the same scene and fuses them into a single image. The resultant image should have higher quality than noisy images.

Suppose we have S different gray scale pictures with size of $I \times J$ for the same scene, which can be taken from different or the same sensor. The normalized pixels of those images form S matrices denoted by $N_s(i,j)$ where $s = 1, 2, \ldots, S$; $i = 1, 2, \ldots, I; j = 1, 2, \ldots, J$. Then we row-wisely vectorize N_s into the sth column of $Z \in \mathbb{R}^{L \times S}$, where $L = I \times J$. After defining Z_s as the sth column of Z, we have $Z_s((i-1)J + j) = N_s(i,j)$. Consider pixels in Z that come from the same picture N_s, we assume they satisfy decompose equation $Z_s = \alpha \circ N_s + \mathcal{N}_s$ where $\alpha \in \mathbb{R}^L$ denotes a scaling vector, $N_s \in \mathbb{R}^L$ is obtained by row-wisely vectoring N_s and $s = 1$, $\ldots, S$. In addition, $\mathcal{N}_s \in \mathbb{R}^L$ stands for zero-mean Gaussian noise randomly produced during imaging. Under the previous decompose equation, the best fused image is derived from

$$z^* = \sum_{s=1}^{S} Z_s u^*(s) = Z u^*,$$

where u^* is the optimal solution of the following QP problem according to [1, 2]:

$$\min x^T G x / 2, \tag{8.32}$$

$$\text{s.t. } A^T x = 1, \ 0 \le x, \tag{8.33}$$

where $A = [1, 1, \ldots, 1]^T \in \mathbb{R}^S$ and $G = (\sum_{l=1}^{L} r_l r_l^T)/L \in \mathbb{R}^{S \times S}$ with $r_l^T \in \mathbb{R}^{1 \times S}$ representing the lth row of Z. By transforming (8.32) and (8.33) into the standard QP problem, U-FTZNN model (8.10) is then used to acquire its optimal solution u^*. Eventually, the fused image $N^*(i,j)$ is reconstructed via $N^*(i,j) = z^*((i-1)J + j)$.

To perform image fusion using U-FTZNN model (8.10), we select a gray scale picture with size of 512×512 which is shown in Figure 8.6a and has the highest quality. Then, a certain number of independent noisy pictures with Gaussian noises are simulatively generated, their sizes are 512×512 while their signal-to-noise (SNR) ratios are 1 dB. One example of noisy images can be found in Figure 8.6b. Moreover, we have tested fusion on different number of noisy images, and the final optimal fused images obtained by U-FTZNN model (8.10) are demonstrated

(a)   (b)

(c)   (d)

Figure 8.6 Results of image fusion on a 512×512 gray scale picture using U-FTZNN model (8.10). (a) Original image. (b) Noisy image with SNR = 1 dB. (c) Fused image when $S = 20$. (d) Fused image when $S = 50$.

in Figure 8.6c,d. Evidently, this application has notably improved the quality of input noised images, and the denoising effect becomes better with larger S.

Noting we set $\gamma_1 = \gamma_2 = 5, r_1 = 2, r_2 = 0.5$ in U-FTZNN model (8.9) for showing that the predefined-time convergence of such neural network can be accelerated by adopting larger γ_1, γ_2. As can be seen in Figure 8.7, when $S = 20$ or $S = 50$, $\|y(t)\|_2$ drops to 0 before the time upper bound 0.6 second that we calculated according to Theorem 8.6. Besides, the matrix G in (8.32) is a high dimensional matrix when $S = 20$ and $S = 50$. However our novel U-FTZNN model (8.9) has successfully solved such a high dimensional QP problem. Image fusion denoising

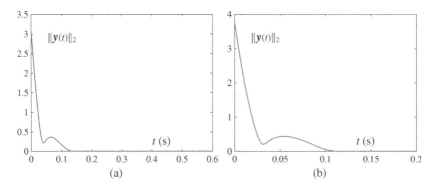

(a)　　　　　　　　　　　(b)

Figure 8.7 Computation error $\|\mathbf{y}(t)\|_2$ synthesized by U-FTZNN model (8.9) during image fusion with different S. (a) $S = 20$. (b) $S = 50$.

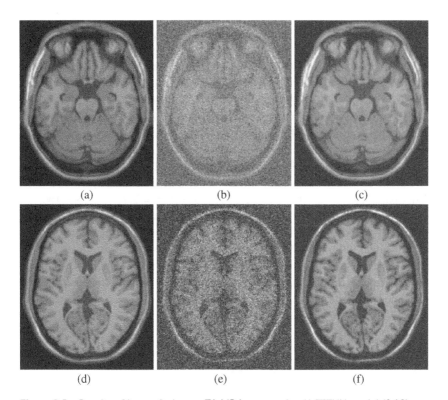

Figure 8.8 Results of image fusion on T1-MR images using U-FTZNN model (8.10). (a) Slice 50 of T1-MR. (b) Slice 50 polluted by Gaussian noise. (c) Fused image of noise-polluted slice 50 when $S = 100$. (d) Slice 80 of T1-MR. (e) Slice 80 polluted by the Rician noise. (f) Fused image of noise-polluted slice 80 when $S = 100$.

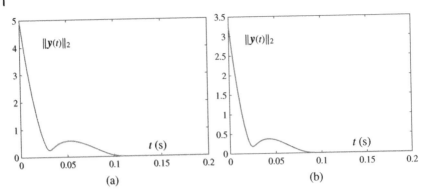

Figure 8.9 Residual error $\|y(t)\|_2$ synthesized by U-FTZNN model (8.10) during image fusion when using different T1-MR images. (a) Using Gaussian noise polluted Slice 50. (b) Using Rician noise polluted Slice 80.

method can be used in more practical industrial applications. For this reason we have tested our U-FTZNN model based image fusion method in magnetic resonance (MR) image denoising tasks. In this experiment, we use high quality MR images of human brain downloaded from online database BrainWeb, https:// brainweb.bic.mni.mcgill.ca/brainweb. The downloaded MR image dataset are T1-MR with slice sickness being 1mm, and they have 181 slices size of 217×181. Then, two different types of noises are applied to original MR images: one is the aforementioned zero-mean Gaussian noise, and the other is the Rician noise (because it appears in MR images more frequently). The Rician noise is synthesized from Gaussian noise but it happens in complex domain [13]. For other model parameters, we set the same as $\gamma_1 = \gamma_2 = 5, r_1 = 2, r_2 = 0.5, S = 100$. We can see in Figure 8.8 that when the applied noise level is 20%, both the Gaussian polluted MR images or Rician polluted MR images have bad image quality and are unrecognizable. However, Figure 8.8c,f demonstrate that our U-FTZNN model based image fusion have improved qualities of noisy MR images a lot and the fused images are recognizable. In addition, the corresponding errors $\|y(t)\|_2$ are plotted in Figure 8.9, whose decreasing trajectories match our expectation perfectly.

8.8 Application to Robot Control

Like the image fusion shown in Section 8.7, there are still many applications can take advantage of our U-FTZNN model (8.10) including controlling redundant robotic manipulators. Generally speaking, extra degrees of freedom (DOFs) make the redundant robot manipulators capable of avoiding obstacles while accomplishing tasks of the end effector. However, such characteristic makes the inverse-kinematics control of a redundant robotic manipulator a difficult job, especially when considering joint limits of the manipulator. In this section, we will use our U-FTZNN model (8.10) to control a redundant robot arm PUM560 in the simulation experiments.

Inspired by Li *et al.* [9], we adopt the repetitive motion planning method that is solved in velocity-level with joint limits considered. This scheme is based on the TVQPEI (8.27)–(8.29) problem and is expressed as follows:

$$
\begin{aligned}
&\min \dot{\theta}(t)^{\mathrm{T}}\dot{\theta}(t)/2 + \boldsymbol{q}^{\mathrm{T}}(t)\dot{\theta}(t), \\
&\text{s.t. } W_J(\theta(t))\dot{\theta}(t) = \dot{\boldsymbol{r}}_d(t) + \sigma(\boldsymbol{r}_d(t) - \mathscr{F}(\theta(t))), \\
&\quad \theta^-(t) \le \theta(t) \le \theta^+(t), \\
&\quad \dot{\theta}^-(t) \le \dot{\theta}(t) \le \dot{\theta}^+(t),
\end{aligned}
\tag{8.34}
$$

where $\theta(t) \in \mathbb{R}^6, \dot{\theta}(t) \in \mathbb{R}^6$ are respectively the joint angle vector and joint velocity vector of PUM560, $\boldsymbol{q}(t) = \xi(\theta(t) - \theta(0))$ denotes the joint drift between current and initial state with $\xi > 0$. Besides, $\boldsymbol{r}_d(t) \in \mathbb{R}^3$ is given nonstationary desired path vector of end effector in three dimensional space, $\mathscr{F}(\cdot) \in \mathbb{R}^6 \to \mathbb{R}^3$ is end effector position calculation function and $W_J(t) = W_J(\theta(t)) = \partial\mathscr{F}(\theta)/\partial\theta$ represents the Jacobian matrix. Then, $\sigma(\boldsymbol{r}_d(t) - \mathscr{F}(\theta(t)))$ with $\sigma > 0$ is used for feedback control. In addition, $\theta^+(t), \theta^-(t) \in \mathbb{R}^6$ and $\dot{\theta}^+(t), \dot{\theta}^-(t) \in \mathbb{R}^6$ denote upper and low bounds of joint angle and joint velocity, respectively. In our TVPQEI problem (8.1)–(8.3), only one unknown vector $U(t)$ is allowed, so limitation of $\theta(t)$ is integrated into $\dot{\theta}(t)$ limit. Finally, the control scheme (8.34) is rewritten into standard TVPQEI problems (8.1)–(8.3) with input coefficients defined as $\boldsymbol{u}(t) = \dot{\theta}(t), S(t) = I_6, \boldsymbol{k}(t) = \boldsymbol{q}(t), A(t) = W_J(t), \boldsymbol{b}(t) = \dot{\boldsymbol{r}}_d(t) + \sigma(\boldsymbol{r}_d(t) - \mathscr{F}(t)), C(t) = [I_6, -I_6]^{\mathrm{T}}$, where I_n stands for the $n \times n$ identity matrix size. We define the last coefficient as $\boldsymbol{d}(t) = [\boldsymbol{\eta}^{+\mathrm{T}}, \boldsymbol{\eta}^{-\mathrm{T}}]^{\mathrm{T}}$ with

$$
\eta_i^+ = \begin{cases} \dot{\theta}_i^+, & \theta_i(t) \in [\theta_i^-, \theta_r], \\ \phi_1(\theta_i(t)), & \theta_i(t) \in [\theta_r, \theta_i^+], \end{cases}
$$

$$
\eta_i^- = \begin{cases} \dot{\theta}_i^-, & \theta_i(t) \in [\theta_l, \theta_i^+], \\ \phi_2(\theta_i(t)), & \theta_i(t) \in [\theta_i^-, \theta_l], \end{cases}
$$

where $\phi_1(\theta_i) = -\dot{\theta}_i^+(\theta_i - \theta_r)^2/(\theta_i^+ - \theta_r)^2 + \dot{\theta}_i^+$, $\phi_2(\theta_i) = -\dot{\theta}_i^-(\theta_i - \theta_l)^2/(\theta_i^- - \theta_l)^2 + \dot{\theta}_i^-$. In the previous equations, $\theta_i, \dot{\theta}_i, \eta_i$ are ith ($\forall i \in 1, 2, \ldots, 6$) element of vector $\theta, \dot{\theta}, \eta$ respectively, $\theta_r, \theta_l \in [\theta_i^-, \theta_i^+]$ satisfying $\theta_r > \theta_l$ are design parameters. Therefore, relationships between θ_i and $\dot{\theta}_i$ have been shown in Figure 8.10a.

We now use the aforementioned U-FTZNN model (8.10) based inverse kinematics control method to control PUM560 to track a rotated Lissajous curve path in 3D space. Parameters of U-FTZNN model (8.10) are selected as $\gamma_1 = \gamma_2 = 1, r_1 = 2, r_2 = 0.8, \delta^+ = 10^8$. Specifically, joint limits in $d(t)$ are set to be

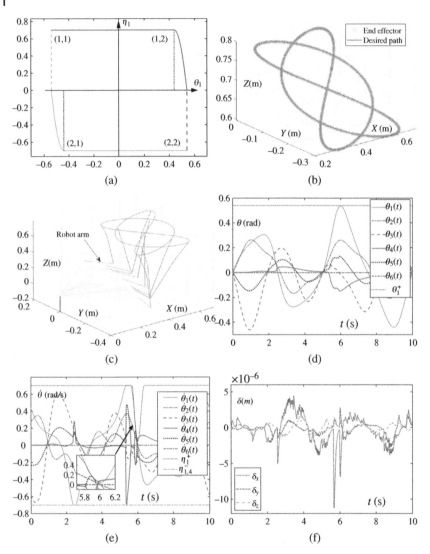

Figure 8.10 Simulation results of using U-FTZNN model (8.10) to control PUM560 robot manipulator to track the Lissajous curve path. (a) Relationship between θ_1 and η_1. (b) Trajectory of end effector and desired path. (c) Full view of path tracking with robot arm in Cartesian space. (d) Traces of joint angles. (e) Traces of joint velocities. (f) Position errors of the end effector in three dimensions.

$\theta^+ = [0.54, 1, 1, 1, 1, 1]$ rad, $\dot{\theta}^+ = 0.7 * [1, 1, 1, 1, 1, 1]$ rad/s, $\theta_r = \theta_i^+ - 0.1$ rad, and $\theta^- = -\theta^+, \dot{\theta}^- = -\dot{\theta}^+, \theta_l = \theta_r$. The results of path tracking in 10 seconds are depicted in Figure 8.10. From Figure 8.10a, taking θ_1 and η_1 for example, it is clearly that two functions $\phi_1(\cdot), \phi_2(\cdot)$ have smoothed boundaries of $\dot{\theta}(t)$, making $d(t)$ differentiable which is required by our U-FTZNN model. Then, let us see Figure 8.10d, there is a time period when joint angle θ_1 is very close to the limit $\theta_1^+ = 0.54$ rad and drops back at about $t = 6$ seconds. Correspondingly, we find in Figure 8.10e that the actual joint velocity limit η_1^+ begins decreasing when θ_1 approaches θ_r and decreases nearly to zero at about $t = 6$ seconds, preventing θ_1 from crossing the bound. Apart from $\dot{\theta}_1$, $\dot{\theta}_4$ also hit the velocity limit η_4^- at about $t = 5.5$ seconds. But in Figure 8.10d,e, limits of joint angle and joint velocity have all been satisfied well. Then, the end effector trajectory and desired path are illustrated in Figure 8.10b while the positions of all arms are shown in Figure 8.10c, where actual path and desired path overlaps very well. As in Figure 8.10f, the end effector position errors of three coordinates are at level of 10^{-6} m. Thus, we conclude that the PUM560 tracks the Lissajous curve path with high precision even with strict limits. The superiorities of our U-FTZNN model (8.10) have now been proved by the aforementioned robot control simulation results.

8.9 Chapter Summary

In this chapter, by designing the special PPAF and combining it with the noise tolerance enhanced ZNN model, we have proposed a U-FTZNN model that solves different branches of QP problems in a unified model. Theoretical analysis on the predefined-time convergence and the noise suppression ability against different time-varying noises have been discussed and proved. Results of simulation experiments have validated that the U-FTZNN model can obtain accurate solutions of TVQP problems in designated finite time and maintain high accuracy when facing with large perturbations. In summary, our proposed U-FTZNN model (8.10) is broadly suitable for various QP problems with tunable and elastic convergence time, and it is also reliable in complex noisy environments. Besides, the U-FTZNN model can handle real world applications like image fusion and robotic manipulators control.

References

1 A. Nazemi, A capable neural network framework for solving degenerate quadratic optimization problems with an application in image fusion, *Neural Process. Lett.*, 47(1) (2018) 167–192.

2 A. Nazemi and M. Nazemi, A gradient-based neural network method for solving strictly convex quadratic programming problems, *Cognit. Comput.*, 6(3) (2014) 484–495.

3 S. Li, Y. Zhang, and L. Jin, Kinematic control of redundant manipulators using neural networks, *IEEE Trans. Neural Netw. Learn. Syst.*, 28(10) (2017) 2243–2254.

4 Z. Zhang and L. Kong *et al.*, Robustness analysis of a power-type varying-parameter recurrent neural network for solving time-varying QM and QP problems and applications, *IEEE Trans. Syst. Man Cybern. Syst.*, 50(12) (2020) 5106–5118.

5 L. Xiao and Y. Zhang *et al.*, Performance benefits of robust nonlinear zeroing neural network for finding accurate solution of Lyapunov equation in presence of various noises, *IEEE Trans. Ind. Inform.*, 15(9) (2019) 5161–5171.

6 D. Guo and Y. Zhang, Li-function activated ZNN with finite-time convergence applied to redundant-manipulator kinematic control via time-varying Jacobian matrix pseudoinversion, *Appl. Soft. Comput.*, 24 (2014) 158–168.

7 S. Boyd, S. P. Boyd, and L. Vandenberghe, *Convex optimization*, Cambridge University Press, (2004).

8 X. Huang, X. Lou, and B. Cui, A novel neural network for solving convex quadratic programming problems subject to equality and inequality constraints, *Neurocomputing*, 214 (2016) 23–31.

9 W. Li and X. Ma *et al.*, A strictly predefined-time convergent neural solution to equality-and inequality-constrained time-variant quadratic programming, *IEEE Trans. Syst. Man Cybern. Syst.*, 51(7) (2021) 4028–4039.

10 L. Xiao, K. Li, and M. Duan, Computing time-varying quadratic optimization with finite-time convergence and noise tolerance: A unified framework for zeroing neural network, *IEEE Trans. Neural Netw. Learn. Syst.*, 30(11) (2019) 3360–3369.

11 D. Chen and Y. Zhang, Robust zeroing neural-dynamics and its time-varying disturbances suppression model applied to mobile robot manipulators, *IEEE Trans. Neural Netw. Learn. Syst.*, 29(9) (2018) 4385–4397.

12 S. Li, S. Chen, and B. Liu, Accelerating a recurrent neural network to finite-time convergence for solving time-varying Sylvester equation by using a sign-bi-power activation function, *Neural Process. Lett.*, 37(2) (2013) 189–205.

13 S. Li, H. Yin, and L. Fang, Group-sparse representation with dictionary learning for medical image denoising and fusion, *IEEE Trans. Biomed. Eng.*, 59(12) (2012) 3450–3459.

9

FTZNN for Nonlinear Minimization

9.1 Introduction

Nonlinear minimization is one of the most important branches of optimization for many scientific and engineering applications [1–9]. For example, optimal path tracking of robot manipulators was usually formulated as nonlinear minimization problems solving [1, 4, 7, 9]. Other practical applications (e.g. multiagent systems, image processing, and restoration) can also be handled by modeling and solving nonlinear minimization problems [3, 8].

In this chapter, we aim to modify the comprehensive property of zeroing neural network (ZNN) models by devising a different formula from a viewpoint of continuous-time systems. As we know, robustness and convergence are two important features, which influence the performance of solving practical time-dependent nonlinear minimizations, and external disturbances or noises are not considered in the existing ZNN models for time-dependent nonlinear minimization. In this work, based on ZNN, a new robust finite-time zeroing neural network (R-FTZNN) is devised and presented to solve time-dependent nonlinear minimization in front of external disturbances. Different from previous ZNN models for this problem [10–12], R-FTZNN model can simultaneously achieve finite-time convergence and suppression of external disturbances. Besides, rigorous theoretical analyses are given to prove the superior performance of the R-FTZNN model when adopted to solve time-dependent nonlinear minimization under external disturbances. Comparative results also substantiate the effectiveness and advantages of R-FTZNN via solving a time-dependent nonlinear minimization problem.

9.2 Problem Formulation and ZNN Models

This part of the chapter provides problem description of time-dependent nonlinear minimization, which is obviously different from static nonlinear minimization.

Zeroing Neural Networks: Finite-time Convergence Design, Analysis and Applications,
First Edition. Lin Xiao and Lei Jia.

Next, two different ZNN models from previous work are presented for solving time-dependent nonlinear minimization for comparison purpose.

9.2.1 Problem Formulation

We are concerned with the following time-dependent nonlinear minimization problem solving [10–12]:

$$\min_{\boldsymbol{u}(t)\in\mathbb{R}^n} g(\boldsymbol{u}(t),t), \quad \forall t \in [0,\infty), \tag{9.1}$$

where t represents time and $g(\cdot,\cdot) : \mathbb{R}^n \times \mathbb{R} \to \mathbb{R}$ represents a smooth nonlinear objective function. The goal of the current work is to compute unknown $\boldsymbol{u}(t) \in \mathbb{R}^n$ at each time instant t under external disturbances so that the value of nonlinear objective function at each time instant achieves the minimum within finite time, which constitutes the dynamic minimum motion trajectory of $g(\boldsymbol{u}(t),t)$ for all t. In order to assure that Eq. (9.1) has only one optimal solution, we consider the situation that $g(\cdot,\cdot)$ is a convex function at each time instant in this work.

From previous studies on nonlinear minimization [10–12], we conclude that the optimal solution of Eq. (9.1) can be obtained via zeroing the partial derivative of nonlinear objective function $g(\boldsymbol{u}(t),t)$ with respective to $\boldsymbol{u}(t)$ at time instant. In this case, we introduce a new function $\boldsymbol{z}(\boldsymbol{u}(t),t)$ such that it satisfies the following condition:

$$\boldsymbol{z}(\boldsymbol{u}(t),t) = \frac{\partial g(\boldsymbol{u}(t),t)}{\partial \boldsymbol{u}(t)} = \boldsymbol{0} \in \mathbb{R}^n, \tag{9.2}$$

where $\frac{\partial g(\boldsymbol{u}(t),t)}{\partial \boldsymbol{u}(t)} = [\frac{\partial g(\boldsymbol{u}(t),t)}{\partial u_1}, \frac{\partial g(\boldsymbol{u}(t),t)}{\partial u_2}, \ldots, \frac{\partial g(\boldsymbol{u}(t),t)}{\partial u_n}]^{\mathrm{T}} = \boldsymbol{0}$. Thus, the optimal solution of Eq. (9.1) is equivalent to the solution of the aforementioned system of nonlinear equations. In other words, via the aforementioned transform, we only need to solve Eq. (9.2) to equivalently find the optimal solution of time-dependent nonlinear minimization (9.1).

9.2.2 ZNN Model

For completeness of this work, ZNN was developed for such time-dependent nonlinear minimization [11–15]. How it has been designed is simply illustrated via equivalently solving the previous nonlinear equation system (9.2).

In the first place, based on the transformation of time-dependent nonlinear minimization (9.2), we are capable of defining a monitor error function as follows:

$$\boldsymbol{y}(t) = \left[\frac{\partial g(\boldsymbol{u}(t),t)}{\partial u_1}, \frac{\partial g(\boldsymbol{u}(t),t)}{\partial u_2}, \ldots, \frac{\partial g(\boldsymbol{u}(t),t)}{\partial u_n}\right]^{\mathrm{T}}, \tag{9.3}$$

where $y(t)$ is a vector-valued error function, and the time-dependent behavior of each element itself can be monitored. If $y(t) = 0$ is checked, the corresponding solution is what we want.

Next, the following first-order nonlinear dynamic system is designed to make sure $y(t)$ converge to zero:

$$\dot{y}(t) + \varpi\Phi(y(t)) = 0, \tag{9.4}$$

where $\varpi > 0$ is a design parameter exploited to adjust the aforementioned dynamic system to converge to the equilibrium point, and $\Phi(\cdot)$ stands for a nonlinear activation function array with each element denoted by $\phi(\cdot)$.

Substituting (9.3) into (9.4), we are further capable of deriving the following expression:

$$\begin{cases} \dfrac{\partial^2 g(u(t),t)}{\partial u_1 \partial t} + \varpi\phi\left(\dfrac{\partial g(u(t),t)}{\partial u_1}\right) = 0, \\ \dfrac{\partial^2 g(u(t),t)}{\partial u_2 \partial t} + \varpi\phi\left(\dfrac{\partial g(u(t),t)}{\partial u_2}\right) = 0, \\ \qquad\qquad\vdots \\ \dfrac{\partial^2 g(u(t),t)}{\partial u_n \partial t} + \varpi\phi\left(\dfrac{\partial g(u(t),t)}{\partial u_n}\right) = 0. \end{cases} \tag{9.5}$$

In addition, $\forall i = 1, 2, \ldots, n$, we have

$$\frac{\partial^2 g}{\partial u_i \partial t} = \frac{\partial^2 g}{\partial u_i \partial u_1}\dot{u}_1(t) + \frac{\partial^2 g}{\partial u_i \partial u_2}\dot{u}_2(t) + \cdots + \frac{\partial^2 g}{\partial u_i \partial u_n}\dot{u}_n(t) + \frac{\partial^2 g}{\partial u_i \partial t},$$

where g is used to denote $g(u(t), t)$ for presentation convenience.

After combining the aforementioned derivation results and considering $\partial g(u(t), t)/\partial u(t) = z(u(t), t)$, we obtain the following ZNN for calculating time-dependent nonlinear minimization (9.1) and the resultant nonlinear equation system (9.2):

$$Q(u(t), t)\dot{u}(t) = -\varpi\Phi(z(u(t), t)) - \frac{\partial z(u(t), t)}{\partial t}, \tag{9.6}$$

where coefficient matrix $Q(u(t), t)$ and vector $\frac{\partial z(u(t),t)}{\partial t}$ are defined as

$$Q(u(t), t) = \begin{bmatrix} \dfrac{\partial^2 g}{\partial u_1 \partial u_1} & \dfrac{\partial^2 g}{\partial u_1 \partial u_2} & \cdots & \dfrac{\partial^2 g}{\partial u_1 \partial u_n} \\ \dfrac{\partial^2 g}{\partial u_2 \partial u_1} & \dfrac{\partial^2 g}{\partial u_2 \partial u_2} & \cdots & \dfrac{\partial^2 g}{\partial u_2 \partial u_n} \\ \vdots & \vdots & \ddots & \vdots \\ \dfrac{\partial^2 g}{\partial u_n \partial u_1} & \dfrac{\partial^2 g}{\partial u_n \partial u_2} & \cdots & \dfrac{\partial^2 g}{\partial u_n \partial u_n} \end{bmatrix},$$

$$\frac{\partial z(u(t), t)}{\partial t} = \begin{bmatrix} \dfrac{\partial^2 g}{\partial u_1 \partial t} & \dfrac{\partial^2 g}{\partial u_2 \partial t} & \cdots & \dfrac{\partial^2 g}{\partial u_n \partial t} \end{bmatrix}^{\mathrm{T}}.$$

Besides, it has been proved that such a ZNN model (9.6) is capable of converging to the optimal solution of nonlinear minimization as well as nonlinear equation system (9.2).

9.2.3 RZNN Model

Note that the aforementioned ZNN model (9.6) for time-dependent nonlinear minimization does not consider the impact of external disturbances, and may lose efficacy when external noises are injected. For modifying the robustness of ZNN model (9.6), in 2015, an inherent noise-tolerance design formula for ZNN was presented in [16, 17], which is repeated as follows for easy reading:

$$\dot{y}(t) + \gamma_1 y(t) + \gamma_2 \int_0^t y(\tau)\mathrm{d}\tau = 0, \tag{9.7}$$

where $\gamma_1 > 0$ and $\gamma_2 > 0$ stand for two different scaling factors. It has been proved that design formula (9.7) possesses the inherent noise-tolerance ability, even in front of dynamic noises. However, in design formula (9.7), nonlinear activation function $\Phi(\cdot)$ is deleted, which makes (9.7) only achieve the exponential convergence (i.e. infinite-time convergence) [18–20], although the inherent noise tolerance is considered for the design of ZNN.

Based on the inherent noise-tolerance design formula (9.7), we are capable of gaining the robust zeroing neural network (RZNN) for time-dependent nonlinear minimization (9.1) via substituting (9.3) into it:

$$Q\dot{U} = -\gamma_1 z - \gamma_2 \int_0^t z\mathrm{d}\tau - \frac{\partial z}{\partial t}, \tag{9.8}$$

where independent variable t is omitted for presentation convenience; and coefficient matrix Q and vector $\frac{\partial z}{\partial t}$ are defined as the same ones of ZNN model (9.6). In addition, it has been proved that RZNN model (9.8) is capable of solving time-dependent nonlinear minimization (9.1) under various additive noises [16, 17]. However, due to elimination of nonlinear activation function $\Phi(\cdot)$, such an RZNN model (9.8) is not able to reach limited-time convergence [18–20].

9.3 Design and Analysis of R-FTZNN

Considering the limitations of the previous two ZNN models, in this part, the R-FTZNN model is devised and studied to solve time-dependent nonlinear minimization (9.1) as well as the equivalent nonlinear equation system (9.2). Before that, a new second-order nonlinear dynamic system is developed and analyzed in details, which is used to establish the R-FTZNN model. Compared to ZNN model (9.6) and RZNN model (9.8) for time-dependent nonlinear minimization (9.1), the proposed R-FTZNN model simultaneously possesses the limited-time convergence and inherent noise tolerance.

9.3.1 Second-Order Nonlinear Formula

The aforementioned first-order nonlinear formula (9.4) purely considers the convergence property, which may confine its real-time applications when external disturbances exist; while the nonlinear formula (9.7) only considers the inherent noise-tolerance property, which may confine its online computing applications. That is to say, such two nonlinear formulas have either limited-time convergence or noise suppression property [16–20]. In order to overcome this limitation, a new second-order nonlinear system is devised to realize limited-time convergence and noise tolerance. The specific expression is formulated as the following second-order nonlinear system:

$$\dot{\boldsymbol{y}}(t) + \gamma_1 \Phi(\boldsymbol{y}(t)) + \gamma_2 \Phi\left(\boldsymbol{y}(t) + \gamma_1 \int_0^t \Phi(\boldsymbol{y}(\tau))\mathrm{d}\tau\right) = 0, \tag{9.9}$$

where $\gamma_1 > 0$, $\gamma_2 > 0$, and $\Phi(\cdot)$ are defined the same as before. In addition, the following theoretical results are given to demonstrate the advantages of the proposed second-order nonlinear system (9.9).

Theorem 9.1 *The second-order nonlinear system (9.9) is globally stable as long as $\Phi(\cdot)$ is a monotonic increasing odd function.*

Proof: Note that (9.9) is a vector-valued function. We first consider the jth subsystem of (9.9), which is described as ($\forall j \in 1, 2, \ldots, n$):

$$\dot{y}_j(t) + \gamma_1 \phi(y_j(t)) + \gamma_2 \phi\left(y_j(t) + \gamma_1 \int_0^t \phi(y_j(\tau))\mathrm{d}\tau\right) = 0, \tag{9.10}$$

where $\phi(\cdot)$ is the element of $\Phi(\cdot)$. Then, we are capable of defining an auxiliary variable $s_j(t)$, and its expression is described as

$$s_j(t) = y_j(t) + \gamma_1 \int_0^t \phi(y_j(\tau))\mathrm{d}\tau. \tag{9.11}$$

Taking a derivative of (9.11) with respect to time t, we have

$$\dot{s}_j(t) = \dot{y}_j(t) + \gamma_1 \phi(y_j(t)). \tag{9.12}$$

Combining (9.10), (9.11), and (9.12) yields to the following fact:

$$\dot{s}_j(t) + \gamma_2 \phi(s_j(t)) = 0, \tag{9.13}$$

which is exactly the jth subsystem of (9.4). Based on the previous conclusion [11, 12, 14, 15, 21], we know that such a subsystem (9.13) is capable of converging to its equilibrium point, even within finite time provided that $\phi(\cdot)$ is selected appropriately.

Next, let us consider the following Lyapunov function candidate $p_j(t)$ for the jth subsystem (9.10):

$$p_j(t) = \frac{1}{2}\zeta y_j^2(t) + \frac{1}{2}s_j^2(t), \tag{9.14}$$

where $\zeta > 0$ and $p_0 = p_j(0) = \zeta y_j^2(0)/2 + s_j^2(0)/2$ with $y_j(0)$ and $s_j(0)$ known. Its time derivative is derived as

$$
\begin{aligned}
\frac{dp_j(t)}{dt} &= \zeta y_j(t)\dot{y}_j(t) + s_j(t)\dot{s}_j(t) \\
&= \zeta y_j(t)[\dot{s}_j(t) - \gamma_1\phi(y_j(t))] - \gamma_2 s_j(t)\phi(s_j(t)) \\
&= -\zeta\gamma_2 y_j(t)\phi(s_j(t)) - \zeta\gamma_1 y_j(t)\phi(y_j(t)) - \gamma_2 s_j(t)\phi(s_j(t)).
\end{aligned} \tag{9.15}
$$

Since $\phi(\cdot)$ is a monotonic increasing odd function, we can apply the mean-value theorem to further simplify the aforementioned expression. Thus, we have

$$\phi(s_j(t)) - \phi(0) = (s_j(t) - 0)\frac{\partial\phi(s_j(\vartheta))}{\partial s_j}\Big|_{s_j(\vartheta)\in R}. \tag{9.16}$$

In addition, in a similar way, we can also conclude $\phi(0) = 0$ and $\partial\phi(s_j(t))/\partial s_j > 0$. Thus, from (9.16), the following result can be further derived as

$$|\phi(s_j(t))| \le a_0|s_j(t)|,$$

where $a_0 = \max\{\partial\phi(s_j(t))/\partial s_j\}|_{s_j(t)\in R} > 0$. Furthermore, we have

$$
\begin{aligned}
|y_j(t)\phi(s_j(t))| &\le |y_j(t)| \cdot |\phi(s_j(t))| \\
&\le a_0|y_j(t)| \cdot |s_j(t)|.
\end{aligned} \tag{9.17}
$$

Let us substitute (9.17) back into (9.15), and the following fact is gained:

$$
\begin{aligned}
\frac{dp_j(t)}{dt} &= -\zeta\gamma_2 y_j(t)\phi(s_j(t)) - \zeta\gamma_1 y_j(t)\phi(y_j(t)) \\
&\quad - \gamma_2 s_j(t)\phi(s_j(t)) \\
&\le \zeta\gamma_2|y_j(t)\phi(s_j(t))| - \zeta\gamma_1 y_j(t)\phi(y_j(t)) \\
&\quad - \gamma_2 s_j(t)\phi(s_j(t)) \\
&\le \zeta\gamma_2 a_0|y_j(t)| \cdot |s_j(t)| - \zeta\gamma_1 a_1 y_j^2(t) - \gamma_2 a_2 s_j^2(t) \\
&= -\zeta\left(\sqrt{\gamma_1 a_1}|y_j| - \frac{\gamma_2 a_0}{2\sqrt{\gamma_1 a_1}}|s_j(t)|\right)^2 - \zeta\left(\frac{\gamma_2 a_2}{\zeta} - \frac{\gamma_2^2 a_0^2}{4\gamma_1 a_1}\right)s_j^2(t),
\end{aligned} \tag{9.18}
$$

where coefficients $a_1 = \min\{\partial\phi(y_j(t))/\partial y_j\}|_{y_j(t)\in R}$ and $a_2 = \min\{\partial\phi(s_j(t))/\partial s_j\}|_{s_j(t)\in R}$ that are gained by applying the mean-value theorem two times. As seen from (9.18), we can easily draw a conclusion $\dot{p}_j(t) \le 0$ provided that

$$\frac{\gamma_2 a_2}{\zeta} - \frac{\gamma_2^2 a_0^2}{4\gamma_1 a_1} \ge 0 \text{ and } \zeta > 0, \text{ i.e. } 0 < \zeta \le \frac{4\gamma_1 a_1 a_2}{\gamma_2 a_0^2}. \tag{9.19}$$

Based on Lyapunov stability theory, we know that the jth subsystem (9.10) is globally stable. Since the second-order nonlinear system (9.9) is consist of n subsystems of (9.10), we conclude that the second-order nonlinear system (9.9) is globally stable as long as $\Phi(\cdot)$ is a monotonic increasing odd function. This completes the proof. ∎

Theorem 9.2 *The second-order nonlinear system (9.9) is capable of converging to the equilibrium point within finite time, and its convergence upper bound t_f is*

$$t_f < \frac{\gamma_1 + \gamma_2}{\gamma_1 \gamma_2 (1 - \alpha)} \max\left\{ |y^-(0)|^{1-\alpha}, |y^+(0)|^{1-\alpha} \right\},$$

provided that $\phi(y) = \left(|y|^\alpha + |y|^{1/\alpha} \right) \operatorname{sgn}(y)$ with $0 < \alpha < 1$, where $\operatorname{sgn}(\cdot)$ denotes the sign function, and the initial errors $y^+(0) = \max\{y(t)\}$ and $y^-(0) = \min\{y(t)\}$.

Proof: For the jth subsystem of (9.9), via introducing $s_j(t) = y_j(t) + \gamma_1 \int_0^t \phi(y_j(\tau))\mathrm{d}\tau$, we are capable of gaining $\dot{s}_j(t) = -\gamma_2 \phi(s_j(t))$. Especially, when $t = 0$, we can obtain $s_j(0) = y_j(0)$. Besides, the Lyapunov function candidate $p_j(t) = s_j^2(t)$ is selected to compute finite convergence time of nonlinear dynamic system $\dot{s}_j(t) = -\gamma_2 \phi(s_j(t))$ [18–20]. Its time derivative is computed as follows:

$$\dot{p}_j(t) = 2s_j(t)\dot{s}_j(t)$$
$$= -2\gamma_2 s_j(t)\phi(s_j(t))$$
$$= -2\gamma_2 \left(|s_j(t)|^{\alpha+1} + |s_j(t)|^{\frac{1}{\alpha}+1} \right)$$
$$\leq -2\gamma_2 |s_j(t)|^{\alpha+1}$$
$$= -2\gamma_2 p_j(t)^{\frac{\alpha+1}{2}},$$

where $\phi(s_j) = \left(|s_j|^p + |s_j|^{1/\alpha} \right) \operatorname{sgn}(s_j)$. Then, solving inequality $\dot{p}_j(t) \leqslant -2\gamma_2 p_j(t)^{\frac{\alpha+1}{2}}$ with $p_j(0) = |s_j(0)|^2 = |y_j(0)|^2$, one can obtain:

$$p_j(t)^{\frac{1-\alpha}{2}} \begin{cases} \leq |s_j(0)|^{1-\alpha} - \gamma_2 t(1 - \alpha), & \text{if } \ t \leq \frac{|s_j(0)|^{1-\alpha}}{\gamma_2(1-\alpha)}, \\ = 0, & \text{if } \ t > \frac{|s_j(0)|^{1-\alpha}}{\gamma_2(1-\alpha)}, \end{cases}$$

which shows that s_j converges to zero when $t > |s_j(0)|^{1-\alpha}/\gamma_2(1 - \alpha)$. Owing to $p_j(t) = s_j^2(t)$ and $s_j(0) = y_j(0)$, it can also be concluded that $s_j(t)$ converges to zero after $t > |y_j(0)|^{1-\alpha}/\gamma_2(1 - \alpha)$.

Since all elements in $s(t)$ have the same dynamics $\dot{s}_j(t) = -\gamma_2 \phi(s_j(t))$, $s(t)$ converges to zero when $t > \max\left\{ |y^-(0)|^{1-\alpha}, |y^+(0)|^{1-\alpha} \right\}/\gamma_2(1 - \alpha)$, where $y^+(0) = \max\{y(t)\}$ and $y^-(0) = \min\{y(t)\}$. Therefore, the upper bound t_1 for $s(t)$ is calculated as

$$t_1 < \frac{1}{\gamma_2(1 - \alpha)} \max\left\{ |y^-(0)|^{1-\alpha}, |y^+(0)|^{1-\alpha} \right\}.$$

The convergence upper bound for $s(t)$ is thus completed.

From the aforementioned discussion, when $t > t_1$, $\boldsymbol{u}(t)$ converges to the equilibrium point, and thus $\dot{\boldsymbol{u}}(t) = 0$. Based on (9.12), when $t > t_1$, we have

$$\dot{y}_j(t) + \gamma_1 \phi(y_j(t)) = 0, \tag{9.20}$$

which is exactly the same form of $\dot{s}_j(t) + \gamma_2 \phi(s_j(t)) = 0$. Considering the different parameters of these two dynamic systems, we are able to compute the convergence upper bound t_2 as follows:

$$t_2 < \frac{1}{\gamma_1(1-\alpha)} \max \left\{ |y^-(0)|^{1-\alpha}, |y^+(0)|^{1-\alpha} \right\},$$

where $y^+(0)$ and $y^-(0)$ are defined as before.

All in all, by generalizing the aforementioned two conclusions, one can conclude that the second-order nonlinear system (9.9) is capable of converging to the equilibrium point in a limited time, and its convergence upper bound t_f is

$$t_f < t_1 + t_2 = \frac{\gamma_1 + \gamma_2}{\gamma_1 \gamma_2 (1-\alpha)} \max \left\{ |y^-(0)|^{1-\alpha}, |y^+(0)|^{1-\alpha} \right\}.$$

This completes the proof. ∎

In order to study the robustness property of the second-order nonlinear system (9.9) when external disturbances are injected into this system, we consider an unknown additive constant noise v. Thus, the noise-disturbed second-order nonlinear dynamic system can be described as

$$\dot{\boldsymbol{y}}(t) = -\gamma_1 \Phi(\boldsymbol{y}(t)) - \gamma_2 \Phi \left(\boldsymbol{y}(t) + \gamma_1 \int_0^t \Phi(\boldsymbol{y}(\tau)) \mathrm{d}\tau \right) + v, \tag{9.21}$$

where v represents an unknown additive constant noise. Next, let us prove the inherent noise tolerant property of the aforementioned noise-disturbed nonlinear dynamic system (9.21).

Theorem 9.3 *The noise-disturbed second-order nonlinear dynamic system (9.21) is capable of globally convergent to zero under additive constant noise v.*

Proof: Let us consider the jth subsystem of (9.21), which is described as

$$\dot{y}_j(t) = -\gamma_1 \phi(y_j(t)) - \gamma_2 \phi \left(y_j(t) + \gamma_1 \int_0^t \phi(y_j(\tau)) \mathrm{d}\tau \right) + v. \tag{9.22}$$

As the same as Theorem 9.1, we also introduce a new variable $s_j(t)$, which is defined as the same with (9.11). Its time derivative is thus gained as $\dot{s}_j(t) = \dot{y}_j(t) + \gamma_1 \phi(y_j(t))$. Then, substituting the expressions of $s_j(t)$ and $\dot{s}_j(t)$ into (9.22), we have the fact:

$$\dot{s}_j(t) = -\gamma_2 \phi(s_j(t)) + v. \tag{9.23}$$

According to the aforementioned results, we are capable of defining the following Lyapunov function for the jth subsystem (9.22):

$$p_j(t) = \left(\gamma_2\phi(s_j(t)) - v\right)^2/2.$$

Its time derivative $\dot{p}_j(t)$ is gained as follows:

$$
\begin{aligned}
\frac{dp_j(t)}{dt} &= \left(\gamma_2\phi(s_j(t)) - v\right)\gamma_2\frac{\partial\phi(s_j(t))}{\partial s_j}\dot{s}_j(t) \\
&= -\gamma_2\frac{\partial\phi(s_j(t))}{\partial s_j}\left(\gamma_2\phi(s_j(t)) - v\right)^2.
\end{aligned}
\tag{9.24}
$$

Since $\phi(\cdot)$ is a monotonic increasing odd activation function, we have $\frac{\partial\phi(s_j(t))}{\partial s_j} > 0$. Therefore, we can obtain $\dot{p}_j(t) \leq 0$, and $\lim_{t\to\infty}p_j(t) = 0$. At this time, $\lim_{t\to\infty}\gamma_2\phi(s_j(t)) - v = 0$ and $\lim_{t\to\infty}s_j(t) = \phi_2^{-1}(v/\gamma_2)$. Thus, we have $\lim_{t\to\infty}\dot{s}_j(t) = -\gamma_2\phi(s_j(t)) + v = 0$.

On the other hand, due to $\dot{s}_j(t) = \dot{y}_j(t) + \gamma_1\phi(y_j(t))$ and $\lim_{t\to\infty}\dot{s}_j(t) = 0$, and basis on Lasalle's invariant set principle [22–24], it can be concluded that $\dot{s}_j(t) = \dot{y}_j(t) + \gamma_1\phi(y_j(t))$ reduces to

$$\dot{y}_j(t) + \gamma_1\phi(y_j(t)) = 0, \tag{9.25}$$

which is the aforementioned nonlinear system. In addition, it has been proved that this nonlinear dynamic system is capable of converging to its equilibrium point exponentially.

According to the aforementioned analyses, we conclude that, under unknown additive constant noise v, the noise-disturbed second-order nonlinear dynamic system (9.21) is capable of globally converging to zero. This completes the proof. ■

9.3.2 R-FTZNN Model

Based on the aforementioned proposed second-order nonlinear dynamic formula (9.9), a robust finite-time zeroing neural network (R-FTZNN) has been established and analyzed for time-dependent nonlinear minimization (9.1) and its equivalent nonlinear equation system (9.2). The detailed design process and theoretical analysis are presented as follows.

At first, we are capable of defining the following monitor error function similarly:

$$\boldsymbol{y}(t) = \left[\frac{\partial g\left(\boldsymbol{u}(t), t\right)}{\partial u_1}, \frac{\partial g\left(\boldsymbol{u}(t), t\right)}{\partial u_2}, \ldots, \frac{\partial g\left(\boldsymbol{u}(t), t\right)}{\partial u_n}\right]^{\mathrm{T}}. \tag{9.26}$$

Then, according to error function (9.26), the proposed second-order nonlinear dynamic formula is adopted to establish the R-FTZNN model. For maintaining the coherence of reading, such a second-order nonlinear dynamic formula is presented again as follows:

$$\dot{y}(t) + \gamma_1 \Phi(y(t)) + \gamma_2 \Phi \left(y(t) + \gamma_1 \int_0^t \Phi(y(\tau)) d\tau \right) = \mathbf{0}.$$

Substituting (9.26) into the aforementioned second-order nonlinear dynamic formula and considering $y(t) = \partial g(u(t), t) / \partial u(t) = z(u(t), t)$, we are capable of gaining the R-FTZNN model for solving time-dependent nonlinear minimization (9.1) and its equivalent nonlinear equation system (9.2) as follows:

$$Q\dot{u} = -\gamma_1 \Phi(z) - \gamma_2 \Phi \left(z + \gamma_1 \int_0^t \Phi(z) d\tau \right) - \frac{\partial z}{\partial t}, \tag{9.27}$$

where independent variable t is omitted for presentation convenience; and coefficient matrix Q and vector $\frac{\partial z}{\partial t}$ are defined as the same ones of RZNN model (9.8).

If external disturbances are injected in R-FTZNN model (9.27), the noise-tolerant R-FTZNN model is directly given next via considering the noise-disturbed second-order nonlinear dynamic system (9.21):

$$Q\dot{u} = -\gamma_1 \Phi(z) - \gamma_2 \Phi \left(z + \gamma_1 \int_0^t \Phi(z) d\tau \right) - \frac{\partial z}{\partial t} + v. \tag{9.28}$$

After proposing the aforementioned R-FTZNN models, we proceed to prove the superior finite-convergence and noise-tolerant properties via the following theorems.

Theorem 9.4 *The neural output $u(t)$ of R-FTZNN model (9.27) is capable of converging to the optimal solution $u^*(t)$ of time-dependent nonlinear minimization (9.1).*

Proof: As observed in the design process of R-FTZNN model (9.27), we can conclude that R-FTZNN model (9.27) is an equivalent extended form of the second-order nonlinear formula (9.9) via defining $y(t) = \frac{\partial g(u(t), t)}{\partial u(t)} = z(u(t), t)$. Then, according to Theorem 9.1, it follows that R-FTZNN model (9.27) is globally stable. Therefore, neural output $u(t)$ of R-FTZNN model (9.27) globally converges to the optimal solution $u^*(t)$ of time-dependent nonlinear minimization (9.1). This completes the proof. ∎

Theorem 9.5 *The neural output $u(t)$ of R-FTZNN model (9.27) is capable of converging to the optimal solution $u^*(t)$ of time-dependent nonlinear minimization (9.1) within finite time, with the convergence upper bound t_f being*

$$t_f < \frac{\gamma_1 + \gamma_2}{\gamma_1 \gamma_2 (1 - \alpha)} \max \left\{ |y^-(0)|^{1-\alpha}, |y^+(0)|^{1-\alpha} \right\},$$

as long as $\phi(y) = \left(|y|^\alpha + |y|^{1/\alpha} \right) \text{sgn}(y)$ with $0 < \alpha < 1$, where $\text{sgn}(\cdot)$ denotes the sign function, and $y^+(0) = \max\{y(t)\}$ and $y^-(0) = \min\{y(t)\}$.

Proof: We can complete the proof in a similar way according to previous theorems. ∎

Theorem 9.6 *The neural output $\boldsymbol{u}(t)$ of the noise tolerant R-FTZNN model (9.28) is capable of converging to the optimal solution $\boldsymbol{u}^*(t)$ of time-dependent nonlinear minimization (9.1) even in the presence of unknown additive constant noises.*

Proof: We can complete the proof in a similar way according to previous theorems. ∎

9.4 Illustrative Verification

To demonstrate the superior property of R-FTZNN model (9.27) for time-dependent nonlinear minimization (9.2), ZNN model (9.6) and RZNN model (9.8) are also applied to solve a time-dependent nonlinear minimization problem under various different noises. Note that ZNN (9.6) and R-FTZNN (9.27) are activated by the sign-bi-power function $\phi(y) = \left(|y|^\alpha + |y|^{1/\alpha}\right) \text{sgn}(y)$ with $\alpha = 0.8$. Now, we consider the following solvable nonlinear minimization example:

$$\min_{\boldsymbol{u}(t)\in\mathbb{R}^4} g\left(\boldsymbol{u}(t), t\right), \quad \forall t \in [0, \infty), \tag{9.29}$$

where $\boldsymbol{u}(t) = [u_1(t), u_2(t), u_3(t), u_4(t)]^{\text{T}}$ and the expression of $g\left(\boldsymbol{u}(t), t\right)$ is defined as

$$
\begin{aligned}
g = &(u_1 + t)^2 + (u_2 + t)^2 + (u_3 - \exp(-t))^2 \\
&+ (u_4 - \exp(-t))^2 + (u_1 + \sin(t))u_3 \\
&- (u_1 + \ln(0.1t + 1))(u_2 + \sin(t)) + 0.1(t - 1)u_3 u_4
\end{aligned}
$$

with independent variable t deleted for presentation convenience. Furthermore, $\boldsymbol{z}(\boldsymbol{u}(t), t)$ can be obtained as

$$
\boldsymbol{z} = \begin{cases}
2(u_1 + t) + u_3 - (u_2 + \sin(t)) = 0, \\
2(u_2 + t) - (u_1 + \ln(0.1t + 1)) = 0, \\
2(u_3 - \exp(-t)) + (u_1 + \sin(t)) + 0.1(t - 1)u_4 = 0, \\
2(u_4 - \exp(-t)) + 0.1(t - 1)u_3 = 0.
\end{cases}
$$

In this example, we consider different situations according to the types of external disturbances. In general, constant and dynamic noises are two kinds of major representatives of external disturbances. Therefore, in the following simulations, we mainly consider the constant and dynamic noises as external disturbances.

9.4.1 Constant Noise

First, the constant noise $v = 0.5$ is taken into account. From a starting point located in $\boldsymbol{u}(0) \in [-4, 4]^4$, such three neural-network models are explored to address the aforementioned nonlinear minimization problem under the same conditions. Computer simulative results are comparatively displayed in Figures 9.1–9.3. Figure 9.1 displays the computing results generated by ZNN (9.6) under design parameter $\varpi = 5$. Because ZNN model (9.6) is activated by the sign-bi-power function, the residual error decreases quickly at first. However, $\|z(u(t), t)\|_2$ does not converge to 0 finally. That is to say, ZNN model (9.6) cannot suppress external noises so that it generates a relatively large error. Figure 9.2 shows the computing results generated by RZNN model (9.8) with design parameters $\gamma_1 = \gamma_2 = 5$. As seen from this figure, the residual error $\|z(u(t), t)\|_2$ can converge to 0 but it needs about five seconds. The convergence time is relatively longer. At last, under the same conditions, Figure 9.3 shows the computing results generated by

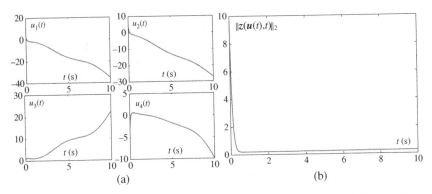

Figure 9.1 Computing nonlinear minimization problem by ZNN model (9.6) using the sign-bi-power activation function with $\varpi = 5$ in front of constant noise $v = 0.5$. (a) Neural output $U(t)$. (b) Residual error $\|z(u(t), t)\|_2$.

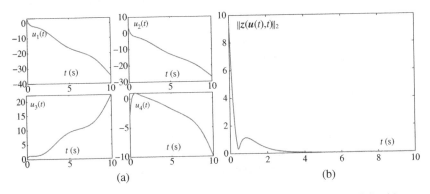

Figure 9.2 Computing nonlinear minimization problem by RZNN model (9.8) with $\gamma_1 = \gamma_2 = 5$ in front of constant noise $v = 0.5$. (a) Neural output $U(t)$. (b) Residual error $\|z(u(t), t)\|_2$.

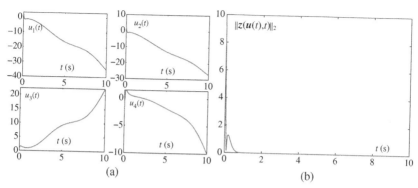

Figure 9.3 Computing nonlinear minimization problem by R-FTZNN model (9.27) using the sign-bi-power activation function with $\gamma_1 = \gamma_2 = 5$ in front of constant noise $v = 0.5$. (a) Neural output $U(t)$. (b) Residual error $\|z(u(t), t)\|_2$.

R-FTZNN model (9.27) with design parameters $\gamma_1 = \gamma_2 = 5$. It follows from this figure that $\|z(u(t), t)\|_2$ can decrease to 0 quickly within limited time 0.8 second. The convergence speed of residual error $\|z(u(t), t)\|_2$ solved by R-FTZNN model (9.27) is about six times faster than that by RZNN model (9.8). The results show that R-FTZNN model (9.27) is a best model for solving time-dependent nonlinear minimization (9.2) under constant noise, compared to ZNN model (9.6) and RZNN model (9.8).

9.4.2 Dynamic Noise

In this part, a more general situation is considered: dynamic noise, which exists more frequently in practical engineering fields. Without losing generality, such a dynamic noise is set as $v = 2\sin(t)$. Then, we apply ZNN (9.6), RZNN (9.8), and R-FTZNN (9.27) to compute the aforementioned example under dynamic noise $v = 2\sin(t)$. With design parameters $\varpi = \gamma_1 = \gamma_2 = 10$, and from a starting point located in $u(0) \in [-4, 4]^4$, simulative results are comparatively generated in Figures 9.4–9.6, from which we are able to draw a conclusion that the residual error generated by ZNN (9.6) is always changing with the direction of the dynamic noise $v = 2\sin(t)$; the residual error generated by RZNN (9.8) can decrease to 0 but its convergence speed is slow; and the residual error generated by R-FTZNN model (9.27) is capable of decreasing to zero with finite time 0.5 second and the convergence time is the shortest. Although the additive noise is dynamic, R-FTZNN model (9.27) is still capable of suppressing the external disturbance. In addition, the convergence speed still achieves finite time. These facts further demonstrate the advantage of R-FTZNN model (9.27) for solving time-dependent nonlinear minimization problems.

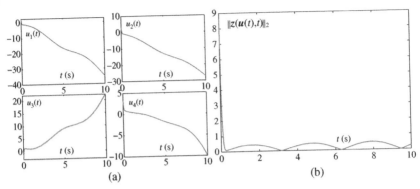

Figure 9.4 Computing nonlinear minimization problem by ZNN model (9.6) using the sign-bi-power activation function with $\varpi = 10$ under constant noise $v = 2\sin(t)$. (a) Neural output $u(t)$. (b) Residual error $\|z(u(t), t)\|_2$.

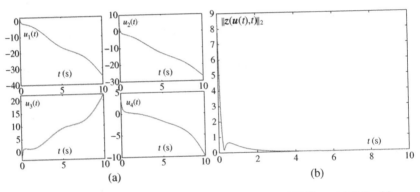

Figure 9.5 Computing nonlinear minimization problem by RZNN model (9.8) with $\gamma_1 = \gamma_2 = 10$ under dynamic noise $v = 2\sin(t)$. (a) Neural output $u(t)$. (b) Residual error $\|z(u(t), t)\|_2$.

We conduct further simulations by using such three models with other conditions unchanged under different types of noises. The bounded additive noise is considered firstly, which is set as $v = 15$. With the other conditions unchanged, the convergence behavior of residual error $\|z(u(t), t)\|_2$ produced by R-FTZNN (9.27), ZNN (9.6), and RZNN (9.8) is shown in Figure 9.7a. When disturbed by the bounded noise, R-FTZNN model (9.27) can still achieve noise suppression and limited-time convergence, while ZNN model (9.6) and RZNN model (9.8) cannot converge to 0 within limited time. Besides, we further investigate the linearly increasing noise, which is set as $v = 3t$. With other conditions unchanged, the corresponding convergence behavior of residual error $\|z(u(t), t)\|_2$ is shown in Figure 9.7b, which demonstrates that R-FTZNN model (9.27) is still effective, while the other models completely lose efficacy.

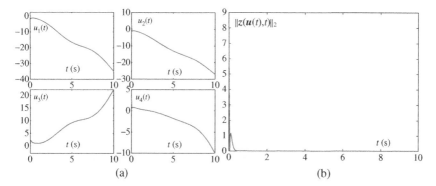

(a)   (b)

Figure 9.6 Computing nonlinear minimization problem by R-FTZNN model (9.27) using the sign-bi-power activation function with $\gamma_1 = \gamma_2 = 10$ in front of dynamic noise $v = 2\sin(t)$. (a) Neural output $\boldsymbol{u}(t)$. (b) Residual error $\|\boldsymbol{z}(\boldsymbol{u}(t), t)\|_2$.

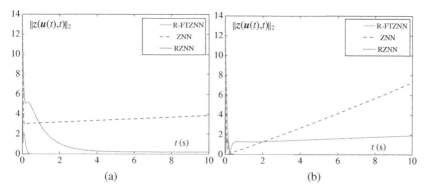

(a)   (b)

Figure 9.7 Residual error $\|\boldsymbol{z}(\boldsymbol{u}(t), t)\|_2$ generated by R-FTZNN model (9.8), ZNN model (9.6), and RZNN model (9.8) with $\varpi = \gamma_1 = \gamma_2 = 10$ in front of different types of noises. (a) Bounded additive noise $v = 15$. (b) Linearly increasing noise $v = 3t$.

In brief, we reach a decision that R-FTZNN model (9.27) is the best model for solving time-dependent nonlinear minimization problem even under various external disturbances.

9.5 Chapter Summary

Based on the second-order nonlinear design formula, the R-FTZNN model has been established according to the method of the ZNN for time-dependent nonlinear minimization. Rigorous theoretical analyses have been given to simultaneously achieve limited-time convergence and inherently noise suppression by the R-FTZNN model. In order to highlight the outstanding advantage of the R-FTZNN model, ZNN model and its improved model have been applied to time-dependent nonlinear minimization solving. Comparative numerical results have further validated the efficacy and advantage of the R-FTZNN model for nonlinear minimization. This work solves time-dependent nonlinear minimization in noisy environments by devising the R-FTZNN model with limited-time convergence and noise tolerance simultaneously, making a progress in theory.

References

1 Y. Zhang and H. Gong *et al.*, Stepsize range and optimal value for Taylor-Zhang discretization formula applied to zeroing neurodynamics illustrated via future equality-constrained quadratic programming, *IEEE Trans. Neural Netw. Learn. Syst.*, 30(3) (2019) 959–966.

2 H. Wang and P. X. Liu *et al.*, Adaptive neural output-feedback control for a class of nonlower triangular nonlinear systems with unmodeled dynamics, *IEEE Trans. Neural Netw. Learn. Syst.*, 29(8) (2018) 3658–3668.

3 L. Xiao, Z. Zhang, and S. Li, Solving time-varying system of nonlinear equations by finite-time recurrent neural networks with application to motion tracking of robot manipulators, *IEEE Trans. Syst. Man Cybern. Syst.*, 49(11) (2019) 2210–2220.

4 Z. Zhang and L. Zheng *et al.*, A new varying-parameter recurrent neural-network for online solution of time-varying Sylvester equation, *IEEE Trans. Cybern.*, 48(11) (2018) 3135–3148.

5 X. Xu and Z. Huang *et al.*, Manifold-based reinforcement learning via locally linear reconstruction, *IEEE Trans. Neural Netw. Learn. Syst.*, 28(4) (2017) 934–947.

6 J. Xu and B. Tang *et al.*, Semisupervised feature selection based on relevance and redundancy criteria, *IEEE Trans. Neural Netw. Learn. Syst.*, 28(9) (2017) 1974–1984.

7 D. Chen and Y. Zhang, Robust zeroing neural-dynamics and its time-varying disturbances suppression model applied to mobile robot manipulators, *IEEE Trans. Neural Netw. Learn. Syst.*, 29(9) (2018) 4385–4397.

8 Y. Zhang and S. Li, Predictive suboptimal consensus of multiagent systems with nonlinear dynamics, *IEEE Trans. Syst. Man Cybern. Syst.*, 47(7) (2017) 1701–1711.

9 W. Li and B. Liao *et al.*, A recurrent neural network with predefined-time convergence and improved noise tolerance for dynamic matrix square root finding, *Neurocomputing*, 337 (2019) 262–273.

10 D. Guo and Y. Zhang, Neural dynamics and Newton-Raphson iteration for nonlinear optimization, *J. Comput. Nonlinear Dynam.*, 9(2) (2014) 021016.

11 L. Jin and Y. Zhang, Continuous and discrete Zhang dynamics for realtime varying nonlinear optimization, *Numer. Algor.*, 73 (2016) 115–140.

12 L. Jin and Y. Zhang, Discrete-time Zhang neural network for online time-varying nonlinear optimization with application to manipulator motion generation, *IEEE Trans. Neural Netw. Learn. Syst.*, 26(7) (2015) 1525–1531.

13 Y. Zhang, D. Jiang, and J. Wang, A recurrent neural network for solving Sylvester equation with time-varying coefficients, *IEEE Trans. Neural Netw.*, 13(5) (2002) 1053–1063.

14 Y. Zhang and S. S. Ge, Design and analysis of a general recurrent neural network model for time-varying matrix inversion, *IEEE Trans. Neural Netw.*, 16(6) (2005) 1477–1490.

15 W. Li, L. Xiao, and B. Liao, A finite-time convergent and noise-rejection recurrent neural network and its discretization for dynamic nonlinear equations solving, *IEEE Trans. Cybern.*, 50(7) (2020) 3195–3207.

16 L. Jin, Y. Zhang, and S. Li, Integration-enhanced Zhang neural network for real-time-varying matrix inversion in the presence of various kinds of noises, *IEEE Trans. Neural Netw. Learn. Syst.*, 27(12) (2016) 2615–2627.

17 L. Xiao and S. Li *et al.*, Co-design of finite-time convergence and noise suppression: A unified neural model for time varying linear equations with robotic applications, *IEEE Trans. Syst. Man Cybern. Syst.*, 50(12) (2020) 5233–5243.

18 Y. Zhang and Y. Ding *et al.*, Signum-function array activated ZNN with easier circuit implementation and finite-time convergence for linear systems solving, *Inf. Process. Lett.*, 124 (2017) 30–34.

19 S. Li, S. Chen, and B. Liu, Accelerating a recurrent neural network to finite-time convergence for solving time-varying Sylvester equation by using a sign-bi-power activation function, *Neural Process. Lett.*, 37 (2013) 189–205.

20 L. Xiao, and R. Lu, Finite-time solution to nonlinear equation using recurrent neural dynamics with a specially-constructed activation function, *Neurocomputing*, 151 (2015) 246–251.

21 C. Yi, Y. Chen, and Z. Lu, Improved gradient-based neural networks for online solution of Lyapunov matrix equation, *Inf. Process. Lett.*, 111(16) (2011) 780–786.

22 L. Jin and S. Li *et al.*, Cooperative motion generation in a distributed network of redundant robot manipulators with noises, *IEEE Trans. Syst. Man Cybern. Syst.*, 48(10) (2018) 1715–1724.

23 Z. Tan and L. Xiao *et al.*, Noise-tolerant and finite-time convergent ZNN models for dynamic matrix Moore-Penrose inversion, *IEEE Trans. Ind. Inform.*, 16(3) (2020) 1591–1601.

24 L. Xiao, K. Li, and M. Duan, Computing time-varying quadratic optimization with finite-time convergence and noise tolerance: A unified framework for zeroing neural network, *IEEE Trans. Neural Netw. Learn. Syst.*, 30(11) (2019) 3360–3369.

10

FTZNN for Quadratic Optimization

10.1 Introduction

Quadratic optimization arises in diverse fields of science and engineering including communication processing [1], image processing [2], nonlinear control [3], motion planning and obstacle avoidance in robotics [4, 5], etc. In addition, several of realistic issues can be addressed by turning initial problems into quadratic optimization problems subject to equality constraints. For instance, the least square problem with linear-equality constraints can be regarded as a basic analytical form that is extensively exploited for system design and modeling [6, 7]. It is evident that the quadratic optimization has great importance both from the mathematical and practical viewpoints. This is reflected in the large number of approaches that have been proposed for solving quadratic optimization problems in real-time [6–11].

In this chapter, we propose a nonlinear finite-time zeroing neural network (N-FTZNN) model activated by a novel function, which is named weighted sign-bi-power activation function, for real-time solution of the equality-constrained quadratic optimization with nonstationary coefficients. The N-FTZNN model possesses much superior finite-time convergence. Furthermore, the upper bound of the finite convergence time is derived analytically according to Lyapunov theory. Now, in order to better show the advantages of the N-FTZNN model, the main differences between the N-FTZNN model and Ref. [12] are compared and listed in Table 10.1. As seen from the table, it can be concluded that only the weighted sign-bi-power activation function is an improved version from the original sign-bi-power activation function.

Zeroing Neural Networks: Finite-time Convergence Design, Analysis and Applications,
First Edition. Lin Xiao and Lei Jia.
© 2023 The Institute of Electrical and Electronics Engineers, Inc. Published 2023 by John Wiley & Sons, Inc.

Table 10.1 The main differences between this chapter and Ref. [12].

#	Item	Reference [12]	This chapter
1	Problem formulation	Sylvester equation	Quadratic optimization
2	Activation function	Sign-bi-power	Weighted sign-bi-power
3	Convergence	Finitely	Finitely (accelerated)
4	Proof method	More conservative	Less conservative

10.2 Problem Formulation

Let us discuss the following nonstationary quadratic optimization which is subject to the nonstationary equality constraint $f(\boldsymbol{u}(t), t) = 0 \in \mathbb{R}^m$:

$$\text{minimize} \quad \frac{1}{2}\boldsymbol{u}^{\mathrm{T}}(t)Q(t)\boldsymbol{u}(t) + \boldsymbol{q}^{\mathrm{T}}(t)\boldsymbol{u}(t), \tag{10.1}$$

$$\text{subject to} \quad f(\boldsymbol{u}(t), t) = 0, \tag{10.2}$$

where variable $\boldsymbol{u}(t) \in \mathbb{R}^n$ is unknown at time instant $t \in [0, +\infty)$ and needs to be found (with $\boldsymbol{u}^{\mathrm{T}}(t)$ denoting the transpose of $\boldsymbol{u}(t)$). In nonstationary quadratic optimization depicted in Eqs. (10.1) and (10.2), Hessian matrix $Q(t) \in \mathbb{R}^{n \times n}$ and coefficients $\boldsymbol{q}(t) \in \mathbb{R}^n$ are smoothly nonstationary. Besides, $f(\cdot)$ denotes a mapping function which can be linear or nonlinear. This chapter aims at proposing a nonlinearly activated neurodynamic model for solving the aforementioned nonstationary quadratic optimization problem and finding the finite-time solution $\boldsymbol{u}(t)$ in real time t. In order to illustrate the complexity of the interesting nonstationary quadratic optimization (10.1) and (10.2) as well as for better readability, the following nonstationary quadratic optimization is taken as an example:

$$\text{minimize} \quad \frac{1}{8}\left(sin(t) + 8\right)u_1^2(t) + \frac{1}{8}\left(cos(t) + 8\right)u_2^2(t)$$

$$+ cos(t)u_1(t)u_2(t) + sin(5t)u_1(t) + cos(5t)u_2(t), \tag{10.3}$$

$$\text{subject to} \quad sin(2t)u_1^2(t) + cos(2t)u_2(t) = cos(4t).$$

Figure 10.1 shows the three-dimension snapshots of the example at different time instants. As observed from the figure, we know that the objective-function surface and the nonlinear-constraint plane are both "moving" with time t. That is to say, the nonstationary optimization problem is a quite difficult problem because the optimal solution is also "moving" with time t due to the "moving" effects of the nonlinear-constraint plane and the objective-function surface.

Therefore, for the purposes of simplicity and clarity, and also to guarantee the solution uniqueness, we limit the discussion to the situation where $f(\boldsymbol{u}(t), t) = A(t)\boldsymbol{u}(t) - \boldsymbol{b}(t) = 0$ and Hessian matrix $Q(t) \in \mathbb{R}^{n \times n}$ is positive-definite, although

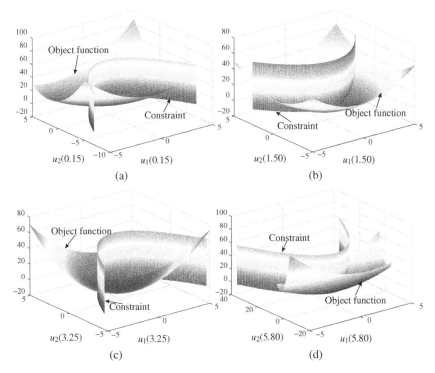

Figure 10.1 "Moving" nonlinear constraint, "Moving" objective function, and "Moving" optimal solution of nonstationary quadratic optimization (10.1) and (10.2). (a) Snapshot at $t = 0.15$ second. (b) Snapshot at $t = 1.50$ seconds. (c) Snapshot at $t = 3.25$ seconds. (d) Snapshot at $t = 5.80$ seconds.

the extension for more general nonstationary quadratic optimization is possible. Thus, the aforementioned nonstationary quadratic optimization can be rewritten as follows:

$$\text{minimize} \quad \frac{1}{2}\boldsymbol{u}^{\mathrm{T}}(t)Q(t)\boldsymbol{u}(t) + \boldsymbol{q}^{\mathrm{T}}(t)\boldsymbol{u}(t), \tag{10.4}$$

$$\text{subject to} \quad A(t)\boldsymbol{u}(t) - \boldsymbol{b}(t) = 0, \tag{10.5}$$

where coefficient $A(t) \in \mathbb{R}^{m \times m}$ and $\boldsymbol{b}(t) \in \mathbb{R}^m$ are smoothly nonstationary.

It is well known that the most common approach for solving equality-constrained QP problems in the real domain is to use a Lagrange multiplier and minimize a suitable cost function [6–10]. Thus, for solving nonstationary quadratic optimization (10.4) and (10.5) [9, 10], its related Lagrangian is presented as follows:

$$\begin{aligned} H(\boldsymbol{u}(t), \lambda(t), t) &= \boldsymbol{u}^{\mathrm{T}}(t)Q(t)\boldsymbol{u}(t)/2 + \boldsymbol{q}^{\mathrm{T}}(t)\boldsymbol{u}(t) \\ &+ \lambda^{\mathrm{T}}(t)\left(A(t)\boldsymbol{u}(t) - \boldsymbol{b}(t)\right), \end{aligned} \tag{10.6}$$

where $\lambda(t) \in \mathbb{R}^m$ denotes the multiplier variable.

It is well-known that solving the quadratic optimization (10.4) and (10.5) could be achieved by zeroing the following equations:

$$\begin{cases} \frac{\partial H(\boldsymbol{u}(t),\lambda(t),t)}{\partial \boldsymbol{u}(t)} = Q(t)\boldsymbol{u}(t) + \boldsymbol{q}(t) + A^{\mathrm{T}}(t)\lambda(t) = 0, \\ \frac{\partial H(\boldsymbol{u}(t),\lambda(t),t)}{\partial \lambda(t)} = A(t)\boldsymbol{u}(t) - \boldsymbol{b}(t) = 0. \end{cases} \tag{10.7}$$

Let

$$C(t) := \begin{bmatrix} Q(t) & A^{\mathrm{T}}(t) \\ A(t) & 0_{m \times m} \end{bmatrix} \in \mathbb{R}^{(n+m) \times (n+m)},$$

$$\boldsymbol{g}(t) := \begin{bmatrix} \boldsymbol{u}(t) \\ \lambda(t) \end{bmatrix} \in \mathbb{R}^{n+m}, \quad \boldsymbol{d}(t) := \begin{bmatrix} -\boldsymbol{q}(t) \\ \boldsymbol{b}(t) \end{bmatrix} \in \mathbb{R}^{n+m}.$$

In addition, the previous linear equation system is further rewritten as a Matrix–vector form as follows:

$$C(t)\boldsymbol{g}(t) = \boldsymbol{d}(t). \tag{10.8}$$

As $Q(t)$ is the positive-definite matrix and $A(t)$ is the full-row-rank matrix, $C(t)$ is nonsingular, which ensures the uniqueness of the solution to Eq. (10.8). In addition, for comparison purposes, the nonstationary theoretical solution of (10.8) can be presented as follows:

$$\boldsymbol{g}^*(t) = [\boldsymbol{u}^{*\mathrm{T}}(t), \lambda^{*\mathrm{T}}(t)]^{\mathrm{T}} := C^{-1}(t)\boldsymbol{d}(t) \in \mathbb{R}^{n+m}. \tag{10.9}$$

Note that, for a small dimensional matrix $C(t)$, the theoretical solution $\boldsymbol{g}^*(t)$ of (10.8) can be exploited to verify the efficacy of the nonlinearly activated neurodynamic model. However, for a large-scale dimensional matrix $C(t)$, the theoretical solution $\boldsymbol{g}^*(t)$ of (10.8) is not easy to be obtained, so we can also use $\|C(t)\boldsymbol{g}(t) - \boldsymbol{d}(t)\|_2$ as a standard to judge the effectiveness of the proposed neurodynamic model.

10.3 Related Work: GNN and ZNN Models

In this section, for completeness of this chapter and for comparative purposes, we present the two of the most relevant works: the gradient neural network (GNN) and zeroing neural network (ZNN) models. The GNN method is widely used to solve constant problems and the ZNN method is recently proposed to solve nonstationary problems. Next, such two methods are developed and exploited to solve the equality-constrained quadratic optimization with nonstationary coefficients.

10.3.1 GNN Model

In this subsection, the GNN model is developed for solving online nonstationary quadratic optimization (10.4) and (10.5), and its design process is provided as follows [6–10].

According to the GNN method, a norm-based energy function is design as follows:

$$\mathcal{E}(t) = \frac{1}{2}\|C(t)\mathbf{g}(t) - \mathbf{d}(t)\|_2^2. \tag{10.10}$$

Evidently, its minimum nonstationary trajectory can be achieved if and only if the neuro-solution $\mathbf{g}(t)$ of nonstationary quadratic optimization (10.4) and (10.5) is equal to $\mathbf{g}^*(t)$.

Then, a calculation strategy could be developed to evolve along a descent way of $\|C(t)\mathbf{g}(t) - \mathbf{d}(t)\|_2^2/2$ until the minimum nonstationary trajectory is reached. The common descent direction is the negative gradient of this energy function. Thus, we have

$$-\frac{\partial \mathcal{E}(t)}{\partial \mathbf{g}} = -\frac{1}{2}\frac{\partial \|C(t)\mathbf{g}(t) - \mathbf{d}(t)\|_2^2}{\partial \mathbf{g}}$$
$$= -C^{\mathrm{T}}(t)\,(C(t)\mathbf{g}(t) - \mathbf{d}(t))\,. \tag{10.11}$$

Finally, according to the aforementioned negative gradient, we can obtain the following gradient-based explicit dynamics of a GNN model:

$$\dot{\mathbf{g}}(t) = -\gamma\frac{\partial \mathcal{E}(t)}{\partial \mathbf{g}}$$
$$= -\gamma C^{\mathrm{T}}(t)\,(C(t)\mathbf{g}(t) - \mathbf{d}(t))\,, \tag{10.12}$$

where $\mathbf{g}(t) \in \mathbb{R}^{n+m}$, from an initial state $\mathbf{g}(0)$ to start, is the neural state corresponding to $\mathbf{g}^*(t)$, and $\gamma > 0$ is exploited to adjust the convergence rate of GNN model (10.12).

10.3.2 ZNN Model

As discussed before, during the processes of solving nonstationary quadratic optimization (10.4) and (10.5), GNN model (10.12) cannot make the error converge to zero even after infinitely long time. Therefore, the ZNN method has been proposed recently and has been proven to converge ideally when time goes to infinity. In this subsection, the ZNN model is developed for solving online nonstationary quadratic optimization (10.4) and (10.5), and its design procedure is also presented as follows [9, 10].

First, to monitor and control the process of nonstationary quadratic optimization (10.4) and (10.5) solving, an indefinite vector-valued error function $\mathbf{y}(t)$ is defined as follows (instead of the norm-based energy function in the GNN model):

$$\mathbf{y}(t) = C(t)\mathbf{g}(t) - \mathbf{d}(t). \tag{10.13}$$

Then, the ZNN formula is adopted so that $\mathbf{y}(t)$ decreases to zero as time goes to infinity. That is

$$\frac{\mathrm{d}\mathbf{y}(t)}{\mathrm{d}t} = -\gamma\Phi\,(\mathbf{y}(t))\,, \tag{10.14}$$

where $\gamma > 0$ is used to adjust the convergence rate of the ZNN formula. Besides, $\Phi(\cdot) : \mathbb{R}^{n+m} \to \mathbb{R}^{n+m}$ denotes a vector array of activation functions.

Finally, expanding Eq. (10.14) and in view of $\dot{\boldsymbol{y}}(t) = \dot{C}(t)\boldsymbol{g}(t) + C(t)\dot{\boldsymbol{g}}(t) - \dot{\boldsymbol{d}}(t)$, we have the following implicit dynamics of a ZNN model:

$$C(t)\dot{\boldsymbol{g}}(t) = -\dot{C}(t)\boldsymbol{g}(t) + \dot{\boldsymbol{d}}(t) - \gamma\Phi\left(C(t)\boldsymbol{g}(t) - \boldsymbol{d}(t)\right), \tag{10.15}$$

where $\boldsymbol{g}(t) \in \mathbb{R}^{n+m}$ denotes the neural state of ZNN model (10.15). Furthermore, we have the following lemma to ensure the global and exponential convergence of ZNN model (10.15) for nonstationary quadratic optimization (10.4) and (10.5) solving [9, 10].

Lemma 10.1 *Take into account nonstationary equality-constrained quadratic optimization (10.4) and (10.5) and the corresponding nonstationary linear system (10.8). If monotonically increasing odd activation function $\Phi(\cdot)$ is used, starting from randomly generated initial state $\boldsymbol{g}(0) \in \mathbb{R}^{n+m}$, state vector $\boldsymbol{g}(t)$ of ZNN model (10.15) always converges to $\boldsymbol{g}^*(t)$ of nonstationary linear system (10.8), of which the first n elements constitute the nonstationary theoretical solution of nonstationary quadratic optimization (10.4) and (10.5).*

10.4 N-FTZNN Model

Because of the in-depth study on neural dynamics, we found that the convergence rate of neural-dynamic models can be thoroughly improved by an elaborate design of the activation function $\Phi(\cdot)$. In addition, taking advantage of the nonlinearity, a properly designed nonlinear activation function often outperforms the linear one in convergence rate. Therefore, in this section, we aim at developing a nonlinear activation function, which can endow ZNN model (10.15) with a finite-time convergence for solving nonstationary quadratic optimization (10.4) and (10.5). Motivated by the investigation on finite-time control of autonomous systems and finite-time convergence of recurrent neural networks [13–16], we propose a weighted sign-bi-power activation function to accelerate ZNN model (10.15) to finite-time convergence to the theoretical solution of nonstationary quadratic optimization (10.4) and (10.5). The weighted sign-bi-power activation function wspb($\cdot$) is defined as follows:

$$\text{wspb}(x) = \frac{1}{2}k_1\text{sgn}^r(x) + \frac{1}{2}k_2\text{sgn}^{1/r}(x) + \frac{1}{2}k_3 x, \tag{10.16}$$

where k_1, k_2, k_3, and $r \in (0, 1)$ are tunable positive parameters. In addition, sign-bi-power function $\text{sgn}^r(\cdot)$ has the following expression:

$$\text{sgn}^r(x) = \begin{cases} |x|^r, & \text{if } x > 0; \\ 0, & \text{if } x = 0; \\ -|x|^r, & \text{if } x < 0; \end{cases} \tag{10.17}$$

where $x \in \mathbb{R}$ and $|x|$ denotes the absolute value of x. Thus, we can obtain the following N-FTZNN model for nonstationary quadratic optimization (10.4) and (10.5):

$$C(t)\dot{g}(t) = -\dot{C}(t)g(t) + \dot{d}(t) - \gamma \text{WSBP}\left(C(t)g(t) - d(t)\right), \tag{10.18}$$

where WSBP($\cdot$) denotes the array of the weighted sign-bi-power activation function with each element defined as wsbp($\cdot$).

10.4.1 Models Comparison

Now, three different models for nonstationary quadratic optimization (10.4) and (10.5) are presented. In this subsection, the following facts are provided for comparing GNN model (10.12), ZNN model (10.15), and N-FTZNN model (10.18).

(1) A specially constructed nonlinear function (i.e. the weighted sign-bi-power activation function) is developed and exploited in N-FTZNN model (10.18), which makes its form totally different from these of GNN model (10.12) and ZNN model (10.15).

(2) The design of ZNN model (10.15) and N-FTZNN model (10.18) is ground on the removal of every entry of a vector-valued indefinite error function. By contrast, the design of GNN model (10.12) is based on the removal of a scalar-valued nonnegative energy function.

(3) ZNN model (10.15) and N-FTZNN model (10.18) adopt an exponential-design formula (i.e. design formula (10.14)) for the nonstationary quadratic optimization problem solving. Thus, they can possess the exponential convergence performance. In contrast, GNN model (10.12) adopts a negative-gradient descent rule, which is intrinsically for handling the quadratic optimization problem with static/constant coefficients only.

(4) Similar to ZNN model (10.15), N-FTZNN model (10.18) is depicted in implicit dynamics that coincides better with the systems in practice and in nature. By contrast, GNN model (10.12) is depicted in an explicit dynamics that is generally related to classic Hopfield neural networks.

(5) ZNN model (10.15) and N-FTZNN model (10.18) systematically use the time-derivative information of nonstationary coefficients (i.e. $\dot{Q}(t)$, $\dot{q}(t)$, $\dot{A}(t)$, and $\dot{b}(t)$). This is one main reason why the state vector of ZNN model (10.15) and N-FTZNN model (10.18) can exactly converge to the nonstationary theoretical solution of the nonstationary quadratic optimization. In contrast, GNN model (10.12) does not use this important information, and thus is not efficient enough for solving online the nonstationary quadratic optimization.

(6) It can be theoretically proved that N-FTZNN model (10.18) achieves superior finite-time convergence performance as compared with GNN model (10.12)

and ZNN model (10.15). It is worth pointing out that convergence rate of ZNN model (10.15) is related to design parameter γ, while GNN model (10.12) cannot guarantee its convergence theoretically.

Before ending this subsection, we would like to mention that the implicit dynamical systems usually arise in analog circuit systems based on Kirchhoff's rules. In addition, implicit dynamical systems have greater abilities in representing dynamical systems due to preserving physical parameters by using matrix coefficients, e.g. $C(t)$ on the left-hand side of N-FTZNN model (10.18) and ZNN model (10.15). Furthermore, the implicit dynamical systems can be transformed mathematically to explicit dynamical systems. From this point of view, owing to the merits of implicit dynamical systems, the proposed N-FTZNN model (10.18) and ZNN model (10.15) are superior to GNN model (10.12).

10.4.2 Finite-Time Convergence

As we know, the applications of neural networks rely generally on the dynamical performance of their models. Therefore, in this subsection, we present the main theorem to reveal the finite-time convergence performance of N-FTZNN model (10.18) by using the weighted sign-bi-power activation function.

Theorem 10.2 *Consider nonstationary quadratic optimization (10.4) and (10.5) and the nonstationary linear system (10.8). From randomly generated initial vector $g(0) \in \mathbb{R}^{n+m}$ to start, neural state $g(t)$ of N-FTZNN model (10.18) globally converges to $g^*(t)$ of nonstationary linear system (10.8) within finite time, where the first n elements of $g^*(t)$ are the nonstationary theoretical solution $u^*(t)$ to nonstationary quadratic optimization (10.4) and (10.5). Besides, the upper bound of convergence time is derived as*

$$
t_{\mathrm{f}} \leqslant
\begin{cases}
\dfrac{2\ln\left[1+\frac{k_1}{k_3}y^+(0)^{1-r}\right]}{\gamma k_3 (1-r)}, & \text{if } |y^+(0)| < 1; \\[4ex]
\dfrac{2r\ln\left[\frac{k_2+k_3}{k_3}y^+(0)^{\frac{1-r}{r}}+k_2\right]}{\gamma k_3 (1-r)} + \dfrac{2r\ln\left[1+\frac{k_3}{k_1}\right]}{\gamma k_3 (1-r)}, & \text{if } |y^+(0)| \geqslant 1;
\end{cases}
\tag{10.19}
$$

where $y^+(0) = \max\{|y_j(0)|\}$ for all possible j.

Proof: Let $\tilde{g}(t) = g(t) - g^*(t)$ denote the difference between the nonstationary solution $g(t)$ obtained by the proposed N-FTZNN model (10.18) and the nonstationary theoretical solution $g^*(t)$ of nonstationary linear system (10.8). Thus, we can obtain

$$
g(t) = \tilde{g}(t) + g^*(t) \in \mathbb{C}^{n+m}.
\tag{10.20}
$$

Substituting the aforementioned equation to N-FTZNN model (10.18); and in view of equation $C(t)g^*(t) - d(t) = 0$ and $C(t)\dot{g}^*(t) + \dot{C}(t)g^*(t) - \dot{d}(t) = 0$, we further know that $\tilde{g}(t)$ is the solution to the following dynamics:

$$C(t)\dot{\tilde{g}}(t) = -\dot{C}(t)\tilde{g}(t) - \gamma \text{WSBP}(C(t)\tilde{g}(t)). \tag{10.21}$$

On the other hand, since $y(t) = C(t)g(t) - d(t) = C(t)[\tilde{g}(t) + g^*(t)] - d(t) = C(t)\tilde{g}(t)$, Eq. (10.21) can be expressed equivalently as

$$\frac{dy(t)}{dt} = -\gamma \text{WSBP}(y(t)). \tag{10.22}$$

Entry-wisely, we have

$$\dot{y}_j(t) = -\gamma \left(\frac{1}{2}k_1 \text{sgn}^r \left(y_j(t) \right) + \frac{1}{2}k_2 \text{sgn}^{1/r} \left(y_j(t) \right) + \frac{1}{2}k_3 y_j(t) \right), \tag{10.23}$$

where $y_j(t)$ is the jth entry of $y(t)$.

Since $y^+(0) = \max\{|y_j(0)|\}$, $-y^+(0) \leqslant y_j(0) \leqslant y^+(0)$. Note that every $y_j(t)$ in $y(t)$ have identical dynamics $\dot{y}_j(t) = -\gamma \text{wsbp}(y_j(t))$ and the same the weighted sign-bi-power activation function. Then, according to the Comparison Lemma, we know that $-y^+(t) \leqslant y_j(t) \leqslant y^+(t)$ with $t \geqslant 0$ for all possible j. This means that $y_j(t)$ converges to zero for all possible j when $y^+(t)$ reach zero. In other words, the convergence time of N-FTZNN model (10.18) is bounded by t_f^+ of the dynamics of $y^+(t)$, where t_f^+ represent the convergence time of the dynamics of $y^+(t)$.

To estimate t_f^+, we can begin with the following formula:

$$\dot{y}^+(t) = -\gamma \text{wsbp}(y^+(t)) \text{ with } y^+(0) = \max\{y(0)\}, \tag{10.24}$$

where wsbp($\cdot$) is the weighted sign-bi-power activation function.

Then, by defining a Lyapunov function candidate $p(t) = |y^+(t)|^2$, the time-derivative of $p(t)$ is thus obtained:

$$\begin{aligned}
\dot{p}(t) &= -2\gamma y^+ \text{wsbp}(y^+(t)) \\
&= -\gamma \left(k_1 |y^+(t)|^{r+1} + k_2 |y^+(t)|^{\frac{1}{r}+1} + k_3 |y^+(t)|^2 \right) \\
&= -\gamma \left(k_1 p(t)^{\frac{r+1}{2}} + k_2 p(t)^{\frac{1+r}{2r}} + k_3 p(t) \right).
\end{aligned} \tag{10.25}$$

For such a differential equation, if $p(0) = |y^+(0)|^2 \leqslant 1$, according to the Lemma 3 of [17], there exists t_f^+ satisfying

$$t_f^+ \leqslant \frac{2\ln\left[1 + \frac{k_1}{k_3}p(0)^{\frac{1-r}{2}}\right]}{\gamma k_3(1-r)}, \tag{10.26}$$

such that all $y_j(t) = 0$ when $t_f > t_f^+$.

If $p(0) = |y^+(0)|^2 \geqslant 1$, according to the Lemma 3 of [17], there exists t_f^+ satisfying

$$t_f^+ \leqslant \frac{2r\ln\left[\frac{k_2+k_3}{k_3}p(0)^{\frac{1-r}{2r}} + k_2\right]}{\gamma k_3(1-r)} + \frac{2r\ln\left[1 + \frac{k_3}{k_1}\right]}{\gamma k_3(1-r)}, \tag{10.27}$$

such that all $y_j(t) = 0$ when $t_f > t_f^+$.

The aforementioned results mean that, if the weighted sign-bi-power activation function (10.16) is adopted, neural state $g(t)$ of N-FTZNN model (10.18) converges to the theoretical solution $g^*(t)$ of nonstationary linear system (10.8) in finite time t_f, of which the first n elements of $g^*(t)$ are the nonstationary theoretical solution to nonstationary quadratic optimization (10.4) and (10.5). ■

From the aforementioned comparison and analysis results, it can be concluded that GNN model (10.12) always has a lagging error for solving nonstationary quadratic optimization (10.4) and (10.5), and that ZNN model (10.15) converges exponentially to the nonstationary theoretical optimal solution of quadratic optimization (10.4) and (10.5) when time goes to infinity. However, they never converge to the theoretical optimal solution of quadratic optimization (10.4) and (10.5) within finite time, which may limit their applications in real-time processing. In contrast, N-FTZNN model (10.18) possesses the desired finite-time convergent performance. Evidently, N-FTZNN model (10.18) is superior to GNN model (10.12) and ZNN model (10.15), which theoretically ensures that N-FTZNN model (10.18) can realize superior convergence property.

10.5 Illustrative Verification

In the aforementioned section, N-FTZNN model (10.18) is proposed for solving nonstationary quadratic optimization (10.4) and (10.5) by adding a specially constructed nonlinear activation function. In addition to detailed design process, the excellent finite-time convergence performance is analyzed in details. Besides, two of the most relevant works (i.e. the GNN and ZNN models) are presented for comparative purposes. In this section, one illustrative example is provided for substantiating the efficacy and superiority of N-FTZNN model (10.18), as compared with GNN model (10.12) and ZNN models (10.15). It is worth pointing out that, in this chapter, the abscissa axis denotes the x-axis and the vertical axis denotes y-axis for all 2-D figures.

Now, without loss of generality, the following nonstationary coefficients for nonstationary quadratic optimization (10.4) and (10.5) are selected:

$$Q(t) = \begin{bmatrix} 0.5\sin(t) + 2 & \cos(t) \\ \cos(t) & 0.5\sin(t) + 2 \end{bmatrix}, \quad q(t) = \begin{bmatrix} \sin(3t) \\ \cos(3t) \end{bmatrix},$$

$$A(t) = \begin{bmatrix} \sin(4t), \cos(4t) \end{bmatrix}, \quad \text{and} \quad b(t) = \cos(2t).$$

It follows from the definitions of Eq. (10.8) that $P(t)$ is equal to

$$\begin{bmatrix} 0.5\sin(t) + 2 & \cos(t) & \sin(4t) \\ \cos(t) & 0.5\sin(t) + 2 & \cos(4t) \\ \sin(4t) & \cos(4t) & 0 \end{bmatrix},$$

and

$$\boldsymbol{d}(t) = \begin{bmatrix} -\sin(3t), -\cos(3t), \cos(2t) \end{bmatrix}^{\mathrm{T}}.$$

It is evident that the nonstationary theoretical solution $\boldsymbol{g}^*(t)$ of (10.8) in this situation can be given as

$$\begin{bmatrix} 0.5\sin(t) + 2 & \cos(t) & \sin(4t) \\ \cos(t) & 0.5\sin(t) + 2 & \cos(4t) \\ \sin(4t) & \cos(4t) & 0 \end{bmatrix}^{-1} \begin{bmatrix} -\sin(3t) \\ -\cos(3t) \\ \cos(2t) \end{bmatrix}.$$

Since we have got the nonstationary theoretical solution of (10.8), we can use it as a criterion to verify the effectiveness of such three neurodynamic models. Simulative results are discussed as follows.

As shown in Figure 10.2a, from 20 randomly generated initial states $\boldsymbol{g}(0) \in \mathbb{R}^3$ to start, state vectors $\boldsymbol{g}(t) \in \mathbb{R}^3$ of GNN model (10.12) do not meet well with the nonstationary theoretical optimal solution of nonstationary linear system (10.8). In addition, Figure 10.2b presents the corresponding transient convergence behavior of $\|C(t)\boldsymbol{g}(t) - \boldsymbol{d}(t)\|_2$ synthesized by GNN model (10.12) for real-time solution of nonstationary linear system (10.8). From the subfigure, we see that $\|C(t)\boldsymbol{g}(t) - \boldsymbol{d}(t)\|_2$ is rather large, and more importantly, does not converge to zero. The results verify that GNN model (10.12) is not effective for real-time solution of nonstationary linear system (10.8) and nonstationary quadratic optimization (10.4) and (10.5).

While ZNN model (10.15) is applied to real-time solution of nonstationary linear system (10.8) under the same conditions, state vector $\boldsymbol{g}(t)$ of ZNN model (10.15) can converge to the nonstationary theoretical solution of nonstationary linear system (10.8) about five seconds, which is demonstrated in Figure 10.3a. In addition,

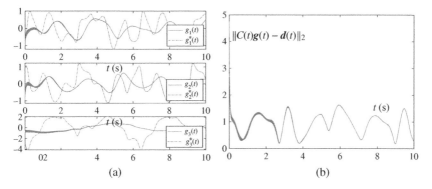

Figure 10.2 Simulative results of real-time solution to nonstationary quadratic optimization (10.4) and (10.5) synthesized by GNN model (10.12) with $\gamma = 1$. (a) Transient behavior of neural state $\boldsymbol{g}(t)$. (b) Transient behavior of $\|C(t)\boldsymbol{g}(t) - \boldsymbol{d}(t)\|_2$.

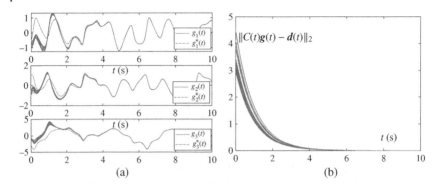

(a)   (b)

Figure 10.3 Simulative results of real-time solution to nonstationary quadratic optimization (10.4) and (10.5) synthesized by ZNN model (10.15) with $\gamma = 1$. (a) Transient behavior of neural state $\boldsymbol{g}(t)$. (b) Transient behavior of $\|C(t)\boldsymbol{g}(t) - \boldsymbol{d}(t)\|_2$.

it is observed from Figure 10.3b that $\|C(t)\boldsymbol{g}(t) - \boldsymbol{d}(t)\|_2$ synthesized by ZNN model (10.15) decreases to zero within five seconds. Thus, the efficacy of ZNN model (10.15) solving for nonstationary linear system (10.8) and nonstationary complex quadratic optimization (10.4) and (10.5) is verified primarily.

Now, in order to verify the efficacy and superiority of N-FTZNN model (10.18) for solving nonstationary linear system (10.8) and nonstationary quadratic optimization (10.4) and (10.5), under the same conditions, Figure 10.4 provides the simulative results of N-FTZNN model (10.18). It is seen from Figure 10.4a that, from 20 randomly generated initial states $\boldsymbol{g}(0) \in \mathbb{R}^3$ to start, state vector $\boldsymbol{g}(t) \in \mathbb{R}^3$ of N-FTZNN model (10.18) converges directly to the nonstationary theoretical solution of (10.8) within a rather short time. In addition, Figure 10.4b shows the transient convergence behavior of $\|C(t)\boldsymbol{g}(t) - \boldsymbol{d}(t)\|_2$ synthesized by N-FTZNN

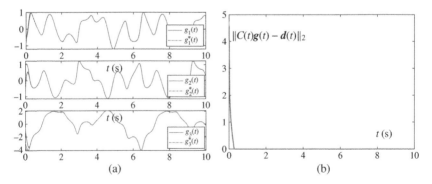

(a)   (b)

Figure 10.4 Simulative results of real-time solution to nonstationary quadratic optimization (10.4) and (10.5) synthesized by N-FTZNN model (10.18) with $\gamma = 1$. (a) Transient behavior of neural state $\boldsymbol{g}(t)$. (b) Transient behavior of $\|C(t)\boldsymbol{g}(t) - \boldsymbol{d}(t)\|_2$.

model (10.18). As presented in Figure 10.4b, $\|C(t)g(t) - d(t)\|_2$ synthesized by N-FTZNN model (10.18) decreases to zero within 0.2 seconds, which is about 25 times faster than that of ZNN model (10.15).

On the whole, from the aforementioned simulative results depicted in the example, we draw a conclusion that ZNN model (10.15) and N-FTZNN model (10.18) are both efficacious for real-time solution of nonstationary linear system (10.8) and nonstationary quadratic optimization (10.4) and (10.5); and that GNN model (10.12) is not suitable for solving online nonstationary linear system (10.8) and nonstationary quadratic optimization (10.4) and (10.5) because the change of nonstationary coefficients is hard to track for it. More importantly, by comparison, N-FTZNN model (10.18) has a superior convergence performance to ZNN model (10.15) for real-time solution of such a nonstationary quadratic optimization problem. In a word, the effectiveness and superiority of N-FTZNN model (10.18) are substantiated in this section.

10.6 Chapter Summary

In this chapter, by adopting a specially constructed nonlinear activation function, a N-FTZNN model has been proposed and studied for real-time solution of nonstationary quadratic optimization problems. The finite-time convergence performance of the proposed model has been analyzed and presented with the convergence upper bound also estimated. We not only have made a comparison among the GNN model, the ZNN model, and the proposed N-FTZNN model theoretically, but also made a comparison among them using illustrative examples. Computer-simulation results have further verified and demonstrated the theoretical analysis, efficacy and superiority of the proposed N-FTZNN model for real-time solution of the nonstationary quadratic optimization problem, as compared with the GNN and ZNN models.

References

1 R. Fantacci and M. Forti *et al.*, A neural network for constrained optimization with application to CDMA communication systems, *IEEE Trans. Circuits Syst. II, Exp. Briefs*, 50(8) (2003) 484–487.

2 Q. Marashdeh and W. Warsito *et al.*, A nonlinear image reconstruction technique for ECT using a combined neural network approach, *Meas. Sci. Technol.*, 17(8) (2006) 2097–2103.

3 T. A. Johansen, T. I. Fsosen, and S. P. Berge, Constrained nonlinear control allocation with singularity avoidance using sequential quadratic programming, *IEEE Trans. Control Syst. Technol.*, 12(1) (2004) 211–216.

4 Y. Zhang and X. Lv *et al.*, Repetitive motion planning of PA10 robot arm subject to joint physical limits and using LVI-based primal-dual neural network, *Mechatronics*, 18(9) (2008) 475–485.

5 D. Guo and Y. Zhang, Li-function activated ZNN with finite-time convergence applied to redundant-manipulator kinematic control via time-varying Jacobian matrix pseudoinversion, *Appl. Soft Comput.*, 24 (2014) 158–168.

6 M. Avriel, *Nonlinear programming: Analysis and methods*, Courier Corporation, 2003.

7 M. S. Bazaraa, H. D. Sherali, and C. M. Shetty, *Nonlinear programming: Theory and algorithms*, John Wiley & Sons, 2013.

8 X. Hu and J. Wang, An improved dual neural network for solving a class of quadratic programming problems and its κ-winners-take-all application, *IEEE Trans. Neural Netw.*, 19(12) (2008) 2022–2031.

9 Y. Zhang and Z. Li, Zhang neural network for online solution of time-varying convex quadratic program subject to time-varying linear-equality constraints, *Phys. Lett. A*, 373(18–19) (2009) 1639–1643.

10 Y. Zhang and G. Ruan *et al.*, Robustness analysis of the Zhang neural network for online time-varying quadratic optimization, *J. Phys. A: Math. Theor.*, 43 (2010) 245202.

11 Y. Maldonado, O. Castillo, and P. Melin, Particle swarm optimization of interval type-2 fuzzy systems for FPGA applications, *Appl. Soft Comput.*, 13(1) (2013) 496–508.

12 S. Li, S. Chen, and B. Liu, Accelerating a recurrent neural network to finite-time convergence for solving time-varying Sylvester equation by using a sign-bi-power activation function, *Neural Process. Lett.*, 37 (2013) 189–205.

13 S. P. Bhat and D. S. Bernstein, Finite-time stability of continuous autonomous systems, *SIAM J. Control Optim.*, 38(3) (2000) 751–766.

14 M. Forti, M. Grazzini, and P. Nistri, Generalized Lyapunov approach for convergence of neural networks with discontinuous or non-Lipschitz activations, *Physica D*, 214(1) (2006) 88–99.

15 W. Lu and T. Chen, Dynamical behaviors of delayed neural network systems with discontinuous activation functions, *Neural Comput.*, 18(3) (2006) 683–708.

16 M. D. Marco, M. Forti, and M. Grazzini, Robustness of convergence in finite time for linear programming neural networks, *Int. J. Circuit Theory Appl.*, 34(3) (2006) 307–316.

17 Y. Shen and P. Miao *et al.*, Finite-time stability and its application for solving time-varying Sylvester equation by recurrent neural network, *Neural Process. Lett.*, 42 (2015) 763–784.

Part V

Application to the Lyapunov Equation

11

Design Scheme I of FTZNN

11.1 Introduction

Lyapunov equation is widely appeared in many scientific and engineering fields, e.g. linear algebra [1], disturbance decoupling [2], and multi-agent systems [3]. In addition, Lyapunov equation plays an important role in controller design and robustness analysis of nonlinear systems [4, 5]. Therefore, many iterative algorithms or approaches are designed and presented to solve Lyapunov equation [1, 4, 6]. However, discrete iterative algorithms have a time complexity $O(n^3)$ to compute the solution of linear matrix equation [7]. That is to say, the serial-processing iterative algorithms may not be efficient enough in large-scale applications and related real-time processing.

In the past three decades, recurrent neural networks, as powerful computational tools [8–11], have found important applications, particularly in the fields of system identification, optimization, speech processing and robotics, after the seminal work on Hopfield neural network [12]. As compared with the numerical iterative algorithms, recurrent neural networks possess the hardware-implementation ability and parallel distributed nature in real-time applications [13–15]. In addition, recurrent neural networks also play an important role in solving Lyapunov equations. In this chapter, a finite-time zeroing neural network (FTZNN) model is proposed and investigated for solving Lyapunov equation by adopting a specially selected nonlinear activation function (termed the sign-bi-power activation function) [16–18]. It is theoretically proved that the convergence speed of the FTZNN model can reach the finite-time convergence, instead of asymptotic or exponential convergence. That is to say, the convergence performance of the FTZNN model is increased remarkably (i.e. from infinite to finite time).

Zeroing Neural Networks: Finite-time Convergence Design, Analysis and Applications,
First Edition. Lin Xiao and Lei Jia.

11.2 Problem Formulation and Related Work

In mathematics, the well-known Lyapunov equation can be generally formulated as

$$A^T U(t) + U(t)A = -C \in \mathbb{R}^{n \times n}, \tag{11.1}$$

where $A \in \mathbb{R}^{n \times n}$ is a constant coefficient matrix; $C \in \mathbb{R}^{n \times n}$ is a symmetric positive-definite matrix; and $U(t) \in \mathbb{R}^{n \times n}$ denotes an unknown matrix to be obtained. Without loss of generality, let $U^* \in \mathbb{R}^{n \times n}$ stand for the theoretical solution of Lyapunov equation (11.1). The target of this chapter is to develop a convergence-accelerated neural network for solving such a Lyapunov equation and find the theoretical solution $U^* \in \mathbb{R}^{n \times n}$ within finite time. In addition, for completeness of this chapter and for comparative purposes, two of the most relevant work (i.e. GNN and zeroing neural network [ZNN] models) are presented to solve online Lyapunov equation (11.1) in the following.

11.2.1 GNN Model

The gradient neural network (GNN) is widely used to solve constant problems. In this part, following the GNN design method [14], we can correspondingly develop a GNN model for solving Lyapunov equation (11.1), and the design process of the GNN model is presented as follows.

First, based on Lyapunov equation (11.1), a norm-based energy function can be constructed as

$$\Delta = \|A^T U(t) + U(t)A + C\|_F^2 / 2, \tag{11.2}$$

such that its minimum value is the theoretical solution of (11.1), where $\| \cdot \|_F$ denotes the Frobenius norm of a matrix.

Second, a strategy is presented to evolve along a descent direction of this energy function until the minimum value is reached. Thus, the negative gradient information of the energy function is adopted and derived as follows:

$$-\frac{\partial \Delta}{\partial U} = -A(A^T U(t) + U(t)A + C) - (A^T U(t) + U(t)A + C)A^T.$$

Third, by using the aforementioned negative gradient to solve Lyapunov equation (11.1), we can obtain the following GNN model:

$$\dot{U}(t) = -\gamma A(A^T U(t) + U(t)A + C) - \gamma(A^T U(t) + U(t)A + C)A^T, \tag{11.3}$$

where design parameter $\gamma > 0$ is used to scale the convergence rate of GNN model (11.3), and state matrix $U(t) \in \mathbb{R}^{n \times n}$, starting from initial state $U(0) \in \mathbb{R}^{n \times n}$, corresponds to the theoretical solution $U^* \in \mathbb{R}^{n \times n}$ of (11.1).

11.2.2 ZNN Model

Following Zhang *et al.*' design method [13], we can define the following matrix-valued error function to monitor the solution process of Lyapunov equation (11.1), instead of the norm-based energy function in GNN model (11.3):

$$Y(t) = A^{\mathrm{T}}U(t) + U(t)A + C \in \mathbb{R}^{n \times n}, \tag{11.4}$$

of which each element can be negative, positive, zero, or lower-unbounded.

Then, starting with the $Y(t)$ earlier, we have the following theorem to construct the ZNN model for solving Lyapunov equation (11.1).

Theorem 11.1 *Given constant matrices $A \in \mathbb{R}^{n \times n}$ and $C \in \mathbb{R}^{n \times n}$ in (11.1), and in view of the definition of $Y(t)$ as well as the design formula $\mathrm{d}Y(t)/\mathrm{d}t = -\gamma\Phi(Y(t))$, the dynamic equation of the ZNN model for solving online Lyapunov equation (11.1) is derived as follows:*

$$A^{\mathrm{T}}\dot{U}(t) + \dot{U}(t)A = -\gamma\Phi(A^{\mathrm{T}}U(t) + U(t)A + C), \tag{11.5}$$

where $\Phi(\cdot)$ denotes an activation function array, design parameter $\gamma > 0$, and state matrix $U(t) \in \mathbb{R}^{n \times n}$, starting from initial state $U(0) \in \mathbb{R}^{n \times n}$, corresponds to the theoretical solution $U^* \in \mathbb{R}^{n \times n}$ of (11.1).

Proof: Let us focus on the matrix-valued error function $Y(t)$ in Eq. (11.4). It can be concluded evidently that the theoretical solution of (11.1) is equivalent to finding a zero point of (11.4).

In order to make each element $y_{ij}(t)$ of $Y(t)$ converge to zero ($i, j = 1, 2, \ldots, n$), the following design formula is exploited [13]:

$$\frac{\mathrm{d}Y(t)}{\mathrm{d}t} = -\gamma\Phi(Y(t)), \tag{11.6}$$

where design parameter $\gamma > 0$ is defined as before and $\Phi(\cdot) : \mathbb{R}^{n \times n} \to \mathbb{R}^{n \times n}$ denotes an activation function array.

Then, by substituting error function (11.4) into the previous design formula and in view of $\dot{Y}(t) = A^{\mathrm{T}}\dot{U}(t) + \dot{U}(t)A$, the following differential equation can be derived:

$$A^{\mathrm{T}}\dot{U}(t) + \dot{U}(t)A = -\gamma\Phi(A^{\mathrm{T}}U(t) + U(t)A + C),$$

which is exactly ZNN model (11.5). This completes the proof. ∎

11.3 FTZNN Model

In Section 11.2, for comparison purposes, two related models (i.e. GNN and ZNN) for Lyapunov equation (11.1) are presented. Though such two models can be successfully applied to online solution of Lyapunov equation (11.1), the convergence performance does not satisfy some real-time requirements in large-scale applications because the GNN and ZNN models cannot converge to the theoretical solution within finite time. In this part, based on the previous work [16–19], a FTZNN model is proposed and investigated for solving Lyapunov equation (11.1). In addition, the convergence speed of the FTZNN model can reach the finite-time convergence, instead of asymptotic or exponential convergence.

It is worth pointing out that the adoption of different activation functions can give rise to different convergence performance for a recurrent neural network. In addition, the convergence speed can be remarkably accelerated by adding a nonlinear activation function. Keeping this point in mind, a specially selected nonlinear activation function (called the sign-bi-power activation function [19]) is adopted to enable ZNN model (11.5) to converge within finite time. Specifically, the sign-bi-power activation function is defined and presented as follows [16, 17, 19]:

$$\phi(y_{ij}) = \text{sgn}^{1/\alpha}(y_{ij}) + \text{sgn}^{\alpha}(y_{ij}), \tag{11.7}$$

where design parameter $\alpha \in (0, 1)$, y_{ij} denotes the ijth element of $Y(t)$, and the function $\text{sgn}^{1/\alpha}(\cdot)$ is defined as

$$\text{sgn}^{1/\alpha}(y_{ij}) = \begin{cases} |y_{ij}|^{1/\alpha}, & \text{if } y_{ij} > 0, \\ 0, & \text{if } y_{ij} = 0, \\ -|y_{ij}|^{1/\alpha}, & \text{if } y_{ij} < 0. \end{cases}$$

Therefore, by adding the sign-bi-power activation function array to ZNN model (11.5), the FTZNN model can be proposed as follows:

$$A^{\text{T}}\dot{U}(t) + \dot{U}(t)A = -\gamma\text{SGN}^{1/\alpha}(A^{\text{T}}U(t) + U(t)A + C)$$
$$- \gamma\text{SGN}^{\alpha}(A^{\text{T}}U(t) + U(t)A + C), \tag{11.8}$$

where $\text{SGN}^{1/\alpha}(\cdot)$ denotes the sign-bi-power activation function array, and its each element is denoted by $\text{sgn}^{1/\alpha}(\cdot)$. For such an FTZNN model (11.8), we have the following theorem to guarantee its finite-time convergence.

Theorem 11.2 *Given constant matrices $A \in \mathbb{R}^{n \times n}$ and $C \in \mathbb{R}^{n \times n}$ in (11.1), if the sign-bi-power activation function array is used, then state matrix $U(t)$ of FTZNN model (11.8), starting from any randomly generated initial state $U(0) \in \mathbb{R}^{n \times n}$, converges to the theoretical solution of (11.1) within finite time*

$$t_{\text{f}} < \max\left\{ \frac{|y^+(0)|^{1-\alpha}}{\gamma(1-\alpha)}, \frac{|y^-(0)|^{1-\alpha}}{\gamma(1-\alpha)} \right\},$$

where $y^-(0)$ and $y^+(0)$ denote the smallest and the largest elements of the initial error matrix $Y(0)$, respectively.

Proof: Let us define $y^-(t)$ to be the element in $Y(t)$ with the smallest initial value $y^-(0) = \min\{Y(0)\}$, and define $y^+(t)$ to be the element in $Y(t)$ with the largest initial value $y^+(0) = \max\{Y(0)\}$. Thus, we can obtain $y^+(0) \geqslant y_{ij}(0)$ and $y^-(t) \leqslant y_{ij}(0)$ for all possible $i, j \in \{1, 2, \dots, n\}$. Since all elements in $Y(t)$ have identical dynamic system $\dot{y}_{ij}(t) = -\gamma \operatorname{sgn}^{1/\alpha}(y_{ij}(t)) - \gamma \operatorname{sgn}^\alpha(y_{ij}(t))$, we can obtain that $y^+(t) \geqslant y_{ij}(t)$ and $y^-(t) \leqslant y_{ij}(t)$ for all possible $i, j \in \{1, 2, \dots, n\}$. By summarizing the aforementioned two situations, we have $y^-(t) \leqslant y_{ij}(t) \leqslant y^+(t)$ for all possible i and j with time. This result shows that $y_{ij}(t)$ converges to zero for all possible i and j if both $y^+(t)$ and $y^-(t)$ reach zero. That is to say, the convergence time of FTZNN model (11.8) is bounded by the larger one between the dynamics of $y^+(t)$ and $y^-(t)$, i.e. $t_f \leqslant \max\{t_f^+, t_f^-\}$ where t_f^+ and t_f^- stand for the convergence time of the dynamics of $y^+(t)$ and $y^-(t)$, respectively.

In order to compute the value of t_f, we have to calculate the values of t_f^+ and t_f^- first. As for t_f^+, we have

$$\dot{y}^+(t) = -\gamma \operatorname{sgn}^{1/\alpha}(y^+(t)) - \gamma \operatorname{sgn}^\alpha(y^+(t)) \text{ with } y^+(0) = \max\{Y(0)\}. \quad (11.9)$$

Next, we can make use of Lyapunov approach to investigate the convergence performance of the aforementioned dynamic system (11.9). Thus, by defining a Lyapunov function candidate $p(t) = |y^+(t)|^2$, its time derivative can be derived as follows:

$$\dot{p}(t) = -2\gamma y^+ \left(\operatorname{sgn}^{1/\alpha}(y^+(t)) + \operatorname{sgn}^\alpha(y^+(t)) \right)$$
$$= -2\gamma \left(|y^+(t)|^{\frac{1}{\alpha}+1} + |y^+(t)|^{\alpha+1} \right)$$
$$\leqslant -2\gamma |y^+(t)|^{\alpha+1}$$
$$= -2\gamma p(t)^{\frac{\alpha+1}{2}}.$$

Furthermore, by solving the differential inequality $\dot{p}(t) \leqslant -2\gamma p(t)^{\frac{\alpha+1}{2}}$ with the initial condition $p(0) = |y^+(0)|^2$, the following result can be derived:

$$p(t)^{\frac{1-\alpha}{2}} \begin{cases} \leqslant |y^+(0)|^{1-\alpha} - \gamma t(1-\alpha), & \text{if } t \leqslant |y^+(0)|^{1-\alpha}/\gamma(1-\alpha), \\ = 0, & \text{if } t > |y^+(0)|^{1-\alpha}/\gamma(1-\alpha), \end{cases}$$

which shows $p(t)$ can converge to zero after a time period $|y^+(0)|^{1-\alpha}/\gamma(1-\alpha)$. So, $y^+(t) = 0$ for $t > |y^+(0)|^{1-\alpha}/\gamma(1-\alpha)$, i.e. $t_f^+ < |y^+(0)|^{1-\alpha}/\gamma(1-\alpha)$. On the other hand, we can obtain that $y^-(t)$ is equal to zero in the same way for $t > |y^-(0)|^{1-\alpha}/\gamma(1-\alpha)$, i.e. $t_f^- < |y^-(0)|^{1-\alpha}/\gamma(1-\alpha)$. Therefore, it follows from the aforementioned two situations that

$$t_f < \max \left\{ \frac{|y^+(0)|^{1-\alpha}}{\gamma(1-\alpha)}, \frac{|y^-(0)|^{1-\alpha}}{\gamma(1-\alpha)} \right\},$$

which shows that, if the sign-bi-power activation function array is used, state matrix $U(t)$ of FTZNN model (11.8), starting from any randomly generated initial state $U(0)$, converges to the theoretical solution of Lyapunov equation (11.1) in finite time t_f. The proof is thus completed. ∎

11.4 Illustrative Verification

In Section 11.2, two related models (i.e. GNN and ZNN) are presented for solving online Lyapunov equation (11.1). For improving the convergence, in Section 11.3, FTZNN model (11.8) is further proposed and investigated. In this section, for illustrative and comparative purposes, let us consider the Lyapunov equation (11.1) with the following coefficient matrices (which are the same as Example 3 in [6]):

$$A = \begin{bmatrix} -3 & 4 \\ -1 & 1 \end{bmatrix} \text{ and } C = \begin{bmatrix} 1 & 0 \\ 0 & 0 \end{bmatrix}.$$

In addition, from Ref. [6], the theoretical solution U^* of the aforementioned Lyapunov equation can be obtained as follows:

$$U^* = \begin{bmatrix} 1/2 & -1 \\ -1 & 4 \end{bmatrix},$$

which can be used as a criterion to verify the solution effectiveness of three models presented in this chapter. Without loss of generality, we set design parameters $\gamma = 10$ and $r = 0.25$ for previous models.

First, starting from 10 randomly generated initial states $U(0) \in \mathbb{R}^{2\times2}$, we apply GNN model (11.3) and ZNN model (11.5) to online solution of the aforementioned Lyapunov equation. The corresponding simulation results are shown in Figures 11.1 and 11.2. From Figure 11.1a, we can observe that neural-state matrices $U(t) \in \mathbb{R}^{2\times2}$ synthesized by GNN model (11.3) can converge to the theoretical solution of the Lyapunov equation, but need about 18 seconds. However, as seen from Figure 11.1b, neural-state matrices $U(t) \in \mathbb{R}^{2\times2}$ synthesized by ZNN model (11.5) only need about 0.7 second to converge to the theoretical solution of the Lyapunov equation. In addition, Figure 11.2 displays the transient behavior of the residual error $\|A^{\mathsf{T}}U(t) + U(t)A + C\|_{\mathrm{F}}$ corresponding to neural-state matrices $U(t) \in \mathbb{R}^{2\times2}$ synthesized by GNN model (11.3) and ZNN model (11.5). From Figure 11.2, we can also obtain that residual errors of GNN model (11.3) can decrease to zero about 18 seconds, and residual errors of ZNN model (11.5) can decrease to zero about 0.7 second. The results agree with these of Figure 11.1 and verify the superior of ZNN (11.5) to GNN model (11.3). Specifically, by comparison with GNN model (11.3), the convergence speed of ZNN model (11.5) is increased about 25 times.

Second, for showing the effectiveness and superiority of FTZNN model (11.8), we apply it to solving the aforementioned Lyapunov equation under the same conditions. As seen from Figure 11.3a, neural-state matrices $U(t) \in \mathbb{R}^{2\times2}$ converge to the theoretical solution precisely within a very short finite time. In other words, $U(t) \in \mathbb{R}^{2\times2}$ synthesized by FTZNN model (11.8) is an exact solution

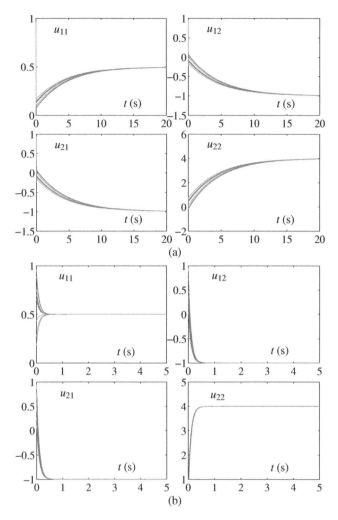

Figure 11.1 Transient behavior of $U(t)$ synthesized by GNN model (11.3) and ZNN model (11.5) starting from randomly generated initial state matrices $U(0) \in \mathbb{R}^{2\times2}$. (a) By GNN model (11.3) and (b) by ZNN model (11.5).

of the aforementioned Lyapunov equation. Besides, Figure 11.3b displays the transient behavior of the residual error $\|A^{\mathrm{T}}U(t) + U(t)A + C\|_{\mathrm{F}}$ corresponding to neural-state matrix $U(t) \in \mathbb{R}^{2\times2}$ synthesized by FTZNN model (11.8). It can be concluded from Figure 11.3b that the residual errors can decrease directly to zero within finite time 0.3 second instead of converging zero exponentially

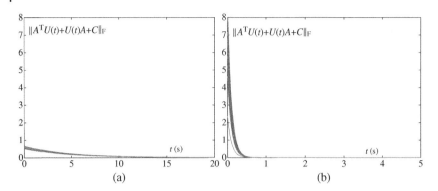

Figure 11.2 Transient behavior of $\|A^{\mathrm{T}}U(t) + U(t)A + C\|_{\mathrm{F}}$ synthesized by GNN model (11.3) and ZNN model (11.5) starting from randomly generated initial state matrices $U(0) \in \mathbb{R}^{2\times2}$. (a) By GNN model (11.3) and (b) by ZNN model (11.5).

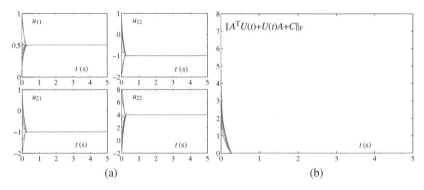

Figure 11.3 Simulative results synthesized by FTZNN model (11.8) starting from randomly generated initial state matrices $U(0) \in \mathbb{R}^{2\times2}$. (a) Transient behavior of state matrices and (b) transient behavior of residual errors.

(usually associated with ZNN model (11.5)). As compared with the previous results of ZNN (11.5) and GNN model (11.3), the convergence speed of FTZNN model (11.8) is the fastest, which verifies the superiority of FTZNN model (11.8) to other models.

It is worth pointing out that, as shown in Figure 11.4, the convergence time of FTZNN model (11.8) can be decreased from 0.3 to 0.03 second, and even to 3×10^{-3} second when the value of design parameter γ increases from 10 to 100 and to 10^3. That is to say, design parameter γ plays an important role in FTZNN model (11.8) and should be selected appropriately large to satisfy the convergence rate needed in fact. In summary, from the aforementioned simulation results, it can be concluded that FTZNN model (11.8) is effective on solving online

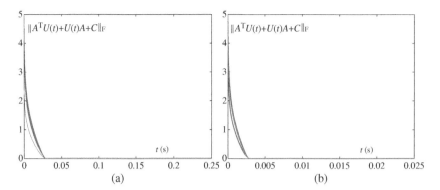

Figure 11.4 Transient behavior of $\|A^T U(t) + U(t)A + C\|_F$ synthesized by FTZNN model (11.8) starting with a randomly generated initial state. (a) With $\gamma = 100$ and (b) With $\gamma = 1000$.

Lyapunov equation (11.1). Furthermore, as compared with ZNN model (11.5) and GNN model (11.3), superior finite-time convergence to theoretical solution can be reached for FTZNN model (11.8).

11.5 Chapter Summary

In this chapter, an FTZNN has been proposed and investigated for online solution of Lyapunov equation. In addition, the upper bound of convergence time of the FTZNN model has been derived analytically. For comparative purposes, the conventional GNN and the original ZNN have been developed and used for solving such a Lyapunov equation. The illustrative results have further verified the efficacy and the superiority of the FTZNN model, as compared with the GNN and ZNN models for solving online Lyapunov equation.

References

1 Z. Luo and H. Sun, Extended Hamiltonian algorithm for the solution of discrete algebraic Lyapunov equations, *Appl. Math. Comput.*, 234 (2014) 245–252.

2 A. Wu, L. Lv, and M. Hou, Finite iterative algorithms for extended Sylvester-conjugate matrix equations, *J. Comput. Appl. Math.*, 54(9–10) (2011) 2363–2384.

3 H. Zhang and Z. Li *et al.*, On constructing Lyapunov functions for multi-agent systems, *Automatica*, 58 (2015) 39–42.

4 B. Zhou, G. Duan, and Z. Li, Gradient based iterative algorithm for solving coupled matrix equations, *Syst. Control Lett.*, 58(5) (2009) 327–333.

5 S. V. Raković and M. Lazar, The Minkowski-Lyapunov equation for linear dynamics: Theoretical foundations, *Automatica*, 50(8) (2014) 2015–2024.

6 G. R. Duan and R. J. Patton, Explicit and analytical solutions to Lyapunov algebraic matrix equations, Proceedings of IEE UKACC International Conference on Control, (1998) 1397–1402.

7 J. H. Mathews and K. D. Fink, *Numerical methods using MATLAB*, Upper Saddle River, NJ: Pearson Prentice Hall, 4 (2004).

8 H. Zhao and J. Zhang, Nonlinear dynamic system identification using pipelined functional link artificial recurrent neural network, *Neurocomputing*, 72(13–15) (2009) 3046–3054.

9 Y. Zhang and W. Ma *et al.*, MATLAB Simulink modeling and simulation of LVI-based primal-dual neural network for solving linear and quadratic programs, *Neurocomputing*, 72(7–9) (2009) 1679–1687.

10 S. M. Siniscalchi, T. Svendsen, and C. H. Lee, An artificial neural network approach to automatic speech processing, *Neurocomputing*, 140 (2014) 326–338.

11 S. Yahya, M. Moghavvemi, and H. A. Mohamed, Artificial neural networks aided solution to the problem of geometrically bounded singularities and joint limits prevention of a three dimensional planar redundant manipulator, *Neurocomputing*, 137 (2014) 34–46.

12 D. Tank and J. J. Hopfield, Simple 'neural' optimization networks: An A/D converter, signal decision circuit, and a linear programming circuit, *IEEE Trans. Circuits Syst.*, 33(5) (1986) 533–541.

13 Y. Zhang, D. Jiang, and J. Wang, A recurrent neural network for solving Sylvester equation with time-varying coefficients, *IEEE Trans. Neural Netw.*, 13(5) (2002) 1053–1063.

14 D. Guo, C. Yi, and Y. Zhang, Zhang neural network versus gradient-based neural network for time-varying linear matrix equation solving, *Neurocomputing*, 74(17) (2011) 3708–3712.

15 L. Xiao and Y. Zhang, Two new types of Zhang neural networks solving systems of time-varying nonlinear inequalities, *IEEE Trans. Circuits Syst. I*, 59(10) (2012) 2363–2373.

16 L. Xiao and Y. Zhang, From different Zhang functions to various ZNN models accelerated to finite-time convergence for time-varying linear matrix equation, *Neural Process. Lett.*, 39 (2014) 309–326.

17 L. Xiao, A finite-time convergent neural dynamics for online solution of time-varying linear complex matrix equation, *Neurocomputing*, 167 (2015) 254–259.

18 L. Xiao, A nonlinearly-activated neurodynamic model and its finite-time solution to equality-constrained quadratic optimization with nonstationary coefficients, *Appl. Soft Comput.*, 40 (2016) 252–259.

19 S. Li, S. Chen, and B. Liu, Accelerating a recurrent neural network to finite-time convergence for solving time-varying Sylvester equation by using a sign-bi-power activation function, *Neural Process. Lett.*, 37 (2013) 189–205.

12

Design Scheme II of FTZNN

12.1 Introduction

Lyapunov equation arises in a wide variety of scientific and engineering applications [1, 2], and especially plays a notable role in robustness analysis of various control systems [3]. There are tremendous amounts of methods that have been developed for the real-time solution of Lyapunov equations [4–9], which show the great importance of Lyapunov equation from both the theoretical and practical viewpoints.

In this chapter, we focus on adopting a novel evolution formula for the error function. Then, based on this new evolution formula, the corresponding FTZNN model is further presented and studied for solving online nonstationary Lyapunov equation. In comparison with the original zeroing neural network (ZNN) model, the output of the FTZNN model for nonstationary Lyapunov equation can coincide with the theoretical nonstationary solution within finite time. Finally, the proposed design strategy is successfully applied to online tracking control of a wheeled mobile manipulator.

12.2 Problem Formulation and Preliminaries

This chapter is concerned with the following nonstationary Lyapunov matrix equation [10–12]:

$$A^{\mathrm{T}}(t)U(t) + U(t)A(t) = -C(t) \in \mathbb{R}^{n \times n}, \tag{12.1}$$

where $A(t) \in \mathbb{R}^{n \times n}$ and $C(t) \in \mathbb{R}^{n \times n}$ stand for nonstationary coefficient matrices that are satisfied with the unique solution condition [11]; and $U(t) \in \mathbb{R}^{n \times n}$ stands for an unknown nonstationary matrix to be solved. For convenience, let $U^*(t) \in \mathbb{R}^{n \times n}$ denote the theoretical nonstationary solution of (12.1). The goal of this chapter is to present the FTZNN model for handling such a nonstationary Lyapunov equation.

Zeroing Neural Networks: Finite-time Convergence Design, Analysis and Applications,
First Edition. Lin Xiao and Lei Jia.

In the literature, gradient-based methods and other traditional algorithms have been presented to solve stationary Lyapunov equation and further developed in nonstationary case with large lagging errors [10, 11]. To remove these errors in real-time, the original ZNN model has been proposed for handling the nonstationary Lyapunov equation with the globally exponential convergence [12]. For comparative purposes, the original ZNN model for solving online nonstationary Lyapunov equation (12.1) is presented and designed in the following three-step procedure.

(1) The following error function is defined to supervise the solution process of (12.1):

$$Y(t) = A^{\mathrm{T}}(t)U(t) + U(t)A(t) + C(t) \in \mathbb{R}^{n \times n}, \tag{12.2}$$

where each element can be positive, zero, negative, or even lower-unbounded.

(2) The following evolution formula for $Y(t)$ is designed:

$$\mathrm{d}Y(t)/\mathrm{d}t = -\gamma Y(t), \tag{12.3}$$

where design parameter $\gamma > 0$,

(3) The following dynamic equation is obtained by substituting (12.2) into (12.3) (i.e. the original ZNN model):

$$\begin{aligned} A^{\mathrm{T}}(t)\dot{U}(t) + \dot{U}(t)A(t) = &- \dot{A}^{\mathrm{T}}(t)U(t) - U(t)\dot{A}(t) - \dot{C}(t) \\ &- \gamma \left(A^{\mathrm{T}}(t)U(t) + U(t)A(t) + C(t) \right), \end{aligned} \tag{12.4}$$

where state matrix $U(t) \in \mathbb{R}^{n \times n}$, starting from initial state $U(0) \in \mathbb{R}^{n \times n}$, corresponds to the theoretical nonstationary solution $U^*(t) \in \mathbb{R}^{n \times n}$ of (12.1).

Note that the following lemma [12] can make sure the global exponential convergence of original ZNN model (12.4) for online solution of nonstationary Lyapunov equation (12.1).

Lemma 12.1 *Given nonstationary matrices $A(t) \in \mathbb{R}^{n \times n}$ and $C(t) \in \mathbb{R}^{n \times n}$ in (12.1), starting from any randomly generated initial state $U(0) \in \mathbb{R}^{n \times n}$, the output $U(t)$ of original ZNN model (12.4) decreases to the theoretical nonstationary solution of (12.1) exponentially with time.*

12.3 FTZNN Model

After deep investigation for RNNs, we found that, by selecting an appropriate activation function, the convergence speed of neural-networks can be accelerated [13–15]. Differing from the thought of choosing nonlinear activation functions, we focus on adopting a novel evolution formula for the error function $Y(t)$, and thus present the novel FTZNN model for solving nonstationary Lyapunov equation (12.1). Specifically, in order to solve the nonstationary Lyapunov equation in finite time, the novel evolution formula and its corresponding FTZNN model are proposed. Then, the finite-time convergence upper bound of the proposed FTZNN model is estimated.

12.3.1 Design of FTZNN

As discussed before, during the processes of solving nonstationary Lyapunov equation (12.1), the output of original ZNN model (12.4) has been proven to decrease to the theoretical solution with time. In this subsection, according to the novel evolution formula for $Y(t)$, the FTZNN model is further proposed and its design procedure is presented as follows.

At first, the error function $Y(t)$ is defined as follows:

$$Y(t) = A^{\mathrm{T}}(t)U(t) + U(t)A(t) + C(t) \in \mathbb{R}^{n \times n},$$

which is the same with that of the original ZNN model.

Next, a new evolution formula for $Y(t)$ is presented as follows (which has a clear difference, as compared with the conventional evolution formula (12.3)):

$$\frac{\mathrm{d}Y(t)}{\mathrm{d}t} = -\gamma \left(\kappa_1 Y(t) + \kappa_2 Y^{\sigma/\rho}(t) \right), \tag{12.5}$$

where design parameters ρ and σ denote positive odd integer and satisfy $\rho > \sigma$; $\kappa_1 > 0$; $\kappa_2 > 0$; and γ is defined as before. More importantly, the following theorem is presented to demonstrate the superior of evolution formula (12.5) to conventional evolution formula (12.3).

Theorem 12.2 *Considering new evolution formula (12.5) for error function $Y(t)$, then $Y(t)$ can converge to zero in finite-time t_{f}:*

$$t_{\mathrm{f}} = \frac{\rho}{\beta_1(\rho - \sigma)} \ln \frac{\beta_1 Y(0)^{(\rho-\sigma)/\rho} + \beta_2}{\beta_2},$$

where $\beta_1 = \gamma \kappa_1 > 0$, $\beta_2 = \gamma \kappa_2 > 0$, and $Y(0)$ denotes any randomly generated initial error matrix.

Proof: For solving the dynamic response of new evolution formula (12.5), its differential equation is rewritten as follows:

$$Y^{-\sigma/\rho}(t) \diamond \frac{\mathrm{d}Y(t)}{\mathrm{d}t} + \beta_1 Y^{(\rho-\sigma)/\rho}(t) = -\beta_2 I, \tag{12.6}$$

where I denotes a $n \times n$ identity matrix; and the matrix-multiplication operator $\diamond$ is defined as follows:

$$W \diamond V = \begin{bmatrix} w_{11}v_{11} & w_{12}v_{12} & \cdots & w_{1n}v_{1n} \\ w_{21}v_{21} & w_{21}v_{21} & \cdots & w_{2n}v_{2n} \\ \vdots & \vdots & \ddots & \vdots \\ w_{m1}v_{m1} & w_{m2}v_{m2} & \cdots & w_{mn}v_{mn} \end{bmatrix} \in \mathbb{R}^{m \times n}.$$

In order to solve Eq. (12.6), let us define $H(t) = Y^{(\rho-\sigma)/\rho}(t)$. It follows that

$$\frac{dH(t)}{dt} = \frac{\rho - \sigma}{\rho} Y^{-\sigma/\rho}(t) \diamond \frac{dY(t)}{dt}. \tag{12.7}$$

Therefore, Eq. (12.6) is equal to

$$\frac{dH(t)}{dt} + \frac{\rho - \sigma}{\rho} \beta_1 H(t) = -\frac{\rho - \sigma}{\rho} \beta_2 I. \tag{12.8}$$

Then, according the first order differential theory, we have:

$$H(t) = \left(\frac{\beta_1}{\beta_2} + H(0) \right) \exp \left(-\frac{\rho - \sigma}{\rho} \beta_1 t \right) - \frac{\beta_1}{\beta_2} I. \tag{12.9}$$

In this case, $H(t)$ decreases to zero in finite time t_f, i.e. $H(t_f) = 0$. Therefore, one can obtain

$$\left(\frac{\beta_1}{\beta_2} I + H(0) \right) \exp \left(-\frac{\rho - \sigma}{\rho} \beta_1 t_f \right) = \frac{\beta_1}{\beta_2} I. \tag{12.10}$$

Thus, the output of new evolution formula (12.5) only requires the finite time t_f to reach the equilibrium state (i.e. $Y(t_f) = 0$):

$$t_f = \frac{\rho}{\beta_1(\rho - \sigma)} \ln \frac{\beta_1 Y(0)^{(\rho-\sigma)/\rho} + \beta_2}{\beta_2},$$

where initial error matrix $Y(0)$ is randomly generated. This result is a great breakthrough, in comparison with infinite time convergence. The proof is thus completed. ∎

Thirdly, we now keep on discussing novel evolution formula (12.5) for error function $Y(t)$. Expanding it, we can obtain the following FTZNN model for online solution of nonstationary Lyapunov equation (12.1):

$$\begin{aligned} A^T(t)\dot{U}(t) + \dot{U}(t)A(t) = &-\dot{A}^T(t)U(t) - U(t)\dot{A}(t) - \dot{C}(t) \\ &- \beta_1 \left(A^T(t)U(t) + U(t)A(t) + C(t) \right) \\ &- \beta_2 \left(A^T(t)U(t) + U(t)A(t) + C(t) \right)^{\sigma/\rho}, \end{aligned} \tag{12.11}$$

where design parameters $\beta_1 = \gamma \kappa_1 > 0$ and $\beta_2 = \gamma \kappa_2 > 0$.

12.3.2 Analysis of FTZNN

In Section 12.3.1, novel evolution formula (12.5) is studied and its corresponding FTZNN model (12.11) is proposed for solving nonstationary Lyapunov equation (12.1). In this part, the finite-time convergence of FTZNN model (12.11) is verified by the following main theorem.

Theorem 12.3 *Given nonstationary matrices $A(t) \in \mathbb{R}^{n \times n}$ and $C(t) \in \mathbb{R}^{n \times n}$ in (12.1), state matrix $U(t)$ of FTZNN model (12.11), starting from any randomly* *generated initial state* $U(0) \in \mathbb{R}^{n \times n}$, *converges to the theoretical nonstationary solution of Lyapunov equation (12.1) in finite time* t_f:

$$t_f \leqslant \max \left\{ \frac{\rho}{\beta_1(\rho - \sigma)} \ln \frac{\beta_1 y^+(0)^{(\rho-\sigma)/\rho} + \beta_2}{\beta_2}, \frac{\rho}{\beta_1(\rho - \sigma)} \ln \frac{\beta_1 y^-(0)^{(\rho-\sigma)/\rho} + \beta_2}{\beta_2} \right\},$$

where $y^-(0)$ *and* $y^+(0)$ *are the smallest and largest elements in* $Y(0)$, *respectively.*

Proof: Let $\tilde{U}(t) = U(t) - U^*(t)$ stand for the difference between the nonstationary solution $U(t)$ generated by proposed FTZNN model (12.11) and the theoretical nonstationary solution $U^*(t)$ of nonstationary Lyapunov equation (12.1). Therefore, we have

$$U(t) = \tilde{U}(t) + U^*(t) \in \mathbb{R}^{n \times n}. \tag{12.12}$$

Then, according to $A^T(t)U^*(t) + U^*(t)A(t) + C(t) = 0$ and its time-derivative form, we further obtain the following dynamic equation by substituting Eq. (12.12) into Eq. (12.11):

$$\begin{aligned} A^T(t)\dot{\tilde{U}}(t) + \dot{\tilde{U}}(t)A(t) = &- \dot{A}^T(t)\tilde{U}(t) - \tilde{U}(t)\dot{A}(t) \\ &- \beta_1 \left(A^T(t)\tilde{U}(t) + \tilde{U}(t)A(t) \right) \\ &- \beta_2 \left(A^T(t)\tilde{U}(t) + \tilde{U}(t)A(t) \right)^{\sigma/\rho}. \end{aligned}$$

Besides, since $Y(t) = A^T(t)U(t) + U(t)A(t) + C(t) = A^T(t)\tilde{U}(t) + \tilde{U}(t)A(t)$, the aforementioned equation can be rewritten equivalently as

$$\frac{dY(t)}{dt} = -\beta_1 Y(t) - \beta_2 Y^{\sigma/\rho}(t).$$

Entry-wisely, one can obtain

$$\dot{y}_{ij}(t) = -\beta_1 y_{ij}(t) - \beta_2 y_{ij}^{\sigma/\rho}(t), \tag{12.13}$$

where $y_{ij}(t)$ denotes the ijth element of $Y(t)$ with $i, j = 1, 2, 3, \ldots, n$.

According to the first order differential Eq. (12.13), we define $y^+(t)$ to be the element in $Y(t)$ with the largest initial value $y^+(0) = \max\{y_{ij}(0)\}$ for all possible i and j; and define $y^-(t)$ to be the element in $Y(t)$ with the smallest initial value $y^-(0) = \min\{y_{ij}(0)\}$ for all possible i and j. Note that every $y_{ij}(t)$ in $Y(t)$ has the same dynamics (12.13). It follows that

$$y^-(t) \leqslant y_{ij}(t) \leqslant y^+(t),$$

for all possible i and j and all $t > 0$. This means that $y_{ij}(t)$ decreases to zero for all possible i and j when both $y^+(t)$ and $y^-(t)$ converge to zero. Therefore, the convergence time of FTZNN model (12.11) is bounded by the larger one between the dynamics of $y^+(t)$ and $y^-(t)$, i.e. $t_f \leqslant \max\{t_f^+, t_f^-\}$ where t_f^+ and t_f^- stand for the convergence time of the dynamics of $y^+(t)$ and $y^-(t)$, respectively.

To estimate t_f, t_f^+, and t_f^- should be first calculated. For t_f^+, according to the analysis of Theorem 12.2, there exists t_f satisfying

$$t_f \leqslant \frac{\rho}{\beta_1(\rho - \sigma)} \ln \frac{\beta_1 y^+(0)^{(\rho-\sigma)/\rho} + \beta_2}{\beta_2},$$

such that $y^+(t_f) = 0$ when $t > t_f$. In the same way, for t_f^-, there exists t_f satisfying

$$t_f \leqslant \frac{\rho}{\beta_1(\rho - \sigma)} \ln \frac{\beta_1 y^-(0)^{(\rho-\sigma)/\rho} + \beta_2}{\beta_2},$$

such that $y^-(t_f) = 0$ when $t > t_f$.

Therefore, it can be concluded that the convergence upper bound of FTZNN model (12.11) is estimated as

$$t_f \leqslant \max \left\{ \frac{\rho}{\beta_1(\rho - \sigma)} \ln \frac{\beta_1 y^+(0)^{(\rho-\sigma)/\rho} + \beta_2}{\beta_2}, \frac{\rho}{\beta_1(\rho - \sigma)} \ln \frac{\beta_1 y^-(0)^{(\rho-\sigma)/\rho} + \beta_2}{\beta_2} \right\},$$

which implies that the output $U(t)$ of FTZNN model (12.11) reaches the theoretical solution of Lyapunov equation (12.1) after a period finite time t_f. The proof is thus completed. ∎

12.4 Illustrative Verification

In the previous section, FTZNN model (12.11) is presented for online solution of nonstationary Lyapunov equation (12.1) by designing a new evolution formula for $Y(t)$. In addition, the design process and the finite-time convergence analysis are provided. In this part, we present one illustrative example to demonstrate the effectiveness and the superiority of FTZNN model (12.11) to original ZNN model (12.4).

For comparison convenience, the illustrative example is chosen with

$$A(t) = \begin{bmatrix} -1 - \frac{1}{2}\cos(2t) & \frac{1}{2}\sin(2t) \\ \frac{1}{2}\sin(2t) & -1 + \frac{1}{2}\cos(2t) \end{bmatrix}, \quad C(t) = \begin{bmatrix} \sin(2t) & \cos(2t) \\ -\cos(2t) & \sin(2t) \end{bmatrix}.$$

The theoretical nonstationary solution of $U(t)$ for the aforementioned problem can be obtained by simple algebraic operations, and the elements of $U^*(t)$ are denoted as follows:

$$u_{11}^*(t) = -\sin(2t)(\cos(2t) - 2)/3,$$
$$u_{12}^*(t) = -(2\cos(2t) - 1)(\cos(2t) + 2)/6,$$
$$u_{21}^*(t) = -(2\cos(2t) + 1)(\cos(2t) - 2)/6,$$
$$u_{22}^*(t) = (\cos(2t) + 2)\sin(2t)/3.$$

This can be validated by substituting the theoretical solution into the left side of (12.1). Thus, we can use the theoretical solution to validate the accuracy of such two ZNN models. It is worth pointing out that, as proved in Theorem 12.3, the convergence upper bound of FTZNN model (12) is related to design parameters γ, κ_1 κ_2, ρ, and σ. In addition, we can conclude that, for FTZNN model (12), the smaller the upper bound, the faster the convergence speed. According to this principle, parameters $\beta_1 = \gamma\kappa_1$ and $\beta_2 = \gamma\kappa_2$ can be chosen as large as hardware permits (e.g. in analog circuits) or selected appropriately for experimental and/or simulative purposes. Besides, as the ratio ρ/σ deceases, the convergence speed of FTZNN model (12) can also be accelerated. Therefore, the ratio ρ/σ should be set as small as hardware permits. Without any loss of generality, design parameters $\gamma = 1$, $\kappa_1 = \kappa_2 = 1$, and $\rho/\sigma = 0.2$. The computer simulation results are shown in Figures 12.1–12.3.

Figure 12.1 displays the transient behavior of neural state $U(t)$ synthesized by original ZNN model (12.4), where dash curves stand for theoretical nonstationary solution $U^*(t)$, and solid curves stand for neural state $U(t)$. From Figure 12.1, it can be observed that, starting from randomly generated initial states $U(0) \in [-3, 3]^{2 \times 2}$, neural states $U(t) \in \mathbb{R}^{2 \times 2}$ of original ZNN model (12.4) can approach to the theoretical nonstationary solution after about five seconds. To validate the superiority of FTZNN model (12.11) for online solution of the nonstationary Lyapunov

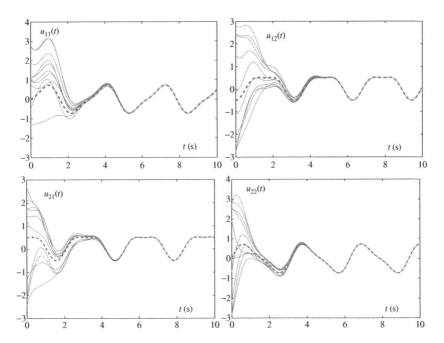

Figure 12.1 Transient behavior of neural state $U(t)$ synthesized by original ZNN model (12.4).

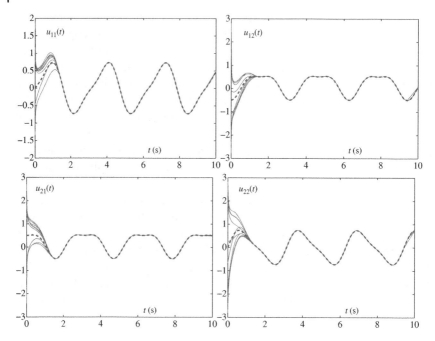

Figure 12.2 Transient behavior of neural state $U(t)$ synthesized by FTZNN model (12.11).

equation, we apply FTZNN model (12.11) to solve the same problem under the same conditions, and the corresponding the transient behavior of neural state $U(t)$ is plotted in Figure 12.2. From this figure, we can see that neural states $U(t) \in \mathbb{R}^{2 \times 2}$ of FTZNN model (12.11) reach the theoretical nonstationary solution only after about 1.5 seconds. This result demonstrates the superiority of FTZNN model (12.11) to original ZNN model (12.4).

On the other hand, we can use the Frobenius norm $\|A^T(t)U(t) + U(t)A(t) + C(t)\|_F$ to measure the residual error and compare the performance between such two ZNN models under the same conditions. Figure 12.3a,b shows the transient behavior of residual error $\|A^T(t)U(t) + U(t)A(t) + C(t)\|_F$ synthesized by the original ZNN model (12.4) and FTZNN model (12.11) separately. From Figure 12.3, starting from 10 randomly generated initial states $U(0) \in [-3, 3]^{2 \times 2}$, we can observe contrastively that the residual error can converge to zero after about five seconds for the original ZNN model (12.4), and about 1.5 seconds for FTZNN model (12.11). The simulative results are fit with these of Figures 12.1 and 12.2, which further validate the advantage of FTZNN model (12.11), as compared with original ZNN model (12.4).

In summary, from the previous comparison results, we know that original ZNN model (12.4) and FTZNN model (12.11) are feasible to handle nonstationary

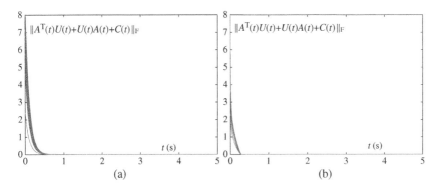

Figure 12.3 Transient behavior of residual error $\|A^T(t)U(t) + U(t)A(t) + C(t)\|_F$ corresponding to the neural state $U(t)$ synthesized by original ZNN model (12.4) and FTZNN model (12.11). (a) By the original ZNN model (12.4) and (b) by FTZNN model (12.11).

Lyapunov equation (12.1). In addition, it can be concluded by comparison that the original ZNN model (12.4) can exponentially decrease to the theoretical nonstationary solution with time. However, original ZNN model (12.4) never converges to the theoretical nonstationary solution of (12.1) within finite time, which may limit its real-time calculations. In contrast, FTZNN model (12.11) owns the excellent convergent performance (i.e. finite-time convergence) for solving such a Lyapunov equation. In short, FTZNN model (12.11) is superior to original ZNN model (12.4), which is substantiated through the theoretical analysis and computer-simulation results.

12.5 Application to Tracking Control

To verify the application ability of FTZNN model (12.11), a mobile manipulator is introduced in this section to show the feasibility of the proposed strategy. The model and the corresponding geometric graph of the mobile manipulator can be seen in [16]. In addition, only the end-effector position is considered for simplicity purposes. From [16], we can obtain the kinematics model of the wheeled mobile manipulator, which is expressed in following simple form:

$$r_w(t) = f(\Theta(t)) \in \mathbb{R}^m, \tag{12.14}$$

where $\Theta = [\varphi^T, \theta T]^T \in \mathbb{R}^{n+2}$ denotes the combined angle vector of the mobile platform $\varphi = [\varphi_1, \varphi_r]^T$ and the manipulator $\theta = [\theta_1, \theta_2, \ldots, \theta_n]^T$, $r_w(t)$ denotes the end-effector position vector with respect to the world coordinate system, and $f(\cdot)$ is a smooth nonlinear mapping function.

Then, according to the design process of FTZNN model (12.11), we can obtain the following dynamic model to track control of the mobile manipulator:

$$J(\Theta(t))\dot{\Theta} = \dot{r}_w(t) + \beta_1 \left(r_w(t) - f(\Theta(t)) \right) + \beta_2 \left(r_w(t) - f(\Theta(t)) \right)^{\rho/\sigma}, \quad (12.15)$$

where $J(\Theta(t))$ is defined as $J(\Theta(t)) = \partial f(\Theta(t))/\partial\Theta \in \mathbb{R}^{m\times(n+2)}$. For further verifying the feasibility of the strategy to track control of the mobile manipulator, an ellipse path is expected to track control by the mobile manipulator. The major axis of the ellipse path is 2 m and the minor axis is 1 m. Besides, we set $\beta_1 = \beta_2 = 1$, initial state $\Theta(0) = [0, 0, \pi/3, \pi/12, \pi/12, \pi/12, \pi/12, \pi/12]^T$, and task duration $\Gamma = 10$ seconds. The corresponding simulation results are displayed in Figures 12.4 and 12.5.

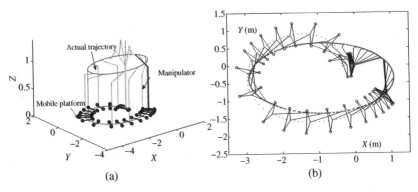

(a) (b)

Figure 12.4 Tracking ellipse-path results of the mobile manipulator synthesized by the proposed model (12.15). (a) Whole tracking motion trajectories and (b) top graph of tracking motion trajectories.

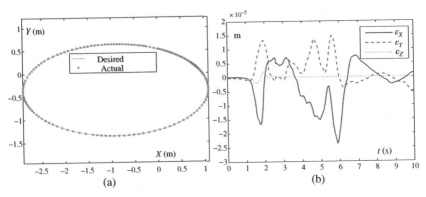

(a) (b)

Figure 12.5 Tracking ellipse-path results of the mobile manipulator synthesized by the proposed model (12.15). (a) Desired path and actual trajectory and (b) tracking errors at the joint position level.

Figure 12.4a plots the tracking process of the mobile manipulator synthesized by the proposed model (12.15), and Figure 12.4b plots the corresponding top graph of tracking trajectories. From Figure 12.4, we can conclude that the mobile manipulator's end-effector performs the tracking task well. Besides, as observed from Figure 12.5a, the actual end-effector motion trajectory overlaps with the desired ellipse path. More importantly, Figure 12.5b plots the tracking errors $\varepsilon := r_w(t) - f(\Theta(t))$ at joint position level, which are less than 3×10^{-5} m. This simulation further validates the feasibility of the proposed model (12.15) by applying the mobile manipulator to perform the ellipse path tracking task.

12.6 Chapter Summary

For the sake of solving online nonstationary problems more efficiently, a new evolution formula has been proposed in this chapter. The corresponding theoretical analysis has been presented to verify its superiority to the previously proposed evolution formula. Then, the novel FTZNN model has been presented and studied for online solution of nonstationary Lyapunov equation based on the new evolution formula, with the upper bound of convergence time derived analytically. In comparison with the original ZNN model for nonstationary Lyapunov equation, the FTZNN model can reach the desired nonstationary solution within finite time. Numerical results have further demonstrated the efficacy and superiority of the FTZNN model to the original ZNN model for handling nonstationary Lyapunov equation. In addition, the proposed strategy for the FTZNN model has been successfully applied to online tracking control of a wheeled mobile manipulator.

References

1 B. Zhou, G. Duan, and Z. Lin, A parametric periodic Lyapunov equation with application in semi-global stabilization of discrete-time periodic systems subject to actuator saturation, *Automatica*, 47(2) (2011) 316–325.

2 H. Zhang and Z. Li *et al.*, On constructing Lyapunov functions for multi-agent systems, *Automatica*, 58 (2015) 39–42.

3 M. S. De Queiroz and D. M. Dawson *et al.*, *Lyapunov-based control of mechanical systems*, Berlin: Springer-Verlag, (2000).

4 Z. Li and B. Zhou, Positive operator based iterative algorithms for solving Lyapunov equations for Itô stochastic systems with Markovian jumps, *Appl. Math. Comput.*, 217(21) (2011) 8179–8195.

5 A. Wu, L. Tong, and G. Duan, Finite iterative algorithm for solving coupled Lyapunov equations appearing in continuous-time Markov jump linear systems, *Int. J. Syst. Sci.*, 44(11) (2013) 2082–2093.

6 V. Druskin, L. Knizhnerman, and V. Simoncini, Analysis of the rational Krylov subspace and ADI methods for solving the Lyapunov equation, *SIAM J. Numer. Anal.*, 49(5) (2011) 1875–1898.

7 G. M. Flagg and S. Gugercin, On the ADI method for the Sylvester equation and the optimal-H_2 points, *Appl. Numer. Math.*, 64 (2013) 50–58.

8 L. Xiao and B. Liao, A convergence-accelerated Zhang neural network and its solution application to Lyapunov equation, *Neurocomputing*, 193 (2016) 213–218.

9 L. Knizhnerman and V. Simoncini, Convergence analysis of the extended Krylov subspace method for the Lyapunov equation, *Numer. Math.*, 118(3) (2011) 567–586.

10 Y. Zhang and K. Chen, Simulink modeling and comparison of Zhang neural networks and gradient neural networks for time-varying Lyapunov equation solving, 2008 4th International Conference on Natural Computation, 3 (2008) 521–525.

11 C. Yi, Y. Chen, and Z. Lu, Improved gradient-based neural networks for online solution of Lyapunov matrix equation, *Inform. Process. Lett.*, 111(16) (2011) 780–786.

12 C. Yi, Y. Chen, and X. Lan, Comparison on neural solvers for the Lyapunov matrix equation with stationary & nonstationary coefficient, *Appl. Math. Model.*, 37(4) (2013) 2495–2502.

13 S. Li, S. Chen, and B. Liu, Accelerating a recurrent neural network to finite-time convergence for solving time-varying Sylvester equation by using a sign-bi-power activation function, *Neural Process. Lett.*, 37 (2013) 189–205.

14 L. Xiao, A nonlinearly-activated neurodynamic model and its finite-time solution to equality-constrained quadratic optimization with nonstationary coefficients, *Appl. Soft Comput.*, 40 (2016) 252–259.

15 L. Xiao and R. Lu, Finite-time solution to nonlinear equation using recurrent neural dynamics with a specially-constructed activation function, *Neurocomputing*, 151 (2015) 246–251.

16 L. Xiao and Y. Zhang, A new performance index for the repetitive motion of mobile manipulators, *IEEE Trans. Cybern.*, 44(2) (2014) 280–292.

13

Design Scheme III of FTZNN

13.1 Introduction

Lyapunov equation has a wide spectrum of applications in nonlinear systems, and many solving methods are given to address this problem in control community [1–6]. In the past decades, static Lyapunov equation was extensively investigated due to the simplicity of the structure [7]. Recently, dynamic Lyapunov equation was appeared more frequently in the literature [8–10]. Generally, the dynamic Lyapunov equation is written as follows [8–10]:

$$C^{\mathrm{T}}(t)U(t) + U(t)C(t) = -G(t), \tag{13.1}$$

where $C(t) \in \mathbb{R}^{n \times n}$ and $G(t) \in \mathbb{R}^{n \times n}$ represent known dynamic matrices; and $U(t) \in \mathbb{R}^{n \times n}$ represents an unknown dynamic matrix. From the point of view of control, solving the dynamic Lyapunov equation earlier is to find $U(t)$ via different control mechanisms such that (13.1) holds under the assumption of existence of the theoretical solution $U^*(t) \in \mathbb{R}^{n \times n}$ [8].

The main work of this chapter is to design and analyze a nonlinear zeroing neural network (ZNN) from the proportional integral derivative (PID) control viewpoint. We particularly address three important aspects in the design: (i) the global stability, to guarantee the effectiveness of the solution; (ii) the robustness against additive noises, to ensure the capability of nonlinear finite-time zeroing neural network (N-FTZNN) for using in harsh environments; (iii) the finite-time convergence, to endow N-FTZNN for real-time solution of dynamical problems. In a word, we aim at establishing a N-FTZNN model with finite-time convergence and inherently noise tolerance based on the efficient solution of dynamic Lyapunov equation in a unified framework of ZNN. In addition, these theoretical conclusions of the N-FTZNN model are validated by solving dynamic Lyapunov equation in the simulation and experiment parts.

Zeroing Neural Networks: Finite-time Convergence Design, Analysis and Applications,
First Edition. Lin Xiao and Lei Jia.
© 2023 The Institute of Electrical and Electronics Engineers, Inc. Published 2023 by John Wiley & Sons, Inc.

13.2 N-FTZNN Model

Keeping the aforementioned consideration in mind, in this section, we first aim at establishing a novel N-FTZNN model with finite-time convergence and inherently noise tolerance based on the efficient solution of dynamic Lyapunov equation (13.1) in a unified framework of ZNN. Then, we show the established N-FTZNN model is essentially a nonlinear PID control law from nonlinear PID perspective.

13.2.1 Design of N-FTZNN

Then, based on the design process of ZNN [11–13], the specific design procedure of the N-FTZNN model for dynamic Lyapunov equation is presented in a unified framework as follows.

At first, based on the description of the dynamic Lyapunov equation, the error function is chosen as

$$Y(t) = C^{\mathrm{T}}(t)U(t) + U(t)C(t) + G(t). \tag{13.2}$$

In order to realize noise tolerance and finite-time convergence, a novel evolution formula activated by nonlinear functions is proposed as follows:

$$
\begin{aligned}
\frac{\mathrm{d}Y(t)}{\mathrm{d}t} = &- \gamma_1 \Phi_1(Y(t)) \\
&- \gamma_2 \Phi_2 \left(Y(t) + \gamma_1 \int_0^t \Phi_1(Y(\tau)) \mathrm{d}\tau \right),
\end{aligned}
\tag{13.3}
$$

where $\gamma_1 > 0$ and $\gamma_2 > 0$; $\Phi_1(\cdot)$ and $\Phi_2(\cdot)$ stand for two monotone increasing odd nonlinear activation function arrays.

In the end, based on the previous design method, by combining (13.2) and (13.3), the following N-FTZNN model is established for computing dynamic Lyapunov equation:

$$
\begin{aligned}
C^{\mathrm{T}}\dot{U} + \dot{U}C = &-\dot{C}^{\mathrm{T}}U - U\dot{C} - \gamma_1\Phi_1\left(C^{\mathrm{T}}U + UC + G\right) \\
&- \dot{G} - \gamma_2\Phi_2\left(\left(C^{\mathrm{T}}U + UC + G\right) \right. \\
&\left. + \gamma_1 \int_0^t \Phi_1\left(C^{\mathrm{T}}U + UC + G\right)\mathrm{d}\tau \right),
\end{aligned}
\tag{13.4}
$$

where argument t is omitted due to space limitation, and the other parameters are defined as before. In the ensuing section, we will theoretically prove the stability and finite-time convergence of N-FTZNN model (13.4). In addition, in order to investigate the inherently noise-tolerance of N-FTZNN model (13.4) for computing dynamic Lyapunov equation, the following noise-polluted N-FTZNN model is directly extended by adding an unknown additive noise ς:

$$C^{\mathrm{T}}\dot{U} + \dot{U}C = -\dot{C}^{\mathrm{T}}U - U\dot{C} - \gamma_1 \Phi_1 \left(C^{\mathrm{T}}U + UC + G \right)$$
$$- \dot{G} - \gamma_2 \Phi_2 \left(\left(C^{\mathrm{T}}U + UC + G \right) \right.$$
$$\left. + \gamma_1 \int_0^t \Phi_1 \left(C^{\mathrm{T}}U + UC + G \right) \mathrm{d}\tau \right) + \varsigma. \tag{13.5}$$

Note that noise-polluted N-FTZNN model (13.5) is a simple extension to noise-free N-FTZNN model (13.4) via adding an additive noise ς. The purpose for this is to study the impact of an unknown additive noise to noise-free N-FTZNN model (13.4).

For comparative purposes, the conventional ZNN for dynamic Lyapunov equation (13.1) is presented

$$C^{\mathrm{T}}\dot{U} + \dot{U}C = - \dot{C}^{\mathrm{T}}U - U\dot{C} - \gamma_1 \left(C^{\mathrm{T}}U + UC + G \right) - \dot{G}, \tag{13.6}$$

where argument t is also omitted. If this model is polluted by unknown additive noise, we can directly exploit the aforementioned processing method by adding an unknown additive noise ς to ZNN model (13.6).

13.2.2 Re-Interpretation from Nonlinear PID Perspective

In this part, we show established N-FTZNN model (13.4) is essentially a non-linear PID control law [14]. In addition, this control law features both nonlinear dynamics and finite time convergence.

At first, the error function can be seen as output error between the true value and the reference. Thus, it can be reformulated as

$$Y(t) = \mathbf{0} - (C^{\mathrm{T}}(t)U(t) + U(t)C(t) + G(t)), \tag{13.7}$$

where $\mathbf{0}$ is used to denote zero matrix corresponding to the value of $C^{\mathrm{T}}(t)U^*(t) + U^*(t)C(t) + G(t)$. To compute dynamic Lyapunov equation (13.1), from the non-linear PID perspective, we can design a control law to make error function $Y(t)$ converge to zero. Thus, with $U(t)$ as an input of such a system, $U(t)$ as a state variable and $Y(t)$ as an output, the following dynamic system can be used to formulate this problem:

$$\frac{\mathrm{d}U(t)}{\mathrm{d}t} = \mathrm{R}(t),$$
$$C^{\mathrm{T}}(t)U(t) + U(t)C(t) + G(t) = -Y(t). \tag{13.8}$$

Through the aforementioned equivalent transformation from the point of control, solving dynamic Lyapunov equation (13.1) is converted to find a control law $\mathrm{R}(t)$

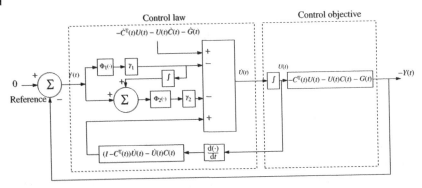

Figure 13.1 Block diagram of the control architecture of N-FTZNN model (13.4) for solving dynamic Lyapunov from the nonlinear PID perspective.

to regulate $Y(t)$ to zero. Now, let us review novel evolution formula (13.3) from the viewpoint of nonlinear PID control. Obviously, expanding evolution formula (13.3) leads to N-FTZNN model (13.4). Besides, based on the formulation of (13.8) and vectorization technique, we can obtain the control law $R(t)$ from N-FTZNN model (13.4) as (expressed in the vector form):

$$r = \dot{u} = -D^{-1}\left(Hu + \dot{g} + \gamma_1 \Phi_1 (Du + g)\right)$$
$$- \gamma_2 D^{-1}\Phi_2 \left((Du + g) + \gamma_1 \int_0^t \Phi_1 (Du + g)\,d\tau\right), \tag{13.9}$$

where $D := I \otimes C^T + C^T \otimes I \in \mathbb{R}^{n^2 \times n^2}$ with $\otimes$ being the Kronecker product operator, $H := I \otimes \dot{C}^T + \dot{C}^T \otimes I$, $r = \text{vec}(R) \in \mathbb{R}^{n^2}$ with $\text{vec}(\cdot)$ being the vectorization operation function by putting all the column vectors of a matrix into one new column vector, $g = \text{vec}(G)$, and $u = \text{vec}(U)$. In addition, $\dot{g}$ and $\dot{u}$ are used to denote the time derivatives of $g = \text{vec}(G)$ and $u = \text{vec}(U)$, respectively. From the expression of the control law $U(t)$, we easily know N-FTZNN model (13.4) can be explained as a nonlinear PID controller because it includes the nonlinear activations and units of the proportional, the integral and the derivative [14]. For easy understanding of N-FTZNN model (13.4) from the nonlinear PID perspective, the block diagram for the realization of N-FTZNN model (13.4) is presented in Figure 13.1 to show the control architecture.

13.3 Theoretical Analysis

In this section, the main theoretical results of N-FTZNN model (13.4) are presented. At first, the global stability and finite-time convergence of N-FTZNN model (13.4) are proved in theory. Then, with unknown additive noises considered, the robustness property of N-FTZNN model (13.4) is discussed by analyzing noise-polluted N-FTZNN model (13.5).

Theorem 13.1 *Given dynamic coefficient matrices $C(t) \in \mathbb{R}^{n \times n}$ and $G(t) \in \mathbb{R}^{n \times n}$ that satisfy the condition of the unique solution of (13.1). N-FTZNN model (13.4) is globally stable in sense of Lyapunov as long as $\Phi_1(\cdot)$ and $\Phi_2(\cdot)$ are monotone increasing odd activation function arrays.*

Proof: First of all, we will show N-FTZNN model (13.4) is a simple expansion of novel evolution formula (13.3). In this work, we focus on the dynamic Lyapunov equation solving. In order to solve dynamic Lyapunov equation, we equivalently transform this problem solving to zero error function (13.2). If this error function is equal to 0, the resultant solution is what we need for dynamic Lyapunov equation. Now, let us compute the time derivative of the error function, and we have

$$\dot{Y}(t) = \dot{C}^{\mathrm{T}}(t)U(t) + C^{\mathrm{T}}(t)\dot{U}(t) + \dot{U}(t)C(t) + U(t)\dot{C}(t) + \dot{G}(t).$$

Then, substituting the expressions of $Y(t)$ and $\dot{Y}(t)$ to novel evolution formula (13.3), we can obtain N-FTZNN model (13.4). Thus, we can directly analyze novel evolution formula (13.3), of which its ijth subsystem is written as follows ($\forall i, j \in 1, 2, \ldots, n$):

$$\dot{y}_{ij}(t) = -\gamma_1 \phi_1(y_{ij}(t)) - \gamma_2 \phi_2 \left(y_{ij}(t) + \gamma_1 \int_0^t \phi_1(y_{ij}(\tau)) \mathrm{d}\tau \right), \tag{13.10}$$

where $y_{ij}(t)$ represents the ijth element of $Y(t)$; and $\phi_1(\cdot)$ and $\phi_2(\cdot)$ respectively stand for the elements of $\Phi_1(\cdot)$ and $\Phi_2(\cdot)$. For the ijth subsystem (13.10), we are able to define the following intermediate variable $a_{ij}(t)$:

$$a_{ij}(t) = y_{ij}(t) + \gamma_1 \int_0^t \phi_1(y_{ij}(\tau)) \mathrm{d}\tau, \tag{13.11}$$

from which, we compute its time derivative as

$$\dot{a}_{ij}(t) = \dot{y}_{ij}(t) + \gamma_1 \phi_1(y_{ij}(t)). \tag{13.12}$$

Synthesizing the results of (13.10), (13.11) and (13.12), we have

$$\dot{a}_{ij}(t) = -\gamma_2 \phi_2(a_{ij}(t)). \tag{13.13}$$

Thus, the following Lyapunov function candidate $p_{ij}(t)$ is designed for analyzing the stability of the ijth subsystem (13.10):

$$p_{ij}(t) = \frac{1}{2} \xi y_{ij}^2(t) + \frac{1}{2} a_{ij}^2(t), \tag{13.14}$$

where $\xi > 0$ and $v_0 = p_{ij}(0) = \xi y_{ij}^2(0)/2 + a_{ij}^2(0)/2$ with $y_{ij}(0)$ and $a_{ij}(0)$ known. Obviously, in this situation, $p_{ij}(t)$ is positive-definite because $p_{ij}(t) > 0$ for any

$y_{ij}(t) \neq 0$ or $a_{ij}(t) \neq 0$; and $p_{ij}(t) = 0$ only for $y_{ij}(t) = a_{ij}(t) = 0$. Besides, the time derivative of $p_{ij}(t)$ is computed as

$$
\begin{aligned}
\dot{p}_{ij}(t) &= \xi y_{ij}(t)\dot{y}_{ij}(t) + a_{ij}(t)\dot{a}_{ij}(t) \\
&= \xi y_{ij}(t)[\dot{a}_{ij}(t) - \gamma_1\phi_1(y_{ij}(t))] \\
&\quad - \gamma_2 a_{ij}(t)\phi_2(a_{ij}(t)) \\
&= -\xi\gamma_2 y_{ij}(t)\phi_2(a_{ij}(t)) - \xi\gamma_1 y_{ij}(t)\phi_1(y_{ij}(t)) \\
&\quad - \gamma_2 a_{ij}(t)\phi_2(a_{ij}(t)).
\end{aligned}
\tag{13.15}
$$

To prove $\dot{p}_{ij}(t) \leq 0$, we can adopt the mean-value theorem in the region $\mathbb{R}$ for $\phi_2(\cdot)$, which yields to the following fact:

$$
\phi_2(a_{ij}(t)) - \phi_2(0) = (a_{ij}(t) - 0)\frac{\partial\phi_2(a_{ij}(\bar{\xi}))}{\partial a_{ij}}\bigg|_{a_{ij}(\bar{\xi})\in\mathbb{R}}.
\tag{13.16}
$$

In addition, from the given conditions, we know $\phi_2(\cdot)$ is a monotone increasing odd function, so $\phi_2(0) = 0$ and $\partial\phi_2(a_{ij}(t))/\partial a_{ij} > 0$. Thus, based on (13.16), we are able to get the following conclusion:

$$
|\phi_2(a_{ij}(t))| \leq A_0|a_{ij}(t)|,
$$

where $A_0 = \max\{\partial\phi_2(a_{ij}(t))/\partial a_{ij}\}|_{a_{ij}(t)\in\mathbb{R}} > 0$. Hence, we further have

$$
\begin{aligned}
|y_{ij}(t)\phi_2(a_{ij}(t))| &\leq |y_{ij}(t)| \cdot |\phi_2(a_{ij}(t))| \\
&\leq A_0|y_{ij}(t)| \cdot |a_{ij}(t)|.
\end{aligned}
\tag{13.17}
$$

Substituting (13.17) back into (13.15), we have

$$
\begin{aligned}
\frac{dp_{ij}(t)}{dt} &= -\xi\gamma_2 y_{ij}(t)\phi_2(a_{ij}(t)) - \xi\gamma_1 y_{ij}(t)\phi_1(y_{ij}(t)) \\
&\quad - \gamma_2 a_{ij}(t)\phi_2(a_{ij}(t)) \\
&\leq \xi\gamma_2|y_{ij}(t)\phi_2(a_{ij}(t))| - \xi\gamma_1 y_{ij}(t)\phi_1(y_{ij}(t)) \\
&\quad - \gamma_2 a_{ij}(t)\phi_2(a_{ij}(t)) \\
&\leq \xi\gamma_2 A_0|y_{ij}(t)| \cdot |a_{ij}(t)| - \xi\gamma_1 A_1 y_{ij}^2(t) - \gamma_2 A_2 a_{ij}^2(t) \\
&= -\xi\left(\sqrt{\gamma_1 A_1}|y_{ij}| - \frac{\gamma_2 A_0}{2\sqrt{\gamma_1 A_1}}|a_{ij}(t)|\right)^2 \\
&\quad - \xi\left(\frac{\gamma_2 A_2}{\xi} - \frac{\gamma_2^2 A_0^2}{4\gamma_1 A_1}\right)a_{ij}^2(t),
\end{aligned}
\tag{13.18}
$$

where $A_1 = \min\{\partial\phi_1(y_{ij}(t))/\partial y_{ij}\}|_{y_{ij}(t)\in\Omega_1} > 0$ and $A_2 = \min\{\partial\phi_2(a_{ij}(t))/\partial a_{ij}\}$ $|_{a_{ij}(t)\in\Omega_2} > 0$ that are obtained by applying the mean-value theorem two times. From the previous discussion, we have $\dot{p}_{ij}(t) \leq 0$ provided that

$$0 < \xi \leq \frac{4\mu_1 A_1 A_2}{\mu_2 A_0^2}. \tag{13.19}$$

The aforementioned result is able to make sure the negative definiteness of $\dot{p}_{ij}(t)$. Hence, according to Lyapunov stability theory, we come to a conclusion that the ijth subsystem (13.10) of the novel evolution formula is globally stable.

In addition, based on the conclusion of $\dot{p}_{ij}(t) \leq 0$, it is easy to conclude that $p_{ij}(t) \leq p_0$. Thus, we can further shrink the range when applying the mean-value theorem. Specifically, in this situation, we can gain the following conclusions:

$$\frac{1}{2}\xi y_{ij}^2(t) \leq p_0 \quad \text{and} \quad \frac{1}{2}a_{ij}^2(t) \leq p_0, \tag{13.20}$$

from which we can further derive

$$|y_{ij}(t)| \leq \sqrt{2p_0/\xi} \quad \text{and} \quad |a_{ij}(t)| \leq \sqrt{2p_0}. \tag{13.21}$$

Let us denote respectively the set Ω_1 for $y_{ij}(t)$ and the set Ω_2 for $a_{ij}(t)$. Then, we have

$$\Omega_1 = \left\{ y_{ij}(t) \in R, \; |y_{ij}(t)| \leq \sqrt{2p_0/\xi} \right\},$$
$$\Omega_2 = \left\{ a_{ij}(t) \in R, \; |a_{ij}(t)| \leq \sqrt{2p_0} \right\}. \tag{13.22}$$

Thus, we can replace the set $\mathbb{R}$ with Ω_1 for $y_{ij}(t)$ and the set Ω_2 for $a_{ij}(t)$, i.e. $A_0 = \max\{\partial\phi_2(a_{ij}(t))/\partial a_{ij}\}|_{a_{ij}(t)\in\Omega_2}$, $A_1 = \min\{\partial\phi_1(y_{ij}(t))/\partial y_{ij}\}|_{y_{ij}(t)\in\Omega_1}$ and $A_2 = \min\{\partial\phi_2(a_{ij}(t))/\partial a_{ij}\}|_{a_{ij}(t)\in\Omega_2}$.

Since novel evolution formula (13.3) is globally stable in sense of Lyapunov, starting from randomly generated initial error $Y(0)$, error function $Y(t)$ will converge to the equilibrium point with time. That is to say, $\lim_{t\to\infty}Y(t) = 0$. Based on the definition of error function $Y(t)$, the solution of $\lim_{t\to\infty}Y(t) = 0$ will make $\lim_{t\to\infty}C^T(t)U(t) + U(t)C(t) + G(t) = 0$ hold. Therefore, N-FTZNN model (13.4) is globally stable in sense of Lyapunov because the output of N-FTZNN model (13.4) will converge to its equilibrium point with time and make the error function $Y(t)$ converge to zero. In addition, since initial values are globally generated, the proposed N-FTZNN model (13.4) is globally stable. The proof is thus completed. ∎

Theorem 13.2 *Given dynamic coefficient matrices $C(t) \in \mathbb{R}^{n\times n}$ and $G(t) \in \mathbb{R}^{n\times n}$ that satisfy the condition of the unique solution of (13.1). Starting from arbitrary* *initial state $U(0)$, state output $U(t)$ of N-FTZNN model (13.4) is convergent to theoretical solution $U^*(t)$ of dynamic Lyapunov equation (13.1) within finite time t_f:*

$$t_f < \frac{\gamma_1 + \gamma_2}{\gamma_1 \gamma_2 (1 - \alpha)} \max \left\{ |y^-(0)|^{1-\alpha}, |y^+(0)|^{1-\alpha} \right\},$$

provided that $\phi_1(y_{ij}) = \phi_2(y_{ij}) = \phi^\alpha(y_{ij}) + \phi^{1/\alpha}(y_{ij})$ with $\alpha \in (0,1)$ and $\phi^\alpha(\cdot)$ defined as

$$\phi^\alpha(y_{ij}) = \begin{cases} |y_{ij}|^\alpha, & \text{if } y_{ij} > 0, \\ 0, & \text{if } y_{ij} = 0, \\ -|y_{ij}|^\alpha, & \text{if } y_{ij} < 0, \end{cases}$$

where $y^-(0) = \min\{Y(0)\}$ and $y^+(0) = \max\{Y(0)\}$.

Proof: From Theorem 13.1, it is easy to derive $\dot{a}_{ij}(t) = -\gamma_2 \phi_2(a_{ij}(t))$ via defining $a_{ij}(t) = y_{ij}(t) + \gamma_1 \int_0^t \phi_1(y_{ij}(\tau)) d\tau$, of which we have $a_{ij}(0) = y_{ij}(0)$ when $t = 0$. For the first-order dynamic system $\dot{a}_{ij}(t) = -\gamma_2 \phi_2(a_{ij}(t))$, we are able to design the Lyapunov function candidate $p_{ij}(t) = a_{ij}^2(t)$, and its time derivative is computed as follows:

$$\begin{aligned} \dot{p}_{ij}(t) &= 2 a_{ij}(t) \dot{a}_{ij}(t) \\ &= -2\gamma_2 a_{ij}(t) \phi_2(a_{ij}(t)) \\ &= -2\gamma_2 \left(|a_{ij}(t)|^{\alpha+1} + |a_{ij}(t)|^{\frac{1}{\alpha}+1} \right) \\ &\leq -2\gamma_2 |a_{ij}(t)|^{\alpha+1} \\ &= -2\gamma_2 p_{ij}(t)^{\frac{\alpha+1}{2}}. \end{aligned}$$

When the initial value $p_{ij}(0) = |a_{ij}(0)|^2 = |y_{ij}(0)|^2$ is given, we are able to derive the following fact by solving $\dot{p}_{ij}(t) \leq -2\gamma_2 p_{ij}(t)^{\frac{\alpha+1}{2}}$:

$$p_{ij}(t)^{\frac{1-\alpha}{2}} \begin{cases} \leq |a_{ij}(0)|^{1-\alpha} - \gamma_2 t (1-\alpha), & \text{if } t \leq \frac{|a_{ij}(0)|^{1-\alpha}}{\gamma_2(1-\alpha)}, \\ = 0, & \text{if } t > \frac{|a_{ij}(0)|^{1-\alpha}}{\gamma_2(1-\alpha)}, \end{cases}$$

which suggests that $p_{ij}(t)$ decreases to zero if $t > |a_{ij}(0)|^{1-\alpha}/\gamma_2(1-\alpha)$. Because of $p_{ij}(t) = a_{ij}^2(t)$ and $a_{ij}(0) = y_{ij}(0)$, we can also conclude that $a_{ij}(t)$ converges to zero after $t > |y_{ij}(0)|^{1-\alpha}/\gamma_2(1-\alpha)$.

Next, let us estimate the upper bound of convergence time t_1 for $U(t)$. Since every element in $U(t)$ have the same dynamics $\dot{a}_{ij}(t) = -\gamma_2 \phi_2(a_{ij}(t))$, $U(t)$ is able to converge to zero when

$$t > \max \left\{ |y^-(0)|^{1-\alpha}, |y^+(0)|^{1-\alpha} \right\} / \gamma_2 (1-\alpha),$$

where $y^+(0) = \max\{Y(0)\}$ and $y^-(0) = \min\{Y(0)\}$. Thus, the upper bound of convergence time t_1 for $z(t)$ is estimated as

$$t_1 < \frac{1}{\gamma_2(1-\alpha)} \max\left\{|y^-(0)|^{1-\alpha}, |y^+(0)|^{1-\alpha}\right\}.$$

After the time period t_1, one can obtain $U(t) = 0$ and $\dot{U}(t) = 0$. Thus, from (13.12), we further gain:

$$\dot{y}_{ij}(t) = -\gamma_1\phi_1(y_{ij}(t)), \tag{13.23}$$

which has the same expression with $\dot{a}_{ij}(t) = -\gamma_2\phi_2(a_{ij}(t))$. In addition, $\phi_1(\cdot) = \phi_2(\cdot)$ is a given known condition. Therefore, we can directly derive the upper bound of convergence time t_2 for $Y(t)$ in the similar way as follows:

$$t_2 < \frac{1}{\gamma_1(1-\alpha)} \max\left\{|y^-(0)|^{1-\alpha}, |y^+(0)|^{1-\alpha}\right\}.$$

In summary, by combining the two conclusions, it can be concluded that, starting from an arbitrary initial state, state output $U(t)$ of N-FTZNN model (13.4) converges to the theoretical solution $U^*(t)$ of (13.1) within finite time $t_f = t_1 + t_2$. That is,

$$t_f < \frac{\gamma_1 + \gamma_2}{\gamma_1\gamma_2(1-\alpha)} \max\left\{|y^-(0)|^{1-\alpha}, |y^+(0)|^{1-\alpha}\right\}.$$

The proof is thus completed. ∎

In the following, the robustness theorem of N-FTZNN model (13.4) is presented by analyzing noise-polluted N-FTZNN model (13.5) in front of unknown additive constant noises, which indicates N-FTZNN model (13.4) is inherently noise-tolerant.

Theorem 13.3 *Given dynamic coefficient matrices $C(t) \in \mathbb{R}^{n \times n}$ and $G(t) \in \mathbb{R}^{n \times n}$ that satisfy the condition of the unique solution of (13.1). Starting from an arbitrary initial value, state output $U(t)$ of noise-polluted N-FTZNN model (13.5) is globally convergent to $U^*(t)$ in front of unknown additive constant noises provided that $\Phi_1(\cdot)$ and $\Phi_2(\cdot)$ are monotone increasing odd activation function arrays.*

Proof: It can be obtained that the ijth subsystem of noise-polluted N-FTZNN model (13.5) is derived from following second-order nonlinear dynamic system:

$$\dot{y}_{ij}(t) = -\gamma_1\phi_1(y_{ij}(t)) - \gamma_2\phi_2\left(y_{ij}(t) + \gamma_1\int_0^t \phi_1(y_{ij}(\tau))d\tau\right) + \varsigma. \tag{13.24}$$

Hence, by defining the same $a_{ij}(t)$ as (13.11), we can derive its time derivative as $\dot{a}_{ij}(t) = \dot{y}_{ij}(t) + \gamma_1\phi_1(y_{ij}(t))$. Furthermore, substituting the expressions of $a_{ij}(t)$ and $\dot{a}_{ij}(t)$ into (13.24), we have

$$\dot{a}_{ij}(t) = -\gamma_2\phi_2(a_{ij}(t)) + \varsigma. \tag{13.25}$$

Thus, we can design the following Lyapunov function candidate to analyze the stability of the ijth noise-disturbed subsystem (13.24):

$$p_{ij}(t) = \left(\gamma_2 \phi_2(a_{ij}(t)) - \varsigma\right)^2 / 2,$$

which ensures the positive definiteness of $p_{ij}(t)$. Its time derivative $\dot{p}_{ij}(t)$ is solved as follows:

$$
\begin{aligned}
\frac{\mathrm{d}p_{ij}(t)}{\mathrm{d}t} &= \left(\gamma_2 \phi_2(a_{ij}(t)) - \varsigma\right) \gamma_2 \frac{\partial \phi_2(a_{ij}(t))}{\partial a_{ij}} \dot{a}_{ij}(t) \\
&= -\gamma_2 \frac{\partial \phi_2(a_{ij}(t))}{\partial a_{ij}} \left(\gamma_2 \phi_2(a_{ij}(t)) - \varsigma\right)^2.
\end{aligned}
\tag{13.26}
$$

Because $\phi_2(\cdot)$ is a monotone increasing odd function, $\partial \phi_2(a_{ij}(t))/\partial a_{ij} > 0$. Hence, we conclude $\dot{p}_{ij}(t)$ is negative definite; i.e. $\dot{p}_{ij}(t) < 0$ for any $\gamma_2 \phi_2(a_{ij}(t)) - \varsigma \neq 0$ and $\dot{p}_{ij}(t) = 0$ only for $\gamma_2 \phi_2(a_{ij}(t)) - \varsigma = 0$. Thus, $p_{ij}(t)$ is convergent to zero. At the same time, $\lim_{t\to\infty} \gamma_2 \phi_2(a_{ij}(t)) - \varsigma = 0$, i.e. $\lim_{t\to\infty} a_{ij}(t) = \phi_2^{-1}(\varsigma/\gamma_2)$. That is to say, $a_{ij}(t)$ converges to $\phi_2^{-1}(\varsigma/\gamma_2)$ and $\lim_{t\to\infty} \dot{a}_{ij}(t) = 0$.

Besides, according to $\dot{a}_{ij}(t) = \dot{y}_{ij}(t) + \gamma_1 \phi_1(y_{ij}(t))$ and $\lim_{t\to\infty} \dot{a}_{ij}(t) = 0$, one can have $\dot{y}_{ij}(t) = \dot{a}_{ij}(t) - \gamma_1 \phi_1(y_{ij}(t))$ and even have

$$\lim_{t\to+\infty} \left(\dot{y}_{ij}(t) + \gamma_1 \phi_1(y_{ij}(t))\right) = 0. \tag{13.27}$$

Now, let us prove $\lim_{t\to\infty} y_{ij}(t) = 0$ from this conclusion. Based on this result, when $t \to \infty$, we have:

$$\dot{y}_{ij}(t) + \gamma_1 \phi_1(y_{ij}(t)) = 0 \quad \text{or} \quad \dot{y}_{ij}(t) = -\gamma_1 \phi_1(y_{ij}(t)).$$

For proving $\lim_{t\to\infty} y_{ij}(t) = 0$, based on this dynamic system, we can directly choose the Lyapunov function candidate as $p_{ij}(t) = y_{ij}^2(t)/2 \geq 0$. Besides, its time derivative is derived as

$$
\begin{aligned}
\dot{p}_{ij}(t) &= y_{ij}(t)\dot{y}_{ij}(t) \\
&= -\gamma_1 y_{ij}(t)\phi_1(y_{ij}(t)).
\end{aligned}
$$

If $\phi_1(\cdot)$ is a monotone increasing odd function, we have

$$
\phi_1(y_{ij}(t)) \begin{cases} > 0, & \text{if } y_{ij}(t) > 0, \\ = 0, & \text{if } y_{ij}(t) = 0, \\ < 0, & \text{if } y_{ij}(t) < 0. \end{cases}
$$

Thus, we can further conclude

$$
y_{ij}(t)\phi_1(y_{ij}(t)) \begin{cases} > 0, & \text{if } y_{ij}(t) \neq 0, \\ = 0, & \text{if } y_{ij}(t) = 0, \end{cases}
$$

which ensures the negative definiteness of $\dot{p}_{ij}(t)$. By Lyapunov theory, we can easily conclude that $\lim_{t\to\infty} y_{ij}(t) = 0$, provided that $\phi_1(\cdot)$ is a monotone increasing odd function.

In summary, from previous analysis, we can draw a conclusion that $Y(t)$ generated by noise-polluted N-FTZNN model (13.5) globally converges to zero even in front of unknown additive constant noises provided that $\Phi_1(\cdot)$ and $\Phi_2(\cdot)$ are monotone increasing odd function arrays. That is to say, starting from an arbitrary initial value, state output $U(t)$ of noise-polluted N-FTZNN model (13.5) is globally convergent to $U^*(t)$ of (13.1) in front of unknown additive constant noises. The proof on the robustness property of N-FTZNN model (13.4) is completed by analyzing noise-polluted N-FTZNN model (13.5). ∎

13.4 Illustrative Verification

Via solving dynamic Lyapunov equation (13.1), N-FTZNN model (13.5) is proposed in Section 13.2 by designing a novel evolution formula. In addition, the stability, convergence, and robustness are proved in Section 13.3. In this section, numerical comparative results based on N-FTZNN model (13.5) and ZNN model (13.6) are first presented to validate the effectiveness and robustness of the proposed model for dynamic Lyapunov equation (13.1). Then, based on the design methods of N-FTZNN model (13.5) and ZNN model (13.6), the N-FTZNN-based and ZNN-based control laws are established to comparatively control a planar six-link manipulator for achieving the repetitive motion task. Both of them validate the high accuracy and the superior of N-FTZNN model (13.5) to ZNN model (13.6).

13.4.1 Numerical Comparison

In the example, the coefficients of dynamic Lyapunov equation (13.1) is simply chosen as

$$C(t) = \begin{bmatrix} -2 + \cos(3t) & \sin(2t) \\ 0.5\sin(3t) & -1 + \cos(2t) \end{bmatrix},$$

$$G(t) = \begin{bmatrix} \exp(-0.5t) & 1 + \cos(t) \\ 1 - \cos(2t) & 1 + 2\sin(3t) \end{bmatrix}$$

which satisfy the condition of the unique solution of (13.1). For simplicity, we set $\phi_1(y_{ij}) = \phi_2(y_{ij}) = \phi^\alpha(y_{ij}) + \phi^{1/\alpha}(y_{ij})$ with $\alpha = 0.4$.

For comparative purposes, both N-FTZNN model (13.5) and ZNN model (13.6) are used to calculate the mentioned dynamic Lyapunov equation. First, we set $\gamma_1 = \gamma_2 = 1$ and assume such two models are polluted by additive constant noise $\varsigma = 1$. From an randomly generated initial state $U(0) \in [-2, 2]^{2\times2}$, the state trajectories of N-FTZNN model (13.5) are depicted in Figure 13.2, which clearly demonstrate each element of state output $U(t)$ is convergent to the one of theoretical solution

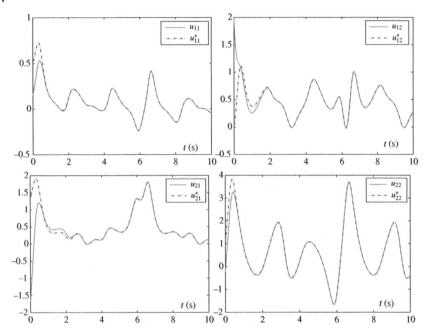

Figure 13.2 Convergence property of each element of state output $U(t)$ corresponding to the one of theoretical solution $U^*(t)$ synthesized by N-FTZNN model (13.5) with $\gamma_1 = \gamma_2 = 1$ in the presence of additive constant noise $\varsigma = 1$.

$U^*(t)$ after a shot time even in the presence of the additive constant noise. Under the same conditions, the simulation results based on ZNN model (13.6) are plotted in Figure 13.3, from which, it can be concluded that ZNN model (13.6) cannot solve the dynamic Lyapunov equation effectively when polluted by the additive constant noise. This is because each element of state output $U(t)$ cannot converge to the one of theoretical solution $U^*(t)$ with time. There exist some errors between $U(t)$ and $U^*(t)$ due to the pollution of the additive constant noise.

Figure 13.4 further plots the trajectories of the residual errors $\|A(t)U(t) - U(t)B(t) + C(t)\|_F$ corresponding to state outputs $U(t)$ of N-FTZNN model (13.5) and ZNN model (13.6). From Figure 13.4a, we can further conclude that the residual error produced by N-FTZNN model (13.5) decreases to zero within finite time three seconds. That is, the finite convergence time of N-FTZNN model (13.5) for the dynamic Lyapunov equation is about three seconds even in the presence of additive constant noise $\varsigma = 1$. In contrast, the residual error produced by ZNN model (13.6) cannot converge to zero and tend to about 2 steadily due to the pollution of the additive noise.

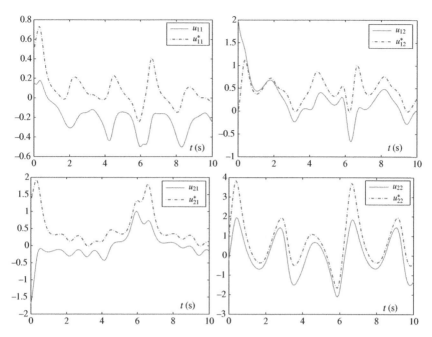

Figure 13.3 Convergence property of each element of state output $U(t)$ corresponding to the one of theoretical solution $U^*(t)$ synthesized by ZNN model (13.6) with $\gamma_1 = \gamma_2 = 1$ in the presence of additive constant noise $\varsigma = 1$.

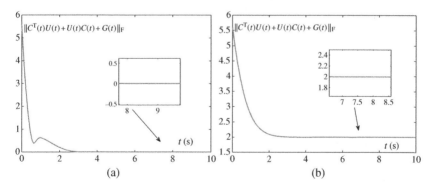

Figure 13.4 Convergence of residual error $\|C^T(t)U(t) + U(t)C(t) + G(t)\|_F$ produced by two different models with $\gamma_1 = \gamma_2 = 1$ in the presence of additive constant noise $\varsigma = 1$. (a) By N-FTZNN model (13.5). (b) By ZNN model (13.6).

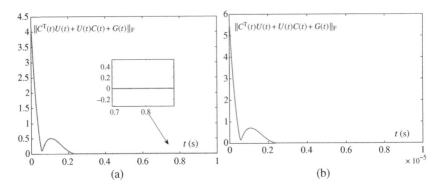

Figure 13.5 Convergence of residual error $\|C^{\mathrm{T}}(t)U(t) + U(t)C(t) + G(t)\|_F$ produced by N-FTZNN model (13.5) with different values of parameters γ_1 and γ_2 in the presence of additive constant noise $\varsigma = 1$. (a) $\gamma_1 = \gamma_2 = 10$. (b) $\gamma_1 = \gamma_2 = 10^6$.

In Figure 13.5, we show the convergence property of N-FTZNN model (13.5) with different values of parameter γ_1 and γ_2 for the dynamic Lyapunov equation in the presence of additive constant noise $\varsigma = 1$. First, we set $\gamma_1 = \gamma_2 = 10$. The convergence time of the residual error $\|A(t)U(t) - U(t)B(t) + C(t)\|_F$ is decreased to 0.23 second. In addition, when $\gamma_1 = \gamma_2 = 10^6$, the convergence time of the residual error is further shorten to 2.3×10^{-6} seconds. These results are enough to illustrate the finite-time convergence and robustness property of N-FTZNN model (13.5) for dynamic Lyapunov equation in the presence of additive constant noises. In addition, it can be concluded that design parameters in N-FTZNN model (13.5) play an accelerated and noise-tolerant role in computing dynamic Lyapunov equation.

Now, let us study the impact of different kinds of additive noises on N-FTZNN model (13.5) and ZNN model (13.6), instead of the previously investigated additive constant noises. In this part, we set $\gamma_1 = \gamma_2 = 10$ for consistency and the difference is that we consider the bounded additive noise $\varsigma = 10$ and the time-varying additive noise $\varsigma = 5U(t)$ successively.

First, let us consider the bounded additive noise $\varsigma = 10$. Starting from an arbitrary initial state $U(0) \in [-2, 2]^{2 \times 2}$, N-FTZNN model (13.5) and ZNN model (13.6) are applied to computing the dynamic Lyapunov equation. The simulation results are depicted in Figure 13.6a, from which, we can conclude that the residual error $\|C^{\mathrm{T}}(t)U(t) + U(t)C(t) + G(t)\|_F$ of N-FTZNN model (13.5) is still convergent to zero within finite time 0.3 second, while the one of ZNN model (13.6) cannot decrease to zero. The state trajectories of such two models are similar to the ones of Figures 13.2 and 13.3, and not presented again due to space limitation. Then, let us consider the time-varying additive noise $\varsigma = 5U(t)$. The convergence trajectories of the residual error for such two models are plotted in Figure 13.6b. Due to the dynamic property of time-varying additive noise, the

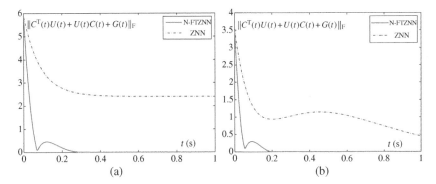

Figure 13.6 Convergence of residual error $\|C^{\mathrm{T}}(t)U(t) + U(t)C(t) + G(t)\|_{\mathrm{F}}$ produced by N-FTZNN model (13.5) and ZNN model (13.6) with $\gamma_1 = \gamma_2 = 10$ in the presence of different kinds of additive noises. (a) Bounded random additive $\varsigma = 10$. (b) Time-varying additive $\varsigma = 5U(t)$.

residual error $\|(C^{\mathrm{T}}(t)U(t) + U(t)C(t) + G(t))\|_{\mathrm{F}}$ of ZNN model (13.6) approaches to 1 about 0.2 second, and then slowly varies with time-varying additive noise. This convergence situation keeps pace with the variation tendency of the time-varying additive noise $\varsigma = 5U(t)$. In contrast, even in the presence of the time-varying additive noise $\varsigma = 5U(t)$, N-FTZNN model (13.5) is still effective and generates the desired solution of the dynamic Lyapunov equation, which can be validated by Figure 13.6b. In this subfigure, the residual error $\|C^{\mathrm{T}}(t)U(t) + U(t)C(t) + G(t)\|_{\mathrm{F}}$ generated by N-FTZNN model (13.5) in presence of the dynamic additive noise $\varsigma = 5U(t)$ is able to converge to zero within a short finite time 0.2 second.

At last, in order to further illustrate the superiority of proposed N-FTZNN model (13.5), some comparisons among existing neural network models are summarized in Table 13.1. In [7, 9], Xiao *et al.* presented an improved Zhang neural network model to accelerate the convergence speed of solution to static or time-varying Lyapunov equations. However, such neural-network models are designed in the ideal conditions and does not consider the impact of various additive noises. In [8], a noise-tolerant Zhang neural network model was developed to solve time-varying zero-finding problems in the presence of additive noises. However, such a neural model requires infinite time for convergence, which may confine the real-time applications. Recurrent neural network model proposed in [15, 16] can only handle static Lyapunov equations and achieve the asymptotical convergence. From the aforementioned comparisons among existing neural network models for Lyapunov equations, there are no existing design methods to simultaneously deal with finite-time convergence and inherently noise-tolerance in the field of ZNN at present. In order to fill this gap in this field, a novel N-FTZNN is designed and established to solve dynamic Lyapunov equation, which possesses simultaneously the stability, finite-time convergence, and robustness.

Table 13.1 The main differences of the N-FTZNN model from existing neural network models for Lyapunov equations.

#	Item	Model in [7]	Model in [8]	Model in [9]	Model in [15]	Model in [16]	Model in this work
1	Solution problems	Static	Time-varying	Time-varying	Static	Static	Time-varying
2	Theoretical errors	Zero	Zero	Zero	Non-zero	Non-zero	Zero
3	Activation functions	Yes	No	No	Yes	No	Yes
4	Dynamic forms	Implicitly	Implicitly	Implicitly	Explicitly	Explicitly	Implicitly
5	Convergence	Finitely	Exponent-ially	Finitely	Asymptot-ically	Asymptot-ically	Finitely
6	Robustness	No	Yes	No	No	No	Yes

13.4.2 Application Comparison

In this part, we comparatively apply N-FTZNN model (13.5) and ZNN model (13.6) as a control law to realize the repetitive motion of the planar six-link manipulator (the length of each link being 1 m). The repetitive motion scheme [17–19] at the acceleration level can be formulated as

$$\text{minimize} \quad (\ddot{\vartheta}(t) + s)^{\mathrm{T}}(\ddot{\vartheta}(t) + s)/2, \tag{13.28}$$

$$\text{subject to} \quad J(\vartheta(t))\ddot{\vartheta}(t) = \ddot{r}_a(t), \tag{13.29}$$

where $s := 2\lambda\dot{\vartheta}(t) + \lambda^2(\vartheta(t) - \vartheta(0))$ with $\lambda > 0$, and $\vartheta(t)$, $\dot{\vartheta}(t)$, and $\ddot{\vartheta}(t)$ respectively denoting the vectors of the joint-angle, joint-velocity, and joint-acceleration, respectively; $J(\vartheta(t))$ denotes Jacobian matrix of the manipulator; and $\ddot{r}_a(t) := \ddot{r}(t) - \dot{J}(\vartheta(t))\dot{\vartheta}(t)$. By introducing the Lagrangian multiplier $\omega(t)$, the repetitive motion scheme can be equivalently converted as the following dynamic system:

$$A(t)z(t) = v(t), \tag{13.30}$$

where

$$A(t) := \begin{bmatrix} I & J^{\mathrm{T}}(t) \\ J(t) & 0 \end{bmatrix}, \quad z(t) := \begin{bmatrix} \ddot{\vartheta}(t) \\ \omega(t) \end{bmatrix}, \quad v(t) := \begin{bmatrix} -q \\ \ddot{r}_a(t) \end{bmatrix}.$$

Thus, we can adopt the design methods of N-FTZNN model (13.5) and ZNN model (13.6) to control the repetitive motion of the planar six-link manipulator in the presence of the additive constant noise $\varsigma = 4$. Without loss of generality, the planar six-link manipulator is located at the origin point, the initial angle of each link is

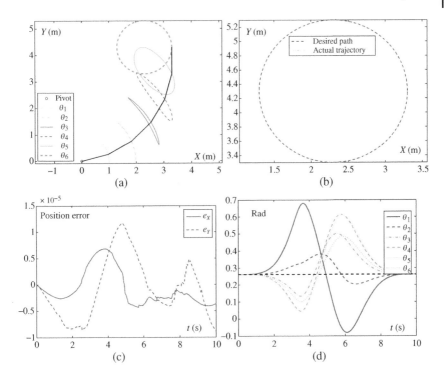

Figure 13.7 Circular tracking results of the planar six-link manipulator synthesized by the N-FTZNN-based control law with $\gamma_1 = \gamma_2 = 100$ in the presence of additive constant noise $\varsigma = 5$. (a) Joint motion trajectories of planar six-link manipulator. (b) Comparison between the desired path and the actual trajectory. (c) Position error between the desired path and the actual trajectory. (d) Dynamic behavior of joint angle.

set as $\pi/12$, and $\lambda = 2$. The given tacking task is a circle with the radius being 1 m and time duration is 10 seconds. The tracking circular results synthesized by the N-FTZNN-based control law are depicted in Figure 13.7, and synthesized by the ZNN-based control law are depicted in Figure 13.8.

In Figure 13.7a, the whole joint motions of the planar six-link manipulator are plotted, which is synthesized by the N-FTZNN-based control law. As seen from this subfigure, the motion process is stable, and the final state overlaps the initial state. That is to say, the planar six-link manipulator successfully realizes the repetitive motion in the presence of the additive constant noise $\varsigma = 5$. Specific details are shown in Figure 13.7b–d. Figure 13.7b shows the comparison of the desired path and the actual trajectory. From this comparison, we can clearly see the actual trajectory coincides with the desired path. In addition, from Figure 13.7c, the position error is less than 1.5×10^{-5} m, and the accuracy is accepted in practice. Figure 13.7d shows the dynamic behavior of joint angle, of which the initial

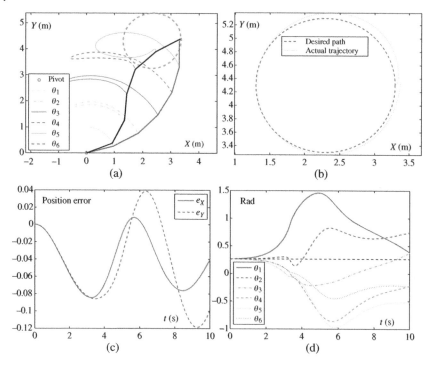

Figure 13.8 Circular tracking results of the planar six-link manipulator synthesized by the ZNN-based control law with $\gamma_1 = \gamma_2 = 100$ in the presence of additive constant noise $\varsigma = 5$. (a) Joint motion trajectories of planar six-link manipulator. (b) Comparison between the desired path and the actual trajectory. (c) Position error between the desired path and the actual trajectory. (d) Dynamic behavior of joint angle.

state returns back the final state. These results show the effectiveness and high accuracy of the N-FTZNN-based control law to achieve the optimization task of the planar six-link manipulator in the presence of additive constant noise.

In contrast, from Figure 13.8, we can see the whole motion process of the planar six-link manipulator is non-stable and the joint-angle drift appears after task duration. Specific details can be seen in Figure 13.8b–d. As seen from Figure 13.8b, the actual trajectory does not overlaps the desired path at some place, which means the failure of the circular tracking task. In addition, Figure 13.8c shows the position error, where the maximum is about 0.12 m. Besides, the final state of joint angle does not returns to its initial state. That is to say, the repetitive motion also fails. These results show the ZNN-based control law is not effective to realize the optimization task in the presence of the additive noise.

In summary, from the previous theoretical analysis to simulation verifications, we conclude that the N-FTZNN model possesses the global stability, finite-time convergence and robustness property for solving dynamic Lyapunov equation (13.1).

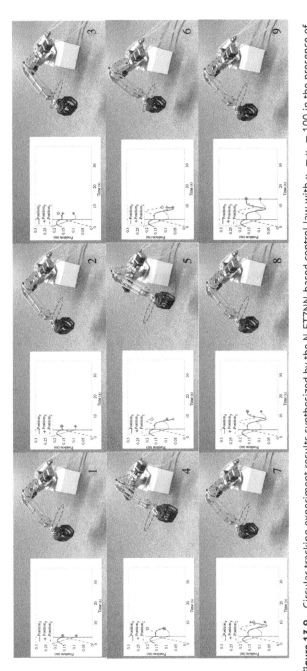

Figure 13.9 Circular tracking experiment results synthesized by the N-FTZNN-based control law with $\gamma_1 = \gamma_2 = 100$ in the presence of additive constant noise $\varsigma = 1$.

13.4.3 Experimental Verification

In this part, a real 3-axis manipulator is presented to further validate the effectiveness of the N-FTZNN-based control law. The forward kinematic equation of this manipulator is directly given as follows:

$$r(t) = f(\theta) = \begin{bmatrix} \cos\theta_1(32\cos\theta_3 + 27\sin\theta_2 + 3)/200 \\ \sin\theta_1(32\cos\theta_3 + 27\sin\theta_2 + 3)/200 \\ 27\cos\theta_2/200 - 4\sin\theta_3/25 + 103/1000 \end{bmatrix}.$$

In the experiment, the additive constant noise is $\varsigma = 1$, and the initial angle of each link is set as $\pi/4$. The given tacking task is a circle in a three-dimensional space, which has a 30° with X–Y plane. The radius is 5 cm, time duration is 10 seconds, and the parameters of the proposed N-FTZNN control law is set to $\gamma_1 = \gamma_2 = 100$. Note that, in the experiment, we run 3 cycles for the circular path to show the repetitive motion of the real 3-axis manipulator, but due to similarity, only the first cycle results are shown in the following.

The snapshots of during the circular tracking experiment in the first cycle synthesized by the N-FTZNN-based control law are shown in Figure 13.9 and the corresponding data profiles are shown in Figure 13.10. As seen from Figure 13.9,

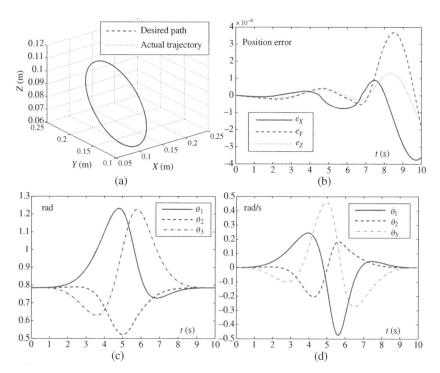

Figure 13.10 Data profiles during the circular tracking experiment of the 3-axis physical manipulator. (a) Comparison between the desired path and the actual trajectory. (b) Position error between the desired path and the actual trajectory. (c) Dynamic behavior of joint angle. (d) Dynamic behavior of joint velocity.

the middle bolts of the end-effector align with an "ellipse" from camera perspective but is actually the given circle in 3-D space. In addition, the related data profiles during the circular tracking experiment of the 3-axis physical manipulator shown in Figure 13.10a,b further verify that the real manipulator successfully completes the given circular tracking task, and the corresponding position error is always small, which is less than 4×10^{-6} m. In addition, as seen from Figure 13.10c,d, the dynamic behavior of θ and $\dot{\theta}$ is continuous and even smooth, which ensures the control performance of the real manipulator. The results validate the efficacy and physical realizability of the N-FTZNN-based control law.

13.5 Chapter Summary

The seeking of constructive tools for control law design has long been a focus in control. Although this problem can be mostly converted to the solution of Lyapunov equations, solving Lyapunov equations, especially when the equations are time-varying, is itself a challenging issue. Practical solution of it imposes further concerns including stability, robustness, and real-time performance. In this chapter, by simultaneously considering the global stability and finite-time convergence and robustness, a N-FTZNN model has been proposed for computing dynamic Lyapunov equation in the presence of various different kinds of additive noises. Both theoretical analysis and illustrative examples have been presented to validate the effectiveness and superior property of the N-FTZNN model for dynamic Lyapunov equation. In addition, by comparing the ZNN with existing solutions, the advantages of the N-FTZNN model have been clearly demonstrated, i.e. finite-time convergence and inherently noise tolerance.

References

1 C. Yang and Y. Jiang, Neural control of bimanual robots with guaranteed global stability and motion precision, *IEEE Trans. Ind. Inform.*, 13(3) (2017) 1162–1171.

2 L. Xiao and Y. Zhang, Solving time-varying inverse kinematics problem of wheeled mobile manipulators using Zhang neural network with exponential convergence, *Nonlinear Dyn.*, 76(2) (2014) 1543–1559.

3 F. Ding and T. Chen, Gradient based iterative algorithms for solving a class of matrix equations, *IEEE Trans. Autom. Control*, 50(8) (2005) 1216–1221.

4 F. Ding and H. Zhang, Gradient-based iterative algorithm for a class of coupled matrix equations related to control systems, *IET Control Theory Appl.*, 8(15) (2014) 1588–1595.

5 B. Zhou, G. Duan, and Z. Lin, A parametric periodic Lyapunov equation with application in semi-global stabilization of discrete-time periodic systems subject to actuator saturation, *Automatica*, 47(2) (2011) 316–325.

6 H. Zhang and Z. Li, On constructing Lyapunov functions for multi-agent systems, *Automatica*, 58 (2015) 39–42.

7 L. Xiao and B. Liao, A convergence-accelerated Zhang neural network and its solution application to Lyapunov equation, *Neurocomputing*, 193 (2016) 213–218.

8 L. Jin and Y. Zhang *et al.*, Noise-tolerant ZNN models for solving time-varying zero-finding problems: A control-theoretic approach, *IEEE Trans. Autom. Control*, 62(2) (2017) 992–997.

9 L. Xiao and B. Liao *et al.*, Design and analysis of FTZNN applied to real-time solution of nonstationary Lyapunov equation and tracking control of wheeled mobile manipulator, *IEEE Trans. Ind. Inform.*, 14(1) (2018) 98–105.

10 M. S. De Queiroz and D. M. Dawson, *Lyapunov-based control of mechanical systems*, Berlin: Springer-Verlag, (2012).

11 L. Jin, Y. Zhang, and S. Li, Integration-enhanced Zhang neural network for real-time-varying matrix inversion in the presence of various kinds of noises, *IEEE Trans. Neural Netw. Learn. Syst.*, 27(12) (2016) 2615–2627.

12 S. Li, S. Chen, and B. Liu, Accelerating a recurrent neural network to finite-time convergence for solving time-varying Sylvester equation by using a sign-bi-power activation function, *Neural Process. Lett.*, 37 (2013) 189–205.

13 D. Guo, Z., Nie, and L. Yan, The application of noise-tolerant ZD design formula to robots' kinematic control via time-varying nonlinear equations solving, *IEEE Trans. Syst. Man Cybern. Syst.*, 48(12) (2018) 2188–2197.

14 D. Guo, F. Xu, and L. Yan, New pseudoinverse-based path-planning scheme with PID characteristic for redundant robot manipulators in the presence of noise, *IEEE Trans. Control. Syst. Technol.*, 26(6) (2018) 2008–2019.

15 C. Yi, Y. Chen, and Z. Lu, Improved gradient-based neural networks for online solution of Lyapunov matrix equation, *Inform. Process. Lett.*, 111(16) (2011) 780–786.

16 C. Yi, Y. Chen, and X. Lan, Comparison on neural solvers for the Lyapunov matrix equation with stationary & nonstationary coefficients, *Appl. Math. Model.*, 37(4) (2013) 2495–2502.

17 Z. Zhang and Y. Zhang, Acceleration-level cyclic-motion generation of constrained redundant robots tracking different paths, *IEEE Trans. Syst. Man Cybern. Part B Cybern.*, 42(4) (2012) 1257–1269.

18 Z. Zhang and T. Fu *et al.*, A varying-parameter convergent-differential neural network for solving joint-angular-drift problems of redundant robot manipulators, *IEEE/ASME Trans. Mechatron.*, 23(2) (2018) 679–689.

19 D. Chen and Y. Zhang, A hybrid multi-objective scheme applied to redundant robot manipulators, *IEEE Trans. Autom. Sci. Eng.*, 14(3) (2017) 1337–1350.

Part VI

Application to the Sylvester Equation

14

Design Scheme I of FTZNN

14.1 Introduction

Due to the important role played in nonlinear dynamic systems, much effort has been made toward solving Sylvester equation in the past decades [1–5]. In addition, many research results regarding Sylvester equation have been obtained from theory to industrial applications [6–10].

In this chapter, a novel integral design formula with finite-time convergence and denoising property is presented for dynamic Sylvester equation in front of additive noises. Then, based on the design procedure of zeroing neural networks (ZNNs), a novel finite-time zeroing neural network (N-FTZNN) model is proposed in a unified framework to solve dynamic Sylvester equation. When applied to the dynamic Sylvester equation solving in front of different additive noises, the N-FTZNN model is able to converge to the theoretical solution within finite time, while the ZNN model only approximates the theoretical solution with a relatively large lagging error. In order to better show the novelties and differences, we would like to compare the proposed N-FTZNN model with the other models (i.e. GRNN model, ZNN model, and FTZNN model) through summarizing the related papers (i.e. [11–13]). The corresponding comparative results are shown in Table 14.1. As seen from the table, we can conclude that the N-FTZNN model has a strong robustness for dynamic Sylvester equation solving in front of different additive noises.

14.2 Problem Formulation and ZNN Model

Without loss of generality, the following general dynamic Sylvester equation is considered in this chapter [6, 12, 13]:

$$A(t)U(t) - U(t)B(t) = -C(t) \in \mathbb{R}^{n \times n}, \tag{14.1}$$

Zeroing Neural Networks: Finite-time Convergence Design, Analysis and Applications,
First Edition. Lin Xiao and Lei Jia.

Table 14.1 The main novelties and differences of the N-FTZNN model from the other models (i.e. GRNN model [11], ZNN model [12], and FTZNN model [13]) for Sylvester equation.

#	Item	GRNN	ZNN	FTZNN	N-FTZNN
1	Objects	Static	Varying	Varying	Varying
2	Errors	Yes	Yes	No	No
3	Functions	No	Yes	Yes	Yes
4	Dynamics	Explicitly	Implicitly	Implicitly	Implicitly
5	Convergence	Asymptotically	Exponentially	Finitely	Finitely
6	Robustness	Very weak	Weak	Weak	Strong

where t represents time; $U(t) \in \mathbb{R}^{n \times n}$ represents an unknown matrix and is varying with time; $A(t) \in \mathbb{R}^{n \times n}$, $B(t) \in \mathbb{R}^{n \times n}$, and $C(t) \in \mathbb{R}^{n \times n}$ represent known coefficient matrices and are varying with time. Throughout the whole chapter, it is assumed that $A(t)$ and $B(t)$ at each time t have no common eigenvalues to ensure the unique solution of dynamic Sylvester equation (14.1) [6]. For easy reading, $U^*(t) \in \mathbb{R}^{n \times n}$ is used to denote the theoretical solution of (14.1). The goal of the current work is to devise a new design formula to establish a N-FTZNN model for solving dynamic Sylvester equation in front of additive noises. Before that, the design process of ZNN for dynamic Sylvester equation (14.1) is directly given as follows for comparative purposes [14–16].

Step 1: The following indefinite error function is chosen to oversee the solving process of dynamic Sylvester equation (14.1):

$$Y(t) = A(t)U(t) - U(t)B(t) + C(t) \in \mathbb{R}^{n \times n}. \tag{14.2}$$

Step 2: The ZNN design formula is selected for $Y(t)$ such that the error function $Y(t)$ is able to converge to zero exponentially:

$$\frac{dY(t)}{dt} = -\gamma Y(t), \tag{14.3}$$

where design parameter $\gamma > 0$.

Step 3: Substituting (14.2) into (14.3), we gain the following ZNN model for solving dynamic Sylvester equation (14.1):

$$A\dot{U} - \dot{U}B = -\dot{A}U + U\dot{B} - \dot{C} - \gamma(AU - UB + C), \tag{14.4}$$

where argument t is omitted for easy reading. In addition, from the previous study on the ZNN model (14.4), we can draw a conclusion that, starting from arbitrary initial state $U(0) \in \mathbb{R}^{n \times n}$, state output $U(t) \in \mathbb{R}^{n \times n}$ of the ZNN model (14.4) is able to converge to $U^*(t) \in \mathbb{R}^{n \times n}$ of dynamic Sylvester equation (14.1) exponentially as time goes [6, 13].

Note that ZNN model (14.4) only achieves the exponential convergence, and does not consider the pollution of additive noises. Therefore, ZNN model (14.4) has several limitations. To study the denoising property of ZNN model (14.4), the noise-polluted ZNN model is extended as follows:

$$A\dot{U} - \dot{U}B = -\dot{A}U + U\dot{B} - \dot{C} - \gamma\,(AU - UB + C) + \varepsilon, \tag{14.5}$$

where ε denotes an additive noise. In the simulation part, for comparative purposes, we will investigate the denoising property of ZNN model (14.4) for dynamic Sylvester equation (14.1) by analyzing noise-polluted ZNN model (14.5).

14.3 N-FTZNN Model

In order to establish a N-FTZNN for dynamic Sylvester equation (14.1), in this section, a nonlinearly activated integral design formula is proposed in this chapter, which is quite different from the one depicted in (14.3). Then, based on such a novel design formula, the N-FTZNN model for dynamic Sylvester equation is proposed with finite-time convergence and additive noises considered.

14.3.1 Design of N-FTZNN

The specific design procedure of the N-FTZNN model for dynamic Sylvester equation is provided as follows.

At the beginning, the chosen error function is the same as (14.2), and not presented again due to the similarity.

Then, differing from the one depicted in (14.3), a completely different integral design formula activated by nonlinear functions is proposed as follows:

$$\frac{dY(t)}{dt} = -\gamma_1\Phi_1(Y(t)) - \gamma_2\Phi_2\left(Y(t) + \gamma_1\int_0^t \Phi_1(Y(\tau))d\tau\right), \tag{14.6}$$

where $\gamma_1 > 0$ and $\gamma_2 > 0$ are used to scale the convergence speed of $\lim_{t\to\infty} Y(t) = 0$; and $\Phi_1(\cdot)$ and $\Phi_2(\cdot)$ represent two monotone increasing odd nonlinear activation function arrays, of which each element has the same mapping expression. As we know, the hardware implementation is a basic issue in the field of neural networks. Thus, the hardware implementation of integral design formula (14.6) can be discussed and presented as follows.

The ijth subsystem of integral design formula (14.6) is presented as follows ($\forall i,j \in 1, 2, \ldots, n$):

$$\dot{y}_{ij}(t) = -\gamma_1\phi_1(y_{ij}(t)) - \gamma_2\phi_2\left(y_{ij}(t) + \gamma_1\int_0^t \phi_1(y_{ij}(\tau))d\tau\right), \tag{14.7}$$

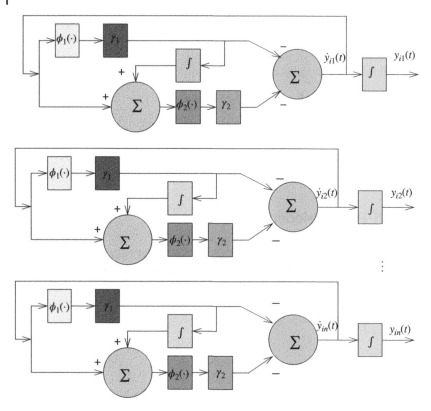

Figure 14.1 The circuit topology of design formula (14.6) for hardware implementation.

where $y_{ij}(t)$ represents the ijth element of error function $Y(t)$; and $\phi_1(\cdot)$ and $\phi_2(\cdot)$ respectively represent the elements of $\Phi_1(\cdot)$ and $\Phi_2(\cdot)$. Based on the ijth subsystem of design formula (14.6), the circuit topology of the ith row of neurons in design formula (14.6) can be illustrated as Figure 14.1. As well as the neuron input is given, via connecting analog adders, multipliers, integrators, and limiters (realizing activation functions), this hardware circuit will work and make $Y(t)$ converge to zero.

In the end, via considering the error function and the aforementioned nonlinearly activated integral design formula, i.e. substituting (14.2) into (14.6), we can establish the following N-FTZNN model for dynamic Sylvester equation:

$$A\dot{U} - \dot{U}B = -\dot{A}X + X\dot{B} - \dot{C} - \gamma_1\Phi_1(AU - UB + C)$$
$$- \gamma_2\Phi_2\left((AU - UB + C) + \gamma_1\int_0^t\Phi_1(AU - UB + C)\,\mathrm{d}\tau\right),$$

(14.8)

where argument t is also omitted, and the other parameters are defined as before. As we know, a recurrent neural network (RNN) is a class of artificial neural network where connections between nodes form a directed cycle. Nodes are either input nodes, output nodes, or hidden nodes. In mathematics, such an RNN can be formulated as a dynamic differential equation. Thus, in the field of neural networks, a dynamic differential equation is directly called a RNN model without any further explanation. That is why (14.8) is called as the RNN model. Besides, in order to study the outstanding robustness of N-FTZNN model (14.8), the noise-polluted N-FTZNN model is directly extended as follows by adding an additive noise ε:

$$
A\dot{U} - \dot{U}B = -\dot{A}U + U\dot{B} - \dot{C} - \gamma_1 \Phi_1 (AU - UB + C)
$$
$$
- \gamma_2 \Phi_2 ((AU - UB + C) \tag{14.9}
$$
$$
+ \gamma_1 \int_0^t \Phi_1 (AU - UB + C)\,\mathrm{d}\tau \Bigg) + \varepsilon.
$$

It is noted that, in implementations of RNNs, we usually assume that it is free of all kinds of noises or external errors. However, there always exist some realization errors in hardware implementation, which can be deemed as the constant noises. For example, the model-implementation error appears most frequently in the hardware realization. Moreover, the environmental interference as well as other external errors can be viewed as the random noises. Simply speaking, all those noises have significant impacts on the solving accuracy of RNNs, and in some cases, these noises cause failure of the solving task [17]. Therefore, an additive noise term is introduced in noise-polluted N-FTZNN model (14.9). The physical meaning of such an additive noise term can be deemed as the constant implementation error, the time-varying bias error, the fast varying noises, the random noises, or their superposition. In addition, noise-polluted N-FTZNN model (14.9) is a simple extension to noise-free N-FTZNN model (14.8) via adding an additive noise ε. The purpose for this is to investigate the impact of an unknown additive noise to ideal N-FTZNN model (14.8). That is to say, we can study the robustness of ideal N-FTZNN model (14.8) via analyzing noise-polluted N-FTZNN model (14.9).

14.3.2 Theoretical Analysis

In this part, we present the main theoretical results of N-FTZNN model (14.8) for dynamic Sylvester equation (14.1) solving. At first, the global stability and finite-time convergence of N-FTZNN model (14.8) are proved in theory. Then, with unknown additive noises considered, the denoising property of N-FTZNN model (14.8) is discussed by analyzing noise-polluted N-FTZNN model (14.9).

Theorem 14.1 *Given dynamic $A(t) \in \mathbb{R}^{n \times n}$, $B(t) \in \mathbb{R}^{n \times n}$, and $C(t) \in \mathbb{R}^{n \times n}$ which satisfy the condition of the unique solution of (14.1). N-FTZNN model (14.8) is globally stable in sense of Lyapunov stability theory as long as $\Phi_1(\cdot)$ and $\Phi_2(\cdot)$ are monotone increasing odd activation function arrays, with error function $Y(t)$ globally converging to zero.*

Proof: From design procedure of N-FTZNN model (14.8), it is easy to conclude that N-FTZNN model (14.8) is a simple expansion of the integral design formula (14.6) by substituting into the error function. So, N-FTZNN model (14.8) is derived from (14.6). Thus, we can directly analyze integral design formula (14.6), of which its ijth subsystem is the same as (14.7). In addition, for the ijth subsystem (14.7), we are able to define the following intermediate variable $z_{ij}(t)$:

$$z_{ij}(t) = y_{ij}(t) + \gamma_1 \int_0^t \phi_1(y_{ij}(\tau)) \mathrm{d}\tau. \tag{14.10}$$

Computing the time derivative on both sides of Eq. (14.10), we gain

$$\dot{z}_{ij}(t) = \dot{y}_{ij}(t) + \gamma_1 \phi_1(y_{ij}(t)). \tag{14.11}$$

Thus, via synthesizing the results of (14.7), (14.10), and (14.11), it follows

$$\dot{z}_{ij}(t) = -\gamma_2 \phi_2(z_{ij}(t)). \tag{14.12}$$

Based on the aforementioned results, we can design the following Lyapunov function candidate $p_{ij}(t)$ for the ijth subsystem (14.7):

$$p_{ij}(t) = \frac{1}{2} \xi y_{ij}^2(t) + \frac{1}{2} z_{ij}^2(t), \tag{14.13}$$

where $\xi > 0$ and $p_0 = p_{ij}(0) = \xi y_{ij}^2(0)/2 + z_{ij}^2(0)/2$ with $y_{ij}(0)$ and $z_{ij}(0)$ known. In this situation, it is easy to conclude that $p_{ij}(t)$ is positive-definite because $p_{ij}(t) > 0$ for any $y_{ij}(t) \neq 0$ or $z_{ij}(t) \neq 0$, and $p_{ij}(t) = 0$ only for $y_{ij}(t) = z_{ij}(t) = 0$. On the other hand, the time derivative of $p_{ij}(t)$ is derived as follows:

$$\begin{aligned}
\frac{\mathrm{d}p_{ij}(t)}{\mathrm{d}t} &= \xi y_{ij}(t)\dot{y}_{ij}(t) + z_{ij}(t)\dot{z}_{ij}(t) \\
&= \xi y_{ij}(t)[\dot{z}_{ij}(t) - \gamma_1 \phi_1(y_{ij}(t))] - \gamma_2 z_{ij}(t)\phi_2(z_{ij}(t)) \\
&= -\xi \gamma_2 y_{ij}(t)\phi_2(z_{ij}(t)) - \xi \gamma_1 y_{ij}(t)\phi_1(y_{ij}(t)) - \gamma_2 z_{ij}(t)\phi_2(z_{ij}(t)).
\end{aligned} \tag{14.14}$$

To prove $\dot{p}_{ij}(t) \leq 0$, we can adopt the mean-value theorem in the region $\mathbb{R}$ for $\phi_2(\cdot)$, and easily obtain the following result:

$$\phi_2(z_{ij}(t)) - \phi_2(0) = (z_{ij}(t) - 0) \frac{\partial \phi_2(z_{ij}(\bar{\xi}))}{\partial z_{ij}} \Bigg|_{z_{ij}(\bar{\xi}) \in \mathbb{R}}. \tag{14.15}$$

In addition, from the given conditions, we know $\phi_2(\cdot)$ is a monotone increasing odd function, so $\phi_2(0) = 0$ and $\partial \phi_2(z_{ij}(t))/\partial z_{ij} > 0$. Thus, based on (14.15), we are able to get the following conclusion:

$$|\phi_2(z_{ij}(t))| \leq K_0 |z_{ij}(t)|,$$

where $K_0 = \max\{\partial\phi_2(z_{ij}(t))/\partial z_{ij}\}|_{z_{ij}(t)\in\mathbb{R}} > 0$ is bounded. Hence, we further have

$$
\begin{aligned}
|y_{ij}(t)\phi_2(z_{ij}(t))| &\leq |y_{ij}(t)| \cdot |\phi_2(z_{ij}(t))| \\
&\leq K_0|y_{ij}(t)| \cdot |z_{ij}(t)|.
\end{aligned}
\tag{14.16}
$$

Substituting (14.16) back into (14.14), we have

$$
\begin{aligned}
\frac{dp_{ij}(t)}{dt} &= -\xi\gamma_2 y_{ij}(t)\phi_2(z_{ij}(t)) - \xi\gamma_1 y_{ij}(t)\phi_1(y_{ij}(t)) - \gamma_2 z_{ij}(t)\phi_2(z_{ij}(t)) \\
&\leq \xi\gamma_2|y_{ij}(t)\phi_2(z_{ij}(t))| - \xi\gamma_1 y_{ij}(t)\phi_1(y_{ij}(t)) - \gamma_2 z_{ij}(t)\phi_2(z_{ij}(t)) \\
&\leq \xi\gamma_2 K_0|y_{ij}(t)| \cdot |z_{ij}(t)| - \xi\gamma_1 K_1 y_{ij}^2(t) - \gamma_2 K_2 z_{ij}^2(t) \\
&= -\xi\left(\sqrt{\gamma_1 K_1}|y_{ij}| - \frac{\gamma_2 K_0}{2\sqrt{\gamma_1 K_1}}|z_{ij}(t)|\right)^2 - \xi\left(\frac{\gamma_2 K_2}{\xi} - \frac{\gamma_2^2 K_0^2}{4\gamma_1 K_1}\right)z_{ij}^2(t),
\end{aligned}
\tag{14.17}
$$

where $K_1 = \min\{\partial\phi_1(y_{ij}(t))/\partial y_{ij}\}|_{y_{ij}(t)\in\mathbb{R}} > 0$ and $K_2 = \min\{\partial\phi_2(z_{ij}(t))/\partial z_{ij}\}$ $|_{z_{ij}(t)\in\mathbb{R}} > 0$ that are obtained by applying the mean-value theorem two times. From the previous discussion, we have $\dot{p}_{ij}(t) \leq 0$ provided that

$$
0 < \xi \leq \frac{4\gamma_1 K_1 K_2}{\gamma_2 K_0^2}.
\tag{14.18}
$$

The aforementioned result is able to make sure the negative definiteness of $\dot{p}_{ij}(t)$. Hence, according to Lyapunov stability theory, we come to a conclusion that the ijth subsystem (14.7) of the integral design formula is stable and the corresponding $y_{ij}(t)$ is convergent to zero. As a result, we can further derive that the error function $Y(t)$ generated by N-FTZNN model (14.8) is convergent to zero. Since initial values are globally generated, the proposed N-FTZNN model (14.8) is globally stable. This completes the proof. ∎

Remark In the process of proof, based on the conclusion of $\dot{p}_{ij}(t) \leq 0$, it is easy to conclude that $p_{ij}(t) \leq p_0$. Thus, we can further shrink the range when applying the mean-value theorem. Specifically, in this situation, we can gain the following conclusions:

$$
\frac{1}{2}\xi y_{ij}^2(t) \leq p_0, \quad \text{and} \quad \frac{1}{2}z_{ij}^2(t) \leq p_0,
\tag{14.19}
$$

from which we can further derive

$$
|y_{ij}(t)| \leq \sqrt{2p_0/\xi} \quad \text{and} \quad |z_{ij}(t)| \leq \sqrt{2p_0}.
\tag{14.20}
$$

Let us denote respectively the set Ω_1 for $y_{ij}(t)$ and the set Ω_2 for $z_{ij}(t)$. Then, we have

$$
\begin{aligned}
\Omega_1 &= \{y_{ij}(t) \in R, \ |y_{ij}(t)| \leq \sqrt{2p_0/\xi}\}, \\
\Omega_2 &= \{z_{ij}(t) \in R, \ |z_{ij}(t)| \leq \sqrt{2p_0}\}.
\end{aligned}
\tag{14.21}
$$

Thus, we can replace the set $\mathbb{R}$ with Ω_1 for $y_{ij}(t)$ and the set Ω_2 for $z_{ij}(t)$, i.e. $K_0 = \max\{\partial\phi_2(z_{ij}(t))/\partial z_{ij}\}$, $K_1 = \min\{\partial\phi_1(y_{ij}(t))/\partial y_{ij}\}$ and $K_2 = \min\{\partial\phi_2(z_{ij}(t))/\partial z_{ij}\}$. The existence of K_0, K_1, and K_2 are thus guaranteed.

Theorem 14.2 *Given dynamic $A(t) \in \mathbb{R}^{n\times n}$, $B(t) \in \mathbb{R}^{n\times n}$, and $C(t) \in \mathbb{R}^{n\times n}$ which satisfy the condition of the unique solution of (14.1), state output $U(t)$ of N-FTZNN model (14.8), starting from an arbitrary initial state, converges to $U^*(t)$ of dynamic Sylvester equation (14.1) in finite time t_f:*

$$t_f < \frac{\gamma_1 + \gamma_2}{\gamma_1\gamma_2(1-\alpha)} \max\left\{|y^-(0)|^{1-\alpha}, |y^+(0)|^{1-\alpha}\right\},$$

provided that $\phi_1(y_{ij}) = \phi_2(y_{ij}) = \mathrm{sgn}^\alpha(y_{ij}) + \mathrm{sgn}^{1/\alpha}(y_{ij})$ with $\alpha \in (0,1)$ and $\mathrm{sgn}^\alpha(\cdot)$ defined as

$$\mathrm{sgn}^\alpha(y_{ij}) = \begin{cases} |y_{ij}|^\alpha, & \text{if } y_{ij} > 0, \\ 0, & \text{if } y_{ij} = 0, \\ -|y_{ij}|^\alpha, & \text{if } y_{ij} < 0, \end{cases}$$

where $y^-(0) = \min\{Y(0)\}$ stands for the minimum element in $Y(0)$ and $y^+(0) = \max\{Y(0)\}$ stands for the maximum element in $Y(0)$.

Proof: From derivation process of the aforementioned stability analysis, we have $\dot{z}_{ij}(t) = -\gamma_2\phi_2(z_{ij}(t))$ through the intermediate variable $z_{ij}(t) = y_{ij}(t) + \gamma_1\int_0^t\phi_1(y_{ij}(\tau))d\tau$, of which we have $z_{ij}(0) = y_{ij}(0)$ when $t = 0$. For the dynamic system $\dot{z}_{ij}(t) = -\gamma_2\phi_2(z_{ij}(t))$, we are able to design the Lyapunov function candidate $p_{ij}(t) = z_{ij}^2(t)$, and the time derivative of $p_{ij}(t)$ is computed as follows:

$$\dot{p}_{ij}(t) = 2z_{ij}(t)\dot{z}_{ij}(t)$$
$$= -2\gamma_2 z_{ij}(t)\phi_2(z_{ij}(t)).$$

Then, according to the aforementioned specially constructed activation function $\phi_2(\cdot)$, we can obtain the conclusion:

$$\dot{p}_{ij}(t) = -2\gamma_2 z_{ij}(t)\phi_2(z_{ij}(t))$$
$$= -2\gamma_2 z_{ij}(t)\left(\mathrm{sgn}^\alpha(z_{ij}(t)) + \mathrm{sgn}^{1/\alpha}(z_{ij}(t))\right)$$
$$= \begin{cases} -2\gamma_2\left(z_{ij}^{\alpha+1}(t) + z_{ij}^{\frac{1}{\alpha}+1}(t)\right), & \text{if } z_{ij} > 0, \\ -2\gamma_2\left(|z_{ij}|^{\alpha+1}(t) + |z_{ij}|^{\frac{1}{\alpha}+1}(t)\right), & \text{if } z_{ij} < 0, \end{cases} \quad (14.22)$$
$$= -2\gamma_2\left(|z_{ij}|^{\alpha+1}(t) + |z_{ij}|^{\frac{1}{\alpha}+1}(t)\right)$$
$$\leq -2\gamma_2|z_{ij}(t)|^{\alpha+1}$$
$$= -2\gamma_2 p_{ij}^{\frac{\alpha+1}{2}}(t).$$

When the initial value $p_{ij}(0) = |z_{ij}(0)|^2 = |y_{ij}(0)|^2$ is given, we are able to derive the following fact by solving $\dot{p}_{ij}(t) \leqslant -2\gamma_2 p_{ij}^{\frac{\alpha+1}{2}}(t)$:

$$\sqrt{p_{ij}^{1-\alpha}(t)} \begin{cases} \leq |z_{ij}(0)|^{1-\alpha} - \gamma_2 t(1-\alpha), & \text{if } t \leq \frac{|z_{ij}(0)|^{1-\alpha}}{\gamma_2(1-\alpha)}, \\ = 0, & \text{if } t > \frac{|z_{ij}(0)|^{1-\alpha}}{\gamma_2(1-\alpha)}, \end{cases}$$

which suggests that $p_{ij}(t)$ decreases to zero if $t > |z_{ij}(0)|^{1-\alpha}/\gamma_2(1-\alpha)$. Because of $p_{ij}(t) = z_{ij}^2(t)$ and $z_{ij}(0) = y_{ij}(0)$, we can also conclude that $z_{ij}(t)$ converges to zero after $t > |y_{ij}(0)|^{1-\alpha}/\gamma_2(1-\alpha)$.

Now, we continue to estimate the upper bound of convergence time t_1 for $z(t)$. Since every element in $z(t)$ have the same dynamics $\dot{z}_{ij}(t) = -\gamma_2\phi_2(z_{ij}(t))$, $z(t)$ converges to zero when $t > \max\left\{|y^-(0)|^{1-\alpha}, |y^+(0)|^{1-\alpha}\right\}/\gamma_2(1-\alpha)$, where $y^+(0) = \max\{Y(0)\}$ and $y^-(0) = \min\{Y(0)\}$. That is to say, the upper bound of convergence time t_1 for $z(t)$ is estimated as

$$t_1 < \frac{1}{\gamma_2(1-\alpha)} \max\left\{|y^-(0)|^{1-\alpha}, |y^+(0)|^{1-\alpha}\right\}.$$

Therefore, after the time period t_1, we have the fact that $z(t) = 0$ and $\dot{z}(t) = 0$. Now, we review (14.11), from which, based on the aforementioned results, we further obtain

$$\dot{y}_{ij}(t) = -\gamma_1\phi_1(y_{ij}(t)), \tag{14.23}$$

which has the same framework with $\dot{z}_{ij}(t) = -\gamma_2\phi_2(z_{ij}(t))$. In addition, $\phi_1(\cdot) = \phi_2(\cdot)$ is a given known condition. Therefore, we can directly adopt the aforementioned conclusion to estimate the upper bound of convergence time t_2 for $Y(t)$ based on the formulation of $\phi_1(\cdot)$ in the similar way as follows:

$$t_2 < \frac{1}{\gamma_1(1-\alpha)} \max\left\{|y^-(0)|^{1-\alpha}, |y^+(0)|^{1-\alpha}\right\},$$

where $y^-(0)$ and $y^+(0)$ are defined as before.

In summary, by uniting the conclusions of the previous discussions, it is very easy to conclude that, starting from an arbitrary initial state, state output $U(t)$ of N-FTZNN model (14.8) converges to the theoretical solution of (14.1) in finite time $t_f = t_1 + t_2$. That is,

$$t_f < \frac{\gamma_1 + \gamma_2}{\gamma_1\gamma_2(1-\alpha)} \max\left\{|y^-(0)|^{1-\alpha}, |y^+(0)|^{1-\alpha}\right\}.$$

The proof is thus completed. ∎

In the following, we present the robustness result of N-FTZNN model (14.8) in front of unknown additive constant noises by analyzing noise-polluted N-FTZNN model (14.9), which shows N-FTZNN model (14.8) is inherently noise-tolerant.

Theorem 14.3 *Consider noise-polluted N-FTZNN model (14.9) for solving dynamic Sylvester equation (14.1). Starting from an arbitrary initial value, state output U(t) of noise-polluted N-FTZNN model (14.9) is globally convergent to U*(t) in front of unknown additive constant noises provided that $\Phi_1(\cdot)$ and $\Phi_2(\cdot)$ are monotone increasing odd activation function arrays.*

Proof: First, it can be obtained that the ijth subsystem of noise-polluted N-FTZNN model (14.9) is derived from the following design formula:

$$\dot{y}_{ij}(t) = -\gamma_1 \phi_1(y_{ij}(t)) - \gamma_2 \phi_2 \left(y_{ij}(t) + \gamma_1 \int_0^t \phi_1(y_{ij}(\tau))d\tau \right) + \varepsilon. \qquad (14.24)$$

Therefore, we can still introduce the same intermediate variable $z_{ij}(t)$ as (14.10). In addition, the time derivative of $z_{ij}(t)$ is computed as $\dot{z}_{ij}(t) = \dot{y}_{ij}(t) + \gamma_1 \phi_1(y_{ij}(t))$. Then, substituting the results of $z_{ij}(t)$ and $\dot{z}_{ij}(t)$ into (14.24), we have

$$\dot{z}_{ij}(t) = -\gamma_2 \phi_2(z_{ij}(t)) + \varepsilon. \qquad (14.25)$$

Hence, based on the aforementioned result, the following Lyapunov function candidate is designed for the ijth noise-disturbed subsystem (14.24) as follows:

$$p_{ij}(t) = \left(\gamma_2 \phi_2(z_{ij}(t)) - \varepsilon \right)^2 / 2,$$

which can guarantee the positive definiteness of $p_{ij}(t)$. Now, we come to compute $\dot{p}_{ij}(t)$, and the specific solving process is presented as follows:

$$\begin{aligned} \frac{dp_{ij}(t)}{dt} &= \left(\gamma_2 \phi_2(z_{ij}(t)) - \varepsilon \right) \gamma_2 \frac{\partial \phi_2(z_{ij}(t))}{\partial z_{ij}} \dot{z}_{ij}(t) \\ &= -\gamma_2 \frac{\partial \phi_2(z_{ij}(t))}{\partial z_{ij}} \left(\gamma_2 \phi_2(z_{ij}(t)) - \varepsilon \right)^2. \end{aligned} \qquad (14.26)$$

Owing to $\phi_2(\cdot)$ being a monotone increasing odd function, we have that $\frac{\partial \phi_2(z_{ij}(t))}{\partial z_{ij}} > 0$. Therefore, we conclude $\dot{p}_{ij}(t) \leq 0$ and $\dot{p}_{ij}(t)$ is negative definite; i.e. $\dot{p}_{ij}(t) < 0$ for any $\gamma_2 \phi_2(z_{ij}(t)) - \varepsilon \neq 0$ and $\dot{p}_{ij}(t) = 0$ only for $\gamma_2 \phi_2(z_{ij}(t)) - \varepsilon = 0$. Thus, $p_{ij}(t)$ converges to zero with time. At this time, $\lim_{t \to \infty} \gamma_2 \phi_2(z_{ij}(t)) - \varepsilon = 0$, i.e. $\lim_{t \to \infty} z_{ij}(t) = \phi_2^{-1}(\varepsilon/\gamma_2)$. That is to say, $z_{ij}(t)$ converges to $\phi_2^{-1}(\varepsilon/\gamma_2)$. Then we know that $\lim_{t \to \infty} \dot{z}_{ij}(t) = -\gamma_2 \phi_2(z_{ij}(t)) + \varepsilon = 0$.

On the other hand, due to $\dot{z}_{ij}(t) = \dot{y}_{ij}(t) + \gamma_1 \phi_1(y_{ij}(t))$ and $\lim_{t \to \infty} \dot{z}_{ij}(t) = 0$, we now conduct analysis according to Lasalle's invariant set principle by investigating the problem in the largest invariant set formed by $\lim_{t \to \infty} \dot{z}_{ij}(t) = 0$ [18, 19]. In this situation, $\dot{z}_{ij}(t) = \dot{y}_{ij}(t) + \gamma_1 \phi_1(y_{ij}(t))$ reduces to

$$\dot{y}_{ij}(t) = -\gamma_1 \phi_1(y_{ij}(t)). \qquad (14.27)$$

For this dynamic system, we can directly choose the Lyapunov function candidate as $p_{ij}(t) = y_{ij}^2(t)/2 \geq 0$. In addition, its time derivative is derived as

$$\dot{p}_{ij}(t) = y_{ij}(t)\dot{y}_{ij}(t)$$
$$= -\gamma_1 y_{ij}(t)\phi_1(y_{ij}(t)).$$

Since $\phi_1(\cdot)$ is a monotone increasing odd function, we have

$$\phi_1(y_{ij}(t)) \begin{cases} > 0, & \text{if} \quad y_{ij}(t) > 0, \\ = 0, & \text{if} \quad y_{ij}(t) = 0, \\ < 0, & \text{if} \quad y_{ij}(t) < 0. \end{cases}$$

Thus, we can further conclude

$$y_{ij}(t)\phi_1(y_{ij}(t)) \begin{cases} > 0, & \text{if} \quad y_{ij}(t) \neq 0, \\ = 0, & \text{if} \quad y_{ij}(t) = 0, \end{cases}$$

which ensures the negative definiteness of $\dot{p}_{ij}(t)$. By Lyapunov theory, we can easily conclude that $\lim_{t\to\infty} y_{ij}(t) = 0$, provided that $\phi_1(\cdot)$ is a monotone increasing odd function.

Synthesizing the aforementioned results, we can draw a conclusion that the error function $Y(t)$ generated by noise-polluted N-FTZNN model (14.9) globally converges to zero even in front of unknown additive constant noises provided that $\Phi_1(\cdot)$ and $\Phi_2(\cdot)$ are monotone increasing odd function arrays. In other words, starting from an arbitrary initial value, state output $U(t)$ of noise-polluted N-FTZNN model (14.9) is globally convergent to $U^*(t)$ of (14.1) in front of unknown additive constant noises. The proof on the denoising property of N-FTZNN model (14.8) is completed by analyzing noise-polluted N-FTZNN model (14.9). ∎

14.4 Illustrative Verification

In Sections 14.2 and 14.3, both ZNN model (14.4) and N-FTZNN model (14.9) are presented for dynamic Sylvester equation (14.1) solving. For N-FTZNN model (14.9), the global stability, the finite-time convergence and the denoising property are analyzed in details. In this section, numerical comparative results are supplied to further demonstrate the superiority of N-FTZNN model (14.9) to ZNN model (14.4).

Without any loss of generality, the time-varying coefficients of dynamic Sylvester equation (14.1) are simply set as follows:

$$A(t) = \begin{bmatrix} \sin(2t) & \cos(2t) \\ -\cos(2t) & \sin(2t) \end{bmatrix}, \quad B(t) = \begin{bmatrix} 1.5 & 0 \\ 0 & 2 \end{bmatrix}, \quad C(t) = \begin{bmatrix} \sin(t) & \cos(t) \\ -\cos(t) & 2\sin(t) \end{bmatrix}$$

which ensure the unique solution of the dynamic Sylvester equation in this situation. Through the whole simulation part, design parameter α in nonlinear activation functions $\phi_1(\cdot)$ and $\phi_2(\cdot)$ is always equal to 0.5.

First, starting from an arbitrary initial state $U(0) \in [-2, 2]^{2 \times 2}$, we apply N-FTZNN model (14.8) to compute the aforementioned dynamic Sylvester equation with $\gamma_1 = \gamma_2 = 1$ in front of no noise. Figure 14.2 plots the trajectories of state output $U(t)$ generated by N-FTZNN model (14.9), as well as the trajectories of the theoretical solution $U^*(t)$ for verification purposes. From this figure, we conclude that all elements of state output $U(t)$ are able to converge to the ones of the theoretical solution $U^*(t)$ within a short finite time. In addition, in Figure 14.3a, we draw the trajectory of the residual error $\|A(t)U(t) - U(t)B(t) + C(t)\|_F$ corresponding to state output $U(t)$ of N-FTZNN model (14.9) under the condition of $\gamma_1 = \gamma_2 = 1$. The finite convergence time of N-FTZNN model (14.9) for the dynamic Sylvester equation is about 2.8 seconds, which can be validated from the result of Figure 14.3a. Besides, when $\gamma_1 = \gamma_2 = 1000$, it can be concluded that the finite convergence time of N-FTZNN model (14.9) for the dynamic Sylvester equation decreases to about 2.8×10^{-3} seconds. The results demonstrate

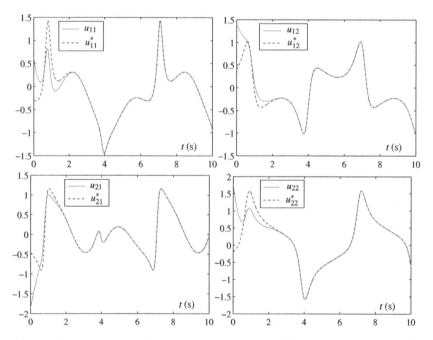

Figure 14.2 Trajectories of theoretical solution $U^*(t)$ and state output $U(t)$ generated by N-FTZNN model (14.9) with $\gamma_1 = \gamma_2 = 1$ in front of no noise, where solid curves denote the elements of state output $U(t)$, and dash curves denotes the elements of $U^*(t)$.

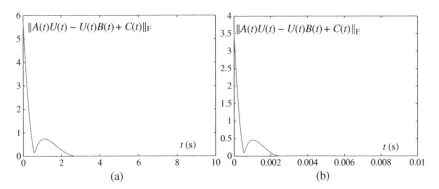

Figure 14.3 Trajectories of residual error $\|A(t)U(t) - U(t)B(t) + C(t)\|_F$ generated by N-FTZNN model (14.9) with different values of γ_1 and γ_2 in front of no noise. (a) With $\gamma_1 = \gamma_2 = 1$. (b) With $\gamma_1 = \gamma_2 = 1000$.

the effectiveness and efficiency of N-FTZNN model (14.9) for solving dynamic Sylvester equation in front of no noise.

On the other hand, for showing the outstanding denoising property of N-FTZNN model (14.9), both ZNN model (14.5), and N-FTZNN model (14.9) are applied to solve the aforementioned dynamic Sylvester equation in front of different additive noises. First, the additive constant noise $\varepsilon = 3$ is considered. Starting from an arbitrary initial state $U(0) \in [-2, 2]^{2\times2}$, the trajectories of state output $U(t)$ generated by ZNN model (14.5) with $\gamma = 1$ are plotted in Figure 14.4. As compared with the elements of the theoretical solution $U^*(t)$, all elements of state output $U(t)$ are always oscillating nearby. In other words, ZNN model (14.5) can not generate an accurate solution of the dynamic Sylvester equation in front of additive constant noises. Besides, the trajectory of the residual error $\|A(t)U(t) - U(t)B(t) + C(t)\|_F$ generated by ZNN model (14.5) in this situation is displayed in Figure 14.5a, from which we can obtain the fact the residual error $\|A(t)U(t) - U(t)B(t) + C(t)\|_F$ stays nearby the additive constant noise $\varepsilon = 3$. This result implies that ZNN model (14.5) is not inherently noise-tolerant. In contrast, under the same conditions, N-FTZNN model (14.9) can generate the desired solution after a short finite time, and the solution trajectories are similar to the ones of Figure 14.2 (and thus not presented). In addition, the trajectory of the residual error $\|A(t)U(t) - U(t)B(t) + C(t)\|_F$ generated by N-FTZNN model (14.9) is plotted in Figure 14.5b, which verify the denoising property of N-FTZNN model (14.9) in front of the additive constant noise $\varepsilon = 3$.

Here, we further investigate the roles of design parameters γ in the ZNN model, γ_1 and γ_2 in the N-FTZNN model. In this part, we set $\gamma = \gamma_1 = \gamma_2 = 10$ and still consider the additive constant noise $\varepsilon = 3$ for consistency. The simulative results are described in Figure 14.6. As seen from this figure, we can conclude that the residual error $\|A(t)U(t) - U(t)B(t) + C(t)\|_F$ generated by ZNN model (14.5) converges

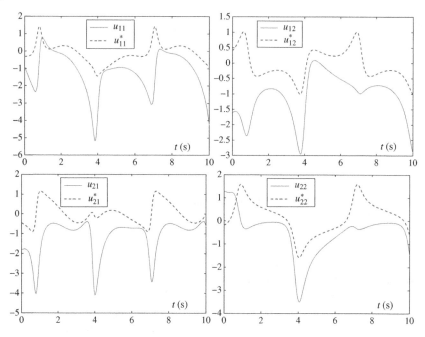

Figure 14.4 Trajectories of theoretical solution $U^*(t)$ and state output $U(t)$ generated by ZNN model (14.4) with $\gamma_1 = \gamma_2 = 1$ in front of the additive constant noise $\varepsilon = 3$, where solid curves denote the elements of state output $U(t)$, and dash curves denotes the elements of $U^*(t)$.

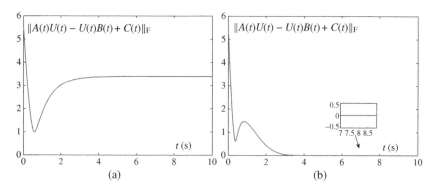

Figure 14.5 Trajectories of residual error $\|A(t)U(t) - U(t)B(t) + C(t)\|_F$ generated by two different models with $\gamma = \gamma_1 = \gamma_2 = 1$ in front of additive constant noise $\varepsilon = 3$. (a) By ZNN model (14.5). (b) By N-FTZNN model (14.9).

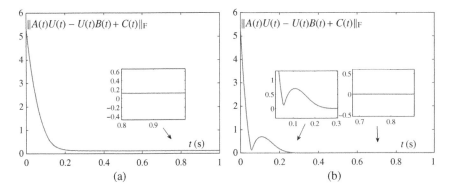

Figure 14.6 Trajectories of residual error $\|A(t)U(t) - U(t)B(t) + C(t)\|_F$ generated by two different models with $\gamma = \gamma_1 = \gamma_2 = 10$ in front of additive constant noise $\varepsilon = 3$. (a) By ZNN model (14.5). (b) By N-FTZNN model (14.9).

to nearby 0.1, and the residual error $\|A(t)U(t) - U(t)B(t) + C(t)\|_F$ generated by N-FTZNN model (14.9) is able to converge to zero within finite time 0.28. The results suggest that design parameters in ZNN model (14.5) and N-FTZNN model (14.9) play an accelerated and noise-tolerant role in solving dynamic Sylvester equation.

At last, we study the impact of additive dynamic noises on ZNN model (14.5) and N-FTZNN model (14.9), instead of the previously investigated additive constant noises. In this situation, we set $\gamma = \gamma_1 = \gamma_2 = 10$ for consistency and the difference is we consider the dynamic additive noise $\varepsilon = 4t$. Starting from an arbitrary initial state $U(0) \in [-2, 2]^{2\times2}$, we apply such two RNN models to compute the dynamic Sylvester equation with simulation results shown in Figure 14.7. It is

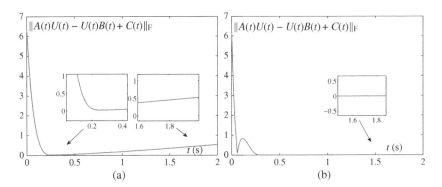

Figure 14.7 Trajectories of residual error $\|A(t)U(t) - U(t)B(t) + C(t)\|_F$ generated by two different models with $\gamma = \gamma_1 = \gamma_2 = 10$ in front of additive dynamic noise $\varepsilon = 4t$. (a) By ZNN model (14.5). (b) By N-FTZNN model (14.9).

worth pointing out that the dynamic additive noise in this situation, i.e. $\varepsilon = 4t$, is increasing from zero with time. Therefore, from Figure 14.7a, we can see that the residual error $\|A(t)U(t) - U(t)B(t) + C(t)\|_F$ of ZNN model (14.5) approaches to zero about 0.2 second, and then slowly increases. This phenomenon keeps pace with the variation tendency of the dynamic additive noise $\varepsilon = 4t$. In contrast, even in front of the dynamic additive noise $\varepsilon = 4t$, N-FTZNN model (14.9) is still effective and generates the desired solution of the dynamic Sylvester equation, which can be validated by Figure 14.7b. In this subfigure, the residual error $\|A(t)U(t) - U(t)B(t) + C(t)\|_F$ generated by N-FTZNN model (14.9) in front of the dynamic additive noise $\varepsilon = 4t$ is able to converge to zero within a short finite time 0.28 second.

Based on the aforementioned discussion in front of different types of noises, we can obtain the following conclusions: (i) N-FTZNN model (14.8) is able to solve dynamic Sylvester equation (14.1) within finite time in front of no noise; (ii) In front of additive constant noises, N-FTZNN model (14.9) is effective on solving dynamic Sylvester equation (14.1) and simultaneously achieves finite-time convergence; and (iii) even in front of additive dynamic noises, N-FTZNN model (14.9) still generates the desired solution of dynamic Sylvester equation (14.1) within finite time.

14.5 Robotic Application

As a hot topic, robots were extensively studied [20, 21]. In this part, we consider the application of the proposed design method to kinematic control of a robotic manipulator in front of additive noises. Besides, the original design method of ZNN model (14.5) is also adopted to complete the same task for comparative purposes. In general, the kinematical equations of manipulators from a joint space (e.g. θ, $\dot{\theta}$) to a Cartesian workspace (e.g. r, $\dot{r}$), at the position and velocity levels can be respectively described as follows [22–24]:

$$r = h(\theta), \tag{14.28}$$

$$\dot{r} = J(\theta)\dot{\theta}, \tag{14.29}$$

where $h(\cdot)$ denotes a differentiable nonlinear function, and $J(\theta) = \partial h(\theta)/\partial \theta \in \mathbb{R}^{m \times n}$ [22–24].

For a robotic manipulator described in (14.29), the kinematical control is to find a control law $u = \dot{\theta}$ to make sure the tracking error $Y(t) = r(t) - r_d(t)$ for a given reference trajectory $r_d(t)$ converges with time even in front of additive noises.

In order to solve the control law $u = \dot{\theta}$, we can apply the proposed design method to establish the novel RNN model to kinematical control of robotic manipulators.

Specifically, based on (14.29) which is used as the error function, we can obtain the following model to generate the control input in front of additive noises ε:

$$
\begin{aligned}
J\dot{u} = &-\gamma_1 \Phi_1 (Ju - \dot{r}_d) - \dot{J}\theta + \ddot{r}_d + \varepsilon \\
&- \gamma_2 \Phi_2 \left((Ju - \dot{r}_d) + \gamma_1 \int_0^t \Phi_1 (Ju - \dot{r}_d) d\tau \right),
\end{aligned} \tag{14.30}
$$

where $\dot{r}_d$ and $\ddot{r}_d$ denote the first order and the second order time derivative of the given reference trajectory $r_d(t)$.

Besides, based on the original design method of ZNN model (14.5), the following model can be established to generate the control input in front of additive noises ε for comparative purposes:

$$
J\dot{u} = -\dot{J}\theta + \ddot{r}_d - \gamma(Ju - \dot{r}_d) + \varepsilon. \tag{14.31}
$$

For the purposes of the easy demonstration, we consider the kinematical control of a simple two-link planar manipulator with each link being 1 m [25]. In this example, we set $\theta(0) = [\pi/4, \pi/3]^{\mathrm{T}}$ rad, $\gamma_1 = \gamma_2 = \gamma = 50$, and $\eta = 2.5$.

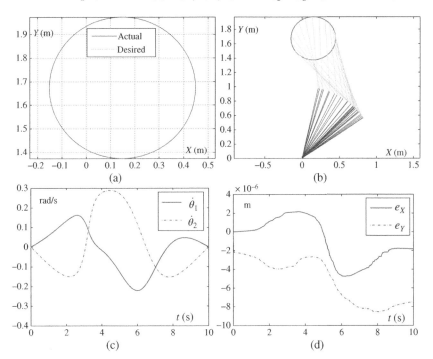

Figure 14.8 Motion trajectories of a two-link planar manipulator synthesized by the N-FTZNN-based model (14.30) with $\gamma_1 = \gamma_2 = 50$ in front of the additive constant noise $\varepsilon = 2.5$. (a) The actual circle trajectory and the desired path. (b) The whole motion process. (c) The control law $u = \dot{\theta}$. (d) The position tracking error $Y(t) = r(t) - r_d(t)$.

The specific tracking task is allocated as a circle path with the radius being 0.3 m, and the task-tracking time is 10 seconds.

First, N-FTZNN-based model (14.30) is applied to the designated the circle-path tracking in front of additive constant noise $\varepsilon = 2.5$, and the simulations are plotted in Figure 14.8. As seen from Figure 14.8a, the actual tracking trajectory is completely fit with the desired path, and the whole tracking process is shown in Figure 14.8b. Figure 14.8c describes the dynamic behavior of the control law $\dot{\theta}$. Especially, from Figure 14.8d, we know that the maximal position tracking error keeps 1.5×10^{-6} order of magnitude. The results are able to demonstrate efficiency of the N-FTZNN-based model (14.30) even in front of additive constant noise $\varepsilon = 2.5$.

On the other hand, simulation results synthesized by ZNN-based model (14.31) are described in Figure 14.9 under the same conditions. From Figure 14.9a, it is concluded that, due to the impact of the additive constant noise, the actual tracking trajectory starts to deviate from its desired motion path with time. Figure 14.9b,c

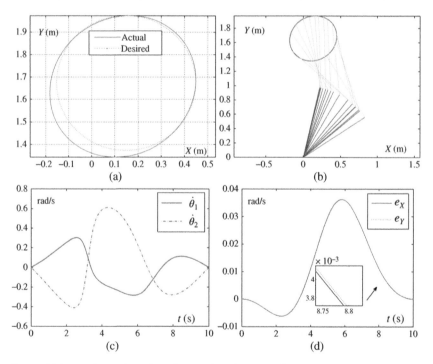

Figure 14.9 Motion trajectories of a two-link planar manipulator synthesized by ZNN-based model (14.31) with $\gamma = 50$ in front of the additive constant noise $\varepsilon = 2.5$. (a) The actual circle trajectory and the desired path. (b) The whole motion process. (c) The control law $u = \dot{\theta}$. (d) The position tracking error $Y(t) = r(t) - r_d(t)$.

show the corresponding the whole tracking process and the dynamic behavior of the control law $\dot{\theta}$. In addition, from Figure 14.9d, we can obtain that the maximal position tracking error reaches about 4 cm. In other words, the planar two-link manipulator is not able to perform successfully the allocated circle-path tracking task due to the impact of the additive constant noise. The results show the invalidity of ZNN-based model (14.31) for kinematical control of robotic manipulators in the presence of the additive noises.

14.6 Chapter Summary

A novel integral design formula activated by nonlinear functions, which is quite different from the ZNN design formula, is presented for solving dynamic Sylvester equation with additive noises considered. On the basis of the integral design formula, a N-FTZNN model with finite-time convergence and inherently noise tolerance is proposed to solve dynamic Sylvester equation in front of various additive noises. In addition, the global stability, finite-time convergence, and denoising property of the N-FTZNN model are proven in theory. Simulative results validate the superiority of the N-FTZNN model for dynamic Sylvester equation in front of various additive noises, as compared with the ZNN model. In addition, the proposed design method for establishing the N-FTZNN model is successfully applied to kinematical control of robotic manipulator in front of additive noises.

References

1 Q. Wang and Z. He, Systems of coupled generalized Sylvester matrix equations, *Automatica*, 50(11) (2014) 2840–2844.

2 Q. Wei, N. Dobigeon, and J. Y. Tourneret, Fast fusion of multi-band images based on solving a Sylvester equation, *IEEE Trans. Image Process.*, 24(11) (2015) 4109–4121.

3 S. Li and Y. Li, Nonlinearly activated neural network for solving time-varying complex Sylvester equation, *IEEE Trans. Cybern.*, 44(8) (2014) 1397–1407.

4 G. Sangalli and M. Tani, Isogeometric preconditioners based on fast solvers for the Sylvester equation, *SIAM J. Sci. Comput.*, 38(6) (2016) A3644–A3671.

5 E. B. Castelan and V. G. Silva, On the solution of a Sylvester equation appearing in descriptor systems control theory, *Syst. Control Lett.*, 54(2) (2005) 109–117.

6 L. Xiao, A finite-time recurrent neural network for solving online time-varying Sylvester matrix equation based on a new evolution formula, *Nonlinear Dyn.*, 90(3) (2017) 1581–1591.

7 M. Darouach, Solution to Sylvester equation associated to linear descriptor systems, *Syst. Control Lett.*, 55(10) (2006) 835–838.

8 F. Ding, P. Liu, and J. Ding, Iterative solutions of the generalized Sylvester matrix equations by using the hierarchical identification principle, *Appl. Math. Comput.*, 197(1) (2008) 41–50.

9 F. Ding and H. Zhang, Gradient-based iterative algorithm for a class of the coupled matrix equations related to control systems, *IET Control Theory Appl.*, 8(15) (2014) 1588–1595.

10 G. Sewell, *Computational methods of linear algebra*, World Scientific Publishing Company, (2014).

11 Y. Zhang, K. Chen, and H. Tan, Performance analysis of gradient neural network exploited for online time-varying matrix inversion, *IEEE Trans. Autom. Control*, 54(8) (2009) 1940–1945.

12 Y. Zhang, D. Jiang, and J. Wang, A recurrent neural network for solving Sylvester equation with time-varying coefficients, *IEEE Trans. Neural Netw.*, 13(5) (2002) 1053–1063.

13 S. Li, S. Chen, and B. Liu, Accelerating a recurrent neural network to finite-time convergence for solving time-varying Sylvester equation by using a sign-bi-power activation function, *Neural Process. Lett.*, 37 (2013) 189–205.

14 L. Jin, Y. Zhang, and S. Li, Integration-enhanced Zhang neural network for real-time-varying matrix inversion in the presence of various kinds of noises, *IEEE Trans. Neural Netw. Learn. Syst.*, 27(12) (2016) 2615–2627.

15 L. Xiao and B. Liao et al., A finite-time convergent dynamic system for solving online simultaneous linear equations, *Int. J. Comput. Math.*, 94(9) (2017) 1778–1786.

16 L. Xiao and Y. Zhang, Zhang neural network versus gradient neural network for solving time-varying linear inequalities, *IEEE Trans. Neural Netw.*, 22(10) (2011) 1676–1684.

17 L. Xiao and S. Li et al., A new recurrent neural network with noise-tolerance and finite-time convergence for dynamic quadratic minimization, *Neurocomputing*, 285 (2018) 125–132.

18 J. P. LaSalle, Stability theory for ordinary differential equations, *J. Differ. Equ.*, 4(1) (1968) 57–65.

19 V. Chellaboina, S. P. Bhat, and W. M. Haddad, An invariance principle for nonlinear hybrid and impulsive dynamical systems, *Nonlinear Anal: Theor. Meth. Appl.*, 53(3–4) (2003) 527–550.

20 D. Guo and Y. Zhang, Acceleration-level inequality-based MAN scheme for obstacle avoidance of redundant robot manipulators, *IEEE Trans. Ind. Electron.*, 61(12) (2014) 6903–6914.

21 Z. Zhang, A. Beck, and N. Magnenat-Thalmann, Human-like behavior generation based on head-arms model for tracking external targets and body parts, *IEEE Trans. Cybern.*, 45(8) (2015) 1390–1400.

22 L. Xiao and Y. Zhang, Solving time-varying inverse kinematics problem of wheeled mobile manipulators using Zhang neural network with exponential convergence, *Nonlinear Dyn.*, 76(2) (2014) 1543–1559.

23 Z. Zhang and Y. Zhang, Acceleration-level cyclic motion generation of constrained redundant robots tracking different paths, *IEEE Trans. Syst. Man Cybern. Part B Cybern.*, 42(4) (2012) 1257–1269.

24 L. Xiao and Y. Zhang, A new performance index for the repetitive motion of mobile manipulators, *IEEE Trans. Cybern.*, 44(2) (2014) 280–292.

25 D. Guo and Y. Zhang, Zhang neural network, Getz-Marsden dynamic system, and discrete-time algorithms for time-varying matrix inversion with application to robots' kinematic control, *Neurocomputing*, 97 (2012) 22–32.

15

Design Scheme II of FTZNN

15.1 Introduction

Solving Sylvester equation is often found in mathematics and control theory and applied to solve various important problems such as eigenvalue assignment [1], and image processing [2]. Therefore, it is a crucial issue to solve the Sylvester equation by designing various different schemes. Numerical methods were usually used to solve the static Sylvester equation in the past [3–14], such as Bartels–Stewart, and Hessenberg–Schur iteration methods [8–14]. However, when faced with the time-variant Sylvester equation, numerical methods (such as Hessenberg–Schur method) may be not suitable due to the high complexity and high sampling in each period.

In this chapter, we are committed to proposing new zeroing neural network (ZNN) models for solving time-variant Sylvester equation, which not only achieves the predefined-time convergence, but also tolerates various different kinds of noises. To do so, two novel nonlinear functions are skillfully devised to activate the ZNN model to establish two noise-tolerant predefined-time zeroing neural network (NT-PTZNN) models for solving time-variant Sylvester equation. It is noted that the design of two novel nonlinear activation functions (AFs) are inspired by referring to the idea of [15–17]. As compared with previous ZNN models activated by some existing AFs (e.g. linear activation function [LAF], bipolar sigmoid activation function [BPAF], power activation function [PAF], sign-bi-power activation function [SBPAF]) the proposed two NT-PTZNN models not only have a predefined-time convergence (i.e. the enhanced finite-time convergence) but also have a better robustness. The main advantage of the predefined-time convergence is independent to initial states of the NT-PTZNN model, which can modify the convergence speed greatly. Furthermore, the convergence upper bounds of the proposed NT-PTZNN models are analytically estimated in theory under different kinds of external noises. Numerical

Zeroing Neural Networks: Finite-time Convergence Design, Analysis and Applications,
First Edition. Lin Xiao and Lei Jia.
© 2023 The Institute of Electrical and Electronics Engineers, Inc. Published 2023 by John Wiley & Sons, Inc.

comparison results further verify the superiority of the proposed NT-PTZNN models to existing ZNN models for time-variant Sylvester equation.

15.2 ZNN Model and Activation Functions

In this part, we first consider the following time-variant Sylvester equation:

$$A(t)U(t) - U(t)B(t) = -C(t) \in \mathbb{R}^{n \times n}, \tag{15.1}$$

where $A(t) \in \mathbb{R}^{n \times n}$, $B(t) \in \mathbb{R}^{n \times n}$, and $C(t) \in \mathbb{R}^{n \times n}$ stand for known time-variant coefficient matrices of appropriate sizes; and $U(t) \in \mathbb{R}^{n \times n}$ stands for an unknown matrix of appropriate size that needs to be obtained. For convenience of presentation, $U^*(t) \in \mathbb{R}^{n \times n}$ is used to denote the theoretical solution of (15.1). In the following, for completeness of this work, the design process of ZNN for time-variant Sylvester equation is given. Then, we review some commonly used AFs that were adopted to activate neural models to modify the performance. At last of this section, two novel nonlinear AFs are presented by following the idea of the predefined-time convergence.

15.2.1 ZNN Model

First, for solving time-variant Sylvester equation (15.1), we can define a matrix-valued error function $Y(t)$:

$$Y(t) = A(t)U(t) - U(t)B(t) + C(t) \in \mathbb{R}^{n \times n}. \tag{15.2}$$

It is obvious that if each element of the error function $Y(t)$ converges to 0, the corresponding $U(t)$ is what we want to find. That is, solving time-variant Sylvester equation (15.1) is equivalently transformed into forcing $Y(t)$ converging to 0.

Then, to make error function (15.2) decrease to 0, the following ZNN design formula is employed [18–20]:

$$\frac{\mathrm{d}Y(t)}{\mathrm{d}t} = -\gamma \Phi(Y(t)), \tag{15.3}$$

where $\Phi(\cdot) : \mathbb{R}^{n \times n} \to \mathbb{R}^{n \times n}$ stands for an AF array and $\gamma > 0$ stands for a known adjustable parameter.

Then, by substituting error function (15.2) into ZNN design formula (15.3) and considering the time derivative of error function $Y(t)$ is $\dot{Y}(t) = A(t)\dot{U}(t) + \dot{A}(t)U(t) - \dot{U}(t)B(t) - U(t)\dot{B}(t) + \dot{C}(t)$, the following ZNN model for time-variant Sylvester equation (15.1) is established:

$$A(t)\dot{U}(t) - \dot{U}(t)B(t) = \dot{A}(t)U(t) + \dot{U}(t)B(t) - \gamma \Phi(A(t)U(t)$$
$$- U(t)B(t) + C(t)) - \dot{C}(t). \tag{15.4}$$

For such a ZNN model, which can be regarded as an ordinary differential equation, if an initial value $U(0)$ is given, it can converge to its equilibrium point and output the accurate solution of time-variant Sylvester equation (15.1).

15.2.2 Commonly Used AFs

In the past decade, various different types of AFs have widely been proposed and investigated to modify the performance of neural networks [21–24]. These survey results indicate different AFs would lead to different performance of neural models, and most of nonlinear AFs have a positive effect on the convergence speed of neural models. Similarly, for ZNN model (15.4), choosing a better AF can further modify its comprehensive performance when applied to solving time-variant Sylvester equation (15.1) even in the presence of external disturbances. Considering the importance of AFs, in this part, several commonly used AFs are reviewed and presented as follows [21–24].

(1) Linear activation function (LAF): $\phi(x) = x$;
(2) Bipolar sigmoid activation function (BPAF): $\phi(x) = (1 - \exp(-\xi x))/(1 + \exp(-\xi x))$ with $\xi > 1$;
(3) Power activation function (PAF): $\phi(x) = x^\alpha$ with $\alpha > 3$ indicating an odd integer;
(4) Power-sigmoid activation function (PSAF):

$$\phi(x) = \begin{cases} x^\alpha, & \text{if } |x| \geq 1, \\ \dfrac{1+\exp(-\xi)}{1-\exp(-\xi)} \cdot \dfrac{1-\exp(-\xi x)}{1+\exp(-\xi x)}, & \text{otherwise,} \end{cases}$$

with $\alpha > 3$ indicating an odd integer and $\xi > 1$;
(5) Hyperbolic sine activation function (HSAF): $\phi(x) = (\exp(\xi x) - \exp(-\xi x))/2$ with $\xi > 1$;
(6) Sign-bi-power activation function (SBPAF): $\phi(x) = (|x|^\alpha + |x|^{1/\alpha})\mathrm{sgn}(x)/2$ with $0 < \alpha < 1$ and $\mathrm{sgn}(\cdot)$ denoting the signum function.

It is worth noting that the aforementioned all nonlinear AFs have been used to accelerate the convergence speed of previous ZNN models and the results are better than that using the LAF. In addition, if SBPAF is used, finite-time convergence can be realized for ZNN models. However, these nonlinear AFs are only used in the ideal conditions (i.e. no external noises exist).

15.2.3 Two Novel Nonlinear AFs

As mentioned earlier, nonlinear AFs can improve the convergence rate even to finite-time convergence performance of ZNN models, but the noise disturbances are essentially not taken into account. That is to say, the aforementioned nonlinear AFs activated ZNN models may no longer work effectively when the noise is disturbed. Therefore, on basis of these AFs, inspired by the idea of the predefined-time stability for nonlinear dynamic systems [15–17, 25], two novel nonlinear AFs have been developed to activate ZNN model (15.4), which can make it not only converge to the equilibrium point in a predefined time, but also tolerate various different external disturbances. Specifically, such two novel nonlinear AFs are presented as follows:

$$\phi_1(x) = (a_1|x|^\eta + a_2|x|^w)\text{sgn}(x) + a_3 x + a_4\text{sgn}(x), \tag{15.5}$$

$$\phi_2(x) = b_1\exp(|x|^\alpha)|x|^{1-\alpha}\,\text{sgn}(x)/\alpha + b_2 x + b_3\text{sgn}(x), \tag{15.6}$$

where design parameters $0 < \eta < 1$, $w > 1$, $a_1 > 0$, $a_2 > 0$, $a_3 \geqslant 0$, $a_4 \geqslant 0$, $0 < \alpha < 1, b_1 > 0, b_2 \geqslant 0$, and $b_3 \geqslant 0$.

In the simulation part, for the purposes of comparison, three typical AFs (i.e. LAF, PSAF, and SBPAF) will be used to activate ZNN model (15.4) for finding the solution of time-variant Sylvester equation (15.1) under different noise disturbances.

15.3 NT-PTZNN Models and Theoretical Analysis

On the basis of two novel AFs (15.5) and (15.6), NT-PTZNN models are proposed to solve time-variant Sylvester equation (15.1). In addition, the detailed theoretical analyses of predefined-time convergence for two NT-PTZNN models are discussed in the presence of various different kinds of external disturbances.

15.3.1 NT-PTZNN1 Model

In the previous section, two novel AFs are presented to modify the comprehensive performance of ZNN model (15.4) when applied to time-variant Sylvester equation (15.1) solving. Note that AFs (15.5) and (15.6) are standardly scalar-valued functions, while ZNN model (15.4) is a matrix-valued neural model. Therefore, AFs (15.5) and (15.6) are needed to be extended to matrix-valued ones. To do so, we use $\Phi_1(x) \in \mathbb{R}^{n \times n}$ to denote the matrix-valued AF array, which is consist of $n \times n$ AF (15.5). Therefore, when AF array $\Phi_1(x) \in \mathbb{R}^{n \times n}$ is used to activate ZNN model (15.4), we can obtain the NT-PTZNN1 model:

$$A(t)\dot{U}(t) - \dot{U}(t)B(t) = \dot{A}(t)U(t) + \dot{U}(t)B(t) - \gamma\Phi_1(A(t)U(t)$$
$$- U(t)B(t) + C(t)) - \dot{C}(t). \tag{15.7}$$

For easy presentation, this model is called the NT-PTZNN1 model. As compared with ZNN model (15.4) activated by existing AFs, NT-PTZNN1 model (15.7) has a superior predefined-time convergence regardless of whether there exist external disturbances, which can be calculated as a priori and is independent of initial conditions of NT-PTZNN1 model (15.7). This feature is important for some practical models where their initial conditions are hard to be regulated or even impossible to be evaluated.

Before the main theoretical results of NT-PTZNN1 model (15.7) are given, the following lemma is presented as a basis for further discussion [15–17].

Lemma 15.1 *For a nonlinear dynamic system $\dot{x}(t) = g(x(t), t)$, $t \in [0, +\infty)$ where $g(\cdot)$ denotes a nonlinear function, if there exists a continuous radially unbounded function $V: \mathbb{R}^n \to \mathbb{R}_+ \cup \{0\}$ such that $V(\zeta) = 0$ and any solution $\zeta(t)$ satisfies*

$$\dot{V}(t) \leqslant -\tau V^{\varsigma}(\zeta(t)) - \rho V^{\mu}(\zeta(t)),$$

where parameters $\tau > 0$, $\rho > 0$, $0 < \varsigma < 1$, and $\mu > 1$ are constants, then the predefined convergence time for this system is

$$T_{\max} = \frac{1}{\tau(1 - \varsigma)} + \frac{1}{\rho(\mu - 1)}.$$

Then, we have the following theorem to ensure the predefined-time convergence of NT-PTZNN1 model (15.7) under the ideal conditions.

Theorem 15.2 *Beginning with a random initial matrix $U(0) \in \mathbb{R}^{n \times n}$, NT-PTZNN1 model (15.7) outputs an accurate solution of time-variant Sylvester equation (15.1) in a predefined time t_f:*

$$t_f \leqslant \frac{1}{\gamma a_1(1 - \eta)} + \frac{1}{\gamma a_2(w - 1)},$$

where design parameters $\gamma, a_1, a_2, \eta, w$ are defined as before.

Proof: First, we can conclude that NT-PTZNN1 model (15.7) is equivalent to $\dot{Y}(t) = -\gamma \Phi_1(Y(t))$ with $Y(t)$ denoting error function (15.2), of which the ijth subsystem is written as

$$\dot{y}_{ij}(t) = -\gamma \phi_1(y_{ij}(t)) \text{ with } i, j \in \{1, 2, \dots, n\}, \tag{15.8}$$

where $y_{ij}(t)$ and $\dot{y}_{ij}(t)$ are the ijth elements of matrices $Y(t)$ and $\dot{Y}(t)$, respectively.

If this subsystem (15.8) is proved to be the predefined-time stability, it can be concluded that NT-PTZNN1 model (15.7) is also the predefined-time stability. To prove the predefined-time stability of the ijth subsystem (15.8), a Lyapunov function candidate is first defined as

$$p(t) = |y_{ij}(t)|.$$

Its time derivative is computed as follows:

$$\dot{p}(t) = \dot{y}_{ij}(t)\mathrm{sgn}(y_{ij}(t)) = -\gamma\phi_1(y_{ij}(t))\mathrm{sgn}(y_{ij}(t)).$$

Since AF (15.5) is used, we have

$$\dot{p}(t) = -\gamma(a_1|y_{ij}(t)|^\eta + a_2|y_{ij}(t)|^w + a_3|y_{ij}(t)| + a_4)$$
$$\leqslant -\gamma(a_1|y_{ij}(t)|^\eta + a_2|y_{ij}(t)|^w)$$
$$= -\gamma(a_1p^\eta(t) + a_2p^w(t)).$$

By comparing it with the conclusion of Lemma 15.1, the predefined convergence time of NT-PTZNN1 model (15.7) is directly given by

$$t_f \leqslant \frac{1}{\gamma a_1(1-\eta)} + \frac{1}{\gamma a_2(w-1)}.$$

Since this convergence time t_f is independent of the initial states, NT-PTZNN1 model (15.7) outputs an accurate solution of time-variant Sylvester equation (15.1) in a predefined time. The proof is thus completed. ∎

Considering that various external disturbances exist during the model hardware implementation, we further investigate the following noise-perturbed NT-PTZNN1 model:

$$A(t)\dot{U}(t) - \dot{U}(t)B(t) = \dot{A}(t)U(t) + \dot{U}(t)B(t) - \gamma\Phi_1(A(t)U(t) \\ - U(t)B(t) + C(t)) - \dot{C}(t) + D(t), \tag{15.9}$$

where $D(t)$ denotes an additive noise. In the following, we mainly study two kinds of additive noises: one is the dynamic bounded vanishing noise, and the other is the dynamic bounded non-vanishing noise.

15.3.1.1 Case 1

When the additive noise $D(t)$ is a dynamic bounded vanishing noise, we have the following result for noise-perturbed NT-PTZNN1 model (15.9).

Theorem 15.3 *If $D(t)$ is a dynamic bounded vanishing noise with its ijth element satisfying $|d_{ij}(t)| \leqslant \delta|y_{ij}(t)|$ where $\delta \in (0, +\infty)$ and $|y_{ij}(t)|$ denotes the absolute value of the ijth element of error function $Y(t)$, beginning with a random initial matrix $U(0) \in \mathbb{R}^{n\times n}$, noise-perturbed NT-PTZNN1 model (15.9) outputs an accurate solution of time-variant Sylvester equation (15.1) in a predefined time t_f:*

$$t_f \leqslant \frac{1}{\gamma a_1(1-\eta)} + \frac{1}{\gamma a_2(w-1)},$$

as long as $\gamma a_3 \geqslant \delta$.

Proof: Similarly, noise-perturbed NT-PTZNN1 model (15.9) can be simplified as $\dot{Y}(t) = -\gamma\Phi_1(Y(t)) + D(t)$ with the ijth subsystem formed by

$$\dot{y}_{ij}(t) = -\gamma\phi_1(y_{ij}(t)) + d_{ij}(t), \tag{15.10}$$

where $d_{ij}(t)$ denotes the ijth element of matrix $D(t)$.

To prove the predefined-time stability of this noise-perturbed subsystem, the following Lyapunov function candidate is chosen:

$$p(t) = |y_{ij}(t)|^2.$$

Besides, $\dot{p}(t)$ is computed as follows:

$$\dot{p}(t) = 2y_{ij}(t)\dot{y}_{ij}(t) = 2y_{ij}(t)(-\gamma\phi_1(y_{ij}(t)) + d_{ij}(t)).$$

Since AF (15.5) is used and $\gamma a_3 \geqslant \delta$, we have

$$\begin{aligned}
\dot{p}(t) &= -2\gamma(a_1|y_{ij}(t)|^{\eta+1} + a_2|y_{ij}(t)|^{w+1}) - 2\gamma a_4|y_{ij}(t)| \\
&\quad + 2(y_{ij}(t)d_{ij}(t) - \gamma a_3|y_{ij}(t)|^2) \\
&\leqslant -2\gamma(a_1|y_{ij}(t)|^{\eta+1} + a_2|y_{ij}(t)|^{w+1}) \\
&\quad + 2(\delta|y_{ij}(t)|^2 - \gamma a_3|y_{ij}(t)|^2) \\
&\leqslant -2\gamma(a_1|y_{ij}(t)|^{\eta+1} + a_2|y_{ij}(t)|^{w+1}) \\
&= -2\gamma(a_1 p(t)^{\frac{\eta+1}{2}} + a_2 p(t)^{\frac{w+1}{2}}).
\end{aligned}$$

According to Lemma 15.1, the predefined time of the noise-perturbed NT-PTZNN1 model (15.9) is calculated as

$$t_f \leqslant \frac{1}{\gamma a_1(1-\eta)} + \frac{1}{\gamma a_2(w-1)}.$$

That is to say, if $\gamma a_3 \geqslant \delta$, noise-perturbed NT-PTZNN1 model (15.9) outputs an accurate solution of time-variant Sylvester equation (15.1) in a predefined time under a dynamic bounded vanishing noise. ∎

15.3.1.2 Case 2

When the additive noise $D(t)$ is a dynamic bounded non-vanishing noise, we have the following result for noise-perturbed NT-PTZNN1 model (15.9).

Theorem 15.4 *If $D(t)$ is a dynamic bounded non-vanishing noise with its ijth element satisfying $|d_{ij}(t)| \leqslant \delta$ where $\delta \in (0, +\infty)$, beginning with a random initial matrix $U(0) \in \mathbb{R}^{n\times n}$, noise-perturbed NT-PTZNN1 model (15.9) outputs an accurate solution of time-variant Sylvester equation (15.1) in a predefined time t_f:*

$$t_f \leqslant \frac{1}{\gamma a_1(1-\eta)} + \frac{1}{\gamma a_2(w-1)},$$

as long as $\gamma a_4 \geqslant \delta$.

Proof: Compared with Theorem 15.3, only the additive noise $D(t)$ is different. As a result, according to the subsystem (15.10), the following Lyapunov function candidate is constructed as

$$p(t) = |y_{ij}(t)|^2.$$

Similarly, $\dot{p}(t)$ is computed as follows:

$$\dot{p}(t) = 2y_{ij}(t)\dot{y}_{ij}(t) = 2y_{ij}(t)(-\gamma\phi_1(y_{ij}(t)) + d_{ij}(t)).$$

Since AF (15.5) is used and $\gamma a_4 \geqslant \delta$, we have

$$\begin{aligned}
\dot{p}(t) &= -2\gamma(a_1|y_{ij}(t)|^{\eta+1} + a_2|y_{ij}(t)|^{w+1}) - 2\gamma a_3|y_{ij}(t)|^2 \\
&\quad + 2(y_{ij}(t)d_{ij}(t) - \gamma a_4|y_{ij}(t)|) \\
&\leqslant -2\gamma(a_1|y_{ij}(t)|^{\eta+1} + a_2|y_{ij}(t)|^{w+1}) \\
&\quad + 2(\delta|y_{ij}(t)|^2 - \gamma a_4|y_{ij}(t)|) \\
&\leqslant -2\gamma(a_1|y_{ij}(t)|^{\eta+1} + a_2|y_{ij}(t)|^{w+1}) \\
&= -2\gamma(a_1 p(t)^{\frac{\eta+1}{2}} + a_2 p(t)^{\frac{w+1}{2}}).
\end{aligned}$$

According to Lemma 15.1, the predefined time of noise-perturbed NT-PTZNN1 model (15.9) in this case is calculated as

$$t_f \leqslant \frac{1}{\gamma a_1(1-\eta)} + \frac{1}{\gamma a_2(w-1)}.$$

That is to say, if $\gamma a_4 \geqslant \delta$, the noise-perturbed NT-PTZNN1 model (15.9) outputs an accurate solution of time-variant Sylvester equation (15.1) in a predefined time under a dynamic bounded non-vanishing noise. ∎

15.3.2 NT-PTZNN2 Model

In this part, AF (15.6) is explored to activate ZNN model (15.4). For obtaining the new neural model, AF (15.6) has to be extended to matrix-valued one. Similar with AF (15.5), we use $\Phi_2(x) \in \mathbb{R}^{n \times n}$ to denote the corresponding AF matrix array of $\phi_2(x)$. So, for emphasizing the importance of this AF, the following NT-PTZNN2 model is presented as follows:

$$\begin{aligned}
A(t)\dot{U}(t) - \dot{U}(t)B(t) &= \dot{A}(t)U(t) + \dot{U}(t)B(t) - \gamma\Phi_2(A(t)U(t) \\
&\quad - U(t)B(t) + C(t)) - \dot{C}(t).
\end{aligned} \tag{15.11}$$

For easy presentation, the previous new neural model is termed the NT-PTZNN2 model. Furthermore, we can obtain the following theoretical result about the predefined-time convergence of NT-PTZNN2 model (15.11).

Theorem 15.5 *Beginning with a random initial matrix $U(0) \in \mathbb{R}^{n \times n}$, NT-PTZNN2 model (15.11) outputs an accurate solution of time-variant Sylvester equation (15.1) in a predefined time t_f:*

$$t_f \leqslant \frac{1}{\gamma b_1},$$

where design parameters γ and b_1 are defined as before.

Proof: Similarly, we can also conclude that NT-PTZNN2 model (15.11) is equivalent to $\dot{Y}(t) = -\gamma\Phi_2(Y(t))$, of which the ijth subsystem is written as

$$\dot{y}_{ij}(t) = -\gamma\phi_2(y_{ij}(t)) \text{ with } i,j \in \{1, 2, \ldots, n\}. \tag{15.12}$$

According to the Lyapunov theory, for proving the stability of the ijth subsystem (15.12), the following Lyapunov function candidate is chosen:

$$p(t) = |y_{ij}(t)|.$$

In addition, $\dot{p}(t)$ is calculated as follows:

$$\dot{p}(t) = \dot{y}_{ij}(t)\text{sgn}(y_{ij}(t)) = -\gamma\phi_2(y_{ij}(t))\text{sgn}(y_{ij}(t)).$$

Since AF (15.6) is used, we have

$$\dot{p}(t) = -\gamma(b_1 \exp(|y_{ij}(t)|^\alpha)|y_{ij}(t)|^{1-\alpha}/\alpha + b_2|y_{ij}(t)| + b_3)$$
$$\leqslant -\gamma b_1 \exp(|y_{ij}(t)|^\alpha)|y_{ij}(t)|^{1-\alpha}/\alpha$$
$$= -\gamma b_1 \exp(p^\alpha(t))p^{1-\alpha}(t)/\alpha.$$

For obtaining the predefined convergence time, calculate $\dot{p}(t) \leqslant -\gamma b_1 \exp(p^\alpha(t))\frac{p^{1-\alpha}(t)}{\alpha}$. Therefore, for the ijth subsystem (15.12), we have

$$t_{ij} \leqslant \frac{1 - \exp(-p^\alpha(0))}{\gamma b_1}.$$

Because $\exp(-p^\alpha(0)) = \exp(-|y_{ij}(0)|^\alpha) \in (0, 1]$, for NT-PTZNN2 model (15.11), we finally obtain:

$$t_f = \max(t_{ij}) \leqslant \frac{1}{\gamma b_1}.$$

That is to say, the upper bound of the convergence time for NT-PTZNN2 model (15.11) is a constant and independent of the initial states, so NT-PTZNN2 model (15.11) outputs an accurate solution of time-variant Sylvester equation (15.1) in a predefined time. The proof is thus completed. ∎

Considering that various external disturbances exist during the model hardware implementation, we further investigate the following noise-perturbed NT-PTZNN2 model:

$$A(t)\dot{U}(t) - \dot{U}(t)B(t) = \dot{A}(t)U(t) + \dot{U}(t)B(t) - \gamma\Phi_2(A(t)U(t)$$
$$- U(t)B(t) + C(t)) - \dot{C}(t) + D(t), \tag{15.13}$$

where $D(t)$ denotes an additive noise. In the following, we also mainly study two kinds of additive noises: one is the dynamic bounded vanishing noise, and the other is the dynamic bounded non-vanishing noise.

15.3.2.1 Case 1

When the additive noise $D(t)$ is a dynamic bounded vanishing noise, we have the following result for noise-perturbed NT-PTZNN2 model (15.13).

Theorem 15.6 *If $D(t)$ is a dynamic bounded vanishing noise with its ijth element satisfying $|d_{ij}(t)| \leqslant \delta|y_{ij}(t)|$ where $\delta \in (0, +\infty)$ and $|y_{ij}(t)|$ denotes the absolute value of the ijth element of error function $Y(t)$, beginning with a random initial matrix $U(0) \in \mathbb{R}^{n \times n}$, noise-perturbed NT-PTZNN2 model (15.13) outputs an accurate solution of time-variant Sylvester equation (15.1) in a predefined time t_f:*

$$t_f \leqslant \frac{1}{\gamma b_1},$$

as long as $\gamma b_2 \geqslant \delta$.

Proof: First, NT-PTZNN2 model (15.13) is also equivalent to $\dot{Y}(t) = -\gamma \Phi_2(Y(t)) + D(t)$, and its ijth subsystem is the same as

$$\dot{y}_{ij}(t) = -\gamma \phi_2(y_{ij}(t)) + d_{ij}(t).$$

To prove the predefined-time stability of this subsystem, the following Lyapunov function candidate is selected:

$$p(t) = |y_{ij}(t)|^2.$$

Besides, $\dot{p}(t)$ is calculated as follows:

$$\dot{p}(t) = 2y_{ij}(t)\dot{y}_{ij}(t) = 2y_{ij}(t)(-\gamma \phi_2(y_{ij}(t)) + d_{ij}(t)).$$

Because AF (15.6) is used and $\gamma b_2 \geqslant \delta$, one further can obtain:

$$\begin{aligned}
\dot{p}(t) &= -2\gamma b_1 \exp(|y_{ij}(t)|^\alpha)|y_{ij}(t)|^{2-\alpha}/\alpha - 2\gamma b_3 |y_{ij}(t)| \\
&\quad + 2(y_{ij}(t)d_{ij}(t) - \gamma b_2 |y_{ij}(t)|^2) \\
&\leqslant -2\gamma b_1 \exp(|y_{ij}(t)|^\alpha)|y_{ij}(t)|^{2-\alpha}/\alpha + 2(\delta|y_{ij}(t)|^2 - \gamma b_2 |y_{ij}(t)|^2) \\
&\leqslant -\gamma b_1 \exp(p^{\frac{\alpha}{2}}(t))p^{\frac{2-\alpha}{2}}(t)/(\alpha/2).
\end{aligned}$$

In a same way, the predefined convergence time of NT-PTZNN2 model (15.13) can be computed by solving $\dot{p}(t) \leqslant -\gamma b_1 \exp(p^{\frac{\alpha}{2}}(t))p^{\frac{2-\alpha}{2}}(t)/(\alpha/2)$, and the result is

$$t_{ij} \leqslant \frac{1 - \exp(-p^{\frac{\alpha}{2}}(0))}{\gamma b_1}.$$

As $\exp(-p^{\frac{\alpha}{2}}(0)) = \exp(-|y_{ij}(0)|^{\frac{\alpha}{2}}) \in (0, 1]$, it can also be concluded that:

$$t_{ij} \leqslant \frac{1 - \exp(-p^{\frac{\alpha}{2}}(0))}{\gamma b_1} \leqslant \frac{1}{\gamma b_1},$$

which suggests that the upper bound of the convergence time for the ijth subsystem is a constant and independent of initial states when $\gamma b_2 \geqslant \delta$. Therefore, if $\gamma b_2 \geqslant \delta$, noise-perturbed NT-PTZNN2 model (15.13) outputs an accurate solution of time-variant Sylvester equation (15.1) in a predefined time under a dynamic bounded vanishing noise. In addition, the predefined convergence time of NT-PTZNN2 model (15.13) is

$$t_f = \max(t_{ij}) \leqslant 1/\gamma b_1.$$

The proof is thus completed. ∎

15.3.2.2 Case 2
When the additive noise $D(t)$ is a dynamic bounded vanishing noise, we have the following result for noise-perturbed NT-PTZNN2 model (15.13).

Theorem 15.7 *If $D(t)$ is a dynamic bounded non-vanishing noise with its ijth element satisfying $|d_{ij}(t)| \leqslant \delta$ where $\delta \in (0, +\infty)$, beginning with a random initial matrix $U(0) \in \mathbb{R}^{n \times n}$, noise-perturbed NT-PTZNN2 model (15.13) outputs an accurate solution of time-variant Sylvester equation (15.1) in a predefined time t_f:*

$$t_f \leqslant 1/\gamma b_1,$$

as long as $\gamma b_3 \geqslant \delta$.

Proof: Similar to Theorem 15.6, the Lyapunov function candidate $p(t) = |y_{ij}(t)|^2$ is first chosen for the ijth subsystem of NT-PTZNN2 model (15.13), and $\dot{p}(t)$ is computed as follows:

$$\dot{p}(t) = 2y_{ij}(t)\dot{y}_{ij}(t) = 2y_{ij}(t)(-\gamma \phi_2(y_{ij}(t)) + d_{ij}(t)).$$

Since AF (15.6) is used and $\gamma b_3 \geqslant \delta$, one can obtain:

$$
\begin{aligned}
\dot{p}(t) &= -2\gamma b_1 \exp(|y_{ij}(t)|^\alpha)|y_{ij}(t)|^{2-\alpha}/\alpha - 2\gamma b_2 |y_{ij}(t)|^2 \\
&\quad + 2(y_{ij}(t)d_{ij}(t) - \gamma b_3 |y_{ij}(t)|) \\
&\leqslant -2\gamma b_1 \exp(|y_{ij}(t)|^\alpha)|y_{ij}(t)|^{2-\alpha}/\alpha + 2(\delta|y_{ij}(t)|^2 - \gamma b_3 |y_{ij}(t)|^2) \\
&\leqslant -2\gamma b_1 \exp(|y_{ij}(t)|^\alpha)|y_{ij}(t)|^{2-\alpha}/\alpha \\
&= -\gamma b_1 \exp(p^{\frac{\alpha}{2}}(t))p^{\frac{2-\alpha}{2}}(t)/(\alpha/2).
\end{aligned}
$$

Similar to the proof process of Theorem 15.6, we can also conclude that the predefined convergence time for NT-PTZNN2 model (15.13) in this case is

$$t_f \leqslant 1/\gamma b_1.$$

Hence, if $\gamma b_3 \geqslant \delta$, the noise-perturbed NT-PTZNN2 model (15.13) outputs an accurate solution of time-variant Sylvester equation (15.1) in a predefined time under a dynamic bounded vanishing noise. The proof is thus completed. ∎

15.4 Illustrative Verification

In Section 15.3, two NT-PTZNN models and the corresponding noise-perturbed ones (i.e. NT-PTZNN1 model (15.9) and NT-PTZNN2 model (15.13)) are proposed for solving time-variant Sylvester equation (15.1). Different from the previous existing AFs, when AF (15.5) and AF (15.6) are used to activate ZNN, the predefined-time convergence can be achieved even if there are noise interruptions. In addition, the predefined-time convergence analyses are provided according to different kinds of noises. In this section, to verify the superior performance of the proposed neural models, three different time-variant Sylvester equation examples are used to test the efficiency.

15.4.1 Example 1

Without loss of generality, design parameters are set as $\gamma = a_1 = a_2 = a_3 = a_4 = b_1 = b_2 = b_3 = 1, \eta = p = 0.25, w = 4$ and the coefficient matrices of time-variant Sylvester equation (15.1) as follows:

$$A(t) = \begin{bmatrix} \sin(2t) & \cos(2t) \\ -\cos(2t) & \sin(2t) \end{bmatrix}, \quad B(t) = 0, \quad \text{and } C(t) = -I.$$

Obviously, the predefined time of NT-PTZNN1 model (15.9) for solving time-variant Sylvester equation (15.1) can be calculated as $t_c = 5/3 \approx 1.67$ seconds, and the one for NT-PTZNN2 model (15.13) can be calculated as $t_c = 1$ seconds. In addition, the theoretical solution $U^*(t)$ of the given example can be calculated as

$$U^*(t) = \begin{bmatrix} \sin(2t) & -\cos(2t) \\ \cos(2t) & \sin(2t) \end{bmatrix},$$

which can be used as a criterion for measuring the correctness of each model to solve the time-variant Sylvester equation (15.1). First, NT-PTZNN1 model (15.9) and NT-PTZNN2 model (15.13) are used to solve the time-variant Sylvester equation (15.1) problem without noises (i.e. $d_{ij}(t) = 0$), and the main simulation results are plotted in Figures 15.1–15.2. When AF (15.5) is activated, the state solution $U(t)$ of NT-PTZNN1 model (15.9) for time-variant Sylvester equation is plotted in Figure 15.1a. From it, we can see that the solid line coincides with the dotted line in a very short time, where the solid line represents each element of the state solution $U(t)$ from the starting point $U(0) \in [-3, 3]^{2 \times 2}$, while the dashed line represents each element of the theoretical solution $U(t)$. When AF (15.6) is activated, the state solution $U(t)$ of NT-PTZNN2 model (15.13) for time-variant Sylvester equation is plotted in Figure 15.1b, which also show that the convergence time required is also very short for coinciding between the solid line and the dotted line.

Figure 15.1 Transient behavior of state solutions $U(t)$ generated by NT-PTZNN1 model (15.9) and NT-PTZNN2 model (15.13) when solving time-variant Sylvester equation of Example 1 with noise $Y(t) = 0$. (a) By NT-PTZNN1 model (15.9). (b) By NT-PTZNN2 model (15.13).

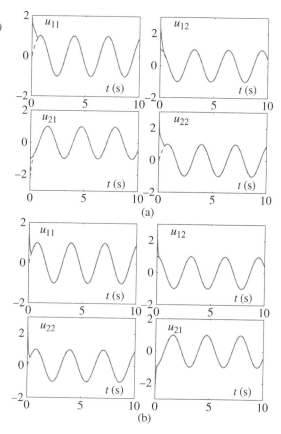

In addition, the residual errors $\|A(t)U(t) - U(t)B(t) + C(t)\|_F$ synthesized by NT-PTZNN1 model (15.9) and NT-PTZNN2 model (15.13) are plotted in Figure 15.2. As shown in Figure 15.2a, the residual error of NT-PTZNN1 model (15.9) converges to zero about 0.6 seconds. This means that NT-PTZNN1 model (15.9) only needs about 0.6 seconds to solve time-variant Sylvester equation of Example 1 accurately, and this convergence time satisfies the requirement of the predefined time $t_c \leq 1.67$ seconds. Besides, as shown in Figure 15.2b, the residual error of NT-PTZNN2 model (15.13) converges to zero in a shorter time (about 0.3 seconds), which also satisfies the requirement of the predefined time $t_{c+} \leq 1$ seconds.

For comparison purposes, ZNN model (15.4) activated by other AFs (such as LAF, PSAF, and SBPAF) are also used to solve time-variant Sylvester equation of Section 15.4.1 under different noises, and all comparison results are shown in Figure 15.3. If noise $d_{ij}(t) = 0$, all residual errors can converge to 0, but NT-PTZNN2 model (15.13) has the fastest convergence rate (approximately

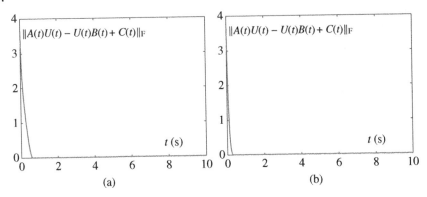

Figure 15.2 Transient behavior of residual errors $\|A(t)U(t) - U(t)B(t) + C(t)\|_F$ generated by NT-PTZNN1 model (15.9) and NT-PTZNN2 model (15.13) when solving time-variant Sylvester equation of Example 1 with noise $d_{ij}(t) = 0$. (a) By NT-PTZNN1 model (15.9). (b) By NT-PTZNN2 model (15.13).

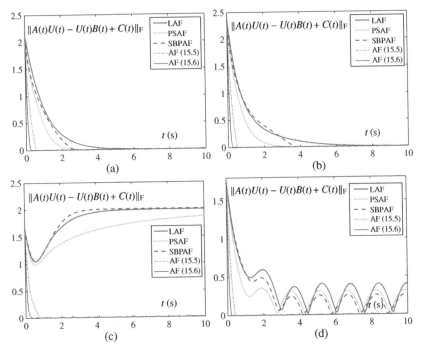

Figure 15.3 Transient behavior of residual errors $\|A(t)U(t) - U(t)B(t) + C(t)\|_F$ synthesized by NT-PTZNN1 model (15.9) activated by AF (15.5), NT-PTZNN2 model (15.13) activated by AF (15.6) and ZNN model (15.4) activated by LAF, PSAF, and SBPAF under different kinds of noises $D(t)$. (a) With noise $d_{ij} = 0$. (b) With noise $d_{ij} = 0.45|y_{ij}(t)|$. (c) With noise $d_{ij} = 1$. (d) With noise $d_{ij} = 0.45\cos(2t)$.

0.3 seconds). Followed by NT-PTZNN1 model (15.9), the time required for the residual error converging to zero is about 0.6 seconds), while ZNN model (15.4) activated by LAF, PSAF, and SBPAF takes longer time to converge to zero (i.e. using SBPAF takes about 2.8 seconds, using PSAF needs about three seconds, and using LAF takes about six seconds). The results verify the advantages of the proposed two neural models for time-variant Sylvester equation in the presence of no noise.

When the external disturbance is a dynamic bounded vanishing noise $d_{ij}(t) = 0.45|y_{ij}|$, comparison results about the residual errors are shown in Figure 15.3b. From it we can see that the convergence time for NT-PTZNN1 model (15.9) and NT-PTZNN2 model (15.13) seems to be unchanged, and the others are correspondingly slower, as compared with the results of Figure 15.3a. When the external disturbance is a constant noise $d_{ij}(t) = 1$, the corresponding residual errors are plotted in Figure 15.3c, which demonstrates residual errors of NT-PTZNN1 model (15.9) and NT-PTZNN2 model (15.13) can still converge to zero quickly, while the residual errors activated by LAF, PSAF, and SBPAF gradually tend to a stable non-zero value that is usually related with the external disturbance. This means that ZNN model (15.4) activated by LAF, PSAF, and SBPAF may be no longer effective in the presence of a constant noise, when applied to time-variant Sylvester equation solving. However, the proposed two NT-PTZNN models can still solve the time-varying Sylvester equation quickly and accurately. When the external disturbance is a dynamic bounded non-vanishing noise $d_{ij}(t) = 0.45\cos(2t)$, the corresponding residual error convergence is shown in Figure 15.3d. It can be seen from Figure 15.3d that the residual errors of NT-PTZNN1 model (15.9) and NT-PTZNN2 model (15.13) can still rapidly drop to zero in a short time, while the residual errors of ZNN model (15.4) activated by LAF, PSAF, SBPAF always fluctuate all the time. In a word, the superiority of NT-PTZNN1 model (15.9) and NT-PTZNN2 model (15.13) is firmly validated in the presence of various external noises.

15.4.2 Example 2

To further validate the superiority of the proposed two NT-PTZNN models, the time-variant Sylvester equation coming from [26] is considered, and its coefficients are described by

$$A(t) = \begin{bmatrix} \sin(4t) & \cos(4t) \\ -\cos(4t) & \sin(4t) \end{bmatrix}, \quad B(t) = \begin{bmatrix} 2 & 0 \\ 0 & 3 \end{bmatrix}, \quad \text{and } C(t) = \begin{bmatrix} \sin(t) & \cos(t) \\ -\cos(t) & \sin(t) \end{bmatrix}.$$

For consistency, in this example, design parameters of all ZNN models are the same with these of Section 15.4.1. According to the theoretical analysis, when NT-PTZNN1 model (15.9) is hired to solve the previous time-variant Sylvester equation, it will converge to the theoretical solution within the predefined time

$t_c = 1.67$ seconds, and when NT-PTZNN2 model (15.13) is hired, the corresponding predefined time t_c equals to one second.

First, NT-PTZNN1 model (15.9) and NT-PTZNN2 model (15.13) are employed to solve the aforementioned time-variant Sylvester equation in the presence of constant noise $d_{ij}(t) = 1$, and the corresponding transient behavior of state solutions is plotted in Figure 15.4. From Figure 15.4a, it can be observed that each element of state solution $U(t)$ for NT-PTZNN1 model (15.9) from a randomly starting point $U(0)$ coincides with the one of the theoretical solution quickly in predefined time one second. In addition, from Figure 15.4b, it follows that the state solution $U(t)$ of NT-PTZNN2 model (15.13) can converge to the theoretical solution $U^*(t)$ under the same conditions in a shorter predefined time (about 0.3 seconds). Note that, in this situation, the convergence time of NT-PTZNN1 model (15.9)

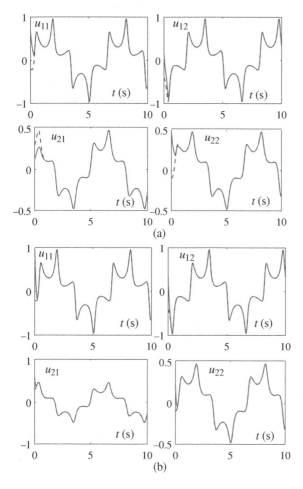

Figure 15.4 Transient behavior of state solution $U(t)$ generated by NT-PTZNN1 model (15.9) and NT-PTZNN2 model (15.13) when solving time-variant Sylvester equation of Example 2 with noise $D(t) = 1$. (a) By NT-PTZNN1 model (15.9). (b) By NT-PTZNN2 model (15.13).

and NT-PTZNN2 model (15.13) can satisfy the requirement of the theoretically computed predefined time.

Figure 15.5 shows some comparison results of the residual errors solved by the proposed two NT-PTZNN models and ZNN model (15.4) activated by existing AFs under different external noise disturbance (including the situation of constant noise $d_{ij}(t) = 1$). First, Figure 15.5a shows the results in the presence of constant noise $d_{ij}(t) = 1$, from which, the residual errors generated by NT-PTZNN1 model (15.9) and NT-PTZNN2 model (15.13) can converge to 0 with the predefined time, while generated by ZNN model (15.4) activated by existing AFs cannot converge to zero over time. Figure 15.5b shows that when a fading noise is added, there is a delay for ZNN model (15.4) activated by existing AFs, as compared with the results of Figure 15.3a, while there is no delay in NT-PTZNN1 model (15.9) and NT-PTZNN2 model (15.13). Besides, time-variant bounded noise $d_{ij}(t) = 0.6\cos(2.5t)$ and time-variant unbounded

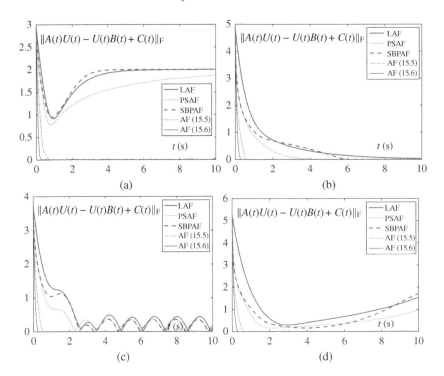

Figure 15.5 Transient behavior of residual errors $\|A(t)U(t) - U(t)B(t) + C(t)\|_F$ synthesized by NT-PTZNN1 model (15.9), NT-PTZNN2 model (15.13), and ZNN model (15.4) activated by LAF, PSAF, and SBPAF under different kinds of noises $D(t)$ with $\gamma = 1$. (a) With noise $d_{ij}(t) = 1$. (b) With noise $d_{ij}(t) = 0.6|y_{ij}(t)|$. (c) With noise $d_{ij}(t) = 0.6\cos(2.5t)$. (d) With noise $d_{ij}(t) = 0.125\exp(0.2t)$.

noise $d_{ij}(t) = 0.125\exp(0.2t)$ are considered, and the corresponding comparison results are plotted in Figure 15.5c,d, respectively. As seen from such two subfigures, the residual errors of NT-PTZNN1 model (15.9) and NT-PTZNN2 model (15.13) can converge to zero in a predefined time, while ZNN model (15.4) activated by existing AFs cannot converge to zero all the time, which means that using existing AFs (such as LAF, PSAF, and SBPAF) may no longer be suitable for solving time-variant Sylvester equation (15.1) when the time-variant noise is injected. In contrast, NT-PTZNN1 model (15.9) and NT-PTZNN2 model (15.13) can still solve the time-variant Sylvester equation accurately within a predefined time.

It is worth noting that the design parameter γ has an important impact on the solution process of the ZNN models. A time-variant non-vanishing noise $d_{ij}(t) = 2.1t$ and a large constant noise $d_{ij}(t) = 18.5$ are both considered when the values of the design parameter γ are adjusted to 10 and 20, respectively. The corresponding comparison results are described in Figure 15.6a,b, respectively. Figure 15.6a demonstrates that the residual errors of NT-PTZNN1 model (15.9) and NT-PTZNN2 model (15.13) can converge to zero. The convergence time for NT-PTZNN1 model (15.9) is reduced to about 0.06 seconds, and for NT-PTZNN2 model (15.13) is reduced to about 0.05 seconds. Considering $\gamma = 10$, the predefined convergence time for NT-PTZNN1 model (15.9) and NT-PTZNN2 model (15.13) is computed as 0.16 and 0.1, respectively. Obviously, both NT-PTZNN1 model (15.9) and NT-PTZNN2 model (15.13) satisfy the predefined time convergence in the presence of $d_{ij}(t) = 2.1t$ when $\gamma = 10$. However, the residual errors of ZNN model (15.4) activated by existing AFs shown in Figure 15.6a have a certain error and cannot converge to zero. This conclusion is also demonstrated by Figure 15.6b conducted in the presence of a large constant noise $d_{ij}(t) = 18.5$ and $\gamma = 20$.

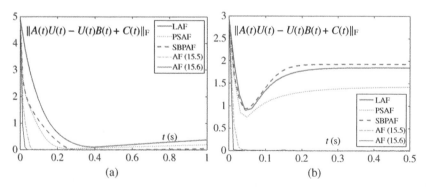

Figure 15.6 Transient behavior of residual errors $\|A(t)U(t) - U(t)B(t) + C(t)\|_F$ synthesized by NT-PTZNN1 model (15.9), NT-PTZNN2 model (15.13), and ZNN model (15.4) activated by LAF, PSAF, and SBPAF under different kinds of noises $D(t)$ with $\gamma = 10$ and $\gamma = 20$. (a) With noise $d_{ij}(t) = 2.1t$ and $\gamma = 10$. (b) With noise $d_{ij}(t) = 18.5$ and $\gamma = 20$.

15.4.3 Example 3

In this example, a three-dimensional time-variant Sylvester equation is considered with coefficients being

$$A(t) = \begin{bmatrix} 2 + \sin(2t) & \cos(2t) & \cos(2t)/2 \\ \cos(2t) & 2 + \sin(2t) & \cos(2t) \\ \cos(2t)/2 & \cos(2t) & 2 + \sin(2t) \end{bmatrix},$$

$B(t) = 0 \in \mathbb{R}^{3\times3}$, and $C(t) = -I \in \mathbb{R}^{3\times3}$.

The value of the design parameters is consistent with the previous two examples. NT-PTZNN1 model (15.9) and NT-PTZNN2 model (15.13) are hired to solve the aforementioned time-variant Sylvester equation in the presence of four different kinds of noise with $\gamma = 1$, and the corresponding transient behavior of residual errors are plotted in Figure 15.7. As seen from Figure 15.7, one can found that all residual errors of NT-PTZNN1 model (15.9) and NT-PTZNN2 model (15.13) can

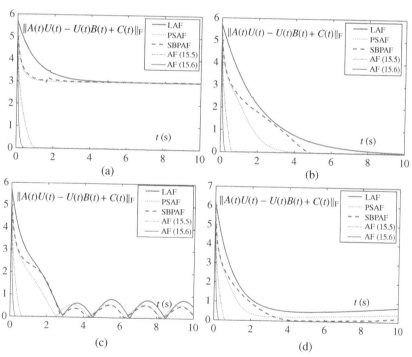

Figure 15.7 Transient behavior of residual errors $\|A(t)U(t) - U(t)B(t) + C(t)\|_F$ synthesized by NT-PTZNN1 model (15.9), NT-PTZNN2 model (15.13), and ZNN model (15.4) activated by LAF, PSAF, and SBPAF under different kinds of noises $D(t)$ with $\gamma = 1$. (a) With noise $d_{ij}(t) = 1$. (b) With noise $d_{ij}(t) = 0.5|y_{ij}(t)|$. (c) With noise $d_{ij}(t) = 0.5 \sin(1.6t)$. (d) With noise $d_{ij}(t) = 0.1 \exp(0.1t)$.

converge to 0 within one second, which satisfying the predefined-time requirement (i.e. $t_c = 1.67$ seconds for NT-PTZNN1 model (15.9) and $t_c = 1$ seconds for NT-PTZNN2 model (15.13)). In contrast, when external noise $d_{ij}(t) = 1$, $d_{ij}(t) = 0.5\sin(1.6t)$ or $d_{ij}(t) = 0.1\exp(0.1t)$ is present, the residual errors of ZNN model (15.4) activated by LAF, PSAF, and SBPAF cannot converge to 0. When a fading noise $d_{ij}(t) = 0.5|y_{ij}|$ is present, all residual errors can converge to 0, but the convergence time of two NT-PTZNN models' residual errors is much shorter, as compared with ZNN model (15.4) activated by LAF, PSAF, and SBPAF.

In summary, according to the aforementioned comparison results, it follows that, as compared with ZNN model (15.4) activated by LAF, PSAF, and SBPAF, NT-PTZNN1 model (15.9) and NT-PTZNN2 model (15.13) have superior predefined-time convergence and noise-tolerant performance when applied to time-variant Sylvester equation (15.1) solving in the presence of various kinds of external disturbances.

15.5 Chapter Summary

By adopting two nonlinear AFs, two NT-PTZNN models are established to solve time-variant Sylvester equation under various external disturbances. Compared with the ZNN model activated by existing AFs for time-variant Sylvester equation, such two NT-PTZNN models have superior the predefined-time convergence and noise-tolerant performance. In addition, the related theorems are rigorously analyzed under no noise, dynamic bounded vanishing noise and dynamic bounded non-vanishing noise. Comparison results further show that the proposed two NT-PTZNN models converge to the accurate solution of the time-variant Sylvester equation in regardless of whether there exist external noises, while the ZNN model activated by LAF, PSAF, and SBPAF cannot converge to the accurate solution under the same conditions.

References

1 S. Brahma and B. Datta, An optimization approach for minimum norm and robust partial quadratic eigenvalue assignment problems for vibrating structures, *J. Sound Vib.*, 324(3–5) (2009) 471–489.

2 D. Calvetti and L. Reichel, Application of ADI iterative methods to the restoration of noisy images, *SIAM J. Matrix Anal. Appl.*, 17(1) (1996) 165–186.

3 L. Bao, Y. Lin, and Y. Wei, A new projection method for solving large Sylvester equations, *Appl. Numer. Math.*, 57(5–7) (2007) 521–532.

4 H. Diao, H. Xian, and Y. Wei, Mixed, componentwise condition numbers and small sample statistical condition estimation of Sylvester equations, *Numer. Linear Algebra Appl.*, 19(4) (2012) 639–654.

5 L. Xiao and B. Liao, A convergence-accelerated Zhang neural network and its solution application to Lyapunov equation, *Neurocomputing*, 193 (2016) 213–218.

6 Y. Lin and Y. Wei, Condition numbers of the generalized Sylvester equation, *IEEE Trans. Autom. Control*, 52(12) (2007) 2380–2385.

7 Y. Lin, L. Bao, and Y. Wei, Matrix sign function methods for solving projected generalized continuous-time Sylvester equations, *IEEE Trans. Autom. Control*, 55(11) (2010) 2629–2634.

8 R. H. Bartels and G. W. Stewart, Solution of the matrix equation $AX + XB = C[F4]$, *Commun. ACM*, 15(9) (1972) 820–826.

9 G. Golub, S. Nash, and C. Van Loan, A Hessenberg-Schur method for the problem $AX + XB = C$, *IEEE Trans. Autom. Control*, 24(6) (1979) 909–913.

10 B. Zhou, G. Duan, and Z. Li, Gradient based iterative algorithm for solving coupled matrix equations, *Syst. Control Lett.*, 58(5) (2009) 327–333.

11 L. Xie, Y. Liu, and H. Yang, Gradient based and least squares based iterative algorithms for matrix equations $AXB + CX^TD = F$, *Appl. Math. Comput.*, 217(5) (2010) 2191–2199.

12 F. Ding and T. Chen, Gradient based iterative algorithms for solving a class of matrix equations, *IEEE Trans. Autom. Control*, 50(8) (2005) 1216–1221.

13 F. Ding and H. Zhang, Gradient-based iterative algorithm for a class of the coupled matrix equations related to control systems, *IET Control Theory Appl.*, 8(15) (2014) 1588–1595.

14 C. Song, and J. Feng *et al.*, Finite iterative method for solving coupled Sylvester-transpose matrix equations, *J. Appl. Math. Comput.*, 46(1) (2014) 351–372.

15 L. Xiao and Y. Zhang *et al.*, A new noise-tolerant and predefined-time ZNN model for time-dependent matrix inversion, *Neural Netw.*, 117 (2019) 124–134.

16 A. Polyakov, D. Efimov, and W. Perruquetti, Finite-time and fixed-time stabilization: Implicit Lyapunov function approach, *Automatica*, 51 (2015) 332–340.

17 W. Li and B. Liao *et al.*, A recurrent neural network with predefined-time convergence and improved noise tolerance for dynamic matrix square root finding, *Neurocomputing*, 337 (2019) 262–273.

18 H. Lu and L. Jin *et al.*, RNN for solving perturbed time-varying underdetermined linear system with double bound limits on residual errors and state variables, *IEEE Trans. Ind. Inform.*, 15(11) (2019) 5931–5942.

19 S. Li, S. Chen, and B. Liu, Accelerating a recurrent neural network to finite-time convergence for solving time-varying Sylvester equation by using a sign-bi-power activation function, *Neural Process. Lett.*, 37(2) (2013) 189–205.

20 Y. Shen and P. Miao, Finite-time stability and its application for solving time-varying Sylvester equation by recurrent neural network, *Neural Process. Lett.*, 42(3) (2015) 763–784.

21 Y. Zhang and S. S. Ge, Design and analysis of a general recurrent neural network model for time-varying matrix inversion, *IEEE Trans. Neural Netw.*, 16(6) (2005) 1477–1490.

22 L. Xiao and Y. Zhang *et al.*, Performance benefits of robust nonlinear zeroing neural network for finding accurate solution of Lyapunov equation in presence of various noises, *IEEE Trans. Ind. Inform.*, 15(9) (2019) 5161–5171.

23 L. Xiao, Design and analysis of robust nonlinear neural dynamics for solving dynamic nonlinear equation within finite time, *Nonlinear Dyn.*, 96(4) (2019) 2437–2447.

24 B. Qiu, Y. Zhang, and Z. Yang, New discrete-time ZNN models for least-squares solution of dynamic linear equation system with time-varying rank-deficient coefficient, *IEEE Trans. Neural Netw. Learn. Syst.*, 29(11) (2018) 5767–5776.

25 W. Li and L. Xiao, A finite-time convergent and noise-rejection recurrent neural network and its discretization for dynamic nonlinear equations solving, *IEEE Trans. Cybern.*, 50(7) (2020) 3195–3207.

26 L. Xiao, A finite-time recurrent neural network for solving online time-varying Sylvester matrix equation based on a new evolution formula, *Nonlinear Dyn.*, 90(3) (2017) 1581–1591.

16

Design Scheme III of FTZNN

16.1 Introduction

The Sylvester equation is a complicated computational problem often encountered in scientific research and engineering applications [1–7]. Especially in the field of control theory, the Sylvester equation is often used to analyze the stability of the dynamics system, such as in robotic application [5, 8] and robot manipulator control [6, 9].

The motivation of this chapter is to improve the convergence performance of zeroing neural network (ZNN) by adding adaptive coefficients during the design process of the model. After analyzing the sign-bi-power function, we discover that the sign-bi-power function can be regarded as a combination of two specially constructed parts that act differently but have the same coefficient as 1/2. For this reason, the ratio of two parts that are activated by these two functions respectively is fixed from beginning to end, despite the constantly changing over time of the error of neuron in ZNN. However, the role of each part played in the sign-bi-power function greatly depends on the computational error of ZNN. In light of this deficiency of the sign-bi-power function, we believe that designing a proper adaptive coefficient correspondingly with the variation of the computational error can accelerate the convergence speed of ZNN. Thereout, three different types of adaptive design coefficients for the sign-bi-power nonlinear activation function are developed and investigated in this chapter for solving the time-varying Sylvester equation. Based on these adaptive coefficients, three new finite-time zeroing neural network (FTZNN) models are proposed to improve the convergence performance of the standard ZNN model. Then the improved finite-time convergence is investigated by analytical theorems and demonstrated by illustrative experiments. Therefore, the validity of the newly proposed models is completely verified.

Zeroing Neural Networks: Finite-time Convergence Design, Analysis and Applications,
First Edition. Lin Xiao and Lei Jia.
© 2023 The Institute of Electrical and Electronics Engineers, Inc. Published 2023 by John Wiley & Sons, Inc.

16.2 ZNN Model and Activation Function

This work concentrates on calculating the following time-varying Sylvester equation of the form [5, 6]:

$$A(t)U(t) - U(t)B(t) = -C(t), \tag{16.1}$$

where $t \in [0, +\infty)$ denotes time, $A(t) \in \mathbb{R}^{n \times n}$, $B(t) \in \mathbb{R}^{n \times n}$, and $C(t) \in \mathbb{R}^{n \times n}$ are given coefficient matrices, and $U(t)$ represents an unknown matrix to be found to obey Eq. (16.1). For the discussion to make sense, we assume there are no common eigenvalues between $A(t)$ and $B(t)$ at any time t. Therefore the Sylvester equation (16.1) has a unique solution for $U(t)$ exactly.

16.2.1 ZNN Model

Aiming to solve the Sylvester equation in real time, this chapter employs the ZNN which has proven to be a competitive approach for handling complex computation. Without loss of generality, the design process of ZNN for calculating the time-varying Sylvester equation is divided into the following three steps.

Step 1: Define an error function in matrix form, and feed its value back to the neuron in each step of calculation:

$$Y(t) = A(t)U(t) - U(t)B(t) + C(t). \tag{16.2}$$

Step 2: In order to make the state of neurons approximate analytic solution quickly, the evolution formula for $Y(t)$ is designed as

$$\frac{dY(t)}{dt} = -\gamma \Phi(Y(t)), \tag{16.3}$$

where $\gamma > 0$ is a scaling design coefficient to adjust the convergence rate of ZNN, and $\Phi(\cdot)$ is the nonlinear activation function array.

Step 3: Based on the two steps earlier, the following implicit dynamic differential equation of ZNN can be obtained:

$$A(t)\dot{U}(t) - \dot{U}(t)B(t) = \dot{A}(t)U(t) + \dot{U}(t)B(t) - \dot{C}(t)$$
$$- \gamma \Phi(A(t)U(t) - U(t)B(t) + C(t)). \tag{16.4}$$

From the aforementioned design steps, it can be seen that the ZNN is a typical recurrent neural network. All connections in the ZNN are symmetric and form a dynamical system with real-time feedback. The evolution formula (16.3) implies that the estimated error is fed back to neurons to enforce the error function (16.2) converge to zero. This allows it to exhibit temporal dynamic behavior that can handle real-time computational problems.

16.2.2 Sign-bi-power Activation Function

From the aforementioned design procedures of ZNN, we can prove that ZNN converges to zero at exponential speed even activated by simple linear function. To further speed up the convergence rate of ZNN, many special constructed nonlinear activation functions were designed. Among these functions, the sign-bi-power function was first proposed by Li *et al.* in [10] to realize the finite-time convergence of ZNN. As reported in Ref. [10], finite-time convergence is that the upper bound of the convergence time can be accurately calculated. Specifically, the upper bound is obtained through theoretical derivation according to the network design parameter γ, the largest initial error $y^+(0)$ and the activation function parameter l. This means that the convergence time has been accelerated from infinite (exponential convergence in standard ZNN) to finite. In the design process of the finite-time convergent ZNN model, using the sign-bi-power function to activate the model is the most critical step. The expression of this specially constructed function is given as

$$\phi_{\text{SBP}}(x) = \frac{1}{2}|x|^{\alpha}\text{sign}(x) + \frac{1}{2}|x|^{\frac{1}{\alpha}}\text{sign}(x), \tag{16.5}$$

with $\alpha > 1$ and sign(x) defined as

$$\text{sign}(x) = \begin{cases} 1, & x > 0; \\ 0, & x = 0; \\ -1, & x < 0. \end{cases}$$

While the sign-bi-power function (16.5) is used in evolution formula (16.3), the following dynamic subsystem for $y(t)$ at element wisely is obtained:

$$\frac{dy(t)}{dt} = -\gamma\left(\frac{1}{2}|y(t)|^{\alpha}\text{sign}(y(t)) + \frac{1}{2}|y(t)|^{\frac{1}{\alpha}}\text{sign}(y(t))\right). \tag{16.6}$$

It can be seen from the previous equation that the item $|y(t)|^{\alpha}\text{sign}(y(t))$ plays a major role in subsystem (16.6) when $|y(t)| \geq 1$, which guarantees $|y(t)|$ decrease to 1 exponentially. Once $|y(t)|$ reaches 1, the term $|y(t)|^{\frac{1}{\alpha}}\text{sign}(y(t))$ plays a major role in subsystem (16.6) and make $|y(t)|$ decrease to 0 in finite time.

Based on the analysis earlier, we further study the convergence performance of ZNN activated by the separate component item of the sign-bi-power function (16.5) mentioned in the previous text. In the rest of this chapter, these two functions are defined as follows:

$$\phi_{\text{SP-1}}(x) = |x|^{\alpha}\text{sign}(x), \text{ with } \alpha > 1, \tag{16.7}$$

$$\phi_{\text{SP-2}}(x) = |x|^{\frac{1}{\alpha}}\text{sign}(x), \text{ with } \alpha > 1. \tag{16.8}$$

For presentation convenience, function (16.7) is called SP-1, and function (16.8) is called SP-2. In addition, two theorems are given to analyze the roles of functions (16.7) and (16.8) played in evolution formula (16.3), which are significant to latter investigation.

Theorem 16.1 *Considering dynamic evolution equation (16.3), if SP-1 function (16.7) is used, then the absolute value $|y(t)|$ of the element with $|y(0)| \geq 1$ in error matrix (16.2) decreases to 1 in finite time:*

$$t_a = \frac{1 - |y(0)|^{1-\alpha}}{\gamma(\alpha - 1)}, \tag{16.9}$$

where $|y(0)| \geq 1$ denotes the initial value of $|y(t)|$ and γ is defined the same as in the evolution equation (16.3).

Proof: According to the previous design principle of the aforementioned ZNN model, each neuron in ZNN can be regarded as a self-autonomous and independent subsystem. Hence, the differential evolution of each neuron error becomes

$$\frac{dy(t)}{dt} = -\gamma |y(t)|^\alpha \text{sign}(y(t)). \tag{16.10}$$

Considering that the aforementioned dynamic equation contains a piecewise expression $\text{sign}(y(t))$, the proof is considered in two cases.

(1) Under the condition of $y(0) \geq 1$, equality (16.10) is rewritten as

$$\frac{dy(t)}{dt} = -\gamma(y(t))^\alpha \text{, with } \alpha > 1$$

which yields to the following equivalent form:

$$(y(t))^{-\alpha} dy(t) = -\gamma dt.$$

Supposing that there exists $t_a \geq 0$ such that $y(t_a) = 1$, let us integrate the previous equation from $t = 0$ to $t = t_a$:

$$\int_{y(0)}^{1} (y(t))^{-\alpha} dy(t) = -\gamma \int_{0}^{t_a} dt. \tag{16.11}$$

Solving (16.11), we compute the time of the error decreasing to 1 as

$$t_a = \frac{1 - (y(0))^{1-\alpha}}{\gamma(\alpha - 1)} = \frac{1 - |y(0)|^{1-\alpha}}{\gamma(\alpha - 1)}. \tag{16.12}$$

(2) Under the condition of $y(0) \leq -1$, the following result can be derived analogous to the proof steps earlier:

$$t_a = \frac{1 - (-y(0))^{1-\alpha}}{\gamma(\alpha - 1)} = \frac{1 - |y(0)|^{1-\alpha}}{\gamma(\alpha - 1)}. \tag{16.13}$$

In summary, the aforementioned discussion leads to the conclusion that, when $|y(t)|$ decreases to 1, the convergence time can be computed as

$$t_a = \frac{1 - |y(0)|^{1-\alpha}}{\gamma(\alpha - 1)}.$$

The proof is completed. ∎

Remark Theorem 16.1 and its proof process theoretically analyze the time required for the computational error of the neurons in the standard ZNN model activated by SP-1 function (16.7) to decrease from the initial value to 1. It paves the theoretical foundation for later introducing adaptive coefficients to improve convergence performance, and also provides a reference for calculating the upper bound of the evolution time when the computational error of the ZNN model is reduced to 1 during the proof of Theorems 16.2, 16.3, and 16.4. The convergence time obtained by solving dynamic differential system (16.10) is a functional value related to the design parameter γ, function parameter α, and initial error $y(0)$. It can be seen from the expression $t_a = (1 - |y(0)|^{1-\alpha})/\gamma(\alpha - 1)$ that when the initial error is constant, the larger the design parameter and function parameter, the shorter the time required for the computational error to decrease to 1.

Theorem 16.2 *Considering dynamic evolution equation (16.3), if SP-2 function (16.8) is used, then the absolute value $|y(t)|$ of the element with $|y(0)| \leq 1$ in the error matrix (16.2) decreases to 0 in finite time:*

$$t_b = \frac{\alpha \cdot |y(0)|^{\frac{\alpha-1}{\alpha}}}{\gamma(\alpha - 1)}, \tag{16.14}$$

where $|y(0)| \leq 1$ denotes the initial value of $|y(t)|$ and γ is defined as before.

Proof: By combining ZNN design formulation (16.3) and SP-2 function (16.8), the following dynamic system can be acquired to depict the evolution of the neuron error $y(t)$:

$$\frac{dy(t)}{dt} = -\gamma |y(t)|^{\frac{1}{\alpha}} \text{sign}(y(t)). \tag{16.15}$$

Considering the sign of $y(0)$, the situation for $y(t)$ is derived into the following three cases.

(1) When $0 < y(0) \leq 1$, equation (16.15) is equivalently expressed as

$$\frac{dy(t)}{dt} = -\gamma(y(t))^{\frac{1}{\alpha}}, \text{ with } \alpha > 1$$

which is equivalent to the following form:

$$(y(t))^{-\frac{1}{\alpha}} dy(t) = -\gamma dt.$$

Supposing that there exists $t_b \geq 0$ such that $y(t_b) = 0$, let us integrate the previous equation from $t = 0$ to $t = t_b$:

$$\int_{y(0)}^{0} (y(t))^{-\frac{1}{\alpha}} dy(t) = -\gamma \int_{0}^{t_b} dt. \tag{16.16}$$

As a result, t_b can be derived by solving equation (16.16):

$$t_b = \frac{\alpha(y(0))^{\frac{\alpha-1}{\alpha}}}{\gamma(\alpha - 1)} = \frac{\alpha|y(0)|^{\frac{\alpha-1}{\alpha}}}{\gamma(\alpha - 1)}. \tag{16.17}$$

(2) When $-1 \le y(0) < 0$, t_b can be obtained in the same way:

$$t_b = \frac{\alpha(-y(0))^{\frac{\alpha-1}{\alpha}}}{\gamma(\alpha-1)} = \frac{\alpha|y(0)|^{\frac{\alpha-1}{\alpha}}}{\gamma(\alpha-1)}. \tag{16.18}$$

(3) When $y(0) = 0$, it is obvious that the following equality holds

$$t_b = 0 = \frac{\alpha|y(0)|^{\frac{\alpha-1}{t}}}{\gamma(\alpha-1)}. \tag{16.19}$$

To sum up the three conditions earlier, t_b can be unified as

$$t_b = \frac{\alpha|y(0)|^{\frac{\alpha-1}{\alpha}}}{\gamma(\alpha-1)}.$$

The proof is completed. ∎

From the aforementioned analysis, it can be concluded that two parts of the well-designed sign-bi-power function have different effects as the error changes dynamically in accelerating the convergence speed of ZNN. In view of this, we design three adaptive coefficients corresponding to varying trend of the computational error to adjust the proportion of two components in ZNN activated by sign-bi-power function.

16.3 FTZNN Models with Adaptive Coefficients

On the basis of discussion in the previous section, three new FTZNN models are proposed to improve the convergence performance of the standard ZNN model (16.4) by designing three adaptive coefficients in the sign-bi-power function (16.5). Then, the improved finite-time convergence of new FTZNN models is theoretically proven, and the corresponding theoretical upper bounds are analytically calculated. For concise expression, three new FTZNN models are respectively called the static adaptive finite-time zeroing neural network (SA-FTZNN) model, the piecewise adaptive finite-time zeroing neural network (PA-FTZNN) model, and the exponential adaptive finite-time zeroing neural network (EA-FTZNN) model according to three different types of adaptive design coefficients for the sign-bi-power function (16.5).

16.3.1 SA-FTZNN Model

Based on the previous analysis results, for the design of static adaptive ZNN model we use $k \in (0,1)$ and $1 - k$ to replace with the fixed $1/2$ respectively in the sign-bi-power function (16.5). Specifically, the following modified sign-bi-power function with static adaptive coefficients is proposed as follows:

$$\begin{aligned}
\phi_{\mathrm{SA}}(x) &= k|x|^{\alpha}\mathrm{sign}(x) + (1-k)|x|^{\frac{1}{\alpha}}\mathrm{sign}(x) \\
&= kf_{\mathrm{SP}\text{-}1}(x) + (1-k)f_{\mathrm{SP}\text{-}2}(x),
\end{aligned} \tag{16.20}$$

which is called the static adaptive sign-bi-power function for convenience. As shown in Eq. (16.20), we can change its proportion about SP-1 function (16.7) and SP-2 function (16.8) by setting different values of k. Especially, when $k = 1/2$, static adaptive sign-bi-power function (16.20) is degenerated into sign-bi-power function (16.5).

Unlike the second step of the standard ZNN design process, static adaptive sign-bi-power function (16.20) is used to replace the general nonlinear function to get following evolution formula:

$$\frac{dY(t)}{dt} = -\gamma \Phi_{SA}(Y(t)), \tag{16.21}$$

where $\Phi_{SA}(\cdot)$ is a new function array consisting of the static adaptive sign-bi-power function $\phi_{SA}(\cdot)$. According to the previous evolution formula, the SA-FTZNN model is derived as

$$A(t)\dot{U}(t) - \dot{U}(t)B(t) = \dot{A}(t)U(t) + \dot{U}(t)B(t) - \dot{C}(t)$$
$$- \gamma \Phi_{SA}(A(t)U(t) - U(t)B(t) + C(t)). \tag{16.22}$$

In order to guarantee the finite-time convergence of SA-FTZNN model (16.22), we first analyze and prove the following theoretical result.

Theorem 16.3 *Given coefficient matrices $A(t) \in \mathbb{R}^{n \times n}$, $B(t) \in \mathbb{R}^{n \times n}$, and $C(t) \in \mathbb{R}^{n \times n}$, the state matrix $U(t) \in \mathbb{R}^{n \times n}$ of SA-FTZNN model (16.22) with any initial state $U(0) \in \mathbb{R}^{n \times n}$ globally converges to the theoretical solution of (16.1) within finite time*

$$t_f \leq \begin{cases} \frac{1 - |\rho(0)|^{1-\alpha}}{\gamma k(\alpha-1)} + \frac{\alpha}{\gamma(1-k)(\alpha-1)}, & |\rho(0)| > 1, \\ \frac{\alpha|\rho(0)|^{(\alpha-1)/\alpha}}{\gamma(1-k)(\alpha-1)}, & |\rho(0)| \leq 1, \end{cases} \tag{16.23}$$

where $|\rho(0)| = \max\{|y_{ij}(0)|\}$ represents the largest absolute value among the elements of error matrix (16.2) in the initial state $Y(0)$.

Proof: Defining $\rho(t)$ being the element in error matrix $Y(t)$ with $|\rho(0)| \geq |y_{ij}(0)|$, $\forall i, j \in 1, 2, \ldots, n$. Because every element in $Y(t)$ shares the same dynamic equation, we conclude that $-|\rho(t)| \leq y_{ij}(t) \leq |\rho(t)|, \forall t > 0$, for all possible i and j. Hence, all $y_{ij}(t)$ converges to 0, when $|\rho(t)|$ decreases to 0. This indicates that the upper bound of the convergence time for SA-FTZNN model (16.22) is determined by the independent subsystems $\rho(t)$ which satisfies the following dynamic evolution:

$$\frac{d\rho(t)}{dt} = -\gamma \phi_{SA}(\rho(t))$$
$$= -\gamma(k|\rho(t)|^{\alpha} \text{sign}(\rho(t)) + (1-k)|\rho|^{\frac{1}{\alpha}} \text{sign}(\rho(t))). \tag{16.24}$$

Considering the aforementioned dynamic system is adjusted by the static adaptive coefficients, we analyze the finite-time convergence of dynamic system (16.24) by enumerating the following two different situations.

(1) If $|\rho(0)| > 1$, on the basis of the previous analysis, we get the following differential inequality from (16.24) when $|\rho(t)| > 1$:

$$\frac{d\rho(t)}{dt} \le -\gamma \cdot k|\rho(t)|^{\alpha}\text{sign}(\rho(t)), \text{ with } |\rho(t)| > 1.$$

By Theorem 16.1, $|\rho(t)|$ decreases to 1 in less than

$$t_a = \frac{1 - |\rho(0)|^{1-\alpha}}{\gamma k(\alpha - 1)}.$$

That is to say, $|\rho(t)| \le 1$, after $t \ge t_a$. When $|\rho(t)| \le 1$, it conforms the ensuing differential inequality:

$$\frac{d\rho(t)}{dt} \le -\gamma \cdot (1 - k)|\rho(t)|^{\frac{1}{\alpha}}\text{sign}(\rho(t)), \text{ with } |\rho(t)| \le 1. \tag{16.25}$$

By Theorem 16.2, substitute $|y(0)| = |\rho(t)| = 1$ into (16.14), we get the upper bound of convergence time when $|\rho(t)|$ from 1 decrease to 0:

$$t_b = \frac{p}{\gamma(1 - k)(\alpha - 1)}.$$

Therefore, if $|\rho(0)| > 1$, SA-FTZNN model (16.22) converges to zero after $t \ge t_a + t_b$, this means that $t_f = t_a + t_b$ is the upper bound of convergence time in this situation.

(2) If $|\rho(0)| \le 1$, the differential inequality (16.25) always holds. By Theorem 16.2, substitute $|y(0)| = |\rho(0)|$ into (16.14), the upper bound of the convergence time can be calculated as follows:

$$t_f \le \frac{\alpha|\rho(0)|^{\frac{\alpha-1}{\alpha}}}{\gamma(1 - k)(\alpha - 1)}.$$

The proof about the finite convergence time for SA-FTZNN model (16.22) is thus completed. ∎

16.3.2 PA-FTZNN Model

After analyzing the analytical result of Theorem 16.3, it can be found that the regulation of k is difficult to balance the two parts of SA-FTZNN model (16.22). Take the case of $\rho(0) > 1$ as an example. If the values of $\rho(0)$, γ, and α are determined, when setting a larger value of k, the first part of the upper bound quickly converges to 1, such that the value of $(1 - |\rho(0)|^{1-\alpha})/\gamma k(\alpha - 1)$ is smaller, but $\alpha/\gamma(1 - k)(\alpha - 1)$ becomes larger. On the contrary, when the value of k is small, $\alpha/\gamma(1 - k)(\alpha - 1)$ is small, but $(1 - |\rho(0)|^{1-\alpha})/\gamma k(\alpha - 1)$ becomes larger. To solve this problem, we design a piecewise adaptive coefficient and the mathematical formulation is given as

$$\psi(x) = \begin{cases} 1, & |x| > 1, \\ 0, & |x| \le 1. \end{cases} \tag{16.26}$$

Make the piecewise adaptive coefficient adjust the sign-bi-power function (16.5), the following piecewise adaptive sign-bi-power function can be obtained:

$$\phi_{PA}(x) = \psi(x)|x|^{\alpha}\text{sign}(x) + (1 - \psi(x))|x|^{\frac{1}{\alpha}}\text{sign}(x)$$
$$= \psi(x)\phi_{SP-1}(x) + (1 - \psi(x))\phi_{SP-2}(x), \tag{16.27}$$

where $\phi_{SP-1}(\cdot)$ and $\phi_{SP-2}(\cdot)$ represent SP-1 function (16.7) and SP-2 function (16.8), respectively.

Then, similar to SA-FTZNN model (16.22) design procedures, the following new evolution formula for the PA-FTZNN model can be obtained by replacing the function array of the standard evolution formula (16.3):

$$\frac{dY(t)}{dt} = -\gamma\Phi_{PA}(Y(t)), \tag{16.28}$$

where $\Phi_{PA}(\cdot)$ is a new function array consisting of the piecewise adaptive sign-bi-power function $\phi_{PA}(\cdot)$.

At last, based on the evolution formula earlier, the PA-FTZNN model is derived as

$$A(t)\dot{U}(t) - \dot{U}(t)B(t) = \dot{A}(t)U(t) + \dot{U}(t)B(t) - \dot{C}(t)$$
$$- \gamma\Phi_{PA}(A(t)U(t) - U(t)B(t) + C(t)). \tag{16.29}$$

In view of aforementioned differential evolution formula (16.28), the improved global finite-time convergence property of PA-FTZNN model (16.29) can be guaranteed by the following theorem.

Theorem 16.4 *Given coefficient matrices $A(t) \in \mathbb{R}^{n \times n}$, $B(t) \in \mathbb{R}^{n \times n}$, and $C(t) \in \mathbb{R}^{n \times n}$, then the state matrix $U(t) \in \mathbb{R}^{n \times n}$ of PA-FTZNN model (16.29) with any initial state $U(0) \in \mathbb{R}^{n \times n}$ globally converges to the theoretical solution of (16.1) within finite time:*

$$t_f = \begin{cases} \dfrac{\alpha+1-|\rho(0)|^{1-\alpha}}{\gamma(\alpha-1)}, & |\rho(0)| > 1, \\[2ex] \dfrac{\alpha|\rho(0)|^{(\alpha-1)/\alpha}}{\gamma(\alpha-1)}, & |\rho(0)| \leq 1. \end{cases} \tag{16.30}$$

where $|\rho(0)| = \max\{|y_{ij}(0)|\}$ is the same as before.

Proof: Defining $\rho(t)$ being the element in $Y(t)$ with $|\rho(0)| \geq |y_{ij}(0)|, \forall i, j \in 1, 2, \ldots, n$. Because every element in $Y(t)$ shares the same dynamic equation, we conclude that $-|\rho(t)| \leq y_{ij}(t) \leq |\rho(t)|, \forall t > 0$, for all possible i and j. Hence, all $y_{ij}(t)$ converges to 0, when $|\rho(t)|$ decreases to 0. This indicates that the convergence time of PA-FTZNN model (16.29) is determined by the independent subsystems $\rho(t)$ which satisfies the following dynamic evolution:

$$\frac{d\rho(t)}{dt} = -\gamma\phi_{PA}(\rho(t))$$
$$= -\gamma(\psi(\rho(t))|\rho(t)|^{\alpha}\text{sign}(\rho(t)) + (1 - \psi(\rho(t)))|\rho|^{\frac{1}{\alpha}}\text{sign}(\rho(t))). \tag{16.31}$$

According to mathematical expression of the coefficient $\psi(x)$ defined in (16.26), Eq. (16.31) can be further rewritten as

$$\frac{d\rho(t)}{dt} = \begin{cases} -\gamma|\rho(t)|^{\alpha}\text{sign}(\rho(t)), & |\rho(t)| > 1, \\ -\gamma|\rho(t)|^{\frac{1}{\alpha}}\text{sign}(\rho(t)), & |\rho(t)| \leq 1. \end{cases} \tag{16.32}$$

Therefore, we finish the proof by enumerating two different situations according to the value of $\rho(t)$.

(1) If $|\rho(0)| > 1$, according to evolution expression (16.32), we get the following dynamic system when $|\rho(t)| > 1$:

$$\frac{d\rho(t)}{dt} = -\gamma|\rho(t)|^{\alpha}\text{sign}(\rho(t)), \text{ with } |\rho(t)| > 1.$$

By Theorem 16.1, the time when $|\rho(t)|$ reduced to 1 can be calculated as

$$t_a = \frac{1 - |\rho(0)|^{1-\alpha}}{\gamma(\alpha - 1)}.$$

That is, $|\rho(t)| = 1$ after $t = t_a$. When $|\rho(t)| \leq 1$, it conforms the ensuing differential equation:

$$\frac{d\rho(t)}{dt} = -\gamma|\rho(t)|^{\frac{1}{\alpha}}\text{sign}(\rho(t)), \text{ with } |\rho(t)| \leq 1. \tag{16.33}$$

By Theorem 16.2, substituting $|y(0)| = |\rho(t)| = 1$ to (16.14), we get the convergence time t_b of $|\rho(t)|$ from 1 to 0:

$$t_b = \frac{\alpha}{\gamma(\alpha - 1)}.$$

Therefore, if $|\rho(0)| > 1$, PA-FTZNN model (16.29) converges to zero when $t_f = t_a + t_b$.

(2) If $|\rho(0)| \leq 1$, the evolution Eq. (16.33) always holds. Based on the analysis in the proof of Theorem 16.2, substitute $|y(0)| = |\rho(0)|$ to (16.14), the convergence time can be calculated as

$$t_f = \frac{\alpha|\rho(0)|^{\frac{\alpha-1}{\alpha}}}{\gamma(\alpha - 1)}.$$

The proof about the finite convergence time for PA-FTZNN model (16.29) is thus completed. ∎

16.3.3 EA-FTZNN Model

Although the piecewise adaptive coefficient has better convergence performance, it makes the first derivative of evolution formula (16.32) not continuous. Moreover, the non-smooth character of the piecewise adaptive coefficient brings difficulties in hardware implementation. In light of this, we design a continuous adaptive coefficient based on an exponential function to approximate piecewise adaptive coefficient smoothly. Its mathematical formulation is designed and given as

$$\phi(x) = 1 - \exp\left(-|x|^q\right), \tag{16.34}$$

where q is a positive integer and $\exp(\cdot)$ represents the exponential function. Let the aforementioned exponential adaptive coefficient act on the sign-bi-power function (16.5), and we get the following piecewise adaptive sign-bi-power function:

$$\begin{aligned}\phi_{\text{EA}}(x) &= \phi(x)|x|^\alpha \text{sign}(x) + (1 - \phi(x))|x|^{\frac{1}{\alpha}} \text{sign}(x) \\ &= \phi(x)f_{\text{SP-1}}(x) + (1 - \phi(x))f_{\text{SP-2}}(x).\end{aligned} \tag{16.35}$$

Using the same method of designing PA-FTZNN model (16.29), we get the following evolution formula:

$$\frac{dY(t)}{dt} = -\gamma\Phi_{\text{EA}}(Y(t)) \tag{16.36}$$

and the corresponding EA-FTZNN model:

$$\begin{aligned}A(t)\dot{U}(t) - \dot{U}(t)B(t) = \dot{A}(t)U(t) + \dot{U}(t)B(t) - \dot{C}(t) \\ - \gamma\Phi_{\text{EA}}(A(t)U(t) - U(t)B(t) + C(t)),\end{aligned} \tag{16.37}$$

where $\Phi_{\text{EA}}(\cdot)$ denotes the exponential adaptive sign-bi-power function $\phi_{\text{EA}}(\cdot)$ array.

According evolution formula (16.36), the following theorem is given to ensure the finite-time convergence property of EA-FTZNN model (16.37).

Theorem 16.5 *Given coefficient matrices $A(t) \in \mathbb{R}^{n\times n}$, $B(t) \in \mathbb{R}^{n\times n}$, and $C(t) \in \mathbb{R}^{n\times n}$, then the state matrix $U(t) \in \mathbb{R}^{n\times n}$ of EA-FTZNN model (16.37) with any initial state $U(0) \in \mathbb{R}^{n\times n}$ globally converges to the theoretical solution of (16.1) within finite time:*

$$t_{\text{f}} \leq \begin{cases} \frac{e(1-|\rho(0)|^{1-\alpha})}{\gamma(e-1)(\alpha-1)} + \frac{e\cdot\alpha}{\gamma(\alpha-1)}, & |\rho(0)| > 1, \\ \frac{e\cdot\alpha|\rho(0)|^{\frac{\alpha-1}{\alpha}}}{\gamma(\alpha-1)}, & |\rho(0)| \leq 1, \end{cases} \tag{16.38}$$

where $e \approx 2.718$ is the mathematical constant, and $|\rho(0)| = \max\{|y_{ij}(0)|\}$ is defined the same as before.

Proof: According to the analysis in the previous proof of Theorems 16.3 and 16.4, it also can be concluded that the upper bound of EA-FTZNN model (16.37) is determined by $\rho(t)$, which is a special element in the error matrix $Y(t)$ with $|\rho(0)| \geq |y_{ij}(0)|$, $\forall i,j \in 1, 2, \dots, n$. Then, the independent subsystem about $\rho(t)$ obeys the following dynamic differential equation:

$$\begin{aligned}\frac{d\rho(t)}{dt} &= -\gamma\phi_{\text{EA}}(\rho(t)) \\ &= -\gamma(\phi(\rho(t))|\rho(t)|^\alpha \text{sign}(\rho(t)) + (1 - \phi(\rho(t)))|\rho|^{\frac{1}{\alpha}} \text{sign}(\rho(t))),\end{aligned} \tag{16.39}$$

which contains two different parts. We can analyze this dynamic system of $\rho(t)$ under the following two conditions.

(1) If $|\rho(0)| > 1$, the following differential inequality can be derived from Eq. (16.39) to find the upper bound when $|\rho(t)|$ is reduced to 1:

$$\frac{d\rho(t)}{dt} \leq -\gamma\phi(\rho(t))|\rho(t)|^{\alpha}\text{sign}(\rho(t)). \tag{16.40}$$

Under the condition that $|\rho(t)|$ is greater than 1, the first derivative of $\phi(|\rho(t)|) = 1 - \exp(-|\rho(t)|^q)$ with respect to $|\rho(t)|$ is $\dot{\phi}(|\rho(t)|) = q \cdot \exp(-|\rho(t)|^q) \cdot |\rho(t)|^{q-1}$, such that $\dot{\phi}(|\rho(t)|) > 0, \forall |\rho(t)| \geq 1$. This means that $\phi(|\rho(t)|)$ is a monotonically increasing function when $|\rho(t)| \in [1, +\infty)$. Hence, $\phi(1) = 1 - 1/e$ is the minimum value of the coefficient function $\phi(|\rho(t)|)$ in interval of $[1, +\infty)$. Therefore, we take $\phi(1) = 1 - 1/e$ instead of $\phi(|\rho(t)|) = 1 - \exp(-|\rho(t)|^q)$ in inequality (16.40) to calculate the upper bound of the convergence time of $\rho(t)$ decreasing to 1, and obtain the following differential inequality:

$$\begin{aligned}\frac{d\rho(t)}{dt} &\leq -\gamma\phi(\rho(t))|\rho(t)|^{\alpha}\text{sign}(\rho(t)) \\ &\leq -\gamma\left(1 - \frac{1}{e}\right)|\rho(t)|^{\alpha}\text{sign}(\rho(t)),\end{aligned} \tag{16.41}$$

where $e \approx 2.718$ is the mathematical constant. According to the analysis in Theorem 16.1, solving the aforementioned differential inequality can obtain the upper bound of $|\rho(t)|$ reducing to 1:

$$t_a = \frac{e(1 - |\rho(0)|^{1-\alpha})}{\gamma(e-1)(\alpha-1)},$$

which implies $|\rho(t)| \leq 1$ after $t \geq t_a$.

When $|\rho(t)| \leq 1$, using the same analysis method, we know that the minimum value of coefficient function $1 - \phi(|\rho(t)|) = \exp(-|\rho(t)|^q)$ in the interval of $[0, 1]$ is $\phi(1) = 1/e$. Hence, we can calculate the upper bound of $|\rho(t)|$ from 1 to 0 by solving the ensuing differential inequality:

$$\begin{aligned}\frac{d\rho(t)}{dt} &\leq -\gamma(1 - \phi(\rho(t)))|x|^{\frac{1}{\alpha}}\text{sign}(\rho(t)) \\ &\leq -\frac{\gamma}{e}|\rho(t)|^{\frac{1}{\alpha}}\text{sign}(\rho(t)).\end{aligned} \tag{16.42}$$

Analogous to the analysis in the proof of Theorem 16.2, we get the upper bound of t_b when $|\rho(t)|$ decreases from 1 to 0:

$$t_b = \frac{e \cdot p}{\gamma(l-1)}.$$

Therefore, if $|\rho(0)| > 1$, the upper bound of EA-FTZNN model (16.37) converges to zero is $t_f = t_a + t_b$.

(2) If $|\rho(0)| \leq 1$, the aforementioned analysis for the upper bound of convergence time under the condition that $|\rho(t)| \leq 1$ is still true. Thus, we get

$$t_f \leq \frac{e \cdot \alpha |\rho(0)|^{\frac{\alpha-1}{\alpha}}}{\gamma(\alpha - 1)}.$$

The proof about the finite convergence time for EA-FTZNN model (16.37) is thus completed. ∎

Before ending this section, we want to discuss the feasibility of applying the newly proposed method to other models. From the aforementioned adaptive coefficient design ideas and the proof process of the improved finite-time convergence, it can be seen that the adaptive coefficients that vary with the computational error are based on the characteristics of sign-bi-power activation function (16.5). Therefore, the adaptive coefficient design method proposed in this chapter can be generalized and applied to any ZNN model activated by the sign-bi-power function. In addition, the adaptive coefficient designed in this work is still in a unified framework of ZNN model. Therefore, the adaptive coefficient design idea can be used as a reference to improve convergence of any complex computing problem using ZNN as a solver.

16.4 Illustrative Verification

In the previous sections, three ZNN models with adaptive coefficients (i.e. SA-FTZNN model (16.22), PA-FTZNN model (16.29), and EA-FTZNN model (16.37)) are proposed and analyzed for solving the Sylvester equation (16.1). To further confirm better convergence performance and verify the theoretical results, an illustrative example is given, solved, and explained in this section. In addition, the proposed three new FTZNN models and the standard ZNN model activated by the sign-bi-power function are simulated by digital computer for comparison.

Without loss of generality, consider a Sylvester equation with the time-varying coefficient matrices chosen as follows:

$$A(t) = \begin{bmatrix} \sin(4t) & \cos(4t) \\ -\cos(4t) & \sin(4t) \end{bmatrix}, \ B(t) = \begin{bmatrix} 2 & 0 \\ 0 & 3 \end{bmatrix}, \ C(t) = \begin{bmatrix} \sin(t) & \cos(t) \\ -\cos(t) & \sin(t) \end{bmatrix}.$$

For better discussion and comparison, the design parameters in the whole simulation part are given as $\alpha = 3$ and $\gamma = 1$.

First, let the initial state of ZNN models start from a randomly generated position $U(0) \in [-1, 1]^{2 \times 2}$. The trajectories of output state $U(t)$ computed by ZNN models and corresponding theoretical solution $U^*(t)$ are plotted in Figure 16.1. It can be seen from this figure that after a short transition, dash-dotted, dashed, and solid curves representing the neural-state solutions of different ZNN models coincide

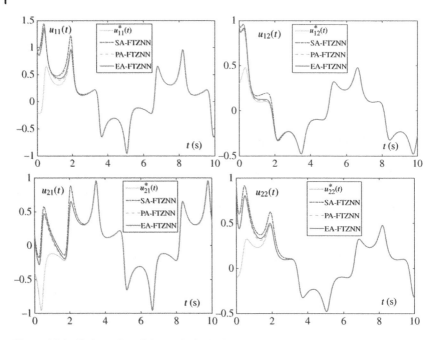

Figure 16.1 Trajectories of theoretical solutions (dotted lines) of the time-varying Sylvester equation and state solutions (dash-dotted, dashed, and solid curves) generated by SA-FTZNN model (16.22), PA-FTZNN model (16.29), and EA-FTZNN model (16.37).

with the dotted lines that paint the time-varying theoretical solution. Therefore, we can conclude that the newly designed models can effectively solve the time-varying Sylvester equation (16.1). On the other hand, to better depict the superior convergence property and further compare the distinction along different models, the Frobenius norm $\|Y(t)\|_F$ describing the error evolution procedure is drawn in

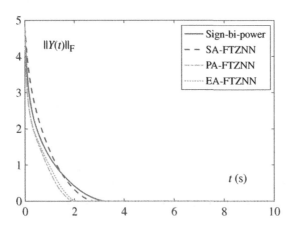

Figure 16.2 Comparisons of the computational errors generated by SA-FTZNN model (16.22), PA-FTZNN model (16.29), EA-FTZNN model (16.37), and the ZNN activated by sign-bi-power function (16.5).

Figure 16.2. As shown in this figure, all the residual errors decrease at exponential speed and converge to zero in finite time. It is worth nothing that, starting from the same initial state, any one of the proposed neural models with adaptive coefficients owns shorter convergence time, as compared with the ZNN model activated by sign-bi-power function. This verifies the effectiveness of dynamically regulating ZNN model by adding adaptive coefficients to speed up the convergence rate.

Remark The first part of the simulation experiment is to validate the efficacy of the newly proposed adaptive ZNN models and make a comparison of the convergence speed with the ZNN model activated by sign-bi-power function. The model generated solutions and the theoretical solution shown in the trajectory figure (i.e. Figure 16.1) can be fitted in a very short time. This ensures that the adaptive models proposed in this chapter can effectively solve time-varying Sylvester equation (16.1). Furthermore, the Frobenius norm $||Y(t)||_F$ plotted in Figure 16.2 compares the convergence speed of the adaptive ZNN models and the state-of-the-art ZNN model (i.e. ZNN model activated by sign-bi-power function). From the simulation experiment results shown in this figure, it can be seen that the new adaptive models have greatly improved the convergence performance.

Second, for SA-FTZNN model (16.22), the proportion of two parts activated by SP-1 function (16.7) and SP-2 function (16.8) can be adjusted by changing the value of k. According to the previous analysis, for setting different values of k to SA-FTZNN model (16.22), the convergence speed is different when the residual error is greater than 1 and less than 1. To verify this, we compare the convergence rate by setting different values of k with the same initial state $U(0)$. Figure 16.3 displays the different evolution trajectories of SA-FTZNN model (16.22) with $k = 0.2$, $k = 0.4$, $k = 0.6$, and $k = 0.8$. It can be seen from the figure that when k is greater than 0.5, the computational error of SA-FTZNN model (16.22) can converge to 1 at a faster rate, but it takes more time to decrease from 1 to 0, and the larger the value of k, the more obvious this situation. Conversely, when k is less than 0.5, the convergence performance of these two parts is just the opposite. Consequently, it verifies the previous analysis that setting different coefficients will affect the convergence speed of SA-FTZNN model (16.22) under the condition of error variation. Furthermore, the possibility of speeding up the convergence speed by setting adaptive coefficients to modify the sign-bi-power function is explained.

Remark The second part of the simulation experiment is to compare the convergence speed of SA-FTZNN model by setting different static coefficient, which is equivalent to using a fixed ratio to combine the two parts of the standard ZNN model activated by the SP-1 function and the SP-2 function. Through this experiment, the previous analysis results that the SP-1 function and the SP-2 function play different roles in accelerating the convergence when the computational error is greater than 1 and less than 1 have been experimentally verified.

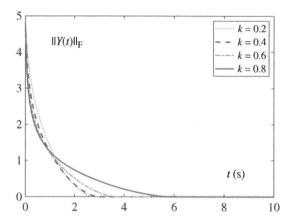

Figure 16.3 Comparisons of the SA-FTZNN model (16.22) with different values of k.

The experimental results show that with a single fixed coefficient, the convergence effect of SA-FTZNN does not reach the best. Especially when setting a larger value of k, the convergence performance of the model decreases obviously. This is consistent with the comparison results in Figure 16.2 where the convergence speed of SA-FTZNN is relatively poor among three adaptive ZNN models.

Third, we set a large initial state and small initial state separately to verify the convergence of new ZNN models with adaptive coefficients under different initial conditions. Moreover, the simulation results are compared with the standard ZNN model only activated by SP-1 function (16.7) or SP-2 function (16.8) to examine the improvement and superiority of the new proposed three ZNN models. Figure 16.4a,b are provided to demonstrate the experimental results. As shown in

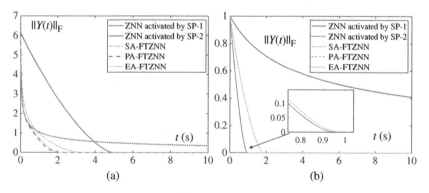

(a)   (b)

Figure 16.4 Comparisons of SA-FTZNN model (16.22), PA-FTZNN model (16.29), EA-FTZNN model (16.37) and the ZNN activated by SP-1 function (16.7) and SP-2 function (16.8) while setting a large and small initial state. (a) Large initial state. (b) Small initial state.

Table 16.1 The convergence time of different ZNN models.

Model	Large initial state	Small initial state
ZNN activated by SP-1	Infinite	Infinite
ZNN activated by SP-2	Finite[a)]	Finite
Adaptive ZNN models	Finite	Finite

a) Although ZNN activated by SP-1 function can achieve finite-time convergence with a large initial state, it can be seen from the Figure 16.4a that the time it takes to reduce to 0 is much longer than all adaptive ZNN models.

Figure 16.4a, when the initial state is large, the computational error of the standard ZNN model activated by SP-1 function (16.7) can quickly decrease, but when the error is reduced to around 1, the convergence speed becomes slower and eventually cannot converge to 0 in a finite time. Correspondingly, the error of the standard ZNN model activated by SP-2 function (16.8) reduces so slowly that it takes a long time to converge in this situation. On the other hand, when the initial error is small, the convergence of these models is plotted in Figure 16.4b. It can be seen that the standard ZNN model activated by SP-2 function (16.8) converges to zero in a finite time, while the standard ZNN model activated by SP-1 function (16.7) has a small error reduction and does not converge. Different from the aforementioned situations, three new models can converge to 0 in a finite time in both cases. In order to display the experimental results more intuitively and further illustrate the superiority of the proposed adaptive ZNN models, the comprehensive comparison results have been listed in Table 16.1. As seen from this table, it can be concluded that three new adaptive ZNN models combine the different convergence advantages of SP-1 function (16.7) and SP-2 function (16.8) by adding adaptive coefficients.

Remark The third part of the simulation experiment is to further validate the superiority of the adaptive ZNN model on the basis of the previous theoretical analysis and experiments. In this part of the experiment, a large and a small initial state are set to compare the convergence performance of different ZNN models in disparate initial states. From the experimental results shown in Figure 16.4, it can be concluded that the standard ZNN model activated by a single SP-1 or SP-2 function may not achieve finite-time convergence under the two initial conditions earlier. However, due to the addition of adaptive coefficients that can automatically adjust the proportion of the model activated by SP-1 and SP-2 functions according to the computational error, the adaptive ZNN models overcome the aforementioned deficiencies in standard ZNN model and improve the model convergence performance.

In summary, based on the aforementioned discussion of numerical comparison experiments, the efficacy and reliability of the proposed adaptive FTZNN models for time-varying Sylvester equation (16.1) are verified. All new models converge to the theoretical solution in finite time. Besides, the new FTZNN models with adaptive coefficients speed up the convergence rate and possess less upper bound, as compared with ZNN model activated by SP-1 function (16.7), SP-2 function (16.8), and sign-bi-power function (16.5).

16.5 Chapter Summary

Three new adaptive FTZNN models with different adaptive coefficients have been proposed for solving time-varying Sylvester equation in this work. For designing better adaptive coefficients, the role of two components of the sign-bi-power function has been studied to impact the convergence speed of the standard ZNN model. Based on the theoretical conclusions, three different adaptive coefficients have been designed to improve the convergence performance of the standard ZNN model. The detailed theoretical results have also been analyzed to show that the proposed FTZNN models have better finite-time convergence upper bound. Furthermore, numerical comparison results have demonstrated the superiority of the FTZNN models for solving time-varying Sylvester equation.

References

1 Q. Wei, N. Dobigeon, and J. Tourneret, Fast fusion of multi-band images based on solving a Sylvester equation, *IEEE Trans. Image Process.*, 24(11) (2015) 4109–4121.

2 G. Sangalli and M. Tani, Isogeometric preconditioners based on fast solvers for the Sylvester equation, *SIAM J. Sci. Comput.*, 38(6) (2016) A3644–A3671.

3 Q. Wei and N. Dobigeon *et al.*, R-FUSE: Robust fast fusion of multiband images based on solving a Sylvester equation, *IEEE Signal Process. Lett.*, 23(11) (2016) 1632–1636.

4 D. C. Sorensen and A. C. Antoulas, The Sylvester equation and approximate balanced reduction, *Linear Algebra Appl.*, 351–352 (2002) 671–700.

5 L. Xiao, Z. Zhang, and Z. Zhang *et al.*, Design, verification and robotic application of a novel recurrent neural network for computing dynamic Sylvester equation, *Neural Netw.*, 105 (2018) 185–196.

6 Z. Zhang, L. Zheng, and J. Weng *et al.*, A new varying-parameter recurrent neural-network for online solution of time-varying Sylvester equation, *IEEE Trans. Cybern.*, 48(11) (2018) 3135–3148.

7 B. Huang and C. Ma, Gradient-based iterative algorithms for generalized coupled Sylvester-conjugate matrix equations, *Comput. Math. Appl.*, 75(7) (2018) 2295–2310.

8 L. Xiao and B. Liao *et al.*, Nonlinear recurrent neural networks for finite-time solution of general time-varying linear matrix equations, *Neural Netw.*, 98 (2018) 102–113.

9 L. Xiao and Y. Zhang *et al.*, A new noise-tolerant and predefined-time ZNN model for time-dependent matrix inversion, *Neural Netw.* 117 (2019) 124–134.

10 S. Li, S. Chen, and B. Liu, Accelerating a recurrent neural network to finite-time convergence for solving time-varying Sylvester equation by using a sign-bi-power activation function, *Neural Process. Lett.*, 37(2) (2013) 189–205.

Part VII

Application to Inequality

17

Design Scheme I of FTZNN

17.1 Introduction

For the past few years, as the inequalities grow in importance in various applications, the approaches based on solving inequalities are widely used to solve various problems in the engineering and science fields [1–5]. Moreover, linear matrix inequalities (LMIs) also have extensive practical application, such as obstacle avoidance for redundant robots [6, 7], motion scheme design based on physical limit avoidance [8, 9], robot speed minimization [10], and robot manipulator control [11].

In this chapter, based on traditional zeroing neural network (ZNN) models, three finite-time zeroing neural network (FTZNN) models are established by suggesting three different sign-bi-power activation functions (AFs) which can make the error functions of various neural network models converge to zero. The first one is the original sign-bi-power AF, the second one is a modification of the first one via amending sign-bi-power AF by adding a linear term, and the third one is activated by tunable sign-bi-power AF, which defines three tunable parameters. Theoretical analysis shows that whatever the initial state is, the error function generated by the proposed FTZNN models always converges to zero in finite time. Compared with the existing algorithms and conventional ZNN models, the main advantage of the proposed FTZNN models lies in the fact that they can offer a faster convergence rate and finite-time convergence property. The numerical simulation results verify the superiority of FTZNN models.

17.2 FTZNN Models Design

In this section, some basic knowledge is presented at first. Then, based on the conventional ZNN model for LMIs, three FTZNN models are designed by applying finite-time AFs.

Zeroing Neural Networks: Finite-time Convergence Design, Analysis and Applications,
First Edition. Lin Xiao and Lei Jia.

17.2.1 Problem Formulation

In this part, the multi-dimensional time-varying LMIs problem is formulated as follows:

$$A(t)U(t)B(t) \le C(t), \tag{17.1}$$

where $A(t) \in \mathbb{R}^{m \times m}$, $B(t) \in \mathbb{R}^{n \times n}$, and $C(t) \in \mathbb{R}^{m \times n}$ denote time-varying matrices. The purpose of this chapter is to find the unknown solution set $U(t)$ which can make (17.1) hold true anytime.

17.2.2 ZNN Model

To monitor the process of solving LMIs, we define the matrix–vector error function as follows:

$$Y(t) = A(t)U(t)B(t) - C(t), \tag{17.2}$$

where $Y(t) \in \mathbb{R}^{m \times n}$.

Based on the efforts which have been done, the ZNN design formula for establishing the neural model is constructed as

$$\dot{Y}(t) = -\gamma \text{STP}(Y(0)) \diamond \Phi(Y(t)), \tag{17.3}$$

where $\Phi(\cdot) : \mathbb{R}^{m \times n} \to \mathbb{R}^{m \times n}$ is a monotonously increasing odd activation function array, γ is a positive parameter and $\text{STP}(\cdot) : \mathbb{R}^{m \times n} \to \mathbb{R}^{m \times n}$ stands for a set of step functions which is defined as

$$\text{stp}(x) = \begin{cases} 1, & x > 0; \\ 0, & x \le 0. \end{cases} \tag{17.4}$$

Besides, the operator $\diamond$ is defined as

$$b \diamond c = \begin{bmatrix} b_1 c_1 \\ b_2 c_2 \\ \vdots \\ b_n c_n \end{bmatrix}. \tag{17.5}$$

Note that the above ZNN design formula can make the error function converge to zero exponentially. Substituting (17.2) into (17.3), we have its implicit dynamic equation of the ZNN model:

$$A(t)\dot{U}(t)B(t) = -\gamma \text{STP}(A(0)U(0)B(0) - C(0)) \diamond \Phi(A(t)U(t)B(t) - C(t))$$
$$- \dot{A}(t)U(t)B(t) - A(t)U(t)\dot{B}(t) + \dot{C}(t). \tag{17.6}$$

17.2.3 Vectorization

According to the implicit dynamic equation of ZNN model (17.6), $U(t)$ can not be calculated directly in Matlab. To address this problem, the Kronecker product is used to convert ZNN model (17.6) from the matrix form to the vector form. Then, ZNN model (17.6) is transformed into the following vector-valued one:

$$
\begin{aligned}
H(t)\dot{\boldsymbol{w}}(t) = {} &-\gamma \mathrm{STP}(H(0)\boldsymbol{w}(0) - \mathrm{vec}(C(0))) \diamond \Phi(H(t)W(t) - \mathrm{vec}(C(t))) \\
&- Q(t)\boldsymbol{w}(t) - R(t)\boldsymbol{w}(t) + \mathrm{vec}(\dot{C}(t)),
\end{aligned}
\tag{17.7}
$$

where $H(t) = B^{\mathrm{T}}(t) \otimes A(t)$ with $H(0) = B^{\mathrm{T}}(0) \otimes A(0)$, $Q(t) = B^{\mathrm{T}}(t) \otimes \dot{A}(t)$, $R(t) = \dot{B}^{\mathrm{T}}(t) \otimes A(t)$ and $\boldsymbol{w}(t) = \mathrm{vec}(U(t))$ with $\boldsymbol{w}(0) = \mathrm{vec}(U(0))$, where $\mathrm{vec}(U(t))$ and $\mathrm{vec}(\dot{C}(t))$ denote the vectorization of $U(t)$ and $\dot{C}(t)$, respectively. In the following part, three finite-time convergent AFs are explored to shorten the convergence time.

17.2.4 Activation Functions

In the past years, the following AFs are widely applied in ZNN models:

(1) the linear activation function:

$$
\phi(x) = x;
\tag{17.8}
$$

(2) the power activation function:

$$
\phi(x) = x^k, k \geq 3;
\tag{17.9}
$$

(3) the bipolar-sigmoid activation function:

$$
\phi(x) = \frac{1 + \exp(-l)}{1 - \exp(-l)} \frac{1 - \exp(-lx)}{1 + \exp(-lx)}, \quad l > 2;
\tag{17.10}
$$

(4) the power-sigmoid activation function:

$$
\phi(x) = \frac{1}{2}x^{l_1} + \frac{1 + \exp(-l_2)}{1 - \exp(-l_2)} \frac{1 - \exp(-l_2 x)}{1 + \exp(-l_2 x)}, \quad l_1 \geq 3, l_2 > 2.
\tag{17.11}
$$

However, the aforementioned AFs only can make the error function of ZNN model (17.6) converge to zero, and they cannot guarantee the finite convergence time in solving time-varying LMIs. To solve this problem, three superior finite-time AFs are applied to ZNN model (17.6), and the corresponding FTZNN models are thus derived.

Specifically, the first sign-bi-power AF is given as follows:

$$
\phi_1(x) = \frac{1}{2}|x|^\alpha \mathrm{sgn}(x) + \frac{1}{2}|x|^{\frac{1}{\alpha}} \mathrm{sgn}(x),
\tag{17.12}
$$

where $0 < r < 1$ and $\mathrm{sgn}(\cdot)$ is defined as

$$
\mathrm{sgn}(x) = \begin{cases} 1, & \text{if } x > 0; \\ 0, & \text{if } x = 0; \\ -1, & \text{if } x < 0. \end{cases}
\tag{17.13}
$$

In order to accelerate convergence, on basis of sign-bi-power AF (17.12), an improved sign-bi-power AF is designed by adding a linear term, and is presented as below:

$$\phi_2(x) = \frac{1}{2}|x|^{\alpha}\operatorname{sgn}(x) + \frac{1}{2}x + \frac{1}{2}|x|^{\frac{1}{\alpha}}\operatorname{sgn}(x). \tag{17.14}$$

To further reduce the theoretical convergence time upper bound, a tunable sign-bi-power AF is presented as below:

$$\phi_3(x) = \frac{1}{2}k_1|x|^{\alpha}\operatorname{sgn}(x) + \frac{1}{2}k_2x + \frac{1}{2}k_3|x|^{\frac{1}{\alpha}}\operatorname{sgn}(x). \tag{17.15}$$

17.2.5 FTZNN Models

In this section, by applying AFs (17.12), (17.14), and (17.15) to ZNN model (17.6), we can obtain the corresponding three FTZNN models to solve time-varying LMIs. Their respective design processes of FTZNN models are presented as below.

(1) FTZNN-1 model: Similar to the design process of (17.6), we can obtain the same error function. Then, the differential formula for this error function is shown as

$$\dot{Y}(t) = -\gamma \operatorname{STP}(Y(0)) \diamond \Phi_1(Y(t)), \tag{17.16}$$

where $\Phi_1(\cdot)$ denotes the sign-bi-power AF (17.12), $Y(0)$ denotes the initial error of $Y(t)$ at $t = 0$, $\operatorname{STP}(\cdot)$, and $\diamond$ are defined as before.

At last, expanding the differential formula (17.16) by substituting $Y(t)$, the dynamic equation corresponding to the FTZNN-1 model is formed by

$$\begin{aligned}
H(t)\dot{\boldsymbol{w}}(t) = &-\gamma \operatorname{STP}(H(0)\boldsymbol{w}(0) - \operatorname{vec}(C(0))) \diamond \Phi_1(H(t)W(t) - \operatorname{vec}(C(t)) \\
&- Q(t)\boldsymbol{w}(t) - R(t)\boldsymbol{w}(t) + \operatorname{vec}(\dot{C}(t)),
\end{aligned} \tag{17.17}$$

where $H(t) = B^{\mathrm{T}}(t) \otimes A(t)$, $Q(t) = B^{\mathrm{T}}(t) \otimes \dot{A}(t)$, $R(t) = \dot{B}^{\mathrm{T}}(t) \otimes A(t)$, and $\boldsymbol{w}(t) = \operatorname{vec}(U(t))$.

(2) FTZNN-2 model: On the basis of FTZNN-1 model (17.17), we change the activation function to the improved sign-bi-power AF (17.14). Then, the differential formula for the error function is obtained as follows:

$$\dot{Y}(t) = -\gamma \operatorname{STP}(Y(0)) \diamond \Phi_2(Y(t)), \tag{17.18}$$

and the corresponding FTZNN-2 model is formed by

$$\begin{aligned}
H(t)\dot{\boldsymbol{w}}(t) = &-\gamma \operatorname{STP}(H(0)\boldsymbol{w}(0) - \operatorname{vec}(C(0))) \diamond \Phi_2(H(t)W(t) - \operatorname{vec}(C(t)) \\
&- Q(t)\boldsymbol{w}(t) - R(t)\boldsymbol{w}(t) + \operatorname{vec}(\dot{C}(t)).
\end{aligned} \tag{17.19}$$

(3) FTZNN-3 model: On the foundation of FTZNN-2 model (17.19), adding the tunable parameters to shorten convergence time, the differential formula for the error function is indicated below:

$$\dot{Y}(t) = -\gamma \mathrm{STP}(Y(0)) \diamond \Phi_3(Y(t)). \tag{17.20}$$

Then, expanding the previous equation, we get the following FTZNN-3 model:

$$H(t)\dot{w}(t) = -\gamma \mathrm{STP}(H(0)w(0) - \mathrm{vec}(C(0))) \diamond \Phi_3(H(t)W(t) - \mathrm{vec}(C(t)))$$
$$- Q(t)w(t) - R(t)w(t) + \mathrm{vec}(\dot{C}(t)). \tag{17.21}$$

17.3 Theoretical Analysis

In this part, we theoretically substantiate the convergent property of the proposed three FTZNN models for solving LMIs. In addition, the finite-time convergence performance of FTZNN models will be proved, with specific upper bound estimated. It is worth mentioning that when the initial state $U(0)$ is inside the solution set, we have $Y(0) = A(0)U(0)B(0) - C(0) \leq 0$. That is, as the time t goes by, $U(t)$ always stays in the solution set. Thus, in the following proofs, we only need to consider the situation when the initial state $U(0)$ is outside the solution set.

17.3.1 Global Convergence

It is the primary goal that we have to demonstrate the global convergence of the proposed three FTZNN models which are activated by three different sign-bi-power activation functions.

Theorem 17.1 *Given smoothly time-varying coefficient matrices $A(t) \in \mathbb{R}^{m \times m}$, $B(t) \in \mathbb{R}^{n \times n}$ and $C(t) \in \mathbb{R}^{m \times n}$, FTZNN-1 model (17.17), FTZNN-2 model (17.19), and FTZNN-3 model (17.21) achieve the global convergence.*

Proof: According to the definitions of the novel AFs, we have

$$\phi_1(-x) = \frac{1}{2}|-x|^\alpha \mathrm{sgn}(-x) + \frac{1}{2}|-x|^{\frac{1}{\alpha}}\mathrm{sgn}(-x)$$
$$= -\frac{1}{2}|x|^\alpha \mathrm{sgn}(x) - \frac{1}{2}|x|^{\frac{1}{\alpha}}\mathrm{sgn}(x) \tag{17.22}$$
$$= -\phi_1(x);$$

$$\phi_2(-x) = \frac{1}{2}|-x|^\alpha \mathrm{sgn}(-x) - \frac{1}{2}x + \frac{1}{2}|-x|^{\frac{1}{\alpha}}\mathrm{sgn}(-x)$$
$$= -\frac{1}{2}|x|^\alpha \mathrm{sgn}(x) - \frac{1}{2}x - \frac{1}{2}|x|^{\frac{1}{\alpha}}\mathrm{sgn}(x) \tag{17.23}$$
$$= -\phi_2(x);$$

$$\phi_3(-x) = \frac{1}{2}k_1| - x|^\alpha \operatorname{sgn}(-x) - \frac{1}{2}k_2 x + \frac{1}{2}k_3| - x|^{\frac{1}{\alpha}}\operatorname{sgn}(-x)$$

$$= -\frac{1}{2}k_1|x|^\alpha \operatorname{sgn}(x) - \frac{1}{2}k_2 x - \frac{1}{2}k_3|x|^{\frac{1}{\alpha}}\operatorname{sgn}(x) \tag{17.24}$$

$$= -\phi_3(x).$$

Therefore, we can know that three AFs are monotonically increasing odd functions.

Then, let us define a Lyapunov function $p_{ij}(t) = y_{ij}^2(t)/2$, where $y_{ij}(t)$ is the element of $Y(t)$ which is defined in (17.2). Since $U(0)$ is outside the solution set, $\operatorname{STP}(Y(0)) = 1$, which means that every element of $\operatorname{STP}(Y(0))$ equals to 1. Therefore, we have $\operatorname{STP}(y_{ij}(0)) = 1$. Thus, $\dot{p}_{ij}(t)$ is computed as

$$\dot{p}_{ij}(t) = \frac{\mathrm{d}p_{ij}(t)}{\mathrm{d}t} = -\gamma y_{ij}(t)\dot{y}_{ij}(t) = -\gamma y_{ij}(t)\phi_k(y_{ij}(t)), \quad k = 1, 2, 3. \tag{17.25}$$

As shown in the previous text, $\phi_k(\cdot)$ is monotonically increasing, so we obtain

$$y_{ij}(t)\phi_k(y_{ij}(t)) \begin{cases} > 0, & \text{if } y_{ij}(t) \neq 0; \\ = 0, & \text{if } y_{ij}(t) = 0; \end{cases} \tag{17.26}$$

which guarantees that $\dot{p}_{ij}(t) < 0$ for $y_{ij}(t) \neq 0$, and $\dot{p}_{ij}(t) = 0$ for $y_{ij}(t) = 0$. That is to say, $y_{ij}(t) \leq 0$ for any i, j, so $Y(t)$ can converge to zero.

The proof is completed. ∎

17.3.2 Finite-Time Convergence

The FTZNN models not only can achieve global convergence but also can accomplish the finite-time convergence. In other word, they have better convergence performance. In this section, we will provide three theorems to show the finite-time convergent property of the proposed three FTZNN models.

Theorem 17.2 *Given smoothly time-varying coefficient matrices $A(t) \in \mathbb{R}^{m \times m}$, $B(t) \in \mathbb{R}^{n \times n}$, and $C(t) \in \mathbb{R}^{m \times n}$, FTZNN-1 model (17.17) can achieve finite-time convergence. The convergence time upper bound T_1 satisfies the following equation:*

$$T_1 \leq \begin{cases} \frac{2\alpha(p(0)^{(\alpha-1)/2\alpha}-1)}{\gamma(\alpha-1)} + \frac{2}{\gamma(1-\alpha)}, & p(0) \geq 1, \\ \frac{2}{\gamma(1-\alpha)}p(0)^{(1-\alpha)/2}, & p(0) < 1, \end{cases} \tag{17.27}$$

where $p(0) = |y^+(0)|^2$ with $y^+(0) = \max\{|y_{ij}(0)|\}$.

Proof: When $U(0)$ is outside the solution set, $\operatorname{STP}(Y(0)) = 1$ which means that every element of $\operatorname{STP}(Y(0))$ equals to 1. Therefore, we have $\operatorname{STP}(y_{ij}(0)) = 1$. From (17.16), we acquire

$$\dot{y}_{ij}(t) = -\gamma \phi_1(y_{ij}(t)), \quad i = 1, 2, \ldots, m \text{ and } j = 1, 2, \ldots, n. \tag{17.28}$$

Then, we define $y^+(t) = \max |(y_{ij}(t))|$ which is used to calculate the convergence time upper bound. By Comparison Lemma, we have $-|y^+(t)| < y_{ij}(t) < |y^+(t)|$. Hence, we just need guarantee that $|y^+(t)|$ achieves finite-time convergence. Substituting the expression of $|y^+(t)|$ into (17.28), we have

$$\dot{y}^+(t) = -\gamma \phi_1(y^+(t)).$$

Define the Lyapunov function $p(t) = |y^+(t)|^2$, whose time derivative along this dynamics is computed as follows:

$$
\begin{aligned}
\dot{p}(t) &= 2y^+(t)\dot{y}^+(t) \\
&= -2\gamma y^+(t)\phi_1(y^+(t)) \\
&= -\gamma(|y^+(t)|^{\alpha+1} + |y^+(t)|^{\frac{1}{\alpha}+1}) \\
&= -\gamma(p(t)^{\frac{\alpha+1}{2}} + p(t)^{\frac{\alpha+1}{2\alpha}}).
\end{aligned}
\tag{17.29}
$$

If $p(0) \geq 1$, from Eq. (17.29), we have the following inequality:

$$\dot{p}(t) \leq -\gamma p(t)^{\frac{\alpha+1}{2\alpha}}, \tag{17.30}$$

from which we can obtain

$$\mathrm{d}p(t) \leq -\gamma p(t)^{\frac{\alpha+1}{2\alpha}}\,\mathrm{d}t. \tag{17.31}$$

Integrating both sides of the formula (17.31) from 0 to t, we have

$$\int_{p(0)}^{p(t)} p(t)^{-\frac{\alpha+1}{2\alpha}}\,\mathrm{d}p(t) \leq -\gamma \int_0^t \mathrm{d}t.$$

Simplify the inequality after integration yields to

$$p(t) \leq \left[\frac{\alpha-1}{2\alpha}(-\gamma t + \frac{2\alpha}{\alpha-1}p(0)^{\frac{\alpha-1}{2\alpha}})\right]^{\frac{2\alpha}{\alpha-1}}. \tag{17.32}$$

Setting the left-hand side of this inequality equal to 1, we get the value of t_1:

$$t_1 = \frac{2\alpha(p(0)^{(\alpha-1)/2\alpha} - 1)}{\gamma(\alpha-1)}. \tag{17.33}$$

Thus, after time t_1, $p(t)$ decreases to 1. When $p(t) \leq 1$, the inequality (17.29) shows that

$$\dot{p}(t) \leq -\gamma p(t)^{\frac{\alpha+1}{2}}. \tag{17.34}$$

Similar to solving for t_1, we compute the remaining convergence time t_2:

$$t_2 = \frac{2}{(1-\alpha)\gamma}. \tag{17.35}$$

Hence, we obtain the convergence time upper bound $T_1 < t_1 + t_2$.

If $p(0) \leq 1$, from Eq. (17.29), we have the following inequality:

$$\dot{p}(t) \leq -\gamma p(t)^{\frac{\alpha+1}{2}}, \text{ and } \mathrm{d}p(t) \leq -\gamma p(t)^{\frac{\alpha+1}{2}}\,\mathrm{d}t.$$

Integrating both sides of the differential inequality $\int_{p(0)}^{p(t)} p(t)^{-\frac{\alpha+1}{2}} \, dp(t) \leq -\gamma \int_0^t \, dt$, the convergence time upper bound t_3 can be computed as

$$t_3 = \frac{2}{\gamma(1-\alpha)} p(0)^{\frac{(1-\alpha)}{2}}. \tag{17.36}$$

The proof is completed. ∎

Theorem 17.3 *Given smoothly time-varying coefficient matrices $A(t) \in \mathbb{R}^{m \times m}$, $B(t) \in \mathbb{R}^{n \times n}$, and $C(t) \in \mathbb{R}^{m \times n}$, FTZNN-2 model (17.19) can accomplish finite-time convergence for solving time-varying LMIs. The convergence time upper bound T_2 is calculated as*

$$T_2 \leq \begin{cases} \dfrac{2\alpha \ln\left[\frac{2}{p(0)^{(\alpha-1)/2\alpha}+1}\right]}{\gamma(1-\alpha)} + \dfrac{2\ln 2}{\gamma(1-\alpha)}, & p(0) \geq 1, \\[4mm] \dfrac{2\ln\left[1+p(0)^{(1-\alpha)/2}\right]}{\gamma(1-\alpha)}, & p(0) < 1, \end{cases} \tag{17.37}$$

where α, γ and $p(0)$ are defined as before.

Proof: Similar to Theorem 17.2, from (17.18), we have

$$\dot{y}_{ij}(t) = -\gamma\phi_2(y_{ij}(t)), \quad i = 1, 2, \ldots, m \text{ and } j = 1, 2, \ldots, n. \tag{17.38}$$

Then, the derivative of the Lyapunov function along time t is computed as follows:

$$\begin{aligned} \dot{p}(t) &= 2y^+(t)\dot{y}^+(t) \\ &= -2\gamma y^+(t)\phi_2(y^+(t)) \\ &= -\gamma(|y^+(t)|^{\alpha+1} + |y^+(t)|^2 + |y^+(t)|^{\frac{1}{\alpha}+1}) \\ &= -\gamma(p(t)^{\frac{\alpha+1}{2}} + p(t) + p(t)^{\frac{\alpha+1}{2\alpha}}). \end{aligned} \tag{17.39}$$

If $p(0) \geq 1$, considering Eq. (17.39), the following inequality is satisfied:

$$\dot{p}(t) \leq -\gamma(p(t) + p(t)^{\frac{\alpha+1}{2\alpha}}), \tag{17.40}$$

which can be rewritten as

$$\frac{dp(t)}{p(t)^{(\alpha+1)/2\alpha} + p(t)} \leq -\gamma dt. \tag{17.41}$$

Integrating the formula (17.41) from 0 to t yields

$$\int_{p(0)}^{p(t)} \frac{1}{p(t)^{(\alpha+1)/2\alpha} + p(t)} \, dp(t) \leq \int_0^t -\gamma \, dt,$$

which can be rewritten as follows:

$$\frac{2\alpha}{\alpha - 1} \int_{p(0)}^{p(t)} \frac{1}{1 + p(t)^{(\alpha-1)/2\alpha}} \, d(p(t)^{(\alpha-1)/2\alpha}) \leq \int_0^t -\gamma \, dt.$$

Let $p(t)$ equal to 1, t_4 satisfies the following equality:

$$t_4 = \frac{2\alpha \ln\left[\frac{2}{p(0)^{(\alpha-1)/2\alpha}+1}\right]}{\gamma(1-\alpha)}. \tag{17.42}$$

When $t \geq t_4$, we have $p(t) \leq 1$. It follows from the condition (17.39) that

$$\dot{p}(t) \leq -\gamma(p(t)^{\frac{\alpha+1}{2}} + p(t)). \tag{17.43}$$

There exists t_5 satisfying the equation:

$$t_5 = \frac{2\ln 2}{\gamma(1-\alpha)}. \tag{17.44}$$

The convergence time upper bound $T_2 < t_4 + t_5$.

If $p(0) \leq 1$, the inequality (17.43) holds and its differential form can be obtained:

$$\frac{dp(t)}{p(t) + p(t)^{(\alpha+1)/2}} \leq -\gamma dt. \tag{17.45}$$

Integrating both sides of the formula from 0 to t, we have

$$\int_{p(0)}^{p(t)} \frac{1}{p(t) + p(t)^{(\alpha+1)/2}}\, dp(t) \leq \int_0^t -\gamma\, dt,$$

which can be rewritten as

$$\frac{2}{1-\alpha} \int_{p(0)}^{p(t)} \frac{1}{1 + p(t)^{(1-\alpha)/2}}\, d(p(t)^{(1-\alpha)/2}) \leq \int_0^t -\gamma\, dt.$$

Thus, the convergence upper bound $T_2 < t_6$ satisfies the following equation:

$$t_6 = \frac{2\ln\left[1 + p(0)^{(1-\alpha)/2}\right]}{\gamma(1-\alpha)}. \tag{17.46}$$

That completes the proof. ∎

Theorem 17.4 *Given smoothly time-varying coefficient matrices $A(t) \in \mathbb{R}^{m\times m}$, $B(t) \in \mathbb{R}^{n\times n}$, and $C(t) \in \mathbb{R}^{m\times n}$, FTZNN-3 model (17.21) can accomplish finite-time convergence and greatly shorten the convergence time. Its upper bound T_3 satisfies the following formula:*

$$T_3 \leq \begin{cases} \dfrac{2\alpha \ln\left[\frac{1+\frac{k_2}{k_3}p(0)^{(\alpha-1)/2\alpha}}{1+\frac{k_2}{k_3}}\right]}{k_2\gamma(\alpha-1)} + \dfrac{2\ln\left[1+\frac{k_2}{k_1}\right]}{k_2\gamma(1-\alpha)}, & p(0) \geq 1, \\[4mm] \dfrac{2\ln\left[1+\frac{k_2}{k_1}p(0)^{(1-\alpha)/2}\right]}{k_2\gamma(1-\alpha)}, & p(0) < 1, \end{cases} \tag{17.47}$$

where α, γ and $p(0)$ are defined as before.

Proof: From (17.20), the ijth element of $Y(t)$ can be rewritten as

$$\dot{y}_{ij}(t) = -\gamma\phi_3(y_{ij}(t)). \tag{17.48}$$

According to the definition of the Lyapunov function as before, its derivative that reflects the dynamic change of the model is obtained as

$$
\begin{aligned}
\dot{p}(t) &= 2y^+(t)\dot{y}^+(t) \\
&= -2\gamma y^+(t)\phi_3(y^+(t)) \\
&= -\gamma(k_1|y^+(t)|^{\alpha+1} + k_2|y^+(t)|^2 + k_3|y^+(t)|^{\frac{1}{\alpha}+1}) \\
&= -\gamma(p(t)^{k_1\frac{\alpha+1}{2}} + k_2p(t) + k_3p(t)^{\frac{\alpha+1}{2\alpha}}).
\end{aligned}
\tag{17.49}
$$

If $p(0) > 1$, the following result is satisfied:

$$
\dot{p}(t) \le -\gamma(k_2p(t) + k_3p(t)^{\frac{\alpha+1}{2\alpha}}),
\tag{17.50}
$$

which can be written as

$$
\frac{2\alpha}{k_3(\alpha-1)} \cdot \frac{d(p(t)^{(\alpha-1)/2\alpha})}{1 + \frac{k_2}{k_3}p(t)^{((\alpha-1)/2\alpha)}} \le -\gamma dt.
\tag{17.51}
$$

Integrating two sides of (17.51) from 0 to t,

$$
\frac{2\alpha}{k_2(\alpha-1)} \int_{p(0)}^{p(t)} \frac{1}{1 + \frac{k_2}{k_3}p(t)^{((\alpha-1)/2\alpha)}} \, d(p(t)^{(\alpha-1)/2\alpha}) \le \int_0^t -\gamma \, dt.
\tag{17.52}
$$

Let $p(t)$ equal to 1, we can get the time t_7:

$$
t_7 = \frac{2\alpha}{k_2\gamma(1-\alpha)} \ln\left[\frac{1 + \frac{k_2}{k_3}p(0)^{(\alpha-1)/2\alpha}}{1 + \frac{k_2}{k_3}} \right].
\tag{17.53}
$$

When $p(0) < 1$, (17.49) satisfies the following equation:

$$
\dot{p}(t) \le -\gamma(k_1p(t)^{\frac{\alpha+1}{2}} + k_2p(t)).
\tag{17.54}
$$

Repeating this process until the $p(t)$ converges to 0, we can get t_8:

$$
t_8 = \frac{2\ln\left[1 + \frac{k_2}{k_1}\right]}{k_2\gamma(1-\alpha)}.
\tag{17.55}
$$

The upper bound of convergence time $T_3 < t_7 + t_8$.

If $p(0) < 1$, analog to the proving course of $p(0) > 1$, the derivative of Lyapunov function can be shown as

$$
\frac{2}{k_2(1-\alpha)} \int_{p(0)}^{p(t)} \frac{1}{1 + \frac{k_2}{k_1}p(t)^{(1-\alpha)/2}} \, d(p(t)^{(1-\alpha)/2}) \le \int_0^t -\gamma \, dt.
$$

In the same way, integrating both sides of the type, we can calculate the convergence time t_9 as

$$
t_9 = \frac{2\ln\left[1 + \frac{k_2}{k_1}p(0)^{(1-\alpha)/2}\right]}{k_2\gamma(1-\alpha)}.
\tag{17.56}
$$

This proof is completed. ∎

17.4 Illustrative Verification

In Section 17.2, three FTZNN models together with their theoretical analysis have been presented. In this part, for illustration and comparison, a numerical example is given to evaluate the performance of the FTZNN models activated by different AFs for solving time-varying LMIs. To testify the superiority of three FTZNN models, some comparative experiments have also been conducted under the same conditions.

For illustration and simulation, let us consider a specific time-varying LMI with the following coefficient matrices $A(t)$, $B(t)$, and $C(t)$:

$$A(t) = \begin{bmatrix} 3 + \sin(4t) & \cos(4t)/2 & \cos(4t) \\ \cos(4t)/2 & 3 + \sin(4t) & \cos(4t)/2 \\ \cos(4t) & \cos(4t)/2 & 3 + \sin(4t) \end{bmatrix},$$

$$B(t) = \begin{bmatrix} \sin(4t) & \cos(4t) \\ -\cos(4t) & \sin(4t) \end{bmatrix} \text{ and }$$

$$C(t) = \begin{bmatrix} \sin(3t) & \cos(3t) \\ \cos(4t) + 1 & \sin(4t) + 1 \\ \sin(5t) + \cos(5t) & \sin(5t)\cos(5t) \end{bmatrix}.$$

Figure 17.1 shows the state trajectories of $U(t)$ by applying FTZNN-1 model (17.17) with $\gamma = 1$ and $\alpha = 0.5$, where the dotted lines represent the theoretical upper bound of the solution set with each element denoted by $u_{ij}^*(t)$, while the solid lines show the actual trajectories with each element denoted by $u_{ij}(t)$. It can be seen that the solid lines gradually coincides with the dotted lines over time. In other words, the simulation results shown in Figure 17.1a–f can constitute the solution of the aforementioned time-varying LMI.

Then, the residual errors $\|H(t)w(t) - \text{vec}(C(t))\|_2 = \|A(t)U(t)B(t) - C(t)\|_F$ (where $\| \cdot \|_2$ denotes two norm of a vector and $\| \cdot \|_F$ denotes Frobenius norm of a matrix) are shown in Figure 17.2. Obviously, the residual error function reflects the whole convergence process. From Figure 17.2, three FTZNN models obviously have shorter convergence time than the conventional ZNN models activated by the linear activation function (17.8), the power function (17.9), the bipolar-sigmoid function (17.10), and the smooth power-sigmoid function (17.11) [12, 13]. Moreover, among them, FTZNN-3 model (17.21) with three tunable parameters obtains the best convergence performance for solving LMIs. In addition, it can be seen that such three FTZNN models can reach zero within three seconds. Meanwhile, the corresponding results of the traditional ZNN models for finding LMIs solution still have some estimation errors at this time.

For the sake of demonstrating the finite-time convergence property of FTZNN models for solving LMIs, a specific initial state $U(0)$ is given. According to the preceding theorems, we can calculate the convergence time upper bound.

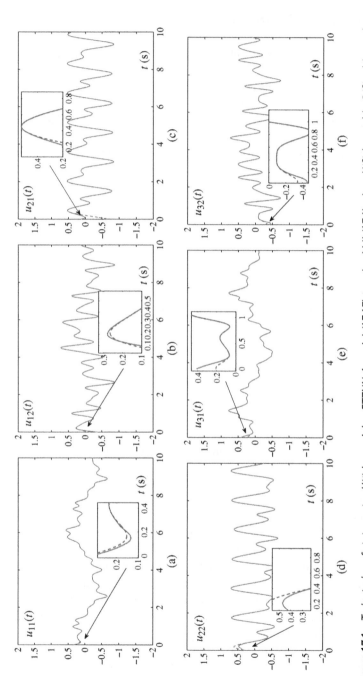

Figure 17.1 Trajectories of state vector $U(t)$ by applying FTZNN-1 model (17.17) to solve LMI (17.1) when $U(0)$ is outside $\Omega(0)$ with $\gamma = 1$ and $\alpha = 0.3$. (a) $u_{11}(t)$, (b) $u_{12}(t)$, (c) $u_{21}(t)$, (d) $u_{22}(t)$, (e) $u_{31}(t)$, and (f) $u_{32}(t)$.

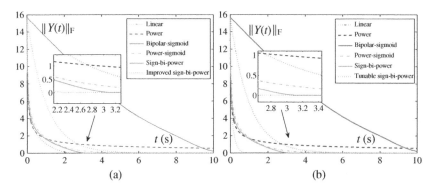

Figure 17.2 Comparisons of three FTZNN models with the conventional ZNN models activated by other AFs with $\gamma = 1$ and $\alpha = 0.3$ when $p(0) > 1$. (a) By FTZNN-1 model (17.17) and FTZNN-2 model (17.19). (b) By FTZNN-1 model (17.17) and FTZNN-3 model (17.21).

Considering that different states can lead to different convergence upper bound, the simulation cases are decomposed into two parts.

Case I Let $U(0) = [-1, -0.5; -3, 2; -1.5, 1]$, which represents that $A(0)U(0)$ $B(0) - C(0) = [-0.5, -7; -8.25, -11.25; -4.5, -7]$, and $p(0) = |y^+(0)|^2 = (11.25)^2 = 126.5625$. The parameters of FTZNN-1 model (17.17) are given as $\alpha = 0.3$ and $\gamma = 1$. By Theorem 17.2, the convergence time upper bound t_a is given as

$$t_a = \frac{2\alpha(p(0)^{(\alpha-1)/2\alpha} - 1)}{\gamma(\alpha - 1)} + \frac{2}{\gamma(1 - \alpha)} \approx 3.7113 \text{ seconds.}$$

Let $\alpha = 0.3$ and $\gamma = 1$. By Theorem 17.3, the convergence time upper bound t_b for FTZNN-2 model (17.19) is given as

$$t_b = \frac{2\alpha \ln\left[\frac{2}{p(0)^{(\alpha-1)/2\alpha}+1}\right]}{\gamma(1 - \alpha)} + \frac{2\ln 2}{\gamma(1 - \alpha)} \approx 2.3942 \text{ seconds.}$$

Keeping α and γ the unchanged, let $k_1 = 1$, $k_2 = 10$, and $k_3 = 1$. According to Theorem 17.4, the convergence time upper bound t_c for FTZNN-3 model (17.21) is computed as

$$t_c = \frac{2\alpha \ln\left[\frac{1+\frac{k_2}{k_3}p(0)^{(\alpha-1)/2\alpha}}{1+\frac{k_2}{k_3}}\right]}{k_3\gamma(1 - \alpha)} + \frac{2\ln\left[1 + \frac{k_2}{k_1}\right]}{k_1\gamma(1 - \alpha)} \approx 1.0227 \text{ seconds.}$$

From Figure 17.2, it can be seen that the actual convergence time is smaller or equal to their corresponding theoretical upper bound of convergence time. Specifically, FTZNN-3 model (17.21) for solving LMIs can converge to zero within 0.75 seconds, FTZNN-2 model (17.19) spends 2.12 seconds, and FTZNN-1 model (17.17) needs 2.95 seconds to complete the process of convergence. Moreover, the distance between the actual time and theoretical analysis value can express the convergence performance. Hence, it can easily be concluded that FTZNN-3 model (17.21) has the best convergence performance, followed by FTZNN-2 model (17.19), and finally FTZNN-1 model (17.17).

Case II Let $U(0) = [0.3, 0.008; 0.1, -0.08; -0.34, -0.3]$, which represents that $A(0)U(0)B(0) - C(0) = [0.71, -0.79; 0.15, -0.004; -0.78, 0.6]$, and $p(0) = |y^+(0)|^2 = (0.79)^2 = 0.6241 < 1$. The parameters of FTZNN-1 model (17.17) are given as $\alpha = 0.3$ and $\gamma = 1$. By Theorem 17.2, the convergence time upper bound t_a is given as

$$t_a = \frac{2}{\gamma(1-\alpha)} p(0)^{(1-\alpha)/2} \approx 2.4225 \text{ seconds.}$$

While using FTZNN-2 model (17.19) to solve (17.1), by Theorem 17.3, the convergence time upper bound t_b is given as

$$t_b = \frac{2\ln\left[1 + p(0)^{(1-\alpha)/2}\right]}{\gamma(1-\alpha)} \approx 1.7544 \text{ seconds.}$$

Let $k_1 = 1, k_2 = 10$, and $k_3 = 1$, by Theorem 17.4, the convergence time upper bound t_c for FTZNN-3 model (17.21) is calculated as

$$t_c = \frac{2\ln\left[1 + \frac{k_2}{k_1} p(0)^{(1-\alpha)/2}\right]}{k_2\gamma(1-\alpha)} \approx 0.6426 \text{ seconds.}$$

Similar to the situation when $p(0) > 1$, from Figure 17.3, three FTZNN models have better convergence performance. In addition, the distance between the theoretical computational time and the actual time using FTZNN-3 model (17.21) is shorter than the other. It demonstrates the superiority of FTZNN-3 model (17.21) with the tunable sign-bi-power AF via numerical simulations.

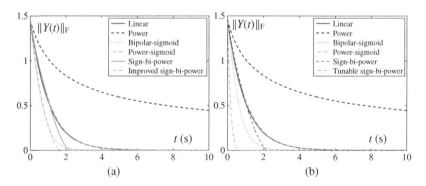

Figure 17.3 Comparisons of three FTZNN models with the conventional ZNN models activated by other AFs with $\gamma = 1$ and $\alpha = 0.3$ when $p(0) < 1$. (a) By FTZNN-1 model (17.17) and FTZNN-2 model (17.19). (b) By FTZNN-1 model (17.17) and FTZNN-3 model (17.21).

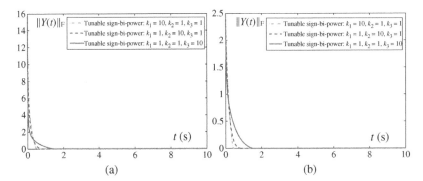

Figure 17.4 Comparisons among three cases of FTZNN-3 model (17.21) with different tunable parameters. (a) $p(0) > 1$. (b) $p(0) < 1$.

For further investigation, we have done a contrast experiment to determine which parameter has the greatest effect on the convergence rate of FTZNN-3 model (17.21). In Figure 17.4, the aforementioned LMI problem can be solved by setting three different cases for FTZNN-3 model (17.21), i.e. $k_1 = 10$, $k_2 = 1$ and $k_3 = 1$; $k_1 = 1$, $k_2 = 10$ and $k_3 = 1$; and $k_1 = 0$, $k_2 = 1$ and $k_3 = 10$. According to the simulation results, we can see that three cases are able to make the residual error achieve to zero rapidly. Under the first case, i.e. $k_1 = 10$, $k_2 = 1$ and $k_3 = 1$, the convergence time is the least. This is consistent with the results of theoretical analysis. Because whatever the initial state $p(0)$ is, there is always a period when $p(0) < 1$. In other words, the time from $p(0) < 1$ to 0 is unavoidable and must be experienced. What determines the length of convergence time for FTZNN-3 model (17.21) is the value of k_1, so the greater k_1, the shorter convergence time.

Furthermore, in Figure 17.5, it is worth pointing out that the convergence time is reduced from 2.17 to 0.425 seconds when the value of k_1 is increased from 1 to 10.

Figure 17.5 Transient behaviors of the error function $\|Y(t)\|_2$ synthesized by FTZNN-3 model (17.21) with $k_2 = 1$, $k_3 = 1$ and different values of k_1.

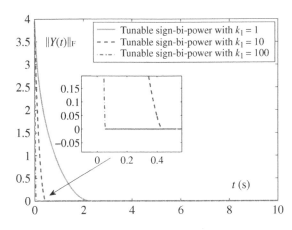

When $k_1 = 100$, the residual error only needs 0.055 seconds to converge to zero. Therefore, the value of k_1 is an important influential factor for the convergence time of FTZNN-3 model (17.21) when applied to solving time-varying LMIs.

17.5 Chapter Summary

For the purpose of solving the time-varying LMIs more faster in finite-time, three FTZNN models are presented and investigated in this chapter by exploring three nonlinear activation functions. It has been proved that three FTZNN models are globally stable according to the Lyapunov theory. Then, the convergence upper bounds of three FTZNN models are estimated to prove the finite-time convergence performance. Numerical comparison results ulteriorly reveal the superiority performance of three FTZNN models for solving LMIs. That is to say, the state solutions by using FTZNN models can converge to the theoretical solution set of time-varying LMIs accurately and rapidly.

References

1 F. Xu and Z. Li *et al.*, Zeroing neural network for solving time-varying linear equation and inequality systems, *IEEE Trans. Neural Netw. Learn. Syst.*, 30(8) (2019) 2346–2357.

2 L. Jin and S. Li *et al.*, Robot manipulator control using neural networks: A survey, *Neurocomputing*, 285 (2018) 23–34.

3 L. Xiao and B. Liao *et al.* Design and analysis of FTZNN applied to the real-time solution of a nonstationary Lyapunov equation and tracking control of a wheeled mobile manipulator, *IEEE Trans. Ind. Inform.*, 14(1) (2018) 98–105.

4 P. Witczak and K. Patan *et al.*, A neural network approach to simultaneous state and actuator fault estimation under unknown input decoupling, *Neurocomputing*, 250(9) (2017) 65–75.

5 B. Huang and G. Hui *et al.*, A projection neural network with mixed delays for solving linear variational inequality, *Neurocomputing*, 125 (2014) 28–32.

6 D. Guo and Y. Zhang, A new inequality-based obstacle-avoidance MVN scheme and its application to redundant robot manipulators, *IEEE Trans. Syst. Man Cybern. Part C Appl. Rev.*, 42(6) (2012) 1326–1340.

7 Y. Zhang and J. Wang, Obstacle avoidance for kinematically redundant manipulators using a dual neural network, *IEEE Trans. Cybern.*, 34(1) (2004) 752–759.

8 L. Xiao and Y. Zhang *et al.*, Performance benefits of robust nonlinear zeroing neural network for finding accurate solution of Lyapunov equation in presence of various noises, *IEEE Trans. Ind. Inform.*, 15(9) (2019) 5161–5171.

9 F. Cheng, T. Chen, and Y. Sun, Resolving manipulator redundancy under inequality constraints, *IEEE Trans. Robot. Autom.*, 10(1) (1994) 65–71.

10 Y. Zhang and B. Cai *et al.*, Bi-criteria velocity minimization of robot manipulators using a linear variational inequalities-based primal-dual neural network and PUMA560 example, *Adv. Robot.*, 22(13–14) (2008) 1479–1496.

11 Y. Zhang and M. Yang *et al.*, New discrete solution model for solving future different-level linear inequality and equality with robot manipulator control, *IEEE Trans. Ind. Inform.*, 15(4) (2019) 1975–1984.

12 Y. Zhang and S. S. Ge, Design and analysis of a general recurrent neural network model for time-varying matrix inversion, *IEEE Trans. Neural Netw.*, 16(6) (2005) 1477–1490.

13 J. Kamruzzaman and S. M. Aziz, A note on activation function in multilayer feedforward learning, IEEE International Joint Conference on Neural Networks, volume 1 (2002) 519–523.

18

Design Scheme II of FTZNN

18.1 Introduction

Solving time-varying linear inequalities occupies an increasingly important position in various applied science and engineering fields [1–3]. For example, based on solving linear variational inequality, the redundant joint drift and repetitive motion of the robot was solved in [4]. As to multiple input multiple output system (such as wind engine), Rahimilarki *et al.* [5] proposed a robust fault analysis system based on linear matrix inequality. In [6], Liu *et al.* obtained the parameters of the controller by solving linear inequalities and designed an output tracking controller. Besides, solving linear inequalities can also be the conditions of the method to a variety of problems, such as quadratic programming problem [7], convex programming problem [8], and finite-time stability [9].

In this chapter, we consider proposing a new finite-time zeroing neural network (FTZNN) model that not only makes error function achieve noise-tolerant convergence, but also accomplishes finite-time and rapid convergence. Inspired by Proportion Integration Differentiation (PID) controller, the integral term in proportional integral and differential control can effectively eliminate the system noise. For the static error in the system, it will be reduced as part of the system error as time increases in the system. When the static error is small, the integral term amplifies the error until it decreases to 0. When solving the linear matrix inequality with noise, the system will define noise as part of the error, so that the influence of noise will gradually decrease to 0 with the error. We give the theoretical analysis of global, finite-time and noise tolerant convergence of noise-tolerance finite-time zeroing neural network (NT-FTZNN) model. The numerical simulative results ulteriorly verify these properties. In addition, in order to verify the noise tolerance performance of NT-FTZNN model, we compared it with the traditional zeroing neural network (ZNN) model. The experiment proves that the NT-FTZNN model can indeed eliminate all kinds of noise, and for the defined parameters, the larger the set parameters are, the better the convergence is.

Zeroing Neural Networks: Finite-time Convergence Design, Analysis and Applications,
First Edition. Lin Xiao and Lei Jia.

18.2 NT-FTZNN Model Deisgn

In this section, we will give the design formulation of the NT-FTZNN model which is based on the conventional ZNN models.

18.2.1 Problem Formulation

Similar to the problem solved by most ZNN models, the main purpose of this chapter is to find the solution set of time-varying linear inequalities, which is shown as follows.

$$A(t)U(t) \le B(t), \tag{18.1}$$

where $A(t) \in \mathbb{R}^{m \times m}$ and $B(t) \in \mathbb{R}^{m \times n}$ denote the time-varying coefficient matrices; and $U(t) \in \mathbb{R}^{m \times n}$ denotes an unknown matrix to be solved.

18.2.2 ZNN Model

To observe the convergence process of solving linear inequalities, we define the error function $Y(t)$ which is formulated as

$$Y(t) = A(t)U(t) - B(t), \tag{18.2}$$

where $Y(t) \in \mathbb{R}^{m \times n}$.

By learning about previous generations, the conventional zeroing neural network (CZNN) model for solving linear inequalities can be constructed as

$$\dot{Y}(t) = -\gamma \text{STP}(Y(0)) \diamond \Phi(Y(t)), \tag{18.3}$$

where $\Phi(\cdot) : \mathbb{R}^{m \times n} \to \mathbb{R}^{m \times n}$ is a monotonously increasing odd activation function (AF) array, γ is a positive parameter and $\text{STP}(\cdot) : \mathbb{R}^{m \times n} \to \mathbb{R}^{m \times n}$ stands for a step function whose decomposition form of each dimension is defined as

$$\text{stp}(x) = \begin{cases} 1, & x > 0; \\ 0, & x \le 0. \end{cases}$$

Besides, the operator $\diamond$ is defined as

$$b \diamond c = \begin{bmatrix} b_1 c_1 \\ b_2 c_2 \\ \vdots \\ b_n c_n \end{bmatrix}.$$

When we need to investigate the noise-tolerance of the CZNN model for solving linear inequalities, the formulation of the CZNN model should be changed to

$$\dot{Y}(t) = -\gamma \text{STP}(Y(0)) \diamond \Phi(Y(t)) + \eta, \tag{18.4}$$

where η represents external additive noise in matrix form.

18.2.3 NT-FTZNN Model

For the sake of the noise reduction, we construct a novel ZNN model, which is inspired by PID control. The main ideal of the NT-FTZNN model is adding an integral item to make full use of its error memory function, which can depress noise effectively. In order to construct this model, we define a new error function at first which is given as follows:

$$\varepsilon(t) = Y(t) + \lambda \int_0^t \Phi(Y(\tau)) \, d\tau. \tag{18.5}$$

The NT-FTZNN model based on the definition of new error function is formulated as

$$\dot{\varepsilon}(t) = -\gamma \text{STP}(\varepsilon(0)) \diamond \Phi(\varepsilon(t)). \tag{18.6}$$

Expand the previous equation to obtain the following formula:

$$\dot{Y}(t) = -\gamma \text{STP}(Y(0)) \diamond \Phi(Y(t) + \lambda \int_0^t \Phi(Y(\tau)) \, d\tau) - \lambda \Phi(\text{STP}(Y(0)) \diamond Y(t)). \tag{18.7}$$

When applying NT-FTZNN model (18.6) to solve linear inequalities with noise, we substitute Eq. (18.2) into formula (18.7). Then, we get the implicit kinetic equation:

$$\begin{aligned}
A(t)\dot{U}(t) = {}& -\gamma \text{STP}(A(0)U(0) - B(0)) \diamond \Phi(A(t)U(t) \\
& - B(t) + \lambda \int_0^t \Phi(A(\tau)U(\tau) - B(\tau)) \, d\tau) \\
& - \lambda \Phi(\text{STP}(A(0)U(0) - B(0)) \diamond (A(t)U(t) \\
& - B(t))) + \dot{B}(t) - \dot{A}(t)U(t) + \eta,
\end{aligned} \tag{18.8}$$

18.2.4 Activation Functions

The AF $\Phi(\cdot)$ mentioned earlier can be any monotone increasing odd function, and it is frequently used as an AF of ZNN models for solving various kinds of equations. There are some typical AFs that are shown as follows:

(1) The linear AF [10]:

$$\phi(x) = x; \tag{18.9}$$

(2) The power AF [11]:

$$\phi(x) = x^l, \quad l \geq 3; \tag{18.10}$$

(3) The bipolar-sigmoid AF [12]:

$$\phi(x) = \frac{1 + \exp(-l_1)}{1 - \exp(-l_1)} \frac{1 - \exp(-l_1 x)}{1 + \exp(-l_1 x)}, \quad l_1 > 2; \tag{18.11}$$

(4) The power-sigmoid AF [13]:

$$\phi(x) = \frac{1}{2}x^{l_2} + \frac{1 + \exp(-l_3)}{1 - \exp(-l_3)}\frac{1 - \exp(-l_3 x)}{1 + \exp(-l_3 x)}, \quad l_2 \geq 3, \; l_3 > 2. \qquad (18.12)$$

Nevertheless, these aforementioned AFs can only guarantee the convergence properties. Hence, a new class of AF, sign-bi-power AF is presented, which is aimed to finite-time convergence.

(1) The sign-bi-power AF:

$$\phi_1(x) = \frac{1}{2}|x|^{\alpha}\mathrm{sign}(x) + \frac{1}{2}|x|^{\frac{1}{\alpha}}\mathrm{sign}(x), \qquad (18.13)$$

where $0 < \alpha < 1$ and $\mathrm{sign}(\cdot)$ is defined as

$$\mathrm{sign}(x) = \begin{cases} 1, & \text{if } x > 0; \\ 0, & \text{if } x = 0; \\ -1, & \text{if } x < 0. \end{cases}$$

(2) The improved sign-bi-power AF:

$$\phi_2(x) = \frac{1}{2}|x|^{\alpha}\mathrm{sign}(x) + \frac{1}{2}x + \frac{1}{2}|x|^{\frac{1}{\alpha}}\mathrm{sign}(x). \qquad (18.14)$$

18.3 Theoretical Analysis

In this part, the proof of global convergence, finite-time convergence and noise-tolerant convergence properties for NT-FTZNN model will be given. It is worth pointing out that when the initial state $U(0)$ satisfies problem (18.1) to be solved, according to the definition of the error function, we can know that the derivative of $Y(t)$ always keeps zero. Therefore, we only need to consider the situation where $U(0)$ is outside of the solution set.

18.3.1 Global Convergence

First of all, we need to prove the global convergence of the noise-free NT-FTZNN model for solving linear inequalities.

Theorem 18.1 *According to the definition of the new error function, we have* $\dot{\varepsilon}(t) = -\gamma STP(\varepsilon(0)) \diamond \Phi(\varepsilon(t))$, *where* γ *is a positive parameter,* $\Phi(\cdot)$ *denotes a monotone increasing odd function. In addition, when* $U(0)$ *is outside of the solution set, the aforementioned formula can be simplified as* $\dot{\varepsilon}(t) = -\gamma\Phi(\varepsilon(t))$. *Then,* $\varepsilon(t)$ *can globally converge to the equilibrium point. That is* $Y(t)$ *achieves global convergence.*

Proof: AFs (18.9)–(18.12) which are frequently used to activate the ZNN models have turned out the monotone increasing odd functions. So, we just have to prove that the sign-bi-power AFs process these properties.

$$\phi_1(-x) = \frac{1}{2}|-x|^\alpha \text{sign}(-x) + \frac{1}{2}|-x|^{\frac{1}{\alpha}} \text{sign}(-x)$$
$$= -\frac{1}{2}|x|^\alpha \text{sign}(x) - \frac{1}{2}|x|^{\frac{1}{\alpha}} \text{sign}(x)$$
$$= -\phi_1(x);$$
$$\phi_2(-x) = \frac{1}{2}|-x|^\alpha \text{sign}(-x) - \frac{1}{2}x + \frac{1}{2}|-x|^{\frac{1}{\alpha}} \text{sign}(-x)$$
$$= -\frac{1}{2}|x|^\alpha \text{sign}(x) - \frac{1}{2}x - \frac{1}{2}|x|^{\frac{1}{\alpha}} \text{sign}(x)$$
$$= -\phi_2(x).$$

Therefore, we can know that the sign-bi-power AFs are monotonically increasing odd functions.

Then, we define Lyapunov function $p_{ij}(t) = \varepsilon_{ij}^2(t)/2$, where $\varepsilon_{ij}(t)$ is the ijth element of $\varepsilon(t)$. On the basis of the simplified derivative of $\varepsilon(t)$, we have

$$\dot{\varepsilon}_{ij}(t) = -\gamma\phi(\varepsilon_{ij}(t)).$$

Thus, the derivative of Lyapunov function is formulated as

$$\dot{p}_{ij}(t) = -\gamma\varepsilon_{ij}(t)\phi(\varepsilon_{ij}(t)),$$

where γ is a positive parameter and $\phi(\cdot)$ monotonically increases.

The following analysis can be divided into two situations.

(1) When $\varepsilon_{ij}(t) = 0$, we can obtain $\dot{y}_{ij}(t) = -\lambda y_{ij}(t)$, where λ is positive and $y_{ij}(t)$ is the ijth element of $Y(t)$. It is obvious that $\dot{y}_{ij}(t) < 0$ which guarantees the error function $Y(t)$ can gradually decline to zero.

(2) When $\varepsilon_{ij}(t) \neq 0$, we can know that $\dot{p}_{ij}(t) < 0$. Then, the Lyapunov function value will decrease inch by inch till it equals to zero. At that time, it means that $\varepsilon_{ij}(t) = 0$ which goes back the first situation.

Hence, the proof is completed. The NT-FTZNN model can achieve global convergence when $Y(t)$ reaches the equilibrium point. To be specific, $Y(t)$ can converge to zero finally. ∎

18.3.2 Finite-Time Convergence

The noise-free NT-FTZNN model without AFs only can accomplish global convergence. Nonetheless, while using two sign-bi-power AFs, the NT-FTZNN model can realize finite-time convergence for solving linear time-varying inequalities. In this part, the exact proof will be given in the following text.

Theorem 18.2 *Given smoothly time-varying coefficient matrices $A(t) \in \mathbb{R}^{m \times m}$ and $B(t) \in \mathbb{R}^{m \times n}$, when activated by sign-bi-power AF, the NT-FTZNN model is shown as follows:*

$$\dot{\varepsilon}(t) = -\gamma \Phi_1(Y(t) + \lambda \int_0^t \Phi_1(Y(\tau)) \, d\tau), \qquad (18.15)$$

where $\Phi_1(\cdot)$ is defined in (18.13).

Proof: The whole proof process is divided in two cases.

Case I When $\varepsilon_{ij}(t) = 0$, we have

$$\dot{y}_{ij}(t) = -\lambda \phi_1(y_{ij}(t)). \qquad (18.16)$$

The convergence time upper bound satisfies the following condition:

$$T_1 \leq \frac{2p(0)^{(1-\alpha)/2}}{\lambda(1-\alpha)},$$

where $p(0) = |y^+(0)|^2$ with $y^+(0) = \max\{|y_{ij}(0)|\}$.

Then, define Lyapunov function as shown next:

$$p(t) = |y^+(t)|^2, \qquad (18.17)$$

where $y^+(t)$ denotes the element of $Y(t)$ with the initial state $y^+(0) = \max\{Y(0)\}$. We can get its derivative easily:

$$
\begin{aligned}
\dot{p}(t) &= 2y^+(t)\dot{y}^+(t) \\
&= -2\lambda\phi_1(y^+(t))y^+(t) \\
&= -\lambda(|y^+(t)|^{\alpha+1} + |y^+(t)|^{\frac{1}{\alpha}+1}) \\
&= -\lambda(p(t)^{\frac{\alpha+1}{2}} + p(t)^{\frac{\alpha+1}{2\alpha}}) \\
&\leq -\lambda p(t)^{\frac{\alpha+1}{2}},
\end{aligned}
\qquad (18.18)
$$

where $0 < \alpha < 1$. Break it up into differential forms:

$$\frac{dp(t)}{p(t)^{(1+\alpha)/2}} \leq -\lambda dt. \qquad (18.19)$$

Integrate both sides of inequality (18.19) from 0 to t and let $p(t)$ equal to 0:

$$\frac{2}{1-\alpha} \int_{p(0)}^0 \frac{dp(t)}{p(t)^{(1-\alpha)/2}} \leq -\lambda \int_0^t dt.$$

Then, we can calculate the time t_1:

$$t_1 = \frac{2p(0)^{(1-\alpha)/2}}{\lambda(1-\alpha)}.$$

Case II $\varepsilon_{ij}(t) \neq 0$, we have

$$\dot{\varepsilon}_{ij}(t) = -\gamma \phi_1(\varepsilon_{ij}(t)). \qquad (18.20)$$

The upper bound of convergence time T_2 satisfies the following inequality:

$$T_2 = T_a + T_b,$$

where $p(0) = |y^+(0)|^2$ with $y^+(0) = \max\{|y_{ij}(0)|\}$ and $p_1(0) = |\varepsilon^+(0)|^2$ with $\varepsilon^+(0) = \max\{|\varepsilon_{ij}(0)|\}$. According the definition of $\varepsilon(t)$, we have $p(0) = p_1(0)$. The definitions of T_a and T_b are given next:

$$T_a = T_1.$$

$$T_b \leq \begin{cases} \dfrac{2\alpha(p(0)^{(\alpha-1)/2\alpha}-1)}{\gamma(\alpha-1)} + \dfrac{2}{(1-\alpha)\gamma}, & p(0) \geq 1; \\ \dfrac{2}{\gamma(1-\alpha)}p(0)^{\frac{(1-\alpha)}{2}}, & p(0) < 1. \end{cases} \tag{18.21}$$

Similar to Case I, the definition of Lyapunov function is shown as follows:

$$p(t) = |\varepsilon^+(t)|^2, \tag{18.22}$$

where $\varepsilon^+(t)$ denotes the element of $\varepsilon(t)$ with the initial state $\varepsilon^+(0) = \max\{\varepsilon(0)\}$. Its derivative is displayed as

$$\begin{aligned} \dot{p}(t) &= 2\varepsilon^+(t)\dot{\varepsilon}^+(t) \\ &= 2\gamma\varepsilon^+(t)\phi_1(\varepsilon(t)) \\ &= -\gamma(|\varepsilon^+(t)|^{\alpha+1} + |\varepsilon^+(t)|^{\frac{1}{\alpha}+1}) \\ &= -\gamma(p(t)^{\frac{\alpha+1}{2}} + p(t)^{\frac{\alpha+1}{2\alpha}}). \end{aligned} \tag{18.23}$$

If $p(0) \geq 1$, from Eq. (18.23), we have the following inequality:

$$\dot{p}(t) \leq -\gamma p(t)^{\frac{\alpha+1}{2\alpha}},$$

from which we can obtain

$$dp(t) \leq -\gamma p(t)^{\frac{\alpha+1}{2\alpha}} dt. \tag{18.24}$$

Integrating both sides of the formula (18.24) from 0 to t, we have

$$\int_{p(0)}^{p(t)} p(t)^{-\frac{\alpha+1}{2\alpha}} dp(t) \leq -\gamma \int_0^t dt.$$

Simplifying the inequality after integration yields to

$$p(t) \leq \left[\frac{\alpha-1}{2\alpha} \left(-\gamma t + \frac{2\alpha}{\alpha-1} p(0)^{\frac{\alpha-1}{2\alpha}} \right) \right]^{\frac{2\alpha}{\alpha-1}}.$$

Setting the left-hand side of this inequality equal to 1, we get the value of t_2:

$$t_2 = \frac{2\alpha(p(0)^{(\alpha-1)/2\alpha} - 1)}{\gamma(\alpha-1)}.$$

Thus, after time t_2, $p(t)$ decreases to 1. When $p(t) \leq 1$, inequality (18.23) shows that:

$$\dot{p}(t) \leq -\gamma p(t)^{\frac{\alpha+1}{2}}.$$

Similar to solving for t_4, we compute the remaining convergence time t_3:

$$t_3 = \frac{2}{(1-\alpha)\gamma}.$$

Since then, the next step to calculate the convergence time goes back to Case I. Hence, we obtain the convergence time upper bound $T_2 < t' + t_2 + t_3$, where t' represents the whole time of Case I.

If $p(0) \leq 1$, from Eq. (18.23), we have the following inequality:

$$\dot{p}(t) \leq -\gamma p(t)^{\frac{\alpha+1}{2}} \quad \text{and} \quad dp(t) \leq -\gamma p(t)^{\frac{\alpha+1}{2}} dt.$$

Integrating both sides of inequality (18.24) $\int_{p(0)}^{p(t)} p(t)^{-\frac{\alpha+1}{2}} dp(t) \leq -\gamma \int_0^t dt$, the convergence time upper bound t_4 can be computed as

$$t_4 = \frac{2}{\gamma(1-\alpha)} p(0)^{\frac{(1-\alpha)}{2}}. \tag{18.25}$$

The convergence time upper bound T_2 of this situation means the sum of the time of Case I and t_4. The proof is completed. ∎

Theorem 18.3 *Given smoothly time-varying coefficient matrices $A(t) \in \mathbb{R}^{m \times m}$ and $B(t) \in \mathbb{R}^{m \times n}$, when activated by the improved sign-bi-power AF, NT-FTZNN model (18.6) is shown as follows:*

$$\dot{\varepsilon}(t) = -\gamma \Phi_2 \left(Y(t) + \lambda \int_0^t \Phi_1(Y(\tau)) d\tau \right), \tag{18.26}$$

where $\Phi_2(\cdot)$ is defined in (18.14).

Proof: The whole proof process is divided in two cases.

Case I When $\varepsilon_{ij}(t) = 0$, it is similar to Case I of Theorem 18.2.

Case II $\varepsilon_{ij}(t) \neq 0$, we have

$$\dot{\varepsilon}_{ij}(t) = -\gamma \phi_2(\varepsilon_{ij}(t)). \tag{18.27}$$

The upper bound of convergence time T_3 satisfies the following inequality:

$$T_3 = T_a + T_c,$$

where $p(0) = |y^+(0)|^2$ with $y^+(0) = \max\{|y_{ij}(0)|\}$ and $p_2(0) = |\varepsilon^+(0)|^2$ with $\varepsilon^+(0) = \max\{|\varepsilon_{ij}(0)|\}$. We have $p(0) = p_2(0)$. T_a is defined in (18.21) and T_c is defined as follows:

$$T_c \leq \begin{cases} \dfrac{2\alpha \ln\left[\frac{2}{p(0)^{(\alpha-1)/2\alpha}+1}\right]}{\gamma(1-\alpha)} + \dfrac{2\ln 2}{\gamma(1-\alpha)}, & p_1(0) \geq 1; \\ \dfrac{2\ln[1+p(0)^{(1-\alpha)/2}]}{\gamma(1-\alpha)}, & p_1(0) < 1. \end{cases}$$

Similar to Case I, the definition of Lyapunov function is shown as follows:

$$p(t) = |\varepsilon^+(t)|^2, \tag{18.28}$$

where $\varepsilon^+(t)$ denotes the element of $\varepsilon(t)$ with the initial state $\varepsilon^+(0) = \max\{\varepsilon(0)\}$. Its derivative is displayed as

$$
\begin{aligned}
\dot{p}(t) &= 2\varepsilon^+(t)\dot{\varepsilon}^+(t) \\
&= 2\gamma\varepsilon^+(t)\phi_2(\varepsilon(t)) \\
&= -\gamma(|\varepsilon^+(t)|^{\alpha+1} + |\varepsilon^+(t)|^2 + |\varepsilon^+(t)|^{\frac{1}{\alpha}+1}) \\
&= -\gamma(p(t)^{\frac{\alpha+1}{2}} + p(t) + p(t)^{\frac{\alpha+1}{2\alpha}}).
\end{aligned}
\tag{18.29}
$$

If $p(0) \geq 1$, from Eq. (18.29), we have the following inequality:

$$\dot{p}(t) \leq -\gamma(p(t) + p(t)^{\frac{\alpha+1}{2\alpha}}), \tag{18.30}$$

from which we can obtain

$$dp(t) \leq -\gamma(p(t) + p(t)^{\frac{\alpha+1}{2\alpha}})dt. \tag{18.31}$$

Integrating both sides of the formula (18.31) from 0 to t, we have

$$\int_{p(0)}^{p(t)} \frac{1}{p(t)^{(\alpha+1)/2\alpha} + p(t)} dp(t) \leq \int_0^t -\gamma \, dt,$$

which can be rewritten as follows:

$$\frac{2\alpha}{\alpha - 1} \int_{p(0)}^{p(t)} \frac{1}{1 + p(t)^{(\alpha-1)/2\alpha}} d(p(t)^{(\alpha-1)/2\alpha}) \leq \int_0^t -\gamma \, dt.$$

Setting the left-hand side of this inequality equal to 1, we get the value of t_4:

$$t_5 = \frac{2\alpha \ln \left[\frac{2}{p(0)^{(\alpha-1)/2\alpha}+1} \right]}{\gamma(1 - \alpha)}. \tag{18.32}$$

Thus, after time t_5, $p(t)$ decreases to 1. When $p_1(t) \leq 1$, the inequality (18.29) shows that:

$$\dot{p}(t) \leq -\gamma(p(t)^{\frac{\alpha+1}{2}} + p(t)). \tag{18.33}$$

Similar to solving for t_7, we compute the remaining convergence time t_5:

$$t_6 = \frac{2 \ln 2}{\gamma(1 - \alpha)}. \tag{18.34}$$

Since then, the next step to calculate the convergence time goes back to Case I. Hence, we obtain the convergence time upper bound $T_2 < t' + t_5 + t_6$, where t' represents the whole time of Case I.

If $p(0) \leq 1$, from Eq. (18.29), we have the following inequality:

$$\dot{p}(t) \leq -\gamma(p(t) + p(t)^{\frac{\alpha+1}{2}}) \quad \text{and} \quad \frac{dp(t)}{p(t) + p(t)^{(\alpha+1)/2}} \leq -\gamma \, dt.$$

Integrate both sides of the differential inequality:

$$\int_{p(0)}^{p(t)} \frac{1}{p(t) + p(t)^{(\alpha+1)/2}}\, dp(t) \le \int_0^t -\epsilon\, dt.$$

The convergence time upper bound t_7 can be computed as

$$t_7 = \frac{2\ln\left[1 + p(0)^{(1-\alpha)/2}\right]}{\gamma(1-\alpha)}. \tag{18.35}$$

The convergence time upper bound T_3 of this situation means the sum of the time of Case I and t_7.

The proof is completed. ∎

18.3.3 Noise-Tolerant Convergence

Compared with the existing algorithms, the main advantage of the proposed NT-FTZNN model lies in the fact that it can offer noise-tolerant properties. In this part, we put forward a theorem to prove the noise-suppression performance of the NT-FTZNN model.

Theorem 18.4 *When the NT-FTZNN model polluted by random constant noise η, we can obtain error function (18.7). Whatever the initial state $U(0)$ is, the actual solution state $U(t)$ can converge to the theoretical solution set $U^*(t)$.*

Proof: According to the definition of error function (18.7) of NT-FTZNN model (18.6), we have the following equation which is the subsystem of each item, i.e. the ijth element of $Y(t)$.

$$\dot{y}_{ij}(t) = -\gamma\phi(y_{ij}(t) + \lambda\int_0^t \phi(y_{ij}(\tau))\, d\tau - \lambda y_{ij}(t) + \eta.$$

Then, because we have $\varepsilon_{ij}(t) = y_{ij}(t) + \lambda\int_0^t y_{ij}(\tau)\, d\tau$, the foregoing equation can be simplified as

$$\dot{\varepsilon}_{ij}(t) = -\gamma\phi(\varepsilon_{ij}(t)) + \eta. \tag{18.36}$$

Let us define the Lyapunov function $p_{ij}(t) = (-\gamma\phi(\varepsilon_{ij}(t)) + \eta)^2/2$. Its derivative is computed as

$$\begin{aligned}
\dot{p}_{ij}(t) &= (-\gamma\phi(\varepsilon_{ij}(t)) + \eta)\gamma\frac{\partial\phi(\varepsilon_{ij}(t))}{\partial\varepsilon_{ij}(t)}\dot{\varepsilon}_{ij}(t) \\
&= -\gamma\frac{\partial\phi(\varepsilon_{ij}(t))}{\partial\varepsilon_{ij}(t)}(-\gamma\phi(\varepsilon_{ij}(t)) + \eta)^2.
\end{aligned} \tag{18.37}$$

On account of $\phi(\cdot)$ is a monotone increasing function, $\partial\Phi(\varepsilon_{ij}(t))/\partial\varepsilon_{ij}(t) \ge 0$. Hence, the derivative $\dot{p}_{ij}(t) > 0$, it means that $p_{ij}(t)$ will gradually decline till

$\partial\Phi(\varepsilon_{ij}(t))/\partial\varepsilon_{ij}(t) = 0$, which signifies $-\gamma\Phi(\varepsilon_{ij}(t)) + \eta = 0$. To sum up, when $\varepsilon_{ij}(t) = \Phi^{-1}(\eta/\gamma)$, $\dot{\varepsilon}_{ij}(t) = 0$. At this time, the situation is same as Theorem 18.1, and it can achieve globally convergence. In other words, NT-FTZNN model (18.6) can become true convergence while polluted by any random constant noise.

That completes the proof. ∎

18.4 Illustrative Verification

This section will accomplish two numerical simulative examples to evaluate the performance of the NT-FTZNN model for solving the time-variant linear inequalities. Primarily, the NT-FTZNN model guarantees the global convergence property of its error function via using monotone increasing odd functions. Then, to demonstrate the noise-tolerant convergence of the NT-FTZNN model, we compare the performance of the NT-FTZNN model with that of the CZNN model under the same noise condition. Furthermore, in order to elucidate the authenticity of finite-time convergence property, the convergence time upper bound of the NT-FTZNN model activated by two sign-bi-power AFs is computed. Additionally, the NT-FTZNN model is proved to solve high-order time-varying inequalities.

For illustration and explanation, we consider the following specific coefficient matrices:

$$A(t) = \begin{bmatrix} \sin(10t) & \cos(10t) \\ -\cos(10t) & \sin(10t) \end{bmatrix} \quad \text{and} \tag{18.38}$$

$$B(t) = \begin{bmatrix} \cos(10t) + 1 & \sin(10t) + 1.5 \\ -\sin(10t) + 1.5 & -\cos(10t) + 1 \end{bmatrix}. \tag{18.39}$$

In the first place, we verify the global convergence of the NT-FTZNN model for solving linear inequalities. We can see that through the NT-FTZNN model activated by linear AF, the arbitrary initial state $U(0)$ could converge to the theoretical solution set after a period of time, which is shown in Figure 18.1. The dashed line represents the theoretical solution set, rather the solid line expresses the actual state of $U(t)$. It is obvious that the solid line finally coincides with the dashed line. To avoid contingency, we select five randomly generated initial values $U(0)$ to observe the variation of the error function, which is shown as Figure 18.2. It can be seen that all the curves converge to zero ultimately, which demonstrates that the NT-FTZNN model can achieve global convergence. In addition, Figure 18.3 shows that NT-FTZNN model performs better than the CZNN model.

In general, we use the Frobenius norm about error function to express the difference between the actual solution set and the theoretical solution set. In order to compare the performance of the NT-FTZNN model with different AFs, we adopt some existing monotone increasing odd functions (e.g. linear activation (18.9),

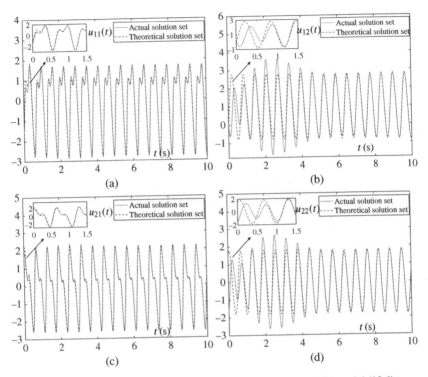

Figure 18.1 Trajectories of state matrix $U(t)$ by applying NT-FTZNN model (18.6) to solve linear inequalities (18.1) when $U(0)$ is outside $\Omega(0)$ with $\gamma = 1$ and $\lambda = 10$. (a) $u_{11}(t)$, (b) $u_{12}(t)$, (c) $u_{21}(t)$, and (d) $u_{22}(t)$.

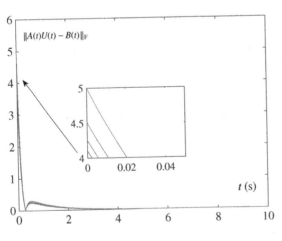

Figure 18.2 Trajectories of five random state matrix $U(t)$ by applying NT-FTZNN model (18.6) with $\gamma = 1$ and $\lambda = 10$ to solve linear inequalities (18.1) when $U(0)$ is outside $\Omega(0)$.

Figure 18.3 Comparisons of the error function generated by NT-FTZNN model (18.6) with $\gamma = 1$ and $\lambda = 1$ and the error function created by the CZNN model with $\gamma = 1$ which are both activated by linear AF.

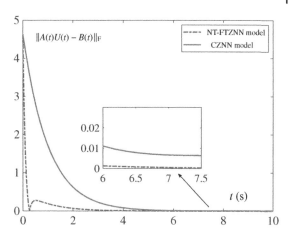

power AF (18.10), bipolar-sigmoid AF (18.11), power-sigmoid AF (18.12), sign-bi-power AF (18.13), and improved sign-bi-power sigmoid (18.14)) as AFs and plot the state curve, respectively. It can be seen from Figure 18.4 that the NT-FTZNN model activated by the aforementioned AF can make its error function gradually converge to 0, which proves the global convergence of the NT-FTZNN model from the experimental aspect in development. Moreover, the NT-FTZNN model activated by the sign-bi-power function can make the error function converge to 0 in about 3.5 seconds, and the time can be reduced to about 2.3 seconds if the AF is changed to the improved sign-bi-power function. However, for other existing AFs, there is still a large error estimate for the error function at this time point. Therefore, the NT-FTZNN model using the sign-bi-power AF has faster convergence rate and shorter convergence time.

Figure 18.4 Comparisons of the error functions generated by NT-FTZNN model (18.6) with $\gamma = 1$ and $\lambda = 1$ which are activated by several of AFs under the same conditions.

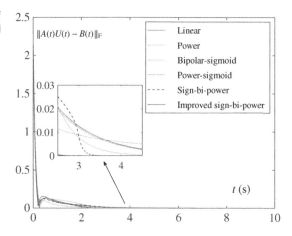

To accomplish finite-time convergence, the NT-FTZNN model is activated by sign-bi-power AFs. Compared to other AFs, the former one has faster convergence rate and finite-time convergence. By Theorems 18.2 and 18.3, the convergence time upper bound has been computed. Then, the correctness of the two theorems earlier will be proved by a concrete example. Considering the different initial state $U(0)$, the calculation of convergence time upper bound can be decomposed into two parts.

Case I Let $U(0) = [-2,0; 2.8, 2.1]$, which expresses that $A(0)U(0) - B(0) = [0.8, 0.6; 0.5, 0]$, we have $\varepsilon(0) = Y(0)$. Then, the Lyapunov function value satisfies the equation that $p_1(0) = p_2(0) = |\varepsilon^+(0)|^2 = 0.8^2 = 0.64 < 1$. The parameters are given as $\alpha = 0.3, \gamma = 1$ and $\lambda = 1$. By Theorem 18.2, the upper bound of the time t_a for the NT-FTZNN model which is used the sign-bi-power AF finding theoretical solution set can be computed as follows:

$$t_a = \frac{2p(0)^{(1-\alpha)/2}}{\lambda(1 - \alpha)} + \frac{2}{\gamma(1 - \alpha)}p(0)^{\frac{(1-\alpha)}{2}} \approx 4.8878 \text{ seconds.}$$

Under the same condition, according to Theorem 18.3, the convergence time upper bound t_b satisfies the following equation:

$$t_b = \frac{2p(0)^{(1-\alpha)/2}}{\lambda(1 - \alpha)} + \frac{2\ln\left[1 + p_2(0)^{(1-\alpha)/2}\right]}{\gamma(1 - \alpha)} \approx 4.2099 \text{ seconds.}$$

As expected, the numerical simulative results are shown in Figure 18.5. When the initial state $p(0) < 1$, the actual convergence time of the NT-FTZNN model with sign-bi-power activation function is approximately 3.81 seconds, which is less than the theoretical upper-bound convergence time that is calculated

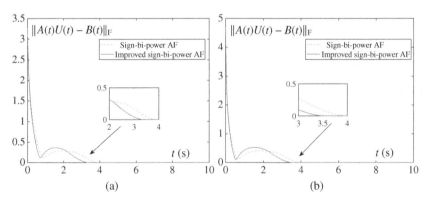

Figure 18.5 Trajectories of the error function generated by NT-FTZNN model (18.6) activated by two sign-bi-power AFs with $\gamma = 1, \lambda = 1$ and $r = 0.3$ to solve linear inequalities (18.1). (a) When the initial state $p(0) < 1$. (b) When the initial state $p(0) > 1$.

according to Theorem 18.2. Under the same condition, when activated by the improved sign-bi-power AF, the error function of the NT-FTZNN model can reach to zero in about 3.25 seconds. It also means that the NT-FTZNN model which uses two sign-bi-power AFs can make its error function achieve finite-time convergence. In addition, the distance between the actual convergence time of the NT-FTZNN model within sign-bi-power AF and its corresponding theoretical convergence time is longer than that of NT-FTZNN model within the improved sign-bi-power AF. Hence, in conclusion, the NT-FTZNN model activated by the improved sign-bi-power AF processes superiority performance when $p(0) < 1$.

Case II Let $U(0) = [-2, -1.5; 3, 2.1]$, which expresses that $A(0)U(0) - B(0) = [1, 0.6; 0.5, 1.5]$, we have $\varepsilon(0) = Y(0)$. Then, the Lyapunov function value satisfies the equation that $p_1(0) = p_2(0) = |\varepsilon^+(0)|^2 = |1.5|^2 = 2.25 > 1$. The parameters are given as $\alpha = 0.3, \gamma = 1$ and $\lambda = 1$. According to Theorem 18.2, the theoretical upper bound of the convergence time t_a is calculated as

$$t_a = \frac{2p(0)^{(1-\alpha)/2}}{\lambda(1-\alpha)} + \frac{2 - 2\alpha(p(0)^{(\alpha-1)/2\alpha} - 1)}{\gamma(\alpha - 1)} \approx 6.3193 \text{ seconds.}$$

The same parameters are given, when used NT-FTZNN model activated by the improved sign-bi-power AF, the convergence time upper bound t_b satisfies

$$t_b = \frac{2p(0)^{(1-\alpha)/2}}{\lambda(1-\alpha)} + \frac{2\ln 2 + 2\alpha \ln\left[\frac{2}{1+p(0)^{\frac{\alpha-1}{2\alpha}}}\right]}{\gamma(1-\alpha)} \approx 6.0883 \text{ seconds.}$$

As Figure 18.5b shown, the actual solution set of the linear inequalities satisfies the convergence limitation of the theoretical solution set when $p(0) > 1$. Moreover, we can obtain the same fact that the distance of the actual and theoretical convergence time for the NT-FTZNN model activated by improved sign-bi-power AF is shorter than used sign-bi-power AF. That is to say, the NT-FTZNN model with improved sign-bi-power AF has better convergence performance.

In addition, it is worth studying the influence of the parameters on the whole NT-FTZNN model. Based on previous work, the parameter γ, which is often used in the CZNN models, plays an important role in solving linear inequalities. When γ increases by an order of magnitude, the convergence time of the CZNN models solving the linear time-variant inequalities will correspondingly decrease by an order of magnitude. Next, we will mainly consider the influence of the parameters α and λ on the NT-FTZNN model system. Let $\alpha = 0.1, \alpha = 0.3, \alpha = 0.5$, and $\alpha = 0.7$ and then, the comparison of the error function state curves of the NT-FTZNN model for solving time-varying inequalities with different α is shown in Figure 18.6. Obviously, it can be seen that with the increase of parameter α, the convergence rate is slower and the convergence time is longer. This is

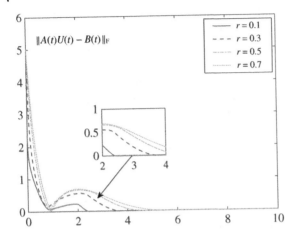

Figure 18.6 Comparisons among three cases of NT-FTZNN model (18.6) with different α to solve linear time-varying inequalities (18.1).

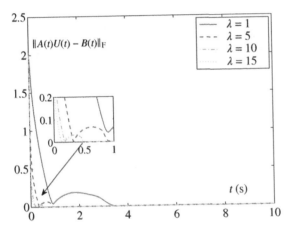

Figure 18.7 Comparisons among three cases of NT-FTZNN model (18.6) with $\alpha = 0.3$ and different λ to solve linear time-varying inequalities (18.1).

consistent with the theoretical derivation of the convergence time upper bound. Therefore, in order to obtain better convergence performance, we should select a smaller α value as far as possible. Next, we let $\alpha = 0.3$ and choose different λ to observe the trajectories development. In Figure 18.7, four curves are displayed the error function of the NT-FTZNN model with $\lambda = 1$, $\lambda = 5$, $\lambda = 10$, and $\lambda = 15$, respectively. It is clear that the convergence rate is accelerated when λ increases. Hence, if the hardware conditions permit, the maximum λ should be selected in order to obtain better performance when the model solves the problem.

In the end, we will use the NT-FTZNN model to solve higher-order linear time-variant inequalities which is demonstrated the advantages and superiorities of the convergence performance about its error function. To be specific, we mainly consider 4×4 time-varying coefficient matrices $A(t)$ and $B(t)$, which are given as follows:

$$A(t) = \begin{bmatrix} 2\sin(t) & 0 & 1 & \sin(t) \\ 0 & \cos(t) & 2\sin(t) & 1 \\ \cos(t) & 1 & 0 & 2\cos(t) \\ 1 & 2\cos(t) & \sin(t) & 0 \end{bmatrix} \text{ and}$$

$$B(t) = \begin{bmatrix} \sin(t) & \cos(t) & \sin(2t)/2 & \cos(2t) \\ \cos(t) & \sin(t) & \sin(t) & \cos(t) \\ \sin(2t)/2 & \cos(t) & \sin(t) & \sin(2t)/2 \\ \cos(2t) & \sin(2t)/2 & \cos(t) & \sin(t) \end{bmatrix}.$$

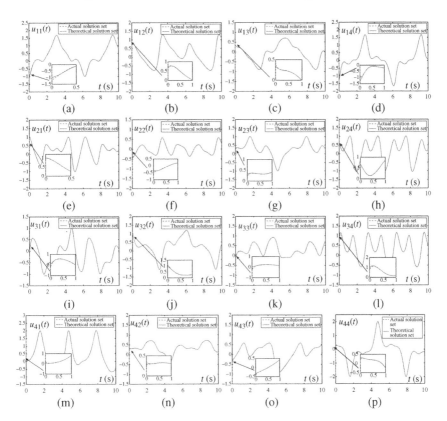

Figure 18.8 Trajectories of theoretical solutions of the higher-order time-varying inequalities and actual solutions starting with random initial state using NT-FTZNN model (18.6) with $\gamma = 1$, $\lambda = 1$, and $\alpha = 0.3$.

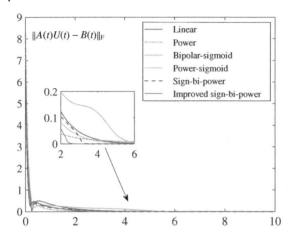

Figure 18.9 Comparisons of the error functions generated by NT-FTZNN model (18.6) with $\gamma = 1$ and $\lambda = 10$ which are activated by different AFs for solving higher-order time-varying inequalities.

We design the parameters $\alpha = 0.3$, $\gamma = 1$ and $\lambda = 1$, and randomly generate the initial state $U(0)$. Firstly, we can obtain each dimension of the theoretical trajectories via computed by the NT-FTZNN model. In Figure 18.8, compared with actual state of $U(t)$, we can see that every element of $U(t)$ can converge to their own theoretical curve $U^*(t)$ in a short time. As a consequence, the global convergence property is also applied to solving higher-order time-varying inequalities. Furthermore, Figure 18.9 displays the comparisons of the error function convergence processes synthesized by the NT-FTZNN model with different AFs. No matter what AF is selected, as long as the time-varying inequality with constant noise is solved through the NT-FTZNN model, its error function can always converge to 0. Therefore, when solving higher-order time-varying inequalities, the noise tolerance performance of the NT-FTZNN model can still be proved. It is worth mentioning that when the NT-FTZNN model is activated by the improved sign-bi-power activation function, the whole system processes the rapid convergence rate and the shortest convergence time. Similar to the first example, the NT-FTZNN model activated by the improved sign-bi-power AF has the superiority and effectiveness for solving higher-order time-varying inequalities.

18.5 Chapter Summary

For sake of solving time-varying linear matrix inequalities with noise-tolerant and finite-time convergence, a novel integral design scheme is proposed. The main idea of the scheme is to construct the NT-FTZNN model, which is introduced by an integral item based on the CZNN model to eliminate errors caused by noise. Firstly, we give the proof of global convergence of the NT-FTZNN model. Then, according to the definition of Lyapunov function, the theoretical convergence time upper bound is calculated. Last, the robustness of NT-FTZNN model is proved and we also can find the equilibrium point of the whole system. Numerical simulative results have verified the better performance of the NT-FTZNN model. It means that the NT-FTZNN model can solve linear time-varying inequalities in finite time and resisting constant noise interference. Furthermore, a higher-order linear time-variant example is considered and it confirms that the global, finite-time and noise tolerant convergence also can be applied to the higher-order problems

References

1 Y. Zhang and M. Yang *et al.*, New discrete-solution model for solving future different-level linear inequality and equality with robot manipulator control, *IEEE Trans. Ind. Inform.*, 15(4) (2019) 1975–1984.

2 L. Jin and S. Li *et al.*, Robot manipulator control using neural networks: A survey, *Neurocomputing*, 285 (2018) 23–34.

3 P. Witczak and K. Patan *et al.*, A neural network approach to simultaneous state and actuator fault estimation under unknown input decoupling, *Neurocomputing*, 250 (2017) 65–75.

4 Z. Zhang and L. Zheng *et al.*, Three recurrent neural networks and three numerical methods for solving repetitive motion planning scheme of redundant robot manipulators, *IEEE ASME Trans. Mechatron.*, 22(3) (2017) 1423–1434.

5 R. Rahimilarki and Z. Gao *et al.*, Robust neural network fault estimation approach for nonlinear dynamic systems with applications to wind turbine systems, *IEEE Trans. Ind. Inform.*, 15(12) (2019) 6302–6312.

6 M. Liu and S. Zhang *et al.*, H_∞ output tracking control of discrete-time nonlinear systems via standard neural network models, *IEEE Trans. Neural Netw. Learn. Syst.*, 25(10) (2014) 1928–1935.

7 L. Jin and S. Li, Nonconvex function activated zeroing neural network models for dynamic quadratic programming subject to equality and inequality constraints, *Neurocomputing*, 267 (2017) 107–113.

8 Y. Hongme, Neural network method for solving convex programming problem with linear inequality constraints, 2016 International Conference on Smart City and Systems Engineering (ICSCSE), Hunan, China, (2016) 521–523.

9 R. Saravanakumar and S. Stojanovic *et al.*, Finite-time passivity-based stability criteria for delayed discrete-time neural networks via new weighted summation inequalities, *IEEE Trans. Neural Netw. Learn. Syst.*, 30(1) (2019) 58–71.

10 Y. Zhang and S. S. Ge, Design and analysis of a general recurrent neural network model for time-varying matrix inversion, *IEEE Trans. Neural Netw.*, 16(6) (2005) 1477–1490.

11 Y. Zhang and C. Yi *et al.*, Comparison on gradient-based neural dynamics and Zhang neural dynamics for online solution of nonlinear equations, International Symposium on Intelligence Computation and Applications, Springer-Verlag, 20(1) (2008) 269–279.

12 D. P. Bertsekas and J. N. Tsitsiklis, *Neuro-dynamic programming*, Athena Scientific, (1996).

13 J. Kamruzzaman and S. M. Aziz, A note on activation function in multilayer feedforward learning, Proceedings of the 2002 International Joint Conference on Neural Networks. IJCNN'02(Cat. No. 02CH37290), (2002) 519–523.

Part VIII

Application to Nonlinear Equation

19

Design Scheme I of FTZNN

19.1 Introduction

It is well known that a wide class of problems, which arise in engineering practices and scientific applications, can be studied via the nonlinear equations using the innovative techniques [1–5]. To solve the nonlinear equation problem in real-time, in mathematics, almost all methods/techniques are based on the following equation [1–11]:

$$f(u) = 0 \in \mathbb{R}, \tag{19.1}$$

where $f(\cdot) : \mathbb{R} \to \mathbb{R}$ denotes a smooth nonlinear function. Due to the nonlinearity of $f(u)$, nonlinear equation (19.1) may have no solutions. Throughout the chapter, we assume that the solution set of (19.1) is nonempty. For presentation convenience, let u^* denote a theoretical solution (or termed, root) of nonlinear equation (19.1). It is worth pointing out that considerable attention has been focused to solve nonlinear equation (19.1) both analytically and numerically. For example, several iterative numerical methods have been developed using quite different techniques such as Taylor's series, quadrature formulas, homotopy, interpolation, decomposition, and its various modification [6–11].

Motivated by further improving the efficacy of the original zeroing neural network (OZNN) model, a finite-time zeroing neural network (FTZNN) model is developed for online nonlinear equation solving. More importantly, the upper bound of the convergence time for the FTZNN model is derived analytically via Lyapunov theory.

19.2 Model Formulation

To facilitate the convergence analysis and to lay a basis for further discussion, the following two dynamical models are presented in this section.

Zeroing Neural Networks: Finite-time Convergence Design, Analysis and Applications,
First Edition. Lin Xiao and Lei Jia.

19.2.1 OZNN Model

To solve online nonlinear equation (19.1), following Zhang and coworkers' design method [12–14], we can develop a neural dynamics expressed as an implicit dynamic system (i.e. the OZNN).

Firstly, to monitor the nonlinear equation solving process, an indefinite error function $y(t)$ is defined next, instead of a square-based energy function associated with the aforementioned gradient neural network (GNN) model:

$$y(t) = f(u). \tag{19.2}$$

Then, the zeroing neural network (ZNN) design formula is adopted such that $y(t)$ converges to zero as time t goes on. That is

$$\frac{dy(t)}{dt} = -\gamma y(t). \tag{19.3}$$

Now, expanding the aforementioned design formula (19.3) and in view of $\dot{y}(t) = f'(u)\dot{u}(t)$, we can obtain the following implicit dynamic equation of the OZNN model:

$$f'(u)\dot{u}(t) = -\gamma f(u), \tag{19.4}$$

where $u(t) \in \mathbb{R}, f'(u)$, and $\gamma > 0 \in \mathbb{R}$ are defined as the before.

19.2.2 FTZNN Model

In this subsection, a FTZNN model is proposed for finding the root of nonlinear equation (19.1) by adding a specially constructed activation function [15–17] (i.e. the sign-bi-power function or the Li function):

$$f'(u)\dot{u}(t) = -\gamma \phi\left(f(u)\right), \tag{19.5}$$

where $\phi(\cdot) : \mathbb{R} \to \mathbb{R}$ denotes a specially constructed nonlinear mapping of neural dynamics and is defined as

$$\phi(x) = \mathrm{sgn}^\alpha(x) + \mathrm{sgn}^{1/\alpha}(x), \tag{19.6}$$

with $\alpha \in (0, 1)$ and $\mathrm{sgn}^\alpha(\cdot)$ defined as

$$\mathrm{sgn}^\alpha(x) = \begin{cases} |x|^\alpha, & \text{if } x > 0; \\ 0, & \text{if } x = 0; \\ -|x|^\alpha, & \text{if } x < 0; \end{cases}$$

where $x \in \mathbb{R}$ and $|x|$ denotes the absolute value of x.

19.2.3 Models Comparison

While the previous subsections present two different models for real-time nonlinear equation solving, in this subsection, the following details are given for comparing OZNN model (19.4) and FTZNN model (19.5), as well as the GNN model.

- A specially constructed nonlinear function is exploited in FTZNN model (19.5), which makes its form totally different from these of the GNN model and OZNN model (19.4).
- The design of OZNN model (19.4) and FTZNN model (19.5) is based on the elimination of an indefinite error function. By contrast, the design of the GNN model is based on the elimination of a square-based positive energy function.
- Similar to OZNN model (19.4), FTZNN model (19.5) is depicted in implicit dynamics that is better consistent with the systems in practice and in nature. By contrast, the GNN model is depicted in an explicit dynamics that is usually associated with classic Hopfield-type recurrent neural networks.
- It can be theoretically proved that FTZNN model (19.5) achieves superior finite-time convergence performance in comparison with the GNN model and OZNN model (19.4). In addition, for the case of a multiple root, with the increase of the order of the multiple root, the neural state of OZNN model (19.4) and FTZNN model (19.5) can still converge well to such a theoretical root. In contrast, the GNN model more probably yields wrong (or approximate) solutions [18, 19].

Before ending this subsection, following the aforementioned third point, we would like to mention that the implicit dynamical systems frequently arise in analog electronic circuits and systems according to Kirchhoff's rules [18, 19]. In addition, implicit dynamical systems have greater abilities in representing dynamical systems because of preserving physical parameters in the coefficient matrices, e.g. $f'(u)$ on the left-hand side of FTZNN model (19.5) and OZNN model (19.4). Besides, the implicit systems could be mathematically transformed to explicit systems if needed. In this sense, owing to the advantages of implicit systems, our FTZNN model (19.5) and OZNN model (19.4) can be much superior to the GNN model in the form of explicit systems.

19.3 Convergence Analysis

In this section, the finite-time convergent performance of FTZNN model (19.5) is investigated. Before that, the lemma [18, 19] about global convergence of OZNN model (19.4) for solving nonlinear equation is presented for comparative purpose.

Lemma 19.1 *Given a solvable smooth nonlinear equation $f(u) = 0 \in \mathbb{R}$, neural state $u(t) \in \mathbb{R}$ of OZNN model (19.4), starting from randomly generated initial state $u(0) \in \mathbb{R}$, can converge globally exponentially to the theoretical root u^* of (19.1) with the exponential convergence rate γ.*

Theorem 19.2 *Given a solvable smooth nonlinear equation $f(x) = 0 \in \mathbb{R}$, neural state $u(t) \in \mathbb{R}$ of FTZNN model (19.5), starting from randomly generated initial state $u(0) \in \mathbb{R}$, can converge globally exponentially to the theoretical root u^* of (19.1) in finite time*

$$t_{\mathrm{f}} < |y(0)|^{1-\alpha}/\gamma(1-\alpha),$$

where $y(0)$ denotes the initial value of $y(t)$.

Proof: By focusing on the definition of $y(t)$ and FTZNN model (19.5), it can be regarded that FTZNN model (19.5) is derived from

$$\frac{\mathrm{d}y(t)}{\mathrm{d}t} = -\gamma\phi(y(t)).$$

Thus, we have

$$\dot{y}(t) = -\gamma\left(\mathrm{sgn}^\alpha(y(t)) + \mathrm{sgn}^{1/\alpha}(y(t))\right). \tag{19.7}$$

To estimate finite time t_{f}, we firstly define a Lyapunov function candidate $p(t) = |y(t)|^2$, the time-derivative of $p(t)$ is thus obtained:

$$\begin{aligned}
\dot{p}(t) &= -2\gamma y(t)\left(\mathrm{sgn}^\alpha(y(t)) + \mathrm{sgn}^{1/\alpha}(y(t))\right) \\
&= -2\gamma\left(|y(t)|^{\alpha+1} + |y(t)|^{\frac{1}{\alpha}+1}\right) \\
&\leqslant -2\gamma|y(t)|^{\alpha+1} \\
&= -2\gamma p(t)^{\frac{\alpha+1}{2}}.
\end{aligned}$$

Solving the aforementioned differential inequality $\dot{p}(t) \leqslant -2\gamma p^{\frac{\alpha+1}{2}}(t)$ with the initial condition $p(0) = |y(0)|^2$ yields

$$p(t)^{\frac{1-\alpha}{2}} \begin{cases} \leqslant |y(0)|^{1-\alpha} - \gamma t(1-\alpha), & \text{if } t \leqslant \frac{|y(0)|^{1-\alpha}}{\gamma(1-\alpha)}, \\ = 0, & \text{if } t > \frac{|y(0)|^{1-\alpha}}{\gamma(1-\alpha)}, \end{cases}$$

which means $p(t)$ can directly decrease to zero after a time period $|y(0)|^{1-\alpha}/\gamma(1-\alpha)$. That is to say, $y(t)$ is zero for $t > |y(0)|^{1-\alpha}/\gamma(1-\alpha)$, i.e. $t_{\mathrm{f}} < |y(0)|^{1-\alpha}/\gamma(1-\alpha)$. Thus, we can conclude that the neural state $u(t)$ of FTZNN model (19.5), starting from randomly generated initial state $u(0)$, can converge to the theoretical root of nonlinear equation (19.1) in finite time t_{f}. This completes the proof. ∎

According to the theoretical analysis earlier, we can draw the conclusion that OZNN model (19.4) can globally and exponentially converge to the theoretical solution of (19.1) when time goes to infinity. However, they never converge to the theoretical root of (19.1) within finite time, which may limit their applications in real-time processing. In contrast, FTZNN model (19.5) possesses the desired finite-time convergent performance. Evidently, FTZNN model (19.5) is superior to OZNN model (19.4), which theoretically guarantees that FTZNN model (19.5) can achieve superior convergence performance. It is worth pointing out that the convergence time of the aforementioned two different dynamical models can be expedited as the value of design parameter γ increases. For example, the convergence time of OZNN model (19.4) decreases in an exponential manner with γ increasing. Consequently, design parameter γ plays an important role in the aforementioned two different dynamical models and thus should be selected appropriately large to satisfy the convergence rate in practice.

19.4 Illustrative Verification

In the previous sections, OZNN model (19.4) and FTZNN model (19.5) have been discussed for solving online nonlinear equation. In addition, the finite-time convergence performance of FTZNN model (19.5) is analyzed in details. In this section, computer-simulation results are provided for substantiating the efficacy of such two neural dynamical models as well as the superiority of FTZNN model (19.5) as compared with OZNN model (19.4). Without loss of generality, we set design parameter $\alpha = 0.25$.

19.4.1 Nonlinear Equation $f(u)$ with Simple Root

In order to illustrate superior finite-time convergence of FTZNN model (19.5) in comparison with OZNN model (19.4), let us consider the following nonlinear equation:

$$f(u) = 0.1u^2 - 0.1u - 0.6.$$

Firstly, we study the situation of $\gamma = 1$ for such two ZNN models. Starting from 50 randomly generated initial states within $[-10, 10]$, we apply such two dynamical models to online solution of the previous nonlinear equation. The corresponding simulative results are shown in Figure 19.1. As seen from Figure 19.1a, neural states $u \in \mathbb{R}$ of OZNN model (19.4) can converge to the theoretical solution u^* about six seconds. Besides, as observed from Figure 19.1b, the convergence time of neural states $u \in \mathbb{R}$ to the theoretical solution u^* synthesized by FTZNN model (19.5) is within 1.5 seconds, which is about four times faster than that of OZNN

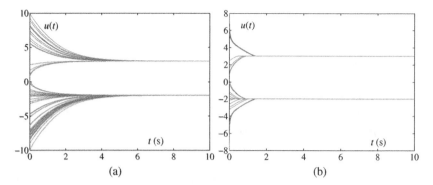

Figure 19.1 Transient behavior of neural states $u(t)$ synthesized by different dynamical models with $\gamma = 1$ and 50 randomly generated initial states within $[-10, 10]$. (a) By OZNN model (19.4). (b) By FTZNN model (19.5).

model (19.4). In addition, the theoretical maximum of the upper bound of FTZNN model (19.5) can be computed as follows:

$$|y(0)|^{1-\alpha}/\gamma(1 - \alpha) = \frac{10.4^{0.75}}{(1 - 0.25)} = 2.3944.$$

Evidently, from the simulation results shown in Figure 19.1b, the convergence time of FTZNN model (19.5) is within finite time 1.5 seconds, which is less than the theoretically computed maximum of the upper bound and agrees well with the theoretical result presented in Theorem 19.2. From the comparative results earlier, we can conclude that our proposed FTZNN model (19.5) is effective and consistent with the theoretical analysis as well as much superior to OZNN model (19.4) for real-time nonlinear equation solving.

It is worth pointing out that the main impacts on the deviation of the convergence time in practical simulations and theoretical maximum of the upper bound are discussed as follows. On one hand, as analyzed in the proof, to estimate finite time t_f, we define a Lyapunov function candidate $p(t) = |y(t)|^2$, and the time-derivative of $p(t)$ can thus be obtained via the shrinkage method. That is, the obtained $\dot{p}(t)$ is less than or equal to the actual $\dot{p}(t)$. In mathematics, $\dot{p}(t) = -2\gamma y(t)(\text{sgn}^\alpha(y(t)) + \text{sgn}^{1/\alpha}(y(t))) = -2\gamma(|y(t)|^{\alpha+1} + |y(t)|^{\frac{1}{\alpha}+1}) \leqslant -2\gamma|y(t)|^{\alpha+1} = -2\gamma p^{\frac{\alpha+1}{2}}(t)$. Evidently, this is one main impact on the deviation of the convergence time in practical simulations and theoretical maximum of the upper bound. On the other hand, the initial states are randomly generated within $[-10, 10]$ in this example. The theoretical maximum of the upper bound is obtained only when $u(0) = 10$ or $u(0) = -10$. However, the convergence time in practical simulations is determined by the actual initial values. Evidently, there is a deviation of the actual initial values and the maximum values in the simulations as well. This is the other main impact on the deviation of the convergence time in practical simulations and theoretical maximum of the upper bound.

To better illustrate the advantages of our proposed FTZNN model (19.5), transient behavior of residual error $|y(t)|$ is a suitable criterion to measure the effectiveness of such two different dynamical models. Corresponding to the neural states $u(t)$ shown in Figure 19.1 under the same conditions, Figure 19.2 shows the transient behavior of residual errors $|y(t)|$ synthesized by OZNN model (19.4) and FTZNN model (19.5) from 50 randomly generated initial states within $[-10, 10]$. Evidently, from Figure 19.2, we know that the convergence time of residual errors $|y(t)|$ synthesized by OZNN model (19.4) is about six seconds, and synthesized by FTZNN model (19.5) is about 1.5 seconds. The comparative results agree with these of Figure 19.1.

It is worth pointing out that, as shown in Figure 19.3, the convergence time of FTZNN model (19.5) can be shortened from 0.15 seconds and even to 1.5 ms, when

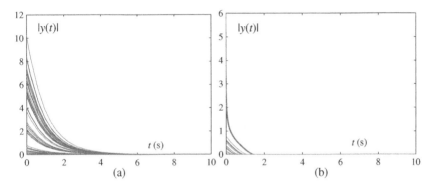

Figure 19.2 Transient behavior of residual functions $|y(t)|$ synthesized by different dynamical models with $\gamma = 1$ and 50 randomly generated initial states within $[-10, 10]$. (a) By OZNN model (19.4). (b) By FTZNN model (19.5).

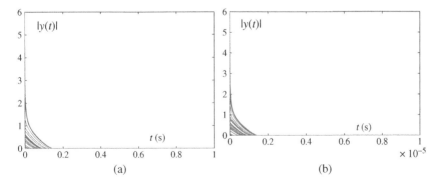

Figure 19.3 Transient behavior of residual functions $|y(t)|$ synthesized by FTZNN model (19.5) with different values of γ and 50 randomly generated initial states within $[-10, 10]$. (a) $\gamma = 10$. (b) $\gamma = 10^6$.

the value of design parameter γ increases from 10 to 10^6. These simulative observations have agreed well with the theoretical analysis presented in Section 19.3, i.e. the convergence rate of such two neural dynamical models being proportional to the design parameter γ.

19.4.2 Nonlinear Equation $f(u)$ with Multiple Root

For further illustrative and comparative purposes, let us consider the same multiple root example as in [20]; that is,

$$f(u) = (u - 3)^{10}(u - 1) = 0.$$

It is worth mentioning that, in [20], OZNN model (19.4) is more efficient using the power-sigmoid activation function than using the linear activation function. So, without loss of generality, OZNN model (19.4) using the power-sigmoid activation function is considered, exploited, and compared in this example.

With $\gamma = 1$, starting from 5 randomly generated initial states within $[-4, 4]$, we apply the power-sigmoid-activated OZNN model and FTZNN model (19.5) to online solution of the previous multiple-root nonlinear equation. Figure 19.4 shows the transient behavior of residual errors $|y(t)|$ synthesized by the power-sigmoid-activated OZNN model and FTZNN model (19.5). As seen from Figure 19.4, we know that the convergence time of residual errors $|y(t)|$ synthesized by the power-sigmoid-activated OZNN model is about three seconds which is about two times faster than that of OZNN model (19.4), and synthesized by FTZNN model (19.5) is still about 1.5 seconds which is about two times faster than that of the power-sigmoid-activated OZNN model instead of four times faster than that of OZNN model (19.4). Simulation results show that the convergence

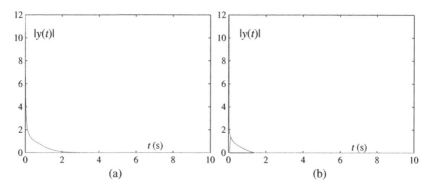

Figure 19.4 Transient behavior of residual functions $|y(t)|$ synthesized by different dynamical models with $\gamma = 1$ and 5 randomly generated initial states within $[-4, 4]$. (a) By OZNN model (19.4). (b) By FTZNN model (19.5).

rate of FTZNN model (19.5) is highest, followed by the power-sigmoid-activated OZNN model, and OZNN model (19.4) lowest. Thus, we can conclude that our FTZNN model is still better than the OZNN model even if using the power-sigmoid activation function.

In summary, from the aforementioned two simulation examples, either simple root or multiple root, such two neural dynamical models are effective on solving online nonlinear equation (19.1). More importantly, compared with OZNN model (19.4), superior finite-time convergence to theoretical solution by our FTZNN model (19.5) can be reached even if OZNN model (19.4) uses the power-sigmoid activation function.

19.5 Chapter Summary

A FTZNN model for solving online nonlinear equation is proposed in this chapter. Finite-time convergent analysis on such a model is investigated and analyzed with the convergence upper bound also estimated. For comparative and illustrative purposes, the OZNN has also been exploited for finding online the root of nonlinear equation. Computer simulation results have substantiated the theoretical analysis and efficacy of our proposed FTZNN model (19.5) for solving online nonlinear equation, as well as its superiority in comparison with recently proposed OZNN model (19.4).

References

1 J. R. Sharma, A. Himani, and S. P. Miodrag, An efficient derivative free family of fourth order methods for solving systems of nonlinear equations, *Appl. Math. Comput.*, 235 (2014) 383–393.

2 X. Yang, A higher-order Levenberg-Marquardt method for nonlinear equations, *Appl. Math. Comput.*, 219(22) (2013) 10682–10694.

3 M. S. Petkovic and B. Neta *et al.*, Multipoint methods for solving nonlinear equations: A survey, *Appl. Math. Comput.*, 226 (2014) 635–660.

4 J. R. Sharma and H. Arora, On efficient weighted-Newton methods for solving systems of nonlinear equations, *Appl. Math. Comput.*, 222 (2013) 497–506.

5 C. Chun and M. Y. Lee, A new optimal eighth-order family of iterative methods for the solution of nonlinear equations, *Appl. Math. Comput.*, 223 (2013) 506–519.

6 S. Abbasbandy, Improving Newton-Raphson method for nonlinear equations by modified Adomian decomposition method, *Appl. Math. Comput.*, 145(2–3) (2003) 887–893.

7 S. Abbasbandy, Y. Tan, and S. J. Liao, Newton-homotopy analysis method for nonlinear equations, *Appl. Math. Comput.*, 188(2) (2007) 1794–1800.

8 C. Chun, Iterative methods improving Newton's method by the decomposition method, *Comput. Math. Appl.*, 50(10–12) (2005) 1559–1568.

9 J. H. He, Some asymptotic methods for strongly nonlinear equations, *Int. J. Mod. Phys. B*, 20(10) (2006) 1141–1199.

10 X. Luo, A note on the new iteration for solving algebraic equations, *Appl. Math. Comput.*, 171(2) (2005) 1177–1183.

11 J. H. Mathews and K. D. Fink *et al.*, *Numerical methods using MATLAB*, Pearson Prentice Hall, Upper Saddle River, NJ, 4 (2004).

12 L. Xiao and Y. Zhang, Different Zhang functions resulting in different ZNN models demonstrated via time-varying linear matrix-vector inequalities solving, *Neurocomputing*, 121 (2013) 140–149.

13 L. Xiao and Y. Zhang, Two new types of Zhang neural networks solving systems of time-varying nonlinear inequalities, *IEEE Trans. Circuits Syst. I Regul. Pap.*, 59(10) (2012) 2363–2373.

14 L. Xiao and Y. Zhang, From different Zhang functions to various ZNN models accelerated to finite-time convergence for time-varying linear matrix equation, *Neural Process. Lett.*, 39 (2014) 309–326.

15 S. Li, S. Chen, and B. Liu, Accelerating a recurrent neural network to finite-time convergence for solving time-varying Sylvester equation by using a sign-bi-power activation function, *Neural Process. Lett.*, 37 (2013) 189–205.

16 S. Li, B. Liu, and Y. Li, Selective positive-negative feedback produces the winner-take-all competition in recurrent neural networks, *IEEE Trans. Neural Netw. Learn. Syst.*, 24(2) (2013) 301–309.

17 S. Li, Y. Li, and Z. Wang, A class of finite-time dual neural networks for solving quadratic programming problems and its κ-winners-take-all application, *Neural Netw.*, 39 (2013) 27–39.

18 Y. Zhang, P. Xu, and N. Tan, Solution of nonlinear equations by continuous- and discrete-time Zhang dynamics and more importantly their links to Newton iteration, Proceedings of the IEEE International Conference on Information, Communications and Signal Processing, (2009) 1–5.

19 Y. Zhang, P. Xu, and N. Tan, Further studies on Zhang neural-dynamics and gradient dynamics for online nonlinear equations solving, Proceedings of the IEEE International Conference on Automation and Logistics, (2009) 566–571.

20 Y. Zhang, C. Yi, and W. Ma, Comparison on gradient-based neural dynamics and Zhang neural dynamics for online solution of nonlinear equations, Proceedings of the International Symposium in Computation and Intelligence, (2008) 269–279.

20

Design Scheme II of FTZNN

20.1 Introduction

Many phenomena in physics and other fields are often described by nonlinear equations in the form of $f(u) = 0$ [1, 2]. When we want to understand the physical mechanism of phenomena in nature, exact solutions for the nonlinear equations have to be explored [3–6]. Thus, considerable attention has been focused to derive exact solutions of nonlinear equations both analytically and numerically [1, 2, 7–9]. For example, several iterative numerical algorithms have been developed using quite different techniques such as quadrature formulas, homotopy, Taylor's series, interpolation, decomposition, and its various modification [7–9]. However, most numerical algorithms may not be efficient enough for real-time computation because of their serial-processing property performed on digital computers.

In this chapter, a nonlinearly activated finite-time zeroing neural network (FTZNN) is proposed and investigated for solving online time-varying nonlinear equations. Different from the existing conventional gradient neural network (GNN) [10, 11] and recently-proposed zeroing neural network [12, 13] for solving time-varying nonlinear equations, the proposed FTZNN model converges in finite time. More importantly, the upper bound of the convergence time for the proposed FTZNN model is derived analytically via Lyapunov theory.

20.2 Problem and Model Formulation

This chapter aims at finding $u(t) \in \mathbb{R}$ in finite time t such that the following smooth time-varying nonlinear equation holds:

$$f(u(t), t) = 0. \tag{20.1}$$

The existence of time-varying theoretical solution $u^*(t)$ is assumed at any time instant $t \in [0, +\infty)$ as a basis of discussion in this chapter. For comparative

Zeroing Neural Networks: Finite-time Convergence Design, Analysis and Applications,
First Edition. Lin Xiao and Lei Jia.
© 2023 The Institute of Electrical and Electronics Engineers, Inc. Published 2023 by John Wiley & Sons, Inc.

purposes, the design procedures of the GNN and OZNN models for solving time-varying nonlinear equation (20.1) are presented in this section.

20.2.1 GNN Model

For solving time-varying nonlinear equation (20.1), according to the gradient-based design method [10, 11, 14], the GNN model requires us to define a norm- or square-based energy function such as $\varepsilon(t) = f^2(u(t), t)/2$. Then, a typical continuous-time adaptation rule based on the negative-gradient information can obtain the following linearly activated differential equation (termed linearly activated gradient-based neural dynamics [10, 11, 14]):

$$\dot{u}(t) = -\gamma \frac{\partial \varepsilon}{\partial u} = -\gamma f(u(t), t) \frac{\partial f}{\partial u}, \tag{20.2}$$

where $u(t)$, starting from a randomly generated initial state $u(0) \in \mathbb{R}$, denotes the neural state corresponding to time-varying theoretical solution $u^*(t)$, and $\gamma > 0$ is a positive design parameter used to scale the convergence rate of neural dynamics.

20.2.2 OZNN Model

Following Zhang *et al.* design method [12, 13], the following indefinite error function $y(t)$ is designed to construct the OZNN model for solving online time-varying nonlinear equation (20.1):

$$y(t) = f(u(t), t).$$

Then, we can exploit the following design formula for $\dot{y}(t)$ (i.e. the time-derivative of $y(t)$) such that the error function $y(t)$ can converge to zero exponentially:

$$\frac{\mathrm{d}y(t)}{\mathrm{d}t} = -\gamma \phi(y(t)), \tag{20.3}$$

where $\gamma > 0$ is defined the same as that of GNN model (20.2) and $\phi(\cdot)$ denotes a nonlinear activation function. In view of $y(t) = f(u(t), t)$ and then expanding the aforementioned design formula (20.3), we have

$$\frac{\partial f}{\partial u} \frac{\mathrm{d}u}{\mathrm{d}t} + \frac{\partial f}{\partial t} = -\gamma \phi(f(u(t), t)),$$

which further leads to the following differential equation (termed the original zeroing neural network, OZNN):

$$\frac{\partial f}{\partial x} \dot{u}(t) = -\gamma \phi(f(u(t), t)) - \frac{\partial f}{\partial t}. \tag{20.4}$$

It is worth pointing out that any monotonically increasing odd activation function $\phi(\cdot)$ can be used for the construction of OZNN model (20.4). In addition, the following four basic types of activation functions have been investigated in OZNN model (20.4) [12, 13]:

- linear activation function $\phi(x) = x$;
- bipolar-sigmoid activation function (with $\xi > 2$)

$$\phi(x) = (1 - \exp(-\xi x)) / (1 + \exp(-\xi x));$$

- power activation function $\phi(x) = x^l$ with odd integer $l \geqslant 3$;
- power-sigmoid activation function (with $\xi \geqslant 1$ and $l \geqslant 3$)

$$\phi(x) = \begin{cases} x^l, & \text{if } |x| \geqslant 1, \\ \frac{1+\exp(-\xi)}{1-\exp(-\xi)} \cdot \frac{1-\exp(-\xi x)}{1+\exp(-\xi x)}, & \text{otherwise.} \end{cases} \tag{20.5}$$

Furthermore, based on such four basic types of activation functions, we have the following lemmas to guarantee the global exponential convergence of OZNN model (20.4) for the real-time solution of time-varying nonlinear equation (20.1) [12, 13].

Lemma 20.1 *Consider a solvable smooth time-varying nonlinear equation (20.1), i.e. $f(u(t), t) = 0$. If a monotonically increasing odd function $\phi(\cdot)$ is used, neural state $u(t)$ of OZNN model (20.4), starting from a randomly generated initial state $u(0) \in \mathbb{R}$, can converge to a time-varying theoretical solution $u^*(t)$ of $f(u(t), t) = 0$.*

Lemma 20.2 *In addition to Lemma 20.1, OZNN model (20.4) possesses the following properties when using different types of activation functions.*

- (1) *If the linear activation function is used, the exponential convergence with rate γ is achieved for ZNN model (20.4).*
- (2) *If the bipolar-sigmoid activation function is used, the superior convergence can be achieved for error range $y(t) = f(u(t), t) \in [-\delta, \delta]$, $\exists \delta > 0$, as compared to the situation of using the linear activation function.*
- (3) *If the power activation function is used, then the superior convergence can be achieved for error ranges $(-\infty, -1)$ and $(1, \infty)$, as compared with the situation of using the linear activation function.*
- (4) *If the power-sigmoid activation function is used, the superior convergence can be achieved for the whole error range $(-\infty, \infty)$, as compared with the situation of the linear activation function.*

20.3 FTZNN Model and Finite-Time Convergence

As discussed in Section 20.2, we found that the convergence rate of neural-dynamic models can be thoroughly improved by an elaborate design of the activation function $\phi(\cdot)$. In addition, taking advantage of the nonlinearity, a properly designed nonlinear activation function often outperforms the linear one in convergence rate. However, this OZNN model (20.4) with the suggested activation functions cannot converge to the time-varying theoretical solution of time-varying nonlinear equation (20.1) in finite time, which may limit its applications in real-time calculation. Therefore, in this section, we aim at developing a specially constructed nonlinear activation function, which can endow OZNN model (20.4) with a finite-time convergence for solving time-varying nonlinear equation (20.1). Inspired by the study on finite-time control of autonomous systems and finite-time convergence of recurrent neural dynamics [15–20], we present a weighted sign-bi-power activation function [21, 22] to accelerate OZNN model (20.4) to finite-time convergence to the time-varying theoretical solution of nonlinear equation (20.1). The weighted sign-bi-power activation function $\phi(\cdot)$ is defined as follows [21, 22]:

$$\phi(x) = \frac{1}{2}k_1 \text{sgn}^{\alpha}(x) + \frac{1}{2}k_2 \text{sgn}^{1/\alpha}(x) + \frac{1}{2}k_3 x, \qquad (20.6)$$

where k_1, k_2, k_3, and $\alpha \in (0, 1)$ are tunable positive parameters. In addition, sign-bi-power function $\text{sgn}^{\alpha}(\cdot)$ has the following expression:

$$\text{sgn}^{\alpha}(x) = \begin{cases} |x|^{\alpha}, & \text{if } x > 0; \\ 0, & \text{if } x = 0; \\ -|x|^{\alpha}, & \text{if } x < 0; \end{cases}$$

where $x \in \mathbb{R}$ and $|x|$ denote the absolute value of x. Thus, we can obtain the following FTZNN for online solution of time-varying nonlinear equations:

$$\frac{\partial f}{\partial u}\dot{u}(t) = -\gamma \phi\left(f\left(u(t), t\right)\right) - \frac{\partial f}{\partial t}. \qquad (20.7)$$

It is worth pointing out that the applications of neural dynamics depend crucially on the dynamical behavior of their models. Thus, now and here, we present the main theorem to reveal the finite-time convergence performance of FTZNN model (20.7) by using the weighted sign-bi-power activation function.

Theorem 20.3 *Given a solvable time-varying nonlinear equation $f(u(t), t) = 0 \in \mathbb{R}$, neural state $u(t) \in \mathbb{R}$ of FTZNN model (20.7), starting from randomly generated initial state $u(0) \in \mathbb{R}$, can converge to the time-varying theoretical solution $u^*(t)$ of (20.1) in finite time*

$$t_{\mathrm{f}} \leqslant \begin{cases} \dfrac{2\ln[1+\frac{k_1}{k_3}y(0)^{1-\alpha}]}{\gamma k_3(1-\alpha)}, & \text{if } |y(0)| < 1; \\[4mm] \dfrac{2\alpha\ln[\frac{k_2+k_3}{k_3}y(0)^{\frac{1-\alpha}{\alpha}}+k_2]}{\gamma k_3(1-\alpha)} + \dfrac{2\alpha\ln[1+\frac{k_3}{k_1}]}{\gamma k_3(1-\alpha)}, & \text{if } |y(0)| \geqslant 1; \end{cases}$$

where $y(0)$ denotes the initial value of $y(t)$.

Proof: According to the definition $y(t) := f(u(t), t)$, we know that $y(t)$ is an infinite nonlinear time-varying error function with regard to variables t and $u(t)$. Evidently, the time derivative of $y(t)$ (i.e. $dy(t)/dt$) can be solved as follows:

$$\frac{dy(t)}{dt} = \frac{\partial f}{\partial u}\frac{du}{dt} + \frac{\partial f}{\partial t}.$$

Then, by focusing on the definitions of $y(t)$ and $dy(t)/dt$, it can be concluded that FTZNN model (20.7) is derived from the following equation:

$$\frac{dy(t)}{dt} = -\gamma\phi(y(t)).$$

Thus, we have

$$\dot{y}(t) = -\gamma\left(\frac{1}{2}k_1\text{sgn}^\alpha(y(t)) + \frac{1}{2}k_2\text{sgn}^{1/\alpha}(y(t)) + \frac{1}{2}k_3 y(t)\right). \tag{20.8}$$

To estimate finite time t_f, we first define a Lyapunov function candidate $p(t) = |y(t)|^2$, the time derivative of $p(t)$ is thus obtained:

$$\dot{p}(t) = -\gamma y(t)\left(k_1\text{sgn}^\alpha(y(t)) + k_2\text{sgn}^{1/\alpha}(y(t)) + k_3 y(t)\right)$$
$$= -\gamma\left(k_1|y(t)|^{\alpha+1} + k_2|y(t)|^{\frac{1}{\alpha}+1} + |y(t)|^2\right)$$
$$= -\gamma\left(k_1 p(t)^{\frac{\alpha+1}{2}} + k_2 p(t)^{\frac{1+\alpha}{2\alpha}} + k_3 p(t)\right).$$

For such a differential equation, if $p(0) = |y(0)|^2 < 1$, according to the Lemma 3 of [21], there exists t_f satisfying

$$t_f \leq \frac{2\ln\left[1 + \frac{k_1}{k_3}p(0)^{\frac{1-\alpha}{2}}\right]}{\gamma k_3(1-\alpha)},$$

such that $y(t) = 0$ when $t > t_f$.

If $p(0) = |y(0)|^2 \geq 1$, according to the Lemma 3 of [21], there exists t_f satisfying

$$t_f \leq \frac{2\alpha\ln\left[\frac{k_2+k_3}{k_3}p(0)^{\frac{1-\alpha}{2r}} + k_2\right]}{\gamma k_3(1-\alpha)} + \frac{2\alpha\ln\left[1 + \frac{k_3}{k_1}\right]}{\gamma k_3(1-\alpha)},$$

such that $y(t) = 0$ when $t > t_f$.

The previous results mean $p(t)$ can directly converge to zero at most after a time period

$$t_f \leq \begin{cases} \dfrac{2\ln\left[1 + \frac{k_1}{k_3}y(0)^{1-\alpha}\right]}{\gamma k_3(1-\alpha)}, & \text{if} \quad |y(0)| < 1; \\[4ex] \dfrac{2\alpha\ln\left[\frac{k_2+k_3}{k_3}y(0)^{\frac{1-\alpha}{\alpha}} + k_2\right]}{\gamma k_3(1-\alpha)} + \dfrac{2\alpha\ln\left[1 + \frac{k_3}{k_1}\right]}{\gamma k_3(1-\alpha)}, & \text{if} \quad |y(0)| \geq 1. \end{cases}$$

Thus, we can conclude that the neural state $u(t)$ of FTZNN model (20.7), starting from randomly generated initial state $u(0)$, can converge to the time-varying theoretical solution of nonlinear equation (20.1) in finite time t_f. The proof is completed.

∎

20.4 Illustrative Verification

In the previous sections, we present GNN model (20.2), OZNN model (20.4), and FTZNN model (20.7); and the theoretical result about the finite-time convergence is discussed. In this section, the computer-simulation results and the corresponding observations are provided to substantiate the effectiveness and superiority of FTZNN model (20.7) for solving time-varying nonlinear equation (20.1).

For comparative and illustrative purposes, such three neural dynamics (i.e. GNN model (20.2), OZNN model (20.4), and FTZNN model (20.7)) are used to solve online the time-varying nonlinear equation $f(u(t), t) = 0$. Without loss of generality, the following illustrative example is exploited:

$$f(u(t), t) = u^2(t) - 2\cos(2t)u + \cos^2(2t) - 1 = 0. \tag{20.9}$$

Evidently, the time-varying nonlinear equation earlier is actually equal to $f(u(t), t) = (u(t) - \cos(2t) - 1)(u(t) - \cos(2t) + 1) = 0$, and its time-varying theoretical solutions can be written down as $u_1^*(t) = \cos(2t) + 1$ and $u_2^*(t) = \cos(2t) - 1$. The corresponding simulation results are shown in Figures 20.1–20.3.

First, we present the solution-performance comparison of GNN model (20.2) and OZNN model (20.4) with design parameter $\gamma = 1$. Specifically, Figure 20.1 shows the transient behaviors of neural states $u(t)$ of GNN model (20.2) and OZNN model (20.4) during the solution process of time-varying nonlinear equation (20.9). As seen from Figure 20.1a, starting from 20 randomly generated initial states within $[-5, 5]$, neural states $u(t)$ of GNN model (20.2) do not fit well with any one of the time-varying theoretical solutions $u_1^*(t)$ and $u_2^*(t)$. In contrast,

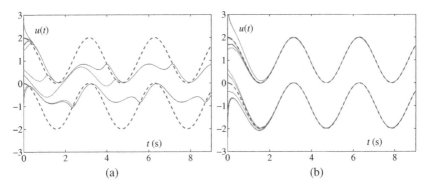

Figure 20.1 Transient behavior of neural states $u(t)$ solved by GNN model (20.2) and OZNN model (20.4) starting with 20 randomly generated initial states and with $\gamma = 1$, where solid curves correspond to neural state $u(t)$, and dash curves correspond to time-varying theoretical solutions $u^*(t)$. (a) By GNN model (20.2). (b) By OZNN model (20.4).

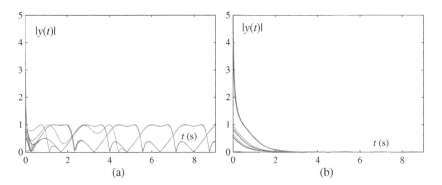

Figure 20.2 Transient behavior of residual errors $|y(t)|$ synthesized by GNN model (20.2) and OZNN model (20.4) starting with 20 randomly generated initial states and with $\gamma = 1$. (a) By GNN model (20.2). (b) By OZNN model (20.4).

under the same conditions, neural states $u(t)$ of OZNN model (20.4) can converge to one of the time-varying theoretical solutions (i.e. $u_1^*(t)$ or $u_2^*(t)$), which is shown evidently in Figure 20.1b. Furthermore, Figure 20.2 shows their corresponding transient behavior of residual errors $|y(t)|$ under the same conditions. As seen from the figure, residual errors $|y(t)|$ synthesized by GNN model (20.2) are always oscillating and never converge to zero stably; while residual errors $|y(t)|$ synthesized by OZNN model (20.4) can converge to zero closely about three seconds. The aforementioned simulation results can illustrate the effectiveness of OZNN model (20.4) and the ineffectiveness of GNN model (20.2) for solving online time-varying nonlinear equations.

However, as discussed before, OZNN model (20.4) can not converge to time-varying theoretical solution within finite time, which may limit its applications in real-time computation. Motivated by this point, now, let us verify the finite-time convergence of FTZNN model (20.7) for solving time-varying nonlinear equation (20.1), which improves the efficacy of the OZNN model greatly. Specifically, by applying FTZNN model (20.7) to solving time-varying nonlinear equation (20.9) under the same simulation conditions with $k_1 = k_2 = 10$, $k_3 = 0$, and $r = 0.25$, neural states $u(t)$ of FTZNN model (20.7) converge to one of the time-varying theoretical solutions (i.e. $u_1^*(t)$ or $u_2^*(t)$) rapidly, which is shown evidently in Figure 20.3a. In addition, residual errors $|y(t)|$ synthesized by FTZNN model (20.7) converge to zero directly, which only needs 0.3 seconds and has 10 times faster than OZNN model (20.4).

In summary, GNN model (20.2) cannot converge to the time-varying theoretical solution of nonlinear equation (20.9), and OZNN model (20.4) can converge exponentially as time goes to infinity. In contrast, the proposed FTZNN model (20.7) can converge to the time-varying theoretical solution within finite time, which increases the convergence performance remarkably (i.e. from infinite to

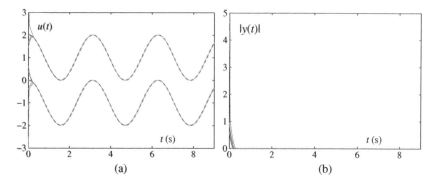

Figure 20.3 Transient behavior of simulation results synthesized by FTZNN model (20.7) starting with 20 randomly generated initial states and with $\gamma = 1$. (a) Neural state $u(t)$. (b) Residual error $|y(t)|$.

finite time). The simulation results (i.e. Figures 20.1–20.3) have also illustrated this fact. Thus, we can conclude that FTZNN model (20.7) is much more efficient for solving online time-varying nonlinear equations, as compared with conventional GNN model (20.2) and the recently proposed OZNN model (20.4).

20.5 Chapter Summary

In this chapter, a nonlinearly activated FTZNN model has been proposed and investigated for solving time-varying nonlinear equations in real time. Different from most existing neural dynamics for solving time-varying nonlinear equations, the proposed neural dynamics has been elegantly introduced by adding a specially constructed nonlinear activation function rather than the usually used linear or nonlinear activation function. As compared with conventional gradient-based neural dynamics and recently proposed Zhang neural dynamics, the proposed neural dynamics has a finite-time convergence performance. In addition, the upper bound of convergence time has been estimated analytically in theory. Simulation results have further illustrated the effectiveness and superiority of the finite-time convergent neural dynamics for solving time-varying nonlinear equations in real time.

References

1 M. A. Z. Raja and Z. Sabir *et al.*, Design of stochastic solvers based on genetic algorithms for solving nonlinear equations, *Neural Comput. & Appl.*, 26 (2015) 1-23.

2 A. Margaris and K. Goulianas, Finding all roots of 2×2 nonlinear algebraic systems using back-propagation neural networks, *Neural Comput. & Appl.*, 21 (2012) 891–904.

3 C. Mead, *Analog VLSI and neural systems*, Addison-Wesley Longman Publishing Co., Inc. (1989).

4 M. M. Fateh and S. Khorashadizadeh, Optimal robust voltage control of electrically driven robot manipulators, *Nolinear Dyn.*, 70 (2012) 1445–1458.

5 J. Peng, J. Wang, and W. Wang, Neural network based robust hybrid control for robotic system: An H_∞ approach, *Nolinear Dyn.*, 65 (2011) 421–431.

6 J. Fei and F. Ding, Adaptive sliding mode control of dynamic system using RBF neural network, *Nolinear Dyn.*, 70 (2012) 1563–1573.

7 J. R. Sharma, A composite third order Newton-Steffensen method for solving nonlinear equations, *Appl. Math. Comput.*, 169(1) (2005) 242–246.

8 C. Chun, Construction of Newton-like iteration methods for solving nonlinear equations, *Numer. Math.*, 104 (2006) 297–315.

9 N. Ujevic, A method for solving nonlinear equations, *App. Math. Comput.*, 174(2) (2006) 1416–1426.

10 S. Yahya, M. Moghavvemi, and H. A. Mohamed, Artificial neural networks aided solution to the problem of geometrically bounded singularities and joint limits prevention of a three dimensional planar redundant manipulator, *Neurocomputing*, 137 (2014) 34–46.

11 S. M. Siniscalchi, T. Svendsen, and C. H. Lee, An artificial neural network approach to automatic speech processing, *Neurocomputing*, 140 (2014) 326–338.

12 Y. Zhang and C. Yi *et al.*, Comparison on Zhang neural dynamics and gradient-based neural dynamics for online solution of nonlinear time-varying equation, *Neural Comput. & Appl.*, 20 (2011) 1–7.

13 Y. Zhang and Z. Li *et al.*, Discrete-time ZD, GD and NI for solving nonlinear time-varying equations, *Numer. Algor.*, 64 (2013) 721–740.

14 L. Xiao and Y. Zhang, Different Zhang functions resulting in different ZNN models demonstrated via time-varying linear matrix-vector inequalities solving, *Neurocomputing*, 121 (2013) 140–149.

15 S. P. Bhat and D. S. Bernstein, Finite-time stability of continuous autonomous systems, *SIAM J. Control Optim.*, 38(3) (2000) 751–766.

16 M. Forti and M. Grazzini *et al.*, Generalized Lyapunov approach for convergence of neural networks with discontinuous or non-Lipschitz activations, *Phys. D Nonlinear Phenom.*, 214(1) (2006) 88–99.

17 W. Lu and T. Chen, Dynamical behaviors of delayed neural network systems with discontinuous activation functions, *Neural Comput.*, 18(3) (2006) 683–708.

18 L. Xiao and R. Lu, Finite-time solution to nonlinear equation using recurrent neural dynamics with a specially-constructed activation function, *Neurocomputing*, 151 (2015) 246–251.

19 Y. Shen and X. Xia, Semi-global finite-time observers for nonlinear systems, *Automatica*, 44(12) (2008) 3152–3156.

20 Y. Shen and Y. Huang, Global finite-time stabilisation for a class of nonlinear systems, *Int. J. Syst. Sci.*, 43(1) (2012) 73–78.

21 Y. Shen and P. Miao *et al.*, Finite-time stability and its application for solving time-varying Sylvester equation by recurrent neural network, *Neural Process. Lett.*, 42(3) (2015) 763–785.

22 P. Miao, Y. Shen, and X. Xia, Finite time dual neural networks with a tunable activation function for solving quadratic programming problems and its application, *Neurocomputing*, 143 (2014) 80–89.

21

Design Scheme III of FTZNN

21.1 Introduction

Recurrent neural networks (RNNs) have a long history in optimization computation, and the first RNN model can be traced to Hopfield neural network [1, 2]. After that, RNNs have been extensively applied in various areas, such as algebraic computation [3–6], state estimation [7], fault tolerant control [8, 9], speech recognition [10], and robotic control [11–15]. In algebraic computation, there exist two kinds of RNNs: gradient neural networks (GNNs) [16–19] and zeroing neural networks (ZNNs) [20–25], which are paid attention by lots of researchers.

In order to simultaneously realize the properties of the superior convergence and tolerating the external noises, in this chapter, by suggesting a new nonlinear activation function, a robust and fixed-time zeroing neural network (R-FTZNN) model is proposed and analyzed for time-variant nonlinear equation (TVNE), which can tolerate external noises and even achieve a faster convergence speed (i.e. fixed-time convergence). Note that the fixed-time convergence is the best convergence performance, as compared with the previous mentioned exponential and finite-time convergence, because it does not depend on initial states of systems and the upper bound can be calculated in advance when system parameters are set. In addition, the theoretical analyses about robustness and fixed-time convergence of the R-FTZNN model are presented in detail. Simulative results demonstrate that the R-FTZNN model combines such two merits.

21.2 Problem Formulation and ZNN Models

In this section, as a basis for study, the research problem is described in mathematics, and ZNN for this problem is developed for comparative purpose.

Zeroing Neural Networks: Finite-time Convergence Design, Analysis and Applications,
First Edition. Lin Xiao and Lei Jia.
© 2023 The Institute of Electrical and Electronics Engineers, Inc. Published 2023 by John Wiley & Sons, Inc.

21.2.1 Problem Formulation

We consider the following TVNE to be solved in this work:

$$f(u(t), t) = 0 \in \mathbb{R}, \tag{21.1}$$

where t represents time; $u(t) \in \mathbb{R}$ represents an unknown dynamic variable; and $f(\cdot, \cdot)$ represents a time-variant nonlinear function mapping. The goal of this work is to find a $u(t)$ within a fixed time to make TVNE (21.1) hold under external disturbances. For achieving this purpose, it is assumed that there exists at least one theoretical solution $u^*(t)$ for TVNE (21.1). Besides, for maintaining the coherence and consistency of this work, ZNN for the aforementioned TVNE is developed and presented as following.

21.2.2 ZNN Model

ZNN is a kind of effective method to solve time-variant algebraic problems. The main design flow of ZNN can be summarized as three steps [16, 26]. Now, we take TVNE (21.1) solving as an example to show the detailed three-step procedures.

Step 1: According to the specific express of TVNE (21.1), we can construct an equivalent error function $y(t)$, which is formed by

$$y(t) = f(u(t), t). \tag{21.2}$$

If $y(t) = 0$, the corresponding $u(t)$ will make $f(u(t), t) = 0$. That is to say, TVNE (21.1) holds. Now, solving TVNE (21.1) is transformed to make $y(t)$ equal to zero.

Step 2: To achieve the aforementioned purpose, an exponential-convergence design formula about the dynamic evolution of $y(t)$ is established as

$$\dot{y}(t) = -\gamma \phi(y(t)), \tag{21.3}$$

where $\dot{y}(t)$ stands for the time derivative of $y(t)$, $\gamma > 0$ stands for an adjusting factor, and $\phi(\cdot)$ stands for a nonlinear activation function.

Step 3: Because of $y(t) = f(u(t), t)$, we can obtain $\dot{y}(t) = \frac{\partial f}{\partial u}\frac{du}{dt} + \frac{\partial f}{\partial t}$. Hence, by plugging (21.2) into (21.3), the following ZNN model for TVNE (21.1) is obtained as

$$\frac{\partial f}{\partial u}\frac{du}{dt} = -\gamma \phi(f(u(t), t)) - \frac{\partial f}{\partial t}. \tag{21.4}$$

Remark Nonlinear activation functions play an important role in ZNN model (21.4), it has been proved that such a model is stable when activation functions are monotonically increasing. Therefore, as long as this condition is satisfied, any monotonically increasing activation functions are potentially used in ZNN model (21.4).

Note that ZNN model (21.4) has been proved to be stable when external environment is ideal [19]. In addition, in the past several years, various different activation functions were developed to speed up the convergence rate of ZNN model (21.4), such as bipolar-sigmoid function, power function, and power-sigmoid (PS) function. Especially, in 2015, sign-bi-power (SBP) function was explored to make ZNN model (21.4) achieve finite-time stability [27]. However, the aforementioned work does not consider external noises. When injected by various external noises, ZNN model (21.4) is still effective for TVNE (21.1). Besides, the finite-time convergence depends on initial states of ZNN seriously, which will limit some practical applications since the knowledge of initial conditions is generally unavailable in advance.

21.3 Robust and Fixed-Time ZNN Model

Robustness and fixed-time convergence are two important indexes for nonlinear systems. In addition, the fixed-time convergence is much superior than finite-time convergence, because the former is dependent of initial states of nonlinear systems, whereas the latter depends on initial states of nonlinear systems seriously. On the other hand, nonlinear activation functions play an important role in ZNN model (21.4). As discussed in Section 21.2, SBP activation function even accelerates ZNN model (21.4) to finite-time convergence. Inspired by this point, we have the following question: can we devise a new nonlinear activation to make ZNN model (21.4) achieve the fixed-time convergence and even reject external disturbances simultaneously?

To realize the aforementioned purposes, in this part, we suggest a new nonlinear activation to modify the comprehensive performance of ZNN model (21.4) for solving TVNE (21.1). In order to distinguish ZNN model (21.4), the new function activated ZNN model is called the R-FTZNN model because it can achieve the fixed-time convergence under external disturbances. On the other hand, we will provide the complete theoretical analysis of the R-FTZNN model from the aspect of stability, convergence, and robustness.

Based on SBP activation function and the fixed-time stability of nonlinear systems [28, 29], the new activation function is constructed as follows:

$$\phi(x) = b_1 \text{sgn}^l(x) + b_2 \text{sgn}^q(x) + b_3 x + b_4 \, \text{sgn}(x), \tag{21.5}$$

where design parameters $0 < l < 1, q > 1, b_1 > 0, b_2 > 0, b_3 \geqslant 0, b_4 \geqslant 0$ and $\text{sgn}(\cdot)$ denotes the signum function. Besides, the sign-power function $\text{sgn}^\alpha(\cdot)$ is defined as follows:

$$\text{sgn}^\alpha(x) = \begin{cases} |x|^\alpha, & \text{if } x > 0; \\ 0, & \text{if } x = 0; \\ -|x|^\alpha, & \text{if } x < 0. \end{cases}$$

Hence, by suggesting the aforementioned new activation function, the R-FTZNN model for solving TVNE (21.1) is proposed as follows:

$$\frac{\partial f}{\partial u}\dot{u}(t) = -\gamma\phi\left(f\left(u(t),t\right)\right) - \frac{\partial f}{\partial t}. \tag{21.6}$$

Note that the essential distinguish between the R-FTZNN model (21.6) and ZNN model (21.4) is the adoption of different nonlinear activation functions. Because of this, the comprehensive performance of the R-FTZNN model (21.6) has been greatly improved, as compared ZNN model (21.4) with the previous mentioned activation functions. In the following section, the complete theoretical analysis of the R-FTZNN model (21.6) will be provided in details. Before that, for studying the robustness of the R-FTZNN model (21.6), the noise-polluted R-FTZNN model is developed by introducing an additive noise $n(t)$, and is presented as follows:

$$\frac{\partial f}{\partial u}\dot{u}(t) = -\gamma\phi\left(f\left(u(t),t\right)\right) - \frac{\partial f}{\partial t} + n(t), \tag{21.7}$$

where $n(t)$ denotes an additive noise, which can be regarded as the constant noise, the time-variant noise, or the mixed one.

21.4 Theoretical Analysis

Before presenting the complete theoretical analysis, the following lemma [30] is given as a basis of discussion.

Lemma 21.1 *Consider a dynamic nonlinear inequality system:*

$$\dot{u}(t) \leqslant -k_1 u^w(t) - k_2 u^r(t),$$

where design parameters $k_1 > 0$, $k_2 > 0$, $0 < w < 1$, and $r > 1$. Then, the inequality system is globally fixed-time stable and the settling time is bounded by

$$T_{\max} = \frac{1}{k_1(1-w)} + \frac{1}{k_2(u-1)}.$$

Note that the aforementioned settling time $T_{\max}$ is independent of initial states of the system, and only depends on the design parameters of the system. Hence, the settling time $T_{\max}$ can be calculated in advance when system parameters are fixed. At present, this convergence property is called the fixed-time convergence, which makes much progress, as compared with the finite-time convergence.

21.4.1 Case 1: No Noise

In this part, we will show the superior fixed-time convergence of the R-FTZNN model (21.6) for solving TVNE (21.1) under the ideal conditions (i.e. no external noises are injected).

Theorem 21.2 *Assume TVNE (21.1) at least exists one time-variant theoretical solution for $t \in [0, +\infty)$. From an arbitrary starting point, the output of the R-FTZNN model (21.6) converges to one of theoretical solutions of TVNE (21.1) within a fixed time t_f:*

$$t_f \leqslant \frac{1}{\gamma b_1 (1-l)} + \frac{1}{\gamma b_2 (q-1)}.$$

Proof: As seen from the design flow of ZNN model (21.4), R-FTZNN model (21.6) can be transformed as

$$\dot{y}(t) = -\gamma \phi(y(t)).$$

Since new activation function $\phi(\cdot)$ is adopted, we can select the Lyapunov function candidate $p(t) = |y(t)|$ to prove the fixed-time stability of the system earlier. In addition, $\dot{p}(t)$ can be calculated as

$$
\begin{aligned}
\dot{p}(t) &= \dot{y}(t)\text{sign}(y(t)) \\
&= -\gamma \phi(y(t))\text{sign}(y(t)) \\
&= -\gamma (b_1 |y(t)|^l + b_2 |y(t)|^q + b_3 |y(t)| + b_4) \\
&\leqslant -\gamma (b_1 |y(t)|^l + b_2 |y(t)|^q) \\
&= -\gamma (b_1 p^l(t) + b_2 p^q(t)).
\end{aligned}
$$

Therefore, on basis of Lemma 21.1, the settling time for R-FTZNN model (21.6) can be directly computed as follows:

$$t_f \leqslant \frac{1}{\gamma b_1 (1-l)} + \frac{1}{\gamma b_2 (q-1)}.$$

Since the upper bound is independent of initial states of R-FTZNN model (21.6) and time t, R-FTZNN model (21.6) possesses a fixed-time convergence property when no external noises are injected. ∎

21.4.2 Case 2: Under External Noises

In this part, we will consider the robustness of R-FTZNN model (21.6) when external additive noises are injected during its practical implementation. Thus, noise-polluted R-FTZNN model (21.7) will be discussed. In the following, different kinds of external noises will be discussed to demonstrate the superior robustness of R-FTZNN model (21.6).

First, when disturbed by a time-variant bounded vanishing additive noise $n(t)$, we have the following theoretical result for noise-polluted R-FTZNN model (21.7) to ensure the fixed-time stability.

Theorem 21.3 *Assume TVNE (21.1) at least exists one time-variant theoretical solution for $t \in [0, +\infty)$, and R-FTZNN model (21.6) is polluted by a time-variant bounded vanishing additive noise $n(t)$ satisfying $|n(t)| \leqslant \delta |y(t)|$ where $\delta \in (0, +\infty)$ and $|y(t)|$ denotes the absolute of the error function. As long as $\gamma b_3 \geqslant \delta$, from an arbitrary starting point, the output of noise-polluted R-FTZNN model (21.7) converges to one of theoretical solutions of TVNE (21.1) within a fixed time t_f:*

$$t_f \leqslant \frac{1}{\gamma b_1 (1 - l)} + \frac{1}{\gamma b_2 (q - 1)}.$$

Proof: Similar to Theorem 21.2, noise-polluted R-FTZNN model (21.7) can be transformed as

$$\dot{y}(t) = -\gamma \phi(y(t)) + n(t). \tag{21.8}$$

For such a noise-polluted nonlinear dynamic system, we can select the Lyapunov function candidate $p(t) = |y(t)|^2$ to prove the fixed-time stability under a time-variant bounded vanishing additive noise. Then, $\dot{p}(t)$ is derived as

$$\dot{p}(t) = 2y(t)\dot{y}(t) = 2y(t)(-\gamma \phi(y(t)) + n(t)).$$

Since the new activation function $\phi(\cdot)$ is adopted, and $\gamma b_3 \geqslant \delta$, the following result can be obtained:

$$\begin{aligned}
\dot{p}(t) &= -2\gamma(b_1 |y(t)|^{l+1} + b_2 |y(t)|^{q+1}) - 2\gamma b_4 |y(t)| \\
&\quad + 2(y(t)n(t) - \gamma b_3 |y(t)|^2) \\
&\leqslant -2\gamma(b_1 |y(t)|^{l+1} + b_2 |y(t)|^{q+1}) + 2(\delta |y(t)|^2 - \gamma b_3 |y(t)|^2) \\
&\leqslant -2\gamma(b_1 |y(t)|^{l+1} + b_2 |y(t)|^{q+1}) \\
&= -2\gamma(b_1 p(t)^{\frac{l+1}{2}} + b_2 p(t)^{\frac{q+1}{2}}).
\end{aligned}$$

From the aforementioned derivation and based on Lemma 21.1, we can conclude that the upper bound of the fixed-time convergence for noise-polluted R-FTZNN model (21.7) is computed as

$$t_f \leqslant \frac{1}{\gamma b_1 (1 - l)} + \frac{1}{\gamma b_2 (q - 1)}.$$

In a word, the output of noise-polluted R-FTZNN model (21.7) converges to one of theoretical solutions of TVNE (21.1) within a fixed time t_f under a time-variant bounded vanishing additive noise. This completes the proof. ∎

Second, when the external noise is a time-variant bounded non-vanishing additive noise $n(t)$, we have the following theoretical result for noise-polluted R-FTZNN model (21.7) to ensure the fixed-time stability.

Theorem 21.4 *Assume TVNE (21.1) at least exists one time-variant theoretical solution for $t \in [0, +\infty)$, and R-FTZNN model (21.6) is polluted by a time-variant* *bounded non-vanishing additive noise* $|n(t)| \leqslant \delta$ *where* $\delta \in (0, +\infty)$. *As long as* $\gamma b_4 \geqslant \delta$, *from an arbitrary starting point, the output of noise-polluted R-FTZNN model (21.7) converges to one of theoretical solutions of TVNE (21.1) within a fixed time* t_f:

$$t_f \leqslant \frac{1}{\gamma b_1(1-l)} + \frac{1}{\gamma b_2(q-1)}.$$

Proof: Since only the noise type is different from Theorem 21.3, we can also select the Lyapunov function candidate $p(t) = |y(t)|^2$ for the system (21.8) in a similar way. Besides, since the new activation function $\phi(\cdot)$ is adopted, and $\gamma b_3 \geqslant \delta$, $\dot{p}(t)$ is derived as

$$\begin{aligned}
\dot{p}(t) &= 2y(t)\dot{y}(t) = 2y(t)(-\gamma\phi(y(t)) + n(t)) \\
&= -2\gamma(b_1|y(t)|^{l+1} + b_2|y(t)|^{q+1}) - 2\gamma b_3|y(t)|^2 \\
&\quad + 2(y(t)n(t) - \gamma b_4|y(t)|) \\
&\leqslant -2\gamma(b_1|y(t)|^{l+1} + b_2|y(t)|^{q+1}) + 2(\delta|y(t)| - \gamma b_4|y(t)|) \\
&\leqslant -2\gamma(b_1|y(t)|^{l+1} + b_2|y(t)|^{q+1}) \\
&= -2\gamma(b_1 p(t)^{\frac{l+1}{2}} + b_2 p(t)^{\frac{q+1}{2}}).
\end{aligned}$$

On basis of Lemma 21.1, the fixed convergence time of noise-polluted R-FTZNN model (21.7) in this situation is derived as

$$t_f \leqslant \frac{1}{\gamma b_1(1-l)} + \frac{1}{\gamma b_2(q-1)}.$$

Therefore, the output of noise-polluted R-FTZNN model (21.7) converges to one of theoretical solutions of TVNE (21.1) within a fixed time t_f under a time-variant bounded non-vanishing additive noise. ∎

In the last condition, we consider a large constant noise n, which can be encountered in neural model implementation. In addition, we have the following theoretical result for noise-polluted R-FTZNN model (21.7) to ensure the fixed-time stability.

Theorem 21.5 *Assume TVNE (21.1) at least exists one time-variant theoretical solution for* $t \in [0, +\infty)$, *and R-FTZNN model (21.6) is polluted by a large constant noise* n *satisfying* $|n| \leqslant \delta < +\infty$. *Even if* $\delta \gg \gamma$ *or at least* $\delta \geqslant \gamma$, *then steady-state error function* $y(t)$ *of noise-polluted R-FTZNN model (21.7) is bounded by*

$$\lim_{t \to +\infty} |y(t)| \leqslant \sqrt{\frac{1}{(256\kappa_1^2\kappa_2^2\kappa_3^2\kappa_4^2)^{\frac{1}{l+q+1}}} \left(\frac{\delta}{\gamma}\right)^{\frac{8}{l+q+1}}}.$$

Proof: First, we can choose the Lyapunov function candidate as $p(t) = |y(t)|^2/2$ for system (21.8), and its time derivative $\dot{p}(t)$ is

$$
\begin{aligned}
\dot{p}(t) &= |y(t)||\dot{y}(t) \\
&= |y(t)|(-\gamma\phi(y(t)) + n) \\
&\leqslant |y(t)|(-\gamma\phi(y(t)) + \delta).
\end{aligned}
$$

Based on the aforementioned equality, the dynamic evolution $y(t)$ can be divided the following three cases.

(1) When $\delta - \gamma\phi(y(t)) < 0$, then $\dot{p}(t) < 0$. Based on Lyapunov theory, $y(t)$ will converge to 0 with time.

(2) When $\delta - \gamma\phi(y(t)) = 0$, then $\dot{p}(t) \leqslant 0$ suggests that $y(t)$ decreases to 0 or $\phi(y(t)) = \delta/\gamma$.

(3) When $\delta - \gamma\phi(y(t)) > 0$, $\dot{p}(t)$ will be less than a positive value, and thus $|y(t)|$ may be not convergent to 0. The worst situation is $0 < \dot{p}(t) \leqslant |y(t)|$ $(-\gamma\phi(y(t)) + \delta)$, which suggests $p(t)$ and $|y(t)|$ will become large. As a result, $\delta - \gamma\phi(y(t))$ will decrease with time, until $\delta - \gamma\phi(y(t)) = 0$ from a positive value, which returns to the second situation $\dot{p}(t) \leqslant 0$. At this time, $\phi(y(t)) = \delta/\gamma$.

From the previous discussion, it can be concluded that

$$
\lim_{t \to +\infty} \phi(|y(t)|) \approx \frac{\delta}{\gamma}.
$$

Based on the previous result, we further have

$$
\begin{aligned}
\lim_{t \to +\infty} \phi^2(|y(t)|) &= \lim_{t \to +\infty} (b_1|y(t)|^l + b_2|y(t)|^q + b_3|y(t)| + b_4)^2 \\
&\geqslant \lim_{t \to +\infty} (b_1^2|y(t)|^{2l} + b_2^2|y(t)|^{2q} + b_3^2|y(t)|^2 + b_4^2) \\
&\geqslant \lim_{t \to +\infty} 4(b_1^2 b_2^2 b_3^2 b_4^2 |y(t)|^{2l+2q+2})^{\frac{1}{4}},
\end{aligned}
$$

which further yields to

$$
\lim_{t \to +\infty} |y(t)|^2 \leqslant \frac{1}{(256 b_1^2 b_2^2 b_3^2 b_4^2)^{\frac{1}{l+q+1}}} \left(\frac{\delta}{\gamma}\right)^{\frac{8}{l+q+1}}.
$$

Hence, we have

$$
\lim_{t \to +\infty} |y|(t) \leqslant \sqrt{\frac{1}{(256 b_1^2 b_2^2 b_3^2 b_4^2)^{\frac{1}{l+q+1}}} \left(\frac{\delta}{\gamma}\right)^{\frac{8}{l+q+1}}}.
$$

The proof is thus completed. ∎

21.5 Illustrative Verification

By suggesting a new activation function, Section 21.3 proposes R-FTZNN model (21.6) and its noise-polluted model (21.7) for solving TVNE (21.1). Section 21.4 details related theoretical analyses according to different noise background. In this section, one illustrative example will be provided to demonstrate the superior convergence and robustness of R-FTZNN model (21.6) by comparing ZNN model (21.4) with the PS and SBP activation functions. Besides, design parameters $l = 1/4$, $q = 4$, and $b_1 = b_2 = b_3 = b_4 = 1$.

Now, consider the following TVNE:

$$f(u(t), t) = u^2(t) - 2\sin(3t)u(t) + \sin^2(3t) - 4 = 0. \tag{21.9}$$

In addition, two theoretical solutions of this example are calculated as $u_1^*(t) = \sin(3t) + 2$ and $u_2^*(t) = \sin(3t) - 2$, which can be used to validate the model solving accuracy. In the following, we first show the effectiveness of R-FTZNN model (21.6) for the previous example under no external noises, and then we are concerned with different types noises mentioned in the previous section to show the advantage of noise-polluted R-FTZNN model (21.7).

The results obtained under no external noises are displayed in Figures 21.1–21.3. These three figures show state solutions and residual errors of TVNE (21.9) generated by ZNN model (21.4) with the PS and SBP activation functions as well as R-FTZNN model (21.6). It follows from these three figures that such three ZNN models are all effective on solving TVNE (21.9), but convergence time is different. Specifically, ZNN model (21.4) with the PS activation function spends about two seconds to make the residual error converge to 0, ZNN model (21.4) with the SBP activation function needs about 1.5 seconds, while R-FTZNN model (21.6) only

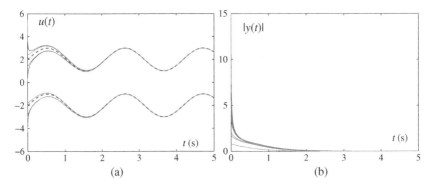

Figure 21.1 Simulative results of solving nonlinear equation (21.9) by ZNN model (21.4) with the power-sigmoid activation function from 18 different initial states. (a) State trajectories. (b) Error trajectories.

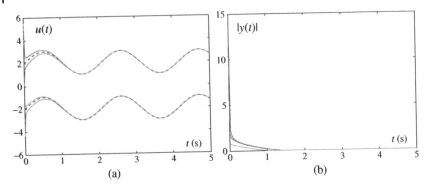

Figure 21.2 Simulative results of solving nonlinear equation (21.9) by ZNN model (21.4) with the SBP activation function from 18 different initial states. (a) State trajectories. (b) Error trajectories.

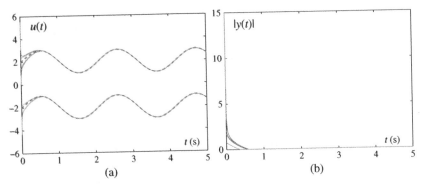

Figure 21.3 Simulative results of solving nonlinear equation (21.9) by R-FTZNN model (21.6) from 18 different initial states and with $\gamma = 1$. (a) State trajectories. (b) Error trajectories.

needs 0.5 seconds. The convergence speed of R-FTZNN model (21.6) is proved to be best under no external noises.

Next, we will show the error results obtained under constant noise $n(t) = 1$ and $\gamma = 5$. Due to similarity, Figure 21.4 only plots transient behavior of residual errors generated by ZNN model (21.4) with the SBP activation function and noise-polluted R-FTZNN model (21.7). It can be concluded that, when injected by external constant noise $n(t) = 1$, noise-polluted R-FTZNN model (21.7) still makes the residual error decrease to 0, while ZNN model (21.4) with the SBP activation cannot. This comparison demonstrates the robustness of noise-polluted R-FTZNN model (21.7) for solving TVNE (21.9).

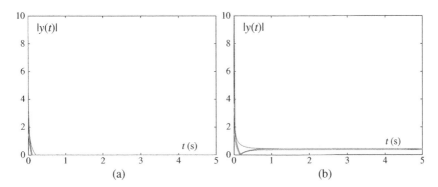

Figure 21.4 Transient behavior of residual errors $|y(t)|$ by different ZNN models from 18 different initial states and with $\gamma = 5$ and constant noise $n(t) = 1$. (a) By R-FTZNN model (21.6). (b) By ZNN model (21.4) with SBP function.

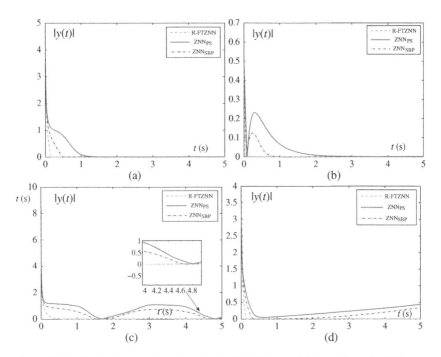

Figure 21.5 Residual errors $|y(t)|$ synthesized by different ZNN models under different types of external noises with $\gamma = 5$. (a) By the vanishing noise $n(t) = y(t)$. (b) By the vanishing noise $n(t) = \exp(-2t)$. (c) By the periodic noise $n(t) = 1.8\cos(t)$. (d) By the non-vanishing noise $n(t) = 0.2t$.

At last, some more simulations are conducted under different types of external noises. Specifically, we consider the following four types noises: the vanishing noise $n(t) = y(t)$, the vanishing noise $n(t) = \exp(-2t)$, the periodic noise $n(t) = 1.8\cos(t)$, and the non-vanishing noise $n(t) = 0.2t$. The corresponding comparison results are plotted in Figure 21.5, from which we can conclude that, when injected by the vanishing noise $n(t) = y(t)$ or the vanishing noise $n(t) = \exp(-2t)$, such three ZNN model are effective on solving TVNE (21.9), but noise-polluted R-FTZNN model (21.7) is a best neural model according to the convergence time; and when injected by the periodic noise $n(t) = 1.8\cos(t)$ or the non-vanishing noise $n(t) = 0.2t$, only noise-polluted R-FTZNN model (21.7) is still effective. These facts further validate the superior robustness of noise-polluted R-FTZNN model (21.7) under various different external noises.

Remark In general, the parameters of novel activation function (21.5) represent the values of capacitance or inductance in the circuit implementation. Therefore, the values of these parameters cannot be set arbitrary large first. Specifically, the values of these parameters can be set according to specific practical requirements to ensure a timely convergence. Besides, parameters b_2 and b_3 are significant to reject bounded disturbances. Therefore, the values of these parameters can be selected based on the upper bound of the disturbances. Specific guidance for choosing parameters of activation functions can be seen in Theorems 21.2–21.5.

In a word, R-FTZNN model (21.6) and its noise-polluted model (21.7) are effective on solving TVNE (21.1) even under various different external noises. Compared with ZNN model (21.4) with existing activation functions, R-FTZNN model (21.6) is proved to be a better model, and combines the robust and fixed-time convergent merits.

21.6 Chapter Summary

By suggesting a new nonlinear activation function, in this work, a R-FTZNN model is developed for TVNE. It has been theoretically proved that the R-FTZNN model can achieve a fixed-time convergence under no external noises with upper bound calculated. In addition, when external noises are injected, the R-FTZNN model has been proved to be fixed-time convergence under weak conditions. That is, the R-FTZNN model possesses a good robust property. As compared with previous ZNN with existing activation functions, the R-FTZNN model has been demonstrated to be a better neural model for solving TVNE in terms of solving accuracy and robustness.

References

1 J. J. Hopfield and D. W. Tank, "Neural" computation of decisions in optimization problems, *Biol. Cybern.*, 52 (1985) 141–152.

2 D. W. Tank and J. J. Hopfield, Simple neural optimization networks: An A/D converter, signal decision circuit, and a linear programming circuit, *IEEE Trans. Circuits Syst.*, 33(5) (1986) 533–541.

3 S. Qin, X. Le, and J. Wang, A neurodynamic optimization approach to bilevel quadratic programming, *IEEE Trans. Neural Netw. Learn. Syst.*, 28(11) (2017) 2580–2591.

4 S. Qin and X. Yang *et al.*, A one-layer recurrent neural network for pseudo-convex optimization problems with equality and inequality constraints, *IEEE Trans. Cybern.*, 47(10) (2017) 3063–3074.

5 Q. Liu and T. Huang *et al.*, One-layer continuous-and discrete-time projection neural networks for solving variational inequalities and related optimization problems, *IEEE Trans. Neural Netw. Learn. Syst.*, 25(7) (2014) 1308–1318.

6 L. Xiao, A nonlinearly-activated neurodynamic model and its finite-time solution to equality-constrained quadratic optimization with nonstationary coefficients, *Appl. Soft Comput.*, 40 (2016) 252–259.

7 F. E. Alsaadi and Y. Luo *et al.*, State estimation for delayed neural networks with stochastic communication protocol: The finite-time case, *Neurocomputing*, 281 (2018) 86–95.

8 L. Xiao and B. Liao *et al.*, Design and analysis of FTZNN applied to the real-time solution of a nonstationary Lyapunov equation and tracking control of a wheeled mobile manipulator, *IEEE Trans. Ind. Inform.*, 14(1) (2018) 98–105.

9 Z. Wang, L. Liu, and H. Zhang, Neural network based model-free adaptive fault tolerant control for discrete-time nonlinear systems with sensor fault, *IEEE Trans. Syst. Man Cybern. Syst.*, 47(8) (2017) 2351–2362.

10 S. M. Siniscalchi, T. Svendsen, and C. H. Lee, An artificial neural network approach to automatic speech processing, *Neurocomputing*, 140 (2014) 326–338.

11 D. Chen, Y. Zhang, and S. Li, Zeroing neural-dynamics approach and its robust and rapid solution for parallel robot manipulators against superposition of multiple disturbances, *Neurocomputing*, 275 (2018) 845–858.

12 D. Chen, and Y. Zhang, Robust zeroing neural-dynamics and its time-varying disturbances suppression model applied to mobile robot manipulators, *IEEE Trans. Neural Netw. Learn. Syst.*, 29(9) (2018) 4385–4397.

13 Z. Zhang and Z. Li *et al.*, Neural-dynamic-method-based dual-arm CMG scheme with time-varying constraints applied to humanoid robots, *IEEE Trans. Neural Netw. Learn. Syst.*, 26(12) (2015) 3251–3262.

14 L. Jin and S. Li *et al.*, Dynamic neural networks aided distributed cooperative control of manipulators capable of different performance indices, *Neurocomputing*, 291 (2018) 50–58.

15 D. Chen, Y. Zhang, and S. Li, Tracking control of robot manipulators with unknown models: A Jacobian-matrix-adaption method, *IEEE Trans. Ind. Inform.*, 14(7) (2018) 3044–3053.

16 Y. Zhang and C. Yi *et al.*, Comparison on Zhang neural dynamics and gradient-based neural dynamics for online solution of nonlinear time-varying equation, *Neural Comput. & Appl.*, 20 (2011) 1–7.

17 C. Yi, Y. Chen, and Z. Lu, Improved gradient-based neural networks for online solution of Lyapunov matrix equation, *Inf. Process. Lett.*, 111(16) (2011) 780–786.

18 Y. Zhang, Y. Yang, and G. Ruan, Performance analysis of gradient neural network exploited for online time-varying quadratic minimization and equality-constrained quadratic programming, *Neurocomputing*, 74(10) (2011) 1710–1719.

19 L. Xiao, K. Li, and M. Duan, Computing time-varying quadratic optimization with finite-time convergence and noise tolerance: A unified framework for zeroing neural network, *IEEE Trans. Neural Netw. Learn. Syst.*, 30(11) (2019) 3360–3369.

20 Y. Zhang, D. Jiang, and J. Wang, A recurrent neural network for solving Sylvester equation with time-varying coefficients, *IEEE Trans. Neural Netw.*, 13(5) (2002) 1053–1063.

21 Y. Zhang and S. S. Ge, Design and analysis of a general recurrent neural network model for time-varying matrix inversion, *IEEE Trans. Neural Netw.*, 16(6) (2005) 1477–1490.

22 Y. Zhang and Z. Li, Zhang neural network for online solution of time-varying convex quadratic program subject to time-varying linear-equality constraints, *Phys. Lett. A*, 373(18–19) (2009) 1639–1643.

23 Z. Li and Y. Zhang, Improved Zhang neural network model and its solution of time-varying generalized linear matrix equations, *Expert Syst. Appl.*, 37(10) (2010) 7213–7218.

24 Y. Zhang and G. Ruan *et al.*, Robustness analysis of the Zhang neural network for online time-varying quadratic optimization, *J. Phys. A: Math. Theor.*, 43 (2010) 245202.

25 L. Xiao and Y. Zhang, Different Zhang functions resulting in different ZNN models demonstrated via time-varying linear matrix-vector inequalities solving, *Neurocomputing*, 121 (2013) 140–149.

26 Y. Zhang, Z. Li, and D. Guo, Discrete-time ZD, GD and NI for solving nonlinear time-varying equations, *Numer. Algor.*, 64 (2013) 721–740.

27 L. Xiao and R. Lu, Finite-time solution to nonlinear equation using recurrent neural dynamics with a specially-constructed activation function, *Neurocomputing*, 151 (2015) 246–251.

28 L. Xiao and Y. Zhang *et al.*, Performance benefits of robust nonlinear zeroing neural network for finding accurate solution of Lyapunov equation in presence of various noises, *IEEE Trans. Ind. Inform.*, 15(9) (2019) 5161–5171.

29 W. Li and B. Liao *et al.*, A recurrent neural network with predefined-time convergence and improved noise tolerance for dynamic matrix square root finding, *Neurocomputing*, 337 (2019) 262–273.

30 Z. Zuo and L. Tie, Distributed robust finite-time nonlinear consensus protocols for multi-agent systems, *Int. J. Syst. Sci.* 47(6) (2016) 1366–1375.

Index

Zeroing Neural Networks: Finite-time Convergence Design, Analysis and Applications,
First Edition. Lin Xiao and Lei Jia.
© 2023 The Institute of Electrical and Electronics Engineers, Inc. Published 2023 by John Wiley & Sons, Inc.

Printed and bound by CPI Group (UK) Ltd, Croydon, CR0 4YY

27/10/2024